Knox County, Tennesse

MARRIAGES

1792–1837

WPA Records

Heritage Books
2024

HERITAGE BOOKS

AN IMPRINT OF HERITAGE BOOKS, INC.

Books, CDs, and more—Worldwide

For our listing of thousands of titles see our website
at
www.HeritageBooks.com

A Facsimile Reprint
Published 2024 by
HERITAGE BOOKS, INC.
Publishing Division
5810 Ruatan Street
Berwyn Heights, MD 20740

December 15, 1938

— Publisher's Notice —
In reprints such as this, it is often not possible to remove blemishes from the original. We feel the contents of this book warrant its reissue despite these blemishes and

International Standard Book Number
Paperbound: 978-0-7884-8808-5

TENNESSEE

RECORDS OF KNOX COUNTY

MARRIAGE RECORDS
1792 -- 1837

COPYING HISTORICAL RECORDS PROJECT
OFFICIAL PROJECT No. 465-44-3-115

COPIED UNDER WORKS PROGRESS ADMINISTRATION

MRS. JOHN TROTWOOD MOORE
STATE LIBRARIAN & ARCHIVIST, SPONSOR

MRS. ELIZABETH D. COPPEDGE
DIRECTOR OF WOMEN'S & PROFESSIONAL PROJECTS

MRS. PENELOPE JOHNSON ALLEN
STATE SUPERVISOR

MRS. MARGARET HELMS RICHARDSON
PROJECT SUPERVISOR

PREPARED BY
C. J. CULLEN
MRS. ELIZABETH CHAUVET
MRS. ALVA LEWIS
MISS ANNA LOU BRAY

TYPED BY
MRS. ELIZABETH CHAUVET

DECEMBER 15, 1938.

TENNESSEE

KNOX COUNTY

MARRIAGE RECORDS

1792 -- 1837

INDEX

A

ASHLEY, THOS. M., 47
ATHEAN, EDMON, 222
ATKIN, CHARLES W., 211
ATKIN, GEORGE, 116, 136, 142, 169, 174, 175, 178, 179, 183, 184, 185, 189, 193, 196, 199, 202, 203, 205, 211, 214, 217, 221, 223
ATKIN, JAS. 162
ATKINS, CHARLES W., 360
ATKINS, GEO. 150
ATKINS, JOSEPH, 195
ATKINS, SUSAN, 348
ATKINSON, ABSALOM, 93
ATKINSON, JESSE, 93
ATKINSON, WILLIAM, 15
AULT, ANDREW J., 360
AULT, BETSY, 157
AULT, CHARITY, 91
AULT, CONRAD, 44
AULT, FREDERICK, 158
AULT, HENRY, 285, 299
AULT, JASON, 39
AULT, JOHN, 47, 104, 265
AULT, JACOB, 54, 76, 265
AULT, MARGARET, 76
AULT, MICHAEL, 220
AULT, THOMAS, 52
AUTRY, PEGGY ANN, 186
AYERS, FRANKY, 171
AYERS, MARY, 336
AYLER, WILLIAM PRESTON, 234
AYLES, WILLIAM PORTER, 234
AYERS, CHARLOTTE, 139
AYERS, D. B., 78
AYERS, ELIZABETH, 259
AYRES, JESSE, 116, 190
AYRES, JONATHAN, 86, 100, 102, 110
AYRES, JOSEPH, 343
AYRES, PHERRIBA, 184
AYRES, POLLY, 44
AYRES, SAMUEL, 154

B

BABER, LEWIS, 250
BABER, WOODSON, 181
BABRING, JOHN, 360
BADGETT, FANNY, 340
BADGETT, FRANCIS, 252
BADGETT, JAMES, 118, 130, 144, 155,
BADGETT, NANCY F. 292
BADGETT, RANSOM, 265
BADGETT, ROBERT D., 284, 250
BADGETT, SAMUEL, 145
BAGWELL, ALLEN, 76
BAILS, ASHER, 181
BAKER, CHARITY, 30, 144
BAKER, CHARLES, 104
BAKER, CHRISTIAN, 266
BAKER, CHRISTOPHER, 266
BAKER, DICE, 180
BAKER, HENRY, 10, 166
BAKER, ISAAC, 291
BAKER, JANE, 341
BAKER, JOHN, 266
BAKER, LEONIDAS W., 250
BAKER, LEWIS, 250
BAKER, MARY, 47
BAKER, PEGGY, 52
BAKER, SOLOMON, 155
BAKER, THOMAS W., 71
BAKER, WILLIAM, 155
BAKER, WILLIAM J., 222
BALDIE, WM., 27
BALDWIN, DARCUS, 230
BALDWIN, FRANCIS J., 298
BALDWIN, HENRY, 250
BALDWIN, MOSES, 93
BALDWIN, POLLY ANN, 298
BALDWIN, WILLIAM 47
BALES, AARON, 54
BALES, KALEB, 28
BALES, LYDIA, 269, 332,
BALES, NATHAN, 291
BALES, POLLY, 288
BALES, RUTH, 326
BALES, SOLOMON, 329
BALEW, MICAJAH B., 281
BALINGER, SARAH, 308
BALL, ANN, 24
BALL, THOMAS, 234
BALLARD, ANDREW J., 360
BALLINGER, JAMES, 211, 222
BALLINS, NANCY, 74
BALLUE, WILLIAM, 349

BAMBLE, J. N., 92
BANDY, THOMAS, 251
BANK, ISAAC, 84
BARBER, UNIA, 370
BARBER, WILLIAM, 181
BARCLAY, BETSY, 244
BARCLAY, FELIX, 22
BARGER, BARBARA, 46
BARGER, ELIZABETH, 307
BARGER, FREDERICK, 341
BARGER, JACOB, 304
BARGER, JOHN, 69
BARGER, NICHOLAS, 195, 307, 337,
BARGER, PEGGY, 42
BARKER, HARDIN, 166
BARKETT, NEWMAN, 360
BARNES, MELINDA, 348
BARNES, THOMAS, 17
BARNES, WM. O., 347
BARNETT, HANNAH, 271
BARNETT, JAMES M., 196
BARNETT, JOHN W., 93
BARNETT, MARGOT, 20
BARNETT, ROBERT, 54
BARNETT, SARAH, 374
BARNETT, WILLIAM, 37
BARNWELL, JANE, 116
BARNWELL, MARTHA, 278
BARNWELL, ROBT. H., 116, 319
BARNWELL, WILLIAM, 268
BARNWELL, WILLIAM L., 266
BARR, JOHN, 52
BARRY, HYRAM, 264, 302
BARRY, WILLIAM, 251
BARTHOLMEW, JOSEPH, 305
BARTLETT, JOSEPH, 17, 196
BARTLETT, JESSE, 208
BARTLETT, JOSEPH, 196
BARTLETT, PRICE, 63
BARTON, C. T., 204. 207
BARTON, HANNAH, 22
BARTON, ISAAC, 144
BASHER, BAZIL, 28
BASHURS, PATSY, 16
BASKETT, NEWMAN, 360
BASS, JOHN, 45
BASS, JUDA, 125
BATES, JOHN, 8
BATKIN, RACHEL, 36
BAYLES, BETSY, 103
BAYLES, SARAH, 107
BAYLESS, ANNE, 72
BAYLESS, ELIZABETH, 284
BAYLESS, ISAAC, 130, 144, 222, 307, 312, 318, 323, 324, 340
BAYLESS, JOHN, 88, 86, 91. 94, 96, 97, 98, 99, 100, 102, 105, 106, 107, 109, 110, 114, 116, 119, 121. 124, 126, 127, 128, 134, 135, 139, 140, 147, 149, 150, 151, 152, 155, 157, 158, 162, 167, 169, 172, 184, 191, 192, 199, 195, 198, 201, 205, 207, 210, 211, 213, 215, 225, 227, 238, 244, 245, 247, 248, 252, 255, 256, 263, 271, 284
BAYLESS, NANCY, 286
BAYLESS, RACHEL, 68
BAYLESS, REESE, 266
BAYLESS, ROBERT, 48, 51
BAYLESS, SAMUEL, 211, 222
BAYLESS, SUSANNAH, 155
BEADLEY, MARY, 354
BEAL, ANNE, 126
BEALES, WILLIAM, 10
BEALL, LOYD, 217
BEALL, SAM'L, 84
BEANY, ANDREW, 329
BEAN, JAMES, 319
BEAN, JOHN I. 360
BEAN, SALLY, 374
BEANE, PEGGY, 217
BEARD, HULDAH, 212
BEARD, JOHN J., 360
BEARD, POLLY, 86
BEARD, WILLIAM, 60
BEARDEN, JOHN, 251
BEARDEN, MARIA, 286
BEARDEN, RICHARD, 292
BEARDEN, SARAH, 307
BEASLEY, ABRAHAM, 99
BEATTIE, MICHAEL, 146
BEDSOLT, DANIEL, 104
BEESON, ABNER, 37
BEIELY, JACOB, 196
BELEW, ELIZABETH, 290

BELEW, JANE, 283
BELL, CHARLOTTE, 109
BELL, DAVID, 241, 251, 265
BELL, EDMUND G., 319
BELL, ELIZABETH, 65, 69
BELL, HARRIET JANE, 318
BELL, JAMES, 130
BELL, JAMES G., 281
BELL, JAMES S., 47, 166
BELL, JENNY, 47
BELL, JOSEPH, 104
BELL, LEVINA, 306
BELL, LOYD, 211
BELL, MARGARET, 104
BELL, MARY A. H., 322
BELL, MARY E., 197
BELL, NANCY, 39
BELL, NEBUCHADNEZAR S., 292
BELL, PHILIP D., 222
BELL, POLLY, 46, 144
BELL, REBECKA, 261
BELL, ROSANA, 314
BELL, ROBERT, 187, 218, 260, 343
BELL, SAMUEL, 314
BELL, SAMUEL N., 329
BELL, SAMUEL P., 390
BELL, SARAH ANN, 343
BELL, THOMAS, 35, 70, 179, 278
BELL, WILLIAM, 39, 46, 47
BELL, WILLIAM M., 196
BELL, WILLIAM W., 181
BELTON, WILLIAM 11
BEMAN, MARY, 30
BENNETT, DAVID, 339
BENNETT, JAMES D., 281
BENNETT, J. D., 344, 348, 360, 365, 372, 373
BENNETT, POLLY D., 92
BENNETT, PRESLEY, 167
BENKLY, POLLY, 139
BENSON, MATTHIAS, 211
BENTON, ISAAC, 222
BENTON, MATTY, 68
BERRY, GEORGE C., 196, 254, 256
BERRY, HUGH L., 223
BERRY, JO. D., 266
BERRY, JOHN S., 251
BERRY, MARY, 89
BERRY, WILLIAM, 116
BEST, GEORGE C., 266
BIBBS, FRANCIS, 293
BIBBS, JOHN, 211
BILDERBACH, JACOB, 52
BILDERBACK, JACOB, 142
BILLUE, WILLIAM, 321, 357, 369
BINLY, LUCY, 220
BIRD, ABRAHAM, 5
BIRD, AMOS, 5
BIRD, AMOS, JUNR., 5
BIRD, THOMAS, 329
BIRDIN, WILLIAM, 5
BIRDWELL, ELIZABETH, 74
BIRDWELL, G., 292
BIRDWELL, GEORGE, 76
BIRDWELL, RACHEL, 33, 96, 171
BIRDWELL, RUSSELL, 283, 301, 303
BIRKLY, LUCY, 220
BISHOP, ABIGALE, 26
BISHOP, ELIZABETH, 109, 288
BISHOP, H. G., 197
BISHOP, HARRIS G., 196
BISHOP, JACOB, 10
BISHOP, JOSEPH, 26
BISHOP, LEWIS, 267
BISHOP, MILLY, 112
BISHOP, POLLY, 12
BISHOP, SARAH W., 198
BISHOP, STEPHEN, 12
BITCHBOARD, DINAH, 165
BIVENS, WILLIAM, 223
BLACK, MARY, 45
BLACK, SARAH, 15
BLACKBURN, ALEXANDER, 305
BLACKBURN, JAMES, 251
BLACKBURN, JEAN, 3
BLACKBURN, MARGARET, 7
BLACKBURN, MARY, 5
BLACKBURN, SALATHIAL, 251
BLACKLEY, JOSEPH, 48
BLACKWELL, JENNY, 57
BLACKWELL, JOHN E. S., 287
BLACKWELL, PEGGY, 185
BLAIN, ROBERT W., 319
BLAINE, ALEXANDER, 343

BLAIR, ELIZA, 255
BLAIR, JOSEPH, 84
BLAIR, ROBERT W., 319
BLAKE, ADAM, G., 181
BLAKE, MERINA, 148
BLAKELEY, ALEXANDER, 22
BLAKELEY, CHARLES, 60
BLAKELY, CHARLES, 76
BLAKELY, FRANCIS, 108
BLAKELY, JOHN, 93
BLAKELY, POLLY, 218
BLALOCK, HENRY, 196
BLANG, GEORGE, 104, 149
BLANG, P. L., 343
BLANK, PATSY, 74
BLANKENSHIP, REUBEN, 76
BLEDSOE, ANY, 80
BLEDSOE, GILES, J., 97
BLEDSOE, PHILADELPHIA, 39, 104
BLEDSOE, SARAH, 63
BLEDSOE, TALITHA, 162
BLEDSOE, UNITY, 97
BLIZZARD, MARY, 23
BLIZZARD, NANCY, 24
BLOUNT, ELIZA INDIANNA, 93
BLOUNT, W. G., 139
BLOUNT, WM. C., 31
BLUNT, SALITA, 190
BOAZ, OBADIAH, 167
BODIE, MATHS, 24
BODKIN, HUGH, 59
BODKIN, PEGG, 12
BODKIN, PEGGY, 186
BODY, MOLTIS, 19
BOGAN, WILLIAM, 12
BOGGES, HENRY, 305
BOHAN, BETSY, 226
BOHANNAN, TABBY, 25
BOHANNON, DIDAMY, 8
BOILER, JACOB, 22
BOLEN, NATHAN, 223
BOLTON, BETSY, 262
BOLTON, REBECKA, 266
BOND, BETSY, 82
BOND, C ---, 149
BOND, ISAAC, 38, 306
BOND, MARGARET F., 187
BOND, NANCY, 202
BOND, POLLY, 275
BOND, REBECKA, 340
BOND, WILLIAM, 47
BOOKER, ELIZABETH, 289
BOOKER, IBBY, 169
BOOKER, JAMES, 305
BOOKER, JANE, 156
BOOKOUT, ELIZABETH, 295
BOOKOUT, JOHN, 281
BOOKOUT, JOHN M., 130, 251
BOOKOUT, THOMAS, 251
BOOMER, PETER, 28
BOOTH, EDWIN E., 50
BOOTH, SALLY, 241
BOOTH, ZACHARIAH, 71
BOOTHE, JAMES, 280
BOOTHE, JANE, 328
BOOTHE, ZAC, 319, 325
BORING, M., 223
BOSWORTH, JAMES M., 267
BOTKIN, HUGH, 30
BOUNDS, AMANDA A., 368
BOUNDS, ELIZA, 353
BOUNDS, ELIZABETH, 115
BOUNDS, FRANCIS, 22
BOUNDS, FRANCIS H., 325
BOUNDS, JOHN, 22
BOUND, JOHN W., 252
BOUNDS, NANCY, 6
BOUNDS, W. M., 347
BOUNDS, WASHINGTON WILLIAM, 292
BOWEN, ABNER, 35
BOWEN, C. G., 252, 278
BOWEN, CHARLES, 31, 243
BOWEN, CHARLES G., 248
BOWEN, JOHN, 8
BOWEN, NANCY, 31
BOWEN, REESE, 50
BOWEN, WILLIAM, 35, 104, 243
BOWEN, WILLIAM R., 361, 372
BOWER, WILLIAM, 60
BOWERS, CHARLES, 159
BOWIE, LANGDON, 252
BOWLING, LYDIA, 281
BOWLING, NATHAN, 256
BOWLING, NOBLE, 211
BOWMAN, ANNE, 202
BOWMAN, BETSY, 190
BOWMAN, CARTER, 252

BURKHART, PETER, 298
BURMAN, OWEN, 131
BURNETT, ABSALOM, 361
BURNETT, ANDERSON, 267, 329
BURNETT, ANNIE, 55
BURNETT, BENJAMIN, 131 235
BURNETT, BERRY, 197, 219
BURNETT, BETSY, 168, 198, 200
BURNETT, ELLY, 58
BURNETT, HOWELL, 197
BURNETT, JOSEPH, 156, 177, 200, 235, 267
BURNETT, MARIA, 178
BURNETT, MARION, 229
BURNETT, MATILDA, 282
BURNETT, MICHAEL, 305
BURNETT, NANCY, 59, 128 129, 178
BURNETT, SAMUEL, 223
BURNETT, VINCENT, 191
BURNETT, ZACHARIAH, 267
BURNETTE, LEMUEL, 144
BURNHAM, HEZEKIAH, 212
BURNHAM, MARY ANN, 169
BURNHAM, SALLY, 172
BURNS, BETSY, 187
BURNS, PATRICK, 11
BURNWOTT, DEBBY, 126
BURROWS, JANE, 34
BURTON, ISAAC, 223
BURUM, HENRY, 223
BUSH, JOHN, 305
BUTLER, EDWARD, 131
BUTLER, JACOB M., 167, 227
BUTLER, VALENTINE, 28
BUTLER, WM. D., 131
BYERLEY, DAVID, 93
BYERLEY, JACOB, 182
BYERLEY, MARTIN, 344
BYERLY, ISAAC, 319
BYERLY, JAMES, 267
BYRAM, EBENEZER, 167
BYRAM, LEVI, 167
BYRD, ABRAHAM, 6
BYRD, AMOS, 6
BYRD, IZEL, 77
BYRD, JOHN, 11
BYRD, NATHANIEL, 344, 345
BYRD, STEPHEN, 6

C

CABLE, ELIZA, 347
CAHOE, MARGARET, 93
CAIN, ALEXANDER, 256, 264
CALDWELL, ABSALOM, 44
CALDWELL, ALEX, 150
CALDWELL, BENJ. 72
CALDWELL, BERTHA, 345
CALDWELL, DAVID, 4, 6
CALDWELL, ENGLISH, 305
CALDWELL, HU. 197
CALDWELL, JAMES, 44, 318, 340
CALDWELL, JAMES, A., 79, 116,
CALDWELL, JANE, 150
CALDWELL, JESSE, 116
CALDWELL, JOHN, 105, 238
CALDWELL, MARGARET, 47, 292
CALDWELL, NANCY, 86
CALDWELL, ROBERT, 361
CALDWELL, RUTHA, 345
CALDWELL, SAMUEL, 2
CALDWELL, THOMAS, 2
CALDWELL, THOMAS J., 212
CALDWELL, WILL R., 178
CALFEE, HENRY, 131
CALLAN, ARCHIBALD, 191
CALLEN, ARCHIBALD, 160
CALLEN, EDWARD, 182
CALLEN, ELIZABETH, 160
CALLEN, MARY, 230
CALLET, REUBEN, 144
CALLISON, JAMES, 6
CALLOWAY, ALEY, 257
CALLOWAY, BETSY, 192
CALLOWAY, CAROLINE, 254
CALLOWAY, CYNTHIA, 215
CALLOWAY, J., 124
CALLOWAY, JNO., 80, 90
CALLOWAY, JOSEPH, 90
CALLOWAY, MARY W., 307
CALLOWAY, NANCY, 221
CALLOWAY, POLLY, 42
CALLOWAY, REBECKA, 96
CALLOWAY, REBECCA E., 312
CALLOWAY, SARAH C., 240

CALLOWAY, SHADRACK, 330
CALLOWAY, THOMAS, 330
CALLOWAY, THOMAS F., 307, 336, 361
CALLUM, ELEANOR, 243
CALLUM, JOHN, 2
CALVERT, ELLEN, 341
CAMERON, ALEXANDER, 37
CAMERON, MARGARET, 37
CAMP, JAMES, 282
CAMP, SARAH A., 357
CAMPBELL, ALEXANDER, 197
CAMPBELL, ANNA, 134
CAMPBELL, ANNY, 64
CAMPBELL, BETSY, 143
CAMPBELL, BETSY L., 69
CAMPBELL, CYNTHIA, 177
CAMPBELL, DAVID, 28, 93, 51, 71, 102, 143, 167
CAMPBELL, E. R., 156, 197
CAMPBELL, HARRIET, 305
CAMPBELL, ISAAC, 54, 67
CAMPBELL, ISABELLA, 95
CAMPBELL, JAMES, 15, 37, 47, 156, 182, 197, 198, 208, 338
CAMPBELL, JAMES W., 252
CAMPBELL, JANE, 80, 119, 320
CAMPBELL, JANE S., 79
CAMPBELL, JOHN, 48, 55, 60, 156, 200, 237, 259, 365
CAMPBELL, JOHN S., 295
CAMPBELL, MARGARET M., 338
CAMPBELL, MARGERY, 138
CAMPBELL, MARY, 365
CAMPBELL, MARY HAMILTON, 28
CAMPBELL, NANCY, 101
CAMPBELL, PATSY, 69, 301
CAMPBELL, PEGGY, 219
CAMPBELL, POLLY, 98
CAMPBELL, ROBERT, 55, 122, 365
CAMPBELL, SUSAN J., 269
CAMPBELL, W. A., 323
CAMPBELL, WM., 55, 96, 99, 76, 102, 122, 128, 197
CAMPBELL, WM. A., 119
CANNON, A. E. 281
CANNON, B. B., 268, 273, 278, 282, 190
CANNON, BENJAMIN, B., 296
CANNON, GEO. R., 166, 182
CANNON, JOHN D., 282
CANNON, JOHN C., 224
CANNON, MARY E., 281
CANNON, THOMAS, 228
CAPP, CALEB, 106
CAPPS, MARY ANN, 357
CAPSHAW, JNK. 66
CAPSHAW, THOMAS, 156
CAPSHAW, WEST WALKER, 268
CARDEN, AMOS T., 95
CARDWELL, JAMES H., 267, 320
CARDWELL, JOHN, 179
CARDWELL, MARGARET W., 179
CARDWELL, MARIAH W., 335
CARDWELL, SUSAN, 301
CARDWELL, THOMAS G., 236
CARITHERS, ANDREW, 52
CARITHERS, JOHN, 52
CARLASS, LUCY, 331
CARLESS, POLLY, 72
CARLISLE, ELIZABETH, 21
CARLISLE, JAMES, 21
CARMICHAEL, CATHARINE C., 237
CARMICHAEL, HUGH, 30
CARMICHAEL, ISABELLA, 196
CARMICHAEL, PEGGY, 35
CARMICHAEL, PUMROY, 39
CARNES, EVE, 61
CARNES, (KARNES) EVE, 61
CARNES, JAMES, 33
CARNES, WM. B. 177
CARNS, ALEXANDER C., 320
CARNS, CATHARINE ANN, 268
CARNS, POLLY, 124
CARNS, ROBT., 345
CARNS, WILLIAM B., 105, 107, 130, 135, 137, 141, 142, 144, 150, 151, 155, 156, 159, 162, 169, 170, 181, 189, 186, 188, 196, 202, 203, 204, 210, 219, 220, 225, 226, 231, 233, 244, 247, 250, 257, 262
CAROL, WILY, 114
CARPENTER, GEORGE, 30
CARPENTER, JACOB, 198

CHURCHWELL, GEORGE W., 198, 199, 344
CISER, MICHAEL, 37
CLAIBORNE, EMELINE, 330
CLAIBORNE, LEONARD, 330
CLAIBOURNE, EPHRAIM, 48
CLAIR, HENRY, 60
CLAMPIT, SALLIE, 3
CLAP, ADAM, 157
CLAP, SALLY, 204
CLAPP, BOSTON, 117
CLAPP, DANIEL, 95
CLAPP, DAVID, 94
CLAPP, ELIZABETH, 361
CLAPP, HANNA, 184
CLAPP, HENRY, 248
CLAPP, MALINDA, 321
CLAPP, NANCY, 89
CLAPP, PHEBE, 178
CLAPP, POLLY, 172
CLAPP, SARAH, 85
CLAPP, SOLOMON, 77
CLAPP, SOPHIA, 261
CLARK, ELIZABETH, 52
CLARK, HUGH M., 194, 224
CLARK, ISAAC, 6
CLARK, JAMES P., 131
CLARK, JOHN, 71, 265
CLARK, JOHN M., 132
CLARK, POLLY, 174
CLARK, SAMUEL, 40
CLARK, SARAH, 26
CLARK, SUSAN, 362
CLARK, THOMAS, 253
CLARK, THOMAS N., 22
CLARK, WILLIAM, 65, 189, 212, 352, 362
CLARK, WM. J., 178, 344
CLARKE, JANE, 265
CLARKE, JOSEPH M., 65
CLARKE, PATSY, 188
CLAYTON, DAVID, 306
CLAYTON, ELIZABETH, 84
CLAYTON, MARY, 161
CLAYTON, MATILDA, 173
CLAYTON, RACHEL, 129
CLAYTON, ROBERT, 306
CLAYTON, TABITHA, 114
CLEVELAND, JOHN, 40
CLIBORN, LARENZO D., 168
CLIBORNE, JUBAL, 242
CLIBOURN, JUBEL, 328
CLIBOURNE, ELIZA, 292
CLIBOURNE, M., 342
CLIBOURNE, MILENDER, 292
CLIBURN, HENDERSON, 253
CLIBURN, JAMES, 253
CLIBURN, JOHN, 254
CLIBURN, JONES, 253
CLIBURN, LASLEY, 145
CLIBURN, MALINDER, 254
CLIFT, ALEE ARENCE, 272
CLIFT, ANNE, 208
CLIFT, BETSY, 206
CLIFT, JAMES SR., 306
CLIFT, JOSEPH, 212
CLIFT, KATTY, 211
CLIFT, WM., 168
CLINE, JOHN, 65
CLINE, MARTHA, 316
CLINE, REBECKA, 246
CLINE, SUSAN, 110
CLOSE, WILLIAM, 40
CLOUD, JOHN, 83
CLOUD, REUBEN, 320
CLOUSE, GEO. 345
CLOWDIS, RADFORD R., 306
COALMAN, DANIEL, 52
COATS, DAVID, 52, 84
COATS, DELPHIA, 287
COATS, NANCY, 276
COATS, REBECCA, 352
COATS, THOMAS, 60
COATS, WILLIAM, 276
COBB, AUGERONA, 210
COBB, ASA, 20
COBB, DIANA, 309
COBB, ELIZABETH, 316
COBB, JAMES, 55
COBB, MALINDA B., 370
COBB, MARGARET ALVIRA, 227
COBB, MARTHA, 263
COBB, MARTHA J., 372
COBB, MILTON, 236
COBB, SALLY, 26
COBB, SARAH, 44
COBB, SARAH D., 240, 196
COCHRAN, ABNER, 40

COEN, JOHN W., 168
COFFIN, CHARLES, 233, 241, 242, 243, 249, 252
COFFIN, CHARLES A., 362
COFFIN, CHARLES H., 362
COFFIN, ELIZA, 252
COFFIN, LEAH, 337
COFFMAN, JAMES, 306
COFFMAN, LEAH, 337
COFFMAN, POLLY, 296
COKER, CHARLES, 196
COKER, ELIZA, 263
COKER, ELIZABETH, 196
COKER, FANNY, 201
COKER, JAMES, 117, 118, 236
COKER, JAMES R., 363
COKER, JOEL, 40, 44, 358
COKER, JOHN, 141, 152, 212, 277
COKER, JNO. P., 345
COKER, LEONARD, 236, 345
COKER, MAHALA, 276
COKER, MALINDA, 236
COKER, MARGARET, 357
COKER, MARY, 93
COKER, NANCY, 345
COKER, SARAH, 141
COKER, WARREN, 44
COKER, WILLIE, 94
COLE, ALEXANDER, 19, 20
COLE, BENJAMIN, 145
COLE, CALEB, 77
COLE, ELEANOR, 189
COLE, ELIZABETH, 166
COLE, JOHN, 132, 345
COLE, LUCINDA, 289
COLE, POLLY, 179
COLE, R., 86, 95, 105, 107, 111, 126, 138, 153
COLE, REBECCA, 70
COLE, SALLY, 98
COLE, SARAH G., 279
COLE, SARAH S., 288
COLE, THOMAS, 224
COLE, WM., 344
COLEMAN, ISABELLA, 273
COLEMAN, JAMES, 157
COLEY, BERRY, 224
COLKER, BETSY, 24
COLKER, WILLIAM, 24
COLLINS, JOHN 268
COMBS, HARRIET, 164
COMBS, NANCY, 183
COMER, AARON, 306
COMER, MARTHA, 319
CON, AGNES, 371
CONDRAY, ISAAC, 355, 357, 358
CONK, POLLY, 49
CONLEY, ABRAM, 268
CONLEY, ELIZABETH, 212
CONLEY, JAMES M., 345
CONLEY, RICHARD, 254, 268
CONLEY, SILAS, 212
CONN, CATHARINE, 14
CONN, ELIZABETH, 21
CONN, LETTY, 171
CONN, NANCY, 205
CONN, ROBERT, 171
CONNELLY, JOHN, 293
CONNER, DANIEL, 254
CONNER, ELIZABETH, 297, 342
CONNER, JAMIMA, 366
CONNER, JOHN M., 254
CONNER, MARY C., 243
CONNER, NANCY, 166
CONNER, POLLY, 183
CONNER, SALLY, 317
CONNER, SAMUEL, 117, 199
CONNER, WILLIAM, 36, 52
CONNER, WILLIAM R., 293
CONWAY, CHARLES, 9, 103, 15,
CONWAY, JAMES, 345
CONWAY, POLLY, 275
COOK, POLLY, 56
COOK, SALLY, 249
COOK, TABBY, 5
COOKE, MARGARET R., 294
COOLEY, GEORGE, 132, 216
COOLEY, JOSIAH, 145
COOLY, VITON, 363
COONTZ, CATHARINE, 233
COONTZ, MARY, 88
COOPER, EBENEZER, 77
COOPER, JOHN, 11
COOPER, JOSEPH, 345
COOPER, MARIA, 291
COOPER, SALLY, 39

COPELAND, ANDREW, 65
COPELAND, ANDREW C., 128
COPELAND, BETSEY, 58
COPELAND, DAVID D., 183
COPELAND, HUGH S., 293
COPELAND, WM., 33
COPLEY, WILLIAM, 212
COPPETT, CHARITY, 285
CORD, ELIZABETH, 214
CORKBUND, BETSY, 429
CORNELIUS, JEPTHA, 27
CORTNEY, WILLIAM, 132
COSBY, RACHEL, 231
COTTRELL, FERIBA, 159
COTTRELL, JOSHUA, 213
COTTRELL, NANCY, 210
COTTRELL, SALLY, 67, 170
COTTRELL, SEMUEL, 254
COTTRELL, THOMAS, 145
COTTRELL, WILLIAM, 282
COUCH, DAVID, 157
COUCH, JANE, 76
COUCH, LOIS, 109
COUCH, POLLY, 108
COUCH, SALLY, 148
COUK, GREENBERRY, 390
COULSON, WILLIAM, 282
COULTER, ALEXANDER, 30
COUNCELL, ANN B., 251
COUNCIL, ELIZABETH, 73, 165
COUNCIL, HOWARD, 165
COUNCIL, ISAAC, 262
COUNCIL, JOHN, 43
+ COUNCIL, NANCY, 106
COUNSEL, PEGGY, 61
COUNSELL, NANCY, 72
COUNSILL, ISAAC, 191
COUNTZ, PEGGY, 160
COURTNEY, ANNY, 106
COURTNEY, JAMES, 307, 319,
365
COURTNEY, JOHN, 157, 213
COURTNEY, JONATHAN, 36
COURTNEY, SAMUEL, 117
COURTNEY, WM. 157
COVENTON, SALLY, 68
COVEY, WM., 30
COVINGTON, BETSEY, 89
COVINGTON, DANIEL, 331
COVINGTON, HIRAM, 199
+ COUNSEL, MARY B., 231

COWAN, BETSY, 210
COWAN, EVELINE, 365
COWAN, JAMES H., 237, 266, 268
COWAN, JANE G., 71
COWAN, JENNY, 39
COWAN, JOHN, 6
COWAN, MARGARET, C., 147
COWAN, MARY E., 156
COWAN, SAM'L. 25
COWAN, WILLIAM WALLACE, 37
COWARD, JOHNY 224
COX, ABRAHAM, 307
COX, ALEXANDER, 66
COX, C., 371
COX, C. C., 391
COX, ELISHA, 236
COX, ELIZABETH, 123
COX, ELIZABETH G., 311
COX, GEORGE, 34
COX, HENRY, 132
COX, JAMES, 52
COX, JANE, 241
COX, JESSE, 60
COX, JOHN, 77, 145
COX, JONATHAN, 118
COX, JOSEPH M., 363
COX, LEAH, 268
COX, LEWIS, 48
COX, MARY, 335
COX, MARY ANN, 222
COX, MILLY, 186
COX, MOSES, 183
COX, MYRA, 371
COX, POLLY, 126, 361
COX, R., 254
COX, RACHEL, 111
COX, RICHARD, 199
COX, SALLY, 149, 248
COX, SAMUEL, 40
COX, THOMAS B., 254, 302, 363
COX, WHITNER, 157
COXE, BETSY, 81
COXE, JOHN, 36
COZART, PATSY ANN, 366
COZBY, ANNE, 95
COZBY, JOHN, 45
CRABB, ANN, 236
CRABB, JOSEPH, 94, 236
CRABB, POLLY, 94
CRAIG, DAVID, 3, 5
CRAIG, ELIZABETH, 29, 253

CRAIG, GILBERT C., 345
CRAIG, JAMES W., 237
CRAIG, JOHN, 260, 261
CRAIG, RACHEL, 327
CRAIG, ROBERT, 19, 237
CRAIG, SALLY, 161
CRAIG, SUSANNAH, 6
CRAIG, THOS., 345
CRAIG, WILLIAM, 331
CRAIGHEAD, ELIZA H., 221
CRAIGHEAD, HANNAH M., 233
CRAIGHEAD, JOHN, 132, 181,
206
CRAIGHEAD, RACHEL, 52
CRAIGHEAD, ROBERT, 33
CRAIGHEAD, T. G., 346,
361, 370
CRAIGHEAD, THOMAS, 33
CRAIGHEAD, THOMAS G., 237
CRAIGHEAD, TINSEY, 294
CRAIGHEAD, WM., 314, 319,
322, 326, 327
CRAIN, BENJIMIN, 30
CRANE, NANCY, 13, 24
CRANE, POLLY, 10
CRANE, REBECCAH, 45
CRANK, ELIZABETH, 236
CRANK, JAMES, 213
CRANK, JESSE, 255
CRANK, LEVINA, 278
CRANK, THOMAS, 132, 213
CRASSAN, WM., 320
CRAWFORD, ADAM, 307
CRAWFORD, ANDREW, 169
CRAWFORD, ARTHUR, 255
CRAWFORD, BARNES, 212, 369
CRAWFORD, EDWIN, 307
CRAWFORD, ELLEN, 278
CRAWFORD, HENRY, 346
CRAWFORD, HUGH, 224
CRAWFORD, J. Y., 219
CRAWFORD, JAMES Y., 207,
210, 215, 218
CRAWFORD, JANE, 8
CRAWFORD, JOSEPH, 22
CRAWFORD, MICAJAH, 363
CRAWFORD, NANCY, 111
CRAWFORD, PEGGY, 33
CRAWFORD, POLLY, 170
CRAWFORD, REBECKA W., 132

CRAWFORD, SALLIE, 242
CRAWFORD, SALLY, 248
CRAWFORD, SIMS, 343, 348
CRAWFORD, THOMAS, 199
CRAWFORD, W. W. 337
CRAWFORD, WILLIAM, 31, 183
CRAWFORD, WM. H., 307
CREELY, ISBEL, 32
CRESWELL, POLLY, 148
CREVAT, MOSES, 255
CREW, BETSY, 123
CREW, PLEASANT, 118, 193, 259
331
CREW, SALLY, 148
CREW, SARAH ANN, 306
CREWS, ARCHIBALD, 346
CREWS, DAVID, 169
CREWS, GIDEON, 287
CREWS, NANCY, 148, 167
CREWS, ROBERT, 169
CREWS, WALTER, 145
CREWSE, WILLIAM, 64, 199
CRIPPEN, JAMES, 45, 321, 330,
332, 335, 358
CRIPPEN, JOHN, 48
CRIPPEN, MARGARET, 40
CRIPPEN, WILLIAM, 266
CRIPPENS, WM. P., 307
CRIPPIN, LEONA, 309
CRISMAN, ISAAC JR., 199
CRISTENBERRY, GREEN, 241
CRONK, ELIZABETH, 52
CROSS, ELIZABETH, 334
CROW, NANCY, 57
CROW, THOMAS, 237
CROWDER, POLLY, 58
CROZIER, C. W., 311
CROZIER, E. JANE, 282
CROZIER, ELIZABETH, 334
CROZIER, ELIZABETH JANE, 282
CROZIER, H. G., 212
CROZIER, JOHN, 22
CROZEER, MARGARET B., 152
CRUISE, SARAH ANN, 306
CRUIZE, JOHN, 85
CRUIZE, HARDEMAN, 40
CRUIZE, HARDIMAN, 42
CRUIZE, RUTHY, 154
CRUMBLEY, MARY, 52
CRUSE, EDWARD, 66
CRUSE, GILBERT, 85

CRUSE, JAMES, 85
CRUSE, LUCY, 338
CRUSE, WALTER, 118
CRUSE, WILLIAM, 66
CRUSH, JOHN, 269
CRUSH, SUSAN, 244
CRUTCHFIELD, CLARISSA, 242
CRUZE, ELISON, 48, 73
CRUZE, MINERVA, 366
CRUZE, NANCY, 148
CULLEN, JNO. M., 52
CULSON, SARAH, 333
CULTON, NANCY, 143
CUMMING, JAMES, 232
CUMMINGS, SARAH, 332, 347
CUMMINGS, URIAH, 293
CUMMINS, MARY, 318
CUMMINS, URIAH, 318
CUMSTOCK, JASPER W., 132
CUNDIFF, THOMAS, 375
CUNNINGHAM, ANDREW, 183, 371
CUNNINGHAM, BETSY, 112
CUNNINGHAM, DAVID, 18
CUNNINGHAM, FRANCIS, 18
CUNNINGHAM, ISAAC, 2
CUNNINGHAM, J., 160, 161,
190, 207, 221, 225
CUNNINGHAM, JAMES, 3, 6,
169, 207, 233
CUNNINGHAM, JANE, 18, 176, 216
CUNNINGHAM, JESSE, 190, 213,
225, 228, 290, 277
CUNNINGHAM, JOHN, 53, 225, 346
CUNNINGHAM, MARNEN, 208
CUNNINGHAM, MOSES, 7, 183
CUNNINGHAM, NANCY, 58
CUNNINGHAM, NELLY, 290
CUNNINGHAM, O. F., 365
CUNNINGHAM, POLLY, 44, 95
CUNNINGHAM, PAUL, 183, 242
CUNNINGHAM, REBECCA, 371
CUNNINGHAM, SAMUEL, 145, 146
176 175
CUNNINGHAM, SAMUEL H., 38 37
CUNNINGHAM, SAMUEL N., 34
CUNNINGHAM, TIMOTHY, 363
CUNNINGHAM, WILLIAM, 9
CURD, JANE MOORE, 209
CURRIER, ADAM, 363
CURRIER, BETSY, 258
CURRIER, BETSY, 258
CURRIER, JAMES, 38, 307
CURRIER, MARGARET, 228
CURRIER, WILLIAM, 38
CURTAIN, SALLY, 15
CUSICK, JOSEPH, 9
CUTHBERTSON, WILLIAM B., 331
CUZZART, SARAH, 209

D

DABNEY, ABRAM, 293
DAIL, ABNER, 70
DAIL, JOHN, 53
DALE, ABNER, 66, 106
DALE, ALEXANDER, 11, 12
DALE, JAMES, 94
DALE, PEGGY, 12
DAMEWOOD, BARBARA, 93
DAMEWOOD, FANNY, 332
DAMEWOOD, HANNAH, 111, 115
DAMEWOOD, ISAAC, 94
DAMEWOOD, JANE, 333
DAMEWOOD, LAVISTA, 307
DAMEWOOD, POLLY, 200
DAMEWOOD, SUSAN, 328
DANIEL, EPHRAIM, 346
DANIEL, EPHRAIM, 320
DANIEL, MARTHA, 109
DANNEL, SALLY, 218
DARDIS, CHARLOTTE, 197, 198
DARDIS, JAMES, 243
DARDIS, LUCY, 212
DARDIS, MARGARET, 263
DARDIS, MARY, 140
DAVENPORT, JOSEPH, 313
DAVENPORT, THOMAS H., 255, 341
DAVID, MICHAEL, 282
DAVIDSON, MARTHA, 27
DAVIDSON, ROBERT, 255
DAVIDSON, SAMUEL, 27, 331
DAVIS, ALEXANDER, 106, 169, 255
DAVIS, ANN A., 289
DAVIS, BETSY, 150, 353
DAVIS, CATHERINE, 19, 20, 350,
354
DAVIS, CHARLES, 71, 258
DAVIS, CLIBORNE, 307
DAVIS, DAVID, 77
DAVIS, E. R., 235, 238, 243

DAVIS, EDMOND, 169
DAVIS, EDMUND, 255
DAVIS, EDWARD, 183
DAVIS, EDWARD R., 227,
229, 239, 252, 260,
271, 283
DAVIS, ELIZA JANE, 293
DAVIS, FRANCIS, 11
DAVIS, GEORGE, 71, 97
DAVIS, HENRY, 200
DAVIS, JAMES, 18, 39,
169, 320
DAVIS, JAMES, L., 293
DAVIS, JANE W., 340
DAVIS, JESSE, 94, 207
DAVIS, JOHN, 23, 29,
132, 133, 145,
334, 354
DAVIS, JOHN M., 183
DAVIS, JOHN R., 308, 360
DAVIS, JOHN S., 56
DAVIS, LACKY, 158
DAVIS, LEWIS, 78
DAVIS, LEVY, 48
DAVIS, MARGARET, 7
DAVIS, MARY, 9
DAVIS, MICHAEL, 89, 266
273, 281, 295, 305
306, 308, 316, 317,
321, 324, 327, 330,
331, 340
DAVIS, NANCY, 139, 312
DAVIS, NATHANIEL, 11
DAVIS, P., 290
DAVIS, POLLY, 169, 200
DAVIS, REBECCA, 18
DAVIS, ROBERT, 60, 118
DAVIS, SALLY, 51, 161,
354
DAVIS, SALLY H., 122
DAVIS, SAMUEL, 18
DAVIS, SARAH C., 321
DAVIS, SOPHIA, 76
DAVIS, SUSAN, 357
DAVIS, SUSANA, 63
DAVIS, THOMAS, 75
DAVIS, TEMPERANCE, 90
DAVIS, WILLIAM, 18, 169,
229, 294
DAVISON, WILLIAM, 21
DAWDY, HOWELL, 11
DAWDY, JOHN, 11
DAWSON, JOHN, 329
DAY, JOHN, 55
DAY, STEPHEN, 255
DEADRICK, DAVID, 282
DEADERICK, DAVID A., 282
DEARMON, ELIZABETH, 216
DEARMOND, CYNTHIA, 71
DEARMOND, D. F., 344
DEARMOND, ESTHER, T., 183
DEARMOND, JOHN, 18, 37, 55,
183, 265
DEARMOND, MATILDA, 245
DEARMOND, RICHARD J., 225
DEARMOND, WILLIAM, 36, 320
DEBUSK, DAVID B., 146
DEFRIESE, JNO. M., 346
DEHART, ANDREW, 200
DELANEY, ELIZABETH, 62
DELANEY, HYRAM F., 237
DELANY, JESSE, 45
DENNIS, WILLIAM, 118
DESAIN, ELISHA, 118
DESUN, ELISHA, 146
DEVAULT, DAVID, 178
DEVAULT, MARGARET, 334
DEWITT, SOPHIA, 60
DIAL, BETSEY, 40
DICK, HENRY, 346
DICK, JACOB, 213
DICKENSON, LUCINDA, 268
DICKEY, DAVID D., 255
DICKEY, JAMES M., 94
DICKEY, JANE H., 296
DICKEY S., 276, 277, 279,
317, 357
DICKEY, SAMUEL, 279, 331, 351
DICKEY, THOMAS, 231
DOAK, MARY, 4
DOBBINS, CORNELIUS, 71
DOBBINS, HENDERSON, 375
DOBBINS, NANCY, 375
DICKSON, ANN, 4
DICKSON, GEORGE, 331
DICKSON, JOHN, 133
DICKSON, STEPHEN, 331
DICKSON, THOMAS, 3
DIDDEP, THOMAS, P., 258
DIGS, JOHN, 363

DIMMIT, DIANNA, 38
DIMMIT, SUSANNAH, 37
DIMMITT, NANCY, 53
DIXON, JAMES, 123, 127, 144
DODD, ELIZABETH, 61
DODD, JAMES, 33
DODD, JOHN, 61
DODD, RICHARD, 61
DODD, WILLIAM, 22
DODD, WILLIS, 169
DODSON, MARGARET, 70
DODSON, NANCY, 25
DODSON, THOMAS, 22
DON CARLOS, ACHILLIS, 200
DONALD, MATTHEW B., 308
DONNELL, GEORGE, 228, 237, 243
DOOLIN, ARCHIBALD, 282
DORAN, BETSY, 253
DORAN, JOSEPH, 237
DORAN, SARAH, 270
DORSE, ELIZABETH, 285
DORSE, MARY, 319
DOSS, WILLIAM, 357
DOTSON, J. M., 294
DOUGHERTY, JOHN, 150
DOUGHERTY, SARAH, 53
DOUGHTY, BENJAMIN, 193
DOUGHTY, REUBEN, 294
DOUGLAS, PHEBE, 108
DOUGLAS, POLLY, 94
DOUGLAS, WM., 94
DOUGLASS, ALEXANDER, 193
DOUGLASS, ELIZABETH, 142
DOUGLASS, FANNY, 23
DOUGLASS, ISABELLA D., 308
DOUGLASS, JNO., 346, 379, 375
DOUGLASS, MARY, 56, 119
DOUGLASS, NANCY, 57
DOUGLASS, PEGGY ANNE, 264
DOUGLASS, SARAH L., 336
DOUGLASS, THOMAS, 85
DOUGLASS, WILLIAM, 3
DOUTY, MARY ANN, 265
DOVE, ANNE, 222
DOVE, ELIZABETH, 140
DOVE, JAMES, 200
DOWY ANNE, 211
DOWEL, ELIJAH, 105
DOWEL, MELINDA, 105
DOWELL, BETSY, 196
DOWELL, COLEBY, 78
DOWELL, ELIZA, 162
DOWELL, FRANCES, 48
DOWELL, NANCY, 116
DOWELL, POLLY, 309
DOWELL, SALLY, 245
DOWELL, TANDY, 308
DOWLEN, WILLIAM, 260
DOWLER, MARY, 123
DOWLER, PEGGY, 81
DOWLER, WILLIAM, 269
DOWLIN, JAMES, 225
DOYALL, ISAAC, 66
DOYLE, BETSY, 158
DOYLE, CATHERINE, 28
DOYLE, DAVID, 179
DOYLE, ISAAC, 66, 170, 219
DOYLE, JAMES P., 308
DOYLE, JOHN, 184, 321
DOYLE, REBECCA JANE, 317
DOYLE, SARAH, 60
DOYLE, WILLIAM, 184
DOZIER, DANIEL, 66
DOZIER, DENNIS, 373
DOZIER, NANCY, 49
DOZIER, PEGGY, 43
DOZIER, PETER, 146
DRAIN, JOHN, 184, 219
DRAKE, JACOB, 32
DRAKE, JOHN, 332
DRAPER, FRANCIS, 266
DRAPER, RUTH, 244
DRAPER, SOLOMON, 225
DUDLEY, BETSY, 303
DUDLEY, F. N. B., 299
DUDLEY, FRANCIS N. B., 255, 346
DUDLEY, JULIA A. M., 267
DUERRETT, EVERETT, 345
DUFFIELD, JAMES, 106
DUNCAN, BENJAMIN, 237
DUNCAN, NANCY, 289
DUNCAN, ROSANAH, 193
DUNHAM, THOMAS, 85
DUNHAM, WM., 152
DUNLAP, ANDERSON, 184
DUNLAP, ANNE A., 138

DUNLAP, GEORGE, 194
DUNLAP, JAMES, 61, 362, 364, 374
DUNLAP, MARY, 89
DUNLAP, MOSES, 18
DUNLAP, NANCY, 60
DUNLAP, NATHANIEL, 193
DUNLAP, R. G., 198
DUNLAP, SALLY, 275
DUNLAP, WILLIAM, 11, 118, 213, 342, 361, 362
DUNN, ANN, 257
DUNN, GEORGE J. G., 321, 332
DUNN, ISABEL, 213
DUNN, ISABELLA, 354
DUNN, JOHN, 200
DUNN, MALINDA, 354
DUNN, MARY, 101, 301
DUNN, SUSAN, 296
DUNN, WILLIAM, 331, 332, 347
DUNN, WILLIAM C., 332
DUNNEKEE, RODY, 50
DUNNINGTON, GUSTINE, 55
DURAN, MARY ANN, 311
DURHAM, SALLY, 166
DYER, JAMES, 96
DYER, JOEL, 269
DYER, WILLIAM, 225
DYER, WILLIAM P., 334
DYKE, JOEL, 269
DYKES, ABNER, 337
DYKES, HARRIETT, 263

E

EAGLETON, E. M., 222
EAGLETON, ELIJAH M., 223, 237, 246, 247, 255
EAGLETON, WILLIAM, 218, 228, 235, 247
EARLEY, MARY, 299
EARLY, ALEXANDER, 94
EARLY, BENJAMIN, 146
EARLY, WILLIAM, 200
EASTERLY, POLLY, 314
EATON, CAMPBELL, 71
EATON, WILLIAM, 78
EBLEN, ELIZA, 25
EBLEN, SAMUEL, 25
EBLIN, SAMUEL, 66
EBLIN, W., 66
EDDINGTON, ELIZA, 354
EDDINGTON, HANNAH, 51
EDDINGTON, JAMES H., 332
EDDINGTON, LOTTIE, 362
EDDINGTON, LOTTY, 369
EDDINGTON, NICHOLAS, 332
EDDINGTON, POLLY, 51
EDDY, GEORGE, 269
EDINGTON, HOLSTON, 256
EDINGTON ISABELLA, 78
EDINGTON, JAMES H., 184, 236, 298
EDINGTON, JANE, 171
EDINGTON, JEMIMA, 123
EDINGTON, JOHN, 219
EDINGTON, LUCINDA, 70
EDINGTON, PHILIP, 71
EDMISTON, BETSY, 228
EDMONDS, WM. F., 346
EDMONDSON, BURNATTA, 270
EDMONDSON, ISAAC, 238, 269
EDMONDSON, JAMES, 238
EDMONDSON, JOHN, 85
EDMONDSON, JOHN B., 170
EDMONDSON, JOHN D., 280
EDMONDSON, LEWIS, 200
EDMONDSON, REBECKA, 269
EDMONDSON, SAMUEL, 225
EDMONDSON, SUSAN, 203, 217
EDMONSON, FRANCIS, 238
EDMONSON, PEGGY, 61
EDMONSON, SAM'L, 146
EDMONSON, STERLING, 85
EDMONSON, WILLIAM, 238
EDMUNDSON, SAMUEL, 67
EDWARDS, JAMES, 200
EDWARDS, MACMY, 82
EDWARDS, MARONY, 57
EDWARDS, SARAH, 3
ELDER, A. W., 269, 285
ELDRIDGE, JESSE, 9
ELDRIDGE, NATHANIEL, 18
ELDRIDGE, STEPHEN, 170
ELDRIGE, JOHN, 9
ELIESON, JOHN O., 347

ELKIN, DAVID, 298
ELKINS, ANNY, 340
ELKINS, JOSEPH, 94
ELKINS, WM., 184
ELLEDGE, ISAAC, 364
ELLIOTT, ANNA, 162
ELLIOTT, HANNAH, 45
ELLIOTT, ISAAC, 170
ELLIOTT, JOHN, 201
ELLIOTT, LUCINDA, 86
ELLIOTT, PATSY, 275
ELLIOTT, POLLY, 89
ELLIOTT, SALLY, 78
ELLIOTT, SAMUEL, 85
ELLIOT, WILLIAM, 38, 347
ELLIOTT, WILLIAM JOHN, 66
ELLIS, FRANCIS, 79
ELLIS, JOHN, 85
ELLIS, MARGARET, 255
ELLIS, NANCY, 49
ELLISON, BETSY, 131
ELLISON, JOHN C., 210
ELLISON, MALINDA, 226
ELSEY, JOSEPH, 347
EMMETT, REUBEN, 273, 290
EMBREE, LEWIS, 214
EMMERSON, ANNE M., 89
EMMETT, CATY, 200
ENGLAND, AARON, 35
ENGLAND, ALFRED, 133
ENGLAND, BETSY, 191
ENGLAND, ELIJAH, 66
ENGLAND, FRANCES, 232, 233
ENGLAND, J. C., 361, 369, 374
ENGLAND, JAMES C., 343, 362, 375
ENGLAND, JOHN, 66, 78, 269
ENGLAND, MARY, 29
ENGLISH, GEORGE W., 308
ENGLISH, JULIAN, 99
EPPES, DRUSILLA, 103
EPPES, THOMAS A., 364
EPPS, MARTHA, 198
EPPS, POLLY, 49, 201
EPPS, SARAH, 277
ERVIN, WILLIAM, 214
ERWIN, JAMES, 225
ERWIN, NATHANIEL, 283
ETTER, GEORGE, 61
EVANS, ANNE, 87
EVANS, DAVID, 7
EVANS, HANNAH, 16
EVANS, HARRIS, 78
EVANS, HENRY, 289, 294
EVANS, JANE, 131, 264
EVANS, JOSEPH, 72, 118
EVANS, MARTHA C., 373
EVANS, MARY, 119
EVANS, REBECCA, 39, 315
EVANS, ROBERT C., 364
EVANS, SAMUEL, 118
EVANS, SUSAN, 270
EVANS, WILLIAM, 72, 119
EVERETT, AQUILLA, 133
EVERETT, BYRD, F., 238
EVERETT, CATHARINE, 288
EVERETT D., 346, 359, 365, 373
EVERETT, DUERRETT, 349
EVERETT, DUERRETT, 367
EVERETT, JOHN C., 184
EVERETT, RACHEL, 127
EVERETT, RALPH, 201
EVERETT, SYLVINUS, 119
EVERETT, WILLIAM, 289
EVERETT, WM. C., 95
EVERETTS, THEO. 61
EVRETT, MAHALA, 74
EWING, JOHN, 269
EWING, RACHEL, 2
EWING, SAMUEL, 119
EZEL, BYRD, 225
EZELL, SALLY, 367

F

FADGETT, ELIJAH, 283
FAIRCHILD, SALLY, 168
FAIRCHILD, KITTY, 72
FALKNER, MAHALY, 322, 323
FALKNER, WILLIAM, 78
FANEN, LUCY, 50
FANNEN, ANNE, 102
FANNON, JANE, 119
FARGUSON, BENJAMIN, 201
FARGUSON, PEGGY, 304
FARGUSON, WILLIAM, 170

FARMER, AGNES, 27
FARMER, ANN, 258
FARMER, HENRY, 23
FARMER, JOHN, 23
FARMER, JUDITH, 99
FARMER, REBECCAH, 28
FARMER, SARAH, 23
FARMON, THOMAS, 106
FARQUHARSON, NANCY, 237
FARR, JAMES, 211
FARR, SELINA, 243
FAUNHULART, MALINDA, 26
FAY, NICHOLAS, 214
FELTS, EMELINE, 296
FELTS, MATILDA, 322
FERGUSON, ANDREW, 332
FERGUSON, BENJAMIN, 326, 328
FERGUSON, BETSY, 99, 120, 294
FERGUSON, CATHARINE, 277
FERGUSON, ELIZABETH, 284
FERGUSON, JAMES, 7
FERGUSON, JOEL, 61
FERGUSON, MARY, 250
FERGUSON, MINT, 95
FERGUSON, OBEDIENT, 280
FERGUSON, REBECCA, 276
FERGUSON, ROBERT, 85
FERGUSON, SALLY, 212
FERGUSON, SAMUEL, 280, 364
FERGUSON, STEPHEN, 94
FERGUSON, SUSAN, 94
FERGUSON, WILLIAM, 66, 270
FERMAULT, JOHN, 3
FERMAULT, THOMAS, 18
FERRELL, ENOCH, 29
FERRILL, ELIZABETH, 33
FERRIS, JNO., 37, 40
FIELDS, WILLIAM, JR., 306
FIKE, HENLAND, 119
FINE, PETER, 86
FINGER, JOHN, 350
FINK, GEORGE, 294
FINLEY, JOHN, 3, 146, 190, 238
FISHER, ARCHIBALD, 11
FISHER, DANIEL, 55
FISHER, EMISLEY, 347
FISHER, GEORGE, 347
FISHER, HANNAH, 19
FISHER, JANE, 144
FISHER, NOAH, 205
FISHER, REBECCA, 292
FISHER, SALLY, 158. 229. 242
FITS, RACHEL, 152
FITZGERALD, GEO. W., 347
FITZGERALD, JNO., 347
FLAKNER, MATILDA, 186
FLANNAGAN, JEAN, 34, 37
FLEMING, D., 292, 301, 306, 309, 311
FLEMING, DAVID, 61
FLEMING, G., 305
FLEMING, JOHN H., 256
FLEMING, M. B., 289
FLEMING, POLLY, 55, 63
FLEMING, R. F. G., 259, 299
FLEMING, R. G., 228
FLEMING, ROBERT F. G., 226
FLEMING, SAMUEL, 23, 61, 134, 136, 177, 188, 209, 212, 214, 231, 233, 236, 242, 257, 260, 269, 273, 275, 277, 281, 282, 288, 299, 301
FLEMING, THOMAS W., 364
FLEMING, WASHINGTON L., 214
FLEMING, WASHINGTON S., 226
FLENAKIN, JOHN, 67
FLENNIKEN, J. W., 170
FLENNIKEN, JNO., 170
+ FLENNIKEN, SAMUEL, 197, 212, 214, 219, 223, 225
FLENNIKEN, SARAH, 241
FLESHART, FRANCIS, 38
FLESHART, SUSAN, 251
FLINN, HEZEKIAH, 12
FLOOD, DANIEL, 298
FLOWERS, THOMAS, 67
FLOYD, JESSE, 106
FORD, ANNE, 104
FORD, BENJAMIN, 106
FORD, BOZE, 300
FORD, CHARLES, 201
FORD, FREDERICK, 283
FORD, JACOB, 133
FORD, JAMES, 206
FORD, JAMES, P., 283
FORD, JAMES V., 283
FORD, JOSEPH M., 273
FORD, JUDY, 63
FORD, M. M., 367

+ FLENNIKEN, POLLY, 37

FORD, MARY, 183, 267
FORD, POLLY, 55, 143
FORD, POLLY ANN, 256
FORD, REBECKA, 337
FORD, SALLY, 227, 323
FORD, WILLIAM, 364
FORGEY, NANCY, 246
FORGUSON, BERSHEBA, 120
FORGUSON, LUCINDA, 242
FORGUSON, MARY, 151, 196
FORGUSON, PATSY, 120
FORGUSON, STEPHEN, 119
FORGUSON, WILLIE C., 214
FORKNER, ELIZABETH, 84
FORKNER, POLLY, 159
FORKNER, SUSAN, 284
FORMAN, JOHN, 119
FORMWALT, ADAM, 333, 343, 364
FORMWATT, ADAM R., 369
FORMWALT, CATHARINE, 159
FORMWALT, EVE, 184
FORMWALT, JOHN H., 406
FORMWALT, MARGARET, 163
FORREST, RICHARD, 12
FORTNER, DAVID, 321, 348
FORTNER, EZEKIEL, 308
FORTNER, FRANKY, 348
FORTNER, GEORGE, 106
FORTNER, JOHN, 348
FORTNER, WILLIAM, 294
FOSTER, ALEXANDER, 23
FOSTER, ANNY, 291
FOSTER, ISAAC, 158
FOSTER, JOHN, 158
FOSTER, PATSY, 107
FOSTER, STEPHEN, 255, 259, 283
FOSTER, SUSANNAH, 403
FOURNIER, N. H. S., 25
FOUST, ABRAM, 284, 294
FOUST, AMANDA, 355
FOUST, BARBARA, 28
FOUST, CATHARINE, 141, 201
FOUST, CHRISTOPHER, 12
FOUST, DANIEL, 226, 256
FOUST, DAVID, 184, 287
FOUST, ELIZABETH, 284
FOUST, HENRY, 348
FOUST, JACOB, 185, 214
FOUST, JOHN, 12, 185, 214, 226, 239, 261, 348
FOUST, LEWIS, 226, 343
FOUST, MARY ANN, 111
FOUST, PHILIP, 201
FOUST, POLLY, 256
FOUST, SARAH, 336
FOUST, SARAH R., 287
FOUSTE, MARY ANNE, 112
FOUTT, DANIEL D., 170
FOWLER, RICHARD, 81
FOWLER, SALLY, 81
FOX, ENOCH, 12
FRAKER, GEORGE, 348
FRAKER, MARGARET, 156
FRAKER, MICHAEL, 270
FRANCIS, MALINDA J., 304
FRANKLIN, BETSY, 182
FRANKLIN, JOHN, 364
FRANKLIN, NANCY, 360
FRANKLIN, PHEBE ANN, 360
FRANKLIN, POLLY, 190
FRANKLIN, SALLY, 480
FRANKLIN, SAMUEL, 348
FRANKLIN, THOS., 185
FRANKLIN, WILLIAM, 55
FRAZIER, BERIAH, 69, 86, 98
FRAZIER, JULIAN, 36, 219
FRAZIER, NANCY, 10, 37
FRAZIER, SAMUEL, 159, 294
FRAZIER, SAMUEL W., 332
FRAZIER, THOMAS, 36, 278, 289, 293, 300, 317, 340, 343
FRAZIER, WILLIAM, 78
FRAZIER, WILLIAM C., 294
FRAZIER, WILLIAM G., 294
FREELLS, THOMAS, 18
FREEMAN, JOSHUA, 61, 144
FRENCH, FREDERICK, 230
FRENCH, GEORGE, 106
FRENCH, KATY, 108
FRENCH, MARY, 257
FRENCH, MARY ANN, 310
FRENCH, PETER JR., 226
FRISBEY, POLLY, 232
FRISBY, JANE, 224
FRISTO, MARKHAM, 67
FRISTOE, MARY ANN 54
FRISTOE, ROBERT, 55, 123
FRISTOE, SARAH, 73
FRITS, ISAAC, 348
FROST, EDWARD, 24
FROST, FRANCES, 14
FROST, JOEL, 158
FROST, JOHN, 14, 149
FROST, JONAS, 48
FROST, MARY, 313
FROST, MCC., 77
FROST, PATSY, 249
FROST, PHOEBE, 16
FROST, POLLY, 290
FROST, SAM, 107
FROST, SUSAN, 373
FROST, THOMAS, 16, 23, 214, 303
FRY, NANCY, 113
FRY, NEWEL C., 332
FRY, NICHOLAS, 146, 214
FRY, RHODES, 158
FRYAR, MARTHA, 38
FRYAR, WILLIAM, 38
FRYE, NICHOLAS, 326
FRYOR, JAMES, 86
FRYOR, WM., 62
FULLER, MARY, 19
FULSHER, FRANCIS, 31
FULTON, HUGH, 308
FULTON, THOMAS, 147
FULTON, WM., 119
FURGASON, JAMES, 7
FUTERELL, ETHELDRED, 364
FUTHY, EMELIN, 292
FUTRIL, ETHELDRED, 365

G

GADDIS, MARGARET, 369
GAILEY, MOSES, 61
GAINES, M. M. 352, 365, 371,
GAINES, MAT. M., 269, 270, 287
GAINS, ARMSTRONG, 283
GAINS, NANCY, 361
GAINS, ROBERT, 95
GALBRAITH, JAMES, 146
GALBRAITH, JOHN, 78
GALBREATH, JOSEPH, 55, 134
GALBREATH, JOSEPH B., 133

GALBREATH, MARY ANN, 289
GALBREATH, THOMAS, 125
GALESPIE, POLLY, 33
GALLAHER, JAS. H., 167
GALLAHER, JOHN, 12
GALLAHER, NANCY, 102
GALLAHER, R., 332
GALLAHER, REBECCA, 56
GALLAHER, ROBERT, 257
GALLAHER, SARAH, 271
GALLAHER, THOMAS, 241, 258, 280
GALLAHER, WILLIAM, 348
GALLAWAY, MARY, 75
GALLIHAN, PRISCILLA, 87
GALLIHER, ALEXANDER, 134
GALLIHER, BETSY, 142
GALLIHER, ELIZABETH, 161
GALLIHER, GEORGE, 271
GALLIHER, MARY ANN, 118
GALLIHER, PEGGY, 192
GALLIHORN, PATIENCE, 84
GALLOWAY, CHARLES, 49
GALLOWAY, JAMES, 42
GALLOWAY, JESSE, 86
GALLOWAY, JOSEPH, 55
GAMBLE, BETSEY, 55
GAMBLE, J. N., 73, 74, 91
GAMBLE, JEAN, 8
GAMBLE, JNO., 39, 40
GAMBLE, JNO. A., 37, 38, 39, 42, 43, 44, 45, 46, 47
GAMBLE, JNO. H., 40
GAMBLE, JNO. M., 56
GAMBLE, JOHN N., 48, 49, 50, 51 52, 56, 57, 59, 62, 63, 64, 65, 67, 82, 323
GAMBLE, NANCY, 335
GAMBLE, REBECCAH, 60
GAMBLE, ROBERT, 332
GAMBLE, WILLIAM, 78
GAMMON, ALICE, 77
GAMMON, ANNE, 10
GAMMON, BETSEY, 52
GAMMON, DICEY, 68
GAMMON, DOZIER, 95
GAMMON, HARRIS, 295
GAMMON, HENRY, JR., 72
GAMMON, LEWIS, 115
GAMMON, MARTHA, 293
GAMMON, SALLY, 97
GAMMON, TABITHA EMERINE, 286
GARDENER, ALICE, 129
GARDENHIRE, WILLIAM, 9
GARDINER, JOHN, 89

GARDNER, CATHERINE, 180
GARDNER, ELIZABETH, 128
GARDNER, JOHN H. R. G., 270
GARNER, ABNER, 79
GARNER, ELIZA, 128
GARNER, JOHN, 49, 77, 265, 281, 283, 316
GARNER, JOHN B., 283
GARRETT, CHRISTIAN, 102
GARRETT, REUBEN, 348
GARRICK, ELIZABETH, 101
GARRISON, JOHN, 79
GASPERSON, BETSY, 207
GASS, J. H., 305, 309
GASS, JAMES H., 240, 296, 317, 336, 346, 352
GASS, JOHN, 122, 123, 126, 130, 132, 161, 166, 172, 174, 175, 176, 180, 183, 186, 194
GASTON, THOMAS, 86
GATEWOOD, IGNATIUS, 72
GAULT, CHRISTINA, 142
GAULT, JOHN, 185
GAULT, LETTY, 238
GAULT, MARY, 335
GAULT, RHODA, 248
GAULT, THOMAS, 239
GEAR, JOHN, 64
GEDION, POLLY, 28
GENTRY, AARON, 308
GENTRY, BETSY, 64
GENTRY, ELEANOR, 174
GENTRY, ELIZABETH, 219
GENTRY, ISAAC, 107, 262
GENTRY, JAMES O., 372
GENTRY, JAMES OVERTON, 215
GENTRY, JOHN T., 185
GENTRY, MARGARET R., 309
GENTRY, MARTIN, 95, 138
GENTRY, RACHEL, 138
GEORGE, EDGAR, 187
GEORGE, ELIZA, 255
GEORGE, ELIZABETH, 65
GEORGE, JESSE, 201
GEORGE, JOSIAH, 309
GEORGE, MARY, 60
GEORGE, NANCY, 213
GEORGE, PARNICK, 119
GEORGE, SAMUEL, 248, 333
GEORGE, SOLOMON, 33
GEORGE, STEPHEN, 255, 270
GEORGE, SUSANNAH, 119, 348
GEORGE, TRAVIS, 61, 134, 324
GERAN, SOLOMON, 13
GEREN, CELIA, 256
GEREN, HIRAM, 201
GEREN, LUCINDA, 248
GERON, ISAAC, 95
GIBBS, DANIEL, 161, 171, 172, 321
GIBBS, DAVID, 295
GIBBS, ELIZABETH, 191, 310
GIBBS, GEORGE, 33
GIBBS, GEORGE W., 284
GIBBS, JOHN, 12, 27, 33, 119, 328, 348
GIBBS, JOHN H., 284
GIBBS, KATY, 100
GIBBS, MARY, 140, 158
GIBBS, NICHOLAS, 169, 201, 321, 349, 200
GIBBS, P., 63
GIBBS, PATSY, 124
GIBBS, REBECCA, 147, 295
GIBBS, SARAH, 112, 259, 284
GIBBS, WILLIAM D., 284, 295
GIBBS, WM. S., 321
GIBSON, BEDA, 228
GIBSON, BETSY, 244
GIBSON, ESTHER, 34
GIBSON, FANNY, 232
GIBSON, HANNA, 260
GIBSON, JOHN, 256
GIBSON, THOMAS, 215, 218
GIDDENS, BENJAMIN H., 256
GIDDENS, RANDOLPH, 47
GIDDEON, CATY, 227
GIDDIAN, NANCY, 59
GIDEON, POLLY, 28
GIDEON, SARAH, 245
GIER, BENJAMIN, 67
GIFFEN, ELIZA JANE, 334
GIFFEN, JANE, 350
GIFFIN, JEFFERSON, 320
GIFFIN, MELINDA, 367
GILBREATH, MARY J., 374
GILBREATH, THOMAS, 19

GILBREATH, WILLIAM, 239
GILL, HARRIET, 211
GILL, SAMUEL, 309
GILLALAND, SARAH, 9
GILLAM, PATSY, 53
GILLAM, WINNEFORD, 13
GILLESPIE, ABRAHAM, 134, 176
GILLESPIE, ANN, 73, 176
GILLESPIE, ANNE, 5, 6
GILLESPIE, ELIZA, 7
GILLESPIE, ELIZABETH, 373
GILLESPIE, ISAAC, 79
GILLESPIE, ISABELLA, 78
GILLESPIE, JANE, 76
GILLESPIE, JENNY, 6
GILLESPIE, MARGARET, 64
GILLESPIE, MARK, 373
GILLESPIE, MARTHA, 217
GILLESPIE, POLLY, 6, 95
GILLESPIE, ROBERT, 120
GILLESPIE, SALLY, 48, 195
GILLESPIE, SUSANNAH, 7
GILLESPIE, THOMAS, 215
GILLESPIE, WILLIAM, 134
GILLIAM, ELIZABETH, 8
GILLIAM, POLLY, 159
GILLILAND, MARY, 9
GILLIM, POLLY, 36
GILLISPY, MARK, 349
GILLUM, ANNA, 343
GILLUM, WINNEFRED, 270
GILMORE, ELEANOR, 90
GILMORE, JAMES, 120
GILMORE, JOHN, 120
GILMORE, THOMAS, 79
GILSTRAP, ISAAC, 158
GINN, JEPTHA, 321
GIRON, JOSEPH, 45
GIVENS, JAMES, 53
GIVENS, REBECKAH, 14
GIVENS, SAMUEL, 37
GIVENS, SOPHIA ANNE PATTERSON, 257
GIVENS, WILLIAM T., 56
GLASS, DAVID, 270
GLASS, HARVEY, 120
GLASS, LEWIS, 120
GLASS, NANCY, 265
GOADUS, MARY, 36
GODDARD, BETSY, 76
GODDARD, CATHARINE, 324
GODDARD, HARRIET C., 305
GODDARD, JOHN, 134, 309
GODDARD, NANCY, 365
GODDARD, SAMUEL M., 333
GODDARD, THORNTON, 95
GODDARD, WILLIAM, 79, 134, 354, 357
GODFREY, JAMES, 236
GODFREY, JOHN, 321
GOINGS, NANCY, 361
GOINS, MALVINA, 329
GOLDEN, NANCY, 31, 41
GOLDEN, WILLIAM, 333
GOLDING, NANCY, 18
GOLDON, MARY, 365
GOLDSON, WILLIAM, 365
GOLLIHER, MELINDA, 294
GOLLIWAY, MALINDA, 14
GOOD, GIMERL, 239
GOOD, MARY, 4
GOODIN, RICHARD, 2
GOODING, JAMES, 86
GOODMAN, JOSEPH, 226
GOODMAN, LYNCH B., 215
GOODMAN, POLLY, 164
GOODRUM, PATSY, 93
GOODSON, JOSEPH, 32
GORDON, MARY, 365
GORDON, ROBERT, 284
GOSS, JAMES H., 240
GOSS, JOHN, 77
GOSSET, JOEL, 215
GOSSETT, POLLY, 305
GOULSTON, JOHN, 3
GOUND, JOHN, 120
GOUNDS, ELIZA R., 336
GOUNDS, NELLY, 149
GOWER, REBECKAH, 26
GRADY, BURREL, 69
GRADY, JOHN, 270
GRAHAM, ASA, 299
GRAHAM, LENORA, 282
GRAHAM, POLLY, 42
GRAHAM, RACHEL, 235, 256
GRAMMER, HENRY, 226
GRAMMER, JAMES, 226
GRANNON, LEWIS, 372
GRANT, TEMPERANCE, 68

GRANTHAM, JOHN, 67
GRAVES, CATHARINE, 204
GRAVES, CLARISSA, 320
GRAVES, DANIEL, 214, 230, 234, 242, 258, 283, 361
GRAVES, DAVID, 95
GRAVES, ELIZABETH, 80
GRAVES, ELLEN, 266
GRAVES, FRANCIS, 323
GRAVES, GEORGE, 49, 222, 224, 226, 231, 246, 247, 248, 261, 272, 280, 285, 286, 289, 294, 295, 300, 302, 316
GRAVES, HENRY, 72, 119, 120, 309, 333, 336, 349, 350, 352, 366, 368, 373
GRAVES, JACOB, 271
GRAVES, JOHN, 271, 333
GRAVES, LUCY, 11
GRAVES, MAHALA, 365
GRAVES, POLLY, 121
GRAVES, RUTH, 286
GRAVES, SOPHIANNA, 271
GRAVES, SUSAN, 294, 345
GRAVES, THOMAS, 295
GRAVES, WILLIAM, 365
GRAVES, WM. C., 365
GRAVIT, THOMAS, 295
GRAVITT, WILLIAM, 356
GRAY, ANN JANE, 368
GRAY, JOSEPH, 271
GRAY, MARGARET ANN, 188
GRAY, NANCY, 227
GRAY, SARAH, 328
GRAYBILL, CHRISTIANA, 112
GRAYBILL, ELIZA, 348
GRAYBILL, JACOB, 86
GRAYHAM, MARY, 29
GRAYSON, BEN, 34
GRAYSON, BENJAMIN, 79
GRAYSON, HANNAH, 194
GRAYSON, JANE, 238
GRAYSON, JOHN, 269
GRAYSON, JOSEPH, 19
GRAYSON, SARAH, 85
GREGG, HARMON, 12
GREGG, MARGARET, 17
GREGGE, HARMON, 12
GREEN, ABNER, 95
GREEN, ELIZABETH, 135
GREEN, MARY, 126
GREEN, SAMUEL, 120
GREEN, SUSSANA, 276
GREEN, WILLIAM, 107
GREENE, PEGGY M., 92
GREENWAY, J. C., 147
GREER, ELIZA, 129
GREER, JOSEPH, 10, 12, 14, 18, 20, 21
GREER, REBECKA, 209
GREYSON, WILLIAM, 239
GRIFFIN, BENJAMIN, 333
GRIFFIN, JEFFERSON, 295
GRIFFIN, SALLY, 54
GRIFFIN, SARAH, 68
GRIFFIS, NANCY, 164
GRIFFIS, WILLIAM, 185, 192
GRIFFY, SALLY, 265
GRILL, PLEASANT R., 309
GRILL, WILLIAM D., 333
GRILLS, BETSY ANN, 72
GRILLS, MARY C., 210
GRILLS, PLEASANT R., 299
GRILLS, THOS. J., 185, 202
GRIMES, MARY A., 186
GRIMES, RACHEL, 257
GRIZZLE, HARRY, 134
GRIZZLE, JOBY, 201
GRIZZLE, JUDA, 195
GRONER, JESSE, 370
GROUNDS, ELIZA R., 336
GROVE, CATHARINE, 67
GROVE, SUSAN, 55
GROVES, MALVINA, 339
GROVES, SUSAN, 294
GRUBB, DIANAH, 240
GUILFORD, NESTER, 325
GUIN, SUSSANNAH, 127
QUINN, JANE, 153
QUINN, PEGGY, 130
QUINN, SUSAN, 153
QUINN, WILLIAM, 349
QUINN, NANCY, 165
GUISS, NATHANIEL, 40
GUM, NORTON, 3
GUNN, POLLY, 164
GUNN, WILLIAM, 349
GUSLING, JOSEPH, 170
GUTHREY, PEYTON HENRY, 239
GUTHRIE, NANCY, 15
GUTRY, GEO., 27

GWIN, ELIZABETH, 132
GWIN, JAMES F., 256

H

HABRUM, HENRY, 121
HACKETT, JEAN, 19
HACKETT, JOHN, 19
HACKNEY, BARTON, 158
HACKNEY, CHARLES, 121
HACKNEY, JACOB, 158, 290
HACKWORTH, AUSTIN, 147
HACKWORTH, JOHN, 95
HACKWORTH, NICHODEMUS, 29
HACKWORTH, POLLY, 19
HACKWORTH, SAMUEL, 185
HADLEY, CASA, 232
HADLEY, JOHN, 239
HAEFLY, BARBARA, 92
HAGAN, JACOB, 239
HAGARD, JOHN, 335
HAGEN, MARY, 349
HAGGARD, WILLIAM, 271
HAGUE, WILLIAM, 147
HAIL, LUKE, 7
HAIN, JAMES A., 104
HAINES, CLINTON, 349
HAINES, SALLY, 202
HAINES, SARAH C., 26
HAINES, SUSAN, 289
HAINEY, AMANDA, 104
HAINEY, ARCHIBALD, 121
HAINEY, POLLY, 128
HAINS, POLLY, 287
HAINS, SALLY, 372
HAIR, JAMES, 240, 261
HAIR, LARKIN, 333
HAIRE, JAMES A., 111, 139
HAIRSE, JAMES A., 115
HAISE, JAMES 118
HAISE, JAMES I., 117
HALBERT, CYNTHY, 355
HALBERT, MARY, 210
HALBERT, STEPHEN, 195
HALEY, CLAIBORNE, 51
HALEY, DOLLY, 51
HALEY, MARTHA, 118
HALFACRE, JACOB, 12, 186
HALL, ABSALOM, 107
HALL, ANDREW, 147
HALL, BETSY, 71
HALL, CHARLES, 305
HALL, DAVID, 67
HALL, EDMOND, 134
HALL, EDMUND, 107
HALL, ELIZA, 310, 358
HALL, HUGH, 185, 202
HALL, JAMES, 158
HALL, JOHN, 67
HALL, MAJOR L., 349
HALL, MATILDA, 351
HALL, NANCY, 41, 48
HALL, OBADIAH, 107, 358
HALL, P. C. I., 350, 353, 355
HALL, PATSY, 45
HALL, SALLY, 52
HALL, THOMAS, 97, 171
HALL, THOS. D., 328
HALL, WIATT, 349
HALL, WM., 309
HALL, ZACHARIAH, 96
HALLMARK, GEORGE, 18, 29
HAMBRIGHT, JOHN W., 240
HAMER, DANIEL, 121
HAMILTON, GENE, 5
HAMILTON, JEAN, 8
HAMILTON, JOSEPH, 147
HAMILTON, LORENZA D., 219
HAMILTON, PEGGY, 36
HAMILTON, ROBERT, 1
HAMILTON, SARAH, 278
HAMILTON, WM., 7, 79
HAMMACK, MARTIN, 61
HAMMER, CHARLOTT, 329
HAMMER, ELLEN, 168
HAMMER, ISAAC, 79
HAMMER, JESSE, 171
HAMMOND, ELIZABETH, 142
HAMMONDS, WILLIS, 160
HAMMONE, WILLIS, 180
HAMONTREE, HARRIS, 68
HAMPTON, ELIZABETH, 145
HANALSON, WILLIAM, 171
HANBY, CHRISTOPHER, 335
HANCOCK, BERRY, 271
HANCOCK, CAROLINE, 294
HANES, JORDAN L., 171
HANEY, SAMUEL, 79
HANKINS, ABEL, 271
HANKINS, ABRAHAM, 349

HEAVNER, JAMES, 23
HEDGECOTH, BAZEL, 272
HEDRICK, ISAAC, 350
HEISKELL, SOPHIA, 124
HELLAM, JONATHAN, 41
HELMS, REBECCA, 114
HELTON, HENRY, 80
HEMBREE, DRURY, 80
HEMBREE, REBECCA, 80
HENDERSON, ALLEN, 365
HENDERSON, ANDREW A., 365
HENDERSON, BETSEY, 279
HENDERSON, ELIZABETH, 266
HENDERSON, ETHELDRED, 296
HENDERSON, HIBEY, 215
HENDERSON, HIRAM, 184
HENDERSON, ISAAC, 107
HENDERSON, JOHN, 186
HENDERSON, MARGARET, 9
HENDERSON, MARY, 390
HENDERSON, POLLY, 34
HENDERSON, ROBERT, 19
HENDERSON, SALLIE, 213
HENDERSON, SARAH, 184
HENDERSON, SUSANNAH, 4
HENDERSON, THATCH, 80, 89
HENDERSON, THOMAS, 171, 334, 350,
HENDERSON, WILLIAM, 7, 96, 227, 365
HENDRIX, AUSTIN H., 322
HENDRIX, LUKE, 19
HENDRIX, MARY, 390
HENDRIX, MORGAN, 147
HENDRIX, RACHAEL, 77
HENDRIX, SQUIRE, 19
HENDRIXON, ELIZABETH, 266
HENDRIXSON, JOHN, 309
HENDRON, JOHN, 287
HENDSON, ELIZABETH, 103
HENLEY, ALFRED, 296
HENNEMAN, POLLY, 34
HENRY, MARGARET, 349
HENRY, MARY, 360
HENRY, SAM'L, 77
HENSHAW, PEGGY, 165
HENSLEY, AGNES, 44
HENSLEY, GEORGE W., 49
HENSLEY, MALINDA, 314
HENSLEY, NANCY, 171
HENSLEY, SAMUEL, 171
HENSON, CATHARINE, 39
HENSON, ELIZABETH, 307
HENSON, JAMES, 240
HENSON, JANE, 137, 150
HENSON, JOSEPH, 216
HENSON, PLEASANT, 240
HENSON, POLLY, 277
HENSON, RICHARD, 365
HENSON, WILLIAM, 159, 284
HEPPENSTALL, BETSY, 167
HERD, STEPHEN, 23
HERNDON, EDWARD, 257
HERNDON, JOHN, 282, 285
HERRELSON, ELIZABETH, 129
HERRON, ELIZA, 40
HESLIT, WILLIAM JR., 7
HESS, MARGARET, 13, 16
HESTER, OWEN, 148
HEWLIN, JAMES, 148
HEWLIN, SILAS, 148
HIBBS, WILLIAM, 209
HICKEY, ANN MARIAH, 374
HICKEY, CORNELIUS, 30, 121
HICKEY, E., 300, 325
HICKEY, ELIJAH, 303, 315, 374
HICKEY, GEORGE, 171, 277
HICKEY, JAMES, 152
HICKEY, JANE, 81, 109
HICKEY, JOHN, 276
HICKEY, JOSEPH, 122
HICKEY, MARY, 336
HICKEY, MILLY, 24
HICKEY, NANCY, 323
HICKEY, PATSY, 117
HICKEY, SALLY, 157
HICKEY, SARAH, 291
HICKLE, ELIZA, 209
HICKLE, GEORGE, 135
HICKLE, JOHN, 195, 199, 208
HICKLE, MARY, 219
HICKLE, NANCY, 208
HICKLE, SALLY, 285
HICKLE, WILLIAM, 227, 319, 324, 327
HICKLIN, JONATHAN, 96
HICKMAN, JNO., 369
HICKMAN, WILLIAM, 362
HICKS, JAMES, 148

HICKS, JAMES E., 350
HICKS, REBECKA, 146
HICKS, R. N. K., 86
HICKSON, BETSY, 346
HIGDON, RHODY, 109
HIGGINS, JOHN, 25
HIGGINS, MARY, 25
HIGHTOWER, DICE, 299
HILL, ABEL, 285
HILL, ABRAHAM, 72
HILL, ALBRED E., 334
HILL, ANDERSON, 96, 269, 272
HILL, BETSY, 86
HILL, BOWEN, 88
HILL, CATHERINE, 15
HILL, ELI, 296
HILL, ELIZABETH, 94, 327
HILL, HANNAH, 280
HILL, HENRY M., 122, 180
HILL, JOANNA, 235
HILL, JANE, 315
HILL, JOHN, 122, 169, 207, 285, 293, 309
HILL, LEWIS, 33, 171
HILL, LUCRETIA, 180
HILL, MARTHA, 324
HILL, MARTIN, 80
HILL, MARVEL, 186
HILL, MASTON, 86
HILL, MIMA, 221
HILL, WILLIAM, 148, 257
HILLIS, STEPHEN, 34, 37, 39
HILLSMAN, ELIZABETH, 337
HILLSMAN, EVELINE, 173
HILLSMAN, JOHN, 261
HILLSMAN, MARY ANN, 334
HILLSMAN, MARY G., 312
HILLSMAN, MATTHEW, 322, 337
HILLSMAN, NANCY, 351
HINAN, JAMES, 296
HINCKLE, JESSE, 186
HINCKLE, PHILIP, 159
HINDES, JOSEPH, 186
HINDMAN, THOS. C. 122
HINDS, BENJ., 49
HINDS, HANNAH, 44
HINDS, ISAAC, 72
HINDS, ISAAC, JR., 350
HINDS, ISABELLA, 225
HINDS, JAMES, 56, 323
HINDS, LUCY, 364
HINDS, MELINDA, 96
HINDS, NELLY, 49
HINDS, PATSEY, 62
HINDS, POLLY, 44, 214
HINDS, ROBERT, 72
HINDS, SAMUEL, 187, 251
HINES, ELIZABETH, 313, 318
HINES, JOSEPH, 62
HINES, NANCY, 344
HINES, SARAH, 13
HINES, SIMON, 62
HINON, BENJAMIN, 227
HINTON, ELIZA, 334
HINTON, JAMES, 240
HITCHCOCK, WILLIAM, 19
HITE, MINERVA, 246
HITHCOTH, ALANSON, 296
HIXON, WILLIAM, 284, 334
HOBBS, JAMES, 41
HOBBS, JOEL, 41
HOBBS, MARTHAY 297
HOBBS, POLLY, 319
HOBBS, SAMMY, 31
HODGE, CHARLES B., 296
HODGE, EDWARD, 49
HODGES, CHARLES B., 240
HODGES, WELCOME, 96
HODGES, WILLIAM O., 56
HODGIN, JOHN, 41
HOFFAR, DANIEL, 36
HOFFAR, HENRY, 216
HOFFAR, WALKER A., 257
HOGGETT, HILA, 118
HOGSHEAD, WILLIAM, 19, 310
HOLBERT, CHARITY, 303
HOLBERT, DICE, 195
HOLBERT, FRANCES, 262
HOLBERT, NANCY, 244
HOLBERT, POLLY, 230
HOLDEN, JANE, 254
HOLLICE, REBECCA, 63
HOLLINSWORTH, ANNA J., 372
HOLLIS, ESTHER, 64
HOLLOWAY, ELIZABETH, 300
HOLLOWAY, MARIAH, 354
HOLLOWAY, POLLY, 80, 95
HOLOWAY, SARAH, 353

Holt, Eleanor, 76
Holt, Emily, 48
Holt, Liley, 238
Holt, Mahala, 182
Holt, Matilda, 351
Holt, Nancy, 31, 131
Holt, Nelly, 44
Holt, Polly, 185
Holt, Rachel, 84
Holt, Sally, 122
Homer, William, 285
Hommel, Elizabeth, 306
Hommel, Ellen, 305
Hommel, Henry, 323
Hon, Jacob, 227
Hon, William, 227
Honeycut, Hyram, 227
Hood, Aaron, 171
Hood, Andrew, 172
Hood, Betsy, 262
Hood, Daniel R., 334
Hood, Elizabeth, 199
Hood, Isaac, 240
Hood, James, 131, 365
Hood, John, 80, 108
Hood, Luke, 87
Hood, Nancy, 219
Hood, Payton, 350
Hood, Peggy, 106
Hood, Polly, 131
Hood, Robert, 227
Hood, Sarah, 178, 349
Hood, Sarah Ann, 325
Hood, Thomas, 56
Hood, Wm., 96
Hooks, David, 251
Hope, David L., 272
Hope, Easter, 88, 89
Hope, Ellender, 240
Hope, Hardin, 365
Hope, John, 177
Hope, Mary, 67
Hope, William, 70
Hopper, Cynthia, 145
Hopper, Sarah, 108
Hord, Lucinda, 314
Horn, George, 216
Horn, William, 235
Horne, Anne, 64
Horne, G., 241
Horner, Mirna, 342
Horner, William, 285, 323, 329
Horton, Daniel, 122
Horton, Peggy, 28
Hoskins, Sally, 268
Hosong, Coonrod, 45
Houk, Margaret, 297
Houk, Sarah, 114, 196
House, Nancy, 34
Householder, Cynthia Ann, 350
Housely, Christian, 350
Houser, Caty, 125
Houser, Daniel, 290
Houser, David, 108
Houser, Jonathan, 285
Houser, Joseph, 288
Houser, P. P., 264
Houser, Philip, 310
Housong, John, 108
Housong, Polly, 96
Houston, Alice, 111
Houston, Amelia, 166
Houston, Eleanor F., 145, 146
Houston, George B., 355
Houston, James, D., 310
Houston, John, 5
Houston, Melinda, 99, 111
Houston, R., 34, 35, 36, 37, 38, 40, 41, 42, 43, 45, 47, 48, 52, 53, 56, 57, 61, 82, 87, 109, 139, 143, 144, 146, 153, 156, 160, 161, 162, 164, 165, 181, 195, 196, 197, 216, 220, 229, 244, 250
Houston, Ro., 160
Houston, Robert, 4, 7, 12, 38, 161
Houston, Rutelia, 310
Houston, Walter, 216
Houston, William, 87
How, Jacob, 187
Howard, Anne, 12
Howard, James, 122
Howard, Jean, 27
Howard, John, 53
Howard, Nancy, 53
Howard, Polly, 277
Howard, Rebecka, 132
Howard, Samuel, 240

Howard, Thomas, 53, 122
Howel, Duke, 241
Howel, Elizabeth, 32
Howel, James, 148
Howell, Anne, 14
Howell, Catharine, 162
Howell, Duke, 216
Howell, Elijah, 67
Howell, Elizabeth, 214
Howell, Lacky, 266
Howell, Locky, 266
Howell, Martha H., 338
Howell, Polly, 39, 326
Howell, Sally, 100
Howell, Sylvanus, 266, 298
Howell, W. S., 173
Howell, William, 87, 216
Howell, Wm. G., 112
Howell, William S., 366
Howry, Sam'l, 323
Howser, Betsy, 106
Howser, Daniel, 187, 290
Howser, Hannah, 190
Howser, Jacob, 155, 159
Howser, Jonathan, 216
Howser, Joseph, 216, 361
Howser, Lydia, 250
Howser, Philip P., 216
Howser, Sally, 170
Howser, Sarah, 155
Hubbard, James, 257
Hubbard, Rebecca, 302
Hubbs, Fanny, 15
Hubbs, John, 280
Hubbs, Polly, 79
Hubbs, Ruth, 280
Hubbs, Sally, 154
Hubbs, Willis, 108
Hudaburg, Catharine, 175
Hudaburg, Malvina, 203
Hudiburg, Elizabeth, 32
Hudiburg, Lewis, 62
Hudiburg, Thomas, 41, 98, 104
Hudson, Elizabeth, 356
Hudson, Obadiah, 202
Huett, Nathaniel, 38
Huffaen, Michael, 187
Huffaker, Amos, 310
Huffaker, Catherine, 42
Huffaker, George, 63
Huffaker, George Jr., 350
Huffaker, Henry, 257
Huffaker, Nancy, 115
Huffane, Henry, 190
Huffan, Daniel, 108
Huffer, George, 285
Hufferman, Ellet, 366
Huffstadler, Barbara, 62
Huffstadler, David, 62
Huffstedler, Jacob, 96
Huffstutler, Henry, 138
Huffstutler, Martin, 202
Huffstutler, Mary, 138
Huges, Theoples, 7
Hughes, John, 24
Human, Anna, 132
Human, Bazell, 13
Human, James, 108, 132, 145
Humbert, Jno. G., 373
Humes, A. R., 362
Humes, And. R., 344
Humes, Elizabeth, 194
Humes, Margaret, 139, 140
Humes, Mary, 221
Humphrey, Anna, 110
Humphrey, Elijah, 227
Humphrey, James, 296
Humphrey, Margaret, 227
Humphrey, William, 228
Humphreys, Alexander, 202, 310
Humphreys, Polly, 239
Humphreys, Samuel, 187
Humphries, William, 42
Humphry, Polly, 234
Hunt, Samuel A., 310
Hunter, Andrew, 46
Hunter, Betsy, 169
Hunter, Casper, 258, 297
Hunter, Catharine, 135
Hunter, Eliphu, 217
Hunter, James, 195
Hunter, Jemima, 46
Hunter, John, 16, 38, 108, 172

JOHNSTON, RACHEL, 249
JOHNSTON, REBECKA, 306
JOHNSTON, RHODA, 103
JOHNSTON, SALLY, 118, 165, 175
JOHNSTON, SAMUEL, 258, 310
JOHNSTON, SARAH, 21
JOHNSTON, THOMAS, 135
JOHNSTON, WILLIAM, 21
JONES, A. T., 240
JONES, ABNER, 68
JONES, ACCA, 144
JONES, ANDREW T., 189
JONES, ANN J., 81
JONES, BETHANA, 303
JONES, ELIZABETH, 297
JONES, FRANCIS K., 159
JONES, GEO. J., 81, 250, 258
JONES, GEORGE M. C., 286
JONES, GEORGE W., 351
JONES, HARRIET, 333
JONES, HENRY, 187
JONES, HUGH, 307, 353
JONES, IBBY, 179
JONES, ISAAC, 27, 56
JONES, JAMES, 53, 135, 201
JONES, JEREMIAH, 187
JONES, JESSE G., 258
JONES, JOHN, 45, 56, 163, 300, 351
JONES, JUDA, 314
JONES, LAYMAN, 371
JONES, LEWIS, 337
JONES, MALINDY, 65
JONES, MARIA, 160
JONES, MARY, 38, 311
JONES, NANCY, 273
JONES, PATSEY, 48
JONES, REBECCA, 102
JONES, REUBEN, 286
JONES, SALLY, 271
JONES, SAMUEL, 241
JONES, SARAH, 85
JONES, SUSAN, 134
JONES, WILLIAM, 303, 323
JONES, THOMAS, 266

JORDAN, JOHN, 149
JORDAN, WILLIS, 272
JORDON, LEWIS, 311
JOUROLMAN, R. D., 335
JULIAN, ABIGAIL, 122
JULIAN, CATHARINE, 342, 359
JULIAN, HULDY, 333
JULIAN, LYDIA, 332
JULIAN, NANCY, 37
JULIAN, POLLY, 199
JULIAN, WILLIAM, 297
JULIEN, JOHN, 13
JUSTICE, REBECKA, 150

K

KAIN, JANE, 59
KAIN, JNO. H., 172
KAIN, MARY, 172
KAIN, NANCY, 90
KAIN, SOLOMON, 108
KAIN, WILLIAM, 80
KARNES, CHARLES, 297
KARNES, EVE, 61
KARNES, HENRY, 366
KARNES, MARY M., 362
KARNES, NANCY, 285
KARNS, AILCY, 352
KARNS, CATHARINE, 279
KARNS, ELIZA H., 333
KARNS, HANNAH, 294
KARNS, HENRY, 366
KARNS, JOHN, 97
KARNS, MICHAEL, 83
KARNS, PHILIP, 297
KARNS, POLLY, 128
KAYHILL, RICHARD, 329
KEAN, JACOB, 56
KEAN, KITTY, 69
KEARNS, ELIZABETH, 246
KEARNS, JAMES, 24
KEARNS, JOHN, 258
KEARNS, ONEY, 178
KEARNS, THENEY, 208
KEEHILL, ELIZABETH, 97
KEENER, ANNE, 45
KEENER, ELIZABETH, 41
KEENER, JACOB B., 241
KEENER, JONATHAN, 41, 88
KEENER, PETER, 159

KEENER, POLLY, 143
KEENER, RACHEL, 30
KEENER, REBECKA, 190
KEENER, ULERY, 241
KEETH, MICAJAH, 24
KEETH, SAMUEL, 24
KEETHE, POLLY, 24
KEGER, MATTHEW, 97
KEINER, ELITHA, 59
KEITH, ANDREW, 172
KEITH, ANN, 361
KEITH, BETSY, 75
KEITH, C. H., 374
KEITH, CATHARINE, 121, 214
KEITH, ELIZABETH L., 368
KEITH, EMELINE, 273
KEITH, EVELINE, 275
KEITH, JOHN, 64
KEITH, POLLY, 35
KEITH, W. J., 368
KELLER, DAVID, 147
KELLER, ELIZABETH, 47
KELLEY, J. N., 329, 338, 361, 363
KELLY, ALEXANDER, 6
KELLY, ELIZABETH, 6
KELLY, JANE, 112, 140
KELLY, JOSEPH, 203
KELLY, MARGARET, 151
KELLY, PEGGY, 74
KELLY, RICHARD, 298
KELLY, SAMUEL, 159, 163, 208
KELLY, WALTHAM, 123
KELSON, DORCAS, 62
KELSON, JAMES B., 203
KEMP, BETSY, 139
KEMP, JAMES, 133
KEMP, POLLY, 133
KENDRICK, MILDRED, 104
KENDRICK, WILLIAM, 85
KENNEDY, ADAM M., 201
KENNEDY, DIANA, 91
KENNEDY, ELIZA ANN, 352
KENNEDY, ELIZABETH, 358
KENNEDY, ISABELLA, 256
KENNEDY, JACOB, 338
KENNEDY, JAMES, 132, 211, 216, 241

KENNEDY, JANE I., 181
KENNEDY, JOHN, 197
KENNEDY, LAVINA, 288, 289
KENNEDY, LUCAS, 172
KENNEDY, MARGARET, 317
KENNEDY, MARIA, 87
KENNEDY, MARTIN, 25
KENNEDY, MARY J., 317
KENNEDY, MIRIAM, 109
KENNEDY, NANCY, 174, 197
KENNEDY, SAMPSON, 3
KENNEDY, SAMUEL, 256
KENNEDY, WILLIAM S., 234, 311
KENNEDY, WM., 109
KENNERS, JAMES, 339
KERSY, ELIZABETH, 265
KERN, HENRY, 53
KERNS, HENRY, 74
KERNS, MAGDALENE, 74
KERR, DAVID, 188
KERR, MARGARET, 3
KERR, MARY, 44
KERR, POLLY, 198
KERR, WILLIAM, 3
KESINGER, MATTHIAS, 149
KEY, MARY, 7
KEY, POLLY, 59
KEYES, ALEXANDER D., 298
KEYHILL, JOHN, 273
KEYHILL, MARGARET, 61
KEYHILL, RICHARD, 10, 320, 323, 327, 332, 334, 346, 350, 351, 361, 369
KEYHILL, THOMAS, 80
KEYS, BETSY, 170, 211
KEYS, HENRY, 160
KEYS, MATTHEW, 62
KEYS, MARY, 198
KEYS, NANCY, 132
KEYS, SALLY, 138
KEYS, WILLIAM, 217
KIDD, EDMUND, 367
KIDD, ELIZABETH, 200
KIDD, HEZEKIAH, 277
KIDD, HORATIO, 97
KIDD, JAMES, 123
KIDD, MAHALA, 355
KIDD, MAHANA, 303
KIDD, MARY ANNE, 97
KIDD, RANDAL, 112

Ledgerwood, Samuel, 242
Ledgerwood, William, 311, 352
Ledsinger, Becka, 110
Lee, Abraham, 94
Lee, Alsey, 60
Lee, Jency, 52
Lee, Jincy, 84
Lee, Permit, 98
Lee, Purmast, 34
Lee, Samuel, 98
Lee, William, 98, 149
Leek, Polly, 80
Leek, Sallie, 61
Lefew, Mary Ann Marthana, 169
Legg, Ellen, 253
Legg, George, 258
Legg, James, 41
Legg, Sally, 193
Legg, Sarah A., 364
Legg, Susanah, 236
Legg, Wesley, 98
Leiper, Hugh, 49
Leister, Isabella, 241
Lender, Isaac, 14
Lenning, Isaac, 80
Leroy, William B., 273
Lester, John, 29
Lethco, Mary, 363
Lethco, William, 352
Letsinger, Allen, 368
Letsinger, Daniel, 286, 302
Letsinger, David, 273
Letsinger, John, 228
Letsinger, Lewis, 286
Letsinger, Philip, 203, 217
Letsinger, Polly, 96
Letsinger, Susan, 302
Lett, Armbrose, 109
Letzinger, Philip, 52
Levi, Elizabeth, 121
Levi, Polly, 126
Levy, Eliza, 336
Lewis, Aurelia, 78
Lewis, Betsy, 88, 151
Lewis, Cornelius, 153
Lewis, Elizabeth, 42, 107
Lewis, Fanny, 153
Lewis, Henry, 56, 88
Lewis, I., 245, 263, 265, 310, 341, 356, 372
Lewis, Isaac, 245, 257, 259, 265, 266, 267, 269, 270, 272, 273, 275, 278, 279, 285, 287, 291, 295, 296, 301, 304, 315, 322, 325, 340, 353
Lewis, J., 235, 371, 250
Lewis, Jesse, 266
Lewis, Loren R., 173
Lewis, Nancy, 98, 158, 242,
Lewis, Polly, 106
Lewis, Richard, 68
Lewis, Susannah, 205
Lewis, William, 109
Likey Andrew, 352, 367
Like, Jacob, 311
Lilburn, Polly, 146
Liles, Henry, 109
Linch, Wiley Y., 374
Lincoln, Jesse, 188
Lincoln, Mordecai, 124
Lindsay, H., 329
Lindsay, John, 141
Lindsay, Moses, 267
Lindsay, R. H., 345
Lindsay, Robert, 73, 89, 92, 94, 112, 114, 124, 158, 202, 210
Lindsay, William, 206, 332, 342, 345, 361, 364, 365
Lindsey, John, 109
Lindsey, Robert, 144
Lineberry, Levi, 298
Lingenfetter, Jacob, 160
Lingo, During, 343
Link, Leah, 258
Linn, Priscilla, 55
Linville, Lisell, 8
Lipford, Mary, 195
Lisbee, Betsy, 125
Lisbey, Mary, 242
Lisby, Betsy, 362, 368
Lisby, James, 367
Lisby, Patsy Ann, 359

Lister, Nancy, 222, 223
Lister, Nanny, 211
Lister, Reuben, 98
Litow, Elizabeth, 370
Litt, Lucy, 57
Little, Adam, 284, 352
Little, Christopher, 368
Little, John, 329
Little, Joseph L., 337
Little, Nancy, 275
Little, Richard, 298
Little, Sarah E., 337
Littleford, Mary, 243
Littleford, Serena, 259
Lively, Biddy, 355
Lively, Thomas, 228
Lonas, Elizabeth, 55
Lonas, George, 68
Lonas, Henry, 124, 331, 342
Lonas, Nancy, 179
Lonas, Polly, 129
Lonas, Samuel, 273
Lonas, Sarah, 273
Lonas, Zabilla, 311
Lones, Amanda, 363
Lones, Charles, 363
Lones, Charlotte, 355
Lones, David, 217
Lones, George W., 353
Lones, Isaac, 242
Lones, Jacob, 81, 157
Lones, Jesse, 109
Lones, John, 173
Lones, Joseph, 173
Lones, Mary, 350, 356
Lones, Nancy, 123
Long, George, 368
Long, Isaac, 262, 303, 319
Long, Job, 335
Long, John, 136
Long, Nancy, 335, 337
Long, William, 20
Longwith, Katy, 126
Longwith, Relay, 222
Longwutt, Betsy, 224
Looney, Alzira, 261
Looney, Benjamin, 150
Looney, Elizabeth, 3
Looney, Hetty, 177, 246
Looney, John, 261, 273
Looney, Joseph M., 285
Looney, Mary, 202
Looney, Matilda, 285
Looney, Peter, 33
Loudermilk, William, 136
Louise, Amanda, 363
Love, Anne, 222
Love, Betsy, 134, 186
Love, Charlotte, 218
Love, George, 273
Love, Jane, 140
Love, Jo, 48
Love, John, 23, 29, 32, 34, 39, 40, 50, 53, 54, 61, 68, 69, 74, 78, 79, 80, 83,
Love, Joseph, 38
Love, Lovy R., 177
Love, Mary Adeline, 298
Love, Mary Ann, 142
Love, Patsy, 73
Love, Pleasant, 286
Love, Robert, 299
Love, S. H., 339
Love, Sally, C., 188
Love, Samuel, 109, 160, 222, 225, 227, 231, 236, 237, 239, 242, 248, 249, 253, 254, 259, 263, 267, 270, 282, 284, 286, 288, 289, 294, 296, 312, 313, 314, 318, 322, 332, 337, 342, 359, 366
Love, Samuel C., 72
Love, Samuel H., 299
Love, Thomas B., 188
Love, William, 81
Lovelace, Sarah, 342
Lovelass, Jane, 169
Low, Aquilla, 98
Low, Catharine, 340
Low, Catherine, 2
Low, David, 18, 228
Low, Eliza, 120
Low, James, 209
Low, John, 20, 124, 228
Low, Margaret, 3, 257

MARTIN, GEORGE JR., 99
MARTIN, JAMES, 110, 153
MARTIN, JANE, 156
MARTIN, JOHN, 45, 110
MARTIN, LUCINDA, 316
MARTIN, M. L., 367
MARTIN, MARY, 40, 105
MARTIN, MARY MIRA, 286
MARTIN, PHOEBE, 92
MARTIN, POLLY, 104
MARTIN, SAMUEL, 66, 73, 92, 137, 149, 160
MARTIN, SIMEON, 57
MARTIN, THOMAS, 294
MARTIN, WILLIAM, 242
MASON, ABRAHAM, 259
MASON, ANN, 316
MASON, CAROLINE, 306
MASON, DAN, 9
MASON, EDWARD, 37
MASON, EVALINA, 205
MASON, JESSE, 218
MASON, JOHN, 144
MASON, NATHANIEL, 31
MASON, REBECCA, 56
MASON, SUSAN H., 234, 235
MASON, WILLIAM, 229
MASON, WINDSOR, 137
MASON, WINSOR, 287
MASSENGILL, MARY C., 71
MASSEY, ABEL, 99
MASSEY, CHARLES, 193
MASSEY, HUGH, 110
MASSEY, JACOB L., 368
MASSEY, JACOMAH, 193
MASSEY, JOHN, 215
MASSEY, SEVIER, 166
MASSEY, SHADRACK, 199
MASSEY, SHERWOOD, 242
MASSEY, THOMAS, 57
MASSEY, THOS. A., 368
MASTERSON, JOHN, 243
MASTERSON, JOHN W., 243
MASTERSON, LUCY, 225
MASTERSON, THOMAS W., 243
MATHEWS, WILLIAM, 9
MATHIS, JAMES J., 287
MATHIS, JOHN, 20
MATLOCK, JOHN, 353
MATLOCK, POLLY, 18
MATTHEW, JAMES J., 287
MATTHEWS, ARCHILLIOUS, 31
MATTHEWS, BRITTON, 31
MATTHEWS, WILLIAM, 229
MATTOCKS, POLLY, 18
MAUPINE, MORGAN G., 160
MAXEY, EDWARD, 259
MAXEY, JUDE, 66, 67
MAXEY, RHODA, 283
MAXEY, SHADRAC, 287
MAXEY, WALTER, 49
MAXWELL, DAVID, 8
MAXWELL, JAMES, 318
MAXWELL, JOHN, 29, 38, 335
MAXWELL, MARY M., 318
MAY, DELILA, 363
MAY, MARY, 139
MAY, WILLIAM, 45
MAYBERRY, ELIZABETH, 58
MAYBERRY, FRANCES, 70
MAYBERRY, JAMES, 137
MAYBERRY, JOSEPH A., 137
MAYBERRY, SALLY 56
MAYBURY, CHARITY, 146
MAYBURY, JOSEPH A., 137
MAYFIELD, MAHALA, 326
MAYFIELD, MALINDA, 168, 198
MAYFIELD, MARIA, 206
MAYFIELD, MINERVA, 194
McAFFEY, ROSANA, 232
McAFFEY, WILLIAM P., 275
McAFFREY, BETSY, 177
McAFFREY, MARY, 364
McAFFRY, TERRENCE, 299
McAFFRY, TERRENCE W., 330
McALISTER, JOSEPH, 29, 31
McALLISTER, ELIZABETH, 336
McANALLY, WM., 88
McAULAY, EDWARD, 49
McBATH, ALEXANDER, 181, 188
McBATH, ANDREW, 49, 130
McBATH, JAMES, 204, 207, 259
McBATH, R., 136
McBATH, ROBERT, 145, 155, 156, 159, 160, 163, 165, 167, 168, 169, 170, 171, 176, 181, 183, 184, 186, 187, 188, 194, 199, 200, 201, 275

McBATH, RUSSELL R., 88
McBATH, WILLIAM, 45
McBEE, ABIGAIL, 45
McBEE, ISAAC M., 336
McBEE, PATSY, 213
McBRIDE, BETSY, 184
McBRIDE, HUGH, 24
McBRIDE, JANE, 151
McBRIDE, JOHN, 110
McBRIDE, NANCY, 109
McBRIDE, PLEASANT, 69
McCABE, ELIZABETH, 290
McCABE, STARKY, 150
McCAHAN, MARTHA, 239
McCALEB, ANDREW, 73
McCALEB, JOHN, 197
McCALEB, POLLY, 56
McCALEB, SAMUEL, 110
McCALL, ANGUS, 111, 250
McCALL, DUNCAN, 336
McCALL, ELIZABETH, 339
McCALL, HUGH, 291
McCALL, JOHN, 229
McCALL, KATY, 111
McCALL, PEGGY, 188
McCALL, POLLY, 250
McCALL, SALLY, 96
McCALL, WILLIAM, 88
McCALLAY, THOS., 368
McCALLUM, ANN, 361
McCAMMON, LETTY, 329, 367
McCAMMON, NANCY, 114
McCAMMON, POLLY, 117
McCAMMON, WILLIAM, 311
McCAMPBELL, ADALINE, 349
McCAMPBELL, BENJ. B., 174
McCAMPBELL, CATHARINE, 195
McCAMPBELL, DRUCILLA C., 360
McCAMPBELL, ELIZA, 176, 204
McCAMPBELL, ELIZABETH W., 240
McCAMPBELL, ISAAC, 229
McCAMPBELL, JAMES, 124, 174, 237
McCAMPBELL, JOHN, 85, 87, 107, 116, 118, 119, 124, 132, 142, 143, 159, 170, 207, 208, 264, 283, 299, 300, 311
McCAMPBELL, JOHN M., 198
McCAMPBELL, MARGARET M., 338
McCAMPBELL, MARY, 116, 352
McCAMPBELL, MARY B., 244
McCAMPBELL, MARY S., 368
McCAMPBELL, NANCY, 35, 65
McCAMPBELL, POLLY, 128
McCAMPBELL, S. S., 87, 201, 259
McCAMPBELL, SAMUEL S., 68, 174, 177, 178, 190, 191, 209, 227, 234, 248, 259, 262, 279
McCAMPBELL, SOLOMON, 81
McCAMPBELL, SUSAN, 40
McCAMPBELL, W. A., 224, 234. 253. 257. 258, 268, 270, 278, 286, 287, 292, 299, 310, 311, 316, 331, 333, 334
McCAMPBELL, WILLIAM A., 88, 98, 116, 132, 133, 145, 149, 163, 222, 235, 244, 252, 253, 268, 269
McCAMPBELL, WILLIAM S., 251
McCANN, HUGH, 368
McCARREL, JOSEPH, 159
McCARREL, WILLIAM, 57
McCARRELL, JOSEPH G., 137
McCARRELL, POLLY, 308
McCARRELL, SIMON, 53
McCARROL, JANE, 360
McCARROLL, JOHN, 324
McCARROLL, JOSEPH G. M., 150
McCARROLL, SALLY, 191
McCARRY, SUSAN, 131
McCARTER, JEREMIAH, 3
McCARTER, POLLY, 41
McCARTNEY, WM., 99
McCARTY, JAMES, 57
McCARTY, JOHN, 353
McCARY, ROBERT W., 124
McCASLAND, ANDREW, 4
McCATHRINE, BETSY, 115
McCATHRINES, BETSY, 111
McCAUGHAN, CATHARINE, 243
McCAUGHAN, JANE, 209
McCAUGHAN, JOHN, 188
McCAUGHEN, SUSAN, 269
McCAVEN, ELIZABETH, 87

McCLAIN, ANNA, 180
McCLAIN, AUSTIN D., 324
McCLAIN, DANIEL C., 110
McCLAIN, ISAAC, 300
McCLAIN, JAMES, 110, 260, 275
McCLAIN, JOHN, 260, 275
McCLAIN, PATSY, 104, 143, 151
McCLAIN, POLLY, 233
McCLAIN, ROBERT, 203
McCLAIN, WILLIAM G., 287
McCLANNAHAN, SALLY, 273
McCLARD, BETSY, 215
McCLARD, WILLIAM, 215
McCLELLAN, ELIZABETH, 17
McCLELLAN, JOHN, 6, 26, 31, 82, 88, 90
McCLELLAN, SAMUEL, 17, 99
McCLELLAN, WM., 46, 90, 99
McCLELLAND, ANNIE, 6
McCLELLAND, JOHN, 7
McCLINE, ISABELLA, 156
McCLINE, SALLY, 328
McCLOUD, ALEXANDER, 150
McCLOUD, ANDREW, 14
McCLOUD, BETSY, 50
McCLOUD, ELIZABETH, 328, 342
McCLOUD, FANNY, 135
McCLOUD, JAMES, 99, 137, 150, 160
McCLOUD, JANE, 181
McCLOUD, JOHN, 88
McCLOUD, LEVI, 160, 169, 188
McCLOUD, PEGGY, 59
McCLOUD, POLLY, 70, 99
McCLOUD, SALLY, 105
McCLOUD, WILLIAM, 275
McCLUNG, BETSY JONES, 138
McCLUNG, CHARLES, 1, 2, 3, 4, 5, 5, 6, 7, 8, 9, 10, 11, 15, 17, 22, 23, 26, 28, 29, 30, 31, 33, 34, 37, 38, 39, 47, 50, 51, 66, 80, 82, 102, 126, 150, 165, 173, 177, 178, 180, 192, 194, 200, 202, 209, 212, 225, 226, 231, 241, 254, 264, 307
McCLUNG, HUGH L., 249
McCLUNG, JAMES W., 103
McCLUNG, MARGARET A. M., 304
McCLUNG, MAT, 88, 199
McCLUNG, MATTHEW, 110
McCLUNG, PEGGY, 11
McCLUNG, WILLIAM M., 29
McCLURE, CHAS. A., 368
McCLURE, MAHALA, 200
McCLURE, MALINDA, 156
McCLURE, MATILDA, 149
McCLURE, PATSY, 63
McCLURE, RACHEL, 132
McCLURE, SALLY, 328
McCLURE, SAMUEL, 156, 188
McCOLLOUGH, HENRY, 68, 151
McCOLLUM, DANIEL, 336
McCOLOUGH, POLLY, 121
McCOMB, JAMES, 88
McCONNEL, THOMAS, 110
McCONNELL, ISABELLA, 154
McCORMACK, ELIZA, 33
McCORMACK, SAMUEL, 229
McCORMACK, WILLIAM, 33
McCORMICK, SUSAN W., 87
McCORRY, ROBERT, 203, 206
McCOWN, MATTHEW, 124, 278
McCOY, A., 17
McCOY, HANNAH, 16
McCOY, PATIENCE, 17, 196
McCOY, RACHEL, 36
McCULLA, JAMES, 99
McCULLOCH, JAMES, 2, 20
McCULLOCH, JEAN, 2
McCULLOUGH, ELIZABETH, 223
McCULLOUGH, JAMES, 4, 31
McCULLOUGH, JOHN, 282
McCULLOUGH, THOMAS, 4
McCULLOUGH, WILLIAM, 262, 336
McDANIEL, JANE, 66, 106
McDANIEL, JOHN, 50
McDANIEL, MARY, 368, 372
McDANIEL, NELLY, 57
McDANIEL, POLLY, 225
McDANIEL, RACHEL, 70
McDANIEL, SUSAN, 284
McDANIEL, WILLIAM, 269
McDONALD, DAN'L, 1
McDONALD, EDWARD, 9
McDONALD, HETTY, 260
McDONALD, NANCY, 94
McDONALD, SUSAN, 136

McDONALD, WILLIAM, 284
McDONOUGH, JOHN, 224, 243
McDONOUGH, MALVINA, 228
McDOWEL, JOHN, 276
McDOWEL, WM., 348
McELWEE, JANE, 30
McENTIRE, JAMES, 9
McFADDIN, JOHN, 182
McFARLAN, GEORGE, 31, 41
McFARLAND, CATHARINE, 299
McFARLAND, JANE, 228
McFARLANE, WM., 73
McFERREN, SAM'L 161
McGHEE, ALEXANDER, 89
McGHEE, JNO., 138
McGHEE, NANCY, 245
McGILTON, ELIZA COATS, 107
McGREW, PLUMLEE, 324
McGRIFF, BETSY, 82
McGRIFF, THOMAS, 41
McGRUFF, MARGARET, 41
McHAFFIE, ANDREW, 94, 174
McHAFFIE, DAVID, 267, 300, 353
McHAFFIE, JAMES, 230
McHAFFIE, JAMES P., 203
McHAFFIE, JANE, 169
McHAFFIE, JOHN, 353
McHAFFIE, JULIA ANN, 267
McHAFFIE, ROBERT, 137
McHENRY, BETSY, 166
McHENRY, NANCY, 78
McINTERF, NANCY, 345
McINTOSH, DONALD, 138
McKAMEY, JOHN, 174
McKEAN, AARON, 125
McKEAN, CATHERINE, 2
McKEAN, EDWARD, 125
McKEE, MARGARET, 5
McKEE, ROBERT, 111
McKINLEY, JAMES, 20
McKINLEY, MARGARET, 342
McKINLEY, NICHOLAS G., 204
McKINLEY, SAMUEL, 368
McKINNEY, JAMES, 3, 5
McKINNEY, JOHN A., 230
McKINNY, SALLY, 143
McLAIN, ANNE, 68
McLAIN, AUSTIN D., 369
McLAIN, CHARLOTTE, 366
McLAIN, ISAAC, 300, 354
McLAIN, JOHN, 275
McLAIN, JOSEPH, 275, 369
McLAIN, PEGGY, 54
McLAIN, SARAH, 74, 295
McLAIN, STEPHEN, 353, 354, 355
McLAIN, WILLIAM, 74, 275
McLAMON, WILLIAM, 204
McLAMORE, GREENE, 230
McLAMORE, PATSY, 126
McLAMORE, WILLIAM, 229
McLEMORE, ARCHIBALD, 90
McLEMORE, JAMES, 260
McLEMORE, NANCY, 90
McLEMORE, RICHARD, 81
McLEMORE, YOUNG, 136
McLIN, SACKFIELD, 270
McLOUD, JANE, 125
McLUSKY, JOHN, 68
McMILLAN, ALEXANDER, 69, 115, 119, 123, 357
McMILLAN, AMELIA A., 290
McMILLAN, ANDREW, 73, 186, 224, 236, 243, 246, 342
McMILLAN, CHARLES, 189, 368
McMILLAN, ELIZABETH, 49, 172, 316, 357
McMILLAN, ESTHER, 71
McMILLAN, EVELINA JANE, 293
McMILLAN, ISABELLA, 296
McMILLAN, JACKSON, 336
McMILLAN, JAMES, 111, 134, 148, 153, 156, 163, 166, 172, 174, 175, 177, 180, 182, 185, 188, 189, 190, 191, 198, 199, 200, 201, 203, 205, 206, 217
McMILLAN, JANE, 239
McMILLAN, JOHN, 223, 233, 246, 253, 255, 261, 264, 265, 288, 290, 328
McMILLAN, MARGARET, 46
McMILLAN, MARGARET A., 235
McMILLAN, MARY, 374
McMILLAN, NANCY, 195
McMILLAN, SALLIE, 55
McMILLAN, SALLY, 153
McMILLAN, THOMAS, 81, 369
McMILLAN, WILLIAM, 50, 150, 153, 218, 248, 331, 364, 367, 370, 374

McMILLEN, ROWLEY, 42
McMILLAN, NANCY, 166
McMOND, REBECCA, 346
McMULLAN, DANIEL, 215, 244, 314
McMULLEN, DANIEL, 239, 327, 363, 371
McMULLEN, ELIZABETH, 21
McMULLEN, WILLIAM, 4
McMULLIN, DANIEL, 243
McMURN, WILLIAM, 111, 300
McNABB, ELI, 73
McNAIR, DAVID, 31
McNAIR, ELIZABETH, 35
McNAIR, MARY, 8
McNAIR, MYRA, 87
McNAIRE, HANNAH, 17
McNAIRE, JOHN, 161
McNALLY, WILLIAM, 89
McNAMEE, WILLIAM, 14
McNAMEY, JOHN, 174
McNAMSEY, FRANCIS, 195
McNANNY, JOHN, 189
McNEIL, DAVID, 271
McNEIL, ISABELLA, 136
McNEIL, JANE, 185
McNEILL, ARCHIBALD, 311
McNIGHT, JENNY, 60
McNUTT, ANN, 309
McNUTT, B., 134, 139, 162, 167, 177, 181, 199, 201, 253, 264, 277, 292, 298, 299, 301, 305, 310, 311, 313, 328, 329, 345, 347, 352, 367
McNUTT, BENJAMIN, 206
McNUTT, CATHARINE, 79
McNUTT, CATY, 154
McNUTT, DEWITT, 287
McNUTT, DORCAS E., 252
McNUTT, GEORGE, 2, 25, 99, 111
McNUTT, JAMES, 7, 63, 164, 360
McNUTT, JOHN, 99, 260
McNUTT, LUCINDA, 312
McNUTT, MARY, 5, 73
McNUTT, PEGGY, 206
McNUTT, PETER, 243
McNUTT, POLLY, 217
McNUTT, REBECKA, 319
McNUTT, ROBERT, 174
McNUTT, SARAH, 347
McNUTT, WILLIAM, 6
McNUTT, WM. B., 35
McPHERAN, JAMES H., 204
McPHERIN, ADALINE, 289
McPHERRIN, JNO., 312
McPHERRIN, NANCY, 175
McPHERRIN, POLLY, 119
McPHERRIN, SAM'L 174
McPHERSON, RICHARD, 191
McPHETRIDGE, C. A., 336
McREE, ROBERT C., 111
McREYNOLDS, ROBERT, 174, 193
McSHERRY, WILLIAM, 69
McSWAN, J. A., 297
McTEER, MARGARET, 4, 363
McTWIFFS, JOHN, 354
McVEY, JAMES, 89
McVEY, JOHN, 89
McWRIGHT, GEO., 111
MEADOWS, FANNY, 291
MEAK, ELIZABETH, 124
MEBANE, NANCY, 15
MEBIN, DAVID, H., 42
MEDARIS, WILSON, F., 369
MEDLOCK, JOHN, 354
MEDLOCK, NICHOLAS, 111
MEDLY, SALLY, 35
MEEK, ADAM C., 336
MEEK, ALEXANDER W., 57
MEEK, DANIEL, 69
MEEK, ELIZABETH, 125, 327
MEEK, JAMES L., 69
MEEK, JANE, 217
MEEK, JANE M. C., 369
MEEK, JO., 321
MEEK, JOSEPH, 73, 305, 314, 321, 322, 323, 326, 330, 337, 348, 358, 359, 362
MEEK, MARGARET, 2, 229
MEEK, RACHEL, 100
MEEK, REBECKA, 175
MEEK, THOMAS, 31
MEEKE, SALLY, 169
MEEKS, JOSEPH, 310, 367
MELTON, HANNAH, 265, 304
MELVINY, JNO., 370
MENEEBY, ISAAC, 29
MENEEBY, MATTY, 29
MENEFEE, JEMIMAH, 23
MENEFEE, JOHN, 40
MENUBY, MOLLY, 22
MERRIMAN, B. H., 238, 245

MERRIMAN, DICK, 155
MERRIMAN, PHEBE, 231
MERRIMAN, WILLIAM, 165, 175
MERRIT, SAMUEL, 260
MERRYMAN, MARTHA, 319
MICHAELS, FREDERIC, 125
MICHAELS, FREDERICK, 218
MICHAELS, ISAAC, 161, 354
MICLES, JOSEPH, 218
MICLES, WILLIAM, 287
MIKELS, JACOB, 260
MIKLES, WESLEY, 369
MILES, BETSY, 247, 313
MILES, CYNTHIA, 334
MILES, JOHN, 243
MILES, WILLIAM, 39, 260
MILIKAN, THOMAS, 8
MILLBRIGHT, ELIZABETH, 136
MILLER, AGNES, 5
MILLER, BETSY, 120, 283
MILLER, CYNTHIA, 333
MILLER, DOUTHULA C., 181
MILLER, ELIZABETH, 61
MILLER, FREEMAN, 260
MILLER, GAVIN, 324
MILLER, GEORGE, 25
MILLER, HIRAM, 340
MILLER, HUGH, 4, 5,
MILLER, ISAAC, 63
MILLER, JAMES P., 218
MILLER, JOHN, 15, 89, 102
MILLER, MALVINA L., 150
MILLER, MARK S., 189
MILLER, MARTIN, 25
MILLER, MICHAEL, 26, 204
MILLER, NANCY, 27, 152
MILLER, PETER, 4, 20
MILLER, PLEASANT, 9, 111, 244
MILLER, RACHEL, 157, 350, 356
MILLER, REBECCA, 56
MILLER, ROBT. G., 100
MILLER, SAMUEL, 14
MILLER, SARAH, 339
MILLER, SILAS, 36
MILLER, SUSANNA, 102
MILLER, THOMAS, 292
MILLER, THOMAS H., 69, 81, 312
MILLICAN, ELIZA JANE, 210
MILLIKEN, ELISHA, 161
MILLIKEN, JNO., 49
MILLIKIN, ARTIMESSA, 47
MILLS, DANIEL, 189
MILLS, ELISHA, 151
MILLS, HUGH, 25
MILLS, ISAAC, 189
MILLS, JNO. N., 369
MILLS, POLLY, 367
MILLS, WM., 312
MILTEBARGER, BETSY, 112
MILTEBARGER, JACOB, 57, 64, 65
MILTEBARGER, POLLY, 65
MILTEBARGER, WILLIAM, 336
MILTEBERGER, BARBARA, 236
MILTEBERGER, JOHN, 161
MILTEN, MOSES, 111
MILTIBARGER, MARY, 357
MINGO, HENRY, 230
MINTER, GREENE W., 204
MINTON, BETSY, 230
MINTON, BIRLY, 230
MINTON, EBENEZER, 230
MINTON, PRESTON, 336
MISER, SOLOMON, 111
MISSIMON, AMANDA, 253
MISSIMON, JOHN, 230, 253
MISSIMON, WILLIAM, 276
MITCHELL, BETSY, 33
MITCHELL, CHARLES, 175, 371
MITCHELL, CHARLOTTE, 357
MITCHELL, CHESLEY, 244
MITCHELL, ELENOR, 319
MITCHELL, ELIZABETH, 251
MITCHELL, HENRY T., 175, 210, 244
MITCHELL, JESSE, 138
MITCHELL, MARTHA, 172
MITCHELL, MORDECAI, 20
MITCHELL, MORRIS, 18
MITCHELL, PAYTON, 354
MITCHELL, PEGGY, 368
MITCHELL, SALLY, 95
MITCHELL, SARAH, 18, 371
MITCHELL, SUKY, 40
MITCHELL, THOMAS, 338
MITCHELL, THOS. M., 369
MITCHELL, WM., 84, 272, 301
MIZER, POLLY, 132

MURPHY, MARIA, 239
MURPHY, MARTHA M., 295
MURPHY, MARY ANN, 260
MURPHY, MORNEN, 180
MURPHY, NANCY, 181
MURPHY, OBEDIAH, 89
MURPHY, PARMELA, 324
MURPHY, PATSY, 185
MURPHY, POLLY, 346
MURPHY, RICHARD S., 300
MURPHY, ROBERT M., 355
MUARPHY, RUTHA, 358
MURPHY, THOS., 370
MURPHY, WM., 175
MURRAY, CHARLES M., 336
MURRAY, EDWARD, 175
MURRAY, ELI, 176
MURRAY, ELIZABETH, 45
MURRAY, ELLEN, 342
MURRAY, J. D., 323
MURRAY, JAMES D., 261, 316, 336, 345, 347, 351, 355, 356, 361, 368
MURRAY, NICHOLAS, 276
MURRAY, R., 162
MURRIAN, PETER, 63
MURRY, LEVINA, 252
MURRY, NANCY, 82
MYERS, NANCY, 255
MYNATT, AMANDA, 319
MYNATT, ANN, 54
MYNATT, ANN ELIZA, 322
MYNATT, CATHARINE, 224
MYNATT, ELIZABETH, 324, 349
MYNATT, GARVAN, 312
MYNATT, H. W., 373
MYNATT, HARDIN W., 313
MYNATT, JAMES, 162
MYNATT, JANE, 299
MYNATT, JOHN, 8, 138, 219, 298, 302, 304, 309, 318, 320, 333, 341, 343, 348, 356, 358, 363, 366
MYNATT, JOSEPH, 219, 231, 337
MYNATT, M. L., 347, 348, 364
MYNATT, MARTIN L., 346
MYNATT, NANCY, 62
MYNATT, PEGGY, 114
MYNATT, RICHARD, 261
MYNATT, RUFUS M., 337
MYNATT, SUSAN, 267
MYNATT, W. C., 220, 317
MYNATT, WILLIAM, 100, 261, 288
MYNATT, WILLIAM A., 355
MYNATT, WILLIAM C., 89, 116, 216

N

NAILL, JOHN, 139, 244
NAIL, SAMUEL, 244
NANCE, ELEANOR, 259
NANCE, ELIZABETH, 70
NANCE, HARRIET, 237
NANCE, JAMES M., 370, 372
NANCE, JOEL, 253
NANCE, LEONARD,C., 337
NANCE, MAHALA, 246
NANCE, OLIVIA, 352, 367,
NANCE, P., 71, 72, 76, 78, 133, 141, 142, 145, 146, 152, 155, 157, 159, 165
NANCE, PERMELIA, 283
NANCE, PETER, 67, 70, 72, 74, 75, 82, 83, 104, 117, 118, 121, 123, 130, 131, 132, 137, 139, 141, 144, 154, 163, 165, 173
NANCE, PRYOR, 319
NANKINS, SPRILL, 313
NARRADYCHE, DANIEL, 25
NASH, WM., 324
NASLER, BASTON, 43
NATTY, JACOB, 315
NAVE, JOANNA, 371
NAVE, SARAH, 341
NAVILLE, MARTHA, 23
NAWSLER, POLLY, 98
NEAL, ESTER, 9
NEAL, JOHN, 15, 362
NEAL, WILLIAM, 370
NEAMOUR, HOLLY, 60
NEATHERING, SAMUEL, 276
NEATHERLIN, ISBEL, 43
NECHESANANHA, ANNY, 74
NEEDHAM, ELIZABETH, 139
NEEDHAM, POLLY, 122
NEELY, JOHN, 32, 220
NEELEY, ROBERT, 15
NEELY, SAMUEL, 313

NEELY, WESTLEY, 300
NELSON, ABRAHAM, 262
NELSON, CAROLINE, 224
NELSON, CHARLES W., 355
NELSON, D., 205, 229
NELSON, DAVID, 163, 176, 178, 187, 197, 206, 210, 213, 216, 218, 221, 233, 239, 355
NELSON, DAVID W., 300, 325
NELSON, E., 195, 209, 210 251, 257, 264, 266, 267, 271, 279,
NELSON, ELIJAH, 281
NELSON, HENRY M., 355
NELSON, JAMES, 64, 262, 313, 356
NELSON, JOHN, 90, 296, 313
NELSON, JOHN M., 244, 355
NELSON, JOHN R., 90
NELSON, LOVE, 227
NELSON, MARTHA, 356
NELSON, MARTIN, 205
NELSON, MARTIN L., 244
NELSON, MATHEW, 76, 187
NELSON, NICHOLAS, 355
NELSON, POLLY, 24, 96
NELSON, REBECKA, 303
NELSON, RICHARD, 176, 204
NELSON, SALLY, 66, 122
NELSON, T. H., 86, 96, 99, 105, 106, 109, 111, 127, 128, 130, 139, 152, 251, 362
NELSON, THO. H., 62, 65, 67, 71, 73, 74, 77, 79, 81, 83, 87, 88, 89, 90, 91, 92, 93, 107, 110, 113, 118, 122, 123, 124, 125, 128, 136, 138, 140, 147, 150, 156, 168, 170, 179, 180, 181, 183, 184, 193, 309, 312, 344,
NELSON, THOMAS H., 187, 188, 191, 192, 194, 195, 198, 203, 205, 206, 207, 211, 212, 216, 221, 222, 224, 233, 235, 237, 239, 250, 251, 257, 261, 262, 264, 269, 272, 273, 276, 279, 282, 287, 290, 292, 293, 299, 303, 304, 310, 311, 315, 326, 333, 338 342, 353
NELSON, DOCTOR W., 126
NELSON, WILLIAM, 310
NESTER, JOHN, 354, 360
NESTER, MALINDA, 353, 354
NESTER, MARY, 372
NESTER, NANCY, 330
NESTER, POLLY, 372
NETHERLIN, ISBEL, 32
NEVILL, NANCY, 23
NEVILLES, MALLINDA, 14
NEWBERRY, EDMOND, 69
NEWBERRY, THOMAS, 64
NEWMAN, BETSY, 213, 225
NEWMAN, CHARLES, 103, 190
NEWMAN, EDMOND, 57, 162
NEWMAN, ELIZABETH, 285
NEWMAN, GEORGE, 325
NEWMAN, H. B., 327
NEWMAN, HENRY, 81
NEWMAN, JESSE, 126
NEWMAN, JOHN, 57, 126
NEWMAN, JOSEPH, 139
NEWMAN, MARGARET, 323
NEWMAN, MARIA, 322
NEWMAN, SALLY, 277
NEWMAN, SARAH, 15
NICHODEMUS, BETSY, 219
NICHODEMUS, FREDERICK, 162, 370
NICHODEMUS, JESSE, 205, 219
NICHODEMUS, REBECKA, 226
NICHODEMUS, SARAH, 365
NICHOLS, ELIZABETH, 308
NICHOLS, POLLY, 217
NICHOLSON, SARAH, 373
NICKLE, WILLIAM, 10
NIPPER, ANNY, 331
NIPPER, JANE, 345
NIPPER, SALLY, 80, 83
NISS, ADAM, 112
NOLEN, ABIGAIL, 32
NOLEN, POLLY, 32
NORIDIKE, DANIEL, 25
NORMAN, AILCY, 172
NORMAN, CASANDRA, 252
NORMAN, COURTNEY, 172
NORMAN, HIRAM, 100
NORMAN, SELINA, 313
NORMAN, THERON, 252
NORMAN, WILLIAM, 64
NORRIS, ALFRED, 162
NORRIS, BROWN, 262
NORRIS, REUBEN, 69
NORRIS, SALLY, 94
NORTON, GEORGE, 29

O

P

Reagan, Timothy, 176
Reagan, William, 207
Reardin, David, 32
Reardon, Robert, 32
Rector, Benjamin, 190
Rector, Ludwell, 190, 191
Rector, Nancy, 159
Rector, Washington, 177
Reed, Abram, 82
Reed, Betsy, 59
Reed, Elizabeth, 50, 116, 130, 157
Reed, Felps, 191
Reed, Isby, 115
Reed, Jacob, 64, 302, 339
Reed, James, 26
Reed, Jane, 60
Reed, Jehu, 315, 369
Reed, Joel, 356
Reed, John, 246
Reed, Joseph, 163
Reed, Liddy, 20
Reed, Lucinda, 171
Reed, Mary, 36, 121
Reed, Mitchell, 154
Reed, Nelly, 100
Reed, Robert, 277, 339
Reed, Sally, 51
Reed, Susan M., 322
Reed, Thomas W., 171
Reed, Thos. B., 372
Reed, William, 195
Reeder, James, 339
Reeder, Thomas, 339
Reeves, George W., 262
Reeves, John, 148
Reice, Kazia, 43
Reid, James, 26
Reid, Thomas, 58, 73
Renfro, Nancy, 75
Renfro, Stephen, 74
Renfrow, Hetty, 134
Rentfro, Mary Ann, 229
Rentfroe, Larkin, 101
Rentfrow, James, 177
Rentfrow, Susan, 193
Rew, Ruth, 10
Reynolds, Betsy, 102
Reynolds, Charlotte, 215
Reynolds, Eliza, 155
Reynolds, Elizabeth, 308
Reynolds, Elizabeth Ann, 299, 300, 311
Reynolds, Fanny Ann, 187
Reynolds, George F., 219
Reynolds, Gideon, 40, 102
Reynolds, James, 44
Reynolds, John, 163
Reynolds, John S., 215
Reynolds, Martin L., 372
Reynolds, Nancy, 251
Reynolds, R. B., 370
Reynolds, Robert, 16
Reynolds, Robert B., 332
Reynolds, William, 246
Rhea, Amy, 290, 291
Rhea, Archibald, 92
Rhea, Jenny, 30
Rhea, John, 339
Rhea, Nancy, 2, 19, 318
Rhea, Robert G., 82
Rhea, Sarah, 21
Rhoads, Hannah, 186
Rhoads, John, 126
Rhodes, Aquilla, 219
Rhodes, Betsy, 205
Rhodes, Charity, 314
Rhodes, Hezekiah, 197, 231
Rhodes, Lewis, 113
Rhodes, Matthews, 302
Rhody, Peter, 219
Rhodes, Polly, 16
Rhody, Mahala, 301
Rice, John, 32
Rice, Isaiah, 326, 356
Rice, Margaret, 356
Rice, Martin, 26
Rice, Sarah, 13
Rice, William N., 356
Richards, Geo., 29
Richards, Sarah, 358
Richards, William, 26
Richardson, Alexander,W., 191
Richardson, Brice, 90
Richey, Abel, 4
Richey, Alexander, 21
Richey, James, 21
Richey, Joseph, 302
Richey, Thomas, 4
Richey, William, 4
Richison, John, 113
Richmond, Alexander, 15
Ridge, Jacob, 334
Riggin, Lloyd, 356
Riggle, Polly Ann, 105
Rigney, Betsy, 147
Rigney, George W., 231
Rigney, Henry, 79

Rigney, Mary, 167
Rigney, Nancy, 79
Rigney, William, 69
Riley, John G., 207
Riley, Samuel, 21, 46
Riseden, William, 207
Risedon, Catherine, 72
Ritchey, James, 21
Ritchey, Sarah, 21
Ritchie, Joseph, 2
Ritchie, William, 207
Ritter, Lucinda, 152
Rively, Francis, 177
Roach, George, 27
Roach, Jesse, 26
Roach, Littleton, 50
Roady, Josiah, 360
Roady, Moses, 177
Roady, Nancy, 327
Roady, Nathaniel, 326
Roady, Thomas, 326
Roane, Ann, 162
Roane, David, 85
Roark, Ivy, 359
Roark, Mahuldah, 372
Roberson, James, 15
Roberson, John, 11, 15
Roberts, Abram, 74
Roberts, Amos, 101, 126
Roberts, Andrew, 140
Roberts, Charles, 354, 357
Roberts, Cynthia, 329
Roberts, Eno., 289
Roberts, Henry, 10, 58, 246, 326
Roberts, Henry G., 337
Roberts, Isabella, 43
Roberts, James, 74, 113, 127, 246
Roberts, John, 69, 90, 285, 302
Roberts, Jozadak, 113, 117, 126
Roberts, Judith, 154
Roberts, Kesiah, 154
Roberts, L. P., 349, 356
Roberts, Margaret, 10, 135
Roberts, Mary Anne, 65
Rogers, Nancy, 54
Roberts, Nathan, 26
Roberts, Peggy, 101
Roberts, Rachel, 1
Roberts, Rebecca, 157
Roberts, Sally, 101, 256
Roberts, Samuel, 76, 185
Roberts, Sarah Catherine, 361
Roberts, Sophia, 352, 367
Roberts, William, 43, 127
Robertson, Arthur, 307
Robertson, Cornelius, 262
Robertson, David, 9, 15
Robertson, Elizabeth, 9
Robertson, Margaret, 206
Robertson, Robert, 53
Robertson, Stephen, 15
Robertson, Willoughby, 4
Robeson, James, 140
Robeson, Peggy, 83
Robeson, Penina, 374
Robinson, James, 140, 191
Robinson, John L., 277
Robinson, Nathaniel, 58
Robinson, Nicholas, 3
Robinson, Thomas, 70
Robison, Benjamin, 276
Robison, Betsy, 276
Robison, Emoline, 325
Robison, Margaret, 153
Robison, Nancy, 157
Robison, Nicholas, 5
Robison, Polly, 262
Roddy, Alexander, 152
Roddy, Gideon, 210
Roddy, Moses, 246
Roddy, Levina, 173
Roddy, Samuel, 208
Roddy, Wm., 163
Rodgers, Andrew, 127
Rodgers, David, 191
Rodgers, Frederick F., 191
Rodgers, James 353, 356, 360, 368, 371
Rodgers, Jas., 344
Rodgers, John, 127, 174
Rodgers, Joseph, 82, 88, 225
Rodgers, Nancy, 109
Rodgers, Sally, 344
Rodgers, Samuel R., 234, 245, 327, 331, 338, 342
Rodgers, Sarah, 225
Rodgers, Thomas, 81, 177, 299

RODGERS, THOS. 82, 127
RODGERS, WILLIAM, 66, 91, 320, 340, 341, 352, 363, 375
RODY, JOSIAH, 315
RODY, NATHANIEL L., 315
ROGAN, DANIEL JR., 289
ROGERS, BETSY, 88
ROGERS, JAMES, 82
ROGERS, JOHN, 196
ROGERS, JOSEPH JR., 277
ROGERS, PETER, 277
ROGERS, REUBEN, 295
ROGERS, THOMAS A., 50
ROGERS, THOS. A., 48, 50, 51
ROHR, PHILIP, 163
ROLIN, LORY, 112
ROLMOND, MARY, 18
ROOKARD, LINDA, 262
ROOP, POLLY, 344
ROPER, WM., 101
RORICK, JANE, 42
ROSE, JOHN, 372
ROSE, POLLY, 201
ROSE, SARAH B., 374
ROSEYGRANT, RICHARD, 48
ROSS, JNO. G., 81
ROSS, LUCRETIA, 137
ROSS, PEGGY, 142
ROSS, RACHEL, 69
ROSS, ROBERT, 375
ROSS, SAMUEL, 15, 137
ROULSTONE, GEORGE, 6
ROUTH, EDWARD, 232
ROUTH, ISAAC, 101
ROUTH, JAMES, 163, 208
ROUTH, JOSEPH, 163, 208
ROWLAND, THOMAS, 101
ROY, FRANCES, 52
RUDDER, CATHARINE, 338
RUDDER, EDWARD, 246
RUDDER, JOEL, 218, 357
RUDDER, LIVIA, 348
RUDER, GERUSHA E., 146
RUDINE, MARTIN, 28
RULE, CHRISTIANA, 227
RULE, GEORGE, 357
RULE, HENRY, 326
RULE, JACOB, 227
RULE, JOHN, 219
RULE, PETER, 357
RULE, ROSANNAH, 108
RUSKIN, PASCAL, 64
RUSSELL, ANDREW, 74, 91
RUSSELL, B. M., 288
RUSSELL, ELIZABETH, 37, 76, 281, 331
RUSSELL, GEORGE, 336, 338, 339, 358, 359
RUSSELL, JOHN, 64, 113
RUSSELL, JOHN P., 339, 340
RUSSELL, JOSEPH, 231
RUSSELL, MARY, 182
RUSSELL, MOSES, 312, 315, 371
RUSSELL, NANCY, 215
RUSSELL, PATSY, 193
RUSSELL, POLLY, 78
RUSSELL, REBECKA, 287
RUSSELL, REUBEN, 127
RUSSELL, WILLIAM, 16, 140
RUSSELL, WM., 121
RUSSOM, JOHN, 310, 341
RUTH, ANN, 315
RUTH, JACOB, 129
RUTH, JAMES, 26
RUTH, MARTHA, 312
RUTH, POLLY, 76
RUTH, RHODA, 193
RUTH, SUSANNA, 371
RUTHERFORD, ABSALOM, 208, 222
RUTHERFORD, AMELIA, 275, 305
RUTHERFORD, ANNY, 49
RUTHERFORD, BETSY, 58, 108
RUTHERFORD, DAVID, 208
RUTHERFORD, EDWARD, 74
RUTHERFORD, ELIZABETH, 348
RUTHERFORD, ESTHER, 199
RUTHERFORD, HOUSTON L., 357
RUTHERFORD, JAMES, 91, 248
RUTHERFORD, JOHN, 54, 58, 177
RUTHERFORD, JOSEPH, 246
RUTHERFORD, LINA, 242
RUTHERFORD, LLOYD, 251, 327
RUTHERFORD, MARK, 315
RUTHERFORD, MARY, 82, 360
RUTHERFORD, NANCY, 227, 258
RUTHERFORD, PEGGY, 231

RUTHERFORD, SARAH, 94, 302
RUTHERFORD, WILLIAM, 140, 332, 341
RYSDON, SOPHY, 100

S

SAMBURG, REASON, 50
SAMPLE, MARTHA, 127
SAMPLE, SAMUEL, 84, 90, 94, 101, 105, 114, 118, 119, 131, 133, 141, 154, 181, 190, 191, 198
SAMPLER, JAMES, 127
SAMPLES, PEGGY, 119
SANDERS, JOHN D., 214
SANDERS, RHODY, 183
SANDERS, SARAH, 115
SANDERSON, LUCY, 57
SANDLAND, ELIZABETH, 204
SANFORD, SIMPSON, 116
SANSKIVER, ANDREW, 16
SARGANT, JOHN H., 45
SARTAIN, DAVID, 16
SARTIN, CLARK, 399
SAUNDERS, JOHN, 74
SAUNDERS, POLLY, 49
SAUNDERS, YOUNG, 101
SAWYERS, JNO. C., 373
SAWYERS, REBECCA, 73
SAWYERS, JAMES, 9
SAWYERS, JOHN, 50
SAWYERS, JOSIAH, 140
SAWYERS, WILLIAM, 110, 111, 112, 115, 120, 132, 138, 140, 141, 145, 236, 147, 148, 151, 159, 239, 174, 178, 182, 183, 242, 184, 185, 186, 187, 246, 197, 200, 201, 204, 247, 208, 222, 227, 234, 249, 256, 258, 261, 262, 284, 285, 287, 291, 294, 305, 308, 313,
SCAGGS, CHARLES, 16
SCAGGS, DEBORAH, 127
SCAGGS, JAMES, 91
SCAGGS, SARAH, 77
SCAGGS, SOLOMON, 70
SCARBORO, ALEY, 121
SCARBOROUGH, ELIJAH, 42, 101
SCARBOROUGH, JAMES, 37
SCARBOROUGH, MARY, 24
SCARBURY, JNO., 372
SCAVITT, SALLY, 113
SCHOOLFIELD, JOSEPH, 277, 313
SCHRIDER, JACOB, 10
SCISSON, NELSON M., 372
SCOTT, ADELINE, 277
SCOTT, ALSE, 137
SCOTT, ANDREW, 305
SCOTT, ARTHUR, 70
SCOTT, BETSY, 72
SCOTT, CATHARINE, 292
SCOTT, CATHRINA, 307
SCOTT, CHARLES, 295, 297, 302, 306, 307, 317,
SCOTT, DONAH, 28
SCOTT, EDWARD, 26, 34
SCOTT, ELSEY, 66
SCOTT, H. T., 306
SCOTT, HAMDEN, 163
SCOTT, HAMDEN S., 141
SCOTT, JAMES, 21, 101, 208, 358, 191
SCOTT, JANE, 183
SCOTT, JNO. N., 113
SCOTT, JOSEPH, 243, 247, 263, 301, 315, 320
SCOTT, LAWRENCE, 26
SCOTT, MALINDA, 167
SCOTT, MARY, 78, 109
SCOTT, MARY ANN, 278, 279
SCOTT, MILLY, 231
SCOTT, MINTY, 243
SCOTT, NANCY, 39
SCOTT, PETER, 232, 277
SCOTT, POLLY, 103
SCOTT, SALLY, 32
SCOTT, SARAH M., 194
SCOTT, TANDY, 263
SCOTT, THOMAS, 127, 327
SCOTT, WILLIAM, 191
SCOTT, WILLIAM P., 232
SCRUGGINS, JOSIAH, 339
SEABOLT, JOHN, 342, 344
SEABOLT, MARY, 269
SEABOLT, SUSANA, 296

SEABOTT, RUSSELL, 315
SEAROEY, RICHARD, 21
SEARS, JOHN, 4
SEATON, ANN A. G., 331
SEATON, JAMES, 73, 271
SEATON, JAMES N., 327
SEAY, ELIZA, 336
SEAY, NANCY W., 272
SEAY, THOMAS, 372
SEAY, WILLIAM F., 355
SEETON, JAMES 284, 300, 301, 303, 314
SEETON, MARGARET, 279
SEITON, JAMES, 58
SENSABAUGH, CATHERINE, 156
SENSABAUGH, JACOB, 141
SENSEBAUGH, ELIZABETH, 187
SENSEBAUGH, MARY MAGDEINE, 268
SENTER, WILLIAM P., 217
SENTER, WILLIAM T., 230, 232
SERET, JAMES, 101
SERTAIN, POLLY, 12
SETLER, ABRAHAM, 21
SEVIER, E. F., 259
SEVIER, ROBERT, 64
SEXTON, MATTHEW, 43
SEYMORE, JAMES, 74
SHADDIN, JOSEPH, 16
SHALL, GEORGE, 43
SHANABERRY, GEORGE, 339
SHANNON, WESTLEY, 357
SHARKEY, PATRICK, 16, 23
SHARP, AMELIA, 244
SHARP, AMOS, 49
SHARP, DANIEL, 26, 27
SHARP, ELIZA, 260
SHARP, ELIZABETH, 11
SHARP, HANNA, 115
SHARP, ISAAC, 208, 216
SHARP, JAMES, 327
SHARP, JAMES B., 58
SHARP, JOHN, 35
SHARP, JONATHAN, 208
SHARP, OSWELL, 327
SHARP, THOMAS, 141
SHARP, WILLIAM, 43
SHARPE, HARIOTT, 443
SHEAFER, POLLY, 27
SHELBY, ELIJA, 373
SHELBY, ELIJAH, 357
SHELHORSE, NANCY, 100
SHELL, ELIZABETH, 159
SHELL, JOHN, 89
SHELL, JULIA, 147
SHELL, LEWIS, 114
SHELL, LILLY, 190
SHELL, NANCY, 50
SHELL, RUTH, 191
SHELLEY, CHARLES, 188
SHELLY, ELIJAH, 373
SHELTON, ELIZABETH, 47
SHELTON, HALL, 58
SHELTON, JENNY, 30
SHELTON, JOHN, 58, 89
SHELTON, LOTTY, 343
SHELTON, LYDIA, 61
SHELTON, SKIRVING, 101
SHERARTZ, ELIZABETH, 197
SHERARTZ, JOHN, 197
SHERERTZ, WILLIAM, 339
SHERET, JAMES D., 152
SHERETZ, JOHN, 164
SHERETZ, MARY, 161
SHERMAN, DAVID A., 208
SHERODD, ELIZABETH, 207, 364
SHERRICK, JACOB, 302
SHERROD, ANNA, 349
SHERROD, JESSE, 345
SHERROD, PHILIP, 357
SHERROD, SUSAN, 353
SHERRODD, CATHARINE, 300
SHERRODD, GEORGE, W., 300
SHERWOOD, BENJAMIN, 127
SHETTERLY, GEORGE, 116, 220, 229, 278
SHIELDS, JAMES, 64
SHIELDS, JOHN, 16
SHIELDS, NATHANIEL, 315
SHIELDS, ROBERT, 131, 192, 312
SHIELDS, WILLIAM, 264, 289
SHINBERRY, JUDY, 348
SHINPACK, HENRY, 302
SHINPATH, POLLY, 273
SHINPOCK, ROSANNAH, 53
SHIPE, ADAM, 70
SHIPE, ELIZABETH, 86
SHIPE, HENRY, 127, 263
SHIPE, MARTHA, 205
SHIPE, MARY, 263

SHIPE, NELSON, 373
SHIPLEY, CHRISTOPHER, 58
SHIPLEY, THOMAS, 70
SHIPP, WILLIS, 278
SHIRK, JOHN, 91
SHIRLEY, BALSAR, 74
SHOOKEY, JOHN, 128
SHOOKEY, MARGARET ANN, 369
SHOEKY, JOHN, 128
SHOOK, ABRAHAM, 10, 14, 46
SHOOK, BECKY, 292
SHOOK, HARMON, 46
SHOOK, JEMIMA, 42
SHOOK, JOHN, 91
SHOOK, MAGDALENA, 14
SHOOK, MARY ANN, 30
SHOOK, SARAH, 10
SHORT, ADAM, 177
SHORT, SARAH, 135
SHOUL, SARAH AGNES, 62
SHRINK, ELIZABETH, 253
SHULER, ABNER, 128
SHUPOCK, JOHN, 58
SIDWELL, ISAAC, 21
SIDWELL, JOSEPH, 21
SIGLER, WM. M., 128
SIMMONS, CATHARINE, 324
SIMMONS, FANNY, 56
SIMMONS, FRANKY, 107
SIMMONS, THOMAS, 56
SIMMONS, WILLIAM, 247, 263
SIMMS, JEAN, 92
SIMPSON, ALEXANDER, 152, 349, 373
SIMPSON, BETSY, 164
SIMPSON, ELIZA, 347
SIMPSON, ELIZA JANE, 349
SIMPSON, JESSE, 374
SIMPSON, JESSE, JR., 357
SIMPSON, JOHN, 70, 152, 278
SIMPSON, LEWIS, 91
SIMPSON, MARY, 7, 281
SIMPSON, MATTHEW, 260, 278, 357
SIMPSON, NANCY, 220
SIMPSON, PEGGY, 4, 20
SIMPSON, POLLY, 295
SIMPSON, REBECCA, 11
SIMPSON, SALLY, 116, 120
SIMPSON, WILLIAM, 232, 278, 340
SIMS, ELY, 32, 38
SINGLETON, JOHN W., 340
SITLU, PHILIP, 74
SKAGGS, CHARLES, 289
SKAGGS, CHARLOTTE, 315
SKAGGS, CLARISSA, 271
SKAGGS, ELI, 263, 289
SKAGGS, ELIZABETH, 186
SKAGGS, JAMES, 221, 290
SKAGGS, MARTHA, 226
SKAGGS, MOSES, 192
SKAGGS, P. H., 348
SKAGGS, PRESTON H., 358
SKAGGS, REBECKA, 230
SKAGGS, S. M., 204, 299
SKAGGS, SOLOMON, 66
SKAGGS, STEPHEN M., 135, 375
SKAGGS, SUSANNA, 110
SKAGGS, URSULA, 285
SKIDMORE, JOHN, 46
SKINNER, WILLIAM, 50
SKIPPER, BNE, 83
SLAGLE, MICHAEL, 358, 371
SLAGLE, REBECCA, 358
SLATER, POLLY, 298
SLATERY, MARGARET, 282
SLATERY, MARGERY, 287
SLATERY, THOMAS, 358
SLOAN, WILLIAM, 4, 5
SLOANE, AMELIA, 35
SMART, JAMES R., 263
SMEDLEY, WILLIAM, 340
SMELSER, DAVID, 12
SMELSER, SUSANNAH, 12
SMILEY, JACOB, 202
SMILEY, PEGGY, 202
SMITH, AARON, 219
SMITH, ADAM, 102
SMITH, ALEE, 287
SMITH, ALEXANDER, 27, 192, 315
SMITH, AMANDA, 202
SMITH, ANDREW, 358
SMITH, ANNE, 28
SMITH, ANNIE, 8
SMITH, BANNISTER, 141, 263
SMITH, BARBARA, 69, 304
SMITH, BETSY, 64, 180, 298, 360, 369, 370, 375

STOUT, MALINDA, 352
STOUT, MOSES, 70
STOUT, ROSANAH, 254
STOW, EDY, 321
STOWELL, ALEXR., 179
STOWELL, JNO., 153
STOWMER, GEORGE, 233
STRANGE, SARAH, 245
STRICKLER, JOSEPH, 21
STRICKLIN, ABIGAIL, 193
STRINGFIELD, MARY, 40
STRINGFIELD, RICHARD, 102
STRINGFIELD, THOMAS, 216, 306, 312, 316, 321
STRONG, JOSEPH C., 59
STRONG, MARTHA A., 207
STRONG, MARY, 333
STUART, ELIZABETH, 20
STUART, JOHN, 102, 161, 192
STUART, JOSEPH, 153
STUART, ROBERT, 102
STUFFLE, ABRAHAM, 290
STUFFLE, GEORGE, 189
STUFFLE, HANNAH, 189
STULCE, ABNER, 129
STURGESS, WESTLEY, 247
SULAN, JOHN A., 165
SULLINS, PATTY, 24
SULLINS, RICHARD, 27
SULLINS, T., 360, 364, 369, 372
SUMMERS, ELIZA, 254
SUMMERS, EMOLINE, 327
SUMMERS, JOHNSTON, 114
SUMMERS, MARY R., 290
SUMMERS, PATSEY, 59
SUMMERS, WILLIAM, 209
SUMPTER, BETSY, 144
SUMPTER, JAMES, 152
SUMPTER, SUSANNAH, 130
SUMPTER, WILLIAM, 91
SUMTER, JAMES, 184
SURRIS, JNO., 40
SUTHERLAND, DAVID, 17
SUTHERLAND, JOHN, 116
SUTHERLAND, JOHN JR., 91, 100
SUTON, JAMES, 254
SUTTLE, JOSEPH, 327
SUTTLE, NANCY, 285
SUTTON, JOHN, 48
SWADDLEY, BETSY, 106
SWADER, FRANCIS, 164
SWADER, POLLY, 100
SWADLEY, JANE, 119
SWADLEY, THOMAS, 102
SWAGERTY, BENJ. A., 179
SWAGERTY, BETSY, 118
SWAGERTY, CLAIBORNE, 263
SWAGERTY, POLLY, 283
SWAGGERTY, D., 167
SWAGGERTY, STOCKLY D., 164
SWAN, ALEXANDER, 247
SWAN, ELIZA, 345
SWAN, J. A., 180, 193, 198, 212, 223, 224, 225, 232, 245
SWAN, JANE, 99
SWAN, JANE H., 141
SWAN, JOHN A., 141, 196, 220
SWAN, JOSEPH L., 316
SWAN, M. M., 269, 344, 352, 355, 358, 360, 362, 363, 364, 365, 367, 369, 370, 371, 372, 373
SWAN, MARGARET, 87
SWAN, MARGARET L. J., 334
SWAN, MARY A., 270
SWAN, MOSES M., 209
SWAN, P. A., 180, 182
SWAN, R. A., 167
SWAN, R. M., 193
SWAN, ROBERT M., 192
SWAN, SAMUEL, 8, 87, 92
SWAN, W., 155
SWAN, W. H., 258
SWAN, WILLIAM, 126, 137, 140, 141, 145, 146, 150, 151, 152, 153, 156, 156, 158, 161, 163, 165, 166, 167, 168, 169, 170, 179, 172, 173, 174, 175, 177, 178, 180, 181, 184, 188, 189, 190, 191, 192, 193, 194, 195, 196, 198, 199, 200, 201, 202, 203, 204, 205, 206, 207, 208, 209, 210, 211, 212, 213, 214, 215, 216, 218, 219, 220, 221, 222, 223, 225, 226, 228,

(SWAN, WILLIAM, CONTINUED TO PAGE 68)

SWAN, WILLIAM, 229, 230, 232, 233, 237, 239, 240, 241, 242, 243, 249, 250, 251, 252, 254, 255, 256, 258, 260, 261, 262, 263, 264, 265, 266, 267, 268, 269, 270, 271, 272, 273, 275, 276, 277, 278, 279, 280, 281, 282, 283, 284, 285, 286, 287, 288, 289, 290, 291, 292, 293, 296, 298, 299, 300, 301, 302, 303, 304, 307, 312, 316, 318, 325, 326
SWAN, WILLIAM H., 247
SWINK, SALLY, 239
SWORD, PHILLIP, 141
SYLAR, PETER, 141

T

TABLER, ANNE, 247
TACKIT, SUSAN, 153
TALBOT, MARY C., 149
TALENT, NANCY, 78
TALLENT, NANCY, 131
TALLENT, ODEM C., 179
TALLEY, MATTHIAS, 40
TALLEY, ROBERT, 336
TANNYHILL, POLLY, 117
TARBET, SAMUEL, 165
TARVER, NANCY, 255
TARVER, RANSOM R., 248
TARWATER, DAVID, 70, 327
TARWATER, FREDERICK, 51
TARWATER, JACOB, 43
TARWATER, MARGARET, 364
TARWATER, NANCY, 279
TARWATER, NANCY J., 326
TARWATER, PETER, 374
TARWATER, TEEWALT, 43, 51
TARWATER, WILLIAM, 64, 156
TAWNYHILL, MARGARET, 58
TAYLOR, ALSO, 220
TAYLOR, ANNE, 84
TAYLOR, ANDREW, 264, 275
TAYLOR, CAWFIELD, 50
TAYLOR, ELIZA, 94
TAYLOR, ELIZABETH, 367
TAYLOR, EZEKIEL, 64
TAYLOR, HANNAH, 201
TAYLOR, HENRY, 43
TAYLOR, JAMES M., 316
TAYLOR, JESSE, 358
TAYLOR, JOHN, 51
TAYLOR, LUCY, 269
TAYLOR, MALVINA, 245
TAYLOR, MARIAH, 147
TAYLOR, MARY, 9
TAYLOR, MARY ANN, 72, 289
TAYLOR, MENCA, 232
TAYLOR, NELLY ANN, 370
TAYLOR, PEGGY, 23
TAYLOR, PHILIP, 40
TAYLOR, REBECCA, 85
TAYLOR, ROBERT S., 316
TAYLOR, SALLEY, 325
TAYLOR, SALLY, 294, 325
TAYLOR, SAMUEL, 102
TAYLOR, THOMAS, 33, 83
TAYLOR, WILLIAM, 54, 248
TAYS, BETSY, 77
TAYS, ROBERT, 70
TEAL, EDWARD, 26
TEDFORD, JOSEPH, 5
TEEL, JOHN, 114
TEEL, SAMUEL, 114
TEENOR, ANNE, 232
TELFORD, JAMES, 3, 5
TELFOUR, GEORGE, 5
TEMPLE, E. S., 348
TEMPLE, JEREMIAH, 220
TEMPLE, PLEASANT J., 374
TEMPLE, THOMAS S., 290
TENOR, JACOB, 34
TERRY, JESSE, 17, 31
TERRY, JOHN, 29
TERRY, MICAJAH, 30
TERRY, SALLY, 31
TERRY, STEPHEN, 32, 43
THARP, DANIEL, 33
THARP, OLIVER C., 209
THATCHER, ELLEN, 259
THATCHER, EMILY, 116
THATCHER, SAMUEL, 233

THOMAS, ADAM, 316, 374
THOMAS, ANDREW, 316
THOMAS, CATHARINE, 184
THOMAS, DAVID, 303
THOMAS, DOUGLASS, 3
THOMAS, HENRY, 142
THOMAS, JACOB, 374
THOMAS, JOHN, 290
THOMAS, MARY, 29
THOMAS, POLLY, 321
THOMAS, SALLY, 255
THOMAS, SAMUEL, 66
THOMAS, SUSAN, 165
THOMASON, JAMES, 193
THOMPSON, BETSY, 141, 201
THOMPSON, BETSY L., 280
THOMPSON, DAVID, 121, 157
THOMPSON, FRANCES, 259
THOMPSON, HARVEY, 114
THOMPSON, ISAAC, 75
THOMPSON, JAMES, 68, 75, 134, 165, 220
THOMPSON, JAMES, H., 374
THOMPSON, JANE, 350
THOMPSON, JENNY, 35
THOMPSON, JOHN, 85, 89, 93, 94, 95, 100, 108, 114, 117
THOMPSON, JONATHAN, 358
THOMPSON, JOSEPH, 193
THOMPSON, LOYAL B., 327
THOMPSON, MAJORY, 369
THOMPSON, MARY, 68
THOMPSON, MARY B., 362
THOMPSON, MATTHEW, 280, 303
THOMPSON, NANCY, 174, 194, 313, 326
THOMPSON, REBECKA, 272
THOMPSON, RICHARD W., 328
THOMPSON, SAMUEL, 103, 114
THOMPSON, SARAH, 133
THOMPSON, SARAH A. M. C., 343
THOMPSON, SUSAN C., 315
THOMPSON, SUSANNAH, 9
THOMPSON, WILLIAM, 10, 27, 43, 75, 153, 279
THOMPSON, YEARLY, 343
THOMPSON, YERBY, 209
THORNBERY, ELLEDGE, 82
THORNHILL, ARMSTEAD, 30
THORNHILL, LOCKY, 233
THORNTON, JAMES A., 114, 290
THORNTON, JOHN, 43
THORNTON, MARGARET, 286
THORNTON, THOMAS D., 316
THREEWITTS, JOHN, 254
THUERRITZ, JOHN, 114
TIDWELL, RACHEL, 17
TILLERY, ELENER, 35
TILLERY, JOHN, 46, 128, 220
TILLERY, LETTY, 128
TILLERY, MARGARET, 224
TILLERY, RICHARD, M., 70
TILLERY, SAMPSON, 71
TILLERY, SAMUEL, 46
TILLERY, THOMAS P., 179
TILLMAN, BARBARA, 26
TIMON, MATTHEW, 193
TINCH, WILEY Y., 374
TINDAL, MILLY, 98
TINDEL, SALLY, 98
TINDALL, ANN, 297
TINDALL, ROBERT, 286
TINDALL, WILLIAM, 35
TINDEL, ROBERT, 199
TINDELL, ABNER, 248, 317
TINDELL, ALFRED, 328
TINDELL, BERIAH, 248
TINDELL, DICK, 307
TINDELL, ELIZA, 231
TINDELL, GEORGE, 209
TINDELL, HIRAM, 328
TINDELL, JAMES, 303
TINDELL, JOHN, 255
TINDELL, MARTIN, 317
TINDELL, MARY, 321
TINDELL, MINERVA, 337
TINDELL, NANCY, 30
TINDELL, NATHAN, 142
TINDELL, RICHARD, 320
TINDELL, ROBERT, 54, 185, 200, 207, 209, 217, 235, 238, 245, 249, 254, 256, 260, 268, 275, 295, 297, 300, 304
TINDELL, SALLY, 99
TINDELL, SUSANNAH, 158
TINDLE, CALVIN, 359
TINER, LEWIS, 5
TINKER, OBADIAH, 153
TINKER, PATSY, 301

TINKER, WILLIAM, 153
TINSLEY, CATHARINE J., 315
TIPTON, ABRAHAM, 51, 152
TIPTON, CHARLOTTE, 313
TIPTON, D. B., 365, 366
TIPTON, DAVID B., 317, 367
TIPTON, ISAAC, 51, 70
TIPTON, JACOB, 75
TIPTON, JONATHAN, 209
TIPTON, JONATHON, 248
TIPTON, NANCY, 337
TIPTON, REUBEN, 36, 142
TIPTON, WILLIAM, 26
TIPTON, WILLIAM C., 317
TITTERO, JACOB, 142
TOBLER, CATHERINE, 75
TOBLER, CHARLOTTE, 107
TOBLER, GEORGE, W., 165
TONKSEY, POLLY, 215
TOOL, JAMES, 50
TOOMY, AMBROSE, 46
TOVERKA, BARTLEY, 317
TOWNSEND, JOHN, 38
TOWNSEND, RACHEL, 38
TRAMMELL, MALINDA, 26
TRAVIS, GEORGE, 61
TRAVIS, MILLER, 276
TREADWAY, JOHN, 34
TRIGG, ANN L., 338
TRIMBLE, ROSANAH, 4
TROOPS, HENRY, 103
TROUT, ISAAC, 317
TROUT, JOHN, 248, 275, 317
TROUT, NANCY, 326
TROUT, NICHOLAS, 341
TROUT, PEGGY, 57
TROUT, WILLIAM, 57, 64, 279, 326, 357
TROUT, JOHN, 44
TROUTT, WILLIAM, 286
TUCKER, CAMPBELL, 359
TUCKER, LAVIN, 118
TUCKER, PATSY, 301
TUCKER, RUSSELL, 359
TUCKER, WILLIAMSON, 359
TUMBLIN, POLLY, 123
TUNNELL, ELIZA, 236
TUNNELL, GEORGE, 215
TUNNELL, JOHN, 17, 30
TUNNELL, MATILDA, 207
TUNNELL, ROBERT, 78, 119, 124, 125, 129, 136, 147, 148, 157, 164, 173, 178
TUNNELL, SUSAN G., 172
TUNNELL, WILLIAM, 17
TURBEVILLE, JAMES, 193
TURBEVILLE, SARAH, 266
TURBEVILLE, WILLIAM, 244
TURBIVILL, LAVINIA V., 95
TURK, GEORGE W., 303
TURNER, ALEXANDER, 374
TURNER, RACHAEL, 80
TURPIN, MARTIN, 37

U

UBANK, JOHN, 165
UMBERSET, DEAVER, 192
UNDERWOOD, ELMIRA, 279
UNDERWOOD, GEO., 83
UNDERWOOD, HIRAM, 171
UNDERWOOD, JAMES, 351
UNDERWOOD, JANE, 143
UNDERWOOD, JOHN, 153
UNDERWOOD, LILAH, 171
UNDERWOOD, MARGARET, 327
UNDERWOOD, MARY, 79
UNDERWOOD, POLLY, 149
UNDERWOOD, SALLY, 283
UNDERWOOD, SUSANNAH, 306
UNDERWOOD, THOMAS, 328
UNDERWOOD, ZILPHA, 69
UPTON, DAVID, 35

V

VANCE, JAMES, 328
VANCE, JOHN, 27, 317
VANCE, JOSEPH, 129
VANCE, SAMUEL, 5, 114, 317
VAN DYKE, JOHN H., 92
VANHOOSER, ISAAC, 27
VANN, DELILAH, 31
VARNER, DRUSILLA, 243
VARNER, HENRY, 293
VARNER, JACOB, 241
VARNER, LOUISA J., 187
VARNER, MARECA JANE, 290
VARNER, MARY C., 243
VARNER, PETER, 290
VARNUM, GEO. 74
VAUGHN, REUBEN, 2
VEAL, MARY, 20
VEALE, J. C., 327, 280
VEALS, MARGARET ANN R., 310
VEALS, MINERVA, 311
VERNON, MILES C., 279

VESTNER, DANIEL, 92
VICKARS, ELIZABETH, 221
VICKERS, KITTY, 56
VICKERS, LILA, 604
VICKERS, POLLY, 245
VICKEY, SAM'L, 372

W

WADDLE, ANNA, 178
WADE, DANIEL, 193
WADE, ELIZABETH, 268
WADE, FLEMING, 233
WADE, HAVEL, 193
WADE, JANE, 275
WADE, NANCY, 219
WADE, SALLY, 225
WAGGONER, GEORGE, 47
WAGGONER, HENRY, 286, 328
WAGGONER, JOHN, 303
WAGGONER, JOHN A., 328
WAGGONER, JNO. A., 325
WAGGONER, PETER, 142
WAGGONER, POLLY, 57
WAGONER, SALLY, 190
WALDROP, ARCHIBALD, 341
WALKER, ----, 109
WALKER, AMANDA M., 323
WALKER, BARCKLY, 264
WALKER, BARKLEY, 175, 211
WALKER, BERSHEBA, 133
WALKER, DALY, 109
WALKER, DAVID, 129
WALKER, ELIZABETH, 271, 351
WALKER, FANNY, 65
WALKER, GEORGE, 75
WALKER, GEORGIA, 164
WALKER, HANNAH, 147, 148
WALKER, HARVEY, 341, 374
WALKER, HENRY, 151, 153
WALKER, HESTER, 105
WALKER, JAMES E., 233, 317
WALKER, JAMES, K., 374
WALKER, JANE, 261
WALKER, JESSE, 209
WALKER, LUCY, 46
WALKER, MARY, 4, 174, 182, 279
WALKER, MARY ANN, 160
WALKER, MARY R., 257
WALKER, MILLY, 170
WALKER, NANCY, 145
WALKER, PATSEY, 60
WALKER, PATSY, 165
WALKER, PEGGY, 79
WALKER, POLLY, 145
WALKER, PRUDENCE, 259
WALKER, RACHEL, 369
WALKER, REUBEN, 193, 142, 209
WALKER, RICHARD, 165
WALKER, SAMUEL K., 341
WALKER, THOMAS H., 340
WALKER, W., 142
WALKER, WEST, 89, 100, 103, 146
WALKER, WILLIAM, 142, 193, 279, 328
WALKER, WM., 168
WALL, JOHN, 220
WALL, WILLIAM, 220, 234
WALLACE, B. M., 221, 251, 268, 275
WALLACE, C., 270
WALLACE, ELIJAH, 318
WALLACE, JOHN, 153
WALLACE, LINDSAY, 303
WALLACE, POLLY, 7
WALLACE, THOMAS, 304
WALLAND, CATHERINE, 364
WALLIN, JAMES M., 374
WALSH, FRANCIS, 341
WANDLESS, POLLY, 36
WARD, AMY, 75
WARD, JOHN, 92, 119
WARD, LEONARD, 92
WARD, NANCY, 79
WARD, SARAH, 92
WARE, JOHN, 50
WARICK, ORANGE, 373
WARNACK, ISAAC E., 179
WARNACK, WILLIAM, 264
WARNICK, ELEANOR, 117
WARREN, MARY, 2
WARREN, NANCY, 256
WARREN, SUSAN, 359

WARREN, WILLIAM, 264
WARRICK, ORANGE, 327
WARWICK, NANCY, 327
WARWICK, ORANGE, 375
WARWICK, PHEBE, 214
WARWICK, SALLY, 222
WARWICK, WESTERN, 65
WARWICK, WIATT, 226
WASHAM, GEORGE J., 248
WASHINGTON, GEORGE, 75
WATERS, P. A., 360
WATKINS, ELIZABETH, 353
WATKINS, JAMES, 267
WATKINS, MATTY, 203
WATKINS, RICHARD, 179
WATKINS, SAMUEL, 220
WATKINS, WM., 344
WATSON, HANNAH, 75
WATSON, SALLY M., 298
WATSON, WILLIAM S., 114
WATT, BETSY, 207
WATT, JAMES, 134, 191, 195, 304
WATT, JANE, 334
WATT, JOSEPH, 248
WATT, MARTHA, 297
WATT, PEGGY, 134
WATT, SAMUEL, 304
WATT, SUSANNAH, 69
WATTS, JOHN, 165
WATTS, POLLY, 347
WEADEN, PEGGY, 217
WEAR, A., 295
WEAR, ABRAHAM, 75
WEAR, BETSY, 75
WEAR, GEORGE, 54
WEAR, JOHN, 17
WEAR, POLLY, 64
WEAR, SAM'L, 59
WEATHERINGTON, ANN, 30
WEATHERTON, ELIZABETH, 16, 17
WEAVER, AMY, 228
WEAVER, DAVID, 180, 290
WEAVER, ELEANOR, 208
WEAVER, JAMES, 180, 209, 356, 359
WEAVER, JNO., 324
WEAVER, MARY, 176
WEAVER, ROBERT, 279
WEAVER, SUSAN, 310
WEAVER, WALTER, 153
WEAVER, WILLIAM, 194, 310
WEAVER, WM., 366
WEBB, ANNE, 288
WEBB, CATHARINE, 289
WEBB, GEORGE, 221
WEBB, JOHN, 290
WEBB, MARY JANE, 324
WEBB, REUBEN, 341
WEBB, ROBERT, 264
WEBB, SARAH, 351
WEBB, SENETH, 204
WEBB, THOMAS, 129
WEBB, TILDA, 366
WEBB, WILLIAM B., 279
WEBSTER, JAMES, 290, 291
WEBSTER, POLLY, 307
WEBSTER, SANDERS, 290, 291, 341
WEBBER, CASPER, 135, 341
WEBBER, TILDA, 366
WEBBER, WILLIAM W., 233
WEEDEN, BETSY, 286
WEIR, HARVEY, 207
WEIR, MARY, 193
WEIR, TELITHA, 321
WEIR, WM. R., 180
WELCH, PETER, 59 ✓
WELKER, CATHARINE, 91
WELKER, MARIAH, 300
WELKER, MARTHA, 259
WELLS, ARCHIBALD, 237
WELLS, CINDRILLA, 197
WELLS, ELIZABETH, 335
WELLS, GEORGE, 75
WELLS, JESSE, 59, 341
WELLS, JNO. T., 372
WELLS, STEPHEN, 51
WELSH, JOHN, 142
WELSH, LUCRETIA, 197
WELSH, MARY E., 272
WERT, JOSEPH, S., 180
WEST, JENNY, 264
WEST, JOHN, 264
WEST, NANCY, 255
WEST, STACY, 54
WESTERFIELD, SARAH A., 364
WEYLAND, ELIZABETH, 298
WHEELER, ALLEN, 210
WHEELER, ANNE, 238
WHEELER, JOHN, 115

WHEELER, NANCY, 187
WHEELER, NEWTON, 375
WHEELER, SAMUEL, 115
WHEELER, SEVIER, 165
WHEELER, THOMAS, 35
WHITCHURCH, WM., 32
WHITE, A., 11, 19, 20, 22, 23, 24, 25, 26, 27, 28, 29, 30, 31, 32, 33, 34, 35, 36, 41
WHITE, A. W., 22
WHITE, ABRAHAM, 59
WHITE, ABRAM D., 142, 145
WHITE, ABSOLEM, 59
WHITE, AMY, 22
WHITE, ANDREW, 8, 9, 10, 11, 13, 19, 20, 21, 23, 24, 25, 27
WHITE, ANNE, 49
WHITE, BECKA, 117
WHITE, BENJAMIN, 75
WHITE, BETSY, 56
WHITE, BETSY M., 113, 115
WHITE, C. A. C., 85
WHITE, CHARLES, 30
WHITE, CLARISSA, 203
WHITE, ELIZA, 209
WHITE, ELIZA H. C., 326
WHITE, ELIZA JANE, 319
WHITE, ELIZABETH, 101
WHITE, FRANCES, 51
WHITE, G. S., 339, 340, 343, 348, 349, 352, 354, 355, 360, 362, 364, 368, 369, 372, 374
WHITE, GEORGE M., 213, 221, 320, 325, 330, 331, 339, 340, 341, 342, 344, 345, 347, 350, 354, 356, 357, 359, 366
WHITE, GEORGE W., 334, 335, 337, 339
WHITE, H.A.M., 185
WHITE, H. L., 3, 4, 6, 11, 12, 13, 14, 15, 16, 17, 18, 19, 20, 21, 22, 23, 25, 26, 27, 29, 30, 41, 196
WHITE, HU. LAW, 9, 10, 12, 13, 14, 15, 16, 17
WHITE, HUGH A. M., 194
WHITE, HUGH L., 4, 5, 6, 375
WHITE, JAMES, 90, 93, 318
WHITE, JAMES, M. M., 194, 221
WHITE, JANE, 136
WHITE, JESSE, 39
WHITE, JOHN, 154, 221
WHITE, JOHN L., 221
WHITE, JOHN, N., 115
WHITE, KATE, MISS, 1
WHITE, MARGARET, 2
WHITE, MARGARET ANN, 249
WHITE, MARGARET E., 264
WHITE, MARTHA, 13
WHITE, NANCY, 65
WHITE, POLLY L., 293
WHITE, RACHEL, 16
WHITE, REBECKA, 225
WHITE, RILEY, 90
WHITE, RUTHY, 116
WHITE, SALLY, 59
WHITE, SAMUEL, 92, 177, 307, 313, 314, 320, 326, 330, 333, 334, 339, 355
WHITE, SARAH, 321
WHITE, SIMON, 221
WHITE, SUKY, 46
WHITE, T., 103,
WHITE, THOMAS, 129, 194
WHITE, WILLIAM, 221
WHITE, WILSON, 120, 158
WHITBERRY, EPHRAIM, 154
WHITECOTTON, LAVINA, 312
WHITECOTTON, LUCINDA, 155
WHITECOTTON, PATSY, 94
WHITHEAD, JANE, 359
WHITEHEAD, JOHN, 359
WHITEHEAD, THOMAS, 359
WHITEMAN, BETHANY, 124
WHITEMAN, JAMES S., 293, 303
WHITEMAN, LOUISA, 340
WHITEMAN, WILLIAM, 32
WHITSON, SALLEY, 50
WHITTLE, CELEY, 84
WHITTLE, GEORGE, 115, 143
WHITTLE, JOHN, 143
WHURLEY, KATY, 106
WIATT, DINAH, 151
WIATT, EDWIN, 138
WIDENER, BETSY, 104

WIDENER, MATHIAS, 115
WIDENER, SAM'L, 372
WIDENER, WM., 103
WIDNER, HENRY, 249
WIDNER, JACOB, 221
WIDNER, PATSY, 238
WIDNER, PEGGY, 205
WIDNER, POLLY, 221
WIDNER, WILLIAM, 249
WIGGINS, MICHAEL, 143
WILES, LUKE, 359
WILEY, JAMES, 279
WILEY, MOSES, 129
WILHITE, GEORGE, 165
WILHITE, JAMES, 71, 244
WILHITE, VINEY, 351
WILKENS, ELIZABETH, 212
WILKENSON, EDMUND, 39
WILKERSON, BENJAMIN, 318
WILKERSON, ELEANOR, 208
WILKERSON, HALL L., 338, 342
WILKERSON, JOHN, 280
WILKERSON, OBADIAH, 129
WILKERSON, REBECKA, 282
WILKERSON, THOMAS, 44, 107, 108, 120, 126, 127, 135, 176, 179, 204, 209, 213, 289, 294, 315
WILKERSON, THOS., 113, 127, 133, 134, 140, 150, 153, 160
WILKERSON, MAJOR WILLIAM, 280
WILKES, MARIAH, 325
WILKES, MARTHA, 253
WILKES, SAMUEL, 342
WILKINS, NANCY, 220
WILKINS, POLLY, 219
WILKISON, CAROLINE, 288
WILLIAMS, ABEL L., 59, 65
WILLIAMS, ALEXANDER, 252, 280, 328
WILLIAMS, BENJAMIN, 264, 291
WILLIAMS, BERRY, 180, 233
WILLIAMS, BETSY, 67, 106
WILLIAMS, DAVID, 32
WILLIAMS, ELIZABETH, 236
WILLIAMS, EPHRAIM, 291
WILLIAMS, FANNY, 155
WILLIAMS, FERIBY, 170
WILLIAMS, ISAAC, 210
WILLIAMS, JAMES, 264
WILLIAMS, JAMES E., 210
WILLIAMS, JASON, 210, 213
WILLIAMS, JEREMIAH, 304,
WILLIAMS, JOEL, 259
WILLIAMS, JOHN, 47, 79, 92, 143
WILLIAMS, JOHN, D., 92
WILLIAMS, JONATHAN, 199
WILLIAMS, JOSEPH, 17, 342
WILLIAMS, JOSHUA S., 154
WILLIAMS, LARKIN, 233
WILLIAMS, LEVINA, 303
WILLIAMS, MALINDA, 259
WILLIAMS, MARY, 287
WILLIAMS, NANCY, 282, 309
WILLIAMS, PATSY, 213
WILLIAMSON, PEGGY, 302
WILLIAMS, POLLY, 240
WILKERSON, REBECCA, 67
WILLIAMS, ROBERT, 84, 302
WILLIAMS, SALLIE, 55
WILLIAMS, SALLY, 114
WILLIAMS, T. L., 169
WILLIAMS, WILLIAM, 308
WILLIAMS, ZACHARIAH, 180
WILLIS, DAVID, 51
WILLIS, HARDIN, 291
WILLOUGHBY, ANDREW, 154
WILLOUGHBY, JOHN, 318
WILLS, CATHERINE, 171
WILLS, DAVID, 258
WILLS, DAVID, S., 342
WILLS, ELIZABETH L., 226
WILLS, JOHN, 133, 154
WILLS, MARGARET, G., 133
WILLS, MARTHA, 226
WILLS, POLLY, 147
WILLS, SARAH, T., 154
WILLSON, THOMAS, 318
WILMOTH, WM., 180
WILSON, ANNE, 79, 300
WILSON, ANNICE, 166
WILSON, BENJAMEN I., 213
WILSON, CATHERINE, 91
WILSON, ELIZABETH, 105,
WILSON, EUNICE, 181
WILSON, FRANCIS T., 280
WILSON, GEO., 72
WILSON, HUGH P., 143

X

Y

Z

TENNESSEE

KNOX COUNTY

MARRIAGE RECORDS

1792 — 1837

KEY:

C. A. REFERS TO ORIGINAL BONDS AND LICENSES NOW ON FILE IN THE COUNTY ARCHIVES ROOM IN THE KNOX COUNTY COURT HOUSE.

O. M. R. REFERS TO RECORDS COLLECTED AND COPIED IN A BOOK CALLED " OLD MARRIAGE RECORD" IN THE COUNTY COURT CLERK'S OFFICE, KNOX COUNTY COURT HOUSE.

T. H. M. REFERS TO MARRIAGE RECORDS COPIED BY MISS KATE WHITE AND PUBLISHED IN THE TENNESSEE HISTORICAL MAGAZINE FROM APRIL 1920 TO JANUARY 1921. AS MANY OF THESE HAVE DISAPPEARED FROM THE COLLECTION OF BONDS AND LICENSES NOW ON FILE IN THE COUNTY ARCHIVES ROOM, MISS WHITE'S COPY HAS BEEN INCLUDED HERE, IN AN EFFORT TO MAKE AS COMPLETE AS POSSIBLE, THE RECORDS OF EARLY MARRIAGES OF KNOX COUNTY.

1792

NAMES: JOHN ANDERSON TO RACHEL ROBERTS
DATE: DEC. 28, 1792
BONDSMAN: DAN'L MCDONALD
WITNESS: CHAS. MCCLUNG, C. K. C.
REFERENCE: C.A., T.H.M. VOL. 6, PG. 10

NAMES: ROBERT HAMILTON TO JEAN HANNAH
DATE: AUG. 30, 1792
BONDSMAN: JOHN HANNAH
WITNESS: CHAS. MCCLUNG, C. K. C.
REFERENCE: C.A., T.H.M. VOL. 6, PG. 10

NAMES: CRAVEN JOHNSON (OR JOHNSTON?) TO PATTY LOWE
DATE: DEC. 21, 1792
REFERENCE: T.H.M. VOL. 6, PG. 10

NAMES: CHARLES MCCLUNG TO MARGARET WHITE
DATE: OCT. 8, 1792
REFERENCE: T.H.M. VOL. 6, PG. 10

NAMES: GEORGE MCNUTT TO CATHERINE MCKEAN
DATE: NOV. 5, 1792
REFERENCE: T.H.M. VOL. 6, PG. 10

NAMES: JOSEPH RITCHIE TO NANCY RHEA
DATE: NOV. 6, 1792
REFERENCE: T.H.M. VOL. 6, PG. 10

NAMES: JAMES STOCKTON TO LIDETHA PRUITT
DATE: _____, 1792 (?)
REFERENCE: T.H.M. VOL. 6, PG. 10

NAMES: REUBEN VAUGHN TO MARY WARREN
DATE: OCT. 4, 1792 (OR 1797)
WITNESS: RAMSEY
REFERENCE: T.H.M. VOL. 6, PG. 10

1793

NAMES: NICHOLAS ALEXANDER TO ANNE SMITH
DATE: DEC. 21, 1793
BONDSMAN: RICHARD GOODIN
WITNESS: CHAS. MCCLUNG, C. K. C.
REFERENCE: C.A.

NAMES: ROBERT BOYD TO MARGARET MEEK
DATE: APR. 3, 1793
REFERENCE: T.H.M. VOL. 6, PG. 10

NAMES: SAMUEL CALDWELL TO RACHEL EWING
DATE: JAN. 26, 1793
REFERENCE: T.H.M. VOL. 6, PG. 10

NAMES: THOMAS CALDWELL TO JEAN MCCULLOCH
DATE: DEC. 16, 1793
BONDSMAN: JAMES MCCULLOCH
WITNESS: CHAS. MCCLUNG, C. K. C.
REFERENCE: C.A.

NAMES: JOHN CALLUM TO CATHRINE LOW
DATE: NOV. 1, 1793
REFERENCE: T.H.M. VOL. 6, PG. 10

NAMES: ISAAC CUNNINGHAM TO MARGARET HANNAH
DATE: APR. 23, 1793
REFERENCE: T.H.M. VOL. 6, PG. 10

Names: James Cunningham to Margaret Hannah
Date: Apr. 3, 1793
Bondsman: James Telford & James McKinney
Witness: David Craig
Reference: C.A.

Names: Joseph Cusick to Jean Blackburn
Date: Jan. 31, 1793
Reference: T.H.M. Vol. 6, Pg. 10

Names: William Douglass to Elizabeth Martin
Date: Dec. 23, 1793
Bondsman: Thomas Douglass
Witness: Chas. McClung, C. K. C.
Reference: C.A., T.H.M. Vol. 6, Pg. 10

Names: John Fermault to Margaret Kerr
Date: 1793
Reference: T.H. M. Vol. 6, Pg. 10

Names: John Finley to Margaret Kerr
Date: Nov. 13, 1793
Bondsman: Jeremiah McCarter
Witness: Chas. McClung, C. K. C.
Reference: C.A., T.H.M. Vol. 6, Pg. 10

Names: John Goulston to Margaret Low
Date: Feb. 5, 1793
Reference: T.H.M. Vol. 6, Pg. 10

Names: Norton Gum to Sallie Clampit
Date: Mar. 23, 1793
Reference: T.H.M. Vol. 6, Pg. 10

Names: Sampson Kennedy to Sarah Edwards
Date: Jany. 30, 1793
Bondsman: Nicholas Robinson
Witness: Chas. McClung, C. K. C.
Reference: C.A., T.H.M. Vol. 6, Pg. 10

Names: William Kerr to Anne Brooks
Date: Sept. 18, 1793
Bondsman: Moses Brooks
Witness: H. L. White, P. C.
Reference: C.A., T.H.M. Vol. 6, Pg. 10

Names: John Mabory to Eliza Brook
Date: Sept. 23, 1793, (?)
Reference: T.H.M. Vol. 6, Pg. 10

Names: Nicholas Mansfield to Elisabeth Looney
Date: Oct. 31, 1793
Bondsman: Thomas Dickson
Reference: C.A; T.H.M. Vol 6, Pg. 10

Names: James McCullough to Susannah Henderson
Date: Jany. 20, 1793
Bondsman: Thomas McCullough
Witness: Hugh L. White
Reference: C.A; T.H.M. Vol 6, Pg. 10

Names: William McMullen to Mary Doak
Date: July 25, 1793 (?)
Reference: T.H.M. Vol. 6, Pg. 10

Names: Hugh Miller to Mary Good
Date: Aug. 27, 1793
Bondsman: Davis Stockton
Witness: Hugh L. White, D: C. K. C.
Reference: C.A; T.H.M. Vol. 6, Pg. 10

Names: Peter Miller to Peggy Simpson
Date: May 20, 1793
Reference: T.H.M. Vol. 6, Pg. 10

Names: Humphrey Montgomery to Mary Walker
Date: Apr. 1, 1793
Bondsman: David Caldwell
Witness: Chas. McClung, C. K. C.
Reference: C.A; T.H.M. Vol. 6, Pg. 10

Names: Abel Richey to Ann Dickson
Date: Oct. 11, 1793
Bondsman: Andrew McCasland
Reference: C.A; T.H.M. Vol. 6, Pg. 10

Names: Thomas Richey to Rosanah Trimble
Date: Oct. 9, 1793
Bondsman: William Richey
Reference: C.A.

Names: Willoughby Robertson to Mary Brook
Date: Sept. 3, 1793
Bondsman: James Brook
Witness: H. L. White
Reference: C.A; T.H.M. Vol. 6, Pg. 10

Names: John Sears to Nancy Brook
Date: Mar. 1, 1793
Bondsman: George Brook
Witness: Chas. McClung & Geo. Brook
Reference: C.A; T.H.M. Vol. 6, Pg. 10

Names: William Sloan to Margaret McTeer
Date: May 26, 1793
Bondsman: Robert Houston
Witness: Chas. McClung, C. K. C.
Reference: C.A; T.H.M. Vol. 6, Pg. 10

NAMES: WILLIAM SLOAN TO MARGARET MCKEE
DATE: MAY 20, 1793 (?)
REFERENCE: T.H.M. VOL. 6, PG. 10

NAMES: WILLIAM STEPHENSON TO GENE HAMILTON
DATE: APR. 17, 1793
REFERENCE: T.H.M. VOL. 6, PG. 10

NAMES: DAVIS STOCKTON TO AGNES MILLER
DATE: AUG. 27, 1793
BONDSMAN: HUGH MILLER
WITNESS: HUGH L. WHITE, D.K.C.
REFERENCE: C.A; T.H.M. VOL. 6, PG. 10

NAMES: HENRY STONE TO PATRENIS SOUTHERLIN
DATE: JANY. 23, 1793
BONDSMAN: PETER KING & NICHOLAS ROBISON
WITNESS: H. RAMSEY
REFERENCE: C.A; T.H.M. VOL. 6, PG. 10

NAMES: JOSEPH TEDFORD TO MARY MCNUTT
DATE: JANY. 11, 1793
BONDSMAN: JOHN HOUSTON
WITNESS: CHAS. MCCLUNG, C.K.C.
REFERENCE: C.A; T.H.M. VOL. 6, PG. 10

NAMES: GEORGE TELFOUR TO JEAN HANNAH
DATE: APR. 3, 1793
BONDSMAN: JAMES TELFORD & JAMES MCKINNEY
WITNESS: DAVID CRAIG
REFERENCE: C.A; T.H.M. VOL. 6, PG. 10

NAMES: LEWIS TINER TO TABBY COOK
DATE: SEPT. 7, 1793 (X)
REFERENCE: T.H.M. VOL. 6, PG. 10

NAMES: SAMUEL VANCE TO MARY BLACKBURN
DATE: JAN. 30, 1793
REFERENCE: T.H.M. VOL. 6, PG. 10

1794

NAMES: AMOS BIRD TO ANNE GILLESPIE
DATE: JANY. 21, 1794
BONDSMAN: AMOS BIRD, JUNR. & ABRAHAM BIRD
WITNESS: CHAS. MCCLUNG
REFERENCE: C.A; T.H.M. VOL. 6, PG. 11

NAMES: WILLIAM BIRDIN TO ELEANOR HUTSON
DATE: JANY. 27, 1794
BONDSMAN: JAMES ANDERSON
WITNESS: CHAS. MCCLUNG, C.K.C.
REFERENCE: C.A; T.H.M. VOL. 6, PG. 11

NAMES: JOHN BRYAN TO ESTHER ANDERSON
DATE: SEPT. 10, 1794
BONDSMAN: JAMES ANDERSON
WITNESS: CHAS. MCCLUNG
REFERENCE: C.A; T.H.M. VOL. 6, PG. 11

NAMES: WILLIAM BRYAN TO JENNY GILLESPIE
DATE: MAY 1, 1794
BONDSMAN: GEORGE ROULSTONE
WITNESS: HU. L. WHITE
REFERENCE: C.A; T.H.M. VOL. 6, PG. 11

NAMES: AMOS BYRD TO ANNE GILLESPIE
DATE: JAN. 21, 1794
WITNESS: (CHAS. MCCLUNG)
REFERENCE: T.H.M. VOL. 6, PG. 11

NAMES: STEPHEN BYRD TO POLLY GILLESPIE
DATE: APR. 1, 1794
BONDSMAN: ABRAHAM BYRD
WITNESS: CHAS. MCCLUNG, C.K.C.
REFERENCE: C.A; T.H.M. VOL. 6, PG. 11

NAMES: DAVID CALDWELL TO ELIZABETH KELLY
DATE: MAY 6, 1794
BONDSMAN: ALEXANDER KELLY
REFERENCE: C.A; T.H.M. VOL. 6, PG. 11

NAMES: JAMES CALLISON TO ANNE GILLESPIE
DATE: JANY. 21, 1794
BONDSMAN: WILLIAM MCNUTT
WITNESS: H. L. WHITE
REFERENCE: C.A; T.H.M. VOL. 6, PG. 11

NAMES: SAMUEL CARRICK TO ANNIE MCCLELLAND
DATE: JAN. 27, 1794
REFERENCE: T.H.M. VOL. 6, PG. 11

NAMES: ISAAC CLARK TO NANCY BOUNDS
DATE: AUG. 6, 1794
REFERENCE: T.H.M. VOL. 6, PG. 11

NAMES: JOHN COWAN TO POLLY KIRKUM (?)
DATE: MCH. 24, 1794
REFERENCE: T.H.M. VOL. 6, PG. 11

NAMES: JAMES CUNNINGHAM TO SUSANNAH CRAIG
DATE: APR. 24, 1794
BONDSMAN: JOHN MCCLELLAN
WITNESS: CHAS. MCCLUNG, C. K. C.
REFERENCE: C.A; T.H.M. VOL. 6, PG. 11

NAMES: MOSES CUNNINGHAM TO MARY SIMPSON
DATE: JUNE 3, 1794
REFERENCE: T.H.M. VOL. 6, PG. 11

NAMES: DAVID EVANS TO MARGARET BLACKBURN
DATE: JUNE 6, 1794
REFERENCE: T.H.M. VOL. 6, PG. 11

NAMES: JAMES FERGUSON TO NANCY CHURCHMAN
DATE: JULY 8, 1794 (?)
REFERENCE: T.H.M. VOL. 6, PG. 11

NAMES: JAMES FURGASON TO MARY CHEESMAN
DATE: JULY 8, 1794
REFERENCE: T.H.M. VOL. 6, PG. 11

NAMES: LUKE HAIL TO MARY KEY
DATE: AUG. 4, 1794
BONDSMAN: WM. HAMILTON
WITNESS: CHAS. MCCLUNG, C. K. C.
REFERENCE: C.A; T.H.M. VOL. 6, PG. 11

NAMES: THEOPLUS HAYES TO POLLY MORGAN
DATE: SEPT. 16, 1794 (?)
REFERENCE: T.H.M. VOL. 6, PG. 11

NAMES: WILLIAM HENDERSON TO SUSANNAH GILLESPIE
DATE: MAY 29, 1794
REFERENCE: T.H.M. VOL. 6, PG. 11

NAMES: WILLIAM HESLIT JR. TO ELIZABETH JACK
DATE: JAN. 28, 1794
REFERENCE: T.H.M. VOL. 6, PG. 11

NAMES: ROBERT HOUSTON TO MARGARET DAVIS
DATE: MCH. 24, (OR 20), 1794
REFERENCE: T.H.M. VOL. 6, PG. 11

NAMES: THEOPLES HUGES TO PEGGY MORGAN
DATE: SEPT. 16, 1794 (?)
REFERENCE: T.H.M. VOL. 6, PG. 11

NAMES: JOHN MCCLELLAND TO POLLY WALLACE
DATE: MAY 13, 1794
REFERENCE: T.H.M. VOL. 6, PG. 11

NAMES: JAMES MCNUTT TO ELIZA GILLESPIE
DATE: JAN. 15, 1794 (?)
REFERENCE: T.H.M. VOL. 6, PG. 11

NAMES: THOMAS MILIKAN TO PRISCILLA BROOK
DATE: JAN. 7, 1794
REFERENCE: T.H.M. VOL. 6, PG. 11

NAMES: DAVID MOORE TO MARY MCNAIR
DATE: JUNE 10, 1794 (?)
REFERENCE: T.H.M. VOL. 6, PG. 11

NAMES: JOHN MYNATT TO LIBELL LINVILLE
DATE: JAN. 28, 1794
REFERENCE: T.H.M. VOL. 6, PG. 11

NAMES: GEORGE RAULSTON TO ELIZABETH GILLIAM
DATE: MAY 1, 1794
REFERENCE: T.H.M. VOL. 6, PG. 11

NAMES: JOHN SOMERVILLE TO ELIZABETH CHISHOLM
DATE: MAY 20, 1794
REFERENCE: T.H.M. VOL. 6, PG. 11

NAMES: WILLIAM STEPHENSON TO JEAN HAMILTON
DATE: APR. 17, 1794
REFERENCE: T.H.M. VOL. 6, PG. 11

NAMES: SAMUEL SWAN TO JEAN GAMBLE
DATE: JUNE 10, 1794
BONDSMAN: JOHN STONE
WITNESS: CHAS. MCCLUNG, C. K. C.
REFERENCE: C.A; T.H.M. VOL. 6, PG. 11

1795

1796

NAMES: NICHOLAS ALEXANDER TO ANNIE SMITH
DATE: DEC. 31, 1796
REFERENCE: T.H.M. VOL. 6, PG. 11

NAMES: WILLIAM ALEXANDER TO MARTHA HASLET
DATE: OCT. 20, 1796
BONDSMAN: WILLIAM HASLET
WITNESS: AND. WHITE
REFERENCE: C.A; T.H.M. VOL. 6, PG. 11

NAMES: JOHN BATES TO DIDAMY (?) BOHANNON
DATE: DEC. 20, 1796
REFERENCE: T.H.M. VOL. 6, PG. 11

NAMES: JOHN BOWEN TO JANE CRAWFORD
DATE: DEC. 28, 1796
BONDSMAN: DAVID MAXWELL
REFERENCE: C.A; T.H.M. VOL. 6, PG. 11

NAMES: THOMAS BRASSFIELD TO MARY DAVIS
DATE: DEC. 25, 1796
REFERENCE: T.H.M. VOL. 6, PG. 11

NAMES: JAMES CHILDERS TO SUSANNAH THOMPSON
DATE: NOV. 15, 1796
BONDSMAN: GEORGE HAYS
REFERENCE: C.A; T.H.M. VOL. 6, PG. 11

NAMES: CHARLES CONWAY TO ELIZABETH ROBERTSON
DATE: OCT. 19, 1796
BONDSMAN: DAVID ROBERTSON
WITNESS: HU. LAW. WHITE
REFERENCE: C.A; T.H.M. VOL. 6, PG. 11

NAMES: JOHN ELDRIGE TO SARAH GILLALAND
DATE: DEC. 2, 1796
BONDSMAN: JESSE ALDRIDGE
WITNESS: ANDREW WHITE
REFERENCE: C.A; T.H.M. VOL. 6, PG. 11

NAMES: WILLIAM GARDENHIRE TO ESTER NEAL
DATE: OCT. 14, 1796
BONDSMAN: JESSE ELDRIDGE
WITNESS: CHAS. MCCLUNG, CLK.
REFERENCE: C.A.

NAMES: DAN MASON TO MARY GILLILAND
DATE: MAY 1796
REFERENCE: T.H.M. VOL. 6, PGS. 11 & 12

NAMES: WILLIAM MATHEWS TO MARY TAYLOR
DATE: NOV. 10, 1796
BONDSMAN: JAMES SAWYERS
WITNESS: HU. LAW. WHITE
REFERENCE: C.A; T.H.M. VOL. 6, PG. 11

NAMES: EDWARD MCDONALD TO NANCY SMITH
DATE: NOV. 22, 1796
BONDSMAN: WILLIAM CUNNINGHAM
WITNESS: ANDREW WHITE
REFERENCE: C.A; T.H.M. VOL. 6, PG. 11

NAMES: JAMES MCENTIRE TO MARGARET HENDERSON
DATE: OCT. 17, 1796
BONDSMAN: GEORGE HAYS
WITNESS: ANDREW WHITE
REFERENCE: C.A; T.H.M. VOL. 6, PG. 11

NAMES: WILLIAM NICKLE TO RACHEL HASLET
DATE: OCT. 21, 1796
BONDSMAN: WILLIAM HASLET
WITNESS: ANDREW WHITE
REFERENCE: C.A; T.H.M. VOL. 6, PG. 11

NAMES: ISAAC WILSON TO SARAH SHOOK
DATE: NOV. 28, 1796
BONDSMAN: ABRAHAM SHOOK
WITNESS: ANDREW WHITE
REFERENCE: C.A; T.HM. VOL. 6, PG. 11

1797

NAMES: WILLIAM ADAMS TO NANCY FRAZIER
DATE: FEBY. 28, 1797
BONDSMAN: WILLIAM THOMPSON
WITNESS: CHAS. MCCLUNG, CLK.
REFERENCE: C.A; T.H.M. VOL. 6, PG. 11

NAMES: ALEXANDER AIKMAN TO PRUDENCE STOCKTON
DATE: DEC. 18, 1797
BONDSMAN: SAMUEL STOCKTON
WITNESS: CHAS. MCCLUNG, CLK.
REFERENCE: C.A.

NAMES: ANDREW ANDERSON TO MARGARET ROBERTS
DATE: DEC. 11, 1797
BONDSMAN: HENRY ROBERTS
WITNESS: JOSEPH GREER
REFERENCE: C.A; T.H.M. VOL. 6, PG. 12

NAMES: DANIEL ANDERSON TO RUTH REW
DATE: APR. 10, 1797
BONDSMAN: RICHARD KEYHILL
WITNESS: HU. LAW. WHITE
REFERENCE: C. A; T.H.M. VOL. 6, PG. 12

NAMES: ROBERT ARMSTRONG TO POLLY CRANE
DATE:
REFERENCE: T.H.M. VOL. 6, PG. 12

NAMES: HENRY BAKER TO JARIDA ALD
DATE: FEBY. 13, 1797
BONDSMAN: JACOB SCHRIDER
REFERENCE: C.A; T.H.M. VOL. 6, PG. 12

NAMES: WILLIAM BEELES TO RACHEL PIERCE
DATE: MCH. 12, 1797
REFERENCE: T.H.M. VOL. 6, PG. 12

NAMES: JACOB BISHOP TO ANNE GAMMON
DATE:
REFERENCE: T.H.M. VOL. 6, PG. 12

Names: James Bray to Rachel Smith
Date: July 29, 1797
Bondsman: John Roberson
Witness: Peggy McClung
Reference: C.A; T.H.M. Vol. 6, Pg. 12

Names: William Brummit to Rebecca Simpson
Date: Sept. 16, 1797
Bondsman: William Dunlap
Witness: Chas. McClung
Reference: C.A; T.H.M. Vol. 6, Pg. 12

Names: Asabel Chapmen to Matty Hart
Date: Sept. 19, 1797
Bondsman: Patrick Burns
Witness: A. White
Reference: C.A.

Names: John Cooper to Lucy Graves
Date: Nov. 1, 1797
Bondsman: John Byrd
Reference: C.A; T.H.M. Vol. 6, Pg. 12

Names: Alexander Dale to Lea Harner
Date: Dec. 30, 1797
Bondsman: William Belton
Witness: H. L. White
Reference: C.A; T.H.M. Vol. 6, Pg. 12

Names: Francis Davis to Eleanor Lyons
Date: Apr. 20, 1797
Reference: T.H.M. Vol. 6, Pg. 12

Names: Nathaniel Davis to Sally Hannah
Date: Apr. 27, 1797
Bondsman: Samuel Hannah
Witness: Andw. White
Reference: C.A; T.H.M. Vol. 6, Pg. 12

Names: John Dawdy to Polly Moss
Date: Sept. 28, 1797
Bondsman: Howell Dawdy & Jepho Moss
Witness: Chas. McClung, Clk.
Reference: C.A; T.H.M. Vol. 6, Pg. 12

Names: Archibald Fisher to Elizabeth Sharp
Date: Dec. 11, 1797
Bondsman: John Steele
Witness: Chas. McClung, Clk.
Reference: C.A; T.H.M. Vol. 6, Pg. 12

Names: Hezekiah Flinn to Elizabeth Cassa
Date: July 25, 1797
Bondsman: William Pruett
Witness: H. L. White
Reference: C.A; T.H.M. Vol. 6, Pg. 12

Names: Richard Forrest to Polly Bishop
Date: Dec. 7, 1797
Bondsman: Stephen Bishop
Witness: H. L. White
Reference: C.A; T.H.M. Vol. 6, Pg. 12

Names: John Foust to Polly Sertain
Date: May 29, 1797
Bondsman: Christopher Foust
Witness: H. L. White
Reference: C.A; T.H.M. Vol. 6, Pg. 12 & 13

Names: Enoch Fox to Peggy Dale
Date: Jany. 9, 1797
Bondsman: Alexander Dale
Witness: Hu. Law. White
Reference: C.A; T.H.M. Vol. 6, Pg. 12

Names: John Gallaher to Salley Harden
Date: Dec. 11, 1797
Bondsman: Robert Houston
Witness: Joseph Greer
Reference: C.A; T.H.M. Vol. 6, Pgs. 11 & 12

Names: John Gibbs to Anne Howard
Date: Aug. 4, 1797
Bondsman: Matthew Harper
Witness: H. L. White
Reference: C.A; T.H.M. Vol. 6, Pg. 12

Names: Harmon Gregg to Susannah Smelser
Date: June 20, 1797
Bondsman: Harmon Gregge & David Smelser
Witness: Hu. Law. White
Reference: C.A; T.H.M. Vol. 6, Pg. 12

Names: Jacob Haleacre to Pegg Bookin
Date: Feb. 4, 1797
Reference: T.H.M. Vol. 6, Pg. 12

Names: John Hankins to Dicey Oliver
Date: Aug. 10, 1797
Bondsman: William Bogan
Witness: Joseph Greer
Reference: C. A.

NAMES: PAUL HARALSON TO MARY FULLER
DATE: DEC. 8, 1797
REFERENCE: T.H.M. VOL. 6, PG. 12

NAMES: JOSEPH HARMAN TO MARGARET HESS
DATE: OCT. 5, 1797
REFERENCE: T.H.M. VOL. 6, PG. 12

NAMES: WILLIE HARP TO SARAH RICE
DATE: JUNE 1, 1797
BONDSMAN: MICAJAH HARP
WITNESS: H. L. WHITE
REFERENCE: C.A; T.H.M. VOL. 6, PG. 12

NAMES: JOSEPH HARRISON TO MARGARET HESS
DATE: OCT. 5, 1797
REFERENCE: T.H.M. VOL. 6, PG. 12

NAMES: BAZELL HUMAN TO WINNEFORD GILLAM
DATE: JANY 28, 1797
BONDSMAN: SOLOMON GERAN
WITNESS: ANDW. WHITE
REFERENCE: C.A; T.H.M. VOL. 6, PG. 12

NAMES: GEORGE INGRAM TO NANCY CRANE
DATE: MCH. 5, 1797
REFERENCE: T.H.M. VOL. 6, PG. 12

NAMES: FRANCIS IRVIN TO ELINOR LYONS
DATE: MAR. 20, 1797
BONDSMAN: JOHN LYON
WITNESS: H. L. WHITE
REFERENCE: C. A.

NAMES: JOHN JACKSON TO MARTHA WHITE
DATE: JAN. 31, 1797
REFERENCE: T.H.M. VOL. 6, PG. 12

NAMES: JOHN JULIEN TO SARAH ALDRIDGE
DATE: MAR. 4, 1797
BONDSMAN: THOMAS ALLRED
WITNESS: HU. LAW. WHITE
REFERENCE: C. A; T.H.M. VOL. 6, PG. 12

NAMES: JACOB KIMBERLIN TO SARAH HINES
DATE: MCH. 6, 1797
REFERENCE: T.H.M. VOL. 6, PG. 12

NAMES: JOHN KIZER TO ROSANNA BRADY
DATE: SEPT. 29, 1797
BONDSMAN: JOHN BRADY
WITNESS: H. L. WHITE
REFERENCE: C.A; T.H.M. VOL. 6, PG. 12

NAMES: ISAAC LENDER TO FRANCES FROST
DATE: DEC. 26, 1797
BONDSMAN: JOHN FROST
WITNESS: H. L. WHITE
REFERENCE: C.A; T.H.M. VOL. 6, PG. 12

NAMES: ANDREW LOWRY TO CATHARINE CONN
DATE: DEC. 20, 1797
REFERENCE: T.H.M. VOL. 6, PG. 12

NAMES: THOMAS LYON TO MARGOT IRWIN
DATE: AUG. 8, 1797
BONDSMAN: FRANCIS IRWIN
WITNESS: JOSEPH GREER
REFERENCE: C.A; T.H.M. VOL. 6, PG. 12

NAMES: ANDREW MCCLOUD TO MALINDA GOLLIWAY
DATE: AUG. 23, 1797
REFERENCE: T.H.M. VOL. 6, PG. 12

NAMES: WILLIAM MCNAMEE TO POLLY WITT
DATE: NOV. 28, 1797
BONDSMAN: CHARLES WITT
WITNESS: H. L. WHITE
REFERENCE: C.A; T.H.M. VOL. 6, PG. 12

NAMES: SAMUEL MILLER TO REBECKAH GIVENS
DATE: FEBY. 21, 1797
BONDSMAN: SAMUEL MILLER - ONLY
WITNESS: HU. LAW. WHITE
REFERENCE: C.A; T.H.M. VOL. 6, PG. 12

NAMES: SAMUEL MONTGOMERY TO MAGDALENA SHOOK
DATE: JULY 19, 1797
BONDSMAN: ABRAHAM SHOOK
WITNESS: H. L. WHITE
REFERENCE: C.A; T.H.M. VOL. 6, PG. 12

NAMES: JOSEPH MOORE TO ANNE HORNE (OR HOWELL?)
DATE: JULY 29, 1797
REFERENCE: T.H.M. VOL. 6, PG. 12

NAMES: COAN MORGAN TO MALLINDA NEVILLES
DATE: DEC. 27, 1797
REFERENCE: T.H.M. VOL. 6, PG. 12

NAMES: WILLIAM MORROW TO NANCY MEBANE
DATE: AUG. 6, 1797
REFERENCE: T.H.M. VOL. 6, PG. 12

NAMES: JOHN NEAL TO JEAN ALLISON
DATE: JANY. 23, 1797
BONDSMAN: JAMES CAMPBELL
WITNESS: HU. LAW. WHITE
REFERENCE: O. A.

NAMES: ROBERT NEELEY TO NANCY OVERSTREET
DATE: DEC. 29, 2797
BONDSMAN: WILLIAM ATKINSON
WITNESS: H. L. WHITE
REFERENCE: O.A; T.H.M. VOL. 6, PG. 12

NAMES: CHARLES OSBORN TO SARAH NEWMAN
DATE: DEC. 28, 1797
BONDSMAN: DANIEL OSBORN
WITNESS: H. L. WHITE
REFERENCE: O. A; T.H.M. VOL. 6, PG. 12

NAMES: JOHN PATE TO FANNY HUBBS
DATE: DEC. 8, 1797
BONDSMAN: JOHN MILLER
WITNESS: H. L. WHITE (?)
REFERENCE: O.A; T.H.M. VOL. 6, PG. 12

NAMES: ALEXANDER RICHMOND TO PRUDENCE STOCKTON
DATE: DEC. 18, 1797
REFERENCE: T.H.M. VOL. 6, PG. 12

NAMES: JAMES ROBERSON TO SARAH BLACK
DATE: JULY 1, 1797
REFERENCE: T.H.M. VOL. 6, PG. 12

NAMES: JOHN ROBERSON TO NANCY OWENS
DATE: SEPT. 13, 1797
BONDSMAN: CHARLES CONWAY
WITNESS: CHAS. MCCLUNG, CLK.
REFERENCE: O.A; T.H.M. VOL. 6, PG. 12

NAMES: DAVID ROBERTSON TO NANCY GUTHRIE
DATE: JAN. 21, 1797
REFERENCE: T.H.M. VOL. 6, PG. 12

NAMES: STEPHEN ROBERTSON TO SALLY CURTAIN
DATE: OCT. 4, 1797
REFERENCE: T.H.M. VOL. 6, PG. 12

NAMES: SAMUEL ROSS TO CATHERINE HILL
DATE: JAN. 9, 1797
REFERENCE: T.H.M. VOL. 6, PG. 12

NAMES: WILLIAM RUSSELL TO ELIZABETH WEATHERTON
DATE: AUG. 11, 1797
REFERENCE: T.H.M. VOL. 6, PG. 12

NAMES: ANDREW SANSKIVER TO HANNAH MCCOY
DATE: OCT. 12, 1797
BONDSMAN: HENRY NULL
WITNESS: H. L. WHITE
REFERENCE: O.A; T.H.M. VOL. 6,PG. 12

NAMES: DAVID SARTAIN TO HENRIETTA STANLEY
DATE: SEPT. 18, 1797
BONDSMAN: RHODES STANLEY
WITNESS: H. L. WHITE
REFERENCE: O. A; T.H.M. VOL. 6, PG. 12

NAMES: CHARLES SCAGGS TO PATSY BASHURS
DATE: JAN. 4, 1797
REFERENCE: T.H.M. VOL. 6, PG. 12

NAMES: JOSEPH SHADDIN TO MARGARET HESS
DATE: OCT. 5, 1797
BONDSMAN: JOHN HUNTER
WITNESS: H. L. WHITE
REFERENCE: O. A.

NAMES: PATRICK SHARKEY TO POLLY RHODES
DATE: AUG. 17, 1797
REFERENCE: T.H.M. VOL. 6, PG. 12

NAMES: JOHN SHIELDS TO HANNAH EVANS
DATE: JANY. 10, 1797
BONDSMAN: ROBERT REYNOLDS
WITNESS: HU. LAW.WHITE
REFERENCE: O. A; T.H.M. VOL. 6, PG. 13

NAMES: WILLIAM SNODGRASS TO RACHEL WHITE
DATE: MCH. 1, 1797
REFERENCE: T.H.M. VOL. 6, PG. 13

NAMES: ISREAL STANDIFORD TO PHOEBE FROST
DATE: DEC. 30, 1797
BONDSMAN: THOMAS FROST
WITNESS: H. L. WHITE
REFERENCE: O.A; T.H.M. VOL. 6, PG. 13

NAMES: JOHN STANTON TO DICIE OLIVER
DATE: AUG. 20, 1797
REFERENCE: T.H.M. VOL. 6, PG. 13

NAMES: GEORGE STEEL TO MARY LEA
DATE: JULY 17, 1797
BONDSMAN: JOHN LEA
REFERENCE: O. A.

NAMES: EPHRAIM STOUT TO JEAN SMITH
DATE: NOV. 29, 1797
BONDSMAN: T. SMITH
WITNESS: H. L. WHITE
REFERENCE: C.A; T.H.M. VOL. 6, PG. 13

NAMES: DAVID SUTHERLAND TO MARGARET GREGG
DATE: APR. 25, 1797 (?)
REFERENCE: T.H.M' VOL. 6, PG. 13

NAMES: JESSE TERRY TO HANNAH MCNAIRE
DATE: MAR. 31, 1797
BONDSMAN: A. MCCOY
WITNESS: CHARLES MCCLUNG
REFERENCE: C.A; T.H.M. VOL. 6, PG. 13

NAMES: WILLIAM TUNNELL TO ELIZABETH WEATHERNTON
DATE: AUG. 19, 1797
BONDSMAN: JOHN TUNNELL
REFERENCE: C.A.

NAMES: JOHN WEAR TO ELIZABETH MCCLELLAN
DATE: FEBY. 14, 1797
BONDSMAN: SAMUEL MCCLELLAN
WITNESS: HU. LAW. WHITE
REFERENCE: C.A; T.H.M. VOL. 6, PG. 13

NAMES: JOSEPH WILLIAMS TO RACHEL TIDWELL
DATE: MAR. 20, 1797
BONDSMAN: JOHN BRYAN
WITNESS: H. L. WHITE
REFERENCE: C.A.

1798

NAMES: THOMAS BARNES TO ALICE BUCHANAN
DATE: JUNE 21, 1798
BONDSMAN: TABITHA BUCHANAN
WITNESS: H. L. WHITE
REFERENCE: C.A; T.H.M. VOL. 6, PG. 13

NAMES: JOSEPH BARTLET TO PATIENCE MCCOY
DATE: APR. 3, 1798
WITNESS: CHAS. MCCLUNG & H. L. WHITE
REFERENCE: C.A; C.M.R. PG. 5

NAMES: HUGH BRAY TO ELIZABETH HAWRY
DATE: MAY 23, 1798
REFERENCE: T.H.M' VOL. 6, PG. 13

NAMES: JOSEPH BRAY TO ELIZABETH HARVEY
DATE: MAY 20, 1798
BONDSMAN: JEREMIAH LEAKEY
WITNESS: JOSEPH GREER
REFERENCE: C.A.

NAMES: DAVID CASTEEL TO SARAH MITCHELL
DATE: MAY 3, 1798
BONDSMAN: MORRIS MITCHELL
WITNESS: H. L. WHITE
REFERENCE: C.A; T.H.M. VOL. 6, PG. 13

NAMES: DAVID CUNNINGHAM TO JANE CUNNINGHAM
DATE: MAY 30, 1798
BONDSMAN: FRANCIS CUNNINGHAM
WITNESS: JOSEPH GREER
REFERENCE: C.A; T.H.M. VOL. 6, PG. 13

NAMES: JAMES DAVIS TO NANCY GOLDING
DATE: OCT. 7, 1798
REFERENCE: T.H.M. VOL. 6, PG. 13

NAMES: SAMUEL DAVIS TO PEGGY PAGE
DATE: DEC. 30, 1798
BONDSMAN: PAUL HARROLSON
WITNESS: H. L. WHITE
REFERENCE: C.A; T.H.M. VOL. 6, PG. 11

NAMES: JOHN DEARMOND TO NELLIE MOORE
DATE: SEPT. 26, 1798
REFERENCE: T.H.M. VOL. 6, PG. 13

NAMES: MOSES DUNLAP TO MARY ROLMOND
DATE: AUG. 8, 1798
BONDSMAN: DAVID LOW
REFERENCE: C.A; T.H.M. VOL. 6, PG. 13

NAMES: NATHANIEL ELDRIDGE TO REBECCA DAVIS
DATE: MAY 12, 1798
BONDSMAN: WILLIAM DAVIS
REFERENCE: C.A; T.H.M. VOL. 6, PG. 13

NAMES: THOMAS FERMAULT TO POLLY MATLOCK
DATE: MAY 28, 1798
REFERENCE: T.H.M. VOL. 6, PG. 13

NAMES: THOMAS FREELLS TO POLLY MATTOCKS
DATE: MAY 23, 1798
BONDSMAN: GEORGE HALLMARK
WITNESS: JOSEPH GREER
REFERENCE: C.A.

Names: Thomas Gilbreath to Sophia Mowry
Date: Aug. 29, 1798
Bondsman: John Brown
Witness: A. White
Reference: C.A; T.H.M. Vol. 6, Pg. 13

Names: Joseph Grayson to Pattie Braizealle
Date: Dec. 10, 1798
Reference: T.H.M. Vol. 6, Pg. 13

Names: Daniel Hare to Hannah Fisher
Date: Sept. 20, 1798
Bondsman: Moltis Body
Witness: H. L. White
Reference: C.A; T.H.M. Vol. 6, Pg. 13

Names: John Harris to Elizabeth ________
Date: July 5, 1798 (or 1790?)
Reference: T.H.M. Vol. 6, Pg. 13

Names: Robert Henderson to Jean Hackett
Date: Nov. 28, 1798
Bondsman: John Hackett
Witness: Andrw. White
Reference: C.A; T.H.M. Vol. 6, Pg. 13

Names: Squire Hendrix to Polly Hackworth
Date: Nov. 24, 1798
Bondsman: Luke Hendrix
Witness: Andrw. White
Reference: C.A; T.H.M. Vol. 6, Pg. 13

Names: William Hitchcock to Nancy Rhea
Date: Mar. 5, 1798
Bondsman: Alexr. Cole
Reference: C. A; T.H.M. Vol. 6, Pg. 13

Names: William Hogshead to A. Kirkpatrick
Date: Jan. 9, 1798
Reference: T.H.M. Vol. 6, Pg. 13

Names: John Irwin to Nancy Adamson
Date: June 15, 1798
Reference: T.H.M. Vol. 6, Pg. 13

Names: Aaron Jenkins to Catherine Davis
Date: Dec. 11, 1798
Bondsman: Robert Craig
Witness: H. L. White
Reference: C.A; T.H.M. Vol. 6, Pg. 13

Names: Anson Jenkins to Catherine Davis
Date: May 11, 1798
Reference: T.H.M. Vol. 6, Pg. 13

Names: Patrick Laten to Mary Veal
Date: Feby. 13, 1798
Bondsman: James McCulloch
Witness: And. White
Reference: C.A; T.H.M. Vol. 6, Pg. 13

Names: Lewis Latham to Laviney Chainey
Date: Feb. 5, 1798
Reference: T.H.M. Vol. 6, Pg. 13

Names: William Long to Mary Annie Stearns
Date: June 29, 1798
Bondsman: Calvin Johnson
Witness: H. L. White
Reference: C.A; T.H.M. Vol. 6, Pg. 13

Names: John Low to Liddy Reed
Date: May 23, 1798
Bondsman: Asa Cobb
Witness: A. White
Reference: C.A; T.H.M. Vol. 6, Pg. 13

Names: James McKinley to Margot Barnett
Date: Aug. 7, 1798
Bondsman: John Stone
Witness: Joseph Greer
Reference: C.A; T.H.M. Vol. 6, Pg. 13

Names: Peter Miller to Peggy Simpson
Date: May 24, 1798
Bondsman: John Mathis
Witness: Joseph Greer
Reference: C. A.

Names: Mordecai Mitchell to Nancy Casteel
Date: June 6, 1798
Bondsman: David Casteel
Witness: H. L. White
Reference: C.A; T.H.M. Vol. 6, Pg. 13

Names: John Raney to Elizabeth Stuart
Date: Dec. 21, 1798
Bondsman: Alexander Cole
Witness: H. L. White
Reference: C.A; T.H.M. Vol. 6, Pg. 13

NAMES: JOHN RAWLINGS TO SARAH RITCHEY
DATE: JULY 4, 1798
BONDSMAN: JAMES RITCHEY
WITNESS: H. L. WHITE
REFERENCE: C.A; T.H.M. VOL. 6, PG. 13

NAMES: ALEXANDER RICHEY TO ELIZABETH MCMULLEN
DATE: SEPT. 12, 1798
BONDSMAN: JAMES RICHEY
WITNESS: ANDREW WHITE
REFERENCE: C.A; T.H.M. VOL. 6, PG. 13

NAMES: SAMUEL RILEY TO SARAH SMITH
DATE: DEC. 11, 1798
REFERENCE: T.H.M. VOL. 6 PG. 13

NAMES: RICHARD SEARCEY TO ELIZABETH CARLISLE
DATE: SEPT. 24, 1798
BONDSMAN: JAMES CARLISLE
WITNESS: H. L. WHITE
REFERENCE: C.A; T.H.M. VOL. 6, PG. 13

NAMES: ABRAHAM SETLER TO SARAH RHEA
DATE: MAY 1, 1798
BONDSMAN: NATHANIEL HAYES
WITNESS: H. L. WHITE
REFERENCE: C.A; T.H.M. VOL. 6, PG. 13

NAMES: JAMES SCOTT TO SARAH JOHNSTON
DATE: JUNE 7, 1798
BONDSMAN: WILLIAM JOHNSTON
WITNESS: JOSEPH GREER
REFERENCE: C.A; T.H.M. VOL. 6, PG. 13

NAMES: ISAAC SIDWELL TO ELIZABETH CONN
DATE: JAN. 27, 1798
REFERENCE: T.H.M. VOL. 6, PG. 13

NAMES: JOSEPH SIDWELL TO MARGARET HUTCHISON
DATE: SEPT. 15, 1798
BONDSMAN: WILLIAM DAVISON
WITNESS: JOSEPH GREER
REFERENCE: C.A; T.H.M. VOL. 6, PG. 13

NAMES: JOSEPH STRICKLER TO MARY CARPENTER
DATE: JAN. 7, 1798
REFERENCE: T.H.M. VOL. 6, PG. 13

1799

NAMES: FELIX BAROLAT TO PRICE BROOK
DATE: JANY. 17, 1799
BONDSMAN: F. A. RAMSEY
WITNESS: CHAS. MCCLUNG, CLK.
REFERENCE: C.A; T.H.M. VOL. 6, PG. 13

NAMES: ALEXANDER BLAKELEY TO SARAH LACKEY
DATE: NOV. 18, 1799
BONDSMAN: WILLIAM DODD
WITNESS: A. W. WHITE
REFERENCE: C.A.

NAMES: FRANCIS BOUNDS TO AMY WHITE
DATE: JANY. 18, 1799
BONDSMAN: JOHN BOUNDS
REFERENCE: C.A; T.H.M. VOL. 6, PG. 13

NAMES: JONOAH BOWMAN TO BETSEY CAVETT
DATE: JANY. 1, 1799
BONDSMAN: THOMAS DODSON
WITNESS: H. L. WHITE
REFERENCE: C.A; T.H.M. VOL. 6, PG. 13

NAMES: JEREMIAH BROWN TO MOLLY MENUBY
DATE: NOV. 26, 1799
BONDSMAN: JACOB BOILER
WITNESS: A. WHITE
REFERENCE: C.A; T.H.M. VOL. 6, PG. 13

NAMES: HENRY BUKERSTAFF TO PEGGY HANNAH
DATE: JUNE 8, 1799
BONDSMAN: DAVID HEAD
WITNESS: H. L. WHITE
REFERENCE: C.A; T.H.M. VOL. 6, PG. 13

NAMES: ARCH CHAPMAN TO MATTIE HART
DATE: SEPT. 19, 1799
REFERENCE: T.H.M. VOL. 6, PG. 13

NAMES: JOSEPH CRAWFORD TO BETSY BROOK
DATE: APR. 10, 1799
BONDSMAN: JAMES BROOK
WITNESS: A. WHITE
REFERENCE: C.A; T.H.M. VOL. 6, PG. 13

NAMES: JOHN CROZIER TO HANNAH BARTON
DATE: JANY. 2, 1799
BONDSMAN: THOMAS N. CLARK
WITNESS: H. L. WHITE
REFERENCE: C.A; T.H.M. VOL. 6, PG. 13

NAMES: JOHN DAVIS TO ELIZABETH JOHNSON
DATE: FEBY. 1, 1799
BONDSMAN: ELIJAH JOHNSON
WITNESS: H. L. WHITE
REFERENCE: C.A; T.H.M. VOL. 6, PG. 13

NAMES: JOHN FARMER TO SARAH FARMER
DATE: NOV. 12, 1799
BONDSMAN: HENRY FARMER
WITNESS: A. WHITE
REFERENCE: C.A; T.H.M. VOL. 6, PG. 13

NAMES: ENOCH FERRELL TO NANCY NEVILL
DATE: FEBY. 5, 1799
BONDSMAN: GOAN MORGAN
WITNESS: H. L. WHITE
REFERENCE: C.A; T.H.M. VOL. 6, PG. 14

NAMES: SAMUEL FLEMING TO PEGGY TAYLOR
DATE: DEC. 2, 1799
BONDSMAN: JOHN LOVE
WITNESS: CHAS. MCCLUNG
REFERENCE: C.A; T.H.M. VOL. 6, PG. 14

NAMES: ALEXANDER FOSTER TO PATSEY PLUMBLEY
DATE: NOV. 29, 1799
BONDSMAN: ISAAC PLUMBLEY
WITNESS: A. WHITE
REFERENCE: C.A; T.H.M. VOL. 6, PG. 14

NAMES: THOMAS FROST TO MARTHA NAVILLE
DATE: OCT. 18, 1799
BONDSMAN: ISRAEL STANIFER
WITNESS: ANDW. WHITE
REFERENCE: C.A; T.H.M. VOL. 6, PG. 14

NAMES: JOSEPH HARDIN TO FANNY DOUGLASS
DATE: JAN. 6, 1799
REFERENCE: T.H.M. VOL. 6, PG. 14

NAMES: JAMES HEAVNER TO MARY BLIZZARD
DATE: NOV. 26, 1799
REFERENCE: T.H.M. VOL. 6, PG. 14

NAMES: STEPHEN HERD TO JEMIMAH MENEFEE
DATE: DEC. 23, 1799
BONDSMAN: PATRICK SHARKEY
WITNESS: A. WHITE
REFERENCE: C.A.

NAMES: JOHN HUGHES TO POLLY NELSON
DATE: SEPT. 16, 1799
BONDSMAN: THOMAS BROWN
WITNESS: A. WHITE
REFERENCE: C.A; T.H.M. VOL. 6, PG. 14

NAMES: JOHN HUTSON TO POLLY KEETHE
DATE: SEPT. 29, 1799
BONDSMAN: WILLIAM BURDEN
WITNESS: A. WHITE
REFERENCE: C.A; T.H.M. VOL. 6, PG. 14

NAMES: GEORGE INGRAM TO NANCY CRANE
DATE: MAR. 5, 1799
BONDSMAN: JOHN PHILLIPS
WITNESS: A. WHITE
REFERENCE: C. A.

NAMES: JOSIAH JENT TO PATTY SULLINS
DATE: AUG. 31, 1799
BONDSMAN: EDWARD FROST
WITNESS: A. WHITE
REFERENCE: C.A; T.H.M. VOL. 6, PG. 14

NAMES: AUGUST JOHNSON TO MARY SCARBOROUGH
DATE: OCT. 16, 1799
REFERENCE: T.H.M. VOL. 6, PG. 14

NAMES: ELIJAH JOHNSON TO BETSY COLKER
DATE: KEBY. 18, 1799
BONDSMAN: WILLIAM COLKER
WITNESS: A. WHITE
REFERENCE: C.A; T.H.M. VOL. 6, PG. 14

NAMES: JAMES JOHNSON TO ANN BALL
DATE: JUNE 1, 1799
BONDSMAN: MATHS BOOIE
REFERENCE: C.A; T.H.M. VOL. 6, PG. 14

NAMES: JAMES KEARNS TO NANCY BLIZZARD
DATE: NOV. 26, 1799
BONDSMAN: HUGH MCBRIDE
WITNESS: A. WHITE
REFERENCE: C.A.

NAMES: MICAJAH KEETH TO MILLY HICKEY
DATE: FEBY. 14, 1799
BONDSMAN: SAMUEL KEETH
WITNESS: ANDW. WHITE
REFERENCE: C.A; T.H.M. VOL. 6, PG. 14

NAMES: MARTIN KENNEDY TO ELIZA EBLEN
DATE: DEC. 16, 1799
BONDSMAN: SAMUEL EBLEN
REFERENCE: C.A; T.H.M. VOL. 6, PG. 14

NAMES: HENRY MANKEY TO KITTY CARPENTER
DATE: NOV. 29, 1799
BONDSMAN: JOHN BRIGHT
WITNESS: A. WHITE
REFERENCE: C.A; T.H.M. VOL. 6, PG. 14

NAMES: JAMES MANFIELD TO PEGGY PARKER
DATE: JULY 1, 1799
BONDSMAN: GEORGE PRESGROVE
WITNESS: H. L. WHITE
REFERENCE: C.A; T.H.M. VOL. 6, PG. 14

NAMES: GEORGE MCNUTT TO GENE ANDERSON
DATE: 1797 (?) SEE 1799
REFERENCE: T.H.M. VOL. 6, PGS. 11 & 14

NAMES: MARTIN MILLER TO JENNY MANFIELD
DATE: JULY 30, 1799
BONDSMAN: GEORGE MILLER
WITNESS: A. WHITE
REFERENCE: C.A; T.H.M. VOL. 6, PG. 14

NAMES: HUGH MILLS TO POLLY MOFFET
DATE: FEBY. 26, 1799
BONDSMAN: N. H. S. FOURNIER
WITNESS: A. WHITE
REFERENCE: C.A; T.H.M. VOL. 6, PG. 14

NAMES: ROBERT MORROW TO NANCY DOBSON
DATE: JANY. 22, 1799
BONDSMAN: SAM'L COWAN
WITNESS: ANDW. WHITE
REFERENCE: C.A; T.H.M. VOL. 6, PG. 14

NAMES: DANIEL NORIDIKE -(NARRADYCHE) TO MARY HIGGINS
DATE: JANY. 18, 1799
BONDSMAN: JOHN HIGGINS
WITNESS: ANDW. WHITE
REFERENCE: C.A; T.H.M. VOL. 6, PG. 14

NAMES: WILLIAM PARKER TO TABBY BOHANNAN
DATE: SEPT. 5, 1799
BONDSMAN: THOMAS WOODWARD
REFERENCE: C.A.

NAMES: JAMES REED TO MALINDA TRAMMELL
DATE: JUNE 19, 1799
BONDSMAN: WILLIAM TIPTON
WITNESS: H. L. WHITE
REFERENCE: C. A.

NAMES: JAMES REID TO MALINDA FAUNNULART
DATE: JUNE 19, 1799
REFERENCE: T.H.M. VOL. 6, PG. 14.

NAMES: MARTIN RICE TO BARBARA TILLMAN
DATE: NOV. 16, 1799
BONDSMAN: DANIEL SHARP
WITNESS: A. WHITE
REFERENCE: C. A; T.H.M. VOL. 6, PG. 13 & 14

NAMES: JESSE ROACH TO SALLY COBB
DATE: MAY 6, 1799
BONDSMAN: EDWARD TEAL
WITNESS: A. WHITE
REFERENCE: C.A; T.H.M. VOL. 6, PG. 14

NAMES: NATHAN ROBERTS TO ABIGALE BISHOP
DATE: NOV. 10, 1799
BONDSMAN: JOSEPH BISHOP
WITNESS: A. WHITE
REFERENCE: C. A; T.H.M. VOL. 6, PG. 14

NAMES: MARTIN RUDINS TO SARAH CLARK
DATE: MAY 2, 1799
BONDSMAN: MICHAEL MILLER
WITNESS: H. L. WHITE
REFERENCE: C.A; T.H.M. VOL. 6, PG. 14

NAMES: JAMES RUTH TO REBECKAH GOWER
DATE: JULY 6, 1799
BONDSMAN: WILLIAM RICHARDS
WITNESS: H. L. WHITE
REFERENCE: C.A; T.H.M. VOL. 6, PG. 14

NAMES: EDWARD SCOTT TO SARAH C. HAINES
DATE: JANY. 17, 1799
BONDSMAN: JOHN MCCLELLAN
WITNESS: CHAS. MCCLUNG, CLK.
REFERENCE: C.A; T.H.M. VOL. 6, PG. 14

NAMES: LAWRENCE SCOTT TO BETSY LOWE
DATE: DEC. 3, 1799
BONDSMAN: JAMES PORTER
WITNESS: CHAS. MCCLUNG
REFERENCE: C.A; T.H.M. VOL. 6, PG. 14

Names: Daniel Sharp to Jean Howard
Date: Apr. 3, 1799
Bondsman: John Gibbs
Witness: A. White
Reference: C.A; T.H.M. Vol. 6, Pg. 14

Names: Alexander Smith to Catherine Lowen
Date: June 25, 1799
Bondsman: John Adair
Witness: H. L. White
Reference: C.A; T.H.M. Vol. 6, Pg. 14

Names: John Stogdon to Polly Sheafer
Date: May 25, 1799
Bondsman: George Roach
Witness: A. White
Reference: C.A; T.H.M. Vol. 6, Pg. 14

Names: Richard Sullins to Agnes Farmer
Date: July 8, 1799
Bondsman: Jeptha Cornelius
Witness: A. White
Reference: C.A; T.H.M. Vol. 6, Pg. 14

Names: William Thompson to Nancy Miller
Date: Mar. 28, 1799
Bondsman: Wm. Baldie
Witness: A. White
Reference: C.A; T.H.M. Vol. 6 Pg. 14

Names: John Vance to Martha Davidson
Date: Mar. 1, 1799
Bondsman: Samuel Davidson
Witness: Andw. White
Reference: C.A; T.H.M. Vol. 6 Pg. 14

Names: Isaac Vanhooser to Polly Poor
Date: Feby. 1, 1799
Bondsman: Isaac Jones
Witness: H. L. White
Reference: C.A; T.H.M. Vol. 6, Pg. 14

Names: John Young to Polly Smith
Date: Mar. 5, 1799
Bondsman: Geo. Gutry (?)
Witness: A. White
Reference: C.A; T.H.M. Vol. 6, Pg. 14

1800

Names: Alexander Adair to Barbara Foust
Date: Dec. 8, 1800
Bondsman: David Adair
Witness: A. White
Reference: C.A; T.H.M. Vol. 6, Pg. 14

Names: Samuel Anderson to Benthing Lowe
Date: Apr. 3, 1800
Reference: T.H.M. Vol. 6, Pg. 15

Names: Kaleb Bales to Anne Smith
Date: Mch. 19, 1800
Reference: T.H.M. Vol. 6, Pg. 14

Names: Bazil Basher to Peggy Horton
Date: July 31, 1800
Reference: T.H.M. Vol. 6, Pg. 14

Names: Peter Boomer to Rebeccah Farmer
Date: Mch. 7, 1800
Reference: T.H.M. Vol. 6, Pg. 14

Names: John Bowman to Peggy Jack
Date: Apr. 21, 1800
Reference: T.H.M. Vol. 6 Pg. 14

Names: John Branon to Donah Scott
Date: Sept. 17, 1800
Reference: T.H.M. Vol. 6, Pg. 14

Names: William Brent to Patty Chisolm
Date: Nov. 4, 1800
Reference: T.H.M. Vol. 6, Pg. 14

Names: Sam (?) Brooks to Catherine Doyle
Date: ________ 13, 1800
Reference: T.H.M. Vol. 6, Pg. 14

Names: Valentine Butler to Polly Gideon (Gedion?)
Date: Sept. 26, 1800
Reference: T.H.M. Vol. 6, Pg. 14

Names: David Campbell to Mary Hamilton Campbell
Date: May 14, 1800
Bondsman: David Campbell
Witness: Chas. McClung
Reference: C.A; T.H.M. Vol. 6, Pg. 14

NAMES: JOHN CAVERT TO MARY GRAYHAM
DATE: MAR. 14, 1800
BONDSMAN: GEORGE HALLMARK
REFERENCE: C.A.

NAMES: JOHN DAVIS TO MATTY MENEESY
DATE: NOV. 25, 1800
BONDSMAN: ISAAC MENEESY
WITNESS: A. WHITE
REFERENCE: C.A; T.H.M. VOL. 6, PG. 14

NAMES: NICHODEMUS HACKWORTH TO MARY ENGLAND
DATE: NOV. 5, 1800
REFERENCE: T.H.M. VOL. 6, PG. 14

NAMES: JOHN LESTER TO POLLY OXYER
DATE: DEC. 30, 1800
BONDSMAN: WILLIAM STANIFER - WILLIAM M. MCCLUNG
REFERENCE: C.A; T.H.M. VOL. 6, PG. 14

NAMES: JOHN MAXWELL TO LUCY SMITH
DATE: APR. 18, 1800
REFERENCE: T.H.M. VOL. 6, PG. 14

NAMES: JOSEPH MCALISTER TO MARGARET STIRLING
DATE: JUNE 17, 1800
REFERENCE: T.H.M. VOL. 6, PG. 14

NAMES: JOHN ORSKINS TO MARY THOMAS
DATE: JUNE 14, 1800
BONDSMAN: GEORGE NORTON
WITNESS: H. L. WHITE
REFERENCE: C.A; T.H.M. VOL. 6, PG. 14

NAMES: GEORGE PEW TO MARGARET ADAMSON
DATE: MAR. 29, 1800
BONDSMAN: ARON ADAMSON
WITNESS: A. WHITE
REFERENCE: C.A; T.H.M. VOL. 6, PG. 14

NAMES: GEO. RICHARDS TO RACHEL MANIFOLD
DATE: OCT. 14, 1800 OR 1801
DATE PER: OCT. 14, 1800 OR 1801
BY: JOHN LOVE, J. P.
REFERENCE: O.M.R. PG. 4

NAMES: JOHN TERRY TO ELIZABETH CRAIG
DATE: DEC. 3, 1800
BONDSMAN: RUBIN BROWN
WITNESS: CHAS. MCCLUNG
REFERENCE: C.A; T.H.M. VOL. 6, PG. 14

NAMES: ARMSTEAD THORNHILL TO RACHEL JOHNSON
DATE: OCT. 1, 1800
BONDSMAN: WILLIAM JOHNSON
WITNESS: A. WHITE
REFERENCE: C.A; T.H.M. VOL. 6, PG. 14

NAMES: JOHN TUNNELL TO ANN WEATHERINGTON
DATE: DEC. 8, 1800
BONDSMAN: (CHAS. MCCLUNG, WITNESS) ALEXANDER COULTER
REFERENCE: C.A; T.H.M. VOL. 6, PG. 15

NAMES: CHARLES WHITE TO JENNY RHEA
DATE: MAY 2, 1800
REFERENCE: T.H.M. VOL. 6, PG. 15

1801

NAMES: HUGH BOTKIN TO RACHEL KEENER
DATE: MCH. 17, 1801
REFERENCE: T.H.M. VOL. 6, PG. 15

NAMES: PETER BOWMER TO MARY BEMAN
DATE: JUNE 10, 1801
REFERENCE: T.H.M. VOL. 6, PG. 15

NAMES: THOMAS BROWN TO JANE MCELWEE
DATE: FEB. 16, 1801
REFERENCE: T.H.M. VOL. 6, PG. 15

NAMES: HUGH CARMICHAEL TO NANCY TINDELL
DATE: DEC. 25, 1801
BONDSMAN: WM. COVEY
WITNESS: A. WHITE
REFERENCE: C.A.

NAMES: THOMAS CARPENTER TO MARY ANN SHOOK
DATE: JUNE 13, 1801
BONDSMAN: GEORGE CARPENTER
WITNESS: H. L. WHITE
REFERENCE: C.A; T.H.M. VOL. 6, PG. 15

NAMES: WILLIAM CARTER TO CHARITY BAKER
DATE: MAR. 25, 1801
BONDSMAN: CORNELIUS HICKEY
WITNESS: A. WHITE
REFERENCE: C.A; T.H.M. VOL. 6, PG. 15

NAMES: BENJIMIN CRAIN TO JENNY SHELTON
DATE: JUNE 13, 1801
BONDSMAN: MICAJAH TERRY
WITNESS: A. WHITE
REFERENCE: C.A; T.H.M. VOL. 6, PG. 15

NAMES: WILLIAM CRAWFORD TO SALLY TERRY
DATE: DEC. 7, 1801
BONDSMAN: JESSE TERRY
WITNESS: WM. C. BLOUNT
REFERENCE: C.A; T.H.M. VOL. 6, PG. 15

NAMES: SAMMY HOBBS TO NANCY HOLT
DATE: MCH. 3, 1801
REFERENCE: T.H.M. VOL. 6, PG. 15

NAMES: NATHANIEL MASON TO PHOEBE BRASHEARS
DATE: JULY 9, 1801
BONDSMAN: FRANCIS FULSHER
WITNESS: CHAS. MCCLUNG, CLK.
REFERENCE: C.A; T.H.M. VOL. 6, PG. 15

NAMES: BRITTON MATTHEWS TO PATSY BROWDER
DATE: SEPT. 26, 1801
BONDSMAN: ARCHILLIOUS MATTHEWS
WITNESS: JOHN MCCLELLAN
REFERENCE: C.A; T.H.M. VOL. 6, PG. 15

NAMES: JOSEPH MCALISTER TO MARGARET STIRLING
DATE: JUNE 17, 1801
BONDSMAN: SAMUEL STIRLING
WITNESS: CHAS. MCCLUNG, CLERK
REFERENCE: C. A.

NAMES: JAMES MCCULLOUGH TO BETSY BRANNUM
DATE: OCT. 11, 1801
BONDSMAN: WILLIAM KNOX
WITNESS: CHAS. MCCLUNG, CLERK
REFERENCE: C. A.

NAMES: GEORGE MCFARLAN TO NANCY GOLDEN
DATE: APR. 20, 1801 (OR 7?)
REFERENCE: T.H.M. VOL. 6, PG. 15

NAMES: DAVID MCNAIR TO DELILAH VANN
DATE: DEC. 30, 1801
BONDSMAN: JOHN MCCLELLAN
REFERENCE: C.A; T.H.M. VOL. 6, PG. 15

NAMES: THOMAS MEEK TO NANCY BOWEN
DATE: MAR. 29, 1801
BONDSMAN: CHARLES BOWEN
WITNESS: A. WHITE
REFERENCE: C.A; T.H.M. VOL. 6, PG. 15

NAMES: STEPHEN TERRY TO ISBEL NETHERLIN (?)
DATE: NOV. 5, 1801
REFERENCE: T.H.M. VOL. 6, PG. 15

NAMES: WM. WHITCHURCH TO ELIZABETH HOWEL
DATE: JUNE 20, 1801
BONDSMAN: JOSEPH GOODSON
REFERENCE: C.A; T.H.M. VOL. 6, PG. 15

NAMES: WILLIAM WHITEMAN TO JEAN SIMMS
DATE: MAR. 2, 1801
BONDSMAN: ELY SIMS
REFERENCE: C. A; T.H.M. VOL. 6, PG. 15 (WIT: A. WHITE)

NAMES: DAVID WILLIAMS TO BETSY MCGRIFF
DATE: NOV. 16, 1801
BONDSMAN: JOHN RICE
WITNESS: A. WHITE
REFERENCE: C. A.

1802

NAMES: JACOB DRAKE TO POLLY NOLEN
DATE: NOV. 13, 1802
BY: JOHN LOVE, ESQ.
REFERENCE: C.A; O?M.R. PG. 5

NAMES: JOHN NEELY TO SALLY SCOTT
DATE: JULY 29, 1802
BY: JOHN LOVE, ESQ.
REFERENCE: C.A; O.M.R. PG. 5

NAMES: DAVID REARDIN TO POLLY BRANNUM
DATE: MAY 3, 1802
BY: JOHN LOVE, ESQ.
REFERENCE: C.A; O.M.R. PG. 5

NAMES: ROBERT REARDON TO ABIGAIL NOLEN
DATE: NOV. 4, 1802
BY: JOHN LOVE, ESQ.
REFERENCE: C.:A; O.M.R. PG. 5

NAMES: MORGAN SNOW TO ELIZABETH HUDIBURG
DATE: OCT. 12, 1802
DATE PER: OCT. 12, 1802
BY: JOHN LOVE, J. P.
REFERENCE: O.M.R. PG. 4

NAMES: CHRISTIAN STICKLEY TO ISBEL CREELY
DATE: OCT. 5, 1802
BY: JOHN LOVE, ESQ.
REFERENCE: C.A; OMR. PG. 5

NAMES: THOMAS TAYLOR TO ELIZABETH FERRILL
DATE: MAR. 23, 1802
BONDSMAN: JOHN GIBBS & GEORGE GIBBS
WITNESS: CHAS. MCCLUNG
REFERENCE: C.A; T.H.M. VOL. 6, PG. 15

NAMES: DANIEL THARP TO CATHARINE HENSON
DATE: DEC. 20, 1802
BONDSMAN: PETER LOONEY - (WIT: CHAS. MCCLUNG, CLERK)
WITNESS: C.A; T.H.M. VOL. 6, PG. 15

1803

NAMES: DAVID CAMPBELL TO JENNY COWAN
DATE: SEPT. 19, 1803
BONDSMAN: SAM'L G. RAMSEY
WITNESS: CHAS. MCCLUNG
REFERENCE: C.A.

NAMES: JAMES CARNES TO BETSY MITCHELL
DATE: AUG. 15, 1803
BONDSMAN: JAMES DODD
WITNESS: CHAS. MCCLUNG, CLERK
REFERENCE: C.A.

NAMES: GEORGE CHRISTIAN TO ELIZA MCCORMACK
DATE: JUNE 1, 1803
BONDSMAN: WILLIAM MCCORMACK
WITNESS: CHAS. MCCLUNG, CLERK
REFERENCE: C.A; T.H.M. VOL. 6, PG. 15

NAMES: THOMAS CRAIGHEAD TO POLLY GALESPIE
DATE: DEC. 23, 1803
BONDSMAN: ROBERT CRAIGHEAD
WITNESS: A. WHITE
REFERENCE: C.A; T.H.M. VOL. 6, PG. 15

NAMES: SOLOMON GEORGE TO PEGGY CRAWFORD
DATE: SEPT. 12, 1803
BONDSMAN: WM. COPELAND
WITNESS: A. WHITE
REFERENCE: C.A; T.H.M. VOL. 6, PG. 15

NAMES: LEWIS HILL TO RACHEL BIRDWELL
DATE: JULY 18, 1803
BONDSMAN: JOHN PICKENS
WITNESS: CHAS. MCCLUNG, CLERK
REFERENCE: C. A.

NAMES: ABRAHAM LEE TO JANE BURROWS
DATE: NOV. 14, 1803
BONDSMAN: PURMAST LEE
BY: JOHN LOVE, J. P.
WITNESS: CHAS. MCCLUNG, CLERK
REFERENCE: C.A; O.M.R. PG. 5; T.H.M. VOL. 6, PG. 15

NAMES: ISAAC PRUITT TO POLLY STICKLEY
DATE: MAR. 25, 1803
BY: JOHN LOVE, ESQ.
WITNESS: CHAS. MCCLUNG
REFERENCE: C.A; O.M.R. PG. 5

NAMES: JACOB TENOR TO ESTHER GIBSON
DATE: JUNE 22, 1803
BONDSMAN: JACOB HUNTSMAN
WITNESS: STEPHEN HILLIS
REFERENCE: C.A; T.H.M. VOL. 6, PG. 15

NAMES: JOHN TREADWAY TO POLLY HAYNES
DATE: JUNE 6, 1803
BONDSMAN: EDWARD SCOTT
WITNESS: A. WHITE
REFERENCE: C.A; T.H.M. VOL. 6, PG. 15

1804

NAMES: OLIVER BREWER TO POLLY HENDERSON
DATE: JAN. 10, 1804
REFERENCE: T.H.M. VOL. 6, PG. 15

NAMES: JOHN BROWN TO NANCY HOUSE
DATE: FEBY. 17, 1804
DATE PER: FEBY 17, 1804
BY: R. HOUSTON, J. P. K. C.
REFERENCE: C.A; O.M.R. PG. 6

NAMES: WILLIAM BUCKLEY TO POLLY HENNEMAN
DATE: JAN. 25, 1804
REFERENCE: T.H.M. VOL. 6, PG. 15

NAMES: GEORGE COX TO RACHEL MORFETT
DATE: JULY 4, 1804
BONDSMAN: BEN GRAYSON
WITNESS: CHAS. MCCLUNG
REFERENCE: C.A; T.H.M. VOL. 6, PG. 15

NAMES: SAMUEL N. CUNNINGHAM TO JEAN FLANNAGAN
DATE: JAN. 15, 1804 (OR 6?)
REFERENCE: T.H.M. VOL. 6, PG. 15

Names: Aaron England to Nancy McCampsell
Date: Aug. 27, 1804
Reference: T.H.M. Vol. 6, Pg. 15

Names: William Tindall to Sally Carpenter
Date: Sept. 22, 1804
Reference: C.A; O.M.R. Pg. 5

Names: David Upton to Peggy Carmichael
Date: Dec. 4, 1804
By: R. Houston, J. P. K. C.
Reference: C.A; O.M.R. Pg. 6.

Names: Thomas Wheeler to Polly Keith L.
Date: Mar. 19, 1804
Reference: C.A; O.M.R. Pg. 5

Names: Sam'l Wilson to Anne Cozby
Date: Mar. 2, 1804
Bondsman: James Wilson & Wm. B. McNutt
Witness: A. White
Reference: C.A; T.H.M. Vol. 6, Pg. 15

1805

Names: John Anderson to Elizabeth McNair
Date: Nov. 11, 1805
Date Per:
By: R. Houston, J.P.K.C.
Reference: C.A; O.M.R. Pg. 6

Names: Thomas Bell to Elener Tillery
Date: Jany. 22, 1805
Reference: T.H.M, Vol. 6, Pg. 15

Names: Abner Bowen to Jenny Thompson
Date: Nov. 27, 1805
Reference: T.H.M. Vol. 6, Pg. 15

Names: William Bowen to Amelia Sloane
Date: Feby. 19, 1805
Date Per: Feby. 19, 1805
By: R. Houston, J.P.K.C.
Reference: C.A; O.M.R. Pg. 6

Names: Peter Carter to Sally Medly
Date: Oct. 12, 1805
Bondsman: John Sharp
Witness: W. Park
Reference: C.A; T.H.M. Vol. 6, Pg. 15

Names: Rueben Casedy to Rachel McCoy
Date: Oct. 14, 1805
Bondsman: William Johnson - Daniel Hoffar
Witness: W. Park
Reference: C.A; T.H.M. Vol. 6, Pg. 15

Names: Robert Childers to Polly Lucas
Date: Nov. 8, 1805
Bondsman: John Childers
Witness: James Park
Reference: C.A; T.H.M. Vol. 6, Pg. 15

Names: William Conner to Sally Case [Cox?]
Date: Dec. 30, 1805
Bondsman: Mordical Yarnell
Witness: W. Park
Reference: C.A; T.H.M. Vol. 6, Pg. 15

Names: Jonathan Courtney to Mary Goadus (?)
Date: Oct. 15, 1805
Bondsman: James Dyer
Witness: A. White
Reference: C.A; T.H.M' Vol. 6, Pg. 15

Names: John Coxe to Peggy Hamilton
Date: Oct. 30, 1805
Reference: T.H.M' Vol. 6, Pg. 15

Names: Wm. Dearmond to Polly Wandless
Date: March 6, 1805
Reference: O.M.R. Pg. 6

Names: Thomas Frazier to Polly Gillim
Date: Aug. 13, 1805
Bondsman: Julian Frazier
Witness: W. Park
Reference: C.A.

Names: Abijah Harris to Nancy Luttrell
Date: Jan. 18, 1805
Date Per: Jan. 18, 1805
By: R. Houston, J.P.
Reference: O.M.R. Pg. 6

Names: Silas Miller to Rachel Batkin
Date: Aug. 29, 1805
Reference: C.A; O.M.R. Pg. 6

Names: Ruben Tipton to Mary Reed
Date: Dec. 3, 1805
Reference: C.A; O.M.R. Pg. 6

NAMES: MARTIN TURPIN TO ELIZABETH RUSSELL
DATE: OCT. 28, 1805
BONDSMAN: JAMES SCARBOROUGH
WITNESS: CHAS. MCCLUNG
REFERENCE: C.A; T.H.M. VOL. 6, PG. 15

NAMES: GEORGE WRINKLE TO NANCY FRAZIER
DATE: MAR. 10, 1805
REFERENCE: C.A; O.M.R. PG. 6

1806

NAMES: JOHN ALLEN TO ELIZABETH MARTIN
DATE: MAR. 12, 1806
DATE PER: MAR. 12, 1806
BY: R. HOUSTON J.P.K.C.
REFERENCE: C.A; O.M.R. PG. 6

NAMES: WILLIAM BARNETT TO ROSANNAH KIRKUM
DATE: NOV. 3, 1806
REFERENCE: T.H.M. VOL. 6, PG. 15

NAMES: ABNER BEESON TO SUSANNAH DIMMIT
DATE: JULY 19, 1806
DATE PER: JULY 19, 1806
BY: R. HOUSTON, J.P.K.C.
REFERENCE: C.A; O.M.R. PG. 7

NAMES: ALEXANDER CAMERON TO MARGARET CAMERON
DATE: FEBY. 1, 1806
BONDSMAN: WILLIAM LEAKEY
WITNESS: JNO. A. GAMBLE
REFERENCE: C.A; T.H.M. VOL. 6, PG. 15

NAMES: MICHAEL CISER TO NANCY JULIAN
DATE: JANY. 11, 1806
BONDSMAN: ABNER PARR
WITNESS: JNO. FERRIS (?)
REFERENCE: C.A.

NAMES: WILLIAM WALLACE COWAN TO POLLY FLENNIKEN
DATE: MAR. 26, 1806
BONDSMAN: JAMES CAMPBELL – SAMUEL GIVENS
WITNESS: STEPHEN HILLIS
REFERENCE: C/A; T.H.M VOL. 6, PG. 15

NAMES: SAMUEL H. CUNNINGHAM TO JEAN FLANNAGAN
DATE: JANY. 15, 1806
BONDSMAN: JOHN DEARMOND – EDWARD MASON
WITNESS: W. PARK
REFERENCE: C.A.

NAMES: JAMES CURRIER TO ANNE STOCKTON
DATE: MAR. 9, 1806
BONDSMAN: ISAAC BOND
WITNESS: CHAS. MCCLUNG, CLK.
REFERENCE: C.A; T.H.M. VOL. 6, PG. 15

NAMES: WILLIAM CURRIER TO MARTHA FRYAR
DATE: NOV. 7, 1806
BONDSMAN: WILLIAM FRYAR
WITNESS: CHAS. MCCLUNG
REFERENCE: C.A.

NAMES: WILLIAM ELLIOT TO DIANNA DIMMIT
DATE: JULY 19, 1806
DATE PER: JULY 19, 1806
BY: R. HOUSTON, J.P.K.C.
REFERENCE: C.A; O.M.R. PG. 7

NAMES: NATHANIEL HUETT TO MARY JONES
DATE: DEC. 30, 1806
BONDSMAN: FRANCIS FLESHART (?)
WITNESS: JNO. A. GAMBLE
REFERENCE: C.A.

NAMES: JOHN HUNTER TO POLLY CAMPBELL
DATE: APR. 29, 1806
BONDSMAN: ROBERT HOUSTON
WITNESS: JNO. A. GAMBLE
REFERENCE: C.A.

NAMES: JOHN MAXWELL TO LUCY SMITH
DATE: APR. 18, 1806
BONDSMAN: JOSEPH LOVE
WITNESS: JNO. A. GAMBLE
REFERENCE: C.A.

NAMES: ELY SIMS TO RACHEL TOWNSEND
DATE: DEC. 26, 1806
BONDSMAN: JOHN TOWNSEND
WITNESS: JNO. A. GAMBLE
REFERENCE: C.A; T.H.M. VOL. 6, PG. 16

NAMES: ELIAS B. SMITH TO JENNY M. MCORE
DATE: SEPT. 4, 1806
BONDSMAN: JOHN A. SMITH
REFERENCE: C.A; O.M.R. PG. 7; T.H.M. VOL. 6, PG. 16

Names:	Thomas Stafford to Nancy Scott
Date:	July 21, 1806
Bondsman:	William Miles
Witness:	Chas. McClung
Reference:	C.A.

Names:	Robert Stevenson to Kitty Stirling
Date:	Nov. 18, 1806
Bondsman:	Samuel Stirling
Witness:	Stephen Hillis
Reference:	C.A.

Names:	Jesse White to Mary Manifee
Date:	June 28, 1806
Bondsman:	Quin Marlow - J. C. Luttrell
Reference:	C.A; T.H.M. Vol. 6, Pg. 16

Names:	Edmund Wilkenson to Sally Cooper
Date:	Jany. 17, 1806
Bondsman:	Jacob Ault
Witness:	William Park
Reference:	C.A.

Names:	John Wright to Crissy Smith
Date:	Sept. 6, 1806
Bondsman:	James Davis
Witness:	Jno. A. Gamble
Reference:	C.A; T.H.M. Vol. 6, Pg. 16

1807

Names:	William Akeman to Jenny Montgomery
Date:	July 31, 1807
Date Per:	Aug. 5, 1807
By:	John Love, Esq.
Reference:	C.A; O.M.R., Pg. 8

Names:	Philadelphia Bledsoe to Polly Howell
Date:	Oct. 9, 1807
Reference:	C.A; O.M.R. Pg. 8

Names:	William Brown to Rebecca Evans
Date:	Sept. 30, 1807
Reference:	C.A; O.M.R. Pg. 8

Names:	Pumroy Carmichael to Nancy Bell
Date:	Nov. 6, 1807
Bondsman:	William Bell
Witness:	Jno. Gamble
Reference:	C.A; T.H.M. Vol. 6, Pg. 16

Names:	Andrew Carthy to Suky Mitchell
Date:	July 13, 1807
Bondsman:	John Menefee
Reference:	C.A; T.H.M. Vol. 6, Pg. 16

Names:	Samuel Clark to Betsey Dial
Date:	Oct. 9, 1807
By:	John Love Esq.
Reference:	C.A; O.M.R. Pg. 8

Names:	John Cleveland to Mary Martin
Date:	May 3, 1807
Bondsman:	James Magee
Date Per:	May 3, 1807
By:	R. Houston, J.P.K.C.
Witness:	Jno. H. Gamble
Reference:	C.A; O.M.R. Pg. 7; T.H.M. Vol. 6, Pg. 16

Names:	William Close to Eliza Herron
Date:	Nov. 19, 1807
Bondsman:	Abner Witt
Witness:	Jno. Ferris (?)
Reference:	C.A; T.H.M. Vol. 6, Pg. 16

Names:	Abner Cochran to Mary Stringfield
Date:	Mar. 16, 1807
Bondsman:	Gideon Reynolds
Witness:	Jno. Gamble
Reference:	C.A; T.H.M Vol. 6, Pg. 16

Names:	Joel Coker to Susan McCampbell
Date:	June 9, 1807
Bondsman:	Philip Taylor
Witness:	Jno. Purris
Reference:	C.A; T.H.M. Vol. 6, Pg. 16

Names:	Samuel Cox to Margaret Crippen
Date:	Dec. 9, 1807
Bondsman:	Matthias Talley
By:	Jno. Surris (?)
Reference:	C.A; T.H.M. Vol. 6, Pg. 16

Names:	Hardeman Guize to Esther Maney
Date:	Apr. 11, 1807
Bondsman:	Wm. Harrelson
Reference:	C.A; T.H.M. Vol. 6, Pg. 16

Names:	Nathaniel Guiss to Patsey Brooks
Date:	Apr. 30, 1807
Reference:	C.A; O.M.R. Pg. 7

NAMES: GEORGE HARLESS ______________
DATE: MAR. 6, 1807
BONDSMAN: THOMAS MCGRIFF
WITNESS: A. WHITE
REFERENCE: C.A.

NAMES: GEORGE HARLESS TO MARGARET MCGRUFF
DATE: MCH. 6, 1801
REFERENCE: T.H.M. VOL. 6, PG. 15

NAMES: JAMES HOBBS TO NANCY HALL
DATE: MAR. 3, 1807
BONDSMAN: JOEL HOBBS
WITNESS: A. WHITE
REFERENCE: C.A.

NAMES: JOHN HODGIN TO ANN CHAPMAN
DATE: AUG. 21, 1807
DATE PER: AUG. 21, 1807
BY: R. HOUSTON, J.P.K.C.
REFERENCE: C.A; O.M.R. PG. 8

NAMES: THOS. HUDIBURG TO POLLY MCCARTER
DATE: NOV. 10, 1807
DATE PER: NOV. 10, 1807
BY: R. HOUSTON, J.P.
REFERENCE: O.M.R. PG. 8

NAMES: JONATHAN KEENER TO ELIZABETH KEENER
DATE: MAR. 2, 1807
REFERENCE: C.A; O.M.R. PG. 7

NAMES: JAMES LEGG TO SALLY LUTTRELL
DATE: SEPT. 14, 1807
DATE PER: SEPT. 14, 1807
BY: R. HOUSTON, J.P.K.C.
REFERENCE: C.A; O.M.R. PG. 8

NAMES: JAMES C. LUTTRELL TO PATSY ARMSTRONG
DATE: OCT. 27, 1807
DATE PER: OCT. 27, 1807
BY: R. HOUSTON, J.P.
REFERENCE: O.M.R. PG. 8

NAMES: GEORGE MCFARLAN TO NANCY GOLDEN
DATE: APR. 20, 1807
BONDSMAN: JONATHAN HELLAM
WITNESS: H. L. WHITE
REFERENCE: C.A.

NAMES: ROWLEY MCMILLEN TO JEMIMA SHOOK
DATE: MAR. 8, 1807
REFERENCE: C.A; O.M.R. PG. 7

NAMES: DAVID H. MEBIN TO SUSANNA CARTER
DATE: DEC. 24, 1807
DATE PER: DEC. 24, 1807
BY: R. HOUSTON, J.P.K.C.
REFERENCE: C.A; O.M.R. PG. 9

NAMES: JOHN OWEN TO POLLY GALLOWAY
DATE: JUNE 16, 1807
BONDSMAN: JAMES GALLOWAY
WITNESSES: JNO. PURRIS
REFERENCE: C. A.

NAMES: ROBERT PALMER TO JANE RORICK
DATE: MAR. 11, 1807
BONDSMAN: WILLIAM PALMER
WITNESS: JOHN A. GAMBLE
REFERENCE: C.A; O.M.R. PG. 7; T.H.M. VOL. 6, PG. 16

NAMES: CHRISTIAN PICKLE TO ELIZABETH LEWIS
DATE: MAY 27, 1807
REFERENCE: C.A; O.M.R. PG. 7

NAMES: HENRY PICKLE TO PEGGY BARGER
DATE: AUG. 8, 1807
BONDSMAN: GEORGE PICKLE
REFERENCE: C.A.

NAMES: JOHN PICKLE TO CATHERINE HUFFAKER
DATE: MAR. 4, 1807
REFERENCE: C.A; O.M.R. PG. 7

NAMES: THOMAS POUNDERS TO POLLY GRAHAM
DATE: JANY. 27, 1807
BONDSMAN: WILLIAM HUMPHRIES
WITNESS: JNO. A. GAMBLE
REFERENCE: C.A.

NAMES: HARRIS PRYOR TO KEZIAH MANEY
DATE: FEBY. 18, 1807
BONDSMAN: HARDIMAN CRUIZE
WITNESS: JNO. A. GAMBLE
REFERENCE: C.A.

NAMES: ELIJAH SCARBOROUGH TO MOLLY ADAMS
DATE: DEC. 27, 1807
REFERENCE: T.H.M. VOL. 6, PG. 16

NAMES: MATTHEW SEXTON TO NANCY ELLIS
DATE: NOV. 4, 1807
BONDSMAN: BENJ. KIMBREL
WITNESS: JNO. A. GAMBLE
REFERENCE: C.A; T.H.M. VOL. 6, PG. 16

NAMES: GEORGE SHALL TO PATSEY HAYNES
DATE: NOV. 23, 1807
BONDSMAN: JOHN BROWN
WITNESS: JNO. PURRIS
REFERENCE: C.A; T.H.M. VOL. 6, PG. 16

NAMES: AMOS SHARP TO SALLY CARTER
DATE: JUNE 15, 1807
DATE PER: JUNE 15, 1807
BY: R. HOUSTON, J.P.K.C.
REFERENCE: C.A; O.M.R. PG. 8

NAMES: WILLIAM SHARP TO ISABELLA ROBERTS
DATE: MAR. 11, 1807
BONDSMAN: WILLIAM ROBERTS
WITNESS: JNO. A. GAMBLE
REFERENCE: C.A.

NAMES: DANIEL STAMPER TO KAZIA REICE
DATE: JUNE 25, 1807
BONDSMAN: WILLIAM MOORE
WITNESS: JNO. PURRIS
REFERENCE: C.A; T.H.M. VOL. 6, PG. 16

NAMES: JACOB TARWATER TO PEGGY DOZIER
DATE: MAY 25, 1807
BONDSMAN: TEEWALT TARWATER
WITNESS: JNO. PURRIS
REFERENCE: C.A; T.H.M. VOL. 6,PG. 16

NAMES: HENRY TAYLOR TO MOLLY NOBLER
DATE: JULY 11, 1807
BONDSMAN: BASTON NASLER
REFERENCE: C.A; T.H.M. VOL. 6, PG. 16

NAMES: STEPHEN TERRY TO ISBEL NEATHERLIN
DATE: NOV. 5, 1807
BONDSMAN: JOHN COUNCIL
WITNESS: NOBLE JOHNSON
REFERENCE: C.A;

NAMES: JOHN THORNTON TO NANCY ALEXANDER
DATE: MAR. 24, 1807
BONDSMAN: WILLIAM THOMPSON
WITNESS: JNO. PURRIS
REFERENCE: C.A; T.H.M. VOL. 6, PG. 16

NAMES: JOHN TROUTT TO MARY KERR
DATE: AUG. 24, 1807
BONDSMAN: JAMES REYNOLDS
WITNESS: JNO. A. GAMBLE
REFERENCE: C.A; T.H.M. VOL. 6, PG. 16

NAMES: THOMAS WILKERSON TO SARAH COBB
DATE: AUG. 18, 1807
BONDSMAN: JOHN N. SMITH
WITNESS: JNO. A. GAMBLE
REFERENCE: C.A.

NAMES: THOMAS WITT TO POLLY WRIGHT
DATE: DEC. 19, 1807
BONDSMAN: GEORGE WITT
WITNESS: PURRIS
REFERENCE: C.A; O.M.R. PG. 9; T.H.M. VOL. 6, PG. 16

NAMES: ISAAC WOOD TO NELLY HOLT
DATE: AUG. 6, 1807
BONDSMAN: CONRAND AULT
REFERENCE: C.A; T.H.M. VOL. 6, PG. 16

NAMES: JOHN WRIGHT TO POLLY HINDS
DATE: AUG. 28, 1807
REFERENCE: C.A; O.M.R. PG. 8

1808

NAMES: ABSALOM CALDWELL TO HANNAH HINDS
DATE: JANY. 11, 1808
BONDSMAN: JAMES CALDWELL
WITNESS: J. PURRIS
REFERENCE: C.A.

NAMES: ABEDNIGO CASTEEL TO AGNES HENSLEY
DATE: APR. 26, 1808
BONDSMAN: DANIEL CASTEEL
WITNESS: JNO. A. GAMBLE
REFERENCE: C.A; T.H.M' VOL. 6, PG. 16

NAMES: JAMES CHILDRESS TO POLLY AYRES
DATE: NOV. 7, 1808
BONDSMAN: JOHN CHILDS
REFERENCE: C.A; T.H.M. VOL. 6, PG. 16

NAMES: WARREN COKER TO POLLY CUNNINGHAM
DATE: SEPT. 28, 1808
BONDSMAN: JOEL COKER
WITNESS: JNO. A. GAMBLE
REFERENCE: C.A; T.H.M. VOL. 6, PG. 16

NAMES: JOHN COZBY TO ABIGAIL MCBEE
DATE: AUG. 10, 1808
BONDSMAN: WM. SMITH
REFERENCE: C.A; T.H.M. VOL. 6, PG. 16

NAMES: JAMES CRIPPEN TO PATSY HALL
DATE: MAR. 28, 1808
BONDSMAN: JOSEPH GIRON
WITNESS: JNO. A. GAMBLE
REFERENCE: C.A; T.H.M. VOL. 6, PG. 16

NAMES: JESSE DELANY TO ANNE KEENER
DATE: SEPT. 7, 1808
REFERENCE: C.A; O.M.R. PG. 9

NAMES: COONROD HOSONG TO MARY BLACK
DATE: DEC. 20, 1808
REFERENCE: O.M.R. PG. 9

NAMES: JOHN JONES TO PATSEY MORRIS
DATE: MAR. 15, 1808
REFERENCE: C.A; O.M.R. PG. 9

NAMES: THOMAS MARSHALL TO HANNAH ELLIOTT
DATE: MAR. 19, 1808
DATE PER: MAR. 20, 1808
BY: WILLIAM CARTY (?)
REFERENCE: C.A; O.M.R. PG. 9

NAMES: JOHN MARTIN TO NANCY ISSEL
DATE: DEC. 28, 1808
DATE PER: DEC. 28, 1808
BY: R. HOUSTON, J.P.K.C.
REFERENCE: C.A; O.M.R. PG. 10

NAMES: WILLIAM MAY TO ELIZABETH MURRAY (OR LUTTRELL?)
DATE: FEB. 22, 1808
REFERENCE: T.H.M. VOL. 6, PG. 16

NAMES: WILLIAM MCBATH TO POLLY JOHNSTON
DATE: FEB. 23, 1808
REFERENCE: C.A; O.M.R. PG. 9

NAMES: BALSER NULL TO FAWNIA PHILLIPS
DATE:: MAY 17, 1808
REFERENCE: C.A; O.M.R. PG. 9

NAMES: JOHN H. SARGANT TO REBECCAH CRANE
DATE: OCT. 13, 1808
BONDSMAN: JOHN BASS
WITNESS: WM. SMITH
REFERENCE: C.A; T.H.M. VOL. 6, PG. 16

NAMES: HARMON SHOOK TO MARGARET MCMILLAN
DATE: FEBY. 16, 1808
BONDSMAN: ABRAHAM SHOOK
REFERENCE: C.A; T.H.M. VOL. 6, PG. 16

NAMES: JOHN SKIDMORE TO POLLY BELL
DATE: NOV. 7, 1808
BONDSMAN: WM. BELL
WITNESS: JNO. A. GAMBLE
REFERENCE: C.A; T.H.M. VOL. 6, PG. 16
(DAU. OF WILLIAM BELL)

NAMES: MOSES SMITH TO JEMIMA HUNTER
DATE: MAY 28, 1808
BONDSMAN: ANDREW HUNTER
REFERENCE: C.A; T.H.M. VOL. 6, PG. 16

NAMES: REUBEN SMITH TO BARBARA BARGER
DATE: DEC. 12, 1808
BONDSMAN: SAMUEL RILEY
REFERENCE: C.A; T.H.M. VOL. 6, PG. 16

NAMES: WILLIAM SMITH TO SUKY WHITE
DATE: JANY. 28, 1808
BONDSMAN: SAMUEL RILEY
REFERENCE: C.A; T.H.M. VOL. 6, PG. 16

NAMES: THOMAS B. SPAIN TO JANE MAISE
DATE: APR. 15, 1808
BONDSMAN: GARDNER MAISE
REFERENCE: C.A; T.H.M. VOL. 6, PG. 16

NAMES: THOMAS STANLEY TO RACHEL LAYKEY
DATE: SEPT. 20, 1808
REFERENCE: C.A; O.M.R. PG. 9

NAMES: ROBERT STEPHENSON TO HETTIE STERLING
DATE: NOV. 18, 1808
REFERENCE: T.H.M. VOL. 6, PG. 16

NAMES: SAMUEL TILLERY TO ANNY PAUL
DATE: MAY 9, 1808
BONDSMAN: JOHN TILLERY
WITNESS: JNO. A. GAMBLE
REFERENCE: C.A; T.H.M. VOL. 6, PG. 16

NAMES: AMBROSE TOOMY TO LUCY WALKER
DATE: JANY. 13, 1808
BONDSMAN: WM. MCCLELLAN
WITNESS: JNO. PURRIS
REFERENCE: C.A; T.H.M. VOL. 6, PG. 16

NAMES: GEORGE WAGGONER TO MARY BAKER
DATE: OCT. 26, 1808
DATE PER: OCT. 26, 1808
BY: R. HOUSTON, J.P.K.C.
REFERENCE: C.A; O.M.R. PG. 9

NAMES: JOHN WILLIAMS TO ARTIMESSA MILLIKIN
DATE: JULY 16, 1808
BONDSMAN: THOMAS JOHNSON
REFERENCE: C.A; T.H.M. VOL. 6, PG. 16

NAMES: JOHN WILLIAMS TO MARGARET CALDWELL
DATE: MAY 26, 1808
BONDSMAN: RANDOLPH GIDDENS
WITNESS: JNO. A. GAMBLE
REFERENCE: C.A; T.H.M. VOL. 6, PG. 16

1809

NAMES: THOS. M. ASHLEY TO ELIZABETH SHELTON
DATE: NOV. 2, 1809
BONDSMAN: THOS. BROWN
WITNESS: JNO. N. GAMBLE
REFERENCE: C.A; T.H.M. VOL. 6, PG. 16

NAMES: JOHN AULT TO PEGGY HASTINGS
DATE: NOV. 22, 1809
REFERENCE: T.H.M. VOL. 6, PG. 16

NAMES: WILLIAM BALDWIN TO BETSEY LUTTRELL
DATE: MAR. 25, 1809
BONDSMAN: ABIJAH HARRIS
DATE PER: MAR. 25, 1809
BY: R. HOUSTON, J.P.K.C.
REFERENCE: C.A; O.M.R. PG. 4; T.H.M. VOL. 6, PG. 16

NAMES: JAMES S. BELL TO JENNY BELL
DATE: NOV. 21, 1809
BONDSMAN: WILLIAM BELL
REFERENCE: C.A; T.H.M. VOL. 6, PG. 16

NAMES: WILLIAM BOND TO ELIZABETH KELLER
DATE: 1809
REFERENCE: T.H.M. VOL. 6, PG. 16

NAMES: JAMES CAMPBELL TO PEGGY RAMSEY
DATE: SEPT. 20, 1809
BONDSMAN: SAM'L G. RAMSEY
WITNESS: CHAS. McCLUNG
REFERENCE: C.A; T.H.M. VOL. 6, PG. 16

NAMES: JOEL CARTER TO HANNAH STOCKTON
DATE: NOV. 6, 1809
BONDSMAN: JOHN CAMPBELL
REFERENCE: C.A; T.H.M. VOL. 6, PG. 16

NAMES: THOMAS CHAPMAN TO PATSEY JONES
DATE: JUNE 13, 1809
BONDSMAN: RICHARD ROSEYGRANT
WITNESS: JNO. N. GAMBLE
REFERENCE: C.A; T.H.M. VOL. 6, PG. 16

NAMES: MITCHELL CHILDRESS TO FRANCES DOWELL
DATE: SEPT. 28, 1809
BONDSMAN: JOSIAH ARMSTRONG
REFERENCE: C.A; T.H.M. VOL. 6, PG. 16

NAMES: EPHRAIM CLAIBOURNE TO POLLY BROWN
DATE: DEC. 20, 1809
BONDSMAN: JOSEPH BLACKLEY
REFERENCE: C.A; T.H.M. VOL. 6 PG. 16

NAMES: LEWIS COX TO EMILY HOLT
DATE: NOV. 9, 1809
BONDSMAN: WILLIAM PARK
REFERENCE: C.A; T.H.M. VOL. 6, PG. 16

NAMES: JOHN CRIPPEN TO ELIZABETH ALLEN
DATE: DEC. 28, 1809
BONDSMAN: WM. HARRELSON
DATE PER: DEC. 28, 1809
BY: R. HOUSTON, J.P.K.C.
REFERENCE: C.A; OMR. PG. 11; T.H.M. VOL. 6, PG. 17

NAMES: ELISON CRUZE TO SALLY GILLESPIE
DATE: AUG. 3, 1809
BONDSMAN: ROBERT BAYLESS
WITNESS: THOS. A. ROGERS
REFERENCE: C.A; O.M.R. PG. 10; T.H.M. VOL. 6, PG. 17

NAMES: LEVY DAVIS TO SYNTHY HURDLE
DATE: MAR. 23, 1809
BONDSMAN: WM. MORRIS & JOHN SUTTON
WITNESS: JO LOVE
REFERENCE: C.A; T.H.M. VOL. 6 PG. 17

NAMES: JONAS FROST TO NANCY HALL
DATE: NOV. 13, 1809
REFERENCE: C.A; O.M.R. PG. 11

NAMES: CHARLES GALLOWAY TO NELLY HINDS
DATE: JULY 12, 1809
REFERENCE: T.H.M. VOL. 6 PG. 17

NAMES: JOHN GARNER TO POLLY CONK
DATE: MCH. 28, 1809
REFERENCE: T.H.M. VOL. 6, PG. 17

NAMES: GEORGE GRAVES TO ANNY RUTHERFORD
DATE: MAR. 17, 1809
REFERENCE: O.A; O.M.R. PG. 10

NAMES: GEORGE W. HENSLEY TO ANNE WHITE
DATE: JANY. 14, 1809
REFERENCE: O.A; O.M.R. PG. 10

NAMES: BENJ. HINDS TO POLLY CHILDRESS
DATE: OCT. 17, 1809
BONDSMAN: JNO. MILLIKEN
REFERENCE: O. A.

NAMES: EDWARD HODGE TO POLLY EPPS
DATE: SEPT. 28, 1809
REFERENCE: O.A; O.M.R. PG. 11

NAMES: ISHAM JENNINGS TO POLLY SAUNDERS
DATE: SEPT. 25, 1809
REFERENCE: O.A; O.M.R. PG. 10

NAMES: JOSEPH LAWSON TO NANCY MORRIS
DATE: APR. 14, 1809
REFERENCE: O.A; O.M.R. PG. 10

NAMES: HUGH LEIPER TO ELIZABETH MCMILLAN
DATE: NOV. 23, 1809
REFERENCE: O.A; O.M.R. PG. 11

NAMES: WALTER MAXEY TO NANCY DOZIER
DATE: MAR. 8, 1809
REFERENCE: O.A; O.M.R. PG. 10

NAMES: EDWARD MCAULAY TO ESTHER MARTIN
DATE: MAY 30, 1809
BONDSMAN: JAMES BRUSE
WITNESS: JOHN N. GAMBLE
REFERENCE: O.A; T.H.M. VOL. 6 PG. 17

NAMES: ANDREW MCBATH TO LUCINDA JOHNSON
DATE: SEPT. 21, 1809
REFERENCE: O.A; O.M.R. PG. 10

NAMES: JOHN MCDANIEL TO SALLEY WHITSON
DATE: JULY 12, 1809
BONDSMAN: EDWIN E. BOOTH
REFERENCE: O.A; T.H.M. VOL. 6, PG. 17

NAMES: WM. MCMILLAN TO ELIZABETH REED
DATE: JANY. 4, 1809
BONDSMAN: WILLIAM MORROW
REFERENCE: O.A; T.H.M. VOL. 6, PG 17

NAMES: HAMILTON MOFFETT TO NANCY SMITH
DATE: MAR. 8, 1809
BONDSMAN: JAMES TOOL – WM. M. MOFFETT
WITNESS: CHAS. MCCLUNG
REFERENCE: O.A; T.H.M. VOL. 6, PG. 17

NAMES: ALEXANDER MORROW TO ROSANNAH SPENCE
DATE: DEC. 2, 1809
BONDSMAN: JOHN WARE
REFERENCE: O.A; T.H.M. VOL. 6, PG. 17

NAMES: WILLIAM PARK TO JANE CROZIER ARMSTRONG
DATE: NOV. 22, 1809
REFERENCE: T.H.M. VOL. 6, PG. 17

NAMES: LITTLETON ROACH TO LUCY FANEN
DATE: MAR. 20, 1809
BY: JOHN LOVE, ESQ.
REFERENCE: O.A; O.M.R. PG. 10

NAMES: REASON SAMBURG TO RODY DUNNEKEE
DATE: AUG. 31, 1809
BONDSMAN: RICHARD PHILLS
WITNESS: THOMAS A. ROGERS
REFERENCE: C.A; T.H.M. VOL. 6, PG. 17

NAMES: JOHN SAWYERS TO NANCY SHELL
DATE: JUNE 27, 1809
BONDSMAN: REESE BOWEN
WITNESS: JOHN N. GAMBLE
REFERENCE: C.A; T.H.M. VOL. 6, PG. 17

NAMES: WILLIAM SKINNER TO ELIZABETH AIKMAN
DATE: AUG. 15, 1809
BONDSMAN: CAWFIELD TAYLOR
WITNESS: THOS. A. ROGERS
REFERENCE: O.A; T.H.M. VOL. 6, PG. 17

NAMES: HENRY SMITH TO BETSY MCCLOUD
DATE: AUG. 22, 1809
BONDSMAN: JOSEPH SMITH
WITNESS: THOS. A. ROGERS
REFERENCE: C.A; T.H.M. VOL. 6, PG. 17

Names: William Smith to Sally Davis
Date: Aug. 2, 1809
Reference: O.A; O.M.R. Pg. 10

Names: Frederick Tarwater to Sally Reed
Date: Oct. 12, 1809
Bondsman: Jacob Harris
Reference: O.A; T.H.M. Vol. 6, Pg. 17

Names: Teewalt Tarwater to Polly Eddington
Date: June 22, 1809
Bondsman: Robert Bayless
Witness: Jno. N. Gamble
Reference: O.A; T.H.M. Vol. 6, Pg. 17

Names: John Taylor to Amelia A. King
Date: May 29, 1809
Bondsman: David Campbell
Witness: Chas. McClung
Reference: O.A; T.H.M Vol. 6, Pg. 17

Names: Isaac Tipton to Frances White
Date: Oct. 12, 1809
Bondsman: Abraham Tipton
Reference: O.A; T.H.M. Vol. 6, Pg. 17

Names: Stephen Wells to Hannah Eddington
Date: Dec. 20, 1809
Bondsman: William Harrelson
Witness: Thos. A. Rogers
Reference: O.A; T.H.M. Vol. 6, Pg. 17

Names: David Willis to Dolly Haley
Date: Jany. 21, 1809
Bondsman: Claiborne Haley
Witnesses: Jno. N. Gamble
Reference: O.A; T.H.M. Vol. 6, Pg. 17

Names: Thomas Wright to Susannah Pickle
Date: Aug. 11, 1809
Bondsman: Joshua Monday
Reference: O.A; T.H.M Vol. 6, Pg. 17

1810

Names: Francis Agel to Barbara Harner
Date: May 25, 1810
Reference: T.H.M. Vol. 6, Pg. 17

Names: John Alexander to Frances Roy
Date: Oct. 23, 1810
Bondsman: Philip Letzinger
Reference: O.A; T.H.M. Vol. 6, Pg. 17

Names: Thomas Ault to Peggy Baker
Date: July 9, 1810
Reference: T.H.M. Vol. 6, Pg. 17

Names: John Barr to Elizabeth Cronk
Date: Jan. 11, 1810
Reference: T.H.M. Vol. 6, Pg. 17

Names: Jacob Bildersbach to Polly Probst
Date: Mch. 26, 1810
Reference: T.H.M. Vol. 6, Pg. 17

Names: John Carithers to Elizabeth Clark
Date: Apr. 18, 1810
Bondsman: Andrew Carithers
Reference: O.A; T.H.M Vol. 6, Pg. 17

Names: Miles Chapman to Nancy Burk
Date: Jany. 24, 1810
Bondsman: Thomas Chapman
Date Per: Jany. 24, 1810
By: R. Houston, J.P.K.C.
Reference: O.A; O.M.R. Pg. 11; T.H.M. Vol. 6, Pg. 17

Names: Stephen Childress to Sally Hall
Date: June 16, 1810
Bondsman: Mitchell Childress
Reference: O.A; T.H.M. Vol. 6, Pg. 17

Names: Daniel Coalman to Mary Chumbley
Date: Nov. 2, 1810
Reference: T.H.M. Vol. 6, Pg. 17

Names: David Coats to Jency Lee
Date: Dec. 2, 1810
Reference: T.H.M. Vol. 6, Pg. 17

Names: James Cox to Betsey Gammon
Date: Oct. 8, 1810
Bondsman: William Conner
Reference: O.A; T.H.M. Vol. 6, Pg. 17

Names: Jno. M. Cullen to Rachel Craighead
Date: May 30, 1810
Bondsman: Jno. N. Gamble
Reference: O.A; T.H.M. Vol. 6, Pg. 17

Names: John Cunningham to Rosannah Shinpock
Date: Nov. 16, 1810
Bondsman: Wm. Harrelson
Reference: O.A. T.H.M. Vol. 6, Pg. 17

Names: James Givens to Easter Hutchason
Date: Mch. 19, 1810
Reference: T.H.M. Vol. 6, Pg. 17

Names: John Howard to Nancy Howard
Date: Jan. 21, 1810
Reference: T.H.M. Vol. 6, Pg. 17

Names: Thomas Howard to Peggy Price (or Pines)
Date: July 9, 1810
Reference: T.H.M. Vol. 6, Pg. 17

Names: James Jones to Nancy Dimmitt
Date: July 17, 1810
Date Per: July 17, 1810
By: R. Houston, J. P. K. C.
Reference: C.A; O.M.R. Pg. 11

Names: Henry Kern to Bessey Stock
Date: May 17, 1810
Date Per: May 17, 1810
By: R. Houston, J.P.D.C.
Reference: C.A; O.M.R. Pg. 11

Names: Simon McCarrell to Sarah Dougherty
Date: Dec. 26, 1810
Bondsman: John Dail
By: John Love, Esq.
Witness: Wm. Purris
Reference: C.A; O.M.R. Pg. 12; T.H.M. Vol. 6, Pg. 17

Names: William Moffett to Lucinda Smith
Date: Jany. 29, 1810
Date Per: Feby. 3, 1810
By: Jno. Love, Esq.
Reference: C.A; O.M.R. Pg. 11

Names: John Murphy to Patsy Gillam
Date: Dec. 31, 1810
Reference: T.H.M. Vol. 6, Pg. 17

Names: Robert Robertson to Vollis Stennet
Date: Sept. 26, 1810
Reference: C.A; (License marked "executed" only)

Names: John Rutherford to Mary Brooks
Date: Nov. 28, 1810
Reference: C.A; O.M.R. Pg. 11

Names: William Taylor to Stacy West
Date: Oct. 15, 1810
Reference: T.H.M. Vol. 6, Pg. 17

Names: Robert Tindell to Peggy McLain
Date: Jan. 18, 1810
Reference: T.H.M. Vol. 6, Pg. 17

Names: George Wear to Ann Hynatt
Date: Mch. 27, 1810
Reference: T.H.M. Vol. 6, Pg. 17

Names: Thomas Wright to Susannah Pickle
Date: Aug. 25, 1810
Reference: C.A; O.M.R. Pg. 11

Names: Aron York to Nancy Rogers
Date: Apr. 13, 1810
Reference: T.H.M. Vol. 6, Pg. 17

1811

Names: Sam'l Anderson to Barthiny Lowe
Date: Apr. 3, 1811
Bondsman: Henry Porter
Reference: C. A.

Names: Jacob Ault to Sally Griffin
Date: Feb. 3, 1811
Reference: T.H.M. Vol. 6, Pg. 17

Names: Aaron Bales to Else Manifold
Date: Dec. 3, 1811
Reference: C.A.

Names: Aaron Bales to Else Manifold
Date: Dec. 3, 1811
Performed: Dec. 3, 1811
By: John Love, Esq.
Reference: O.M.R. Pg. 13

Names: Robert Barnett to Elizabeth Porter
Date: Apr. 16, 1811
Reference: T.H.M. Vol. 6, Pg. 17

Names: Isaac Campbell to Mary Ann Fristoe
Date: June 8, 1811
Reference: C.A; T.H.M. Vol. 6, Pg. 17

NAMES: JOHN CAMPBELL TO PEGGY BROWN
DATE: OCT. 25, 1811
REFERENCE: C.A; O.M.R. PG. 13

NAMES: ROBERT CAMPBELL TO BETSEY GAMBLE
DATE: AUG. 26, 1811
BONDSMAN: WILLIAM CAMPBELL
REFERENCE: C.A; T.H.M. VOL. 6, PG. 17

NAMES: RICHARD CARTER TO ELIZABETH LONAS
DATE: JAN. 17, 1811
REFERENCE: T.H.M. VOL. 6, PG. 17

NAMES: JAMES COBB TO SALLIE HARPER
DATE: MAY 7, 1811
REFERENCE: T.H.M. VOL. 6, PG. 17

NAMES: JOHN DAY TO POLLY FORD
DATE: AUG. 20, 1811
REFERENCE: T.H.M. VOL. 6, PG. 17

NAMES: JOHN DEARMOND TO ANNIE BURNETT
DATE: JUNE 4, 1811
REFERENCE: T.H.M. VOL. 6, PG. 17

NAMES: GUSTINE DUNNINGTON TO PRISCILLA LINN
DATE: JUNE 15, 1811
REFERENCE: T.H.M. VOL. 6, PG. 17

NAMES: DANIEL FISHER TO BETSEY BOYD
DATE: OCT. 18, 1811
REFERENCE: C.A; O.M.R. PG. 12

NAMES: WILLIAM FRANKLIN TO SALLIE MCMILLAN
DATE: MCH. 11, 1811
REFERENCE: T.H.M. VOL. 6, PG. 17

NAMES: ROBERT FRISTOE TO SUSAN GROVE
DATE: NOV. 8, 1811
REFERENCE: C.A; O.M.R. PG. 13

NAMES: JOSEPH GALBREATH TO POLLY FLEMING
DATE: AUG. 20, 1811
REFERENCE: T.H.M. VOL. 6, PG. 58

NAMES: JOSEPH GALLOWAY TO SALLIE WILLIAMS
DATE: APR. 4, 1811
REFERENCE: T.H.M. VOL. 6, PG. 58

NAMES: WILLIAM T. GIVENS TO SALLY MAYBERRY
DATE: JUNE 27, 1811
BONDSMAN: JOHN S. DAVIS
WITNESS: SAM'L G. RAMSEY
REFERENCE: C.A; T.H.M. VOL. 6, PG. 58

NAMES: PHILIP HARNER TO KITTY VICKERS
DATE: SEPT. 14, 1811
WITNESS: JNO. N. GAMBLE
REFERENCE: C.A; T.H.M. VOL. 6, PG. 58

NAMES: DANIEL HAWKINS TO POLLY COOK
DATE: FEB. 19, 1811
REFERENCE: T.H.M VOL. 6, PG. 58

NAMES: JAMES HINDS TO SALLY PAYNE (?)
DATE: SEPT. 24, 1811
REFERENCE: T.H.M. VOL. 6, PG. 58

NAMES: WILLIAM C. HODGES TO MARY DOUGLASS
DATE: OCT. 7, 1811
REFERENCE: T.H.M. VOL. 6, PG. 58

NAMES: THOMAS HOOD TO FANNY SIMMONS
DATE: DEC. 18, 1811
BONDSMAN: THOMAS SIMMONS
WITNESS: JOHN N. GAMBLE
REFERENCE: C.A; T.H.M. VOL. 6, PG. 58

NAMES: ISAAC JONES TO POLLY MCCALEB
DATE: AUG. 5, 1811
REFERENCE: T.H.M. VOL. 6, PG. 58

NAMES: JOHN JONES TO REBECCA GALLAHER
DATE: APR. 16, 1811
REFERENCE: T.H.M. VOL. 6, PG. 58

NAMES: JACOB KEAN TO REBECCA MASON
DATE: MCH. 4, 1811
REFERENCE: T.H.M. VOL. 6, PG. 58

NAMES: WILLIAM M. KYLE TO BETSY WHITE
DATE: MAY 20, 1811
REFERENCE: T.H.M. VOL. 6, PG. 58

NAMES: HENRY LEWIS TO REBECCA MILLER
DATE: APR. 7, 1811
DATE PER: APR. 7, 1811
BY: R. HOUSTON, J.P.C.
REFERENCE: C.A; O.MR. PG. 12

NAMES: RICHARD MALONE TO LUCY LITT
DATE: FEB. 27, 1811
REFERENCE: T.H.M. VOL. 6, PG. 58

NAMES: PETER MANN TO NELLY MCDANIEL
DATE: JUNE 4, 1811
DATE PER: JUNE 4, 1811
BY: R. HOUSTON, J.P.K.C.
REFERENCE: C.A; O.M.R. PG. 12; T.H.M. VOL. 6, PG. 58

NAMES: SIMEON MARTIN TO LUCY LANDAM
DATE: APR. 30, 1811
BONDSMAN: THOMAS BRASSFIELD
WITNESS: JOHN N. GAMBLE
REFERENCE: C.A.

NAMES: THOMAS MASSEY TO JENNY BLACKWELL
DATE: APR. 9, 1811
BONDSMAN: WILLIAM MCCARREL
REFERENCE: C.A; T.H.M. VOL. 6, PG. 58

NAMES: JAMES MCCARTY TO HANNAH MANSFIELD
DATE: FEB. 5, 1811
REFERENCE: T.H.M. VOL. 6, PG. 58

NAMES: ALEXANDER W. MEEK TO NANCY DOUGLASS
DATE: JANY. 29, 1811
REFERENCE: C.A; O.M.R. PG. 12; T.H.M. VOL. 6, PG. 58

NAMES: JACOB MILTEBARGER TO PEGGY TROUT
DATE: FEBY. 23, 1811
BONDSMAN: WILLIAM TROUT
WITNESS: W. J. L. S. PURRIS
REFERENCE: C.A; T.H.M. VOL. 6, PG. 58

NAMES: SIMON MORTON TO LUCY SANDERSON
REFERENCE: T.H.M. VOL. 6, PG. 58

NAMES: JOHN NEWMAN TO NANCY CROW
DATE: MAY 10, 1811
BONDSMAN: EDMOND NEWMAN
WITNESS: JOHN N. GAMBLE
REFERENCE: C.A; T.H.M. VOL. 6, PG. 58

NAMES: JOHN O'NEILL TO POLLY WAGGONER
DATE: MCH. 30, 1811
REFERENCE: T.H.M. VOL. 6, PG. 58

NAMES: WILLIAM OSBURN TO MARONY EDWARDS
DATE: OCT. ____, 1811
REFERENCE: T.H.M. VOL. 6, PG. 58

NAMES: JESSE PARKER TO BETSEY COPELAND
DATE: FEBY. 5, 1811
BONDSMAN: PURNELL INGRAM
REFERENCE: C.A; T.H.M. VOL. 6, PG. 58

NAMES: EDWARD PRICE TO SALLIE SPAIN
DATE: NOV. 5, 1811
REFERENCE: T.H.M. VOL. 6, PG. 58

NAMES: RICHARD PRICE TO NANCY PRICE
DATE: OCT. 23, 1811
BONDSMAN: DANIEL PRICE
REFERENCE: C.A.

NAMES: PETER REAGAN TO NANCY CUNNINGHAM
DATE: OCT. 27, 1811
REFERENCE: T.H.M. VOL. 6, PG. 58

NAMES: THOMAS REID TO ELLY BURNETT
DATE: AUG. 15, 1811
REFERENCE: T.H.M. VOL. 6, PG. 58

NAMES: NATHANIEL ROBINSON TO MARGARET LYONS
DATE: OCT. 22, 1811
REFERENCE: T.H.M. VOL. 6, PG. 58

NAMES: JOHN RUTHERFORD TO MARGARET TAWNYHILL
DATE: MAR. 1, 1811
BONDSMAN: HENRY ROBERTS
REFERENCE: C.A; O.M.R PG. 12; T.H.M. VOL. 6, PG. 58

NAMES: JAMES SEITON TO ELIZA LOWE
DATE: SEPT. 5, 1811
REFERENCE: T.H.M. VOL. 6, PG. 58

NAMES: JAMES B. SHARP TO LOCKEY M. PETERSON
DATE: NOV. 11, 1811
BONDSMAN: JOHN HAYNIE
REFERENCE: C.A; T.H.M. VOL. 6, PG. 58

NAMES: HALL SHELTON TO ELIZABETH MAYBERRY
DATE: JANY. 15, 1811
BONDSMAN: JOHN SHELTON
REFERENCE: C.A; T.H.M. VOL. 6, PG. 58

NAMES: CHRISTOPHER SHIPLEY TO BETSY RUTHERFORD
DATE: APR. 20, 1811
REFERENCE: C.A; O.M.R. PG. 12; T.H.M. VOL. 6, PG. 58

NAMES: JOHN SHUPOCK TO POLLY CROWDER
DATE: JAN. 10, 1811
REFERENCE: T.H.M. VOL. 6, PG. 58

NAMES: JOHN SMITH TO POLLY MULVANY
DATE: MAR. 19, 1811
BONDSMAN: WILLIAM MULVANY
REFERENCE: C.A; O.M.R. PG. 12

NAMES: JOSEPH SMITH TO PEGGY MCCLOUD
DATE: JUNE 26, 1811
REFERENCE: T.H.M. VOL. 6, PG. 58

NAMES: JOHN STONE TO PATSEY SUMMERS
DATE: DEC. 20, 1811
BONDSMAN: JESSE WELLS
REFERENCE: C.A; T.H.M. VOL. 6, PG. 58

NAMES: JOSEPH C. STRONG TO JANE KAIN
DATE: MAY 22, 1811
REFERENCE: T.H.M. VOL. 6, PG. 58

NAMES: SAM'L WEAR TO SALLY WHITE
DATE: SEPT. 26, 1811
BONDSMAN: ABRAHAM WHITE
WITNESS: JOHN N. GAMBLE
REFERENCE: C.A; T.H.M. VOL. 6, PG. 58

NAMES: PETER WELCH TO NANCY GIDDIAN
DATE: MAY 25, 1811
REFERENCE: T.H.M. VOL. 6, PG. 58

NAMES: ABSOLEM WHITE TO BETSY REED
DATE: JAN. 24, 1811
REFERENCE: T.H.M. VOL. 6, PG. 58

NAMES: ABEL L. WILLIAMS TO ELITHA KEINER
DATE: MAR. 16, 1811
BONDSMAN: HUGH BODKIN
REFERENCE: C.A; O.M.R. PG. 12

NAMES: SOLOMON WILSON TO POLLY KEY
DATE: APR. 8, 1811
WITNESS: W.J.S.L. PURRIS
BONDSMAN: WILLIAM HARRELSON
REFERENCE: C.A; O.M.R. PG. 12

NAMES: LINDSEY WRIGHT TO CYNTHIA CAVITT
DATE: MCH. 5, 1811
REFERENCE: T.H.M. VOL. 6, PG. 58

NAMES: ANDREW WRINKLE TO NANCY BURNETT
DATE: DEC. 24, 1811
REFERENCE: C.A; O.M.R. PG.217; T.H.M. VOL. 6, PG. 58

1812

NAMES: WELLS ADAMSON TO MARY GEORGE
DATE: DEC. 29, 1812
BONDSMAN: CHARLES BLAKELEY
WITNESS: A. HUTCHESON
REFERENCE: C.A.

NAMES: CHRISTIAN ALLBRIGHT TO PATSEY WALKER
DATE: JANY. 6, 1812
REFERENCE: C.A; O.M.R. PG. 13; T.H.M. VOL. 6, PG. 58

NAMES: WILLIAM BEARD TO MOLLY NEAMOUR
DATE: MAY 25, 1812
REFERENCE: C.A; T.H.M. VOL. 6, PG. 58

NAMES: WILLIAM BOWER TO JENNY MCNIGHT
DATE: MAR. 28, 1812
REFERENCE: C.A; O.M.R. PG. 14

NAMES: JOHN BROCKUS TO SOPHIA DEWITT
DATE: OCT. 30, 1812
REFERENCE: T.H.M. VOL. 6, PG. 58

NAMES: JOSEPH BUCKHART TO SALLIE LUMPKIN
DATE: AUG. 11, 1812
REFERENCE: T.H.M. VOL. 6, PG. 58

NAMES: JOHN CAMPBELL TO JANE REED
DATE: JUNE 4, 1812
REFERENCE: T.H.M. VOL. 6, PG. 58

NAMES: ADDISON CARRICK TO REBECCAH GAMBLE
DATE: NOV. 5, 1812
BONDSMAN: WILL PURRIS
REFERENCE: C.A; T.H.M. VOL. 6, PG. 58

NAMES: HENRY CLAIR TO NANCY DUNLAP
DATE: JANY. 25, 1812
BONDSMAN: JAMES HARBISON
REFERENCE: C.A; T.H.M. VOL. 6, PG. 58

NAMES: THOMAS COATS TO ALSEY LEE
DATE: JULY 21, 1812
REFERENCE: T.H.M. VOL. 6, PG. 58

NAMES: JESSE COX TO FEASIBY (?) LEAHY
DATE: JULY 13, 1812
REFERENCE: T.H.M. VOL. 6, PG. 59

NAMES: ROBERT DAVIS TO SARAH DOYLE
DATE: OCT. 8, 1812
REFERENCE: T.H.M. VOL. 6, PG. 59

NAMES: JOHN DODD TO SALLIE LEEK
DATE: FEB. 12, 1812
REFERENCE: T.H.M. VOL. 6, PG. 59

NAMES: RICHARD DODD TO ELIZABETH DODD
DATE: JUNE 23, 1812
REFERENCE: T.H.M. VOL. 6, PG. 59

NAMES: JAMES DUNLAP TO ELIZABETH CASTEELE
DATE: APR. 8, 1812
REFERENCE: C.A; O.M.R. PG. 14

NAMES: GEORGE ETTER TO EVE KARNES (CARNES?)
DATE: MCH. 31, 1812
REFERENCE: T.H.M. VOL. 6, PG. 59

NAMES: THEO. EVERETTS TO PEGGY EDMONSON
DATE: DEC. 6, 1812
REFERENCE: T.H.M. VOL. 6, PG. 59

NAMES: JOEL FERGUSON TO SUSANNAH STOCKTON
DATE: JUNE 2, 1812
REFERENCE: T.H.M. VOL. 6, PG. 59

NAMES: DAVID FLEMING TO LYDIA SHELTON
DATE: SEPT. 1, 1812
BONDSMAN: SAM'L FLEMING
DATE PER: SEPT. 1, 1812
BY: JNO. LOVE, ESQ.
REFERENCE: C.A; O.M.R. PG. 14; T.H.M. VOL. 6, PG. 59

NAMES: JOSHUA FREEMAN TO PEGGY COUNSEL
DATE: MAY 27, 1812
REFERENCE: C.A; O.M.R. PG. 14; T.H.M. VOL. 6, PG. 59

NAMES: MOSES GAILEY TO MARGARET KEYHILL
DATE: JUNE 2, 1812
REFERENCE: C.A; O.M.R. PG. 14

NAMES: TRAVIS GEORGE (OR GEORGE TRAVIS?)
TO
ELIZABETH MILLER
DATE: JAN. ______, 1812
REFERENCE: T.H.M. VOL. 6, PG. 59

NAMES: MARTIN HAMMACK TO SALLY JANUARY
DATE: APR. 24, 1812
DATE PER: APR. 24, 1812
BY: R. HOUSTON, J.P.K.C.
REFERENCE: C.A; O.M.R. PG. 14

NAMES: SOLOMAN HARGUS TO SARAH AGNES SHOUL
DATE: JAN. 30, 1812
REFERENCE: T.H.M. VOL. 6, PG. 59

NAMES: JOHN HARNETT TO REBECCAH WOLF
DATE: NOV. 9, 1812
BONDSMAN: WILLIAM MORRIS
REFERENCE: C.A; T.H.M. VOL. 6, PG. 59

NAMES: R. M. HASSEL TO POLLY HARDIN
DATE: JAN. 29, 1812
REFERENCE: T.H.M. VOL. 6, PG. 59

NAMES: GILBERT HAWKINS TO ELIZABETH DELANEY
DATE: SEPT. 20, 1812
REFERENCE: T.H.M. VOL. 6, PG. 59

NAMES: MARTIN HAYES TO SALLIE JANUARY
DATE: APR. 24, 1812
REFERENCE: T.H.M. VOL. 6, PG. 59

NAMES: JOSEPH HINES TO SUSANNA HAWKINS
DATE: JUNE 9, 1812
REFERENCE: T.H.M. VOL. 6, PG. 59

NAMES: SIMON HINES TO ELIZABETH LARKART
DATE: FEBY. 11, 1812
REFERENCE: C.A; O.M.R. PG. 13; T.H.M. VOL. 6, PG. 59

NAMES: LEWIS HUDIBURG TO DORCAS KELSO
DATE: JAN. 1, 1812
DATE PER: JAN. 1, 1812
BY: THO. H. NELSON, M. G.
REFERENCE: O.M.R. PG. 13; T.H.M. VOL. 6, PG. 59

NAMES: GEORGE JOHNSON TO BARBARA HUFFSTADLER
DATE: OCT. 28, 1812
BONDSMAN: DAVID HUFFSTADLER
REFERENCE: C.A; T.H.M. VOL. 6, PG. 59
WITNESS: JOHN N. GAMBLE

NAMES: JONATHAN JOHNSTON TO PATSEY HINDS
DATE: DEC. 23, 1812
BONDSMAN: WM. FRYOR
REFERENCE: C.A; O.M.R. PG. 15; T.H.M. VOL. 6, PG. 59

NAMES: MATTHEW KEYS TO NANCY MYNATT
DATE: JANY. 3, 1812
REFERENCE: C.A; O.M.R. PG. 13

Names: Matthias Kime to Rachel Ross
Date: Feby. 10, 1812
Bondsman: George Huffaker
Reference: C.A; O.M.R. Pg. 13; T.H.M. Vol. 6, Pg. 59

Names: John King to Judy Ford
Date: June 19, 1812
Reference: C.A; O.M.R. Pg. 14

Names: John Kirkpatrick to Peggy Brown
Date: Sept. 17, 1812
Bondsman: James Kirkpatrick
Witness: John N. Gamble
Reference: C.A; T.H.M' Vol. 6, Pg. 59

Names: Pascal Kusken (?) to Martha Stevenson
Date: Aug. 5, 1812
Reference: T.H.M. Vol. 6, Pg. 59

Names: L. Luttrell to P. Gibbs
Date: Feb. 11, 1812
Reference: T.H.M. Vol. 6, Pg. 59

Names: James McNutt to Polly Fleming
Date: Dec. 23, 1812
Reference: T.H.M. Vol. 6, Pg. 59

Names: Isaac Miller to Susana Davis
Date: July 15, 1812
Bondsman: Presley Buckner
Reference: C.A.

Names: James Montgomery to Hally Lowe
Date: Jan. 1, 1812
Reference: T.H.M. Vol. 6, Pg. 59

Names: Andrew Moore to Rebecca Hollice
Date: Aug. 26, 1812
Reference: C.A; O.M.R. Pg. 14; T.H.M. Vol. 6, Pg. 59

Names: George Moses to Sarah Bledsoe
Date: Sept. 7, 1812
Bondsman: Pleasant McBride
Reference: C.A; T.H.M. Vol. 6, Pg. 59

Names: John Mowrey to Patsy McClure
Date: Feby. 21, 1812
Reference: C.A; O.M.R. Pg. 14

Names: Peter Murrian to Pricy Bartlett
Date: June 5, 1812
Reference: T.H.M. Vol. 6, Pg. 59

Names: James Nelson to ________
Date: July 7, 1812
Reference: T.H.M. Vol. 6, Pg. 59

Names: Thomas Newberry to Polly Peyton
Date: Dec. 24, 1812
Bondsman: John Russell
Witness: A. Hutchison
Reference: C.A; T.H.M. Vol. 6, Pg. 59

Names: William Norman to Nancy King
Date: Aug. 3[illegible], 1812
Bondsman: John Gear
Reference: C.A; T.H.M. Vol. 6, Pg. 59

Names: Joseph Ore to Margaret Gillespie
Date: Dec. 16, 1812
Reference: C.A; O.M.R. Pg. 15; T.H.M. Vol. 6, Pg. 59

Names: Jacob Reed to Esther Hollis
Date: Aug. 10, 1812
Bondsman: Robert Sevier
Reference: C.A; O.M.R. Pg. 14; T.H.M. Vol. 6, Pg. 59

Names: Pascal Ruskin to Martha Stephenson
Date: Aug. 5, 1812
Reference: T.H.M. Vol. 6, Pg. 59

Names: James Shields to Anny Campbell
Date: Jany. 17, 1812
Reference: C.A; O.M.R. Pg. 13

Names: William Smith to Betsy Smith
Date: ________
Bondsman: Jesse Smith
Reference: C.A.

Names: William Tarwater to Judah Childress
Date: July 23, 1812
Bondsman: William Crewse
Reference: C.A; T.H.M. Vol. 6, Pg. 59

Names: Ezekiel Taylor to Betsy Gentry
Date: Oct. 20, 1812
Bondsman: John Keith
Reference: C.A

Names: William Trout to Polly Wear
Date: Jany. 12, 1812
Bondsman: Jacob Mitlebarger
Witness: Jno. N. Gamble
Reference: C.A.

NAMES: WESTERN WARWICK TO FANNY WALKER
DATE: JANY. 6, 1812
REFERENCE: C.A; O.M.R. PG. 13; T.H.M. VOL. 6, PG. 59

NAMES: OBIDIAH WRIGHT TO MALINDY JONES
DATE: APR. 30, 1812
REFERENCE: T.H.M. VOL. 6, PG. 59

1813

NAMES: ROBERT H. ADAMS TO CHARLOTTE MONTGOMERY
DATE: JANY. 19, 1813
BONDSMAN: ANDERSON HUTCHESON
REFERENCE: C.A; T.H.M. VOL. 6, PG. 59

NAMES: DAVID ADAMSON TO MARY ANNE ROBERTS
DATE: NOV. 2, 1813
BONDSMAN: ABEL L. WILLIAMS
WITNESS: A. HUTCHESON
REFERENCE: C.A; O.M.R. PG. 16; T.H.M. VOL. 6, PG. 59

NAMES: LEWIS ADKINS TO ELIZABETH GEORGE
DATE: JULY 8, 1813
REFERENCE: T.H.M. VOL. 6, PG. 59

NAMES: JAMES CHILDRESS TO LOCKEY JOHNSON
DATE: JANY. 20, 1813
DATE PER: JANY. 24, 1813
BY: JEREMIAH KING, M. G.
REFERENCE: C.A; O.M.R. PG. 15; T.H.M. VOL. 6, PG. 59

NAMES: WILLIAM CLARK TO NANCY WHITE
DATE: NOV. 11, 1813
BONDSMAN: JNO. ARMSTRONG
REFERENCE: C.A; T.H.M. VOL. 6, PG. 59

NAMES: JOSEPH M. CLARKE TO NANCY MCCAMPBELL
DATE: JANY. 19, 1813
DATE PER: JANY. 20, 1813
BY: THO. H. NELSON (PRES. CHURCH)
REFERENCE: C.A; O.M.R. PG. 15; T.H.M. VOL. 6, PG. 59

NAMES: JOHN CLINE TO POLLY MILTEBARGER
DATE: MAR. 13, 1813
WITNESS: JOHN N. GAMBLE -- BONDSMAN: JACOB MILTEBARGER
REFERENCE: C.A; T.H.M. VOL. 6, PG. 59

NAMES: ANDREW COPELAND TO ELIZABETH BELL
DATE: DEC. 21, 1813
REFERENCE: T.H.M. VOL. 6, PG. 59

NAMES: ALEXANDER COX TO REBECCA HUTCHISON
DATE: JUNE 3, 1813
BONDSMAN: SAMUEL MARTIN - WILLIAM RODGERS
REFERENCE: C.A; T.H.M. VOL. 6, PG. 59

NAMES: EDWARD CRUSE TO SALLY NELSON
DATE: MAR. 17, 1813
REFERENCE: C.A; O.M.R. PG. 16

NAMES: WILLIAM CRUSE TO LUCY CHILDRESS
DATE: APR. 19, 1813
REFERENCE: T.H.M. VOL. 6, PG. 59

NAMES: ABNER DALE TO JANE MCDANIEL
DATE: APR. 19, 1813
BONDSMAN: SOLOMON SKAGGS
WITNESS: H. HUTCHISON
REFERENCE: C.A; T.H.M. VOL. 6, PG. 59

NAMES: ISAAC DOYALL (DOYLE?) TO JNE CAPSHAW
DATE: DEC. 24, 1813
REFERENCE: T.H.M. VOL. 6, PG. 59

NAMES: DANUL DOZIER TO JUDE MAXEY
DATE: AUG. 25, 1813
REFERENCE: T.H.M. VOL. 6, PG. 59

NAMES: SAMUEL EBLIN TO MARTHA YOUNG
DATE: FEBY. 4, 1813
BONDSMAN: TAPLY YOUNG
WITNESS: W. EBLIN -- CHAS. MCCLUNG
REFERENCE: C.A; T.H.M. VOL. 6, PG. 59

NAMES: WILLIAM JOHN ELLIOTT TO SOPHIA PIERSON
DATE: NOV. 29, 1813
BONDSMAN: WILLIAM BOYD
REFERENCE: C.A; T.H.M. VOL. 6, PG. 59

NAMES: ELIJAH ENGLAND TO ELSEY SCOTT
DATE: APR. 7, 1813
BONDSMAN: JOHN ENGLAND
WITNESS: A. HUTCHESON
REFERENCE: C.A; T.H.M. VOL. 6, PG. 59

NAMES: WM. FERGUSON TO FANNY BOWMAN
DATE: APR. 22, 1813
BONDSMAN: SAMUEL THOMAS
WITNESS: A. HUTCHESON
REFERENCE: C.A; T.H.M. VOL. 6, PG. 59

NAMES: JOHN FLENAKIN TO SALLY COTTRELL
DATE: JULY 1, 1813
REFERENCE: C.A; O.M.R. PG. 16; T.H.M. VOL. 6, PG. 59

NAMES: THOMAS FLOWERS TO NANCY KRUNK
DATE: NOV. 25, 1813
BY: PETER NANCE, J.P.K C.
REFERENCE: C.A; O.M.R. PG. 16; T.H.M. VOL. 6, PG. 60

NAMES: MARKHAM FRISTO TO CATHARINE GROVE
DATE: JANY. 16, 1813
BONDSMAN: ISAAC CAMPBELL
WITNESS: A. HUTCHESON
REFERENCE: C.A; O.M.R. PG. 15; T.H.M. VOL. 6, PG. 60

NAMES: BENJAMIN GIER TO BETSY WILLIAMS
DATE: JUNE 19, 1813
BONDSMAN: BAALAM JACKSON
WITNESS: A. HUTCHESON
REFERENCE: C.A; T.H.M. VOL. 6, PG. 60

NAMES: JOHN GRANTHAM TO SUSANNAH BRANHAM
DATE: NOV. 11, 1813
REFERENCE: T.H.M. VOL. 6, PG. 60

NAMES: DAVID HALL TO REBECCA WILKERSON
DATE: FEB. 10, 1843
REFERENCE: T.H.M. VOL. 6, PG. 60

NAMES: JOHN HALL TO SUSANNA YARNELL
DATE: DEC. 27, 1813
BONDSMAN: SAMUEL EDMUNDSON
REFERENCE: C.A; T.H.M' VOL. 6, PG. 60

NAMES: JACOB HARMON TO POLLY WRIGHT
DATE: FEBY. 1, 1813
BONDSMAN: JNO. N. GAMBLE
DATE PER: FEBY. 1, 1813
BY: THO. H. NELSON
REFERENCE: C.A; O.M.R. PG. 15; T.H.M. VOL. 6, PG. 60

NAMES: WILLIAM HARWICK TO MARY HOPE
DATE: MAY 5, 1813
REFERENCE: T.H.M. VOL. 6, PG. 60

NAMES: ELIJAH HOWELL TO JUDE MAXEY
DATE: AUG. 24, 1813
REFERENCE: T.H.M, VOL. 6, PG. 60

NAMES: BYRON HYNDS TO BETSY CHILDRESS
DATE: OCT. 2, 1813
REFERENCE: T.H.M. VOL. 6, PG. 60

NAMES: BAALAM JACKSON TO PATSY BRADFORD
DATE: JUNE 19, 1813
BONDSMAN: HARRIS HAMONTREE
WITNESS: A. HUTCHESON
REFERENCE: C.A; T.H.M. VOL. 6, PG. 60

NAMES: ABNER JONES TO SARAH GRIFFIN
DATE: JULY 27, 1813
REFERENCE: T.H.M. VOL. 6, PG. 60

NAMES: REUBEN KILINSWORTH TO ANNE MCLAIN
DATE: APR. 16, 1813
BONDSMAN: ANDERSON KILINSWORTH
REFERENCE: C.A; T.H.M. VOL. 6, PG. 60

NAMES: RICHARD KIRBY TO TEMPERANCE GRANT
DATE: APR. 24, 1813
REFERENCE: C.A; O.M.R. PG. 16; T.H.M. VOL. 6, PG. 60

NAMES: ROBERT KIRKPATRICK TO RACHEL BAYLESS
DATE:
REFERENCE: T.H.M. VOL. 6, PG. 60

NAMES: GEORGE LONAS TO SALLY COVENTON
DATE: FEBY. 23, 1813
DATE PER: FEBY. 25, 1813
BY: JOHN LOVE, ESQ.
REFERENCE: C.A; O.M.R. PG. 15

NAMES: WILSON MANLY TO DICEY GAMMON
DATE: JANY. 5, 1813
BONDSMAN: RICHARD LEWIS
WITNESS: ANDW. HUTCHESON
REFERENCE: C.A; T.H.M. VOL. 6, PG. 60

NAMES: SAMUEL S. MCCAMPBELL TO POLLY INGRAM
DATE: JULY 10, 1813
BONDSMAN: SAM'L INGRAM -- WITNESS: A. HUTCHESON
REFERENCE: C.A.

NAMES: HENRY MCCOLLOUGH TO MARY THOMPSON
DATE: JANY. 27, 1813
BONDSMAN: JAMES THOMPSON
WITNESS: A. HUTCHESON
REFERENCE: C.A; T.H.M' VOL. 6, PG. 60

NAMES: JOHN MCLUSKY TO MATTY BENTON
DATE: MAY 15, 1813
BONDSMAN: THOMAS BREWER
WITNESS: A. HUTCHESON
REFERENCE: C.A; T.H.M. VOL. 6, PG. 60

NAMES: ALEXANDER McMILLAN TO SUSANNAH WATT
DATE: JAN. 18, 1813
REFERENCE: T.H.M. VOL. 6, PG. 60

NAMES: WILLIAM McSHERRY TO ELIZABETH PETERSON
DATE: JULY 21, 1813
REFERENCE: T.H.M. VOL. 6, PG. 60

NAMES: DANIEL MEEK TO BETSY L. CAMPBELL
DATE: MARCH 8, 1813
BONDSMAN: JAMES L. MEEK
WITNESS: A. HUTCHESON
REFERENCE: C.A; O.M.R. PG. 15; T.H.M. VOL. 6, PG. 60

NAMES: THOMAS H. MILLER TO ELIZABETH BELL
DATE: APR. 12, 1813
BONDSMAN: BURREL GRADY
REFERENCE: C.A.

NAMES: CHRISTOPHER MULVANEY TO ZILPHA UNDERWOOD
DATE: MAR. 9, 1813
DATE PER: MARCH ____, 1813
BY: JNO. LOVE, ESQ.
REFERENCE: O.M.R. PG. 15

NAMES: EDMOND NEWBERRY TO SARAH ALLEN
DATE: SEPT. 2, 1813
REFERNCE: C.A; O.M.R. PG. 16

NAMES: REUBEN NORRIS TO CATHERINE MORRIS
DATE: MAY 25, 1813
REFERENCE: T.H.M. VOL. 6, PG. 60

NAMES: DAVID PARR TO BARBARA SMITH
DATE: FEBY 16, 1813
BONDSMAN: JOHN BARGER
REFERENCE: C.A.

NAMES: ENOCH PARSONS TO KITTY KEAN
DATE: SEPT. 7, 1813
REFERENCE: T.H.M. VOL. 6, PG. 60

NNAMES: WILLIAM RIGNEY TO PATSY CAMPBELL
DATE: DEC. 28, 1813
REFERENCE: C.A; O.M.R. PG. 16; T.H.M. VOL. 6, PG. 60

NAMES: JOHN ROBERTS TO ELSEY BROWN
DATE: DEC. 27, 1813
BONDSMAN: BERIAH FRAZIER
REFERENCE: C.A; T.H.M. VOL. 6, PG. 60

NAMES: THOMAS ROBINSON TO PEGGY BROADWAY
DATE: DEC. 23, 1813
BONDSMAN: DAVID TARWATER
BY: PETER NANCE, J.P.K.C.
WITNESS: A. HUTCHESON, D.C.
REFERENCE: C.A; O.M.R. PG. 16; T.H.M. VOL. 6, PG. 60

NAMES: SOLOMON SCAGGS TO RACHEL McDANIEL
DATE: APR. 19, 1813
BONDSMAN: ABNER DAIL
WITNESS: A. HUTCHESON
REFERENCE: C.A; T.H.M. VOL. 6, PG. 60

NAMES: ARTHUR SCOTT TO ELIZABETH NANCE
DATE: DEC. 23, 1813
BONDSMAN: ISAAC TIPTON
REFERENCE: C.A; T.H.M. VOL. 6, PG. 60

NAMES: ADAM SHIPE TO FRANCES CARTER
DATE: DEC. 25, 1813
BONDSMAN: JOHN CHUMLEA
REFERENCE: C.A; T.H.M. VOL. 6, PG. 60

NAMES: THOMAS SHIPLEY TO LUCINDA EDINGTON
DATE: FEBY. 25, 1813
REFERENCE: C.A; O.M.R. PG. 15

NAMES: JOHN SIMPSON TO FRANCES MAYBERRY
DATE: AUG. 5, 1813
BONDSMAN: WILLIAM HOPE
WITNESS: A. HUTCHESON
REFERENCE: C.A; T.H.M. VOL. 6, PG. 60

NAMES: MICHAEL SMITH TO POLLY McCLOUD
DATE: SEPT. 9, 1813
BONDSMAN: THOS. WILSON
WITNESS: A. HUTCHESON
REFERENCE: C.A; T.H.M. VOL. 6, PG. 60

NAMES: MOSES STOUT TO MARGARET DODSON
DATE: APR. 24, 1813
REFERENCE: T.H.M. VOL. 6, PG. 60

NAMES: ROBERT TAYS TO ELIZABETH BUCKALEW
DATE: DEC. 7, 1813 -- BONDSMAN: JOSEPH JACKSON
REFERENCE: C.A; O.M.R. PG. 16; T.H.M. VOL. 6, PG. 60

NAMES: RICHARD M. TILLERY TO REBECCA COLE
DATE: NOV. 2, 1813
BONDSMAN: THOMAS BELL
WITNESS: A. HUTCHESON
REFERENCE: C.A; T.H.M. VOL. 6, PG. 60

NAMES: SAMPSON TILLERY TO CATHARINE YOAST
DATE: DEC. 22, 1813
BONDSMAN: ANDREW YOST
REFERENCE: C.A; T.H.M. VOL. 6, PG. 60

NAMES: JAMES WILHITE TO COMFORT STANSBERRY
DATE: DEC. 22, 1813
REFERENCE: C.A; O.M.R. PG. 16

1814

NAMES: THOMAS W. BAKER TO ESTHER MCMILLAN
DATE: OCT. 3, 1814
REFERENCE: T.H.M. VOL. 6, PG. 60

NAMES: ZACHARIAH BOOTH TO MARY C. MASSENGILL
DATE: MAY 12, 1814
BONDSMAN: THO. H. NELSON
REFERENCE: C.A; O.M.R. PG. 17; T.H.M. VOL. 6, PG. 60

NAMES: DAVID CAMPBELL TO JANE G. COWAN
DATE: MAY 30, 1814
DATE PER: MAY 30, 1814
BY: THO. H. NELSON
REFERENCE: O.M.R. PG. 17

NAMES: JOHN CLARK TO CATEY MOATS
DATE: MCH. 14, 1814
REFERENCE: T.H.M. VOL. 6, PG. 60

NAMES: CHARLES DAVIS TO CATHARINE OVERTON
DATE: MAY 30, 1814
BONDSMAN: THOMAS BRASFIELD
REFERENCE: C.A; T.H.M. VOL. 6, PG. 60

NAMES: GEORGE DAVIS TO CYNTHIA DEARMOND
DATE: SEPT. 13, 1814
REFERENCE: C.A; O.M.R. PG. 18; T.H.M. VOL. 6, PG. 60

NAMES: CORNELIUS DOBBINS TO POLLY SMITH
DATE: JUNE 16, 1814
REFERENCE: T.H.M. VOL. 6, PG. 60

NAMES: CAMPBELL EATON TO JANE M. PAUL
DATE: MAY 31, 1814
BONDSMAN: WILLIAM PAUL
REFERENCE: C.A; T.H.M. VOL. 6, PG. 60

NAMES: PHILIP EDINGTON TO BETSY HALL
DATE: FEBY. 12, 1814
BY: P. NANCE, J.P.K.C.
REFERENCE: C.A; OMR. PG. 17; T.H.M. VOL. 6, PG 60

NAMES: WILLIAM EVANS TO NANCY JOHNSON
DATE: JULY 26, 1814
BONDSMAN: JOSEPH EVANS
REFERENCE: C.A; O.M.R. PG. 18; T.H.M. VOL. 6; PG. 60

NAMES: HENRY GAMMON JR., TO POLLY STEPHENSON
DATE: MCH. 28, 1814
REFERENCE: T.H.M. VOL. 6, PG. 60

NAMES: IGNATIUS GATEWOOD TO POLLY PRUITT
DATE: OCT. 14, 1814
REFERENCE: T.H.M. VOL. 6, PG. 60

NAMES: HENRY GRAVES TO BETSY ANN GRILLS
DATE: AUG. 30, 1814
BONDSMAN: GEO. WILSON
REFERENCE: C.A; T.H.M. VOL. 6, PG. 60

NAMES: ABRAHAM HILL TO MARY ANN TAYLOR
DATE: JANY. 26, 1814
BY: R. NANCE, J.P.K.C.
REFERENCE: C.A; O.M.R. PG. 17

NAMES: ISAAC HINDS TO POLLY CARLESS
DATE: MAY 17, 1814
BONDSMAN: ROBERT HINDS
REFERENCE: C.A; O.M.R. PG. 17; T.H.M. VOL. 6, PG 60

NAMES: WILLIAM JOHNSON TO KITTY FAIRCHILDS
DATE: FEBY. 26, 1814
DATE PER:
BY: PETER NANCE, J.P.K.C.
REFERENCE: C.A; T.H.M. VOL. 6, PG. 60

NAMES: MARTIN KIRKPATRICK TO ANNE BAYLESS
DATE: JANY. 25, 1814
BONDSMAN: BENJ. CALDWELL
REFERENCE: C.A; T.H.M. VOL. 6, PG. 60

NAMES: JOHN KYLE TO CATHERINE RISEDON
DATE: JUNE 19, 1814
REFERENCE: T.H.M. VOL. 6, PG. 60

NAMES: SAMUEL C. LOVE TO NANCY COUNSELL (?)
DATE: MAY __, 1814
REFERENCE: T.H.M VOL. 6, PG 60

NAMES: JOHN LOWE TO BETSY SCOTT
DATE: JUNE 16, 1814
BONDSMAN: CANFIELD TAYLOR
DATE PER: W
BY: A. HUTCHESON
REFERENCE: C.A; T.H.M. VOL. 6, PG. 60

NAMES: GEORGE MALCOM TO ANN GILLESPIE
DATE: AUG. 15, 1814
BONDSMAN: ELISON CRUZE
WITNESS: A. HUTCHESON
REFERENCE: C.A; O.M.R. PG. 18; T.H.M. VOL. 6, PG. 61

NAMES: SAMUEL MARTIN TO PATSY LOVE
DATE: FEBY. 24, 1814
BONDSMAN: JAMES SEATON
DATE PER: FEBY 25, 1814
BY: THO. H. NELSON
WITNESS: J. N. GAMBLE
REFERENCE: C.A; O.M.R. PG. 17; T.H.M. VOL. 6, PG. 61

NAMES: ANDREW MCCALEB TO ANN BOYD
DATE: OCT. 8, 1814
REFERENCE: T.H.M. VOL. 6, PG. 60

NAMES: WM. MCFARLANE TO MARY MCNUTT
DATE: SEPT. 14, 1814
BONDSMAN: ROBERT LINDSAY
REFERENCE: C.A; T.H.M. VOL. 6, PG. 60

NAMES: ANDREW MCMILLAN TO PEGGY REAGAN
DATE: AUG. 11, 1814
REFERENCE: T.H.M. VOL. 6, PG. 61

NAMES: JOSEPH MEEK TO REBECCA SAWYER
DATE: MCH. 22, 1814
REFERENCE: T.H.M. VOL. 6, PG. 61

NAMES: JOB R. MONDS TO SARAH SMITH
DATE: OCT. 20, 1814
BONDSMAN: ELI MCNABB
WITNESS: A. HUTCHESON
REFERENCE: C.A; T.H.M. VOL. 6, PG. 61

NAMES: JOHN K. OWENS TO PEGGY WALKER
DATE: MCH. 12, 1814
REFERENCE: T.H.M. VOL. 6, PG. 61

NAMES: CHARLES W. PRICE TO SARAH FRISTOE
DATE: JANY. 19, 1814
REFERENCE: C.A. O.M.R. PG. 17

NAMES: THOMAS REID TO ELIZABETH COUNCIL
DATE: JUNE 27, 1814
REFERENCE: T.H.M. VOL. 6, PG. 61

NAMES: STEPHEN RENFRO TO ELEANOR CHRISTER
DATE: NOV. 3, 1814
REFERENCE: T.H.M. VOL. 6, PG. 61

NAMES: ABRAM ROBERTS TO NANCY BALLINS
DATE: OCT 14, 1814
REFERENCE: T.H.M. VOL. 6, PG. 61

NAMES: JAMES ROBERTS TO MAHALA EVRETT
DATE: JUNE 16, 1814
REFERENCE: T.H.M. VOL. 6, PG. 61

NAMES: ANDREW RUSSELL TO ELIZABETH BIRDWELL
DATE: MAR. 14, 1814
DATE PER: MAR. 15, 1814
BY: JOHN LOVE, ESQ.
REFERENCE: C.A; O.M.R. PG. 17; T.H.M. VOL. 6, PG 61

NAMES: EDWARD RUTHERFORD TO POLLY HARKINSON
DATE: JUNE 16, 1814
REFERENCE: T.H.M. VOL. 6, PG. 61

NAMES: JOHN SAUNDERS TO PATSY BLANK
DATE: MAR. 17, 1814
DATE PER: MAR. 17, 1814
BY: THO. H. NELSON
REFERENCE: C.A; O.M.R. PG. 17

NAMES: JAMES SEYMORE TO PEGGY KELLY
DATE: APR. 11, 1814
REFERENCE: T.H.M. VOL. 6, PG. 61

NAMES: BALSAR SHIRLEY TO MAGDALENE KERNS
DATE: FEBY. 1, 1814
BONDSMAN: HENRY KERNS
REFERENCE: C.A.

NAMES: PHILIP SITLU TO ANNY NEONESANANHA (?)
DATE: OCT. 22, 1814
REFERENCE: T.H.M. VOL. 6, PG. 61

NAMES: ISAAC SMITH TO SARAH MCLAIN
DATE: MARCH (?) 1814
BONDSMAN: WM. MCLAIN
REFERENCE: C.A.

NAMES: WILLIAM SPRADLIN TO MIACKEY KNOX
DATE: FEBY. 19, 1814
BONDSMAN: GEO. VARNUM
BY: PETER NANCE
WITNESS: J. M. GAMBLE
REFERENCE: C.A; O.M.R. PG. 17; T.H.M. VOL. 6, PG. 61

NAMES: JOSEPH STEWART TO SUSAN BUCKALIEU
DATE: DEC. 23, 1814
REFERENCE: C.A; O.M.R. PG. 18

NAMES: ISAAC THOMPSON TO POLLY PETERS
DATE: JULY 4, 1814
BONDSMAN: THOMAS DAVIS
REFERENCE: O.A; T.H.M. VOL. 6, PG. 61

NAMES: JAMES THOMPSON TO NANCY RENFRO
DATE: MCH. 3, 1814
REFERENCE: T.H.M. VOL. 6, PG. 61

NAMES: WILLIAM THOMPSON TO MARY BOYD
DATE: DEC. 17, 1814
REFERENCE: C.A; O.M.R. PG. 18; T.H.M. VOL. 6, PG. 61

NAMES: JACOB TIPTON TO HANNAH WATSON
DATE: SEPT. 6, 1814
BY: PETER NANCE, J.P.K.C.
REFERENCE: O.A; O.M.R. PG. 18; T.H.M. VOL. 6, PG. 61

NAMES: GEORGE WALKER TO BETSY WEAR
DATE: FEBY. 25, 1814
BONDSMAN: ABRAHAM WEAR
REFERENCE: C.A; T.H.M VOL. 6, PG. 61

NAMES: GEORGE WASHINGTON TO CATHERINE TOBLER
DATE: JULY 7, 1814
REFERENCE: T.H.M. VOL. 6, PG. 61

NAMES: GEORGE WELLS TO JANE MURPHY
DATE: JULY 12, 1814
REFERENCE: C.A; O.M.R. PG. 18; T.H.M VOL. 6, PG. 61

NAMES: BENJAMIN WHITE TO MARY GALLAWAY
DATE: NOV. 26, 1814
REFERENCE: T.H.M VOL. 6, PG. 61

NAMES: JAMES WILSON TO BETSY KEITH
DATE: FEBY. 12, 1814
BONDSMAN: ROBERT CHANDLER
REFERENCE: O.A; T.H.M. VOL. 6, PG. 61

1815

NAMES: PETER ABEL TO AMY WARD
DATE: FEBY. 16, 1815
REFERENCE: C.A; O.M.R. PG. 18; T.H.M. VOL. 6, PG. 61

NAMES: WILLIAM ALLEN TO MARGARET AULT
DATE: FEB. 16, 1815
REFERENCE: T.H.M. VOL. 6, PG. 61

NAMES: WILLIAM ANDERSON TO SOPHIA DAVIS
DATE: JANY. 6, 1815
BONDSMAN: MATHEW NELSON
REFERENCE: O.A; T.H.M. VOL. 6, PG. 61

NAMES: JACOB AULT TO SARAH HANNAH
DATE: MAR. 15, 1815
BONDSMAN: JAMES BREESE
WITNESS: A. HUTCHESON
REFERENCE: C.A; T.H.M VOL. 6, PG. 61

NAMES: ALLEN BAGWELL TO SARAH LANCASTER
DATE: OCT. 14, 1815
REFERENCE: T.H.M. VOL. 6, PG. 61

NAMES: GEORGE BIRDWELL TO ELIZABETH RUSSELL
DATE: JULY 31, 1815
BONDSMAN: SAM'L G. RAMSEY
REFERENCE: C.A; T.H.M VOL. 6, PG. 61

NAMES: CHARLES BLAKELY TO POLLY RUTH
DATE: NOV. 27, 1815
REFERENCE: C.A; O.M.R. PG. 21

NAMES: REUBEN BLANKENSHIP TO JANE COUCH
DATE: DEC. 20, 1815
REFERENCE: T.H.M. VOL. 6, PG. 61

NAMES: GEORGE BRANDON TO JANE GILLESPIE
DATE: MAR. 22, 1815
REFERENCE: C.A; O.M.R. PG. 19

NAMES: WILLIAM BUCALLO TO ELEANOR HOLT
DATE: DEC. 16, 1815
REFERENCE: T.H.M. VOL. 6, PG. 61

NAMES: WILLIAM CAMPBELL TO BETSY GOODARD
DATE: JULY 20, 1815
REFERENCE: O.A; OLM.R. PG. 20

NAMES: DAVID CATCHCART TO RHODA ANDERSON
DATE: APR. 28, 1815
BONDSMAN: SAMUEL ROBERTS
DATE PER:
BY: P. NANCE, J.P.K.C.
REFERENCE: O.A; O.M.R. PG. 19; T.H.M. VOL. 6, PG. 61

Names: Jesse Cate to Rachel Pyror
Date: Aug. 8, 1815
Bondsman: Sam'l Henry
Date Per: Aug. 8, 1815
By: Thos. H. Nelson
Reference: C.A; O.M.R. Pg. 20; T.H.M. Vol. 6, Pg. 61

Names: James Chavis to Catharine Chavis
Date: Mar. 14, 1815
Bondsman: John Garner
Witness: A. Hutcheson
Reference: C.A; O.MR. Pg. 19; T.H.M. Vol. 6, Pg. 61

Names: John Chesney to Sarah Scaggs
Date: Nov. 3, 1815
Reference: T.H.M. Vol. 6, Pg. 61

Names: Mitchell Childress to Rachael Hendrix
Date: Mar. 1, 1815
Bondsman: William Morrow
Witness: A. Hutcheson, D. C.
Reference: C.A; T.H.M. Vol. 6, Pg. 61

Names: Solomon Clapp to Teaberry Smith
Date: Sept. 1, 1815
Bondsman: McC. Frost
Reference: C.A; T.H.M. Vol. 6, Pg. 61

Names: Caleb Cole to Polly G. Wright
Date: Mar. 16, 1815
Bondsman: Byrd Izel
Witness: A. Hutcheson
Reference: C.A; T.H.M. Vol. 6, Pg. 61

Names: Ebenezar Cooper to Nancy Brown
Date: June 28, 1815
Date Per: June 28, 1815
By: Tho. H. Nelson
Reference: C.A; O.M.R. Pg. 19

Names: John Cox to Alice Gammon
Date: Oct. 16, 1815
Bondsman: John Goss
Witness: A. Hutcheson, D. C.
Reference: C.A; T.H.M. Vol. 6, Pg. 61

Names: David Davis to Betsy Tays
Date: Oct. 2, 1815
Reference: T.H.M. Vol. 6, Pg. 61

Names: Lewis Davis to Nancy McHenry
Date: Jany. 11, 1815
Bondsman: Geo. Brandon
Reference: C.A; O.M.R. Pg. 18; T.H.M. Vol. 6, Pg. 61

Names: Colesby Dowell to Sally Elliott
Date: Nov. 14, 1815
Reference: T.H.M. Vol. 6, Pg. 61

Names: William Eaton to Isabella Gillespie
Date: July 22, 1815
Reference: T.H.M. Vol. 6, Pg. 61

Names: John England to Mary Scott
Date: Dec. 25, 1815
Bondsman: D. B. Ayres
Date Per: Dec. 28, 1815
By: John Love, J.P.K.C.
Witness: A. Hutcheson
Reference: C.A; O.M.R. Pg. 21; T.H.M. Vol. 6, Pg. 61

Names: Harris Evans to Aurelia Lewis
Date:
Reference: T.H.M. Vol. 6, Pg. 61

Names: William Falkner to Nancy Talent
Date: Apr. 3, 1815
Bondsman: Robert Tunnell
Witness: A. Hutcheson
Reference: C.A; T.H.M. Vol. 6, Pg. 61

Names: William Frazier to Sarah Pickle
Date: Sept. 14, 1815
Reference: C.A; O.M.R. Pg. 20

Names: John Galbraith to Isabella Edington
Date: Dec. 25, 1815
Bondsman: Willis Casteel
By: P. Nance, J.P.K.C.
Witness: A. Hutcheson
Reference: C.A; O.M.R. Pg. 21; T.H.M. Vol. 6, Pg. 61

Names: William Gamble to Polly Russell
Date: Oct. 9, 1815
Bondsman: Jesse Carpenter
Witness: A. Hutcheson
Reference: C.A; T.H.M Vol. 6, Pg. 61

NAMES: ABNER GARNER TO MARGARET HARDEN
DATE: OCT. 26, 1815
DATE PER: OCT. 27, 1815
BY: JOHN LOVE, J.P.K.C.
REFERENCE: C.A; O.M.R. PG. 21; T.H.M. VOL. 6, PG. 61

NAMES: JOHN GARRISON TO POLLY HUBBS
DATE: OCT. 4, 1815
REFERENCE: T.H.M. VOL. 6, PG. 61

NAMES: ISAAC GILLESPIE TO NANCY WARD.
DATE: AUG. 14, 1815
REFERENCE: C.A; O.M.R. PG. 20; T.H.M. VOL. 6, PG. 61

NAMES: THOMAS GILMORE TO ANNE WILSON
DATE: DEC. 31, 1815
REFERENCE: T.H.M. VOL. 6, PG. 61

NAMES: WILLIAM GODDARD TO JANE S. CAMPBELL
DATE: JULY 29, 1815
REFERENCE: C.A; O.M.R. PG. 20

NAMES: BENJAMIN GRAYSON TO NANCY RIGNEY
DATE: MAY 29, 1815
BONDSMAN: HENRY RIGNEY
WITNESSES: A. HUTCHESON, D.C.
REFERENCE: C.A; T.H.M. VOL. 6, PG. 61

NAMES: WM. HAMILTON TO POLLY BREEDLOVE
DATE: MAR. 1, 1815
BONDSMAN: FRANCIS ELLIS
WITNESS: A. HUTCHESON, D.C.
REFERENCE: C.A; T.H.M. VOL. 6, PG. 61

NAMES: ISAAC HAMMER TO MARY UNDERWOOD
DATE: DEC. 8, 1815
BONDSMAN: SIMON ADAMSON
WITNESS: A. HUTCHESON, D. CLERK
REFERENCE: C.A; O.M.R. PG. 21; T.H.M. VOL. 6, PG. 62

NAMES: SAMUEL HANEY TO POLLY BROOKS
DATE: JUNE 20, 1815
BONDSMAN: JOHN WILLIAMS
DATE PER: JUNE 20, 1815
BY: THO. H. NELSON
REFERENCE: C.A; T.H.M. VOL. 6, PG. 60 & 62

NAMES: ALEXANDER HAYS TO CATHARINE MCNUTT
DATE: SEPT. 18, 1815
BONDSMAN: JAMES A. CALDWELL
WITNESS: A. HUTCHESON
REFERENCE: C.A; T.H.M. VOL. 6, PG. 62

NAMES: HENRY HELTON TO RACHAEL TURNER
DATE: DEC. 28, 1815
BONDSMAN: JNO. GALLOWAY
WITNESS: AND. HUTCHESON
REFERENCE: C.A; T.H.M VOL. 6, PG. 62

NAMES: THATCH HENDERSON TO SALLY NIPPER
DATE: DEC. 20, 1815
REFERENCE: T.H.M VOL. 6, PG. 62

NAMES: MARTIN HILL TO POLLY HANSARD
DATE: FEB. 12, 1815
REFERENCE: T.H.M VOL. 6, PG. 62

NAMES: JOHN HOOD TO POLLY HOLLOWAY
DATE: OCT. 11, 1815
DATE PER: OCT. 11, 1815
BY: JOHN LOVE, J.P.K.C.
REFERENCE: C.A; O.M.R. PG. 21

NAMES: SOLOMON JACKSON TO REBECCA HEMBREE
DATE: APR. 3, 1815
BONDSMAN: DRURY HEMBREE
WITNESS: A. HUTCHESON, D. C.
REFERENCE: C.A; T.H.M. VOL. 6, PG. 62

NAMES: SAMUEL JOHNSON TO ELIZABETH STEPHENSON
DATE: JANY. 17, 1815
BONDSMAN: ROBERT STEPHENSON
REFERENCE: C.A; T.H.M VOL. 6, PG. 62

NAMES: WILLIAM KAIN TO ANY BLEDSOE
DATE: JULY 21, 1815
REFERENCE: T.H.M VOL. 6, PG. 62

NAMES: THOMAS KEYHILL TO ELIZABETH GRAVES
DATE: NOV. 21, 1815
BONDSMAN: SAMUEL ANDERSON
WITNESS: AND. HUTCHESON
REFERENCE: C.A; O.M.R. PG. 21; T.H.M. VOL. 6, PG. 62

NAMES: DIMEON LANE TO JANE CAMPBELL
DATE: JULY 25, 1815
WITNESSES: CHAS. MCCLUNG, CLK. - AND. HUTCHESON, DEPUTY
REFERENCE: C.A; O.M.R. PG. 20

NAMES: ISAAC LENNING TO POLLY LEEK
DATE: JUNE 20, 1815
REFERENCE: T.H.M. VOL. 6, PG. 62

Names: Jacob Lones to Jane Hickey
Date: July 5, 1815
Reference: T.H.M. Vol. 6, Pg. 62

Names: Nathan Lyon to Betsy Coxe
Date: July 31, 1815
Reference: T.H.M. Vol. 6, Pg. 62

Names: Solomon McCampbell to Peggy Dowler
Date: Nov. 28, 1815
Reference: T.H.M. Vol. 6, Pg. 62

Names: Richard McLemore to Sally Fowler
Date: Sept. 20, 1815
Bondsman: Richard Fowler
Witness: A. Hutcheson, D.C.
Reference: C.A; T.H.M. Vol. 6, Pg. 62

Names: Thos. McMillan to Sarah Ragan
Date: Jany. 12, 1815
Bondsman: Thomas Rodgers
Date Per: Jany. 12, 1815
By: Tho. H. Nelson
Reference: C.A; C.M.R. Pg. 18; T.H.M. Vol. 6, Pg. 62

Names: Thomas H. Miller to Polly A. Cavett
Date: July 17, 1815
Bondsman: Jno. G. Ross
Date Per: July 18, 1815
By: Tho. H. Nelson
Witness: A. Hutcheson, D.C.K.C.
Reference: C.A; C.M.R. Pg. 19

Names: Wm. Morris to Elizabeth Morris
Date: Sept. 14, 1815
Bondsman: William Love
Witness: A. Hutcheson, D.C.
Reference: C.A; T.H.M. Vol. 6, Pg. 62

Names: John Morrow to Ann J. Jones
Date: June 26, 1815
Bondsman: Geo. J. Jones
Reference: C.A; T.H.M. Vol. 6, Pg. 62

Names: Henry Newman to Priscilla Plumley
Date: Dec. 20, 1815
Date Per: Dec. 20, 1815
By: John Haynie, Deacon
Reference: C.A; C.M.R. Pg. 21; T.H.M. Vol. 6, Pg. 62

Names: Marcus Ore to Susanna Carpenter
Date: Oct. 14, 1815
Reference: C.A; C.M.R. Pg. 21; T.H.M. Vol. 6, Pg. 62

Names: William Osburn to Naomy Edwards
Date: Oct. - 1815
Date Per: Oct. - 1815
By: R. Houston, J.P.K.C.
Reference: C.A; C.M.R. Pg. 20

Names: John Palmer to Nancy Chandler
Date: June 29, 1815
Reference: C.A; C.M.R. Pg. 19

Names: Samuel Payne to Polly Paine
Date: May 16, 1815
Witness: Chas. McClung, Clk. - John N, Gamble, Depty.
Reference: C.A; C.M. R. Pg. 19

Names: Joseph Peterson to Mary Rutherford
Date: May 24, 1815
Reference: T.H.M. Vol. 6, Pg. 62

Names: Abram Reed to Nancy Murry
Date: Sept. 7, 1815
Bondsman: Thornbery Elledge
By: Peter Nance, J.P.K.C.
Witness: A. Hutcheson, D. Clk.
Reference: C.A; C.M.R. Pg. 20; T.H.M. Vol. 6, Pg. 62

Names: Robert G. Rhea to Peggy Majors
Date: Feb. 27, 1815
Reference: T.H.M. Vol. 6, Pg. 62

Names: Thos. Rodgers to Anne Patton
Date: Apr. 3, 1815
Bondsman: Robert Patton
Witness: A. Hutcheson
Reference: C.A; T.H.M. Vod. 6, Pg. 62

Names: James Rogers to Betsy Bond
Date: Dec. 27, 1815
Bondsman: Joseph Rodgers
Date Per: Dec. 28, 1815
By: John McClellan, J.P.K.C.
Witness: A. Hutcheson
Reference: C.A; T.H.M. Vol. 6, Pg. 62

Names: John Shell to Nancy Pursley
Date: Dec. 4, 1815
Bondsman: William Morrow
Witness: A. Hutcheson
Reference: C.A; T.H.M. Vol. 6, Pg. 62

Names: John Shelton to Polly Catchem
Date: May 24, 1815
Bondsman: Jacob Cetchem
Witness: A. Hutcheson
Reference: C.A; O.M.R. Pg. 19; T.H.M. Vol. 6, Pg. 62

Names: Bne Skipper to Charity Chavis
Date: Mar. 21, 1815
Reference: C.A; O.M.R. Pg. 19

Names: John Smith to Betsy Childress
Date: June 21, 1815
Bondsman: John Cloud - Michael Smith
Witness: A. Hutcheson
Reference: C.A.

Names: John A. Smith to Peggy Robeson
Date: Aug. 26, 1815
By: Peter Nance, J.P.K.C.
Reference: C.A; O.M.R. Pg. 20

Names: Daniel Stickley to Betsy Covington
Date: Dec. 22, 1815
Bondsman: Michael Karns
Date Per: Dec. 25, 1815
By: John Love, J.P.K.C.
Witness: A. Hutcheson
Reference: C.A; O.M.R. Pg. 21

Names: Thomas Taylor to Sarah Brown
Date: July 3, 1815
Date Per: July 3, 1815
By: Tho. H. Nelson
Reference: C.A; O.M.R. Pg. 19; T.H.M. Vol. 6, Pg. 62

Names: Henderson Thatch to Sally Nipper
Date: Dec. 20, 1815
Reference: T.H.M. Vol. 6, Pg. 62

Names: Geo. Underwood to Elizabeth Kymes
Date: Sept. 16, 1815
Reference: C.A; O.M.R. Pg. 20; T.H.M. Vol. 6, Pg. 62

Names: Robert Williams to Elizabeth Clayton
Date: Sept. 28, 1815
Bondsman: Wm. Mitchell
Reference: C.A; T.H.M. Vol. 6, Pg. 62

Names: Robert G. Wray to Peggy Majors
Date: Feb. 27, 1815
Reference: T.H.M. Vol. 6, Pg. 62

1816

Names: Francis Able to Barbara Harner
Date: May 25, 1816
Reference: C.A; O.M.R. Pg. 24

Names: James Aikman to Patience Gallihorn
Date: June 27, 1816
Bondsman: James Boyd
Witness: A. Hutcheson
Reference: C.A.

Names: Isaac Bank to Elizabeth Forkner
Date: Oct. 30, 1816
Reference: C.A; O.M.R. Pg. 25

Names: Sam'l Beall to Hanna Luttrell
Date: Oct. 28, 1816
Bondsman: Francis A. Ramsey
Witness: Andw. Hutcheson
Reference: C.A; T.H.M. Vol. 6, Pg. 62

Names: Joseph Blair to Celey Whittle
Date: Sept. 4, 1816
Date Per: Sept. 10, 1816
By: Sam'l Sample, J.P.K.C.
Reference: C.A; O.M.R. Pg. 25

Names: William Brown to Anne Taylor
Date: Jany. 27, 1816
Reference: C.A; O.M.R. Pg. 22

Names: George B[illegible] to Rachel Holt
Date: Aug. 10, 1816
Reference: C.A; O.M.R. Pg. 24

Names: David Coats to Jincy Lee
Date: Dec. 24, 1816
Date Per: Dec. 26, 1816
By: Amos Hardin, J.P.K.C.
Reference: C.A; T.H.M. Vol. 6, Pg. 62

NAMES: GILBERT CRUSE TO SUSAN HAVELY
DATE: DEC. 24, 1816
BONDSMAN: JOHN CRUIZE
DATE PER: DEC. 24, 1816
BY: S. MONTGOMERY
WITNESS: C. A. C. WHITE
REFERENCE: C.A; O.M.R. PG. 26

NAMES: JAMES CRUSE TO LANNICE CHILDRESS
DATE: OCT. 22, 1816
DATE PER: OCT. 22, 1816
BY: JEREMIAH KING, M.G.
REFERENCE: C.A; O.M.R. PG. 25

NAMES: THOMAS DOUGLASS TO BETSY BRYAN
DATE: FEBY. 10, 1816
DATE PER: FEBY. 15, 1816
BY: JOHN MCCAMPBELL, V.D.M.
REFERENCE: C.A; T.H.M. VOL. 6, PG. 62

NAMES: THOMAS DUNHAM TO SARAH JONES
DATE: MAY 18, 1816
WITNESS: DAVID ROANE
REFERENCE: T.H.M. VOL. 6, PG. 62

NAME: JOHN EDMONDSON TO SARAH GRAYSON
DATE: AUG. 13, 1816
REFERENCE: T.H.M. VOL. 6, PG. 62

NAMES: STERLING EDMONSON TO REBECCA TAYLOR
DATE: JULY 27, 1816
BONDSMAN: WILLIAM KENDRICK
WITNESS: A. HUTCHESON
REFERENCE: C.A; T.H.M. VOL. 6, PG. 62

NAMES: SAMUEL ELLIOTT TO JANE MANLY
DATE: APR. 16, 1816
REFERENCE: T.H.M. VOL. 6, PG. 62

NAMES: JOHN ELLIS TO SARAH CLAPP
DATE: SEPT. 14, 1816
DATE PER: SEPT. 26, 1816
BY: JOHN THOMPSON, J.P.K.C.
REFERENCE: C.A; O.M.R. PG. 25; T.H.M. VOL. 6, PG. 62

NAMES: ROBERT FERGUSON TO PATSY STANSBERRY
DATE: NOV. 7, 1816
DATE PER: NOV. 7, 1816
BY: S. MONTGOMERY
REFERENCE: C.A; O.M.R. PG. 26; T.H.M. VOL. 6, PG. 62

NAMES: PETER FINE TO ELIZABETH ALEXANDER
DATE: NOV. 25, 1816
REFERENCE: C.A; O.M.R. PG. 25

NAMES: JAMES FRYOR TO BETSY HILL
DATE: DEC. 17, 1816
DATE PER: DEC. 17, 1816
BY: T. H. NELSON
REFERENCE: C.A; O.M.R. PG. 26; T.H.M. VOL. 6, PG. 62

NAMES: JESSE GALLOWAY TO NANCY CALDWELL
DATE: JULY 29, 1816
DATE PER: JULY 31, 1816
BY: JOHN BAYLESS, J.P.K.C.
REFERENCE: C.A; T.H.M. VOL. 6, PG. 62

NAMES: THOMAS GASTON TO MILLY SPEERS
DATE: NOV. 27, 1816
DATE PER: NOV. 28, 1816
BY: JONATHAN AYRES, J.P.K.C.
REFERENCE: C.A; O.M.R. PG. 25

NAMES: JAMES GOODING TO JANE HARDEN
DATE: APR. 13, 1816
REFERENCE: C.A; T.H.M. VOL. 6, PG. 62

NAMES: JACOB GRAYBILL TO ELIZABETH SHIPE
DATE: MAR. 4, 1816
BONDSMAN: JOHN CHUMLEA
WITNESS: ANDW. HUTCHESON
REFERENCE: C.A; T.H.M. VOL. 6, PG. 62

NAMES: SIMEON HARRIS TO POLLY BEARD
DATE: JULY 26, 1816
DATE PER: JULY 26, 1816
BY: BERIAH FRAZIER, J.P.K.C.
REFERENCE: C.A; O.M.R. PG. 24

NAMES: R. N. K. HICKS TO LUCINDA ELLIOTT
DATE: MAY 20, 1816
DATE PER: MAY 23, 1816
BY: R. COLE, J.P.K.C.
REFERENCE: C.A; O.M.R. PG. 23; T.H.M. VOL. 6, PG. 62

NAMES: MASTON HILL TO POLLY HANSARD
DATE: FEBY. 12, 1816
DATE PER: FEBY. 15, 1816
BY: JOHN BAYLESS, J.P.K.C.
REFERENCE: C.A; O.M.R. PG. 22; T.H.M. VOL. 6, PG. 62

Names: Luke Hood to Elizabeth McCaven
Date: Feb. 25, 1816
Reference: T.H.M. Vol. 6, Pg. 62

Names: William Houston to Margaret Swan
Date: Sept. 23, 1816
Reference: T.H.M. Vol. 6, Pg. 62

Names: William Howell to Myra McNair
Date: Feby. 15, 1816
Date Per: Feby. 15, 1816
By: R. Houston, J.P.K.C.
Reference: C.A; O.M.R. Pg. 22; T.H.M. Vol. 6, Pg. 62

Names: Aaron Ingram to Anne Evans
Date: Aug. 14, 1816
Bondsman: S. S. McCampbell
Date Per: Aug. 15, 1816
By: John McCampbell
Witness: A. Hutcheson
Reference: C.A; T.H.M. Vol. 6, Pg. 63

Names: Solomon D. Jacobs to Susan Young
Date: Jany. 4, 1816
Date Per: Jany. 4, 1816
By: Tho. H. Nelson
Reference: C.A; O.M.R. Pg. 22; T.H.M. Vol. 6, Pg. 63

Names: Josiah Johnson to Priscilla Gallihan
Date: Feby 21, 1816
Bondsman: Edmund Johnson
Date Per: Feby. 22, 1816
By: Samuel Swan, J.P.K.C.
Witness: Andw. Hutcheson
Reference: C.A; O.M.R. Pg. 23; T.H.M. Vol. 6, Pg. 63

Names: Luke Lea to Susan W. McCormick
Date: Feby. 28, 1816
Date Per: Feby. 28, 1816
By: Tho. H. Nelson
Reference: O.M.R. Pg. 23

Names: Pryor Lea to Maria Kennedy
Date: Oct. 6, 1816
Date Per: Oct. 6, 1816
By: Tho. H. Nelson
Reference: O.M.R. Pg. 37

Names: David Lowe to Elizabeth Able
Date: Nov. 15, 1816
Bondsman: Jonathan Keener
Date Per: Nov. 17, 1816
By: John McClellan, J.P.K.C.
Witness: Andw. Hutcheson
Reference: C.A; O.M.R. Pg. 25; T.H.M. Vol. 6, Pg. 63

Names: Jacob Lowe to Betsy Rogers
Date: Feby. 13, 1816
Bondsman: Joseph Rodgers - Bowen Hill
Witness: Mat. McClung
Reference: C.A; O.M.R. Pg. 22; T.H.M. Vol. 6, Pg. 63

Names: Wm. McAnally to Easter Hope
Date: July 11, 1816
Date Per: July 11, 1816
By: Tho. H. Nelson
Reference: O.M.R. Pg. 24

Names: Russell R. McBath to Elizabeth Johnson
Date: July 9, 1816; Date Per: July 10, 1816
By: S. Montgomery, J.P.K.C.
Reference: C.A; O.M.R. Pg. 24

Names: William McCall to Rachel Ragan
Date: Oct. 17, 1816
Bondsman: Peter Reagan
Witness: Andw. Hutcheson
Reference: C.A; T.H.M. Vol. 6, Pg. 63

Names: Wm. A. McCampbell to Mary Shannon Anderson
Date: Nov. 11, 1816
Date Per: Nov. 12, 1816
By: Isaac Anderson
Reference: O.M.R. Pg. 25; T.H.M. Vol. 6, Pg. 63

Names: John McCloud to Mary Coontz
Date: Oct. 7, 1816
Bondsman: Philip Koontz
Date Per: Oct. 11, 1816
By: John Bayless, J.P.K.C.
Witness: A. Hutcheson
Reference: C.A; O.M.R. Pg. 25; T.H.M. Vol. 6, Pg. 63

Names: James McComb to Betsy Lewis
Date: Sept. 26, 1816
Bondsman: Henry Lewis
Witness: Andw. Hutcheson
Reference: C.A; T.H.M. Vol. 6, Pg. 63

NAMES: ALEXANDER MCGHEE TO ANNE M. EMMERSON
DATE: JANY. 11, 1816
BONDSMAN: JOHN GARDINER
WITNESS: ANDW. HUTCHESON
REFERENCE: C.A; O.M.R. PG. 22; T.H.M. VOL. 6, PG. 63

NAMES: WILLIAM MCNALLY TO EASTER HOPE
DATE: JULY 11, 1816
REFERENCE: T.H.M. VOL. 6, PG. 63

NAMES: JOHN MCVEY TO MELINDA QUARLES
DATE: AUG. 26, 1816
BONDSMAN: JAMES MCVEY
WITNESS: ANDW. HUTCHESON
REFERENCE: C.A; O.M.R. PG. 24; T.H.M. VOL. 6, PG. 63

NAMES: JOHN MILLER TO POLLY ELLIOTT
DATE: MAR. 25, 1816
DATE PER: JUNE 1, 1816
BY: ROBERT LINDSAY, J.P.K.C.
REFERENCE: C.A; O.M.R. PG. 23

NAMES: JOHN MCKEE MONTGOMERY TO MARY DUNLAP
DATE: SEPT. 30, 1816
DATE PER: OCT. 1, 1816
BY: SAM'L MONTGOMERY, J.P.K.C.
REFERENCE: C.A; O.M.R. PG. 25; T.H.M. VOL. 6, PG. 63

NAMES: ARNOLD MOSS TO SALLY QUALLS
DATE: FEBY. 13, 1816
DATE PER: FEBY. 15, 1816
BY: WEST WALKER, M.G.
REFERENCE: C.A; O.M.R. PG. 22

NAMES: MOSES MOWRY TO NANCY CLAPP
DATE: DEC. 17, 1816
DATE PER: DEC. 24, 1816
BY: JOHN THOMPSON, J. P. K. C.
REFERENCE: C.A; O.M.R. PG. 26; T.H.M. VOL. 6, PG. 63

NAMES: OBEDIAH MURPHY TO MARY BERRY
DATE: MAR. 18, 1816
BONDSMAN: MICHAEL DAVIS
WITNESS: ANDW. HUTCHESON
REFERENCE: C.A; T.H.M. VOL. 6, PG. 63

NAMES: WILLIAM C. MYNATT TO HARRIET BROWN
DATE: JUNE 27, 1816
DATE PER: JUNE 27, 1816
BY: THO. H. NELSON
REFERENCE: C.A; O.M.R. PG. 24

NAMES: JOHN NELSON TO LUCINDA PAYNE
DATE: MAR. 26, 1816
BONDSMAN: WM. MCCLELLAN
DATE PER: MAR. 26, 1816
BY: THO. H. NELSON
WITNESS: ANDW. HUTCHESON
REFERENCE: C.A; O.M.R. PG. 23; T.H.M. VOL. 6, PG. 63

NAMES: PETER PARSONS TO NANCY KAIN
DATE: APR. 11, 1816 — PERFORMED: APR. 11, 1816
BY: ISAAC ANDERSON
REFERENCE: C.A; O.M.R. PG. 23

NAMES: WILLIAM PAUL TO REBECCA CARUTHERS
DATE: AUG. 27, 1816
BONDSMAN: AUDLAY PAUL
DATE PER: AUG. 27, 1816
BY: JAMES WHITE
WITNESS: ANDW. HUTCHESON
REFERENCE: C.A; T.H.M. VOL. 6, PG. 63

NAMES: WILLIAM PLUMLEE TO NANCY MCLEMORE
DATE: SEPT. 26, 1816
BONDSMAN: ARCHIBALD MCLEMORE
WITNESS: A. HUTCHESON
REFERENCE: C. A.

NAMES: JAMES RAY TO ELIZABETH CAVIN
DATE: FEBY. 13, 1816
BONDSMAN: JOSEPH CALLOWAY
WITNESS: A. HUTCHESON
REFERENCE: C.A; T.H.M VOL. 6, PG. 63

NAMES: JOHN RAY TO RILEY WHITE
DATE: APR. 22, 1816
BONDSMAN: JOHN CALLOWAY
WITNESS: ANDW. HUTCHESON
REFERENCE: C.A; O.M.R. PG. 23; T.H.M. VOL. 6, PG. 63

NAMES: BRICE RICHARDSON TO TEMPERANCE DAVIS
DATE: OCT. 23, 1816
BONDSMAN: JOHN R. NELSON
DATE PER: OCT. 21, 1816
BY: JOHN MCCLELLAN, J.P.K.C.
REFERENCE: C.A; T.H.M. VOL. 6, PG. 63

NAMES: JOHN ROBERTS TO ELEANOR GILMORE
DATE: AUG. 10, 1816
DATE PER: AUG. 13, 1816
BY: SAM'L SAMPLE, J.P.K.C.
REFERENCE: C.A; O.M.R. PG. 24; T.H.M. VOL. 6, PG. 63

Names: William Rodgers to Mahala Lowe
Date: Aug. 13, 1816
Bondsman: Andrew Russell
Witness: J. N. Gamble
Reference: C.A; T.H.M. Vol. 6, Pg. 63

Names: James Rutherford to Nancy Owens
Date: Feby. 3, 1816
Bondsman: Wm. Owens
Witness: A. Hutcheson
Reference: C.A; T.H.M. Vol. 6, Pg. 63

Names: James Scaggs to Nancy Majors
Date: July 20, 1816
Bondsman: Pleasant Miller
Date Per: July 25, 1816
By: John Bayless, J.P.K.C.
Witness: Andw. Hutcheson
Reference: C.A; T.H.M. Vol. 6, Pg. 63
(Signed Pleasant Miller)

Names: John Shirk to Catharine Welker
Date: Aug. 7, 1816
Bondsman: Wm. Morrow
Witness: Andw. Hutcheson
Reference: C.A.

Names: John Shook to Catherine Wilson
Date: Aug. 7, 1816
Reference: T.H.M. Vol. 6, Pg. 63

Names: Lewis Simpson to Charity Ault
Date: Aug. 1, 1816
Date Per: Aug. 1, 1816
By: John Haynie, M. G.
Reference: C.A; O.M.R. Pg. 24

Names: William Sumpter to Elizabeth Moad
Date: Jany 9, 1816
Date Per: Jany. 11, 1816
By: John Bayless, J.P.K.C.
Reference: C.A; O.M.R. Pg. 22

Names: John Sutherland, Jr. to Diana Kennedy
Date: Dec. 31, 1816
Date Per: Dec. 31, 1816
By: Tho. H. Nelson
Reference: C.A; O.M.R. Pg. 26

Names: John H. Van Dyke to Phoebe Martin
Date: Feb. 27, 1816
Witness: Sam'l Martin
Reference: T.H.M. Vol. 6, Pg. 63
(Signed Samuel Martin)

Names: Daniel Vestner to Rutha Sparks
Date: Dec. 3, 1816
Bondsman: Archibald Rhea
Date Per: Dec. 3, 1816
By: J. Anderson
Witness: Hugh Brown, D.C.
Reference: C.A; O.M.R. Pg. 26; T.H.M. Vol. 6, Pg. 63

Names: Leonard Ward to Peggy M. Greene
Date: Jany. 29, 1816
Bondsman: John Ward
Witness: J. N. Gamble
Reference: C.A; O.M.R. Pg. 22; T.H.M. Vol. 6, Pg. 63

Names: John Williams to Rhoda Morgan
Date: Jan. 1, 1816
Reference: T.H.M. Vol. 6, Pg. 63

Names: John D. Williams to Sarah Ward
Date: Oct. 20, 1816
Bondsman: William Morrow
Reference: C.A; T.H.M. Vol. 6, Pg. 63

Names: Samuel White to Polly D. Bennett
Date: Mar. 6, 1816
Date Per: Mar. 6, 1816
By: Tho. H. Nelson
Reference: O.M.R. Pg. 23

Names: James Wolf to Barbara Haefly
Date: Mar. 25, 1816
Bondsman: Jeremiah Wolf
Date Per: Mar. 26, 1816
By: Sam'l Swan, J.P.C.
Witness: A. Hutcheson
Reference: C.A; O.M.R. Pg. 23; T.H.M. Vol. 6, Pg. 63

Names: James Wood to Polly Bradley
Date: Jany. 30, 1816
Bondsman: William Bradley
Date Per: Feby. 1, 1816
By: Rob't. Lindsay, J.P.K.C.
Witness: Andw. Hutcheson
Reference: C.A; O.M.R. Pg. 22; T.H.M. Vol. 6, Pg. 63

NAMES: EDWIN WYATT TO ELIZA INDIANNA BLOUNT
DATE: FEBY. 20, 1816
DATE PER: FEBY. 20, 1816
BY: THO. H. NELSON
REFERENCE: O.M.R. PG. 23

1817

NAMES: WILLIAM ALEXANDER TO ELIZABETH ________
DATE: OCT. 17, 1817
REFERENCE: T.H.M. VOL. 6, PG. 63

NAMES: JESSE ATKINSON TO PATSY GOODRUM
DATE: JANY. 25, 1817
BONDSMAN: ABSALOM ATKINSON
DATE PER: JANY. 25, 1817
BY: JAMES WHITE
REFERENCE: C.A; O.M.R. PG. 26; T.H.M. VOL. 6, PG. 63

NAMES: MOSES BALDWIN TO ELIZA KILLINGSWORTH
DATE: FEBY. 6, 1817
DATE PER: FEBY. 12, 1817
BY: WM. ALLDREDGE, J.P.K.C.
REFERENCE: C.A; O.M.R. PG. 26; T.H.M. VOL. 6, PG. 63

NAMES: MOSES BALDWIN TO MARGARET CAHOE
DATE: JUNE 2, 1817
DATE PER: JUNE 3, 1817
BY: THO. H. NELSON
REFERENCE: C.A; O.M.R. PG. 27; T.H.M. VOL. 6, PG. 63

NAMES: JOHN W. BARNETT TO MARY COKER
DATE: FEBY. 26, 1817
DATE PER: FEBY. 27, 1817
BY: S. MONTGOMERY
REFERENCE: C.A; O.M.R. PG. 27; T.H.M. VOL. 6, PG. 63

NAMES: ABRAHAM BEASLEY TO BARBARA DAMEWOOD
DATE: AUG. 5, 1817
DATE PER: AUG. 7, 1817
BY: JOHN THOMPSON, J.P.K.C.
REFERENCE: C.A; O.M.R. PG. 28; T.H.M. VOL. 6, PG. 63

NAMES: JOHN BLAKELY TO LEVINA BROWN
DATE: JUNE 6, 1817
BONDSMAN: JOSHUA BROWN
REFERENCE: C.A; T.H.M. VOL. 6, PG. 63

NAMES: DAVID BYERLEY TO MARY JOHNSTON
DATE: NOV. 22, 1817
BONDSMAN: JOHN WRIGHT
REFERENCE: C.A; T.H.M. VOL. 6, PG. 63

NAMES: WILLIAM CARTER TO SUSAN FERGUSON
DATE: MAY 26, 1817
BONDSMAN: LEWIS LUTTRELL & STEPHEN FERGUSON
DATE PER: MAY 27, 1817
BY: SAM'L SAMPLE, J.P.K.C.
REFERENCE: C.A; T.H.M. VOL. 6, PG. 63

NAMES: ISAIAH CHAPMAN TO POLLY CRABB
DATE: MAR. 5, 1817
BONDSMAN: JOSEPH CRABB
DATE PER: MAR. 5, 1817
BY: ROBT. LINDSAY, J.P.K.C.
REFERENCE: C.A; T.H.M. VOL. 6, PG. 63

NAMES: DAVID CLAPP TO SARAH RUTHERFORD
DATE: ________ 25, 1817
REFERENCE: T.H.M. VOL. 6, PG. 63

NAMES: WILLIE COKER TO ELIZA TAYLOR
DATE: FEB. 1, 1817
REFERENCE: T.H.M. VOL. 6, PG. 63

NAMES: JAMES DALE TO NANCY MCDONALD
DATE: AUG. 30, 1817
REFERENCE: T.H.M. VOL. 6, PG. 63

NAMES: ISAAC DAMEWOOD TO SALLY NORRIS
DATE: OCT. 7, 1817
DATE PER: OCT. 9, 1817
BY: JOHN THOMPSON, J.P.K.C.
REFERENCE: C.A; O.M.R. PG. 30; T.H.M. VOL. 6, PG. 63

NAMES: JESSE DAVIS TO ELIZABETH HILL
DATE: JANY. 6, 1817
BONDSMAN: ANDREW MCHAFFIE
REFERENCE: C.A; T.H.M. VOL. 6, PG. 63

NAMES: JAMES M. DICKEY TO POLLY DOUGLAS
DATE: NOV. 1, 1817
BONDSMAN: WM. DOUGLAS
DATE PER: NOV. 4, 1817
BY: R. H. KING (?)
REFERENCE: C.A; T.H.M. VOL. 6, PG. 63

NAMES: ALEXANDER EARLY TO LEAMY MOORE
DATE: JUNE 13, 1817
REFERENCE: T.H.M. VOL. 6, PG. 63

NAMES: JOSEPH ELKINS TO PATSY WHITECOTTON
DATE: OCT. 7, 1817
DATE PER: OCT. 28, 1817
BY: JOHN BAYLESS, J.P.K.C.
REFERENCE: C.A; O.M.R. PG. 30; T.H.M. VOL. 6, PG. 63

NAMES: WM. C. EVERETT TO POLLY GILLESPIE
DATE: SEPT. 30, 1817
DATE PER: OCT. 2, 1817
BY: AMOS T. CARDEN, J.P.K.C.
REFERENCE: C.A; O.M.R. PG. 30; T.H.M. VOL. 6, PG. 63

NAMES: MINT FERGUSON TO ELIZABETH STANSBURY
DATE: OCT. 25, 1817
DATE PER: NOV. 6, 1817
BY: S. MONTGOMERY
REFERENCE: C.A; O.M.R. PG. 31

NAMES: ROBERT GAINS TO NANCY PRICE
DATE: DEC. 10, 1817
REFERENCE: T.H.M. VOL. 6, PG. 63

NAMES: COZIER GAMMON TO LAVINIA V. TURBIVILL
DATE: OCT. 13, 1817
REFERENCE: T.H.M. VOL. 6, PG. 64

NAMES: MARTIN GENTRY TO SALLY MITCHELL
DATE: OCT. 6, 1817
DATE PER: OCT. 16, 1817
BY: R. COLE, J.P.K.C.
REFERENCE: C.A; O.M.R. PG. 30; T.H.M. VOL. 6, PG. 64

NAMES: ISAAC GERON TO ANNA HANKINS
DATE: NOV. 18, 1817
BONDSMAN: JOEL KIRKPATRICK
REFERENCE: C.A; T.H.M. VOL. 6, PG. 64

NAMES: THORNTON GODDARD TO POLLY CUNNINGHAM
DATE: FEB. 3, 1817
REFERENCE: T.H.M. VOL. 6, PG. 64

NAMES: DAVID GRAVES TO POLLY HOLLOWAY
DATE: SEPT. 13, 1817
BONDSMAN: DANIEL CLAPP
DATE PER: SEPT. 14, 1817
BY: JOHN THOMPSON, J.P.K.C.
REFERENCE: C.A; O.M.R. PG. 30; T.H.M. VOL. 6, PG. 64

NAMES: ABNER GREEN TO REBECCA JOHNSON
DATE: JAN. 2, 1817
REFERENCE: T.H.M. VOL. 6, PG. 64

NAMES: JOHN HACKWORTH TO ISABELLA CAMPBELL
DATE: APR. 12, 1817
BY: AMOS HARDEN, J.P.K.C.
REFERENCE: C.A; O.M.R. PG. 27

NAMES: ZACHARIAH HALL TO POLLY NELSON
DATE: AUG. 8, 1817
DATE PER: AUG. 12, 1817
BY: JOHN BAYLESS, J.P.K.C.
REFERENCE: C.A; O.M.R. PG. 29

NAMES: JOHN HANKINS TO MELINDA HINDS
DATE: FEBY. 28, 1817
DATE PER: MAR. 6, 1817
BY: JOHN BAYLESS, J.P.K.C.
REFERENCE: C.A; O.M.R. PG. 27; T.H.M. VOL. 6, PG. 64

NAMES: ADAM HARMON TO POLLY HOUSONG
DATE: NOV. 13, 1817
DATE PER: NOV. 13, 1817
BY: JEREMIAH KING, M.G.
REFERENCE: C.A; O.M.R. PG. 31; T.H.M. VOL. 6, PG. 64

NAMES: WILLIAM HENDERSON TO MATILDA KING
DATE: DEC. 11, 1817
BONDSMAN: WM. Y. KING
REFERENCE: C.A; T.H.M. VOL. 6, PG. 64

NAMES: JONATHAN HICKLIN TO MARY MONTGOMERY
DATE: OCT. 8, 1817
BONDSMAN: JAMES MONTGOMERY
DATE:PER: OCT. 8, 1817
BY: R. H. KING
REFERENCE: C.A; O.M.R. PG. 31

NAMES: ANDERSON HILL TO RACHEL BIRDWELL
DATE: MAY 14, 1817
DATE PER: MAY 15, 1817
BY: R. H. KING
REFERENCE: C.A; O.M.R. PG. 27; T.H.M. VOL. 6, PG. 64

NAMES: WELCOME HODGES TO REBECCA CALLOWAY
DATE: FEBY. 15, 1817
DATE PER: FEBY. 16, 1817
BY: AMOS HARDIN, J.P.K.C.
REFERENCE: C.A; O.M.R. PG. 27; T.H.M. VOL. 6, PG. 64

NAMES: WM. HOOD TO SALLY MCCALL
DATE: OCT. 28, 1817 -- PERFORMED: OCT. 28, 1817
BY: T. H. NELSON
REFERENCE: C.A; O.M.R. PG. 31

NAMES: JACOB HUFFSTEDLER TO POLLY LETSINGER
DATE: NOV. 12, 1817
BY: WM. CAMPBELL, J.P.K.C.
REFERENCE: C.A; O.M.R. PG. 31; T.H.M. VOL. 6, PG. 64

Names: Thomas Jarnagin to Unity Bledsoe
Date: Nov. 14, 1817
Bondsman: Giles J. Bledsoe
Reference: C.A; T.H.M. Vol. 6, Pg. 64

Names: Elijah Johnson to Polly Childress
Date: Jan. 13
By: Jeremiah King
Reference: T.H.M. Vol. 6, Pg. 64
(M. by Jeremiah King)

Names: Benjamin Johnston to Nancy Kiltner
Date: Nov. 22, 1817
Reference: T.H.M. Vol. 6, Pg. 64

Names: Elijah Johnston to Polly Childres
Date: Jany. 13, 1817
Bondsman: Thomas Hall
Witness: Hugh Brown
Reference: C.A.

Names: John Karns to Sally Gammon
Date: Aug. 20, 1817
Date Per: Aug. 24, 1817
By: John Bayless, J.P.K.C.
Reference: C.A; O.M.R. Pg. 29; T.H.M. Vol. 6, Pg. 64

Names: Matthew Keger to __________?
Date: Oct. ______, 1817
Reference: T.H.M. Vol. 6, Pg. 64

Names: Horatio Kidd to Mary Anne Kidd
Date: Oct. 23, 1817
Reference: T.H.M. Vol. 6, Pg. 64

Names: Thomas King to Elizabeth Keehill
Date: July 19, 1817
Bondsman: George Davis
Date Per: July 20, 1817
By: John Haynie
Reference: C.A; O.M.R. Pg. 28; T.H.M. Vol. 6, Pg. 64

Names: Wm. King to Elizabeth Anderson
Date: Sept. 1, 1817
Bondsman: John Anderson
Date Per: Sept. 1, 1817
By: John Haynie, Deacon
Reference: C.A; O.M.R. Pg. 29; T.H.M. Vol. 6, Pg. 64

Names: William Y. King to Peggy Larimore
Date: June 19, 1817
Reference: C.A; O.M.R. Pg. 28; T.H.M. Vol. 6, Pg. 64

Names: Jacob Kisinger to Polly Nawsler
Date: Mar. 11, 1817
Date Per: Mar. 11, 1817
By: Beriah Frazier, J.P.K.C.
Reference: C.A; O.M.R. Pg. 27; T.H.M. Vol. 6, Pg. 64

Names: Benjamin Larew to Milly Tindal
Date: Sept. 30, 1817
Date Per: Sept. 30, 1817
By: William A. McCampbell
Reference: C.A; O.M.R. Pg. 30; T.H.M. Vol. 6, Pg. 64

Names: Wm. Larew to Sally Tindal
Date: Sept. 2, 1817
Date Per: Oct. 6, 1817 (?)
By: John Bayless, J.P.K.C.
Reference: C.A; O.M.R. Pg. 29

Names: Permit Lee to Susanna Moats
Date: Nov. 28, 1817
Date Per: Dec. 4, 1817
By: Amos Hardin, J.P.K.C.
Reference: C.A; O.M.R. Pg. 32

Names: Samuel Lee to Polly York
Date: Jany. 16, 1817
Reference: C.A; O.M.R. Pg. 26; T.H.M. Vol. 6, Pg. 64

Names: Wm. Lee to Barbara Moats
Date: Nov. 28, 1817
Date Per: Dec. 4, 1817
By: Amos Hardin, J.P.K.C.
Reference: C.A; O.M.R. Pg. 32; T.H.M. Vol. 6, Pg. 64

Names: Wesley Legg to Price Christian
Date: May 17, 1817
Reference: T.H.M. Vol. 6, Pg. 64

Names: Reuben Lister to Sally Cole
Date: Nov. 20, 1817
Date Per: Nov. 20, 1817
By: John Haynie
Reference: C.A; O.M.R. Pg. 32; T.H.M. Vol. 6, Pg. 64

Names: Aquilla Low to Nancy Lewis
Date: Feby. 20, 1817
Date Per: Feby 20, 1817
By: Thomas Hudiburg
Reference: C.A; O.M.R. Pg. 27; T.H.M. Vol. 6, Pg. 64

Names: William Lucas to Sally Tindell
Reference: T.H.M. Vol. 6, Pg. 64

Names: George Martin, Jr. to Julian English
Date: Dec. 9, 1817
By: Wm. Campbell
Reference: C.A; O.M.R. Pg. 32; T.H.M. Vol. 6, Pg. 64

Names: Abel Massey to Judith Farmer
Date: Aug. 7, 1817
Reference: T.H.M. Vol. 6, Pg. 64

Names: Wm. McCartney to Betsy Ferguson
Date: Nov. 26, 1817
Date Per: Nov. 27; 1817
By: S. Montgomery
Reference: C.A; O.M.R. Pg. 32; T.H.M. Vol. 6, Pg. 64

Names: Samuel McClellan to Eliza Sterling
Date: July 25;
Reference: T.H.M. Vol. 6, Pg. 64

Names: Wm. McClellan to Peggy Sterling
Date: Apr. 8, 1817
Date Per: Apr. 10, 1817
By: T.H. Nelson
Reference: O.M.R. Pg. 27; T.H.M. Vol. 6, Pg. 64

Names: James McCloud to Polly McCloud
Date: Sept. 26, 1817
Date Per: Sept. 30, 1817
By: John Bayless, J.P.K.C.
Reference: C.A; O.M.R. Pg. 30; T.H.M. Vol. 6, Pg. 64

Names: James McCulla to Jane Swan
Date: Nov. 11, L817
Date Per: Nov. 13, 1817
By: R. H. King
Reference: C.A; O.M.R. Pg. 31; T.H.M. Vol. 6, Pg. 64

Names: George McNutt to Melinda Houston
Date: May 21, 1817
Date Per: May 21, 1817
By: T. H. Nelson
Reference: C.A.

Names: John McNutt to Martha Jack
Date: Apr. 14, 1817
Reference: T.H.M. Vol. 6, Pg. 64

Names: Robt. G. Miller to Sophy Rysdon
Date: Aug. 21, 1817
Date Per: Aug. 21, 1817
By: John Haynie, Deacon
Reference: C.A; O.M.R. Pg. 29; T.H.M. Vol. 6, Pg. 64

Names: James Mode to Polly Randal
Date: Aug. 19, 1817
Date Per: Aug. 19, 1817
By: John Bayless, J.P.K.C.
Reference: C.:A; O.M.R. Pg. 29; T.H.M. Vol. 6, Pg. 64

Names: Levi Moore to Nancy Shelhorse
Date: Nov. 15, 1817
Bondsman: James Moore
By: West Walker, M. G.
Reference: C.A; O.M.R. Pg. 32; T.H.M. Vol. 6, Pg. 64

Names: Wm. Mynatt to Nelly Reed
Date: Oct. 29; 1817
Date Per: Oct. 30, 1817
By: John Bayless, J.P.K.C.
Reference: C.A; O.M.R. Pg. 31; T.H.M. Vol. 6, Pg. 64

Names: Hiram Norman to Hanna Yarnell
Date: June 10, 1817
Date Per: June 14, 1817
By: Jonathan Ayres
Reference: C.A; O.M.R. Pg. 28; T.H.M. Vol. 6, Pg. 64

Names: Nicholas Norwood to Rachel Meek
Date: Sept. 11, 1817
Bondsman: John Sutherland, Jr.
Reference: C.A; O.M.R. Pg. 30; T.H.M. Vol. 6, Pg. 64

Names: James Patrick to Katy Gibbs
Date: Aug. 9, 1817
Bondsman: William Morrow
Date Per: Aug. 10, 1817
By: John Thompson, J.P.K.C.
Reference: C.A; O.M.R. Pg. 29; T.H.M. Vol. 6, Pg. 64

Names: Aaron S. Peterson to Sally Howell
Date: Mar. 5, 1817
Reference: T.H.M. Vol. 6, Pg. 64

Names: Wm. Pickle to Polly Swader
Date: Oct. 18, 1817
Date Per: Oct. 30, 1817
By: S. Montgomery, J.P.K.C.
Reference: C.A; O.M.R. Pg. 31; T.H.M. Vol. 6, Pg. 64

NAMES: LARKIN RENTFROE TO ELIZABETH WHITE
DATE: JULY 24, 1817
DATE PER: JULY 24, 1817
BY: JNO. HAYNIE
REFERENCE: O.M.R. PG. 28; T.H.M. VOL. 6, PG. 64

NAMES: AMOS ROBERTS TO SALLY WINES
DATE: JUNE 19, 1817
DATE PER: JUNE 26, 1817
BY: SAM'L MONTGOMERY
REFERENCE: C.A; O.M.R. PG. 28; T.H.M. VOL. 6, PG. 64

NAMES: WM. ROPER TO ELIZABETH BROWN
DATE: JUNE 26, 1817
DATE PER: JUNE 26, 1817
BY: JOHN HAYNIE
REFERENCE: C.A; O.M.R. PG. 28; T.H.M. VOL. 6, PG. 64

NAMES: ISAAC ROUTH TO SALLY ROBERTS
DATE: OCT. 30, 1817
DATE PER: OCT. 23, 1817
BY: SAM'; SAMPLE, J.P.K.C.
REFERENCE: C.A; O.M.R. PG. 31; T.H.M. VOL. 6, PG. 64

NAMES: THOMAS ROWLAND TO MARY DUNN
DATE: AUG. 4, 1817
DATE PER: AUG. 5, 1817
BY: SAM'L MONTGOMERY, J.P.K.C.
REFERENCE: C.A; O.M.R. PG. 28; T.H.M. VOL. 6, PG. 64

NAMES: YOUNG SAUNDERS TO ELIZABETH GARRICK
DATE: AUG. 9, 1817
DATE PER: AUG. 9, 1817
BY: RD. H. KING
REFERENCE: C.A; O.M.R. PG. 29

NAMES: ELIJAH SCARBOROUGH TO MATTY ADAMS
DATE: DEC. 27, 1817
BONDSMAN: JAMES SCOTT
REFERENCE: C.A; T.H.M. VOL. 6, PG. 64

NAMES: JAMES SERET TO NANCY CAMPBELL
DATE: SEPT. 25, 1817
DATE PER: OCT. 7, 1817
REFERENCE: C.A.

NAMES: SKIRVING SHELTON TO PEGGY ROBERTS
DATE: MAY 16, '
REFERENCE: T.H.M. VOL. 6, PG. 64

NAMES: ADAM SMITH TO JANE SMITH
DATE: DEC. 15, 1817
BONDSMAN: JAMES SMITH
DATE PER: DEC. 15, 1817
BY: JOHN BAYLESS, J.P.K.C.
REFERENCE: C.A; O.M.R. PG. 32

NAMES: ELI SMITH TO BETSY REYNOLDS
DATE: NOV. 29, 1817
DATE PER: NOV. 29, 1817
BY: JONATHAN AYRES, J.P.K.C.
REFERENCE: C.A; O.M.R. PG. 32

NAMES: ISAAC SMITH TO VENUS RAMSEY
DATE: MCH. 29, 1817
REFERENCE: T.H.M. VOL. 6, PG. 64

NAMES: WM. STEPHENS TO SUSANNA MILLER
DATE: SEPT. 15, 1817
DATE PER: SEPT. 18, 1817
BY: JOHN BAYLESS, J.P.K.C.
REFERENCE: C.A; O.M.R. PG. 30

NAMES: RICHARD STRINGFIELD TO CHRISTIAN GARRETT
DATE: MAR. 11, 1817
BONDSMAN: GIDEON REYNOLDS
REFERENCE: C.A; O.M.R. PG. 27; T.H.M. VOL. 6, PG. 64

NAMES: JOHN STUART TO NANCY GALLAHER
DATE: SEPT. 8, 1817
BY: WM. CAMPBELL
REFERENCE: C.A; O.M.R. PG. 29

NAMES: ROBERT STUART TO JENNY LAMPKINS
DATE: JANY. 21, 1817
REFERENCE: C.A; O.M.R. PG. 26

NAMES: THOMAS SWADLEY TO ANNE FANNEN
DATE: JULY 29, 1817
BONDSMAN: JOHN MILLER
DATE PER: JULY 30, 1817
BY: R. H. KING
WITNESS: CHAS. MCCLUNG
REFERENCE: C.A; O.M.R. PG. 28

NAMES: SAMUEL TAYLOR TO REBECCA JONES
DATE: JULY 5, 1817
BONDSMAN: DAVID CAMPBELL
DATE PER: JULY 10, 1817
BY: AMOS HARDIN, J.P.K.C.
REFERENCE: C.A; O.M.R. PG. 28; T.H.M. VOL. 6, PG. 64

Names: Sam'l Thompson to Margaret Havins
Date: Oct. 8, 1817
Date Per: Oct. 8, 1817
By: J. Anderson
Reference: C.A.

Names: Henry Troops (?) to Sally Payne
Date: Nov. 27, 1817
Reference: T.H.M. Vol. 6, Pg. 64

Names: Daly Walker to Drusilla Eppes
Date: Aug. 23, 1817
Reference: C.A; O.M.R. Pg. 29; T.H.M. Vol. 6, Pg. 64

Names: T. White to Elizabeth Hendson (?)
Date: July 13,
Reference: T.H.M. Vol. 6, Pg. 65

Names: Wm. Widener to Betsy Bayles
Date: Nov. 6, 1817
Bondsman: Charles Newman
Date Per: Nov. 6, 1817
By: S. Montgomery
Reference: C.A; O.M.R. Pg. 31; T.H.M. Vol. 6, Pg. 65

Names: Ignatius Wilson to Jane C. King
Date: Dec. 1, 1817
Date Per: Dec. 2, 1817
By: I. Anderson, M.G.
Reference: O.M.R. Pg. 32; T.H.M. Vol. 6, Pg. 65

Names: Henry Wicott to Susannah Foster
Date: July 11,
Reference: T.H.M. Vol. 6, Pg. 65

Names: Daniel Yarnell to Polly Scott
Date: Jany. 14, 1817
Bondsman: Charles Conway
Witness: James W. McClung, D. C.
Reference: C.A; T.H.M. Vol. 6, Pg. 95

1818

Names: John B. Abel to Rhoda Johnston
Date: Aug. 29, 1818
Date Per: Sept. 1, 1818
By: West Walker, M.G.
Reference: C.A; O.M.R. Pg. 36; T.H.M. Vol. 6, Pg. 65

Names: Ephraim Alexander to Lucy Parry
Date: Feby. 10, 1818
Bondsman: William Bowen
Reference: C.A; T.H.M. Vol. 6, Pg. 65

Names: James Anderson to Anne Ford
Date: Nov. 3, 1818
Date Per: Nov. 5, 1818
By: Peter Nance, J.P.K.C.
Reference: C.A; O.M.R. Pg. 38; T.H.M. Vol. 6, Pg. 65

Names: John Armstrong to Patsy McClain
Date: Nov. 3, 1818
Bondsman: James C. Luttrell
Reference: C.A; T.H.M. Vol. 6, Pg. 65

Names: John Ault to Amanda Hainey
Date: Sept. 19, 1818
Date Per: Sept. 20, 1818
By: John Haynie, M.G.
Reference: C.A; O.M.R. Pg. 37; T.H.M. Vol. 6, Pg. 65

Names: Charles Baker to Margaret Lowe
Date: Dec. 18,
Reference: T.H.M. Vol. 6, Pg. 65

Names: Daniel Bedsolt to Polly Martin
Date: Apr. 16, 1818
Date Per: Apr. 19, 1818
By: James A. Hain, J.P.K.C.
Reference: C.A; O.M.R. Pg. 34; T.H.M. Vol. 6, Pg. 65

Names: Joseph Bell to Betsy Widener
Date: Nov. 2[illegible],
Reference: T.H.M. Vol. 6, Pg. 65

Names: George Blang to Margaret Bell
Date: Nov. 4,
Reference: T.H.M. Vol. 6, Pg. 65

Names: Philadelphia Bledsoe to Mildred Kendrick
Date: Feby. 24, 1818
Date Per: Feby. 24, 1818
By: Thomas Hudiburg
Reference: C.A; O.M.R. Pg. 34

Names: Jesse Braden to Lila Vickers
Date: Aug. 28, 1818
Date Per: Aug. 31, 1818
By: T. A. Ramsey, J.P.K.C.
Reference: C.A; O.M.R. Pg. 36; T.H.M. Vol. 6, Pg. 65

NAMES: JOHN BRADLEY TO MELINDA DOWEL
DATE: FEBY. 17, 1818
BONDSMAN: ELIJAH DOWEL
DATE PER: FEBY. 24, 1818
BY: JOHN BAYLESS, J.P.K.C.
REFERENCE: C.A; O.M.R. PG. 34; T.H.M. VOL. 6, PG. 65

NAMES: ISAAC BRASHIERS TO ELIZABETH WILSON
DATE: OCT. 6, 1818
BY: R. COLE, J.P.K.C.
REFERENCE: C.A; O.M.R. PG. 37; T.H.M. VOL. 6, PG. 65

NAMES: JAMES BRAY TO MARY MARTIN
DATE: FEBY. 5, 1818
DATE PER: FEBY. 5, 1818
BY: T. H. NELSON
REFERENCE: C.A; O.M.R. PG. 33; T.H.M. VOL. 6, PG. 65

NAMES: JAMES BREESE TO SARAH LAREW
DATE: SEPT. 10, 1818
DATE PER: SEPT. 10, 1818
BY: JOHN HAYNIE, M.G.
REFERENCE: C.A; O.M.R. PG. 37

NAMES: THOMAS G. BRITT TO SALLY MCCLOUD
DATE: JUNE 13, 1818
DATE PER: JUNE 14, 1818
BY: JOHN BAYLESS, J.P.K.C.
REFERENCE: C.A; O.M.R. PG. 36; T.H.M. VOL. 6, PG. 65

NAMES: FRANCIS BROWN TO BETSY BROWING
DATE: DEC. 29, 1818
DATE PER: DEC. 31, 1818
BY: SAM'L SAMPLE, J.P.K.C.
REFERENCE: C.A; O.M.R. PG. 39; T.H.M. VOL. 6, PG. 65

NAMES: JOSHUA BROWN TO FRANCIS BLAKELY
DATE: SEPT. 27, 1818
DATE PER: SEPT. 30, 1818
BY: JOHN BAYLESS, J.P.K.C.
REFERENCE: C.A; O.M.R. PG. 37; T.H.M. VOL. 6, PG. 65

NAMES: WILLIAM BRYAN TO HESTER WALKER
DATE: AUG. 6
REFERENCE: T.H.M. VOL. 6, PG. 65

NAMES: JOHN CALDWELL TO POLLY/ANN RIGGLE
DATE: MAY 16, 1818
DATE PER: MAY 19, 1818
BY: WILLIAM B. CARNS, J.P.K.C.
REFERENCE: C.A; O.M.R. PG. 35

NAMES: CALEB CAPP TO PEGGY HOOD
DATE: JULY 18
REFERENCE: T.H.M. VOL. 6, PG. 65

NAMES: WILY CARROLL TO CLARENDA P ______
DATE: MAY 29
REFERENCE: T.H.M. VOL. 6, PG. 65

NAMES: ABNER DALE TO JANE MCDANIEL
DATE: APR. 19, 1818
REFERENCE: T.H.M. VOL. 6, PG. 65

NAMES: ALEXANDER DAVIS TO ANNY COURTNEY
DATE: APR. 1
REFERENCE: T.H.M. VOL. 6, PG. 65

NAMES: JAMES DUFFIELD TO KATY WHURLEY
DATE: OCT. 27, 1818
DATE PER: OCT. 29, 1818
BY: JOHN BAYLESS, J.P. K. C.
REFERENCE: C.A; O.M.R. PG. 38; T.H.M. VOL. 6, PG. 65

NAMES: THOMAS FARMON (?) TO BETSY SWADDLEY
DATE: OCT. 15
REFERENCE: T.H.M. VOL. 6, PG. 65

NAMES: JESSE FLOYD TO BETSY WILLIAMS
DATE: SEPT. 17, 1818
DATE PER: SEPT. 18, 1818
BY: S. MONTGOMERY
REFERENCE: C.A; O.M.R. PG. 37; T.H.M. VOL. 6, PG. 65

NAMES: BENJAMIN FORD TO RACHEL STEEL
DATE: OCT. 20
REFERENCE: T.H.M. VOL. 6, PG. 65

NAMES: JOHN H. FORMWALT TO NANCY COUNCIL
DATE: JANY. 29, 1818
DATE PER: JANY. 29, 1818
BY: T. H. NELSON
REFERENCE: C.A; O.M.R. PG. 33; T.H.M. VOL. 6, PG. 65

NAMES: GEORGE FORTNER TO POLLY LEWIS
DATE: MCH. 12
REFERENCE: T.H.M. VOL. 6, PG. 65

NAMES: GEORGE FRENCH TO BETSY HOWSER
DATE: JULY 31, 1818
DATE PER: AUG. 4, 1818
BY: JEREMIAH KING, M.G.
REFERENCE: C.A; O.M.R. PG. 36; T.H.M. VOL. 6, PG. 65

NAMES: SAM FROST TO NANCY CHILDRESS
DATE: DEC. 29
REFERENCE: T.H.M. VOL. 6, PG. 65

NAMES: ISAAC GENTRY TO ELIZABETH LEWIS
DATE: SEPT. 20, 1818
BY: R. COLE, J.P.K.C.
REFERENCE: C.A; O.M.R. PG. 37; T.H.M. VOL. 6, PG. 65

NAMES: WILLIAM GREEN TO ELIZA COATS MCGILTON
DATE: JANY. 29, 1818
DATE PER: JANY. 29, 1818
BY: THO. H. NELSON
REFERENCE: C.A; O.M.R. PG. 33; T.H.M. VOL. 6, PG. 65

NAMES: ABSALOM HALL TO NANCY BROWN
DATE: NOV. 26, 1818
DATE PER: NOV. 26, 1818
BY: JOHN BAYLESS, J.P.K.C.
REFERENCE: C.A; O.M.R. PG. 38.C.

NAMES: OBADIAH HALL TO SARAH BAYLES
DATE: APR. 29, 1818
BONDSMAN: EDMUND HALL
DATE PER: APR. 30, 1818
BY: WILLIAM B. CARNS, J.P.K.C.
REFERENCE: C.A; O.M.R. PG. 35; T.H.M. VOL. 6, PG. 65

NAMES: MEREDITH HARRIS TO CHARLOTTE TOBLER (?)
DATE: SEPT. 1
REFERENCE: T.H.M. VOL. 6, PG. 65

NAMES: BENJAMIN HASWELL TO FRANKY SIMMONS
DATE: FEBY. 16, 1818
BONDSMAN: ALEXANDER MURPHY
DATE PER: FEBY. 16, 1818
BY: JOHN MCCAMPBELL, J.P.K.C.
REFERENCE: C.A; O.M.R. PG. 33; T.H.M. VOL. 6, PG. 65

NAMES: WESLEY HANKINS TO PATSY FOSTER
DATE: MAY 23, 1818
BY: THOMAS WILKERSON, M.G.
REFERENCE: C.A; O.M.R. PG. 36; T.H.M. VOL. 6, PG. 65

NAMES: ISAAC HENDERSON TO JANE LEDGERWOOD
DATE: AUG. 6
REFERENCE: T.H.M. VOL. 6, PG. 65

NAMES: JOHN HOOD TO POLLY COUCH
DATE: OCT. 22, 1818
DATE PER: OCT. 26, 1818
BY: WM. MORRIS, J.P.K.C.
REFERENCE: C.A.

NAMES: JNO. HOOD TO POLLY COUCH (CARRICK?)
DATE: OCT. 22, 1818
DATE PER: OCT. 26, 1818
BY: WM. MORRIS, J.P.
REFERENCE: O.M.R. PG. 38; C.A.

NAMES: DAVID HOUSER TO KATY FRENCH
DATE: MAR. 30, 1818
DATE PER: APR. 1, 1818
BY: JEREMIAH KING, M.G.
REFERENCE: C.A; T.H.M. VOL. 6, PG. 65

NAMES: JOHN HOUSONG TO ROSANNAH RULE
DATE: DEC. 10, 1818
BY: JEREMIAH KING, M.G.
REFERENCE: C.A; O.M.R. PG. 39; T.H.M. VOL. 6, PG. 65

NAMES: WILLIS HUBBS TO BETSY RUTHERFORD
DATE: OCT. 1, 1818
DATE PER: OCT. 1, 1818
BY: JOHN THOMPSON, J.P.K.C.
REFERENCE: C.A; O.M.R. PG. 37; T.H.M. VOL. 6, PG. 65

NAMES: DANIEL HUFFAR TO SALLY QUALS
DATE: DEC. 11, 1818
BONDSMAN: JOHN CHUMLEY
DATE PER: " ABOUT TWO WEEKS LATER"
BY: THOMAS WILKERSON, M. G.
REFERENCE: C.A; O.M.R. PG. 39; T.H.M. VOL. 6, PG. 65

NAMES: JAMES HUMAN TO SARAH HOPPER
DATE: JAN. 22
REFERENCE: T.H.M. VOL. 6, PG. 65

NAMES: JOHN HUNTER TO PHEBE DOUGLAS
DATE: JANY. 26, 1818
DATE PER: JANY. 29, 1818
BY: A. S. MORRISON
REFERENCE: C.A; O.M.R. PG. 33; T.H.M. VOL. 6, PG. 65

NAMES: SOLOMON KAIN TO JANE LYONS
DATE: JUNE 13, 1818
BONDSMAN: JOHN MORROW
REFERENCE: C.A; T.H.M. VOL. 6, PG. 65

NAMES: Wm. KENNEDY TO MARY SCOTT
DATE: JANY. 6, 1818
DATE PER: JANY. 6, 1818
BY: T. H. NELSON
REFERENCE: O.M.R. PG. 33

NAMES: THO. KILLENSWORTH TO JANE HICKEY
DATE: JANY. 12, 1818
DATE PER: JANY. 12, 1818
BY: ___ WALKER, M. G.
REFERENCE: C.A; O.M.R. PG. 33; T.H.M. VOL. 6, PG. 65

NAMES: ANDREW KITTS TO NANCY McBRIDE
DATE: DEC. 17, 1818
DATE PER: DEC. 17, 1818
BY: R. HOUSTON
REFERENCE: C.A; O.M.R. PG. 39; T.H.M. VOL. 6, PG. 65

NAMES: PRYOR LEA TO MIRIAH KENNEDY
DATE: OCT. 6
REFERENCE: T.H.M. VOL. 6, PG. 65

NAMES: ARMBROSE LETT TO LOIS COUCH
DATE: AUG. 17
REFERENCE: T.H.M. VOL. 6, PG. 65

NAMES: WILLIAM LEWIS TO RHODY HIGDON
DATE: MCH. 12, 1818
REFERENCE: T.H.M. VOL. 6, PG. 65

NAMES: HENRY LILES TO NANCY RODGERS
DATE: NOV. 9, 1818
DATE PER: NOV. 10, 1818
BY: ABEL PATTY, J.P.K.C.
REFERENCE: C.A; O.M.R. PG. 38

NAMES: JOHN LINDSEY TO ELIZABETH BISHOP
DATE: APR. 9, 1818
DATE PER: APR. 9, 1818
BY: JOHN BAYLESS, J.P.K.C.
REFERENCE: C.A; O.M.R. PG. 34; T.H.M. VOL. 6, PG. 65

NAMES: JESSE LONES TO MARTHA DANIEL
DATE: NOV. 10
REFERENCE: T.H.M. VOL. 6, PG. 65

NAMES: SAM'L LOVE TO CHARLOTTE BELL
DATE: FEBY. 16, 1818
DATE PER: FEBY. 17, 1818
BY: R. HOUSTON, J.P.
REFERENCE: O.M.R. PG. 33; T.H.M. VOL. 6, PG. 65

NAMES: WILLIAM MAJOR TO SUSANNA SKAGGS
DATE: MAR. 16, 1818
DATE PER: MAR. 19, 1818
BY: JOHN BAYLESS, J.P.K.C.
REFERENCE: C.A; O.M.R. PG. 34; T.H.M. VOL. 6, PG. 66

NAMES: JAMES MARTIN TO BECKA LEDSINGER
DATE: SEPT. 24, 1818
BONDSMAN: JOHN MARTIN
REFERENCE: C.A; T.H.M. VOL. 6, PG. 66

NAMES: HUGH MASSEY TO ANNA HUMPHREY
DATE: AUG. 1, 1818
DATE PER: AUG. 4, 1818
BY: JEREMIAH KING, M.G.
REFERENCE: C.A; O.M.R. PG. 36; T.H.M. VOL. 6, PG. 66

NAMES: JOHN McBRIDE TO SUSAN CLINE
DATE: DEC. 3, 1818
DATE PER: DEC. 3, 1818
BY: WILLIAM SAWYERS, J.P.K.C.
REFERENCE: C.A; O.M.R. PG. 39; T.H.M. VOL. 6, PG. 66

NAMES: SAMUEL McCALEB TO JANE SMITH
DATE: MAY 5, 1818
DATE PER: MAY 5, 1818
BY: RD. H. KING
REFERENCE: C.A; O.M.R. PG. 35; T.H.M. VOL. 6, PG. 66

NAMES: DANIEL C. McCLAIN TO MALINDA YARNELL
DATE: DEC. 29, 1818
DATE PER: DEC. 29, 1818
BY: JONATHAN AYRES
REFERENCE: C.A; O.M.R. PG. 39; T.H.M. VOL. 6, PG. 65

NAMES: JAMES McCLAIN TO POLLY YARNELL
DATE: FEBY. 3, 1818
DATE PER: FEBY. 3, 1818
BY: JONATHAN AYRES, J.P.K.C.
REFERENCE: C.A; O.M.R. PG. 33; T.H.M. VOL. 6, PG. 66

NAMES: MATTHEW McCLUNG TO ELIZA J. MORGAN
DATE: JUNE 9, 1818
DATE PER: JUNE 9, 1818
BY: THO. H. NELSON
REFERENCE: O.M.R. PG. 36

NAMES: THOMAS McCONNEL TO KATHARINE HAVENS
DATE: JUNE 25, 1818
DATE PER: JUNE 25, 1818
BY: JOHN HAYNIE, M.G.
REFERENCE: C.A; O.M.R. PG. 36; T.H.M. VOL. 6, PG. 66

NAMES: ROBERT McKEE TO JANE BROOKS
DATE: MCH. 11,
REFERENCE: T.H.M.VOL. 6, PG. 66

NAMES: JAMES McMILLAN TO ALICE HOUSTON
DATE: JAN. 1
REFERENCE: T.H.M. VOL. 6, PG. 66

NAMES: WILLIAM McMUNN TO NANCY CRAWFORD
DATE: SEPT. 1
REFERENCE: T.H.M. VOL. 6, PG. 66

NAMES: GEO. McNUTT TO MELINDA HOUSTON
DATE: MAY 21, 1818
DATE PER: MAY 21, 1818
BY: T. H. NELSON
REFERENCE: O.M.R. PG. 35; T.H.M. VOL. 6, PG. 66

NAMES: ROBERT C. McREE TO JANE BROOKS
DATE: MAY 11, 1818
DATE PER: MAY 12, 1818
BY: T. H. NELSON
REFERENCE: C.A; O.M.R. PG. 35

NAMES: GEO. McWRIGHT TO BETSY McCATHRINESS
DATE: MAY 7, 1818
DATE PER: MAY 8, 1818
BY: JAMES A. HAIRE, J.P.
REFERENCE: O.M.R. PG. 35

NAMES: NICHOLAS MEDLOCK TO KATY McCALL
DATE: APR. 7, 1818
BONDSMAN: ANGUS McCALL
REFERENCE: C.A; T.H.M. VOL. 6, PG. 66

NAMES: PLEASANT MILLER TO RACHEL COX
DATE: FEBY. 16, 1818
DATE PER: FEBY. 25, 1818
BY: R. COLE, J.P.
REFERENCE: O.M.R. PG. 33; T.H.M. VOL. 6, PG. 66

NAMES: MOSES MILTEN TO HANNAH DAMEWOOD
DATE: SEPT. 30, 1818
DATE PER: OCT. 4, 1818
BY: WM. SAWYERS, J. P.
REFERENCE: O.M.R. PG. 37

NAMES: SOLOMON MISER TO MARY ANN FOUST
DATE: FEBY. 26, 1818
DATE PER: MAR. 1, 1818
BY: WM. SAWYERS, J.P.
REFERENCE: O.M.R. PG. 34

NAMES: WM. M. MONROW TO MILLY BISHOP
DATE: OCT. 23, 1818
BONDSMAN: WM. G. HOWELL
REFERENCE: C.A; T.H.M. VOL. 6, PG. 66

NAMES: SOLOMON MOSER TO MARY ANNE FOUSTE
DATE: FEBY. 26, 1818
DATE PER: MAR. 1, 1818
BY: WILLIAM SAWYERS, J.P.K.C.
REFERENCE: C.A; T.H.M. VOL. 6, PG. 66

NAMES: ADAM NISS TO CHRISTIANA GRAYBILL
DATE: DEC. 1, 1818
DATE PER: DEC. 1, 1818
BY: ROBT. LINDSAY, J.P.K.C.
REFERENCE: C.A; O.M.R. PG. 39; T.H.M. VOL. 6, PG. 66

NAMES: ABRAHAM OWENS TO LORY ROLIN
DATE: APR. 18, 1818
BY: JAMES C. LUTTRELL, J.P.K.C.
REFERENCE: C.A; O.M.R. PG. 35; T.H.M. VOL. 6, PG. 66

NAMES: JOHN OWENS TO SARAH GIBBS
DATE: NOV. 21, 1818
BONDSMAN: RANDAL KIDD
DATE PER: DEC. 25, 1818
BY: JEREMIAH KING, M. G.
REFERENCE: C.A; O.M.R. PG. 38; T.H.M. VOL. 6, PG. 66

NAMES: JESSE PARKER TO RHODY ALLEY
DATE: MAY 12, 1818
DATE PER: MAY 12, 1818
BY: WM. ALLDREDGE, J.P.K.C.
REFERENCE: C.A; O.M.R. PG. 35; T.H.M. VOL. 6, PG. 66

NAMES: WILLIAM PARR TO BETSY MILTEBARGER
DATE: OCT. 16, 1818
DATE PER: OCT. 20, 1818
BY: WILLIAM SAWYERS, J.P.K.C.
REFERENCE: C.A; O.M.R. PG. 36; T.H.M. VOL. 6, PG. 66

NAMES: WILLIAM PETERSON TO JANE KELLY
DATE: DEC. 9
REFERENCE: T.H.M. VOL. 6, PG. 66

NAMES: JONATHAN FICKLE TO BETSY CUNNINGHAM
DATE: JUNE 22, 1818
DATE PER: JUNE 23, 1818
BY: S. MONTGOMERY
REFERENCE: C.A; O.M.R. PG. 36; T.H.M. VOL. 6, PG. 65

NAMES: JOSEPH PLUMLEY TO BETSY PERRY
DATE: DEC. 31, 1818
BONDSMAN: JESSE PERRY
DATE PER: DEC. 31, 1818
BY: S. MONTGOMERY
REFERENCE: C.A; O.M.R. PG. 39

NAMES: LEWIS RHODES TO NANCY FRY
DATE: APR. 28, 1818
DATE PER: APR. 28, 1818
BY: JOHN HAYNIE, M.G.
REFERENCE: C.A; O.M.R. PG. 35; T.H.M. VOL. 6, PG. 66

NAMES: JOHN RICHISON TO RHODY LUTTRELL
DATE: JULY 14, 1818
BONDSMAN: J. L. YATES
REFERENCE: C.A; T.H.M. VOL. 6, PG. 66

NAMES: JAMES ROBERTS TO ELIZABETH LUTTRELL
DATE: DEC. 31, 1818
BONDSMAN: WM. LUTTRELL
REFERENCE: C.A.

NAMES: JAMES ROBERTS TO ELIZABETH LUTTRELL
DATE: DEC. 31, 1818
DATE PER: DEC. ____, 1818
BY: THOS. WILKERSON, M. G.
REFERENCE: O.M.R. PG. 217; T.H.M. VOL. 6, PG. 66

NAMES: JOZADAK ROBERTS TO MARY LUTTRELL
DATE: OCT. 22, 1818
BONDSMAN: WILLIAM LUTTRELL
DATE PER: OCT. 22, 1818
BY: JOHN HAYNIE
REFERENCE: C.A; O.M.R. PG. 38; T.H.M. VOL. 6, PG. 66

NAMES: JOHN RUSSELL TO SALLY SCAVITT
DATE: NOV. 26, 1818
DATE PER: NOV. 26, 1818
BY: THO. H. NELSON, M. G. OF PRES. CHURCH
REFERENCE: C.A; O.M.R. PG. 38; T.H.M. VOL. 6, PG. 66

NAMES: JNO. N. SCOTT TO BETSY M. WHITE
DATE: NOV. 26, 1818
DATE PER: NOV. 25, 1818
REFERENCE: O.M.R. PG. 38

NAMES: LEWIS SHELL TO NANCY SOLUST
DATE: MAR. 7, 1818
DATE PER: MAR. 8, 1818
BY: JOHN THOMPSON, J.P.K.C.
REFERENCE: C.A; O.M.R. PG. 34

NAMES: DAVID SMITH TO PEGGY MYNATT
DATE: JUNE 23, 1818
BONDSMAN: WILY CAROL
REFERENCE: C.A.

NAMES: ROBERT STEPHENSON TO UNICE MOOE
DATE: APR. 13, 1818
DATE PER: APR. 14, 1818
BY: JOHN BAYLESS, J.P.K.C.
REFERENCE: C.A; O.M.R. PG. 34; T.H.M. VOL. 6, PG. 65

NAMES: JOHNSTON SUMMERS TO SALLY WILLIAMS
DATE: NOV. 28, 1818
BONDSMAN: JAS. A. THORNTON
DATE: NOV. 29, 1818
BY: SAM'L SAMPLE, J.P.K.C.
REFERENCE: C.A; T.H.M. VOL. 6, PG. 66

NAMES: JOHN TEEL TO REBECCA HELMS
DATE: AUG. 6, 1818
BONDSMAN: SAMUEL TEEL
REFERENCE: C.A.

NAMES: HARVEY THOMPSON TO NANCY MCCAMMON
DATE: MAY 21, 1818
DATE PER: MAY 21, 1818
BY: ROBT. LINDSAY, J.P.K.C.
REFERENCE: C.A; O.M.R. PG. 35; T.H.M. VOL. 6, PG. 66

NAMES: SAMUEL THOMPSON TO ELIZABETH BROOK
DATE: MAY 13
REFERENCE: T.H.M. VOL. 6, PG. 66

NAMES: JOHN THUERRITZ (?) TO TABITHA CLAYTON
DATE: JULY 29
REFERENCE: T.H.M. VOL. 6, PG. 66

NAMES: SAMUEL VANCE TO ELIZABETH BROCK
DATE: MAY 13,
REFERENCE: T.H.M. VOL. 6, PG. 66

NAMES: WILLIAM S. WATSON TO SARAH HOUK
DATE: JUNE 22, 1818
DATE PER: JUNE 24, 1818
BY: JOHN HAYNIE, M. G.
REFERENCE: C.A; O.M.R. PG. 36; T.H.M. VOL. 6, PG. 66

NAMES: JOHN WHEELER TO SARAH SANDERS
DATE: APR. 2, 1818
BONDSMAN: SAMUEL WHEELER
DATE PER: APR. 2, 1818
BY: JEREMIAH KING, M. G.
REFERENCE: C.A; O.M.R. PG. 34; T.H.M. VOL. 6, PG. 66

NAMES: JOHN N. WHITE TO BETSY M. WHITE
DATE: NOV. 27, 1818
BONDSMAN: SPENCER JARNAGIN
REFERENCE: C.A.

NAMES: GEORGE WHITTLE TO NANCY HUFFAKER
DATE: MAR. 23, 1818
DATE PER: MAR. 24, 1818
BY: NICHOLAS NORWOOD, M. G.
REFERENCE: C. A; O.M.R. PG. 34

NAMES: MATHIAS WIDENER TO HANNA SHARP
DATE: SEPT. 16, 1818
DATE PER: SEPT. 20, 1818
BY: WILLIAM SAWYERS, J.P.K.C.
REFERENCE: C.A; O.M.R. PG. 37

NAMES: JAMES WITT TO IBBY REED
DATE: APR. 20, 1818
BONDSMAN: LEWIS GAMMON
REFERENCE: C.A; T.H.M. VOL. 6, PG. 66

NAMES: GEORGE M. WRIGHT TO BETSY MCCATHRINE
DATE: MAY 7, 1818
DATE PER: MAY 8, 1818
BY: JAMES A. HAIRSE
REFERENCE: C.A.

NAMES: MOSES WRITTEN TO HANNAH DAMEWOOD
DATE: SEPT. 30, 1818
DATE PER: OCT. 4, 1818
BY: WILLIAM SAWYERS, J.P.K.C.
REFERENCE: C.A.

1819

NAMES: AARON ARMSTRONG TO ELIZABETH BOUNDS
DATE: FEBY. 3, 1819
BONDSMAN: MOSES ARMSTRONG
DATE PER: FEBY. 4, 1819
BY: ALEXANDER MCMILLAN
REFERENCE: C.A; O.M.R. PG. 40; T.H.M. VOL. 6, PG. 66

NAMES: GEORGE ATKIN TO EMILY THATCHER
DATE: JUNE 29, 1819
BONDSMAN: JOHN SUTHERLAND
REFERENCE: C.A.

NAMES: JESSE AYRES TO ELIZABETH REED
DATE: NOV. 3, 1819
DATE PER: NOV. 5, 1819
BY: WM. MORRIS, J.P.K.C.
REFERENCE: C.A.

NAMES: ROBT. H. BARNWELL TO JANE BARNWELL
DATE: OCT. 7, 1819
BONDSMAN: GEORGE SHETTERLY
DATE PER: OCT. 7, 1819
BY: JOHN HAYNIE
REFERENCE: C.A; O.M.R. PG. 46; T.H.M. VOL. 6, PG. 66

NAMES: WM. BERRY TO RUTHY WHITE
DATE: SEPT. 27, 1819
BONDSMAN: WILLIAM PRICE
DATE PER: SEPT. 27, 1819
BY: WM. A. MCCAMPBELL, ESQ.
WITNESSES: WM. C. MYNATT
REFERENCE: C.A; O.M.R. PG. 45; T.H.M. VOL. 6, PG. 66

NAMES: WILLIAM BERRY TO SALLY SIMPSON
DATE: MAR. 17, 1819
BONDSMAN: SANFORD SIMPSON
REFERENCE: C.A; T.H.M. VOL. 6, PG. 66

NAMES: ACHILLES BRADLEY TO NANCY DOWELL
DATE: JUNE 3, 1819
BONDSMAN: JOHN BRADLEY
DATE PER: JUNE 3, 1819
BY: JOHN BAYLESS, J.P.K.C.
REFERENCE: C.A; O.M.R. PG. 43; T.H.M. VOL. 6, PG. 66

NAMES: JAS. A. CALDWELL TO MARY MCCAMPBELL
DATE: MAR. 11, 1819
DATE PER: MAR. 13, 1819
BY: JNO. MCCAMPBELL, V.D.M.
REFERENCE: O.M.R. PG. 41; T.H.M. VOL. 6, PG. 66

NAMES: JESSE CALDWELL TO MARY MCCAMPBELL
DATE: MAR. 11, 1819
DATE PER: MAR. 18, 1819
REFERENCE: C.A.

NAMES: JOHN CARSON TO CYNTHIA SPILMAN
DATE: AUG. 4, 1819
BONDSMAN: CHRISTOPHER SPILMAN
REFERENCE: C.A.

NAMES: JNO. CARSON TO CYNTHIA SPILMAN
DATE: AUG. 4, 1819
DATE PER: AUG. 5, 1819
BY: JEREMIAH KING, M. G.
REFERENCE: O.M.R. PG. 44; T.H.M. VOL. 6, PG. 66

NAMES: AMOS CARTER TO NANCY LUTTRELL
DATE: MAR. 11, 1819
BONDSMAN: JEHADAK ROBERTS
REFERENCE: C.A; T.H.M. VOL. 6, PG. 66

NAMES: JOHN L. CHAPMAN TO ELEANOR WARNICK
DATE: FEBY. 17, 1819
DATE PER: FEBY. 17, 1819
BY: JOHN HAYNIE, M. G., METHODIST CH.
REFERENCE: C.A; O.M.R. PG. 41; T.H.M. VOL. 6, PG. 66

NAMES: RICHARD CHILDRESS TO BECKA WHITE
DATE: MAY 21, 1819
DATE PER: MAY 25, 1819
BY: JAMES I. HAISE, J.P.K.C.
REFERENCE: C.A; O.M.R. PG. 43; T.H.M. VOL. 6, BG. 66

NAMES: BOSTON CLAPP TO POLLY TANNYHILL
DATE: APR. 13, 1819
DATE PER: APR. 15, 1819
BY: JOHN THOMPSON, J.P.K.C.
REFERENCE: C.A; OLM.R. PG. 42; T.H.M. VOL. 6, PG. 66

NAMES: JAMES COKER TO POLLY MCCAMMON
DATE: OCT. 27, 1819
DATE PER: OCT. 29, 1819
BY: PETER NANCE, J.P.K.C.
REFERENCE: C.A; O.M.R. PG. 46; T.H.M. VOL. 6, PG. 66

NAMES: SAMUEL CONNER TO PATSY HICKEY
DATE: JANY. 12, 1819
BONDSMAN: JOSIAH ARMSTRONG
DATE PER: JANY. 14, 1819
BY: WM. ALLDREDGE, J.P.K.C.
REFERENCE: C.A; T.H.M. VOL. 6, PG. 66

NAMES: SAMUEL COURTNEY TO SUSAN LUTTRELL
DATE: JULY 5, 1819
BONDSMAN: JOHN LUTTRELL
REFERENCE: C.A; T.H.M. VOL. 6, PG. 66

NAMES: JONATHAN COX TO MARY ANN GALLIHER
DATE: OCT. 25, 1819
DATE PER: NOV. 4, 1819
BY: AMOS HARDIN, J.P.K.C.
REFERENCE: C.A; O.M.R. PG. 46; T.H.M. VOL. 6, PG. 66

NAMES: PLEASANT CREW TO MARGARET LAYTON
DATE: JUNE 7, 1819
DATE PER: JUNE 7, 1819
BY: JOHN HAYNIE
REFERENCE: C.A; O.M.R. PG. 43; T.H.M. VOL. 6, PG. 66

NAMES: WALTER CRUSE TO LAVIN TUCKER
DATE: FEBY. 5, 1819
BONDSMAN: JAMES COKER
DATE PER: FEBY. 5, 1819
BY: JAS. HEISE, J.P.K.C.
REFERENCE: C.A; O.M.R. PG. 40; T.H.M. VOL. 6, PG. 66

NAMES: ROBERT DAVIS TO MARTHA HALEY
DATE: MAR. 17, 1819
DATE PER: MAR. 17, 1819
BY: THO. H. NELSON
REFERENCE: C.A; O.M.R. PG. 41; T.H.M. VOL. 6, PG. 66

NAMES: WILLIAM DENNIS TO RUTH PETTIE
DATE: FEB. 29,
REFERENCE: T.H.M. VOL. 6, PG. 67

NAMES: ELISHA DESAIN TO SALLY JOHNSTON
DATE: DEC. 15, 1819
BONDSMAN: JAMES BADGETT
BY: PETER NANCE, J.P.K.C.
REFERENCE: C.A; O.M.R. PG. 47; T.H.M. VOL. 6, PG. 67

NAMES: WM. DUNLAP TO BETSY SWAGERTY
DATE: SEPT. 17, 1819
DATE PER: SEPT. 22, 1819
BY: S. MONTGOMERY
REFERENCE: C.A; O.M.R. PG. 45; T.H.M. VOL. 6, PG. 67

NAMES: JOSEPH EVANS TO HILA HOGGETT
DATE: AUG. 10, 1819
DATE PER: AUG. AUG. 12, 1819
BY: SAM'L SAMPLE, J.P.K.C.
REFERENCE: C.A; O.M.R. PG. 44; T.H.M. VOL. 6, PG. 67

NAMES: SAMUEL EVANS TO SARAH STEEL
DATE: MAR. 17, 1819
DATE PER: MAR. 18, 1819
BY: JOHN MCCAMPBELL, J.P.K.C.
REFERENCE: C.A; O.M.R. PG. 41

NAMES: WILLIAM EVANS, TO MARY EVANS
DATE: MAR. 30, 1819
DATE PER: APR. 1, 1819
BY: JOHN MCCAMPBELL
REFERENCE: C.A; O.M.R. PG. 42; T.H.M. VOL. 6, PG. 67

NAMES: SYLVINUS EVERETT TO MARY DOUGLASS
DATE: AUG. 19, 1819
DATE PER: AUG. 19, 1819
BY: WM. A. CAMPBELL
REFERENCE: C.A; O.M.R. PG. 45; T.H.M. VOL. 6, PG. 67

NAMES: SAMUEL EWING TO SARAH STEEL
DATE: MCH. 17,
REFERENCE: T.H.M. VOL. 6, PG. 67

NAMES: HENLAND FIKE TO JANE CAMPBELL
DATE: JULY 27, 1819
DATE PER: JULY 29, 1819
BY: ROBT. TUNNELL, J.P.K.C.
REFERENCE: C.A; O.M.R. PG. 44; T.H.M. VOL. 6, PG. 67

NAMES: STEPHEN FORGUSON TO ANNE PICKLE
DATE: APR. 5, 1819
DATE PER: APR. 6, 1819
BY: SAM'L SAMPLE, J.P.K.C.
REFERENCE: C.A; O.M.R. PG. 42

NAMES: JOHN FORMAN TO JANE SWADLEY (OR FANNON)
DATE: JULY 27,
REFERENCE: T.H.M. VOL. 6, PG. 67

NAMES: WM. FULTON TO PEGGY SAMPLES
DATE: AUG. 2, 1819 - DATE PER: AUG. 2, 1819
BY: ALEX. MCMILLAN, J.P.K.C.
REFERENCE: C.A; O.M.R. PG. 44; T.H.M. VOL. 6, PG. 67

NAMES: PARNICK GEORGE TO POLLY MCPHERRIN
DATE: DEC. 4, 1819
BONDSMAN: JOHN WARD
DATE PER: DEC. 2, 1819
BY: JOHN BAYLESS, J.P.K.C.
REFERENCE: C.A; O.M.R. PG. 47; T.H.M. VOL. 6, PG. 67

NAMES: JOHN GIBBS TO SUSANNAH GEORGE
DATE: JUNE 19, 1819
BONDSMAN: HENRY GRAVES
DATE PER: JUNE 20, 1819
BY: JOHN BAYLESS, J.P.K.C.
REFERENCE: C.A; O.M.R. PG. 43; T.H.M. VOL. 6, PG. 67

NAMES: ROBERT GILLESPIE TO MARY G. KING
DATE: JUNE 16, 1819
DATE PER: JUNE 17, 1819
BY: ANDW. S. MORRISON
REFERENCE: C.A; O.M.R. PG. 43; T.H.M. VOL. 6, PG. 67

NAMES: JAMES GILMORE TO BERSHEBA FORGUSON
DATE: JUNE 2, 1819
BONDSMAN: JAMES WILSON
REFERENCE: C.A.

NAMES: JOHN GILMORE TO BETSY FERGUSON
DATE: JUNE 20,
REFERENCE: T.H.M. VOL. 6, PG. 67

NAMES: HARVEY GLASS TO REBECCA PAUL
DATE: MAR. 2, 1819
DATE PER: MAR. 4, 1819
BY: RD. H. KING
REFERENCE: C.A; O.M.R. PG. 41; T.H.M. VOL. 6, PG. 67

NAMES: LEWIS GLASS TO SALLY SIMPSON
DATE: OCT. 19, 1819
BONDSMAN: WILSON WHITE
DATE PER: A SHORT TIME AFTER THE DATE OF LICENSE.
BY: THOMAS WILKERSON, M. E. CHURCH
REFERENCE: C.A; O.M.R. PG. 46; T.H.M. VOL. 6, PG. 67

NAMES: JOHN GOUND TO ELIZA LOW
DATE: DEC. 15, 1819
DATE PER: DEC. 16, 1819
BY: RD. H. KING
REFERENCE: C.A; O.M.R. PG. 47; T.H.M. VOL. 6, PG. 67

NAMES: HENRY GRAVES TO BETSY MILLER
DATE: JULY 5, 1819
REFERENCE: C.A.

NAMES: HENRY GRAVES TO BETSY MILLER
DATE: JULY 5, 1819
DATE PER: JULY 5, 1819
BY: WM. SAWYERS, J.P.
REFERENCE: O.M.R. PG. 43; T.H.M. VOL. 6, PG. 67

NAMES: SAMUEL GREEN TO PATSY FORGUSON
DATE: OCT. 4, 1819
BY: S. MONTGOMERY
DATE PER: OCT. 7, 1819
REFERENCE: C.A; O.M.R. PG. 45; T.H.M. VOL. 6, PG. 67

NAMES: HENRY HABRUM (?) TO ALEY SCARBORO
DATE: APR. 5, 1819
DATE PER: APR. 6, 1819
BY: AMOS HARDIN, J.P.K.C.
REFERENCE: O.A; O.M.R. PG. 42 & 48

NAMES: CHARLES HACKNEY TO ELIZABETH LEVI
DATE: MAY 18
REFERENCE: T.H.M. VOL. 6, PG. 67

NAMES: ARCHIBALD HAINEY TO CATHERINE BROWN
DATE: OCT. 2, 1819
REFERENCE: T.H.M. VOL. 6, PG. 67

NAMES: JOHN W. HANSWARD TO NANCY HANSWARD
DATE: APR. 15, 1819
BY: JOHN BAYLESS, J.P.K.C.
REFERENCE: C.A; O.M.R. PG. 42; T.H.M. VOL. 6, PG. 67

NAMES: PLEDGE HARBISON TO POLLY GRAVES
DATE: FEBY. 10, 1819
BONDSMAN: WM. RUSSELL
DATE PER: FEBY. 12, 1819
BY: RD. H. KING
REFERENCE: O.A; O.M.R. PG. 40; T.H.M. VOL. 6, PG. 67

NAMES: DANIEL HARMON (HAMER?) TO POLLY MCCOLOUGH
DATE: APR. 12,
REFERENCE: T.H.M. VOL. 6, PG. 67

NAMES: ARCHIBALD HARRIS TO CATHARINE BROWN
DATE: OCT. 28, 1819
DATE PER: OCT. 28, 1819
BY: JOHN HAYNIE
REFERENCE: O.A; O.M.R. PG. 46

NAMES: BENJ. HAZELWOOD TO MARY REED
DATE: JANY. 1, 1819
BONDSMAN: JNO. REAGAN
DATE PER: JANY. 3, 1819
BY: PETER NANCE, J.P.K.C.
REFERENCE: O.A; O.M.R. PG. 39; T.H.M. VOL. 6, PG. 67

NAMES: CORNELIUS HICKEY TO CATHARINE KEITH
DATE: JULY 6, 1819
BONDSMAN: DAVID THOMPSON
REFERENCE: O.A; T.H.M. VOL. 6, PG. 67

NAMES: JOSEPH HICKEY TO ABIGAIL JULIAN
DATE: NOV. 9, 1819
DATE PER: NOV. 11, 1819
BY: WM. ALLDREDGE, J.P.K.C.
REFERENCE: C.A; O.M.R. PG. 46; T.H.M. VOL. 6, PG. 67

NAMES: HENRY M. HILL TO NANCY IZZARD
DATE: AUG. 28, 1819
DATE PER: AUG. 29, 1819
BY: JOHN GASS, J.P.K.C.
REFERENCE: O.A; O.M.R. PG. 45; T.H.M. VOL. 6, PG. 67

NAMES: JOHN HILL TO SALLY H. DAVIS
DATE: MAR. 30, 1819
DATE PER: MAR. 30, 1819
BY: JOHN HAYNIE, M. G.
REFERENCE: O.A; O.M.R. PG. 42; T.H.M. VOL. 6, PG. 67

NAMES: THOS. C. HINDMAN TO SALLY HOLT
DATE: JANY. 21, 1819
DATE PER: JANY. 25; 1819
BY: RD. H. KING, T.P.C.
REFERENCE: O.A; O.M.R. PG. 40; T.H.M. VOL. 6, PG. 67

NAMES: DANIEL HORTON TO POLLY NEEDHAM
DATE: AUG. 25, 1819
BONDSMAN: JONATHAN PICKEL
REFERENCE: O.A.

NAMES: DANIEL HORTON TO POLLY NEEDHAM
DATE: AUG. 25, 1819
DATE PER: AUG. 26, 1819
BY: F. A. RAMSEY, J.P.
REFERENCE: O.M.R. PG. 45; T.H.M. VOL. 6, PG. 67

NAMES: JAMES HOWARD TO LUCY CHUMNEY
DATE: MAR. 27, 1819
BONDSMAN: ROBERT CAMPBELL
DATE PER: APR. 4, 1819
BY: WM. CAMPBELL
REFERENCE: O.A; O.M.R. PG. 42; T.H.M. VOL. 6, PG. 67

NAMES: THOMAS HOWARD TO POLLY LUMPKIN
DATE: SEPT. 15, 1819
BONDSMAN: RICHARD LUMPKIN
REFERENCE: O.A; T.H.M. VOL. 6, PG. 67

NAMES: TRUMAN HURDLE TO SALLY NELSON
DATE: OCT. 13, 1819
BY: THOS. H. NELSON
REFERENCE: O.A; O.M.R. PG. 46; T.H.M. VOL. 6, PG. 67

Names: Uriah Jackson to Polly Tumblin
Date: July 27, 1819
Bondsman: Robert Fristoe
Reference: C.A; T.H.M. Vol. 6, Pg. 67

Names: Spencer Jarnagan to Clarissa H. Montgomery
Date: Dec. 23, 1819
Date Per: Dec. 23, 1819
By: Tho. H. Nelson
Reference: C.A; O.M.R. Pg. 47; T.H.M. Vol. 6, Pg. 67

Names: John Jett to Elizabeth Cox
Date: Nov. 23, 1819
Date Per: Nov. 23, 1819
By: John Gass, J.P.K.C.
Reference: C.A; O.M.R. Pg. 47; T.H.M. Vol. 6, Pg. 67

Names: Benjamin Johnston to Jemima Edington
Date: Dec. 9, 1819
By: Peter Nance, J.P.K.C.
Reference: C.A; O.M.R. Pg. 47; T.H.M. Vol. 6, Pg. 67

Names: Joseph Johnston to Betsy Crew
Date: Nov. 25, 1819
Date Per: Nov. 25, 1819
By: James Dixon, E.M.E.C.
Reference: C.A; O.M.R. Pg. 47; T.H.M. Vol. 6, Pg. 67

Names: Waltham Kelly to Nancy Lones
Date: Jan. 10,
Reference: T.H.M. Vol. 6, Pg. 67

Names: James Kidd to Franky Childress
Date: Jany. 6, 1819
Bondsman: James Childress
Date Per: Jany. 9, 1819
By: Peter Nance, J.P.K.C.
Reference: C.A; O.M.R. Pg. 40; T.H.M. Vol. 6, Pg. 67

Names: Solomon H. King to Nancy Lawson
Date: Feby. 6, 1819
Bondsman: Wm. Y. King
Reference: C.A; T.H.M. Vol. 6, Pg. 67

Names: James Leak to Mary Dowler
Date: Jany. 16, 1819
Date Per: Jany. 17, 1819
By: Alexander McMillan, J.P.K.C.
Reference: C.A; O.M.R. Pg. 40; T.H.M. Vol. 6, Pg. 67

Names: Mordecai Lincoln to Sophia Heiskell
Date: Apr. 15, 1819
Date:Per: Apr. 15, 1819
By: Tho. H. Nelson
Reference: O.M.R. Pg. 42; T.H.M. Vol. 6, Pg. 67

Names: Henry Lonas to Bethany Whiteman
Date: Dec. 23, 1819
Date Per: Dec. 23, 1819
By: John Haynie
Reference: C.A; O.M.R. Pg. 48; T.H.M. Vol. 6, Pg. 67

Names: John Low to Jane Mowery
Date: Jany. 4, 1819
Bondsman: Martin Low
Date Per: Jany. 7, 1819
By: Rd. H. King, P.P.C.
Reference: C.A; O.M.R. Pg. 39; T.H.M. Vol. 6, Pg. 67

Names: Lewis Luttrell to Patsy Gibbs
Date: Feby. 11, 1819
Bondsman: J. Calloway
Date Per: Feby. 11, 1819
By: John Bayless, J.P.K.C.
Reference: C.A; O.M.R. Pg. 40

Names: Thomas B. Marley to Elizabeth Meak
Date: Dec. 14, 1819
Date Per: Dec. 16, 1819
By: John McCampbell
Reference: C.A; O.M.R. Pg. 47

Names: James McCampbell to Betsy Ingram
Date: Mar. 30, 1819
Date Per: Apr. 1, 1819
By: John McCampbell, V.D.M.
Reference: C.A; O.M.R. Pg. 42; T.H.M. Vol. 6, Pg. 67

Names: Robert W. McCary to Polly Carns
Date: June 22, 1819
Date Per: June 22, 1819
By: Robt. Lindsay, J.P.K.C.
Reference: C.A; O.M.R. Pg. 43

Names: Matthew McCown to Elizabeth Luttrell
Date: Sept. 20, 1819
Date Per: Sept. 23, 1819
By: Robert Tunnell, J.P.K.C.
Reference: C.A; O.M.R. Pg. 45

Names: Aaron McKean _ Caty Houser
Date: Sept. 25,
Reference: T. H. M. Vol. 6, Pg. 67

Names: Edward McKean to Elizabeth Mapes
Date: Aug. 3, 1819
Date Per: Aug. 3, 1819
By: Robert Tunnell, J.P.K.C.
Reference: C.A; O.M.R. Pg. 44; T.H.M. Vol. 6, Pg. 67

Names: Frederic Michaels to Polly Bowman
Date: Mar. 24, 1819
Bondsman: Allen Jack +
Date Per: Mar. 25, 1819
By: F. A. Ramsey, J.P.K.C.
Reference: C.A; O.M.R. Pg. 41; T.H.M. Vol. 6, Pg. 67

Names: Thomas Monday to Elizabeth Meek
Date: Dec. 14.
Reference: T. H.M. Vol. 6, Pg. 67

Names: George Morrow to Nancy Carter
Date: Apr. 7, 1819
Bondsman: James Boyd
Date Per: Apr. 7, 1819
By: Tho. H. Nelson
Reference: C.A; O.M.R. Pg. 42; T.H.M. Vol. 6, Pg. 67

Names: John Morrow to Juda Bass
Date: July 15, 1819
Date Per: July 15, 1819
By: Thos. H. Nelson
Reference: C.A; O.M.R. Pg. 44

Names: Samuel Mowery to Jane McLoud
Date: Mar. 11, 1819
Bondsman: Thomas Galbreath
Reference: C.A; T.H.M. Vol. 6, Pg. 67

Names: Lewis Mowry to Betsy Lissee
Date: Mch. 3, 1819
Reference: T.H.M. Vol. 6, Pg. 67

Names: Archibald Murphy to Polly L. Monday
Date: Nov. 13, 1819
Date Per: Nov. 13, 1819
By: John Haynie
Reference: C.A; O.M.R. Pg. 47; T.H.M. Vol. 6, Pg. 67

Names: Doctor W. Nelson to Sally Bright
Date: July 26, 1819
Date Per: July 29, 1819
By: John Bayless, J.P.K.C.
Reference: C.A; O.M.R. Pg. 44; T.H.M. Vol. 6, Pg. 68

Names: John Newman to Polly Levi
Date: Sept. 9, 1819
Bondsman: Jesse Newman
Reference: C.A; T.H.M. Vol. 6, Pg. 68

Names: John Owen to Debby Burnwott
Date: Oct. 27, 1819
Bondsman: Buckner Issell
Date Per: Oct. 28, 1819
By: R. Cole, J.P.K.C.
Witness: Will Swan
Reference: C.A; O.M.R. Pg. 46; T. H.M. Vol. 6, Pg. 68

Names: Wm. Packett to Katy Longwith
Date: July 10, 1819
Bondsman: Jazedack Roberts
Reference: C.A; T.H.M. Vol. 6, Pg. 67

Names: Robert Palmer to Mary Green
Date: Oct. 4, 1819
Date Per: Oct. 14, 1819
By: S. Montgomery
Reference: C.A; O.M.R. Pg. 46; T.H.M. Vol. 6, Pg. 68

Names: Joseph Perry to Patsy McLamore
Date: Aug. 12, 1819
Date Per: Aug. 13, 1819
By: Sam'l Montgomery
Reference: C.A; O.M.R. Pg. 44

Names: James Pow to Anne Beal
Date: Oct. 25, 1819
Nondsman: Alexander Moorhead
Witness: Chas. McClung
Reference: C. A; T.H.M. Vol. 6, Pg. 68

Names: John Rhoads to Polly Cox
Date: Dec. 28, 1819
Date Per: Dec. 29, 1819
By: John Cass, J.P.K.C.
Reference: C.A; O.M.R. Pg. 48; T.H.M. Vol. 6, Pg. 68

Names: Amos Roberts to Nancy Luttrell
Date: Mar. 11, 1819
By: Thomas Wilkerson, M. G.
Reference: C.A; O.M.R. Pg. 41

NAMES: JAMES ROBERTS TO ELIZABETH LUTTRELL
DATE: DEC. 31, 1819 (?)
DATE PER: DEC. 31, 1819 (?)
BY: THOS. WILKERSON
REFERENCE: O.M.R. PG. 48

NAMES: WILLIAM ROBERTS TO MARTHA SAMPLE
DATE: MAR. 4, 1819
BONDSMAN: WILLIAM LUTTRELL
BY: THOMAS WILKERSON, M. G.
REFERENCE: C.A; O.M.R. PG. 41; T.H.M. VOL. 6, PG. 68

NAMES: ANDREW RODGERS TO SALLY KIRKLAND
DATE: AUG. 24, 1819
BONDSMAN: GEO. W. KIRKLAND
REFERENCE: C.A; T.H.M. VOL. 6, PG. 68

NAMES: JOHN RODGERS TO REBECCA PATTON
DATE: DEC. 23, 1819
BONDSMAN: THOS. RODGERS
DATE PER: DEC. 23, 1819
BY: F. A. RAMSEY, J.P.K.C.
REFERENCE: C.A; O.M.R. PG. 48; T. H.M. VOL. 6, PG. 68

NAMES: REUBEN RUSSELL TO DOCAY OANS
DATE: SEPT. 7,
REFERENCE: T.H.M. VOL. 6, PG. 68

NAMES: JAMES SAMPLER TO SUSSANNAH GUIN
DATE: JAN. 11, 1819
REFERENCE: T.H.M. VOL. 6, PG. 68

NAMES: THOMAS SCOTT TO ELEANOR STIRLING
DATE: FEBY. 15, 1819
DATE PER: FEBY. 15, 1819
BY: T. H. NELSON
REFERENCE: C.A; O.M.R. PG. 41

NAMES: BENJAMIN SHERWOOD TO RACHEL EVERETT
DATE: NOV. 25, 1819
DATE PER: NOV. 25, 1819
BY: JAMES DIXON, E.M.E.C.
REFERENCE: C.A; O.M.R. PG. 47; T.H.M. VOL. 6, PG. 68

NAMES: HENRY SHIPE TO DEBORAH SCAGGS
DATE: OCT. 4, 1819
DATE PER: OCT. 7, 1819
BY: JOHN BAYLESS, J.P.K.C.
REFERENCE: C.A; O.M.R. PG. 46; T.H.M. VOL. 6, PG. 68

NAMES: JOHN SHOOKEY TO POLLY KARNS
DATE: AUG. 23, 1819
DATE PER: AUG. 24, 1819
BY: THO. H. NELSON
REFERENCE: C.A.; O.M.R. PG. 45

NAMES: JOHN SHOCKY (?) TO POLLY HAINEY
DATE: AUG. 2,
REFERENCE: T.H.M. VOL. 6, PG. 68

NAMES: ABNER SHULER TO NANCY BURNETT
DATE: SEPT. 22,
REFERENCE: T.H.M. VOL. 6, PG. 68

NAMES: WM. M. SIGLER TO ELIZA GARNER
DATE: MAY 25, 1819
DATE PER: MAY 25, 1819
BY: T. H. NELSON
REFERENCE: C.A; O.M.R. PG. 43

NAMES: JOHN SMITH TO MARIAH CHRISTIE
DATE: AUG. 2, 1819
DATE PER: JULY 3, 1819
BY: T. H. NELSON
REFERENCE: C.A; O.M.R. PG, 44; T.H.M. VOL. 6, PG. 68

NAMES: PHILIP SMITH TO POLLY MCCAMPBELL
DATE: JANY. 21, 1819
DATE PER: JANY. 21, 1819
BY: THO. H. NELSON
REFERENCE: C.A; O.M.R. PG. 40

NAMES: WM. M. SMITH TO ELIZABETH GARDNER
DATE: JULY 24, 1819
DATE PER: AUG. 5, 1819
BY: WM. CAMPBELL, J.P.K.C.
REFERENCE: C.A; O.M.R. PG. 44; T.H.M. VOL. 6, PG. 68

NAMES: ELIJAH SNODGRASS TO PEGGY SMITH
DATE: MAR. 13, 1819
BONDSMAN: ANDREW C. COPELAND
DATE PER: MAR. 14, 1819
BY: JOHN BAYLESS, J.P.K.C.
REFERENCE: C.A; O.M.R. PG. 41; T.H.M. VOL. 6, PG. 68

NAMES: JOHN STEWART TO LETTY TILLERY
DATE: JANY. 19, 1819
BONDSMAN: JOHN TILLERY
DATE PER: JANY. 19, 1819
BY: J. C. LUTTRELL, J.P.K.C.
REFERENCE: C.A; O.M.R. PG. 40

NAMES: ABNER STULCE TO NANCY BURNETT
DATE: SEPT. 22, 1819
BONDSMAN: JAMES HAZLEWOOD
DATE PER: SEPT. 23, 1819
BY: ROBERT TUNNELL, J.P.K.C.
REFERENCE: C.A; O.M.R. PG. 45

NAMES: JOSEPH VANCE TO ELIZA GREER
DATE: DEC. 27, 1819
DATE PER: DEC. 28, 1819
BY: ISAAC ANDERSON, R. D. M.
REFERENCE: C.A; O.M.R. PG. 48; T.H.M. VOL. 6, PG. 68

NAMES: DAVID WALKER TO MARY CARPENTER
DATE: FEBY. 11, 1819
BONDSMAN: JACOB RUTH
DATE PER: FEBY. 15, 1819
BY: S. MONTGOMERY
REFERENCE: C.A; O.M.R. PG. 40; T.H.M. VOL. 6, PG. 68

NAMES: THOMAS WEBB TO BETSY CORKBUND (?)
DATE: OCT. 18, 1819
REFERENCE: T.H.M. VOL. 6, PG. 68

NAMES: THOMAS WHITE TO ELIZABETH HERRELSON
DATE: JULY 13, 1819
BONDSMAN: JAMES BOYD
REFERENCE: C.A.

NAMES: MOSES WILEY TO ALICE GARDENER
DATE: JUNE 14,
REFERENCE: T.H.M. VOL. 6, PG. 68

NAMES: OBADIAH WILKERSON TO RACHEL CLAYTON
DATE: JULY 24,
REFERENCE: T.H.M. VOL. 6, PG. 68

NAMES: SAM'L WOOD TO SARAH HARRIS
DATE: SEPT. 16, 1819
REFERENCE: O.M.R. PG. 45

NAMES: PETER YOST TO POLLY LONAS
DATE: APR. 15, 1819
DATE PER: APR. 15, 1819
BY: JOHN HAYNIE
REFERENCE: C.A; O.M.R. PG. 43

1820

NAMES: JAMES ARTHUR TO HANNAH HOWSER
DATE: SEPT. 20, 1820
BONDSMAN: ANDREW MCGATH
DATE PER: SEPT. 21, 1820
BY: PETER NANCE, J.P.K.C.
REFERENCE: C.A; O.M.R. PG. 54; T.H.M. VOL. 6, PG. 68

NAMES: JESSE AYRES TO ELIZABETH REED
DATE: NOV. 3, 1820
BONDSMAN: HUGH BROWN
REFERENCE: C.A.

NAMES: JESSE AYRES TO ELIZABETH REED
DATE: NOV. 3, 1820
DATE PER: NOV. 5, 1820
BY: WM. MORRIS, J.P.
REFERENCE: O.M.R. PG. 56; T.H.M. VOL. 6, PG. 68

NAMES: JAMES BADGETT TO SUSAN HARRIS
DATE: NOV. 23,
REFERENCE: T.H.M. VOL. 6, PG. 68

NAMES: ISAAC BAYLESS TO SUSANNAH SUMPTER
DATE: JULY 18, 1820
DATE PER: JULY 27, 1820
BY: WILLIAM B. CARNS, J.P.K.C.
REFERENCE: C.A; O.M.R. PG. 53; T.H.M. VOL. 6, PG. 68

NAMES: JAMES BELL TO NANCY STEPHENSON
DATE: JANY. 13, 1820
BONDSMAN: JAMES STEPHENSON
REFERENCE: C.A.

NAMES: JAMES BELL TO NANCY STEPHENSON
DATE: JANY. 13, 1820
DATE PER: JANY. 13, 1820
BY: T. H. NELSON, M. G.
REFERENCE: O.M.R. PG. 49; T.H.M. VOL. 6, PG. 68

NAMES: JOHN M. BOOKOUT TO PEGGY GUINN
DATE: JUNE 12, 1820
DATE PER: JUNE 16, 1820
BY: JOHN GASS, J.P.K.C.
REFERENCE: C.A; O.M.R. PG. 52; T.H.M. VOL. 6, PG. 68

NAMES: ALEXANDER BOYD TO CATHERINE STARNES
DATE: AUG. 21, 1820
REFERENCE: T.H.M. VOL. 6, PG. 68

Names: Lewis Bryan to Nancy Tallent
Date: Aug. 30, 1820
Date Per: Aug. 31, 1820
By: Amos Hardin, J.P.K.C.
Reference: C.A; O.M.R. Pg. 54

Names: Owen Burman to Polly Hood
Date: Apr. 12, 1820
Bondsman: James Hood
Date Per: Apr. 13, 1820
By: Peter Nance, J.P.K.C.
Reference: C.A; O.M.R. Pg. 51

Names: Benj. Burnett to Betsy Ellison
Date: Jany. 3, 1820
By: Peter Nance, J.P.K.C.
Reference: C.A; O.M.R. Pg. 49

Names: Edward Butler to Nancy Holt
Date: May 13, 1820
Date Per: May 18, 1820
By: Amos Hardin, J.P.K.C.
Reference: C.A; O.M.R. Pg. 52; T.H.M. Vol. 6, Pg. 68

Names: Wm. D. Butler to Elizabeth Cavett
Date: Feby. 4, 1820
Date Per: Feby. 7, 1820
By: Sam'l Sample, J.P.
Reference: O.M.R. Pg. 49; T.H.M. Vol. 6, Pg. 68

Names: Henry Calfee to Tabitha Hazlewood
Date: Aug. 23, 1820
Bondsman: Benj. Hazlewood
Date Per: Aug. 23, 1820
By: Sam'l Montgomery, J.P.
Reference: C.A; O.M.R. Pg. 54; T.H.M. Vol. 6, Pg. 68

Names: Archibald Callan to Jane Evans
Date: Nov. 17, 1820
Bondsman: Robert Shields
Date Per: Dec. 7, 1820
By: Sam'l Sample, J.P.K.C.
Reference: C.A; O.M.R. Pg. 56

Names: James P. Clark to Susan McCarry
Date: June 27, 1820
Date Per: June 27, 1820
By: Isaac Anderson, M. G.
Reference: C.A; O.M.R. Pg. 52; T.H.M. Vol. 6, Pg. 68

Names: John M. Clark to Rebecka W. Crawford
Date: July 29, 1820
Bondsman: James Kennedy
Date Per: Aug. 3, 1820
By: John McCampbell
Reference: C.A; O.M.R. Pg. 53

Names: John Cole to Polly Mizer
Date: Mar. 13, 1820
Bondsman: Wm. Allen
Date Per: Mar. 13, 1820
By: Jno. Haynie, D. M. E.
Reference: C.A; O.M.R. Pg. 50

Names: George Cooley to Rebecka Howard
Date: Nov. 23, 1820
Date Per: Nov. 23, 1820
By: Peter Nance, J.P.
Reference: C.A; O.M.R. Pg. 56

Names: William Cortney to Rachel McClure
Date: Dec. 20. 1820
Bondsman: John Craighead
Date Per: Dec. 20, 1820
By: Peter Nance, J.P.
Reference: C.A; O.M.R. Pg. 57; T.H.M. Vol. 6, Pg. 187

Names: Henry Cox to Elizabeth Gwin
Date: Oct. 2, 1820
Date Per: Oct. 3, 1820
By: Jno. Gass, J.P.
Reference: C.A; O.M.R. Pg. 55; T.H.M. Vol. 6, Pg. 187

Names: Thomas Crank to Anna Human
Date: Apr. 4, 1820
Bondsman: James Human
Date Per: Apr. 5, 1820
By: Wm. A. McCampbell
Reference: C.A; O.M.R. Pg. 51

Names: Jasper W. Cumstock to Nancy Keys
Date: July 27, 1820
Date Per: Aug. 6, 1820
By: William Sawyers, J.P.K.C.
Reference: C.A; O.M.R. Pg. 53; T.H.M. Vol. 6, Pg. 68

Names: John Davis to Nancy Johnston
Date: July 22, 1820
Bondsman: Hugh B. Maget
Reference: C.A.

NAMES: JNO. DAVIS TO NANCY JOHNSTON
DATE: JULY 22, 1820
DATE PER: JULY 22, 1820
BY: THOS. WILKERSON, M.G.
REFERENCE: O.M.R. PG. 53; T.H.M. VOL. 6, PG. 187

NAMES: JOHN DICKSON TO MARGARET G. WILLS
DATE: SEPT. 25; 1820
BONDSMAN: JOHN WILLS
REFERENCE: O.A; T.H.M. VOL. 6, PG. 187

NAMES: BENJAMIN DOUGHTY TO POLLY KEMP
DATE: SEPT. 20, 1820
BONDSMAN: JAMES KEMP
BY: P. NANCE, J.P.
REFERENCE: O.A; O.M.R. PG. 55; T.H.M. VOL. 6, PG. 187

NAMES: ALEXANDER DOUGLASS TO RHODA RUTH
DATE: NOV. 13, 1820
DATE PER: NOV. 14, 1820
BY: SAM. SAMPLE
REFERENCE: C.A; O.M.R. PG. 56; T.H.M. VOL. 6, PG. 187

NAMES: NATHANIEL DUNLAP TO POLLY MONTGOMERY
DATE: MAR. 11, 1820
DATE PER: MAR. 14, 1820
BY: S. MONTGOMERY
REFERENCE: O.A; T.H.M. VOL. 6, PG. 187

NAMES: ALFRED ENGLAND TO BERSHEBA WALKER
DATE: NOV. 11, 1820
BONDSMAN: REUBEN WALKER
REFERENCE: O.A; T.H.M. VOL. 6, PG. 187

NAMES: AQUILLA EVERETT TO SARAH THOMPSON
DATE: JULY 1, 1820
BONDSMAN: SAM'L INGRAM
DATE PER: JULY 1, 1820
BY: WM. A. MCCAMPBELL, J.P.
REFERENCE: O.A; O.M.R. PG. 52; T.H.M. VOL. 6, PG. 187

NAMES: JACOB FORD TO ELIZABETH NEEDHAM
DATE: JULY 12, 1820
DATE PER: JULY 13, 1820
BY: S. MONTGOMERY
REFERENCE: O.A; O.M.R. PG. 53

NAMES: JOSEPH B. GALBREATH TO ABIGAIL STRICKLIN
DATE: MAR. 14, 1820
DATE PER: MAR. 14, 1820
BY: R. HOUSTON
REFERENCE: O.A; O.M.R. PG. 50; T.H.M. VOL. 6, PG. 187

NAMES: JOSEPH GALBREATH TO BETSY LOVE
DATE: APR. 26; 1820
BONDSMAN: SAMUEL FLEMING
DATE PER: APR. 27, 1820
BY: RD. H. KING
REFERENCE: O.A; O.M.R. PG. 52; T.H.M. VOL. 6, PG. 187

NAMES: ALEXANDER GALLIHER TO JANE CARTER
DATE: JUNE 2, 1820
BY: THOS. WILKERSON, M.G.
REFERENCE: C.A; O.M.R. PG. 52; T.H.M. VOL. 6, PG. 187

NAMES: TRAVIS GEORGE TO ELIZABETH JOHNSTON
DATE: APR. 14, 1820
DATE PER: APR. 23, 1820
BY: JNO. BAYLESS, J.P.
REFERENCE: C.A; O.M.R. PG. 51; T.H.M. VOL. 6, PG. 187

NAMES: ABRAHAM GILLESPIE TO PEGGY PAUL
DATE: AUG. 10,
REFERENCE: T.H.M. VOL. 6, PG. 187

NAMES: WILLIAM GILLESPIE TO PEGGY WATT
DATE: AUG. 10, 1820
BONDSMAN: JAMES WATT
DATE PER: AUG. 10, 1820
BY: JAMES MCMILLAN, J.P.
REFERENCE: C.A; O.M.R. PG. 53

NAMES: JOHN GODDARD TO ANNA CAMPBELL
DATE: JANY. 25, 1820
BONDSMAN: WM. GODDARD
DATE PER: JANY. 25, 1820
BY: S. MONTGOMERY
REFERENCE: O.A; O.M.R. PG. 49; T.H.M. VOL. 6, PG. 187

NAMES: HARRY GRIZZLE TO SUSAN JONES
DATE: NOV. 4, 1820
BY: B. MCNUTT, J.P.
REFERENCE: C.A; O.M.R. PG. 56; T.H.M. VOL. 6, PG. 187

NAMES: EDMOND HALL TO HETTY RENFROW
DATE: AUG. 17, 1820
BONDSMAN: JAMES THOMPSON
DATE PER: AUG. 17, 1820
BY: JOHN BAYLESS, J.P.
REFERENCE: C.A; O.M.R. PG. 53

Names: Levi Hankins to Elizabeth Green (?)
Date: Oct. 17, 1820
Bondsman: Stephen M. Skaggs
Date Per: Oct. 17, 1820
By: John Bayless, J.P.
Reference: C.A; O.M.R. Pg. 55; T.H.M. Vol. 6, Pg. 187

Names: George Hickle to Margaret Roberts
Date: Aug. 14, 1820
Bondsman: John Hickle
Reference: C.A; T.H.M. Vol. 6, Pg. 187

Names: James Hunter to Fanny McCloud
Date: Dec. 20, 1820
Bondsman: Casper Webber
Date Per: Dec. 21, 1820
By: Wm. B. Carns, J.P.
Reference: C.A; O.M.R. Pg. 56; T.H.M. Vol. 6, Pg. 187

Names: Elliott Johnston to Susan Luttrell
Date: Aug. 1, 1820
Bondsman: John Abel
Reference: C.A; T.H.M. Vol. 6, Pg. 187

Names: Lorzena Johnston to Catharine Hunter
Date: Jany. 17, 1820
Date Per: Jany. 20, 1820
By: Sam'l Montgomery
Reference: C.A; O.M.R. Pg. 49; T.H.M. Vol. 6, Pg. 187

Names: Thomas Johnston to Nancy Chumley
Date: Apr. 18, 1820
By: Thomas Wilkerson, M. G.
Reference: C.A; O.M.R. Pg. 51

Names: James Jones to Juda Grizzle
Date: Nov. 4, 1820
Date Per: Nov. 4, 1820
By: Sam'l Montgomery
Reference: C.A; O.M.R. Pg. 56

Names: Lewis Kime to Sarah Short
Date: June 21, 1820
Bondsman: William Reed
Date Per: June 22, 1820
By: Sam'l Montgomery
Reference: C.A; O.M.R. Pg. 52; T.H.M. Vol. 6, Pg. 187

Names: James R. King to Isabella McNeil
Date: Feby. 25, 1820
Date Per: Feby. 29, 1820
By: Tho. H. Nelson
Reference: C.A; O.M.R. Pg. 50; T.H.M. Vol. 6, Pg. 187

Names: Geo. W. Kirkland to Louisa Alexander
Date: Aug. 30, 1820
Date Per: Sept. 7, 1820
By: Sam'l Fleming, J.P.
Reference: O.M.R. Pg. 54; T.H.M. Vol. 6, Pg. 187

Names: William Lane to Jane White
Date: Aug. 31, 1820
Date Per: Aug. 31, 1820
By: Sam'l Montgomery
Reference: C.A; O.M.R. Pg. 54

Names: Francis Larew to Nancy Anne Young
Date: Oct. 19, 1820
Bondsman: Young McLemore
Date Per: Oct. 19, 1820
By: George Atkin, M.P.
Reference: C. A; O.M.R. Pg. 55; T.H.M. Vol. 6, Pg. 187

Names: Isham Large to Betsy Large
Date: Dec. 22, 1820
Date Per: Dec. 22, 1820
By: John Haynie
Reference: C.A; O.M.R. Pg. 57

Names: John Long to Betsy Parker
Date: Dec. 2, 1820
Date Per: Dec. 7, 1820
By: R. McBath, Esq.
Reference: C.A; O.M.R. Pg. 56; T.H.M. Vol. 6, Pg. 187

Names: William Loudermilk to Elizabeth Millbright
Date: Feby. 17, 1820
Date Per: Feby. 22, 1820
By: S. Montgomery
Reference: C.A; O.M.R. Pg. 53; T.H.M. Vol. 6, Pg. 187

Names: Samuel Lyle to Susan McDonald
Date: Jany. 31, 1820
Date Per: Feby. 3, 1820
By: Robert Tunnell, J.P.
Reference: C.A; O.M.R. Pg. 49; T.H.M. Vol. 6, Pg. 187

Names: Washington Lyons to Patty Lyons
Date: July 3,
Reference: T.H.M. Vol. 6, Pg. 187

Names: Samuel Martin to Sally Ragan
Date: Oct. 2,
Reference: T.H.M. Vol. 6, Pg. 187

Names: Windsor Mason to Maria Lane
Date: Apr. 1, 1820
Bondsman: Wm. Campbell
Date Per: Apr. 5, 1820
By: S. Montgomery
Reference: C.A; O.M.R. Pg. 51; T.H.M. Vol. 6, Pg. 187

Names: James Mayberry to Lucretia Ross
Date: Sept. 13, 1820
Bondsman: Samuel Ross
Reference: C.A;

Names: James Maybury to Lucretia Rose
Date: Sept. 13, 1820
Date Per: Sept. 13, 1820
By: Wm. Alldridge, J.P.
Reference: O.M.R. Pg. 54; T.H.M. Vol. 6, Pg. 187

Names: Joseph A. Mayberry to Alse Scott
Date: Dec. 4, 1820
Bondsman: Wm. Swan
Reference: C.A.

Names: Joseph A. Maybury to Alse Scott
Date: Dec. 4, 1820
Date Per: Dec. 5, 1820
By: Wm. Morris, J.P.
Reference: O.M.R. Pg. 57; T.H.M. Vol. 6, Pg. 187

Names: Joseph G. McCarrell to Jane Henson
Date: July 10, 1820
Bondsman: Sam'l Flenniken
Date Per: July 10, 1820
By: Peter Nance, J.P.
Reference: C.A; O.M.R. Pg. 52

Names: James McCloud to Peggy Havin
Date: Oct. 11, 1820
Bondsman: Robert McHaffie
Date Per: Oct. 19, 1820
By: William B. Carns
Reference: C.A; O.M.R. Pg. 55

Names: Jno. McGhee to Betsy Jones McClung
Date: Sept. 5, 1820
Date Per: Sept. 5, 1820
By: R. H. King, M.G.
Reference: O.M.R. Pg. 54

Names: Donald McIntosh to Margery Campbell
Date: Feby. 1, 1820
Bondsman: Edwin Wiatt
Reference: C.A.

Names: Donald McIntosh to Margery Campbell
Date: Feby. 1, 1820
Date Per: Feby. 1, 1820
By: Tho. H. Nelson
Reference: O.M.R. Pg. 49; T.H.M. Vol. 6, Pg. 187

Names: Jesse Mitchell to Rachel Gentry
Date: Mar. 6, 1820
Bondsman: Martin Gentry
Date Per: Mar. 16, 1820
By: R. Cole, J.P.
Reference: C.A; O.M.R. Pg. 50; T.H.M. Vol. 6, Pg. 187

Names: John Moats to Mary Huffstutler
Date: Dec. 15, 1820
Bondsman: Henry Huffstutler
Date Per: Dec. 19, 1820
By: Amos Hardin, J.P.
Reference: C.A; O.M.R. Pg. 57; T.H.M. Vol. 6, Pg 187

Names: Tandy Monday to Polly Wood
Date: Sept. 5, 1820
Bondsman: James Alldredge
Date Per: Sept. 5, 1820
By: Wm. Alldredge, J.P.
Reference: C.A; O.M.R. Pg. 54; T.H.M. Vol. 6, Pg. 187

Names: Wm. A. Montgomery to Anne A. Dunlap
Date: Feby. 7, 1820
Bondsman: Isaac Wilson
Date Per: Feby. 8, 1820
By: S. Montgomery
Reference: C.A; O.M.R. Pg. 50

Names: John Mynatt to Sally Keys
Date: Apr. 5, 1820
Bondsman: John Perrin
Date Per: Apr. 16, 1820
By: William Sawyers, J.P.
Reference: C.A; O.M.R. Pg. 51

NAMES: JOHN MAILL TO POLLY BENKLY
DATE: JAN. 19,
REFERENCE: T.H.M. VOL. 6, PG. 187

NAMES: JOSEPH NEWMAN TO KESIAH HATHCOCK
DATE: DEC. 5, 1820
BY: B. MCNUTT, J.P.
REFERENCE: C.A; O.M.R. PG. 57; T.H.M. VOL. 6, PG. 187

NAMES: JOHN OVERTON TO MARY MAY
DATE: JULY 28, 1820
BONDSMAN: W. G. BLOUNT
DATE PER: JULY 28, 1820
BY: T. H. NELSON
REFERENCE: C.A; T.H.M. VOL. 6, PG. 187

NAMES: BRIANT PATRICK TO NANCY DAVIS
DATE: JANY. 13, 1820
DATE PER: JANY 13, 1820
BY: JOHN BAYLESS, J.P.
REFERENCE: C.A; O.M.R. PG. 49

NAMES: EDLEY PAUL TO ELEANOR COLE
DATE: MAR. 23, 1820
DATE PER: MAR. 23, 1820
BY: JAMES C. LUTTRELL, J.P.
REFERENCE: C.A; O.M.R. PG. 50; T.H.M. VOL. 6, PG. 187

NAMES: WM. PETERSON TO ESTHER RUTHERFORD
DATE: JULY 13, 1820
BONDSMAN: SAM'L M. ARMSTRONG
REFERENCE: C.A; T.H.M. VOL. 6, PG. 187

NAMES: JOHN PRICE TO BETSY KEMP
DATE: APR. 19, 1820
BONDSMAN: JOHN STERLING
DATE: APR. 20, 1820
BY: PETER NANCE
REFERENCE: C.A; O.M.R. PG. 51; T.H.M. VOL. 6, PG. 187

NAMES: ELI RAGAN TO CHARLOTTE AYRES
DATE: JANY. 4, 1820
BONDSMAN: JAMES A. HAIRE
REFERENCE: C.A; T.H.M. VOL. 6, PG. 187

NAMES: FRANCIS A. RAMSEY TO MARGARET HUMES
DATE: APR. 13, 1820
BONDSMAN: HUGH BROWN
REFERENCE: C.A;

NAMES: F. A. RAMSEY TO MARGARET HUMES
DATE: APR. 13, 1820
DATE PER: APR. 13, 1820
BY: R. H. KING
REFERENCE: O.M.R. PG. 51; T.H.M. VOL. 6, PG. 187

NAMES: ANDREW ROBERTS TO JANE KELLY
DATE: OCT. 5, 1820
BONDSMAN: WM. SWAN
DATE PER: MAY 31, 1821
BY: JOHN BAYLESS, J.P.
REFERENCE: C.A; O.M.R. PG. 55; T.H.M. VOL. 6, PG. 187

NAMES: JAMES ROBESON TO MARY DARDIS
DATE: AUG. 3, 1820
BONDSMAN: WILLIAM PARK
REFERENCE: C.A.

NAMES: JAMES ROBINSON TO MARY DARDIS ✓
DATE: AUG. 3, 1820
DATE PER: AUG. 3, 1820
BY: THO. H. NELSON, M.G.
REFERENCE: O.M.R. PG. 53; T.H.M. VOL. 6, PG. 187

NAMES: WILLIAM RUSSELL TO JANE LOVE
DATE: MAY 30, 1820
DATE PER: JUNE 1, 1820
BY: RD. H. KING
REFERENCE: C.A; O.M.R. PG. 52

NAMES: WILLIAM RUSSELL TO JANE LOWE
DATE: MAY 30,
REFERENCE: T.H.M. VOL. 6, PG. 187

NAMES: WILLIAM RUTHERFORD TO ELIZABETH DOVE
DATE: FEBY. 15, 1820
DATE PER: FEBY. 22, 1820
BY: WILLIAM SAWYERS, J.P.
REFERENCE: C.A; O.M.R. PG. 50; T.H.M. VOL. 6, PG. 188

NAMES: JOSIAH SAWYERS TO MARY GIBBS
DATE: DEC. 13, 1820
BONDSMAN: SAMUEL IRWIN
DATE PER: DEC. 14, 1820
BY: JOHN BAYLESS, J.P.
REFERENCE: C.A; O.M.R. PG. 57

NAMES: HAMDEN S. SCOTT TO PATSY LAREW
DATE: MAR. 28, 1820
BONDSMAN: JOHN LINDSAY
DATE PER: MAR. 28, 1820
BY: WM. B. CARNS, J.P.
REFERENCE: C.A; O.M.R. PG. 51; T.H.M. VOL. 6, PG. 188

NAMES: JACOB SENSABAUGH TO BETSY THOMPSON
DATE: JANY. 24, 1820
BY: PETER NANCE, J.P.
REFERENCE: C.A; O.M.R. PG. 48; T.H.M. VOL. 6, PG. 188

NAMES: THOMAS SHARP TO CATHARINE FOUST
DATE: OCT. 11, 1820
DATE PER: OCT. 19, 1820
BY: WILLIAM SAWYERS, J.P.
REFERENCE: C.A; O.M.R. PG. 55

NAMES: BANNISTER SMITH TO SARAH COKER
DATE: DEC. 2, 1820
BONDSMAN: JOHN COKER
DATE PER: DEC. 3, 1820
BY: P. NANCE, J.P.
REFERENCE: C.A; O.M.R. PG. 56; T.H.M. VOL. 6, PG. 188

NAMES: JOHN SMITH TO RACHEL MULVANY
DATE: APR. 4, 1820
BONDSMAN: JESSE SMITH
REFERENCE: C.A.

NAMES: JNO. SMITH TO RACHEL MULVANY
DATE: APR. 5, 1820
DATE PER: APRL. 6, 1820
BY: SAMUEL SAMPLE, J.P.
REFERENCE: O.M.R. PG. 51; T.H.M. VOL. 6, PG. 188

NAMES: JOHN A. SWAN TO JANE H. SWAN
DATE: OCT. 13, 1820
BONDSMAN: WM. SWAN
REFERENCE: C.A; T.H.M. VOL. 6, PG. 188

NAMES: PHILLIP SWORD TO NANCY CHEATHAM
DATE: JAN. 21,
REFERENCE: T.H.M. VOL. 6, PG. 188

NAMES: PETER SYLAR TO POLLY ARNOLD
DATE: DEC. 16,
REFERENCE: T.H.M. VOL. 6, PG. 188

NAMES: HENRY THOMAS TO ELIZABETH HAMMON
DATE: JANY. 5, 1820
BONDSMAN: JOHN SMITH
REFERENCE: C.A; O.M.R. PG. 49

NAMES: NATHAN TINDELL TO PEGGY ROSS
DATE: NOV. 30, 1820
BONDSMAN: LINDSAY CHILDRESS
DATE PER: NOV. 30, 1820
BY: WM. ALLDRIDGE, J.P.
REFERENCE: C.A; O.M.R. PG. 56

NAMES: REUBEN TIPTON TO ALEE CHILDRESS
DATE: SEPT. 29, 1820
DATE PER: OCT. 1, 1820
BY: P. NANCE, J.P.
REFERENCE: C.A; O.M.R. PG. 55

NAMES: JACOB TITTERO TO SUSAN PROPES
DATE: JANY. 1, 1820
BONDSMAN: JACOB BILDERBACK
REFERENCE: C.A.

NAMES: PETER WAGGONER TO POLLY M. SMITH
DATE: JUNE 20, 1820
DATE PER: JUNE 20, 1820
BY: GEO. ATKIN, M.G.
REFERENCE: C.A; O.M.R. PG. 52; T.H.M. VOL. 6, PG. 188

NAMES: REUBEN WALKER TO BETSY GALLIHER
DATE: DEC. 22, 1820 -- DATE PER: DEC. 28, 1820
BY: W. WALKER, M.G.
REFERENCE: C.A; O.M.R. PG. 57; T.H.M. VOL. 6, PG. 188

NAMES: WILLIAM WALKER TO MARY ANN LOVE
DATE: OCT. 3, 1820
DATE PER: OCT. 4, 1820
BY: R. H. KING
REFERENCE: C.A; O.M.R. PG. 55

NAMES: JOHN WELSH TO CHRISTINA GUALT
DATE: OCT. 16, 1820
BONDSMAN: WM. MORROW
DATE PER: OCT. 17, 1820
BY: WILLIAM B. CARNS, J.P.
REFERENCE: C.A; O.M.R. PG. 55
NAMES: ABRAM D. WHITE TO ELIZABETH DOUGLASS
DATE: FEBY. 24, 1820
DATE PER: FEBY. 24, 1820
BY: JOHN MCCAMPBELL
REFERENCE: C.A; O.M.R. PG. 50; T.H.M. VOL. 6, PG. 188

NAMES: JOHN WHITTLE TO POLLY KEENER
DATE: AUG. 29, 1820
BONDSMAN: GEORGE WHITTLE
DATE PER: AUG. 31, 1820
BY: SAML. MONTGOMERY
REFERENCE: O.A; O.M.R. PG. 54; T.H.M. VOL. 6, PG. 188

NAMES: MICHAEL WIGGINS TO POLLY FORD
DATE: MAR. 9, 1820
DATE PER: MAR. 3, 1820
BY: JOHN HAYNIE, O.M.C.
REFERENCE: O.A; O.M.R. PG. 50

NAMES: HUGH P. WILSON TO NANCY OULTON
DATE: FEBY. 24, 1820
DATE PER: FEBY. 24, 1820
BY: JOHN MCCAMPBELL
REFERENCE: C.A; O.M.R. PG. 50

NAMES: JOHN W. WILSON TO BETSY CAMPBELL
DATE: JULY 28, 1820
BONDSMAN: DAVID CAMPBELL
DATE PER: JULY 30, 1820
BY: RD. H. KING
REFERENCE: O.A; O.M.R. PG. 53; T.H.M. VOL. 6, PG. 188

1821

NAMES: ISAAC ADAMSON TO JANE UNDERWOOD
DATE: JULY 28,
REFERENCE: T.H.M. VOL. 6, PG. 188

NAMES : PETER ADKINSON TO HARIOTT SHARPE
DATE: SEPT. 11, 1821
BONDSMAN: JOHN WILLIAMS
DATE PER: SEPT. 11, 1821
BY: R. HOUSTON, J.P.
REFERENCE: O.A; O.M.R. PG. 61; T.H.M. VOL. 6, PG. 188

NAMES: WILLIAM ALLDREDGE TO PATSY MCCLAIN
DATE: NOV. 12, 1821
BONDSMAN: WILLIAM OLINGER
REFERENCE: C.A; T.H.M. VOL. 6, PG. 188

NAMES: WILLIAM ALLISON TO SALLY MCKINNY
DATE: AUG. 20, 1821
DATE PER: AUG. 20, 1821
BY: JOHN HAYNIE, M.G.

REFERENCE: C.A; O.M.R. PG. 60; T.H.M. VOL. 6, PG. 188

NAMES: JAMES BADGETT TO MARY ANN MOORE
DATE: SEPT. 8,
REFERENCE: T.H.M. VOL. 6, PG. 188

NAMES: JAMES BADGETT TO SUSAN HARRIS
DATE: NOV. 23, 1821
BONDSMAN: JOSHUA FREEMAN
DATE PER: NOV. 23, 1821
BY: PETER NANCE, J.P.
REFERENCE: O.A; O.M.R. PG. 63

NAMES: ISAAC BARTON TO CHARITY BAKER
DATE: APR. 10, 1821;
BONDSMAN: JOHN MASON
REFERENCE: O.A.

NAMES: ISAAC BARTON TO CHARITY BAKER
DATE: APR. 10, 1821
DATE PER: APR. 10, 1821
BY: JAMES DIXON
REFERENCE: O.M.R. PG. 59; T.H.M. VOL. 6, PG. 188

NAMES: ISAAC BAYLESS TO BETSY SUMPTER
DATE: NOV. 23, 1821
DATE PER: NOV. 28, 1821
BY: WM. B. CARNS
REFERENCE: C.A; O.M.R. PG. 63; T.H.M. VOL. 6, PG. 188

NAMES: JNO. BROOKS TO MARIA ARMSTRONG
DATE: JANY. 9, 1821
DATE:PER: JANY. 9, 1821
BY: R. HOUSTON, J.P.
REFERENCE: O.M.R. PG. 58; T.H.M. VOL. 6, PG. 188

NAMES: FRANCIS G. BROWN TO POLLY BELL
DATE: DEC. 6, 1821
DATE PER: DEC. 6, 1821
BY: ROBERT LINDSEY, J.P.
REFERENCE: C.A; O.M.R. PG. 62; T.H.M. VOL. 6, PG. 188

NAMES: LEMUEL BURNETTE TO JANE FISHER
DATE: JUNE 6, 1821
DATE PER: JUNE 7, 1821
BY: SAM'L MONTGOMERY
REFERENCE: O.A; O.M.R. PG. 60; T.H.M. VOL. 6, PG. 188

NAMES: REUBEN CALLET TO AGGA JONES
DATE: AUG. 20, 1821
BONDSMAN: JAMES PEARSON
DATE PER: AUG. 21, 1821
BY: SAM MONTGOMERY
REFERENCE: C.A; O.M.R. PG. 60

NAMES: WINSTON CARTER TO SUSANNAH LUTTRELL
DATE: JUNE 1, 1821
BONDSMAN: ABRAM O. WHITE
WITNESS: WM. SWAN
REFERENCE: C.A; T.H.M. VOL. 6, PG. 188

NAMES: LASLEY CLIBURN TO CYNTHIA HOPPER
DATE: OCT. 27, 1821
BONDSMAN: JAMES HUMAN
DATE PER: OCT. 27, 1821
BY: WM. A. MCCAMPBELL, J.P.
REFERENCE: C.A; O.M.R. PG. 62; T.H.M. VOL. 6, PG. 188

NAMES: BENJAMIN COLE TO POLLY WALKER
DATE: MCH. 21,
REFERENCE: T.H.M. VOL. 6, PG. 188

NAMES: JOSIAH COOLEY TO NANCY MANEY
DATE: DEC. 26, 1821
BONDSMAN: SAMUEL BADGETT
DATE PER: DEC. 26, 1821
BY: P. NANCE, J.P.
REFERENCE: C.A; O.M.R. PG. 63; T.H.M. VOL. 6, PG. 188

NAMES: THOMAS COTTRELL TO LYDIA CHEESMAN
DATE: DEC. 27, 1821
REFERENCE: T.H.M. VOL. 6, PG. 188

NAMES: THOMAS COTTRELL TO LYDIA CHESHER
DATE: DEC. 27, 1821
BY: P. NANCE, J.P.
REFERENCE: C.A; O.M.R. PG. 63

NAMES: JOHN COX TO ELIZABETH HAMPTON
DATE: FEBY. 2, 1821
BY: WM. SAWYERS, J.P.
REFERENCE: C.A; O.M.R. PG. 58

NAMES: WALTER CREWS TO NANCY WALKER
DATE: APR. 13, 1821
DATE PER: APR. 26, 1821
BY: ROBT. MCBATH, ESQ.
REFERENCE: C.A; O.M.R. PG. 59; T.H.M. VOL. 6, PG. 188

NAMES: SAM'L CUNNINGHAM TO ELEANOR F. HOUSTON
DATE: OCT. 25, 1821
BONDSMAN: JOHN DAVIS
REFERENCE: C.A.

NAMES: SAM'L CUNNINGHAM TO ELEANOR F. HOUSTON
DATE: OCT. 25, 1821
DATE PER: OCT. 25, 1821
BY: R. HOUSTON, J.P.
REFERENCE: O.M.R. PG. 61; T.H.M. VOL. 6, PG. 188

NAMES: DAVID B. DEBUSK TO GERUSHA E. RUDER
DATE: DEC. 28, 1821
BONDSMAN: ELISHA DESUN
DATE PER: DEC. 28, 1821
BY: P. NANCE, J.P.
REFERENCE: C.A; O.M.R. PG. 63; T.H.M. VOL. 6, PG. 188

NAMES: PETER DOZIER TO REBEKA HARRIS
DATE: AUG. 22, 1821
DATE PER: AUG. 22, 1821
BY: JOHN HAYNIE, M.G.
REFERENCE: C.A; O.M.R. PG. 61; T.H.M. VOL. 6, PG. 188

NAMES: BENJAMIN EARLY TO POLLY LILBURN
DATE: JAN. 8, 1821
REFERENCE: T.H.M. VOL. 6, PG. 188

NAMES: SAM'L EDMONDSON TO REBECKA HICKS
DATE: DEC. 21, 1821
DATE PER: DEC. 23, 1821
BY: WM. MORRIS, J.P.
REFERENCE: C.A; O.M.R. PG. 62; T.H.M. VOL. 6, PG. 188

NAMES: JOHN FINDLEY TO PATSY PEAN
DATE: DEC. 8, 1821,
BONDSMAN: JOHN FINDLEY
REFERENCE: C.A; T.H.M. VOL. 6, PG. 188

NAMES: NICHOLAS FRY TO CISSY MOORE
DATE: MAR. 8, 1821
BONDSMAN: MICHAEL BEATTIE
WITNESS: WM. SWAN
REFERENCE: C.A.

NAMES: JAMES GALBRAITH TO CHARITY MAYBERRY
DATE: DEC. 25, 1821
REFERENCE: T.H.M. VOL. 6, PG. 188

NAMES: JAMES GOLLIHER TO CHARITY MAYBURY
DATE: DEC. 25, 1821
DATE PER: DEC. 27, 1821
BY: WEST WALKER, M. G.
REFERENCE: O.M.R. PG. 63

NAMES: THOMAS FULTON TO POLLY WILLS
DATE: JAN. 25,
REFERENCE: T.H.M. VOL. 6, PG. 188

NAMES: J. C. GREENWAY TO MARGARET C. COWAN
DATE: SEPT. 18, 1821
DATE PER: SEPT. 18, 1821
BY: THO. H. NELSON, M. G.
REFERENCE: O.M.R. PG. 61

NAMES: AUSTIN HACKWORTH TO BETSY RIGNEY
DATE: OCT. 24, 1821
BONDSMAN: MORGAN HENDRIX
DATE PER: NOV. 1, 1821
BY: WM. MORRIS, J.P.
REFERENCE: C.A; O.M.R. PG. 61 ; T.H.M. VOL. 6, PG. 188

NAMES: WILLIAM HAGUE TO HANNAH WALKER
DATE: JUNE 2, 1821
DATE PER: JULY 17, 1821
BY: ROBERT TUNNELL, J.P.
REFERENCE: C.A.; O.M.R. PG. 60

NAMES: ANDREW HALL TO JANE HANSARD
DATW: APR. 30, 1821
DATE PER: MAY 3, 1821
BY: JOHN BAYLESS, J. P.
REFERENCE: C.A; O.M.R. PG. 59

NAMES: JOSEPH HAMILTON TO ELIZABETH MOORE
DATE: JANY. 23, 1821
BONDSMAN: DAVID KELLER
DATE PER: JANY. 23, 1821
BY: J. ANDERSON, M.G.
REFERENCE: C.A; O.M.R. PG. 58; T.H.M. VOL. 6, PG. 188

NAMES: MARTIN HARDIN TO MARIAH TAYLOR
DATE: OCT. 10,
REFERENCE: T.H.M.VOL. 6, PG. 188

NAMES: JOSEPH HARRIS TO JULIA SHELL
DATE: NOV. 7, 1821
BONDSMAN: SAMUEL WOOD
BY: WM. SAWYERS, J.P.
REFERENCE: C.A; O.M.R. PG. 63; T.H.M. VOL. 6, PG. 188

NAMES: NATHAN HARRIS TO REBECCA GIBBS
DATE: OCT. 27,
REFERENCE: T.H.M. VOL. 6, PG. 188

NAMES: SILAS HAWKINS TO NANCY CRUZE
DATE: DEC. 24,
REFERENCE: T.H.M. VOL. 6, PG. 188

NAMES: WILLIAM HAZEN TO HANNAH WALKER
DATE: JUNE 2, 1821
BONDSMAN: JOHN REEVES
REFERENCE: C.A; T.H.M. VOL. 6, PG. 188

NAMES: OWEN HESTER TO POLLY CRESWELL
DATE: MAR. 12, 1821
DATE PER: MAR. 12, 1821
BY: JOHN HAYNIE
REFERENCE: C.A; O.M.R. PG. 58; T.H.M. VOL. 6, PG. 188

NAMES: JAMES HEWLIN TO SALLY CREW.
DATE: DEC. 4,
REFERENCE: T.H.M. VOL. 6, PG. 188

NAMES: SILAS HEWLIN TO NANCY CREWS
DATE: DEC. 24, 1821
DATE PER: DEC. 27, 1821
BY: ROBERT TUNNELL, J.P.
REFERENCE: C.A; O.M.R. PG. 62

NAMES: JAMES HICKS TO SALLY COUCH
DATE: OCT. 20, 1821
DATE PER: OCT. 21, 1821
BY: WM. MORRIS, J.P.
REFERENCE: C.A; OMR. PG. 61; T.H.M. VOL. 6, PG. 188

NAMES: WILLIAM HILL TO JULIA ANN WRIGHT
DATE: OCT. 18, 1821
DATE PER: OCT. 18, 1821
BY: JOHN HAYNIE, M.G.
REFERENCE: C.A; O.M.R. PG. 61; T.H.M. VOL. 6, PG. 188

NAMES: JAMES HOWEL TO REBECCA HAVEN
DATE: JUNE 14, 1821
DATE PER: JUNE 14, 1821
BY: WILLIAM SAWYERS, J.P.
REFERENCE: C.A; O.M.R. PG. 60

NAMES: WILLIAM HUNTER TO MERINA BLAKE
DATE: JANY. 15, 1821
DATE PER: JANY. 15, 1821
BY: JAMES MCMILLAN, J.P.
REFERENCE: C.A; O.M.R. PG. 58

NAMES: ANDREW JOHNSTON TO CATHARINE STEPHENSON
DATE: SEPT. 28, 1821
BONDSMAN: ROBERT STEPHENSON
DATE PER: OCT. 2, 1821
BY: JOHN BAYLESS, J.P.
REFERENCE: C.A; O.M.R. PG. 61; T.H.M. VOL. 6, PG. 188

NAMES: JOHN JORDAN TO NELLY GOUNDS
DATE: JULY 17, 1821
BONDSMAN: SAM'L MARTIN
REFERENCE: C.A; T.H.M. VOL. 6, PG. 188

NAMES: MATTHIAS KESINGER TO SALLY COX
DATE: DEC. 24, 1821
BONDSMAN: JOHN FROST
REFERENCE: C.A; T.H.M. VOL. 6, PG. 188

NAMES: WILLIAM KILLINGSWORTH TO MATILDA MCCLURE
DATE: MCH. 30,
REFERENCE: T.H.M. VOL. 6, PG. 188

NAMES: THOMAS KING TO MARY HAGEN
DATE: MAY 17, 1821,
BONDSMAN: GEORGE BLANG
DATE PER: MAY 17, 1821
BY: JOHN HAYNIE
REFERENCE: C.A; O.M.R. PG. 59; T.H.M. VOL. 6, PG. 188

NAMES: JAMES KNOX TO Q______ BOND
DATE: OCT. 20,
REFERENCE: T.H.M. VOL. 6, PG. 189

NAMES: JOSEPH LAREW TO MARY PARKER
DATE: DEC. 18, 1821
DATE PER: DEC. 18, 1821
BY: WM. A. MCCAMPBELL
REFERENCE: C.A; O.M.R. PG. 62

NAMES: THOS. J. LEA TO MARY C. TALBOT
DATE: SEPT. 27, 1821
DATE PER: SEPT. 27, 1821
BY: THOS. WILKERSON
REFERENCE: O.M.R. PG. 61; T.H.M. VOL. 6, PG. 189

NAMES: WILLIAM LEE TO POLLY UNDERWOOD
DATE: JUNE 12, 1821
DATE PER: JUNE 14, 1821
REFERENCE: C.A.

NAMES: BENJAMIN LOONEY TO JANE CALDWELL
DATE: MAR. 16, 1821
BONDSMAN: ALEX. CALDWELL
DATE PER: MAR. 16, 1821
BY: WM. B. CARNS, J.P.
REFERENCE: C.A; O.M.R. PG. 58; T.H.M. VOL. 6, PG. 189

NAMES: RICHARD LUMPKIN TO REBECKA JUSTICE
DATE: DEC. 19. 1821
DATE PER: DEC. 20, 1821
BY: JOHN BAYLESS, J.P.
REFERENCE: C.A; O.M.R. PG. 62; T.H.M. VOL. 6, PG. 189

NAMES: WILSON LYLES TO BETSY PRITCHET
DATE: FEB. 6,
REFERENCE: T.H.M. VOL. 6, PG. 189

NAMES: STARKY MCCABE TO ELIZABETH MURPHY
DATE: MAY 29, 1821
BONDSMAN: JOHN DOUGHERTY
DATE PER: MAY 29, 1821
BY: GEO. ATKINS, M.G.
REFERENCE: C.A; O.M.R. PG. 59; T.H.M. VOL. 6, PG. 189

NAMES: JOSEPH G. M. MCCARROLL TO JANE HENSON
DATE: JULY 10,
REFERENCE: T.H.M. VOL. 6, PG. 189

NAMES: ALEXANDER MCCLOUD TO DICE BAKER
DATE: AUG. 13, 1821
BONDSMAN: JAMES MCCLOUD
REFERENCE: C.A; T.H.M. VOL. 6, PG. 189

NAMES: CHARLES MCCLUNG TO MALVINA L. MILLER
DATE: JULY 2, 1821
BONDSMAN: PRYOR LEA - WILL SWAN
REFERENCE: C.A.

NAMES: CHARLES MCCLUNG TO MALVINA L. MILLER
DATE: JULY 2, 1821
DATE PER: JULY 3, 1821
BY: THO. H. NELSON, M.G.
REFERENCE: O.M.R. PG. 60

NAMES: WM. MCMILLAN TO BETSY DAVIS
DATE: FEBY. 7, 1821
DATE PER: FEBY. 7, 1821
BY: THOS. WILKERSON, M. G.
REFERENCE: O.M.R. PG. 58

NAMES: ELISHA MILLS TO DINAH WIATT
DATE: JULY 18, 1821
DATE PER: JULY 19, 1821
BY: WILLIAM SAWYERS, J.P.
REFERENCE: C.A; O.M.R. PG. 60

NAMES: GEORGE OLINGER TO MARY FORGUSON
DATE: MAY 14, 1821
BONDSMAN: HENRY MCCOLLOUGH
DATE PER: MAY 15, 1821
BY: JAMES C. LUTTRELL, J.P.
REFERENCE: C.A; O.M.R. PG. 59; T.H.M. VOL. 6, PG. 189

NAMES: HENRY OLINGER TO PEGGY STOKES
DATE: AUG. 28, 1821
BONDSMAN: GEO. OLINGER
DATE PER: AUG. 30, 1821
BY: JAMES C. LUTTRELL, J.P.
REFERENCE: C.A; O.M.R. PG. 60; T.H.M. VOL. 6, PG. 189

NAMES: WILLIAM OLINGER TO PATSY MCCLAIN
DATE: NOV. 12, 1820
BONDSMAN: JAMES ALLDREDGE
DATE PER: NOV. 12, 1821
BY: WILLIAM B. CARNS, J.P.
REFERENCE: C.A; O.M.R. PG. 63

NAMES: WILSON PARKER TO MARGARET KELLY
DATE: NOV. 28, 1821
BONDSMAN: JOHN SMITH
DATE PER: NOV. 29, 1821
BY: JOHN BAYLESS, J.P.
REFERENCE: C.A; O.M.R. PG. 64; T.H.M. VOL. 6, PG. 189

NAMES: JAMES PATRICK TO BETSY LEWIS
DATE: JUNE 2, 1821
BONDSMAN: HENRY WALKER
WITNESS: WILL SWAN
REFERENCE: C.A; T.H.M. VOL. 6, PG. 189

NAMES: EDMOND PAYNE TO JANE WRINKLE
DATE: JUNE 20, 1821
BONDSMAN: SAM'L PAYNE
DATE PER: JUNE 21, 1821
BY: SAM'L MONTGOMERY
REFERENCE: C.A; O.M.R. PG. 60; T.H.M. VOL. 6, PG. 189

NAMES: ISAAC PETERSON TO JANE MCBRIDE
DATE: AUG. 4, 1821
BONDSMAN: WILLIAM PETERSON
REFERENCE: C.A; T.H.M. VOL. 6, PG. 189

NAMES: JAMES G. M. G. RAMSEY TO MARGARET B. CROZIER
DATE: MAR. 1, 1821
DATE PER: MAR. 1, 1821
BY: T. H. NELSON, M.G.
REFERENCE: O.M.R. PG. 58; T.H.M. VOL. 6, PG. 189

NAMES: ALEXANDER RODDY TO DICE JOHNSTON
DATE: MAR. 29, 1821
BONDSMAN: ABRAHAM TIPTON
REFERENCE: C.A.

NAMES: ALEXANDER RODDY TO DICE JOHNSTON
DATE: MAR. 29, 1821
DATE PER: MAR. 29, 1821
BY: P. NANCE, J.P.
REFERENCE: O.M.R. PG. 59; T.H.M. VOL. 6, PG. 189

NAMES: JAMES D. SHERET TO POLLY LYON
DATE: DEC. 24, 1821
BONDSMAN: JAMES SUMPTER
DATE PER: DEC. 27, 1821
BY: JOHN BAYLESS, J.P.
REFERENCE: C.A; O.M.R. PG. 62; T.H.M. VOL. 6, PG. 189

NAMES: ALEXANDER SIMPSON TO NANCY MILLER
DATE: MAY 31, 1821
BONDSMAN: WM. DUNHAM
DATE PER: MAY 31, 1821
BY: WM. MORRIS, J.P.
REFERENCE: C.A; O.M.R. PG. 59

NAMES: JOHN SIMPSON TO RACHEL FITS
DATE: SEPT. 28, 1821
BONDSMAN: JAMES HICKEY
REFERENCE: C.A; T.H.M. VOL. 6, PG. 189

NAMES: BEVERLY SMITH TO LUCINDA RITTER
DATE: NOV. 17, 1821
BONDSMAN: JOHN COKER
DATE PER: NOV. 18, 1821
BY: P. NANCE, J.P.
REFERENCE: C.A; O.M.R. PG. 63; T.H.M. VOL. 6, PG. 189

NAMES: JOHN STIRLING TO SALLY ANDERSON
DATE: AUG. 16, 1821
BONDSMAN: SAM'L STIRLING
WITNESS: WM. SWAN
REFERENCE: C.A; T.H.M. VOL. 6, PG. 189

NAMES: JNO. STOWELL TO MARGARET ARMSTRONG
DATE: MAR. 17, 1821
DATE PER: MAR. 25, 1821
BY: WM. MORRIS
REFERENCE: O.M.R. PG. 59; T.H.M. VOL. 6, PG. 189

NAMES: JOSEPH STUART TO SUSAN TACKIT
DATE: DEC. 17, 1821
DATE PER: DEC. 18, 1821
BY: JAMES MCMILLAN, J.P.
REFERENCE: C.A; O.M.R. PG. 62

NAMES: WILLIAM THOMPSON TO SALLY MCMILLAN
DATE: JANY. 17, 1821
BONDSMAN: WM. MCMILLAN
DATE PER: FEBY. 18, 1821
BY: WILLIAM SAWYERS, J.P.
REFERENCE: C.A; O.M.R. PG. 58

NAMES: WILLIAM TINKER TO MARGARET ROBISON
DATE: OCT. 31, 1821
BONDSMAN: OBADIAH TINKER
DATE PER: NOV. 1, 1821
BY: THOS. WILKERSON, ELDER
REFERENCE: C.A; O.M.R. PG. 62; T.H.M. VOL. 6, PG. 189

NAMES: JOHN UNDERWOOD TO JANE GUINN
DATE: APR. 3, 1821
BONDSMAN: RICHARD LUMPKIN
REFERENCE: C.A.

NAMES: JOHN UNDERWOOD TO SUSAN GUINN
DATE: APR. 3,
REFERENCE: T.H.M. VOL. 6, PG. 189

NAMES: HENRY WALKER TO FANNY LEWIS
DATE: JUNE 6, 1821
BONDSMAN: CORNELIUS LEWIS
REFERENCE: C.A;

NAMES: JOHN WALLACE TO REBECKA NORTON
DATE: SEPT. 7, 1821
DATE PER: SEPT. 9, 1821
BY: R. COLE, J.P.
REFERENCE: C.A; O.M.R. PG. 61; T.H.M. VOL. 6, PG. 189

NAMES: WALTER WEAVER TO ELIZABETH MARTIN
DATE: OCT. 27, 1821
BONDSMAN: JAMES MARTIN
DATE PER: OCT. 27, 1821
BY: R. HOUSTON, J.P.
WITNESS: WILL SWAN
REFERENCE: C.A; O.M.R. PG. 62; T.H.M. VOL. 6, PG. 189

NAMES: JNO. WHITE TO CATY MCNUTT
DATE: DEC. 31, 1821
DATE PER: JANY. 1, 1822
BY: SAM'L SAMPLE, J.P.
REFERENCE: O.M.R. PG. 63; T.H.M. VOL. 6, PG. 189

NAMES: EPHRAIM WHITEBERRY TO SARAH T. WILLS
DATE: JULY 30, 1821
BONDSMAN: JOHN WILLS
REFERENCE: C.A.

NAMES: JOSHUA S. WILLIAMS TO JUDITH ROBERTS
DATE: MAR. 24, 1821
BONDSMAN: JAMES PEARSON
DATE PER: MAR. 24, 1821
BY: SAM'L MONTGOMERY
REFERENCE: C.A; O.M.R. PG. 59; T.H.M. VOL. 6, PG. 189

NAMES: SOLOMON YENELL TO SALLY HUBBS
DATE: OCT. 3,
REFERENCE: T.H.M. VOL. 6, PG. 189
REFERENCE: T.H.M. VOL. 6, PG. 189

NAMES: JOHN YOUNG TO RUTHY CRUIZE
DATE: JANY. 1, 1821
BONDSMAN: MITCHELL REED
DATE PER: JANY. 1, 1821
BY: JOHN HAYNIE
REFERENCE: C.A; O.M.R. PG. 58; T.H.M. VOL. 6, PG. 189

1822

NAMES: DAVID ALLISON TO ISABELLA MCCONNELL
DATE: SEPT. 12, 1822
BONDSMAN: ANDREW WILLOUGHBY
REFERENCE: C.A.

NAMES: DAVID ALLISON TO ISABELLA MCCONNELL
DATE: SEPT. 12, 1822
DATE PER: SEPT. 12, 1822
BY: PETER NAHOE, J.P.
REFERENCE: O.M.R. PG. 66; T.H.M. VOL. 6, PG. 189

NAMES: SAMUEL AYRES TO KESIAH ROBERTS
DATE: NOV. 30, 1822
DATE PER: DEC. 12, 1822
BY: SAM'L SAMPLE, J.P.
REFERENCE: C.A; O.M.R. PG. 69; T.H.M. VOL. 6, PG. 189

NAMES: JAMES BADGETT TO FANNY WILLIAMS
DATE: OCT. 5, 1822
DATE PER: OCT. 7, 1822
BY: P. NANCE, J.P.
REFERENCE: C.A; O.M.R. PG. 68; T.H.M. VOL. 6, PG. 189

NAMES: SOLOMON BAKER TO SUSANNAH BAYLESS
DATE: NOV. 25, 1822
BONDSMAN: RO. KIRKPATRICK
DATE PER: NOV. 28, 1822
BY: WM. B. CARNS, J.P.
WITNESS: WM. SWAN
REFERENCE: C.A; O.M.R. PG. 69; T.H.M. VOL. 6, PG. 189

NAMES: WILLIAM BAKER TO SARAH HOWSER
DATE: DEC. 16, 1822
BONDSMAN: JACOB HOWSER
DATE PER: DEC. 17, 1822
BY: ROBERT MCBATH, ESQ.
WITNESS: W. SWAN
REFERENCE: C.A; O.M.R. PG. 70; T.H.M. VOL. 6, PG. 189

NAMES: JOHN BAYLESS TO LUCINDA WHITECOTTON
DATE: MAR. 2, 1822
BONDSMAN: ROBERT SMITH
DATE PER: MAR. 5, 1822
BY: WM. B. CARNS, J.P.
WITNESS: WM. SWAN
REFERENCE: C.A; O.M.R. PG. 65; T.H.M. VOL. 6, PG. 189

NAMES: JOSEPH BOYD TO PEGGY KILBURN
DATE: FEB. 22, 1822
REFERENCE: T.H.M. VOL. 6, PG. 189

NAMES: WILLIAM BOYD TO ELIZA REYNOLDS
DATE: SEPT. 4,
REFERENCE: T.H.M. VOL. 6, PG. 189

NAMES: MICHAEL BRADBERRY TO DICE MERRIMAN
DATE: MAR. 23, 1822
DATE PER: MAR. 26, 1822
BY: WM. MORRIS, J.P.
REFERENCE: C.A; O.M.R. PG. 65

NAMES: ELIAS R. BRIGHT TO DEBORAH HANKINS
DATE: OCT. 4, 1822
DATE PER: OCT. 10, 1822
BY: WM. B. CARNS, J.P.
REFERENCE: C.A; OLM.R. PG. 68; T.H.M. VOL. 6, PG. 189

NAMES: ELISHA BROWN TO JANE BOOKER
DATE: APR. 17,
REFERENCE: T. H.M. VOL. 6, PG. 189

NAMES: JAMES BROWN TO MARGARET FRAKER
DATE: FEBY. 12, 1822
DATE PER: FEBY. 14, 1822
BY: WM. B. CARNS, J.P.
REFERENCE: C.A; O.M.R. PG. 64; T.H.M. VOL. 6, PG. 189

NAMES: JOSEPH BURNETT TO JANE MARTIN
DATE: MAY 16, 1822
DATE PER: MAY 16, 1822
BY: R. HOUSTON
REFERENCE: C.A; O.M.R. PG. 66

NAMES: JAMES CAMPBELL TO PATSY HAZELWOOD
DATE: OCT. 5, 1822
BONDSMAN: JAMES H. REAGAN
REFERENCE: C.A.

NAMES: JOHN CAMPBELL TO MARY E. COWAN
DATE: MAY 23, 1822
BONDSMAN: E. R. CAMPBELL
REFERENCE: C.A.

NAMES: JNO. CAMPBELL TO MARY E. COWAN
DATE: MAY 23, 1822
DATE PER: MAY 23, 1822
BY: THO. H. NELSON, M.G.
REFERENCE: O.M.R. PG. 66; T.H.M. VOL. 6, PG. 189

NAMES: THOMAS CAPSHAW TO CATHERINE SENSABAUGH
DATE: JULY 31, 1822
BONDSMAN: WM. TARWATER
DATE PER: AUG. 1, 1822
BY: ROBERT MCBATH, ESQ.,
WITNESS: WM. SWAN
REFERENCE: C.A; O.M.R. PG. 67

NAMES: WILLIAM CARPENTER TO ISABELLA MCCLINE
DATE: FEBY. 18, 1822
DATE PER: FEBY. 21, 1822
BY: JAMES MCMILLAN, J.P.
REFERENCE: C.A; O.M.R. PG. 64; T.H.M. VOL. 6; PG. 189

NAMES: SAMUEL CATE TO MALINDA MCCLURE
DATE: JUNE 15, 1822
BONDSMAN: SAMUEL MCCLURE
REFERENCE: C.A.

NAMES: DENNIS CHESHER TO BETSY AULT
DATE: FEBY. 28, 1822
BONDSMAN: HENRY HAYRON
DATE PER: FEBY. 28, 1822
BY: JOHN HAYNIE, M.G.-- REF: C.A; O.M.R. PG. 65; & T.H.M. VOL. 6, PG. 189

NAMES: CLAIBORNE CHUMLEY TO ELIZABETH CAVET
DATE: SEPT. 20, 1822
BONDSMAN: DAVID THOMPSON
REFERENCE: C.A.

NAMES: CLAIBORNE CHUMLEY TO ELIZABETH CAVET
DATE: SEPT. 20, 1822
DATE PER: SEPT. 22, 1822
BY: ROB'T TUNNELL, J.P.
REFERENCE: O.M.R. PG. 68; T.H.M. VOL. 6, PG. 189

NAMES: ADAM CLAP TO REBECCA ROBERTS
DATE: SEPT. 17,
REFERENCE: T.H.M. VOL. 6, PG. 189

NAMES: JAMES COLEMAN TO SALLY HICKEY
DATE: MAY 1, 1822
BONDSMAN: JACOB LONES
DATE PER: MAY 2, 1822
BY: JAMES C. LUTTRELL, J.P.
REFERENCE: C.A; O.M.R. PG. 66; T.H.M. VOL. 6, PG. 189

NAMES: DAVID COUCH TO ELIZABETH REED
DATE: JUNE 13, 1822
BONDSMAN: WM. MOORE
DATE PER: JUNE 13, 1822
BY: WM. MORRIS, J.P.
REFERENCE: C.A; O.M.R. PG. 66; T.H.M. VOL. 6, PG. 189

NAMES: JOHN COURTNEY TO NANCY ROBISON
DATE: OCT. 29, 1822
BONDSMAN: WM. COURTNEY
DATE PER: OCT. 30, 1822
BY: P. NANCE, J.P.
REFERENCE: C.A; O.M.R. PG. 69; T.H.M. VOL. 6, PG. 189

NAMES: WHITNER COX TO RACHEL MILLER
DATE: DEC. 16, 1822
DATE PER: DEC. 19, 1822
BY: JOHN BAYLESS, J.P.
REFERENCE: C.A; O.M.R. PG. 70

NAMES: ISAAC FOSTER TO MARY GIBBS
DATE: MAR. 16, 1822
BONDSMAN: JOHN FOSTER
DATE PER: MAR. 21, 1822
BY: JOHN BAYLESS, J.P.
REFERENCE: C.A; O.M.R. PG. 65; T.H.M. VOL. 6, PG. 189

NAMES: JOEL FROST TO SUSANNAH TINDELL
DATE: DEC. 9, 1822
DATE PER: DEC. 10, 1822
BY: JOHN BAYLESS, J.P.
REFERENCE: C.A; O.M.R. PG. 70; T.H.M. VOL. 6, PG. 189

NAMES: RHODES FRY TO BETSY DOYLE
DATE: APR. 17, 1822
BONDSMAN: FREDERICK AULT
DATE PER: APR. 17, 1822
BY: ROB'T. LINDSAY, J.P.
REFERENCE: C.A; O.M.R. PG. 65; T.H.M. VOL. 6, PG. 189

NAMES: ISAAC GILSTRAP TO LACKY DAVIS
DATE: MAR. 22, 1822
BONDSMAN: ELIJAH JOHNSTON
WITNESS: WILL SWAN
REFERENCE: C.A; T.H.M. VOL. 6, PG. 189

NAMES: JACOB HACKNEY TO SALLY FISHER
DATE: JUNE 4, 1822
BONDSMAN: BARTON HACKNEY
DATE PER: JUNE 4, 1822
BY: JOHN HAYNIE
WITNESS: WM. SWAN
REFERENCE: C.A; O.M.R. PG. 66; T.H.M. VOL. 6, PG. 190

NAMES: JAMES HALL TO ELIZABETH PENSLEY
DATE: JUNE 24,
REFERENCE: T.H.M. VOL. 6, PG. 190

NAMES: A. HANSARD TO NANCY LEWIS
DATE: DEC. 24, 1822
DATE PER: DEC. 26, 1822
BY: JOHN BAYLESS, J.P.
REFERENCE: C.A; O.M.R. PG. 70; T.H.M. VOL. 6, PG. 190

NAMES: WILLIAM HEATH TO POLLY PLUMLEY
DATE: OCT. 15, 1822
BONDSMAN: WILSON WHITE
DATE PER: OCT. 15, 1822
BY: JOHN HAYNIE
REFERENCE: C.A; O.M.R. PG. 68

NAMES: WM. HEAVIN TO ELIZABETH SHELL
DATE: JANY. 8, 1822
BONDSMAN: CHARLES BOWERS
REFERENCE: C.A; T.H.M. VOL. 6, PG. 190

NAMES: WILLIAM HENSON TO FERIBA COTTRELL
DATE: AUG. 29, 1822
BONDSMAN: JOSEPH MCCARREL
DATE PER: AUG. 29, 1822
BY: P. NANCE, J.P.
REFERENCE: C.A; O.M.R. PG. 68; T.H.M. VOL. 6, PG. 190

NAMES: PHILIP HINCKLE TO RACHEL SMITH
DATE: JULY 13, 1822
BONDSMAN: SAMUEL FRAZIER
DATE PER: JUNE 25, 1822
BY: WILLIAM B. CARNS, J.P.
REFERENCE: C.A; O.M.R. PG. 67; T.H.M. VOL. 6, PG. 190

NAMES: JACOB HOWSER TO BETSY ANDERSON
DATE: JULY 29, 1822
DATE PER: JULY 30, 1822
BY: ROB'T MCBATH,
REFERENCE: C.A; O.M.R. PG. 67; T.H.M. VOL. 6, PG. 190

NAMES: SAMUEL INGRAM TO POLLY GILLIAM
DATE: JANY. 26, 1822
BONDSMAN: ARMSTRONG MORROW
DATE PER: JANY. 26, 1822
BY: JOHN MCCAMPBELL, J.P.
REFERENCE: C.A; O.M.R. PG. 64; T.H.M. VOL. 6, PG. 190

NAMES: FRANCIS K. JONES TO POLLY FORKNER
DATE: FEBY. 26, 1822
DATE PER: FEBY. 26, 1822
BY: P. NANCE, J.P.
REFERENCE: C.A; O.M.R. PG. 64; T.H.M. VOL. 6, PG. 190

NAMES: PETER KEENER TO NANCY RECTOR
DATE: APR. 1, 1822
DATE PER: APR. 4, 1822
BY: SAM'L MONTGOMERY
REFERENCE: C.A; O.M.R. PG. 65; T.H.M. VOL. 6, PG. 190

NAMES: SAMUEL KELLY TO CATHARINE FORMWALT
DATE: JANY. 24, 1822
BONDSMAN: JOSHUA JACKSON
DATE PER: JANY. 24, 1822
BY: JOHN HAYNIE
REFERENCE: C.A; O.M.R. PG. 64; T.H.M. VOL. 6, PG. 190

NAMES: HENRY KEYS TO REBECKA LYONS
DATE: OCT. 31, 1822
DATE PER: OCT. 31, 1822
BY: THOS. WILKERSON
REFERENCE: O.M.R. PG. 69; T.H.M. VOL. 6, PG. 190

NAMES: J. V. R. KING TO MARY ANN WALKER
DATE: DEC. 2, 1822
BONDSMAN: J.G.M. RAMSEY
REFERENCE: C.A; T.H.M.VOL. 6, PG. 190

NAMES: JACOB LINGENFETTER TO JANE RAY
DATE: DEC. 10, 1822
DATE PER: DEC. 10, 1822
BY: ROB'T. MCBATH, ESQ.
REFERENCE: C.A; O.M.R. PG. 70

NAMES: SAMUEL LOVE TO POLLY SMITH
DATE: JULY 9, 1822
BONDSMAN: RO. HOUSTON
REFERENCE: C.A.

NAMES: SAM'L LOVE TO POLLY SMITH
DATE: JULY 9, 1822
DATE PER: JULY 9, 1822
BY: R. HOUSTON, J.P.
REFERENCE: O.M.R. PG. 67; T.H.M. VOL. 6, PG. 190

NAMES: THOMAS LUTTRELL TO MARIA JONES
DATE: JUNE 26, 1822
DATE PER: JUNE 26, 1822
BY: SAM'L MONTGOMERY
REFERENCE: O.M.R. PG. 66

NAMES: SAMUEL MARTIN TO MARTHA STEWART
DATE: APR. 17, 1822
REFERENCE: C.A; O.M.R. PG. 65; T.H.M. VOL. 6, PG. 190

NAMES: MORGAN G. MAUPINE TO ELIZABETH CALLEN
DATE: MAY 28, 1822
BONDSMAN: ARCHIBALD CALLEN
DATE PER: MAY 30, 1822
BY: J. CUNNINGHAM, M.E.
REFERENCE: C.A; O.M.R. PG. 66; T.H.M. VOL. 6, PG. 190

NAMES: LEVI MCCLOUD TO PEGGY COUNTZ
DATE: OCT. 29, 1822
BONDSMAN: JAMES MCCLOUD
DATE PER: OCT. 31, 1822
BY: WILLIS HAMMONDS, M. G.
REFERENCE: C.A; O.M.R. PG. 69; T.H.M. VOL. 6, PG. 189

Names: John McNaire to Mary Shertz
Date: July 12, 1822
Bondsman: Robert Houston
Date Per: July 12, 1822
By: R. Houston, J.P.
Reference: C.A; T.H.M. Vol. 6, Pg. 190

Names: Isaac Michaels to Sally Davis
Date: Aug. 25, 1822
Reference: C.A.

Names: Elisha Milliken to Mary Clayton
Date: Sept. 24, 1822
Bondsman: Sam'l McFerren
Date Per: Oct. 3, 1822
By: John Gass, J.P.
Reference: C.A; O.M.R. Pg. 68; T.H.M. Vol. 6, Pg. 190

Names: John Milteberger to Sally Craig
Date: Feby. 12, 1822
Bondsman: Joseph Woods
Witness: Will Swan
Reference: C.A.

Names: John Milteberger to Sally Craig
Date: Feby. 12, 1822
Date Per: Feby. 14, 1822
By: Dan'l Gibbs, J.P.
Reference: O.M.R. Pg. 64; T.H.M. Vol. 6, Pg. 190

Names: Jethro W. Mounger to Elizabeth Galliher
Date: Oct. 23, 1822
Bondsman: John Stuart
Reference: C.A.

Names: Jethro W. Mounger to Elizabeth Galliher
Date: Oct. 23, 1822
Date Per: Oct. 31, 1822
By: Robert Hardin
Reference: O.M.R. Pg. 69; T.H.M. Vol. 6, Pg. 190

Names: Jacob Mulvany to Nancy Lane
Date: Nov. 25, 1822
Bondsman: Jesse Smith
Reference: C.A.

Names: Jacob Mulvany to Nancy Lane,
Date: Nov. 25, 1822
Date Per: Nov. 26, 1822
By: J. Cunningham, M.G.
Reference: O.M.R. Pg. 69; T.H.M. Vol. 6, Pg. 190

Names: R. Murray to Anna Elliott
Date: Aug. 6, 1822
Date Per: Aug. 6, 1822
By: James C. Luttrell, J.P.
Reference: C.A; O.M.R. Pg. 67; T.H.M. Vol. 6, Pg. 190

Names: James Mynatt to Nancy Parker
Date: Aug. 6?, 1822
Bondsman: A. M. Brown
Date Per: Aug. 12, 1822
By: John Bayless, J.P.
Reference: C.A; O.M.R. Pg. 67; T.H.M. Vol. 6, Pg. 190

Names: Edmund Newman to Margaret Bowman
Date: Feby. 2, 1822
Bondsman: Samuel Bowman
Date Per: Feby. 5, 1822
By: B. McNutt, J.P.
Reference: C.A; O.M.R. Pg. 64; T.H.M. Vol. 6, Pg. 190

Names: Frederick Nichodemus to Catharine Howell
Date: Dec. 18, 1822
Date Per: Dec. 19, 1822
By: R. Houston, J.P.
Reference: C.A; O.M.R. Pg. 70; T.H.M. Vol. 6, Pg. 190

Names: Alfred Norris to Talitha Bledsoe
Date: Nov. 14, 1822
Date Per: Nov. 14, 1822
By: Jas. Atkin, M. G. Methodist Ch.
Reference: C.A; O.M.R. Pg. 69; T.H.M. Vol. 6, Pg. 190

Names: Peter Ogg to Eliza Dowell
Date: Apr. 18, 1822
Date Per: Apr. 18, 1822
By: William B. Carns, J.P.
Reference: C.A; O.M.R. Pg. 66; T.H.M. Vol. 6, Pg. 190

Names: Reynolds Ramsey to Ann Roane
Date: July 17, 1822
Bondsman: W. B. A. Ramsey
Reference: C.A.

Names: Reynolds Ramsey to Ann Roane
Date: July 17, 1822
Date Per: July 18, 1822
By: R.H. King, M.G.
Reference: O.M.R. Pg. 67; T.H.M. Vol. 6, Pg. 190

NAMES: JOHN RANSOM TO BETSY LUTTRELL
DATE: NOV. 14, 1822
BONDSMAN: JOHN JONES
REFERENCE: C.A;

NAMES: JOHN RANSOM TO BETSY LUTTRELL
DATE: NOV. 14, 1822
DATE PER: NOV. 14, 1822
BY: ROBERT MCBATH, ESQ.
REFERENCE: O.M.R. PG. 69; T.H.M. VOL. 6, PG. 190

NAMES: DANIEL REAGAN TO BETSY CATCHUM
DATE: SEPT. 11, 1822
BONDSMAN: ABSALOM REAGEN
REFERENCE: C.A; T.H.M. VOL. 6, PG. 190

NAMES: JOSEPH REED TO BETSY BREESE
DATE: DEC. 12, 1822
DATE PER: DEC. 12, 1822
BY: JAMES MCMILLAN, J.P.
REFERENCE: C.A; O.M.R. PG. 70; T.H.M. VOL. 6, PG. 190

NAMES: JOHN REYNOLDS TO JANE MCHAFFIE
DATE: APR. 11, 1822
BONDSMAN: SAMUEL KELLY
REFERENCE: C.A; T.H.M. VOL. 6, PG. 190

NAMES: WM. RODDY TO MARTHA CHILDRESS
DATE: JANY. 15, 1822
DATE PER: JANY. 15, 1822
BY: PETER NANCE, J.P.
REFERENCE: O.M.R. PG. 64; T.H.M. VOL. 6, PG. 190

NAMES: PHILIP ROHR TO MARGARET FORMWALT
DATE: DEC. 27, 1822
BONDSMAN: HAMDEN SCOTT & SAM'L M. ARMSTRONG
DATE PER: DEC. 27, 1822
BY: DAVID NELSON, J.P.
WITNESS: WM. SWAN
REFERENCE: C.A; O.M.R. PG. 70; T.H.M. VOL. 6, PG. 190

NAMES: JOSEPH ROUTH TO JANE LOVELASS
DATE: ~~DEC. 24, 1822~~
BONDSMAN: ~~JAMES ROUTH~~ DATE PER: DEC. 24, 1822
BY: WM. ~~A.~~ MCCAMPBELL, J.P.
REFERENCE: C.A; O.M.R. PG. 70; T.H.M. VOL. 6, PG. 190

NAMES: JOHN SHERETZ TO POLLY BRANNER
DATE: SEPT. 2, 1822
DATE PER: SEPT. 3, 1822
BY: R. HOUSTON, J.P.
REFERENCE: C.A; O.M.R. PG. 68

NAMES: JOHN SHERETZ TO GEORGIA WALKER
DATE: SEPT. 2, 1822
REFERENCE: T.H.M. VOL. 6, PG. 190

NAMES: CHARLES SMITH TO BETSY SIMPSON
DATE: AUG. 21, 1822
BONDSMAN: JAMES MCNUTT
BY: R. HOUSTON, J.P.
REFERENCE: C.A; O.M.R. PG. 68; T.H.M. VOL. 6, PG. 190

NAMES: JOHN SMITH TO HARRIET COMBS
DATE: FEBY. 4, 1822
DATE PER: FEBY. 7, 1822
BY: LEWIS LUTTRELL, J.P.
REFERENCE: C.A; O.M.R. PG. 64; T.H.M. VOL. 6, PG. 190

NAMES: ROBERT SMITH TO ELIZA STERLING
DATE: SEPT. 3,
REFERENCE: T.H.M.VOL. 6, PG. 190

NAMES: WILLIAM SMITH TO POLLY GOODMAN
DATE: DEC. 4, 1822
BY: ROBERT TUNNELL, J.P.
REFERENCE: C.A; O.M.R. PG. 69; T.H.M. VOL. 6, PG. 190

NAMES: ARCHIBALD SNOW TO NANCY GRIFFIS
DATE: AUG. 10, 1822
DATE PER: JAN. 7, 1823
BY: WM. MORRIS, J.P.
REFERENCE: C.A; O.M.R. PG. 67; T.H.M. VOL. 6, PG. 190

NAMES: FRANCIS SWADER TO MARY LYONS
DATE: JULY 23, 1822
BONDSMAN: JAMES PEARSON
REFERENCE: C.A; T.H.M. VOL. 6, PG. 190

NAMES: STOCKLY D. SWAGGERTY TO POLLY GUNN
DATE: DEC. 20, 1822
DATE PER: DEC. 20, 1822
BY: SAM'L MONTGOMERY
REFERENCE: C.A; O.M.R. PG. 70; T.H.M. VOL. 6, PG. 190

NAMES: SAMUEL TARBET TO ELIZABETH COUNCIL
DATE: FEBY. 26, 1822
BONDSMAN: HOWARD COUNCIL
DATE PER: FEBY. 28, 1822
BY: RD. H. KING
WITNESS: CHAS. MCCLUNG
REFERENCE: C.A; O.M.R. PG. 65

NAMES: JAMES THOMPSON TO DINAH BITCHBOARD
DATE: JULY 25, 1822
DATE PER: JULY 25, 1822
BY: ROBERT MCBATH, ESQ.
REFERENCE: C.A; O.M.R. PG. 67; T.H.M. VOL. 6, PG. 190

NAMES: GEORGE W. TOBLER TO PEGGY HENSHAW
DATE: MAY 13, 1822
REFERENCE: T.H.M. VOL. 6, PG. 190

NAMES: JOHN UBANK TO PATSY WALKER
DATE: AUG. 24, 1822
BONDSMAN: WM. MERRIMAN
DATE PER: AUG. 25, 1822
BY: JOHN A. SULAN, J.P.
WITNESS: WM. SWAN
REFERENCE: C.A; O.M.R. PG. 68; T.H.M. VOL. 6, PG. 190

NAMES: RICHARD WALKER TO SUSAN THOMAS
DATE: APR. 9, 1822
DATE PER: APR. 12, 1822
BY: ROBERT MCBATH, ESQ.
REFERENCE: C.A; O.M.R. PG. 65; T.H.M. VOL. 6, PG. 190

NAMES: JOHN WATTS TO ANNA WOLF
DATE: MAY 20, 1822
DATE PER: MAY 21, 1822
BY: R. HOUSTON, J.P.
REFERENCE: C.A; O.M.R. PG. 66

NAMES: SEVIER WHEELER TO SALLY JOHNSTON
DATE: MAR. 28, 1822
BONDSMAN: NATHANIEL HARRIS
DATE PER: MAR. 28, 1822
BY: PETER NANCE, J.P.
REFERENCE: C.A; O.M.R. PG. 65; T.H.M. VOL. 6, PG. 190

NAMES: GEORGE WILHITE TO NANCY GUINS
DATE: JULY 2, 1822
DATE PER: JULY 7, 1822
BY: P. NANCE, J.P.
REFERENCE: C.A; O.M.R. PG. 67; T.H.M. VOL. 6, PG. 190

NAMES: MASON WOODS TO ELIZABETH COLE
DATE: OCT. 14, 1822
DATE PER: OCT. 17, 1822
BY: JOHN GASS, J.P.
REFERENCE: C.A; O.M.R. PG. 68; T.H.M. VOL. 6, PG. 190

1823

NAMES: MOSES ABEL TO BETSY MCHENRY
DATE: JULY 1, 1823
BONDSMAN: GEO. R. CANNON
REFERENCE: C.A; T.H.M. VOL. 6, PG. 190

NAMES: JOHN ANDERSON TO SALLY DURHAM
DATE: MAY 1, 1823
BONDSMAN: SEVIER MASSEY
WITNESS: WM. SWAN
REFERENCE: C.A; T.H.M. VOL. 6, PG. 190

NAMES: ADDISON W. ARMSTRONG TO NANCY MCMILLIAN
DATE: MCH. 21,
REFERENCE: T.H.M. VOL. 6, PG. 190

NAMES: DRURY P. ARMSTRONG TO AMELIA HOUSTON
DATE: FEBY. 17, 1823
DATE PER: FEBY. 18, 1823
BY: JAMES MCMILLAN, J.P.
REFERENCE: O.M.R. PG. 72

NAMES: HENRY BAKER TO RHODA HAVIN
DATE: JANY. 24, 1823
BONDSMAN: RICHARD HAVIN
DATE PER: FEBY. 6, 1823
BY: JOHN GASS, J.P.
WITNESS: WM. SWAN
REFERENCE: C.A; O.M.R. PG. 71

NAMES: HARDIN BARKER TO ANNICE WILSON
DATE: NOV. 20, 1823
DATE PER: NOV. 20, 1823
BY: JAMES MCMILLAN, J.P.
REFERENCE: C.A; O.M.R. PG. 78

NAMES: JAMES S. BELL TO NANCY CONNER
DATE: APR. 28, 1823
DATE PER: APR. 29, 1823
BY: J. B. WYNN, M.G.
REFERENCE: C.A; O.M.R. PG. 73; T.H.M. VOL. 6, PG. 191

Names: Ro. Bell to Malinda Scott
Date: Feby. 20, 1823
Date Per: Feby. 21, 1823
By: Jno. Bayless, J.P.
Reference: O.M.R. Pg. 72; T.H.M. Vol. 6, Pg. 191

Names: Presley Bennett to Nancy Crews
Date: July 3, 1823
Bondsman: Walter Childress
Date Per: July 3, 1823
By: Rob't McBath
Witness: Wm. Swan
Reference: C.A; O.M.R. Pg. 75

Names: Obadiah Boaz to Eliza Prudence King
Date: Nov. 18, 1823
Date Per: Nov. 25, 1823
By: Isaac Anderson, M. G.
Reference: C.A; O.M.R. Pg. 78; T.H.M. Vol. 6, Pg. 191

Names: Samuel Bowman to Betsy Heppenstall
Date: Dec. 31, 1823
Date Per: Jany. 1, 1824
By: B. McNutt, J.P.
Reference: C.A; O.M.R. Pg. 79; T.H.M. Vol. 6, Pg. 191

Names: John Brooks to Nancy Kirkland
Date: July 10, 1823
Bondsman: D. Swaggerty
Date Per: July 10, 1823
By: R. A. Swan, J.P.
Reference: C.A; O.M.R. Pg. 75

Names: Jacob M. Butler to Sarah Hardin
Date: Nov. 17, 1823
Bondsman: Jas. H. Gallaher
Reference: C.A; T.H.M. Vol. 6, Pg. 191

Names: Levi Byram to Mary Rigney
Date: Jany. 13, 1823
Bondsman: Ebenezer Byram
Date Per: Jany. 16, 1823
By: Mordecai Yarnell, J.P.
Witness: Wm. Swan
Reference: C.A; O.M.R. Pg. 71

Names: David Campbell to Jane Smith
Date: Nov. 29, 1823
Bondsman: Jno. T. Smith
Date Per: Nov. 29, 1823
By: Rd. H. King
Reference: C.A; O.M.R. Pg. 78; T.H.M. Vol. 6, Pg. 191

Names: Benjamin Cash to Betsy Burnett
Date: Mar. 8, 1823
Bondsman: G. Brown
Witness: Wm. Swan
Reference: C.A.

Names: Elijah Casteel to Sally Fairchild
Date: Aug. 30, 1823
Bondsman: Jeremiah Johnson
Date Per: Sept. 2, 1823
By: Robert McBath
Witness: Wm. Swan
Reference: C.A; O.M.R. Pg. 76; T.H.M. Vol. 6, Pg. 191

Names: George Cheasman to Malinda Mayfield
Date: Apr. 2, 1823
Reference: T.H.M. Vol. 6, Pg. 191

Names: Richard Chinowith to Ellen Hammer
Date: Jany. 14, 1823
Bondsman: Mordecai Yarnell
Date Per: Jany. 14, 1823
By: Mordecai Yarnell, J.P.
Reference: C.A; O.M.R. Pg. 71

Names: Larenzo D. Cliborn to Peggy E. Anderson
Date: Oct. 2, 1823
Bondsman: James Anderson
Witness: Wm. Swan
Reference: C.A; O.M.R. Pg. 77

Names: Wm. Clift to Nancy Brooks
Date: Aprl. 15, 1823
Bondsman: Wm. Walker
Reference: C.A.

Names: Wm. Clift to Nancy Brooks
Date: Apr. 15, 1823
Date Per: Apr. 15, 1823
By: Tho. H. Nelson, M. G.
Reference: O.M.R. Pg. 73; T.H.M. Vol. 6, Pg. 191

Names: John W. Coen to Charlotte Monday
Date: July 1, 1823
Date Per: July 1, 1823
By: Mordecai Yarnell, J.P.
Reference: C.A; O.M.R. Pg. 75

NAMES: ANDREW CRAWFORD TO SALLY MEEKE
DATE: MAY 22, 1823
BONDSMAN: T. L. WILLIAMS
DATE PER: MAY 22, 1823
BY: GEO. ATKIN, M.G.
REFERENCE: C.A; O.M.R. PG. 74

NAMES: DAVID CREWS TO POLLY SMITH
DATE: OCT. 4, 1823
BONDSMAN: LEVI MCCLOUD
DATE PER: OCT. 5, 1823
BY: WILLIAM B. CARNS, J.P.
REFERENCE: C.A; O.M.R. PG. 77; T.H.M. VOL. 6, PG. 191

NAMES: ROBERT CREWS TO MARY ANN BURNHAM
DATE: APR. 3, 1823
DATE PER: APR. 16, 1823
BY: ROB'T MCBATH, ESQ.
REFERENCE: C.A; O.M.R. PG. 73

NAMES: JAMES CUNNINGHAM TO PEGGY ANDERSON
DATE: SEPT. 3, 1823
BONDSMAN: S. JARNAGIN
DATE PER: SEPT. 4, 1823
BY: ROBERT MCBATH
REFERENCE: C.A; O.M.R. PG. 77; T.H.M. VOL. 6, PG. 191

NAMES: EDMOND DAVIS TO MARY ANN MARTHANA LEFEW
DATE: MAY 7, 1823
BONDSMAN: ALEXANDER DAVIS
WITNESS: WM. SWAN
REFERENCE: C.A; T.H.M. VOL. 6, PG. 191

NAMES: JAMES DAVIS TO IBBY BOOKER
DATE: MAY 20, 1823
BONDSMAN: NICHOLAS GIBBS
DATE PER: MAY 22, 1823
BY: JOHN BAYLESS, J.P.
REFERENCE: C.A; O.M.R. PG. 74

NAMES: WM. DAVIS TO BETSY HUNTER
DATE: FEBY. 10, 1823
BONDSMAN: WM. SWAN
REFERENCE: C.A; T.H.M. VOL. 6, PG. 191

NAMES: WILLIS DODD TO POLLY DAVIS
DATE: JULY 15, 1823
BONDSMAN: JOHN HILL
DATE PER: JULY 15, 1823
BY: JOHN HAYNIE
REFERENCE: C.A; O.M.R. PG. 76

NAMES: DAVID DOYLE TO SALLY HOWSER
DATE: MAY 3, 1823
BONDSMAN: ISAAC DOYLE
DATE PER: MAY 5, 1823
BY: ROBERT MCBATH, J.P.
REFERENCE: C.A; O.M.R. PG. 73; T.H.M. VOL. 6, PG. 191

NAMES: JOHN B. EDMONDSON TO POLLY CRAWFORD
DATE: MAY 7, 1823
DATE PER: MAY 8, 1823
BY: JOHN MCCAMPBELL, V.D.M.
REFERENCE: C.A; O.M.R. PG. 73; T.H.M. VOL. 6, PG. 191

NAMES: STEPHEN ELDRIDGE TO MILLY WALKER
DATE: DEC. 18, 1823
BONDSMAN: WM. HAZEN
WITNESS: WM. SWAN
REFERENCE: C.A; T.H.M. VOL. 6, PG. 191

NAMES: ISAAC ELLIOTT TO FERIBY WILLIAMS
DATE: MAY 29, 1823
BONDSMAN: WILSON PARKER
DATE PER: MAY 29, 1823
BY: WM. B. CARNS, J.P.
REFERENCE: C.A; O.M.R. PG. 74; T.H.M. VOL. 6, PG. 191

NAMES: WILLIAM FARGUSON TO PHEBY MORGAN
DATE: JANY. 4, 1823
DATE PER: JANY. 4, 1823
BY: WM. B. CARNS, J.P.
REFERENCE: C.A; O.M.R. PG. 71

NAMES: JNO. FLENNIKEN TO SALLY COTTRELL
DATE: JULY 1, 1823
BONDSMAN: J. W. FLENNIKEN
WITNESS: A. HUTCHESON
REFERENCE: C.A.

NAMES: DANIEL D. FOUT TO DORCAS M. KING
DATE: OCT. 7, 1823
DATE PER: OCT. 7, 1823
BY: THO. H. NELSON (PRESBY. CHURCH)
REFERENCE: C.A; O.M.R. PG. 77; T.H.M. VOL. 6, PG. 191

NAMES: JOSEPH GUSLING TO BETSY KEYS
DATE: JAN. 9
REFERENCE: T.H.M. VOL. 6, PG. 191

NAMES: THOMAS HALL TO JANE EDINGTON
DATE: AUG. 20, 1823
DATE PER: AUG. 21, 1823
BY: ROBERT MCBATH
REFERENCE: C.A; O.M.R. PG. 76

NAMES: JESSE HAMMER TO LILAH UNDERWOOD
DATE: JANY. 18, 1823
BONDSMAN: HIRAM UNDERWOOD
REFERENCE: C.A; O.M.R. PG. 71; T.H.M. VOL. 6, PG. 191

NAMES: WILLIAM HANALSON TO CATHERINE WILLS
DATE: MCH. 31,
REFERENCE: T.H.M. VOL. 6, PG. 191

NAMES: JORDAN L. HANES TO LETTY CONN
DATE: MAR. 5, 1823
BONDSMAN: ROBERT CONN – WILLIS KING
REFERENCE: C.A; T.H.M. VOL. 6, PG. 191

NAMES: JOHN HANNON TO MILLY HUSONG
DATE: DEC. 22, 1823
REFERENCE: C.A; O.M.R. PG. 79; T.H.M. VOL. 6, PG. 191

NAMES: THOMAS HENDERSON TO FRANKY AYERS
DATE: MAR. 21, 1823
BONDSMAN: THOMAS W. REED
REFERENCE: C.A.

NAMES: SAMUEL HENSLEY TO NANCY JOHNSTON
DATE: MAY 28, 1823
BONDSMAN: AARON HOOD
DATE PER: MAY 29, 1823
BY: ROBERT MCBATH, J.P.
REFERENCE: C.A; O.M.R. PG. 74

NAMES: GEORGE HICKEY TO LUCINDA REED
DATE: AUG. 9, 1823
DATE PER: AUG. 13, 1823
BY: MORDECAI YARNELL, J.P.
REFERENCE: C.A; O.M.R. PG. 76

NAMES: LEWIS HILL TO RACHEL BIRDWELL
DATE: JULY 18,
REFERENCE: T.H.M. VOL. 6, PG. 191

NAMES: AARON HOOD TO NANCY HENSLEY
DATE: MAY 28, 1823
DATE PER: MAY 29, 1823
BY: ROBERT MCBATH, J.P.
REFERENCE: C.A; O.M.R. PG. 74; T.H.M. VOL. 6, PG. 191

NAMES: ANDREW HOOD TO SALLY BURNHAM
DATE: MAY 10, 1823
BONDSMAN: NICHOLAS HUSONG
WITNESS: WM. SWAN
REFERENCE: C.A; O.M.R. PG. 73

NAMES: JOHN HUNTER TO ELIZABETH MCMILLAN
DATE: DEC. 23, 1823
DATE PER: JANY. 1, 1824
BY: JAS. MCMILLAN, J.P.
REFERENCE: C.A; O.M.R. PG. 79; T.H.M. VOL. 6, PG. 191

NAMES: ISOM ISRAEL TO NETTY PARR
DATE: MAR. 28, 1823
BONDSMAN: MATTHIAS PARR
REFERENCE: C.A; T.H.M VOL. 6, PG. 191

NAMES: WM. JETT TO AILCY NORMAN
DATE: NOV. 3, 1823
BONDSMAN: COURTNEY NORMAN
DATE PER: NOV. 20, 1823
BY: JOHN GASS, J.P.
REFERENCE: C.A; O.M.R. PG. 78; T.H.M. VOL. 6, PG. 191

NAMES: CASWELL JOHNSTON TO SUSAN G. TUNNELL
DATE: NOV. 6, 1823
DATE PER: NOV. 6, 1823
BY: WM. MORRIS, J.P.
REFERENCE: C.A; O.M.R. PG. 78

NAMES: DAVID JOHNSTON TO POLLY CLAPP
DATE: NOV. 11, 1823
DATE PER: NOV. 11, 1823
BY: DANIEL GIBBS, J.P.
REFERENCE: C.A; O.M.R. PG. 78

NAMES: JOHN JOHNSTON TO ELIZABETH CHRISTIAN
DATE: JANY. 13, 1823
DATE PER: JANY. 23, 1823
BY: JOHN BAYLESS, J.P.
REFERENCE: C.A; O.M.R. PG. 71

NAMES: ANDREW KEITH TO MARTHA MITCHELL
DATE: APR. 16, 1823
DATE PER: APR. 16, 1823
BY: JOSEPH B. WYMES, M. G.
REFERENCE: C.A; O.M.R. PG. 73; T.H.M. VOL. 6, PG. 191

NAMES: LUCAS KENNEDY TO MARY KAIN
DATE: JULY 15, 1823
BONDSMAN: JNO. H. KAIN
REFERENCE: C.A; T.H.M. VOL. 6, PG. 191

NAMES: JOSEPH KIMBROUGH TO MARY L. HASEN
DATE: OCT. 15, 1823
DATE PER: OCT. 15, 1823
BY: JOHN HAYNIE
REFERENCE: C.A; O.M.R. PG. 77; T.H.M. VOL. 6, PG. 191

NAMES: LOREN R. LEWIS TO LEVINA RODDY
DATE: FEBY. 25, 1823
BONDSMAN: W. S. HOWELL
WITNESS: WM. SWAN
REFERENCE: C.A; T.H.M. VOL. 6, PG. 191

NAMES: LOREN R. LEWIS TO LEVINIA RODDY
DATE: FEBY. 25, 1823
DATE PER: FEBY. 25, 1823
BY: PETER NANCE, J.P.
REFERENCE: O.M.R. PG. 72

NAMES: JOHN LONES TO EVELINE HILLSMAN
DATE: JANY. 21, 1823
DATE PER: JANY. 23, 1823
BY: JAMES C. LUTTRELL, J.P.
REFERENCE: C.A; O.M.R. PG. 71

NAMES: JOSEPH LONES TO NANCY CAVETTE
DATE: DEC. 14, 1823
DATE PER: DEC. 14, 1823
BY: JNO. HAYNIE
REFERENCE: O.M.R. PG. 79; T.H.M. VOL. 6, PG. 191

NAMES: ZACHARIA A. LYLE TO MARIA HAYNIE
DATE: NOV. 18, 1823
DATE PER: NOV. 18, 1823
BY: JOHN HAYNIE
REFERENCE: C.A; O.M.R. PG. 78

NAMES: WILLIAM MACLIN TO ANNE STARKY
DATE: FEBY. 5, 1823
DATE PER: FEBY. 6, 1823
BY: ROBERT TUNNELL, J.P.
WITNESS: CHAS. MCCLUNG, CLK.
REFERENCE: C.A; O.M.R. PG. 79

NAMES: SILAS MARPHEE TO MATILDA CLAYTON
DATE: NOV. 11, 1823
BONDSMAN: JOHN JARDEN
WITNESS: CHAS. MCCLUNG
REFERENCE: C.A; T.H.M. VOL. 6, PG. 191

NAMES: BENJ. B. MCCAMPBELL TO MARGARET ANDERSON
DATE: JANY. 27, 1823
DATE PER: JANY. 30, 1823
BY: ISAAC ANDERSON, M. G.
REFERENCE: O.M.R. PG. 71

NAMES: JAMES MCCAMPBELL TO JANE BOYD
DATE: MAR. 27, 1823
BONDSMAN: WM. MARSHALL
DATE PER: MAR. 27, 1823
BY: SAM. S. MCCAMPBELL, J.P.
REFERENCE: C.A; O.M.R. PG. 73; T.H.M. VOL. 6, PG. 191

NAMES: ANDREW MCHAFFIE TO NANCY WOODS
DATE: JULY 4, 1823
DATE PER: JULY 17, 1723
BY: WM. SAWYERS, J.P.
REFERENCE: C.A; O.M.R. PG. 75

NAMES: JOHN MCKAMEY TO POLLY CLARK
DATE: MAY 26, 1823
BONDSMAN: WM. SWAN
REFERENCE: C.A.

NAMES: JAMES MCMILLAN TO NANCY KENNEDY
DATE: DEC. 30,
REFERENCE: T.H.M. VOL. 6, PG. 191

NAMES: JOHN MCNAMEY TO RACHEL SMITH
DATE: JUNE 16, 1823
DATE PER: JUNE 17, 1823
BY: WM. MORRIS, J.P.
REFERENCE: C.A; O.M.R. PG. 75; T.H.M. VOL. 6, PG. 191

NAMES: ROBERT MCNUTT TO NANCY THOMPSON
DATE: JULY 1, 1823
DATE PER: JULY 3, 1823
BY: SAM'L. MONTGOMERY
REFERENCE: C.A; O.M.R. PG. 75

NAMES: SAM'L. MCPHERRIN TO ELEANOR GENTRY
DATE: SEPT. 12, 1823
DATE PER: SEPT. 18, 1823
BY: JOHN GASS, J.P.
REFERENCE: C.A; O.M.R. PG. 77

NAMES: ROBERT MCREYNOLDS TO MARY WALKER
DATE: JUNE 11, 1823
BONDSMAN: JOHN RODGERS
DATE PER: JUNE 11, 1823
BY: GEO. ATKIN, M. G.
REFERENCE: C.A; O.M.R. PG. 74

Names: William Merriman to Catharine Hudaburg
Date: Dec. 15, 1823
Date Per: Dec. 18, 1823
By: Wm. Morris, J.P.
Reference: O.M.R. Pg. 79

Names: William Merriman to Catharine Hudaburg
Date: Dec. 15, 1823
Bondsman: Michael Bradberry
Reference: C.A.

Names: Charles Mitchell to Nancy McPherrin
Date: Oct. 18, 1823
Bondsman: James Hankins
Date Per: Oct. 21, 1823
By: John Gass. J.P.
Witness: Wm. Swan
Reference: C.A; O.M.R. Pg. 77

Names: Henry T. Mitchell to Rebecka Meek
Date: Dec. 16, 1823
Bondsman: Gabrl. Brown
Date Per: Dec. 16, 1823
By: George Atkin, M. G.
Reference: C.A; O.M.R. Pg. 79

Names: John Morgan to Judy Quails
Date: Aug. 28, 1823
Bondsman: Sam'l. Cunningham
Reference: C.A; T.H.M. Vol. 6, Pg. 191

Names: Charles Morrow to Sally Harris
Date: Dec. 18, 1823
Bondsman: Barkley Walker
Date Per: Dec. 18, 1823
By: James McMillan, J.P.
Reference: C.A; O.M.R. Pg. 79; T.H.M. Vol. 6, Pg. 191

Names: Wm. Murphy to Sally Johnston
Date: Mar. 12, 1823
Date Per: Mar. 12, 1823
By: Geo. Atkin, M. G.
Reference: C.A; O.M.R. Pg. 72

Names: Edward Murray to Eliza Hawthorn
Date: Nov. 20, 1823
Bondsman: Jesse Hawthorn
Date Per: Nov. 20, 1823
By: W. B. A. Ramsey, J.P.
Witness: Wm. Swan
Reference: C.A; O.M.R. Pg. 78

Names: Eli Murray to Phebe Hawthorn
Date: May 15, 1823
Bondsman: Timothy Reagan
Date Per: May 15, 1823
By: W. B. A. Ramsey, J.P.
Reference: C.A; O.M.R. Pg. 74; T.H.M. Vol. 6, Pg. 191

Names: Richard Nelson to Eliza McCampbell
Date: June 23, 1823
Date Per: June 26, 1823
By: Isaac Anderson, M. G.
Reference: O.M.R. Pg. 75

Names: Jno. Norwood to Mary Weaver
Date: June 21, 1823 -- Bondsman: Jno. Gass
Date Per: June 22, 1823
By: Jno. Gass, J.P.
Reference: O.M.R. Pg. 75; T.H.M. Vol. 6, Pg. 191; C.A.

Names: John Overton to Anne Parr
Date: Apr. 21, 1823
Bondsman: Joseph Jackson
Reference: C.A.

Names: Jno. Overton to Anne Parr
Date: Apr. 21, 1823
Date Per: Apr. 24, 1823
By: Daniel Gibbs, J.P.
Reference: O.M.R. Pg. 73; T.H.M. Vol. 6, Pg. 191

Names: William Patton to Jane Cunningham
Date: June 11, 1823
Bondsman: David Nelson
Date Per: June 12, 1823
By: Thomas Wilkerson, Elder in M. E. Church
Reference: C.A; O.M.R. Pg. 74; T.H.M. Vol. 6, Pg. 191

Names: Audley Paul to Ann Gillespie
Date: Nov. 4, 1823
Bondsman: Abrham Gillespie
Reference: C.A.

Names: John Reagan to Rebecka Moore
Date: Oct. 30, 1823
Bondsman: James Wilson
Date Per: Nov. 6, 1823
By: Robert McGath, J.P.
Reference: C.A; O.M.R. Pg. 78; T.H.M. Vol. 6, Pg. 191

NAMES: WASHINGTON RECTOR TO NANCY KIRKPATRICK
DATE: JULY 12, 1823
BONDSMAN: JOHN HOPE
DATE PER: JULY 17, 1823
BY: SAM'L S. MCCAMPBELL, J.P.
REFERENCE: C.A; O.M.R. PG. 76; T.H.M. VOL. 6, PG. 191

DATE: JAMES RENTFROW TO SALLY YOST
DATE: DEC. 22, 1823
BONDSMAN: PETER YOAST
DATE PER: DEC. 23, 1823
BY: WM. B. CARNES, J.P.
REFERENCE: C.A; O.M.R. PG. 79; T.H.M. VOL. 6, PG. 191

NAMES: FRANCIS RIVELY TO LOVY R. LOVE
DATE: AUG. 13, 1823
DATE PER: AUG. 14, 1823
BY: SAM'L FLEMING, J.P.
WITNESS: CHAS. MCCLUNG, CLK.
REFERENCE: C.A; O.M.R. PG. 76

NAMES: MOSES ROADY TO HETTY LOONEY
DATE: FEBY. 22, 1823
BONDSMAN: JOSEPH BURNETT
REFERENCE: C.A.

NAMES: THOMAS RODGERS TO CYNTHIA CAMPBELL
DATE: JUNE 19, 1823
BONDSMAN: S. M. ARMSTRONG,
DATE PER: JUNE 19, 1823
BY: B. MCNUTT, J.P.
REFERENCE: C.A; O.M.R. PG. 75; T.H.M. VOL. 6, PG. 191

NAMES: JOHN RUTHERFORD TO BETSY MCAFFREY
DATE: FEBY. 18, 1823
BONDSMAN: SAM'L WHITE - WM. SWAN
DATE PER: FEBY 18, 1823
BY: JOHN HAYNIE, ELDER
REFERENCE: C.A; O.M.R. PG. 72; T.H.M. VOL. 6, PG. 191

NAMES: ADAM SHORT TO POLLY PRATT
DATE: JANY. 22, 1823
BONDSMAN: SAM'L BOWMAN
DATE PER: FEBY. 5, 1823
BY: JAMES MCMILLAN, J.P.
REFERENCE: C.A; O.M.R. PG. 71; T.H.M. VOL. 6, PG. 191

NAMES: ROBERT SMITH TO ELIZA STIRLING
DATE: SEPT. 3, 1823
BONDSMAN: WM. J. CLARK
DATE PER: SEPT. 3, 1823
BY: DAVID NELSON, J.P.
REFERENCE: C.A; O.M.R. PG. 77

NAMES: ROBERT SMITH TO PHEBE CLAPP
DATE: NOV. 25, 1823
BONDSMAN: MICHAEL SMITH
REFERENCE: C.A; T.H.M. VOL. 6, PG. 191

NAMES: SAMUEL SMITH TO ONEY KEARNS
DATE: AUG. 12, 1823
BONDSMAN: WM. SWAN
DATE PER: AUG. 12, 1823
BY: GEO. ATKIN, M.G.
REFERENCE: C.A; O.M.R. PG. 76; T.H.M. VOL. 6, PG. 191

NAMES: WM. SMITH TO NANCY BURNETT
DATE: FEBY. 22, 1823
DATE PER: FEBY. 25, 1823
BY: SAM'L S. MCCAMPBELL, J.P.
REFERENCE: C.A; T.H.M. VOL. 6, PG. 191

NAMES: LEVIN SPEARS TO ANNA WADDLE
DATE: JUNE 12, 1823
BONDSMAN: WILL R. CALDWELL
REFERENCE: C.A; T.H.M. VOL. 6, PG. 191

NAMES: DAVID SPHORE TO MILLY HEAD
DATE: JAN. 29, 1823 - CHAS. MCCLUNG - BY HIS DEP. (WM. SWAN
DATE PER: JANY. 29, 1823
BY: JOHN HAYNIE, ELDER OF M.E.C.
REFERENCE: C.A; O.M.R. PG. 72; T.H.M. VOL. 6, PG. 191

NAMES: WASHINGTON STANTON TO SARAH HOOD
DATE: MAR. 7, 1823
BONDSMAN: DAVID DEVAULT
DATE PER: MAR. 13, 1823
BY: WM. SAWYERS, J.P.
REFERENCE: C.A; O.M.R. PG. 72; T.H.M. VOL. 6, PG. 191

NAMES: SAMUEL STARKY TO MARIA BURNETT
DATE: JANY. 27, 1823
BONDSMAN: FRANCIS MONDAY
DATE PER: JANY. 30, 1823
BY: ROBERT TUNNELL, J.P.
WITNESS: WM. SWAN
REFERENCE: C.A; O.M.R. PG. 71; T.H.M. VOL. 6, PG. 191

NAMES: JAMES STEPHENSON TO MARGARET BROOKS
DATE: MAR. 12, 1823
BONDSMAN: SAM'L STEPHENSON
REFERENCE: C.A.

NAMES: JAMES STEPHENSON TO MARGARET BROOKS
DATE: MAR. 12, 1823
DATE PER: MAR. 12, 1823
BY: THO. H. NELSON, M.G.
REFERENCE: O.M.R. PG. 72; T.H.M. VOL. 6, PG. 192

NAMES: ALEXR. STOWELL TO MARIA STEPHENSON
DATE: OCT. 16, 1823
BONDSMAN: MAHELL BROWN
WITNESS: WM. SWAN
REFERENCE: C.A; T.H.M. VOL. 6, PG. 192

NAMES: BENJ. A. SWAGERTY TO IBBY JONES
DATE: APR. 5, 1823
BONDSMAN: JAMES PEARSON
DATE: APR. 7, 1823
BY: SAM'L MONTGOMERY, J.P.
REFERENCE: C.A; O.M.R. PG. 73

NAMES: ODEM C. TALLENT TO CHRISTIANA HARNER
DATE: APR. 19, 1823
BONDSMAN: JOHN PRITCHETT
WITNESS: WM. SWAN
REFERENCE: C.A.

NAMES: THOMAS P. TILLERY TO POLLY COLE
DATE: MAY 13, 1823
BONDSMAN: THOMAS BELL
DATE PER: MAY 13, 1823
BY: MORDECAI YARNELL, J.P.
REFERENCE: C.A; O.M.R. PG. 74

NAMES: ISAAC E. WARNACK TO NANCY LOHAS
DATE: JUNE 4, 1823
BONDSMAN: JOSEPH JACKSON
DATE PER: JUNE 4, 1823
BY: GEO. ATKIN, M. G.
REFERENCE: C.A; O.M.R. PG. 74; T.H.M. VOL. 6, PG. 192

NAMES: RICHARD WATKINS TO MARGARET W. CARDWELL
DATE: MAR. 4, 1823
BONDSMAN: JOHN CARDWELL
DATE PER: MAR. 4, 823
BY: THOMAS WELKERSON, ELDER
REFERENCE: C.A; O.M.R. PG. 72; T.H.M. VOL. 6, PG. 192

NAMES: DAVID WEAVER TO BETSY SMITH
DATE: AUG. 30, 1823
DATE PER: SEPT. 4, 1823
BY: JNO. GASS, J.P.
REFERENCE: C.A; O.M.R. PG. 76

NAMES: JAMES WEAVER TO ANNA MCCLAIN
DATE: DEC. 22, 1823
DATE PER: DEC. 22, 1823
BY: THO. H. NELSON
REFERENCE: C.A; O.M.R. PG. 79

NAMES: WM. R. WEIR TO MORNEN MURPHY
DATE: SEPT. 4, 1823 - BY WM. SWAN
DATE PER: SEPT. 4, 1823
BY: JOHN HAYNIE ELDER, M.E.C.
REFERENCE: C.A; O.M.R; PG. 77

NAMES: JOSEPH S. WERT TO CATHERINE GARDNER
DATE: NOV. 13, 1823
BONDSMAN: MOSES ABEL
WITNESS: CHAS. MCCLUNG
REFERENCE: C.A; T.H.M. VOL. 6, PG. 192

NAMES: ~~BERRY~~ H WILLIAMS TO LUCRETIA HILL
DATE: MAR. 22, 1823
BONDSMAN: HENRY M. HILL
DATE PER: MAR. 23, 1823
BY: WILLIS HAMMONE, M.G.
REFERENCE: C.A; O.M.R. PG. 72; T.H.M. VOL. 6, PG. 192

NAMES: ZACHARIAH WILLIAMS TO SALLY FRANKLIN
DATE: JULY 31, 1823
DATE PER: JULY 31, 1823
BY: JAMES MCMILLAN, J.P.
REFERENCE: O.M.R. PG. 76

NAMES: WM. WILMOTH TO MARGARET KIRKLAND
DATE: JUNE 29, 1823
BONDSMAN: J.A. SWAN - WM. SWAN
DATE PER: JULY 1, 1823
BY: P. A. SWAN, J.P.
REFERENCE: C.A; O.M.R. PG. 75; T.H.M. VOL. 6, PG. 192

1824

NAMES: PETER AIRHART TO NANCY MURPHY
DATE: NOV. 18, 1824
BONDSMAN: ALEXANDER MCBATH
DATE PER: NOV. 18, 1824
BY: ROBERT MCBATH
WITNESS: WM. SWAN
REFERENCES: C.A; O.M.R. PG. 87

NAMES: SAM'L M. ARMSTRONG TO CHARLOTTE ARMSTRONG
DATE: MAR. 15, 1824
DATE PER: MAR. 16, 1824
BY: R. HOUSTON, J.P.
REFERENCE: C.A; O.M.R. PG. 83

NAMES: WOODSON BABER TO JANE MCCLOUD
DATE: NOV. 17, 1824
BONDSMAN: MICHAEL SMITH
DATE PER: NOV. 21, 1824
BY: WILLIAM B. CARNS, J.P.
REFERENCE: C.A; O.M.R. PG. 87

NAMES: ASHER BAILS TO SALLY KING
DATE: JULY 22, 1824
DATE PER: JULY 22, 1824
BY: B. MCNUTT, J.P.
REFERENCE: C.A; O.M.R. PG. 84; T.H.M. VOL. 6, PG. 192

NAMES: WILLIAM BARBER TO EUNICE WILSON
DATE: SEPT. 29, 1824
DATE PER: SEPT. 30, 1824
BY: SAM'L SAMPLE, J.P.
REFERENCE: C.A; O.M.R. PG. 86

NAMES: WM. W. BELL TO SUSAN LOW
DATE: FEBY. 13, 1824
DATE PER: FEBY. 13, 1824
BY: R. H. KING
REFERENCE: C.A; T. H.M. VOL. 6, PG. 192

NAMES: ADAM B. BLAKE TO JANE I. KENNEDY
DATE: FEBY. 19, 1824
BONDSMAN: JOHN CRAIGHEAD
REFERENCE: C.A.

NAMES: ALEXANDER B. BRADFORD TO DOUTHULA C. MILLER
DATE: SEPT. 10, 1824
DATE PER: SEPT. 16, 1824
BY: THO. H. NELSON
REFERENCE: C.A; O.M.R. PG. 85

NAMES: AARON BRANHAM TO BETSY FRANKLIN
DATE: JANY. 22, 1824
BONDSMAN: JAMES MURPHY
REFERENCE: C.A.

NAMES: THOMAS H. BRYAN TO PATSY MANIFOLD
DATE: NOV. 27, 1824
DATE PER: DEC. 2, 1824
BY: JAMES MCMILLAN, J.P.
REFERENCE: C.A; O.M.R. PG. 89; T.H.M. VOL. 6, PG. 192

NAMES: JAMES BUCKALEW TO MAHALA HOLT
DATE: AUG. 25, 1824
BONDSMAN: JOSHUA JACKSON
REFERENCE: C.A.

NAMES: JACOB BYERLEY TO SALLY BROWN
DATE: NOV. 2, 1824
BONDSMAN: JOHN MCFADDIN
DATE PER: NOV. 3, 1824
BY: P. A. SWAN, J.P.
REFERENCE: C.A; T.H.M. VOL. 6, PG. 192

NAMES: EDWARD CALLEN TO PATSY CATES
DATE: MAR. 11, 1824
BONDSMAN: JOHN CATES
DATE PER: MAR. 11, 1824
REFERENCE: C.A; O.M.R. PG. 81

NAMES: JAMES CAMPBELL TO SALLY SMITH
DATE: MAR. 19, 1824
DATE PER: MAR. 20, 1824
BY: R. H. KING
REFERENCE: C.A; O.M.R. PG. 82

NAMES: GEO. R. CANNON TO MARY RUSSELL
DATE: JANY. 26, 1824
DATE PER: JANY. 28, 1824
BY: R. H. KING
REFERENCE: C.A; O.M.R. PG. 80

NAMES: RICHARD CASSADY TO MARY WALKER
DATE: SEPT. 7, 1824
BONDSMAN: ANDREW CASSADAY
DATE PER: SEPT. 9, 1824
BY: WM. SAWYERS, J.P.
REFERENCE: C.A; O.M.R. PG. 85; T.H.M. VOL. 6, PG. 192

NAMES: DAVID D. COPELAND TO NANCY COMBS
DATE: SEPT. 21, 1824
DATE PER: SEPT. 21, 1824
BY: WM. B. CARNS, J.P.
REFERENCE: C.A; O.M.R. PG. 85

NAMES: MOSES COX TO POLLY CONNER
DATE: OCT. 26, 1824
BONDSMAN: JOHN GASS
DATE PER: OCT. 28, 1824
BY: JOHN GASS, J.P.
REFERENCE: C.A; O.M.R. PG. 86; T.H.M. VOL. 6, PG. 192

NAMES: WM. CRAWFORD TO MATILDA CHURCHMAN
DATE: FEBY. 18, 1824
DATE PER: FEBY. 19, 1824
BY: WM. SAWYERS, J.P.
REFERENCE: C.A; O.M.R. PG. 81

NAMES: ANDREW CUNNINGHAM TO ELIZABETH ANDERSON
DATE: NOV. 11, 1824
BONDSMAN: JOHN STIRLING
REFERENCE: C.A; O.M.R. PG. 87; T.H.M. VOL. 6, PG. 192

NAMES: MOSES CUNNINGHAM TO ESTHER T. DEARMOND
DATE: SEPT. 29, 1824
BONDSMAN: JOHN DEARMOND
DATE PER: SEPT. 29, 1824
BY: GEO. ATKIN, M. G.
REFERENCE: C.A; O.M.R. PG. 86

NAMES: PAUL CUNNINGHAM TO MARY FORD
DATE: NOV. 11, 1824
DATE PER: NOV. 11, 1824
BY: ROBT. MCBATH
REFERENCE: C.A; O.M.R. PG. 87

NAMES: EDWARD DAVIS TO RHODY SANDERS
DATE: APR. 14, 1824
DATE PER: APR. 14, 1824
BY: JOHN HAYNIE
REFERENCE: C.A; O.M.R. PG. 82

NAMES: JOHN M. DAVIS TO JANE SCOTT
DATE: DEC. 23, 1824
DATE PER: DEC. 23, 1824
BY: THO. H. NELSON,
REFERENCE: C.A; O.M.R. PG. 88

NAMES: JOHN DOYLE TO EVE FORMWALT
DATE: NOV. 12, 1824
BONDSMAN: PRYOR LEA
DATE PER: NOV. 12, 1824
BY: THO. H. NELSON
REFERENCE: C.A; O.M.R. PG. 87

NAMES: WILLIAM DOYLE TO CATHARINE THOMAS
DATE: NOV. 25, 1824
DATE PER: NOV. 25, 1824
BY: GEO. ATKIN, M.G.
REFERENCE: C.A; O.M.R. PG. 87; T. H.M. VOL. 6, PG. 192

NAMES: JOHN DRAIN TO SARAH HENDERSON
DATE: DEC. 5, 1824
BONDSMAN: HIRAM HENDERSON
WITNESS: WM. SWAN
REFERENCE: C.A; T.H.M. VOL. 6, PG. 192

NAMES: ANDERSON DUNLAP TO BETSY MCBRIDE
DATE: JANY. 10, 1824
BONDSMAN: JAMES SUMTER
REFERENCE: C.A; T.H.M. VOL. 6, PG. 192

NAMES: JAMES H. EDINGTON TO FANNY JOHNSTON
DATE: AUG. 5, 1824
BONDSMAN: KINZEY SMITH
DATE PER: AUG. 5, 1824
BY: ROBT. MCBATH, J.P.
WITNESS: WM. SWAN
REFERENCE: C.A; O.M.R. PG. 85

NAMES: WM. ELKINS TO SARAH LAREW
DATE: FEBY 26, 1824
BONDSMAN: JOEL KIRKPATRICK
DATE PER: FEBY 26, 1824
BY: JOHN BAYLESS, J.P.
WITNESS: WM. SWAN
REFERENCE: C.A; O.M.R. PG. 81

NAMES: JOHN C. EVERETT TO PHERRISA AYRES
DATE: APR. 30, 1824
DATE PER: MAY 2, 1824
BY: MORDECAI YARNELL, J.P.
REFERENCE: C.A; O.M.R. PG. 83

NAMES: DAVID FOUST TO HANNA CLAPP
DATE: JULY 29, 1824
DATE PER: JULY 29, 1824
BY: WM. SAWYERS, J.P.
REFERENCE: C.A; O.M.R. PG. 84; T. H.M. VOL. 6, PG. 192

NAMES: JACOB FOUST TO AMANDA PATE
DATE: MAR. 6, 1824
DATE PER: MAR. 9, 1824
BY: WM. SAWYERS, J.P.
REFERENCE: C.A; O.M.R. PG. 82

NAMES: JOHN FOUST TO MARIA PATE
DATE: JULY 22, 1824
DATE PER: JULY 24, 1824
BY: WM. SAWYERS, J.P.
REFERENCE: C.A; O.M.R. PG. 84

NAMES: THOS. FRANKLIN TO ELIZA MULVANEY
DATE: DEC. 11, 1824
DATE PER: DEC. 15, 1824
BY: JAMES MCMILLAN, J.P.
REFERENCE: O.M.R. PG. 88

NAMES: JOHN GAULT TO PATSY MURPHY
DATE: FEBY. 4, 1824
DATE PER: FEBY. 4, 1824
BY: GEO. ATKIN, M.G.
REFERENCE: C.A; O.M.R. PG. 80; T.H.M. VOL. 6, PG. 192

NAMES: JOHN T. GENTRY TO JANE MCNEIL
DATE: MAR. 2, 1824,
BONDSMAN: H.A.M. WHITE
DATE PER: MAR. 4, 1824
BY: ROBT. TINDELL, J.P.
REFERENCE: C.A; O.M.R. PG. 81

NAMES: WM. GRIFFIS TO PEGGY BLACKWELL
DATE: DEC. 13, 1824
DATE PER: DEC. 13, 1824
REFERENCE: C.A; O.M.R. PG. 88

NAMES: THOS. J. GRILLS TO MARTHA SMITH
DATE: JANY. 22, 1824
BONDSMAN: HUGH HALL
DATE PER: JANY. 22, 1824
BY: JOHN HAYNIE
REFERENCE: C.A; O.M.R. PG. 80

NAMES: SAM'L HACKWORTH TO POLLY HOLT
DATE: JUNE 16, 1824
BONDSMAN: SAM'L ROBERTS
DATE PER: JUNE 17, 1824
BY: WM. MORRIS, J.P.
REFERENCE: C.A; O.M.R. PG. 84; T.H.M. VOL. 6, PG. 192

NAMES: JACOB HALFACRE TO PEGGY BODKIN
DATE: FEB. 1,
REFERENCE: T.H.M. VOL. 6, PG. 192

NAMES: EDWARD HANKINS TO ELIZABETH SKAGGS
DATE: FEBY. 28, 1824
DATE PER: MAR. 4, 1824
BY: WM. B. CARNS, J.P.
REFERENCE: C.A; O.M.R. PG. 81; T.H.M. VOL. 6, PG. 192

NAMES: JOHN M. HAVRON TO BETSY LOVE
DATE: SEPT. 20, 1824
BONDSMAN: JAMES C. LUTTRELL
REFERENCE: C.A.

NAMES: GEORGE HAWKINS TO MATILDA FLAKNER
DATE: APR. 7,
REFERENCE: T.H.M. VOL. 6, PG. 192

NAMES: JOHN HENDERSON TO PEGGY ANN AUTRY
DATE: NOV. 9,
REFERENCE: T.H.M. VOL. 6, PG. 192

NAMES: JOHN HENDERSON TO ANN CARR
DATE: DEC. 22, 1824
BONDSMAN: ANDREW MCMILLAN
DATE PER: DEC. 23, 1824
BY: ROBT. MCBATH
REFERENCE: C.A; O.M.R. PG. 88; T.H.M. VOL. 6, PG. 192

NAMES: MARVEL HILL TO MILLY COX
DATE: MAR. 15, 1824
BONDSMAN: WM. LOY
DATE PER: MAR. 18, 1824
BY: JOHN GASS, J.P.
REFERENCE: C.A; O.M.R. PG. 82; T.H.M. VOL. 6, PG. 192

NAMES: JESSE HINCKLE TO HANNAH RHOADS
DATE: FEBY. 17, 1824
BONDSMAN: W. M. MORROW
DATE PER: FEBY. 26, 1824
BY: WM. B. CARNS, J.P.
REFERENCE: C.A; O.M.R. PG. 80

NAMES: JOSEPH HINDES TO MARY A. GRIMES
DATE: DEC. 16, 1824
DATE PER: DEC. 30, 1824
BY: WM. SAWYERS, J.P.
REFERENCE: C.A; O.M.R. PG. 88; T.H.M. VOL. 6, PG. 192

Names: Samuel Hinds to Fanny Ann Reynolds
Date: Dec. 22, 1824
Date Per: Jany. 6, 1825
By: Wm. Sawyers, J.P.
Reference: C.A; O.M.R. Pg. 88; T.H.M. Vol. 6, Pg. 192

Names: Jacob How to Elizabeth Sensebaugh
Date: Apr. 23,
Reference: T.H.M. Vol. 6, Pg. 192

Names: Daniel Howser to Louisa J. Varner
Date: Aug. 2, 1824
Bondsman: Matthew Nelson
Date Per: Aug. 5, 1824
By: David Nelson, J.P.
Reference: C.A; O.M.R. Pg. 85

Names: Michael Huffaen to Betsy Burns
Date: May 3, 1824
Date Per: May 4, 1824
By: Tho. H. Nelson
Reference: C.A; O.M.R. Pg. 89

Names: Samuel Humphreys to Margaret F. Bond
Date: Oct. 9, 1824
Date Per: Oct. 12, 1824
By: Tho. H. Nelson
Reference: C.A; O.M.R. Pg. 86

Names: Wm. Ingram to Elizabeth Harris
Date: Jany. 15, 1824
Bondsman: Armstrong Morrow
Reference: C.A.

Names: Lillerbury Johnson to Edg.__ George
Date: Apr.(?) 5,
Reference: T.H.M. Vol. 6, Pg. 192

Names: Henry Jones to Elizabeth Lamporter
Date: Apr. 10, 1824
Date Per: Apr. 10, 1824
By: David Nelson, J.P.
Reference: C.A; O.M.R. Pg. 82

Names: Jeremiah Jones to Nancy Wheeler
Date: Nov. 10, 1824
Date Per: Nov. 10, 1824
By: Robt. McBath
Reference: C.A; O.M.R. Pg. 87

Names: David Kerr to Polly Manifold
Date: July 23, 1824
Date Per: July 27, 1824
By: James McMillan, J.P.
Reference: O.M.R. Pg. 84

Names: Jesse Lincoln to F. Brown
Date: Nov. 22, 1824
By: Tho. H. Nelson
Reference: C.A; O.M.R. Pg. 87

Names: Thos. B. Love to Susan Smith
Date: Feby. 21, 1824
Date Per: Feby. 22, 1824
By: R. H. King
Reference: O.M.R. Pg. 81; T.H.M. Vol. 6, Pg. 192

Names: Wilson Maples to Patsy Clarke
Date: Oct. 19, 1824
Bondsman: Joshua Jacison
Date Per: Oct. 21, 1824
By: Sam'l Fleming, J.P.
Witness: Wm. Swan
Reference: C.A; O.M.R. Pg. 86

Names: Alexander McBath to Peggy McCall
Date: Dec. 30, 1824
Bondsman: Robert McBath
Date Per: Dec. 30, 1824
By: Robt. McBath
Reference: C.A; O.M.R. Pg. 89; T.H.M. Vol. 6, Pg. 192

Names: John McCaughan to Margaret Ann Gray
Date: July 7, 1824
Bondsman: Charles Shelley
Reference: C.A; T.H.M. Vol. 6, Pg. 192

Names: Levi McCloud to Jane Lyons
Date: Oct. 29, 1824
Date Per: Oct. 31, 1824
By: Wm. B. Carns, J.P.
Reference: C.A; O.M.R. Pg. 86

Names: Samuel McClure to Sally G. Love
Date: Sept. 22, 1824
Bondsman: Wm. Killingworth
Date Per: Sept. 29, 1824
By: Sam'l Fleming, J.P.
Reference: C.A; O.M.R. Pg. 35; T.H.M. Vol. 6, Pg. 192

NAMES: CHARLES MCMILLAN TO ROSANNAH HUNTER
DATE: FEBY. 24, 1824
DATE PER: FEBY. 26, 1824
BY: JAS. MCMILLAN, J.P.
REFERENCE: C.A; O.M.R. PG. 81; T.H.M. VOL. 6, PG. 192

NAMES: MARK S. MILLER TO MARY ANN JANE PINKSON
DATE: DEC. 15, 1824 - BONDSMAN: WM. CLARK
DEC. PER: DEC. 16, 1824
BY: TOM RAMSEY, J.P.
WITNESS: WM. SWAN, J.P.
REFERENCE: C.A; O.M.R. PG. 88; T.H.M. VOL. 6, PG. 192

NAMES: DANIEL MILLS TO HANNAH STAFFLE
DATE: JUNE 19, 1824
BONDSMAN: ANDREW T. JONES
REFERENCE: C.A.

NAMES: ISAAC MILLS TO HANNAH STUFFLE
DATE: JUNE 23, 1824
BONDSMAN: GEO. STUFFLE
WITNESS: WM. SWAN
REFERENCE: C.A.

NAMES: WM. MONEYMAKER TO POLLY HEATH
DATE: JULY 29, 1824
BONDSMAN: JACOB SPORE
REFERENCE: C.A.

NAMES: WM. MONEYMAKER TO POLLY HEATH
DATE: JULY 29, 1824
DATE PER: JULY 29, 1824
BY: JAMES C. LUTTRELL, J.P.
REFERENCE: O.M.R. PG. 84

NAMES: AUSTIN MOORE TO MIRANDE HASKEW
DATE: JUNE 28, 1824
BONDSMAN: JOSEPH MOORE
DATE PER: JULY 26, 1824
BY: GEO. ATKIN, M. G.
REFERENCE: C.A; O.M.R. PG. 84

NAMES: WM. MOORE TO KESIAH SMITH
DATE: FEBY. 14, 1824
BONDSMAN: JNO. MCNANNY
DATE PER: FEBY. 15, 1824
BY: WM. MORRIS, J.P.
WITNESS: WM. SWAN
REFERENCE: C.A; O.M.R. PG. 80

NAMES: HENRY MULVANY TO SALLY WAGONER
DATE: JULY 15, 1824
BONDSMAN: JOSEPH SMITH
REFERENCE: C.A.

NAMES: HENRY MULVANEY TO SALLY WAGONER
DATE: JULY 15, 1824
DATE PER: JULY 27, 1824
BY: SAM'L SAMPLE, J.P.
REFERENCE: O.M.R. PG. 84

NAMES: CHARLES NEWMAN TO BETSY BOWMAN
DATE: OCT. 20, 1824
BONDSMAN: SAM'L BOWMAN
DATE PER: OCT. 20, 1824
BY: J. CUNNINGHAM
REFERENCE: C.A; O.M.R. PG. 86

NAMES: JOSEPH PAYNE TO REBECKA KEENER
DATE: JUNE 10, 1824
BONDSMAN: HENRY HUFFANE
BY: JESSE CUNNINGHAM
WITNESS: WM. SWAN
REFERENCE: C.A; O.M.R. PG. 84

NAMES: ELIJAH POWELL TO SALITA BLUNT
DATE: NOV. 12, 1824
BONDSMAN: JNO. FINDLEY
REFERENCE: C.A.

NAMES: ELIJAH POWELL TO SELETA BLUNT
DATE: NOV. 12, 1824
DATE PER: NOV. 14, 1824
BY: SAM'L SAMPLE, J.P.
REFERENCE: O.M.R. PG. 87

NAMES: JOHN PRATT TO POLLY FRANKLIN
DATE: MAR. 24, 1824
BY: JAMES MCMILLAN, J.P.
DATE PER: MAR. 25, 1824
REFERENCE: C.A; O.M.R. PG. 82

NAMES: BENJ. RECTOR TO LILLY SHELL
DATE: OCT. 14, 1824
BONDSMAN: LUDWELL RECTOR
DATE PER: NOV. 7, 1824
BY: SAM'L S. MCCAMPBELL, J.P.
WITNESS: WM. SWAN
REFERENCE: C.A; O.M.R. PG. 86; T.H.M. VOL. 6, PG. 192

NAMES: LUDWELL RECTOR TO RUTH SHELL
DATE: JANY. 10, 1824
BONDSMAN: VINCENT BURNETT
DATE PER: JANY 22, 1824
BY: SAM'L S. MCCAMPBELL, J.P.
REFERENCE: C.A; O.M.R. PG. 80

NAMES: FELPS REED TO BETSY ENGLAND
DATE: MAY 29, 1824
BONDSMAN: ISAAC COUNSILL
DATE PER: MAY 29, 1824
BY: WM. MORRIS, J.P.
REFERENCE: C.A; O.M.R. PG. 83

NAMES: ALEXANDER W. RICHARDSON TO ELIZABETH GIBBS
DATE: MAY 22, 1824
DATE PER: MAY 26, 1824
BY: JOHN BAYLESS, J.P.
REFERENCE: C.A; O.M.R. PG. 83; T.H.M. VOL. 6, PG. 192

NAMES: JAMES ROBINSON TO SALLY MCCARROLL
DATE: MAR. 12, 1824
BONDSMAN: JAS. WATT
DATE PER: MAR. 14, 1824
BY: JEREMIAH KING
REFERENCE: C.A; O.M.R. PG. 81

NAMES: DAVID RODGERS TO LIEUMIMA JACKSON
DATE: MAR. 29, 1824
BONDSMAN: JNO. HAYNIE
DATE PER: MAR. 29, 1824
BY: JOHN HAYNIE
REFERENCE: C.A; O.M.R. PG. 82; T.H.M. VOL. 6, PG. 192

NAMES: FREDERICK F. RODGERS TO CHARITY WOLF
DATE: MAR. 25, 1824
BONDSMAN: RD. MCPHERSON
DATE PER: APR. 1, 1824
BY: JAMES MCMILLAN, J.P.
REFERENCE: C.A; O.M.R. PG. 82

NAMES: SAMUEL SAMPLE TO POLLY KING
DATE: FEBY. 23, 1824
BONDSMAN: QUIN BROWN
WITNESS: WM. SWAN
REFERENCE: C.A.

NAMES: WILLIAM SCOTT TO MARY ANN ODEL
DATE: FEBY. 12, 1824
BONDSMAN: JAMES SCOTT
DATE PER: FEBY. 12, 1824
BY: THO. H. NELSON
REFERENCE: C.A; O.M.R. PG. 80; T.H.M. VOL. 6, PG. 192

NAMES: ROBERT SHIELDS TO PRUDENCE BOYD
DATE: APR. 29, 1824
BONDSMAN: JOSEPH JACKSON
DATE PER: MAY 19, 1824
BY: THO. H. NELSON
REFERENCE: C.A; O.M.R. PG. 83; T.H.M. VOL. 6, PG. 192

NAMES: MOSES SKAGGS TO SALLY MAJOR
DATE: MAR. 25, 1824
BONDSMAN: WM. MAJOR
DATE PER: MAR. 25, 1824
BY: JOHN BAYLESS, J.P.
REFERENCE: C.A; O.M.R. PG. 82

NAMES: ALEXANDER SMITH TO PEGGY GALLIHER
DATE: FEBY. 28, 1824
BONDSMAN: JNO. STUART
REFERENCE: C.A; T.H.M. VOL. 6, PG. 192

NAMES: JOHN SMITH TO BETSY CALLOWAY
DATE: SEPT. 20, 1824
BONDSMAN: HUGH SMITH
DATE PER: SEPT. 20, 1824
BY: WM. MORRIS, J.P.
WITNESS: WM. SWAN
REFERENCE: C.A; O.M.R. PG. 85

NAMES: JAMES SPEARS TO SOPHY RAGSDALE
DATE: DEC. 25, 1824
BONDSMAN: WM. GRIFFIS
DATE PER: DEC. 26, 1824
BY: J.A. MAYBRY, J.P.
WITNESS: CHAS. MCCLUNG
REFERENCE: C.A; O.M.R. PG. 88; T.H.M. VOL. 6, PG. 192

NAMES: LUKE STANSBERRY TO DEAVER UMBERSET
DATE: JUNE [illegible] 1824
DATE PER: JUNE 1, 1824
BY: SAM'L MONTGOMERY
REFERENCE: O.M.R. PG. 83

NAMES: DAVID STERRETT TO BETHIA H. KING
DATE: JANY. 8, 1824
BONDSMAN: JEREMIAH KING
REFERENCE: C.A; O.M.R. PG. 80; T.H.M. VOL. 6, PG. 192
NAMES: ROBERT M. SWAN TO AMELIA RAMSEY
DATE: DEC. 15, 1824
BONDSMAN: WM. SWAN
REFERENCE: C.A.

Names: R. M. Swan to Ann Amelia Ramsey
Date: Dec. 15, 1824
Date Per: Dec. 16, 1824
By: Tho. H. Nelson
Reference: O.M.R. Pg. 88; T.H.M. Vol. 6, Pg. 192

Names: James Thomason to Jacomah Massey
Date: Aug. 12, 1824
Bondsman: Chas. Massey
Date Per: Aug. 15, 1824
By: J.A. Massey, J.P.
Witness: Wm. Swan
Reference: C.A; O.M.R. Pg. 85

Names: Joseph Thompson to Sally Legg
Date: Feb. 12, 1824
Reference: T.H.M. Vol. 6, Pg. 192

Names: Matthew Timon to Rosanah Duncan
Date: Feby. 2, 1824
Date Per: Feby. 5, 1824
By: J.A. Swan, J.P.
Reference: C.A; O.M.R. Pg. 80

Names: James Turbeville to Patsy Landrum
Date: Sept. 15, 1824
Bondsman: Pleasant Crew
Date Per: Sept. 15, 1824
By: John Haynie
Reference: C.A; O.M.R. Pg. 85

Names: Daniel Wade to Susan Rentfrow
Date: Apr. 2[illegible], 1824 - Date Per: Apr. 22, 1824
By: John Haynie
Reference: C.A; O.M.R. Pg. 82

Names: Havel Wade to Patsy Russell
Date: May 19, 1824
Date Per: May 20, 1824
By: Geo. Atkin, M.G.
Reference: C.A; O.M.R. Pg. 83

Names: William Walker to Mary Weir
Date: May 27, 1824
Bondsman: Robt. McReynolds
Date Per: May 27, 1824
By: Geo. Atkin, M.G.
Reference: C.A; O.M.R. Pg. 83

Names: Wm. Weaver to Patsy Izard
Date: Mar. 9, 1824
Bondsman: Reuben Owens
Date Per: Mar. 11, 1824
By: John Gass, J.P.
Witness: Wm. Swan
Reference: C.A; O.M.R. Pg. 81; T.H.M. Vol. 6, Pg. 192

Names: Hugh A. M. White to Elizabeth Humes
Date: Oct. 14, 1824
Date Per: Oct. 14, 1824
By: Tho. H. Nelson
Reference: O.M.R. Pg. 86

Names: Thomas White to Margaret Smith
Date: Nov. 11, 1824
Bondsman: Hugh M. Clark
Date Per: Nov. 11, 1824
By: Wm. Morris, J.P.
Witness: Chas. McClung
Reference: C.A; O.M.R. Pg. 87; T.H.M. Vol. 6, Pg. 192

Names: Calvin Wolf to Minerva Mayfield
Date: Sept. 15, 1824
Date Per: Sept. 16, 1824
By: Sam'l Ramsey, J.P.
Reference: C.A; O.M.R. Pg. 85

Names: Wm. Wolf to Nancy Thompson
Date: May 15, 1824
Date Per: May 15, 1824
By: Robt. McBath
Reference: C.A; O.M.R. Pg. 83

Names: Thos. Yarnell to Hannah Grayson
Date: Mar. 3, 1824
Bondsman: Geo. Dunlap
Date Per: Mar. 4, 1824
By: Wm. Morris, J.P.
Reference: C.A; O.M.R. Pg. 81

Names: George S. Yerger to Sarah M. Scott
Date: Dec. 22, 1824
Bondsman: James M.M. White
Date Per: Dec. 23, 1824
By: Tho. H. Nelson
Witness: Wm. Swan
Reference: C.A; O.M.R. Pg. 88

1825

NAMES: PAYTON ADKINS TO MARY LIFFORD
DATE: MAR. 2, 1825
BONDSMAN: FRANCIS MCNAMSEY
DATE PER: MAR. 3, 1825
BY: JOHN BAYLESS, J.P.
WITNESS: WM. SWAN
REFERENCE: C.A; O.M.R. PG. 91

NAMES: SAMUEL ALLEN TO SALLY GILLESPIE
DATE: MAY 18, 1825
DATE PER: MAY 19, 1825
BY: J. A. MABRY, J.P.
REFERENCE: C.A; O.M.R. PG. 93

NAMES: ROBERT M. ANDERSON TO CATHARINE MCCAMPBELL
DATE: MAR. 31, 1825
DATE PER: MAR. 31, 1825
BY: ISAAC ANDERSON, V.D.M.
REFERENCE: C.A; O.M.R. PG. 92

NAMES: ADDISON W. ARMSTRONG TO NANCY MCMILLAN
DATE: MAR. 26, 1825
DATE PER: MAR. 22, 1825
BY: R. HOUSTON
REFERENCE: C.A; O.M.R. PG. 92

NAMES: WM. C. ARMSTRONG TO HANNAH DENTON LUCAS
DATE: DEC. 28, 1825
BONDSMAN: JOSIAH G. ARMSTRONG
DATE PER: DEC. 29, 1825
BY: WM. MORRIS, J.P.
REFERENCE: C.A; O.M.R. PG. 99

NAMES: JOSEPH ATKINS TO DICE HOLBERT
DATE: OCT. 13, 1825
BONDSMAN: STEPHEN HALBERT
DATE PER: OCT. 20, 1825
BY: E. NELSON, J.P.
WITNESS: WM. SWAN
REFERENCE: C.A; O.M.R. PG. 96

NAMES: NICHOLAS BARGER TO POLLY STERLING
DATE: JANY. 6, 1825
BONDSMAN: JAMES WATT
DATE PER: JANY. 6, 1825
BY: THO. H. NELSON
REFERENCE: C.A; O.M.R. PG. 89

NAMES: JAMES M. BARNETT TO ELIZABETH COKER
DATE: AUG. 16, 1825
BONDSMAN: CHAS. COKER
WITNESS: WM. SWAN
REFERENCE: C.A.

NAMES: JOSEPH BARTLETT TO PATIENCE MCCOY
DATE: 1825
BONDSMAN: IS. BRADLEY
WITNESS: H. L. WHITE
REFERENCE: C.A.

NAMES: JACOB BEIELY TO SALLY BROWN
DATE: NOV. 2, 1825
DATE PER: NOV. 3, 1825
BY: JNO. A. SWAN, J.P.
REFERENCE: O.M.R. PG. 97

NAMES: WM. M. BELL TO SUSAN LOWE
DATE: FEBY. 13, 1825
DATE PER: FEBY. 13, 1825
BY: R. H. KING, M.G.
REFERENCE: O.M.R. PG. 90

NAMES: GEO. C. BERRY TO MARY FORGUSON
DATE: DEC. 21, 1825
BONDSMAN: THOMAS ANDERSON
WITNESS: WM. SWAN
REFERENCE: C.A.

NAMES: HARRIS G. BISHOP TO ISABELLA CARMICHAEL
DATE: JULY 11, 1825
BONDSMAN: ANDREW M. BROWN
DATE PER: JULY 14, 1825
BY: R. HOUSTON, J.P.
REFERENCE: C.A; O.M.R. PG. 95

NAMES: HENRY BLALOCK TO SARAH HOUK
DATE: APR. 11, 1825
BONDSMAN: JNO. ROGERS
DATE PER: APR. 11, 1825
BY: GEO. ATKIN, M. G.
REFERENCE: C.A; O.M.R. PG. 93

NAMES: WILLIA BRADLEY TO BETSY DOWELL
DATE: DEC. 6, 1825
BONDSMAN: ACHILLES BRADLEY
DATE:PER: DEC. 8, 1825
BY: WM. B. CARNS, J.P.
REFERENCE: C.A; O.M.R. PG. 98

NAMES: JAMES W. BRIGHT TO NANCY KENNEDY
DATE: DEC. 1, 1825
BONDSMAN: JOHN KENNEDY
BY: JOSEPH WOOD, J.P.
WITNESS: HU BROWN
REFERENCE: C.A; O.M.R. PG. 98

NAMES: ANDREW M. BROWN TO MARY E. BELL
DATE: JULY 11, 1825
BONDSMAN: H. G. BISHOP
DATE PER: JULY 11, 1825
BY: R. HOUSTON, J.P.
REFERENCE: C.A; O.M.R. PG. 95

NAMES: JOHN BROWN TO SARAH WOOD
DATE: FEBY. 28, 1825
DATE PER: FEBY. 29, 1825
REFERENCE: C.A; O.M.R. PG. 91

NAMES: BERRY BURNETT TO NANCY PAYNE
DATE: OCT. 4, 1825
BONDSMAN: JAMES ALLISON
DATE PER: OCT. 4, 1825
BY: DAVID NELSON, J.P.
REFERENCE: C.A; O.M.R. PG. 96

NAMES: HOWELL BURNETT TO ELIZABETH SHERARTZ
DATE: MAY 31, 1825
BONDSMAN: JOHN SHERARTZ
REFERENCE: C.A.

NAMES: HU CALDWELL TO LUCRETIA WELSH
DATE: FEBY. 5, 1825
BONDSMAN: HEZEKIAH RHODES
DATE PER: FEBY. 6, 1825
BY: WM. SAWYERS, J.P.
REFERENCE: C.A; O.M.R. PG. 90

NAMES: ALEXANDER CAMPBELL TO CINDRILLA WELLS
DATE: JANY. 5, 1825
BONDSMAN: JNO. MCCALEB
DATE PER: JANY. 13, 1825
BY: J. A. MABRY, J.P.
REFERENCE: C.A; O.M.R. PG. 89

NAMES: JAMES CAMPBELL TO CHARLOTTE DARDIS
DATE: AUG. 11, 1825
BONDSMAN: E. R. CAMPBELL
REFERENCE: C.A.

NAMES: JAMES CAMPBELL TO CHARLOTTE DARDIS
DATE: AUG. 11, 1825
DATE PER: AUG. 11, 1825
BY: THO. H. NELSON, M.G.
REFERENCE: O.M.R. PG. 95

NAMES: JACOB CARPENTER TO POLLY KERR
DATE: AUG. 17, 1825
BONDSMAN: ISAAC M. STEEL
DATE PER: AUG. 18, 1825
BY: W.B.A. RAMSEY, J.P.
REFERENCE: C.A; O.M.R. PG. 96

NAMES: MARTIN B. CARTER TO MARTHA EPPS
DATE: OCT. 29, 1825
BONDSMAN: WM. MOLDEN
DATE PER: NOV. 1, 1825
BY: JAMES MCMILLAN, J.P.
REFERENCE: C.A; O.M.R. PG. 97

NAMES: BENJ. CASH TO BETSY BURNETT
DATE: MAR. 8, 1825
DATE PER: MAR. 9, 1825
BY: SAM'L SAMPLE, J.P.
REFERENCE: C.A; O.M.R. PG. 91

NAMES: FAYETTE W. CHAPMAN TO MARY KEYS
DATE: DEC. 26, 1825
BONDSMAN: JOSEPH JACKSON
DATE PER: DEC. 27, 1825
BY: JAMES MCMILLAN, J.P.
REFERENCE: C.A; O.M.R. PG. 99

NAMES: GEORGE CHEATHAM TO MALINDA MAYFIELD
DATE: APR. 2, 1825
DATE PER: APR. 7, 1825
BY: J.A. SWAN, J.P.
REFERENCE: C.A; O.M.R. PG. 92

NAMES: JOHN A. CHRISTIAN TO SARAH W. BISHOP
DATE: DEC. 19, 1825
BONDSMAN: JNO. M. MCCAMPBELL
DATE PER: DEC. 20, 1825
BY: JOHN BAYLESS, J.P.
WITNESS: WM. SWAN
REFERENCE: C.A; O.M.R. PG. 99

NAMES: GEO. W. CHURCHWELL TO R. E. MONTGOMERY
DATE: MAY 26, 1825
BONDSMAN: R. G. DUNLAP
REFERENCE: C.A.

NAMES: GEO. W. CHURCHWELL TO R. E. MONTGOMERY
DATE: MAY 26, 1825
DATE PER: MAY 26, 1825
BY: GEO. ATKIN, M.G.
REFERENCE: O.M.R. PG. 94

NAMES: SAMUEL CONNER TO MARGARET KIME
DATE: NOV. 29, 1825
DATE PER: DEC. 1, 1825
BY: B. MCNUTT, J.P.
REFERENCE: C.A; O.M.R. PG. 98

NAMES: HIRAM COVINGTON TO LUCY PAYNE
DATE: JANY. 19, 1825
BONDSMAN: WM. WYONER
DATE PER: JANY. 20, 1825
BY: SAM'L MONTGOMERY, J.P.
WITNESS: MAT. MCCLUNG
REFERENCE: C.A; O.M.R. PG. 89

NAMES: RICHARD COX TO POLLY JULIAN
DATE: MAY 20, 1825
BONDSMAN: JONATHAN WILLIAMS
DATE PER: MAY 30, 1825
BY: ROBT. TINDEL, J.P.
REFERENCE: C.A; O.M.R. PG. 94

NAMES: THOMAS CRAWFORD TO MARIA HARRIS
DATE: SEPT. 20, 1825
BONDSMAN: JOHN HICKLE
DATE PER: SEPT. 20, 1825
BY: JOHN BAYLESS, J.P.
REFERENCE: C.A; O.M.R. PG. 96; T.H.M. VOL. 6, PG. 192

NAMES: WM. CREWSE TO ELIZABETH HOOD
DATE: APR. 26, 1825
BONDSMAN: SHADRACK MASSEY
DATE PER: APR. 26, 1825
BY: ROBT. MCBATH
WITNESS: WM. SWAN
REFERENCE: C.A; O.M.R. PG. 93

NAMES: ISAAC CRISMAN, JR., TO ISABELLA PURSLEY
DATE: OCT. 27, 1825
BONDSMAN: FLEMING PURSLEY
DATE PER: OCT. 27, 1825
BY: JAMES MCMILLAN, J.P.
REFERENCE: C.A; O.M.R. PG. 97; T.H.M. VOL. 6, PG. 192

NAMES: HENRY DAVIS TO RACHEL HUNTER
DATE: NOV. 21, 1825
BONDSMAN: AMOS CARTER
DATE PER: NOV. 24, 1825
BY: JAMES MCMILLAN, J.P.
REFERENCE: C.A; O.M.R. PG. 98

NAMES: ANDREW DEHART TO CATY EMMETT
DATE: DEC. 31, 1825
DATE PER: JANY. 3, 1826
BY: WM. MORRIS, J.P.
REFERENCE: C.A; O.M.R. PG. 99

NAMES: ACHILLIS DON CARLOS TO ELIZABETH KIDD
DATE: JUNE 23, 1825
BONDSMAN: JOSEPH BURNETT
DATE PER: JUNE 23, 1825
BY: ROBT. MCBATH
REFERENCE: C.A; O.M.R. PG. 94

NAMES: JAMES DOVE TO POLLY DAMEWOOD
DATE: AUG. 15, 1825
BONDSMAN: NICHOLAS GIBBS
DATE PER: AUG. 15, 1825
BY: WM. SAWYERS, J.P.
REFERENCE: C.A; O.M.R. PG. 95

NAMES: JOHN DUNN TO MAHALA MCCLURE
DATE: JULY 25, 1825
DATE PER: JULY 28, 1825
BY: W.B.A/ RAMSEY, J.P.
REFERENCE: C.A; O.M.R. PG. 95; T.H.M. VOL. 6, PG. 192

NAMES: WM. EARLY TO BETSY BURNETT
DATE: JANY. 14, 1825
BONDSMAN: JOHN CAMPBELL
WITNESS: CHAS. MCCLUNG
REFERENCE: C.A.

NAMES: LEWIS EDMONDSON TO POLLY DAVIS
DATE: JULY 26, 1825
BONDSMAN: JAMES EDWARDS
DATE PER: JULY 26, 1825
BY: ROBT. TINDELL, J.P.
WITNESS: WM. SWAN
REFERENCE: C.A; O.M.R. PG. 95

Names: John Elliott to Polly Rose
Date: Dec. 1, 1825
Bondsman: Josiah Armstrong
Date Per: Dec. 1, 1825
By: Wm. Morris, J.P.
Reference: C.A; O.M.R. Pg. 98

Names: Ralph Everett to Betsy Thompson
Date: Mar. 2, 1825
Date Per: Mar. 4, 1825
By: S. S. McCampbell, J.P.
Reference: C.A; O.M.R. Pg. 91

Names: Benj. Farguson to Fanny Coker
Date: Jany. 26, 1825
Date Per: Jany. 26, 1825
By: Robt. McBath
Reference: C.A; O.M.R. Pg. 90

Names: Charles Ford to Joby Grizzle
Date: June 13, 1825
Bondsman: James Jones
Date Per: June 13, 1825
By: B. McNutt, J.P.
Witness: Wm. Swan
Reference: C.A; O.M.R. Pg. 94

Names: Philip Foust to Catharine Foust
Date: Feby 23, 1825
Date Per: Feby. 24, 1825
By: Wm. Sawyers, J.P.
Reference: C.A; O.M.R. Pg. 91

Names: Jesse George to Sally Mulvaney
Date: Jany. 12, 1825
Bondsman: Adam M. Kennedy
Date Per: Jany. 12, 1825
By: James McMillan, J.P.
Reference: C.A; O.M.R. Pg. 89

Names: Hiram Geren to Hannah Taylor
Date: Oct. 31, 1825
Date Per: Nov. 3, 1825
By: John Bayless, J.P.
Reference: C.A; O.M.R. Pg. 97

Names: Nicholas Gibbs to Polly Epps
Date: Dec. 13, 1825
Date Per: Dec. 15, 1825
By: James McMillan, J.P.
Witness: Wm. Swan
Reference: C.A; O.M.R. Pg. 98

Names: Thomas J. Grills to Harriet W. Smith
Date: May 24, 1825
Date Per: May 29, 1825
By: Geo. Atkin, M.G.
Reference: C.A; O.M.R. Pg. 93

Names: Hugh Hall to Mary Looney
Date: Jany. 31, 1825
Date Per: Feby. 1, 1825
By: Wm. B. Carns, J.P.
Reference: C.A; O.M.R. Pg. 90

Names: Wm. Harvey to Sally Haines
Date: July 15, 1825
Bondsman: Henry Lamon
Witness: Wm. Swan
Reference: C.A.

Names: Obadiah Hudson to Anne Bowman
Date: Feby. 10, 1825
Date Per: Feby. 10, 1825
By: John Haynie
Reference: C.A; O.M.R. Pg. 90

Names: Martin Huffstutler to Peggy Smiley
Date: Sept. 14, 1825
Bondsman: Jacob Smiley
Witness: Chas. McClung
Reference: C.A.

Names: Alexander Humphreys to Nancy Bond
Date: Nov. 5, 1825
Date Per: Nov. 8, 1825
By: Isaac Anderson, M.G.
Reference: C.A; O.M.R. Pg. 97; T.H.M. Vol. 6, Pg. 193

Names: James Jackson to Amanda Smith
Date: June 28, 1825
Date Per: June 30, 1825
By: Wm. B. Carns, J.P.
Reference: C.A; O.M.R. Pg. 94

Names: Demsey Johnston to Polly Brown
Date: Dec. 8, 1825
Date Per: Dec. 8, 1825
By: Robt. Lindsay, J.P.
Reference: C.A; O.M.R. Pg. 98

NAMES: JOSEPH KELLY TO POLLY WOLF
DATE: APR. 20, 1825
BONDSMAN: PETER WOLF
WITNESS: WM. SWAN
REFERENCE: C.A.

NAMES: JAMES B. KELSO TO MALVINA HUDABURG
DATE: SEPT. 28, 1825
DATE PER: SEPT. 29, 1825
BY: THO. H. NELSON
REFERENCE: C.A; O.M.R. PG. 96

NAMES: GEORGE LAMMIE (?) TO BETSY LYONS
DATE: FEBY. 9, 1825
DATE PER: FEBY. 10, 1825
BY: WM. B. CARNS, J.P.
REFERENCE: C.A; O.M.R. PG. 90

NAMES: ZACHARIAH LEA TO MATTY WATKINS
DATE: APR. 4, 1825
DATE PER: APR. 4, 1825
BY: J.A. MABRY, J.P.
REFERENCE: C.A; O.M.R. PG. 92

NAMES: PHILIP LETSINGER TO SUSAN EDMONDSON
DATE: JANY. 30, 1825
DATE PER: FEBY. 2, 1825
BY: MORDECAI YARNELL, J.P.
REFERENCE: C.A.

NAMES: JNO. LUTTRELL TO CLARISSA WHITE
DATE: APR. 11, 1825
DATE PER: APR. 14, 1825
BY: W.B/A. RAMSEY, J.P.
REFERENCE: O.M.R. PG. 93

NAMES: ROBERT MCCLAIN TO ELEANOR WEAVER
DATE: DEC. 27, 1825
DATE PER: DEC. 29, 1825
BY: WM. B. CARNS, J.P.
REFERENCE: C.A; O.M.R. PG. 99

NAMES: ROBERT MCCORRY (?) TO ANNE CLIFT
DATE: JUNE 11, 1825
DATE PER: JUNE 22, 1825
BY: JAMES MCMILLAN, J.P.
REFERENCE: C.A; O.M.R. PG. 94

NAMES: JAMES P. MCHAFFIE TO MARY STARNES
DATE: FEBY. 1, 1825
DATE PER: FEBY. 1, 1825
BY: GEO. ATKIN, M.G.
REFERENCE: C.A; O.M.R. PG. 90

NAMES: NICHOLAS G. MCKINLEY TO ELIZABETH SANDLAND
DATE: JANY. 16, 1825
DATE PER: JANY. 16, 1825
BY: JOHN HAYNIE
REFERENCE: C.A; O.M.R. PG. 89

NAMES: WM. MCLAMON TO BETSY LUTTRELL
DATE: FEBY. 16, 1825
BONDSMAN: JOHN LUTTRELL
WITNESS: WM. SWAN
REFERENCE: C.A; T.H.M. VOL. 6, PG. 193

NAMES: JAMES H. MCPHERAN TO SALLY CLAP
DATE: SEPT. 19, 1825
BONDSMAN: S. M. SKAGGS
DATE PER: SEPT. 20, 1825
BY: WM. B. CARNS, J.P.
REFERENCE: C.A; O.M.R. PG. 96

NAMES: MICHAEL MILLER TO CATHARINE GRAVES
DATE: SEPT. 28, 1825
BONDSMAN: JOSEPH JACKSON
DATE PER: SEPT. 29, 1825
BY: WM. SAWYERS, J.P.
REFERENCE: C.A; O.M.R. PG. 96

NAMES: GREENE W. MINTER TO JANE LARGE
DATE: MAY 21, 1825
DATE PER: MAY 22, 1825
BY: THOMAS WILKERSON
REFERENCE: C.A; O.M.R. PG. 94

NAMES: WM. MOLDEN TO CYNTHIA CARTER
DATE: OCT. 11, 1825
BONDSMAN: JAMES MCBATH
REFERENCE: C.A.

NAMES: GEORGE MORRIS TO SENETH WEBB
DATE: NOV. 24, 1825
DATE PER: NOV. 24, 1825
BY: ISAAC ANDERSON, M.G.
REFERENCE: C.A; O.M.R. PG. 98

NAMES: RICHARD NELSON TO ELIZA MCCAMPBELL
DATE: JUNE 23, 1825
BONDSMAN: C.T. BARTON
DATE PER: JUNE 26, 1825
BY: ISAAC ANDERSON, M.G.
REFERENCE: C.A.

Names: Thos. J. Nelson to Susannah Lewis
Date: Mar. 1, 1825
Bondsman: Martin Nelson
Date Per: Mar. 10, 1825
By: John Bayless, J.P.
Witness: Wm. Swan
Reference: C.A; O.M.R. Pg. 91

Names: Jesse Nichodemus to Betsy Rhodes
Date: Mar. 10, 1825
Bondsman: James Murphy
Reference: C.A.

Names: William Car to Peggy Widner
Date: Mar. 18, 1825
Bondsman: Noah Fisher
Date Per: Mar. 18, 1825
By: James McMillan, J.P.
Reference: C.A; O.M.R. Pg. 92

Names: Richard H. Owenby to Martha Shipe
Date: Apr. 21, 1825
Bondsman: John Chumly
Reference: C.A.

Names: Robert Park to Evalina Mason
Date: Feby. 24, 1825
Bondsman: Wm. Swan
Date Per: Feby. 24, 1825
By: Jno. Haynie
Reference: C.A; O.M.R. Pg. 91

Names: James Parr to Nancy Conn
Date: Oct. 31, 1825
Bondsman: D. Nelson
Date Per: Nov. 10, 1825
By: J.A. Mabry, J.P.
Reference: C.A; O.M.R. Pg. 97

Names: Willis H. Patterson to Mary Ann Moore
Date: Mar. 5, 1825
Bondsman: James H. King
Date Per: Mar. 5, 1825
By: Geo. Atkin, M.G.
Reference: C.A; O.M.R. Pg. 91

Names: Elijah Perry to Mira Plumley
Date: Mar. 22, 1825
Bondsman: Joseph Plumley
Date Per: Mar. 23, 1825
By: W.B.A. Ramsey, J.P.
Witness: Wm. Swan
Reference: C.A; O.M.R. Pg. 92

Names: Lewis Perry to Mannen Cunningham
Date: Mar. 29, 1825
Bondsman: James Ford
Witness: Wm. Swan
Reference: C.A.

Names: Robert Pierce to Betsy Clift
Date: July 14, 1825
Bondsman: Robert McCorry
Date Per: July 14, 1825
By: James McMillan, J.P.
Reference: C.A; O.M.R. Pg. 95

Names: Boyd Porter to Peggy McNutt
Date: Nov. 11, 1825
Bondsman: Benj. McNutt
Date Per: Nov. 17, 1825
By: Tho. H. Nelson
Reference: C.A; O.M.R. Pg. 97

Names: Benj. James Powell to Betsy Lumpkins
Date: May 15, 1825
Bondsman: Wm. Lindsay
Reference: C.A.

Names: Fleming Pressley to Margaret Robertson
Date: July 7, 1825
Bondsman: Jno. Craighead
Date Per: July 7, 1825
By: W.B.A. Ramsey, J.P.
Reference: C.A; O.M.R. Pg. 94

Names: Thomas Price to Maria Mayfield
Date: Nov. 16, 1825
Date Per: Nov. 17, 1825
By: David Nelson, J.P.
Reference: C.A; O.M.R. Pg. 98

Names: Edward Pritchett to Catharine Harner
Date: Aug. 16, 1825
Bondsman: Wm. Pritchett
Date Per: Aug. 18, 1825
By: J. A. Mabry, J.P. Witness: Wm. Swan
Reference: C.A; O.M.R. Pg. 95

Names: John Pritchett to Drucilla Perry
Date: July 12, 1825
Date Per: July 14, 1825
By: Henry Soward, M.G.
Reference: C.A; O.M.R. Pg. 95

Names: Andrew Randles to Cassandra Parsley
D te: Dec. 14, 1825
Bondsman: James Cunningham
Date Per: Dec. 15, 1825
By: J. Cunningham, J.P.
Reference: C.A; O.M.R. Pg. 99

Names: Chas. Ready to Martha A. Strong
Date: May 19, 1825
Bondsman: P. N. Smith - C. T. Barton
D^te Per: May 19, 1825
By: Tho. H. Nelson
Reference: C. A.

Names: Wm. Reagan to Matilda Tunnell
Date: Oct. 1, 182 5
Bondsman: James McBath
Date Per: Oct. 4, 1 825
By: Jas. Y. Crawford, M.G.
Reference: C.A; O.M.R. Pg. 96

Names: John G. Riley to Elizabeth Sherodd
Date: Dec. 17, 1825
Bondsman: Harvey Weir
Date Per: Dec. 27, 1825
By: John Bayless, J.P.
Witness: Wm. Swan
Reference: C.A; O.M.R. Pg. 99

Names: Wm. Riseden to Betsy Gasperson
Date: May 20, 1825
Bondsman: Jesse Davis
Date Per: May 22, 1825
By: Robt. Tindell, J.P.
Witness: Wm. Swan
Reference: C.A; O.M.R. Pg. 93

Names: William Ritchie to Betsy Watt
D^te: May 21, 1825
Bondsman: John Hill
Date Per: May 26, 1825
By: John McCampbell, T.D.M.
Reference: C.A; O.M.R. Pg. 93

Names: Samuel Roddy to Milly Johnston
Date: Feby. 14, 1825
Bondsman: Jonathan Sharp
Witness: Wm. Swan
Reference: C.A.

Names: Sam'l Roddy to Milly Johnston
Date: Feby. 14, 1825
Date Per: Feby 15, 1825
By: Jesse Bartlett, J.P.
Reference: O.M.R. Pg. 91

Names: James Routh to Eleanor Wilkerson
Date: Sept. 21, 1825
Bondsman: Joseph Routh
Witness: Wm. Swan
Reference: C.A.

Names: Absalom Rutherford to Theney Kearns
Date: Mar. 15, 1825
Bondsman: Sam'l Kelly
Date Per: Mar. 17, 1825
By: Wm. Sawyers, J.P.
Reference: C.A; O.M.R. Pg. 92

Names: David Rutherford to Nancy Hickle
Date: Dec. 15, 1825
Bondsman: John Hickle
Reference: C.A.

Names: James Scott to Eliza N. J.(?) B.A. Ramsey
Date: Jany. 27, 1825
Date Per: Jany. 27, 1825
By: Jno. McCampbell, V.D.M.
Reference: O.M.R. Pg. 90

Names: Isaac Sharp to Sally Moore
Date: Feby. 9, 1825
Date Per: Feby. 10, 1825
By: Wm. Sawyers, J.P.
Reference: C.A; O.M.R. Pg. 90

Names: David A. Sherman to Jane Wing
Date: May 5, 1825
Bondsman: James Campbell
Witness: Wm. Swan
Reference: C.A.

Names: John Soward to Sarah Ottery
Date: July 26, 1825
Bondsman: Wm. Soward
Reference: C.A.

NAMES: WILLIAM SUMMERS TO BETSY HANKINS
DATE: MAR. 26, 1825
DATE PER: MAR. 30, 1825
BY: THOS. WILKERSON, ELDER
REFERENCE: C.A; O.M.R. PG. 92

NAMES: MOSES M. SWAN TO JANE MCCAUGHAN
DATE: APR. 28, 1825
BONDSMAN: JAMES LOW
DATE PER: APR. 28, 1825
BY: SAM'L FLEMING, J.P.
WITNESS: CHAS. MCCLUNG
REFERENCE: C.A; O.M.R. PG. 93

NAMES: OLIVER C. THARP TO ELIZA WHITE
DATE: SEPT. 28, 1825
REFERENCE: C.A; O.M.R. PG. 96

NAMES: YERBY THOMPSON TO SARAH CUZZART
DATE: JANY. 20, 1825
BONDSMAN: JAMES SPENCE
DATE PER: JANY. 20, 1825
BY: SAM'L S. MCCAMPBELL, J.P.
WITNESS: WM. SWAN
REFERENCE: C.A; O.M.R. PG. 89

NAMES: GEORGE TINDELL TO ELIZA HICKLE
DATE: NOV. 12, 1825
BONDSMAN: JOSEPH LAREW
REFERENCE: C.A; O.M.R. PG. 97

NAMES: JONATHAN TIPTON TO MARY CHILDRESS
DATE: APR. 8, 1825
DATE PER: APR. 10, 1825
BY: ROBT. TINDELL, J.P.
REFERENCE: C.A; O.M.R. PG. 93

NAMES: JESSE WALKER TO REBECKA GREER
DATE: SEPT. 23, 1825
BONDSMAN: REUBEN WALKER
REFERENCE: C.A; T.H.M. VOL. 6, PG. 193

NAMES: JAMES WEAVER TO JANE MOORE CURD
DATE: DEC. 28, 1825
BONDSMAN: WM. HIBBS
DATE PER: JANY. 5, 1826
BY: E. NELSON, J.P.
WITNESS: WM. SWAN
REFERENCE: C.A; O.M.R. PG. 99

NAMES: ALLEN WHEELER TO BETSY COWAN
DATE: NOV. 24, 1825
BONDSMAN: GIDEON RODDY
REFERENCE: C.A.

NAMES: ISAAC WILLIAMS TO ELIZA JANE MILLICAN
DATE: JANY. 5, 1825
BONDSMAN: JNO. C. ELLISON
DATE PER: JAN. 6, 1825
BY: WM. B. CARNS, J.P.
WITNESS: WM. SWAN
REFERENCE: C.A; O.M.R. PG. 89

NAMES: JAMES E. WILLIAMS TO MARTHA WITCHER
DATE: OCT. 17, 1825
BONDSMAN: HENRY T. MITCHELL
DATE PER: OCT. 17, 1825
BY: DAVID NELSON, J.P.
REFERENCE: C.A; O.M.R. PG. 97

NAMES: JASON WILLIAMS TO NANCY COTTRELL
DATE: DEC. 15, 1825
DATE PER: DEC. 15, 1825
BY: ROBT. LINDSAY, J.P.
REFERENCE: C.A; O.M.R. PG. 99; T.H.M. VOL. 6, PG. 193

NAMES: JOEL WRIGHT TO MARY HALBERT
DATE: MAR. 15, 1825
BY: E. NELSON, J.P. – BONDSMAN: MOSES WRIGHT
REFERENCE: C.A; O.M.R. PG. 92

1826

NAMES: CLAYTON C. ABERNATHY TO AUGERONA COBB
DATE: OCT. 24, 1826
BONDSMAN: BARY ABERNATHY
REFERENCE: C.A.

NAMES: ISOM P. ALLEY TO MARY C. GRILLS
DATE: MAR. 14, 1826
BONDSMAN: HARRISON SMITH
DATE PER: MAR. 14, 1826
BY: JAMES Y. CRAWFORD, M.G.
WITNESS: WM. SWAN
REFERENCE: C.A; O.M.R. PG. 102

NAMES: JNO. W. ALLEY TO LUCINDA SMITH
DATE: JANY. 10, 1826
DATE PER: JANY. 11, 1826
BY: JOHN BAYLESS, J.P.
REFERENCE: C.A; O.M.R. PG. 100

NAMES: CHARLES W. ATKIN TO HARRIET GILL
DATE: AUG. 24, 1826
BONDSMAN: JAMES HARE
DATE PER: AUG. 24, 1826
BY: GEO. ATKIN, M. G.
REFERENCE: C.A; O.M.R. PG. 104

NAMES: JAMES BALLINGER TO ANNE DOW
DATE: OCT. 25, 1826
REFERENCE: T.H.M. VOL. 6, PG. 193

NAMES: SAMUEL BAYLESS TO NANNY LISTER
DATE: MCH. 9,
REFERENCE: T.H.M. VOL. 6, PG. 193

NAMES: LOYD BELL TO BETSY KEYS
DATE: APR. 12, 1826
BONDSMAN: BARKLEY WALKER
WITNESS: WM. SWAN
REFERENCE: C.A.

NAMES: MATTHIAS BENSON TO HANNAH SMITH
DATE: AUG. 1, 1826
DATE PER: AUG. 3, 1826
BY: GEO. ATKIN, M.G.
REFERENCE: C.A; O.M.R. PG. 104; T.H.M. VOL. 6, PG. 193

NAMES: JOHN BIBBS TO LEVIOO MANLEY
DATE: SEPT. 11, 1826
DATE PER: SEPT. 12, 1826
BY: JOHN BAYLESS, J.P.
REFERENCE: C.A; O.M.R. PG. 104

NAMES: NOBLE BOWLING TO KATTY CLIFT
DATE: DEC. 8, 1826
BONDSMAN: JAMES FARR
DATE PER: DEC. 14, 1826
BY: ELI KING, J.P.
REFERENCE: C.A; O.M.R. PG. 107

NAMES: BENJ. BOYD TO CYNTHIA BROOKS
DATE: NOV. 9, 1826
BONDSMAN: JAMES KENNEDY
REFERENCE: C.A.

NAMES: BENJ. S. BOYD TO CYNTHIA BROOKS
DATE: NOV. 9, 1826
DATE PER: NOV. 9, 1826
BY: THO. H. NELSON, M. G.
REFERENCE: O.M: R. PG. 106

NAMES: HEZEKIAH BURNHAM TO SUSANNA HUSSONG
DATE: FEBY. 9, 1826
REFERENCE: C.A; O.M.R. PG. 101

NAMES: THOS. J. CALDWELL TO LUCY BARDIS
DATE: NOV. 28, 1826
BONDSMAN: ANDREW PARK - H. G. CROZIER
REFERENCE: C.A.

NAMES: THOS. J. CALDWELL TO LUCY DARDIS
DATE: NOV. 28, 1826
DATE PER: NOV. 28, 1826
BY: THO. H. NELSON, M.G.
REFERENCE: O.M.R. PG. 106

NAMES: BENJAMIN CARR TO HULDAH BEARD
DATE: JULY 29, 1826
BONDSMAN: JNO. OWENS
DATE PER: JULY 31, 1826
BY: SAM FLENNIKEN, J.P.
WITNESS: WM. SWAN
REFERENCE: C.A; O.M.R. PG. 104

NAMES: MICAJAH CHILES TO ELIZABETH WILKENS
DATE: JULY 29,
REFERENCE: T.H.M. VOL. 6, PG. 193

NAMES: WILLIAM CLARK TO ELIZABETH CONLEY
DATE: DEC. 12, 1826
BONDSMAN: SILAS CONLEY
DATE PER: DEC. 12, 1826
BY: SAM'L FLEMING, J.P.
WITNESS: CHAS. MCCLUNG
REFERENCE: C.A; O.M.R. PG. 107

NAMES: JOSEPH CLIFT TO OHRISTIANA HAYWORTH
DATE: NOV. 13, 1826
BONDSMAN: BARNES CRAWFORD
REFERENCE: C.A.

NAMES: JOHN COKER TO SALLY FERGUSON
DATE: DEC. 16, 1826
DATE PER: DEC. 17, 1826
BY: SAM'L FLENNIKEN, J.P.
REFERENCE: C.A; O.M.R. PG. 107; T.H.M. VOL. 6, PG. 193

NAMES: WM. COPLEY TO KATTY PEELER
DATE: NOV. 28, 1826
BONDSMAN: BERRY PEELER
BY: J. A. SWAN, J.P.
REFERENCE: C.A; O.M.R. PG. 106

NAMES: JOSHUA COTTRELL TO BETSY CHESSER
DATE: JANY. 25, 1826
BONDSMAN: JASON WILLIAMS
WITNESS: WM. SWAN
REFERENCE: C.A; O.M.R. PG. 100

NAMES: JOHN COURTNEY TO PATSY WILLIAMS
DATE: NOV. 30, 1826
BONDSMAN: JOHN HASKINS
REFERENCE: C.A.

NAMES: JAMES CRANK TO NANCY GEORGE
DATE: JANY. 17, 1826
BONDSMAN: THOS. CRANK
DATE PER: JANY. 22, 1826
BY: JOHN BAYLESS, J.P.
WITNESS: WM. SWAN
REFERENCE: C.A; O.M.R. PG. 100; T.H.M. VOL. 6, PG. 193

NAMES: JESSE CUNNINGHAM TO BETSY NEWMAN (?)
DATE: JULY 18,
REFERENCE: T.H.M. VOL. 6, PG. 193

NAMES: JACOB DICK TO PATSY MCBEE
DATE: JULY 22, 1826
BONDSMAN: BENJ. I. WILSON
DATE PER: JULY 27, 1826
BY: THOMAS WILKERSON
REFERENCE: C.A; O.M.R. PG. 103

NAMES: ISAAC DOYLE TO PEGGY CAMPBELL
DATE: DEC. 14, 1826
BONDSMAN: GEO. M. WHITE
REFERENCE: C.A; T.H.M. VOL. 6, PG. 193

NAMES: JOHN DRAIN TO SALLIE HENDERSON
DATE: DEC. 5,
REFERENCE: T.H.M. VOL. 6, PG. 193

NAMES: WILLIAM DUNLAP TO PATSY YARNELL
DATE: MAR. 29, 1826
DATE PER: MAR. 30, 1826
BY: WM. MORRIS, J.P.
REFERENCE: C.A; O.M.R. PG. 102

NAMES: JOHN EDINGTON TO ISABEL DUNN
DATE: JULY 18, 1826
BONDSMAN: BERRY BURNETT — WITNESS: WM. SWAN
DATE PER: JULY 19, 1826
BY: DAVID NELSON, J.P.
REFERENCE: C.A; O.M.R. PG. 103

NAMES: LEWIS EMBREE TO PHEBE WARWICK
DATE: SEPT. 28, 1826
BONDSMAN: JNO. F. PATE
DATE PER: SEPT. 1826
BY: DANIEL GRAVES, J.P.
REFERENCE: C.A; O.M.R. PG. 105

NAMES: WILLIAM ERVIN TO POLLY HINDS
DATE: DEC. 6, 1826
BONDSMAN: LAZARUS JOHNSTON
DATE PER: DEC. 6, 1826
BY: J. JOHNSON, J.P.
REFERENCE: C.A; O.M.R. PG. 107

NAMES: NICHOLAS FAY(OR FRY) TO CIBBY MOORE
DATE: MAR. 8, 1826
DATE PER: MAR. 8, 1826
BY: GEO. ATKIN, M. G.
REFERENCE: C.A; O.M.R. PG. 102

NAMES: WASHINGTON L. FLEMING TO RUTH BROWN
DATE: APR. 21,
REFERENCE: T.H.M. VOL. 6, PG. 193

NAMES: SAMUEL FLENNIKEN TO ELIZABETH HOWELL
DATE: FEBY. 15, 1826
BONDSMAN: JEREMIAH KING
REFERENCE: C.A; O.M.R. PG. 101

NAMES: WILLIE C. FORGUSON TO CATHARINE KEITH
DATE: OCT. 30, 1826
DATE PER: OCT. 30, 1826
BY: SAM'L FLEMING, J.P.
REFERENCE: C.A; O.M.R. PG. 106

NAMES: JOHN FOUST TO ELIZABETH CORD
DATE: NOV. 30, 1826
BONDSMAN: JACOB FOUST
WITNESS: WM. SWAN
REFERENCE: C.A.

NAMES: THOMAS FROST TO SALLY D. LUCAS
DATE: APR. 23, 1826
BONDSMAN: JNO. D. SANDERS
DATE PER: APR. 23, 1826
BY: MORDECAI YARNELL, J.P.
WITNESS: WM. SWAN
REFERENCE: C.A. O.M.R. PG. 102

NAMES: JAMES OVERTON GENTRY TO CHARLOTTE REYNOLDS
DATE: JANY. 24, 1826
BONDSMAN: JNO. S. REYNOLDS
DATE PER: JANY. 25, 1826
BY: JAMES Y. CRAWFORD, J.P.
REFERENCE: C.A; O.M.R. PG. 100

NAMES: THOMAS GIBSON TO KESSIAH CASH
DATE: FEBY. 8, 1826
DATE PER: FEBY. 9, 1826
BY: ELI KING, J.P.
REFERENCE: C.A; O.M.R. PG. 101

NAMES: THOMAS GILLESPIE TO NANCY RUSSELL
DATE: JANY. 21, 1826
DATE PER: JANY. 24, 1826
BY: GEO. TUNNELL
REFERENCE: C.A; O.M.R. PG. 100

NAMES: LYNCH B. GOODMAN TO POLLY TONKSEY
DATE: DEC. 12, 1826
BONDSMAN: JNO. MASSEY
DATE PER: DEC. 15, 1826
BY: JOHN BAYLESS, J.P.
WITNESS: WM. SWAN, J.P.
WITNESS: WM. SWAN
REFERENCE: C.A; O.M.R. PG. 107

NAMES: JOEL GOSSET TO MARGARET MURPHY
DATE: FEBY. 2, 1826
BONDSMAN: DANIEL MCMULLAN
REFERENCE: C.A; O.M.R. PG. 101

NAMES: GEORGE HARDEN TO CYNTHIA CALLOWAY
DATE: SEPT. 6, 1826
DATE PER: SEPT. 7, 1826
BY: MORDECAI YARNELL, J.P.
REFERENCE: C.A; O.M.R. PG. 104

NAMES: GEO. HARN TO AMANDA LUTTRELL
DATE: OCT. 11, 1826
BONDSMAN: JAMES KING
REFERENCE: C.A.

NAMES: HIBEY HENDERSON TO BETSY MCCLARD
DATE: DEC. 10, 1826
BONDSMAN: WM. MCCLARD
REFERENCE: C.A.

NAMES: JOSEPH HENSON TO POLLY SMITH
DATE: AUG. 17, 1826
BONDSMAN: GEO. COOLEY
WITNESS: WM. SWAN
REFERENCE: C.A.

NAMES: GEO. HORN TO AMANDA LUTTRELL
DATE: OCT. 11, 1826
DATE PER: OCT. 12, 1826
BY: THO. STRINGFIELD
REFERENCE: O.M.R. PG. 105; T.H.M. VOL. 6, PG. 193

NAMES: WALTER HOUSTON TO JANE CUNNINGHAM
DATE: MAR. 1, 1826
REFERENCE: C.A; O.M.R. PG. 102; T.H.M. VOL. 6, PG. 193

NAMES: DUKE HOWELL TO ELIZABETH DEARMON
DATE: MAR. 9, 1826
BONDSMAN: HENRY HOFFAR
DATE PER: MAR. 9, 1826
BY: THOS. H. NELSON
REFERENCE: C.A; O.M.R. PG. 102

NAMES: WILLIAM HOWELL TO SALLY PHELPS
DATE: SEPT. 6, 1826
BONDSMAN: ISAAC SHARP
DATE PER: SEPT. 8, 1826
BY: JOSEPH WOODS, ESQ.
WITNESS: WM. C. MYNATT
REFERENCE: C.A; O.M.R. PG. 104

NAMES: JONATHAN HOWSER TO POLLY HARMON
DATE: AUG. 15,
REFERENCE: T.H.M. VOL. 6, PG. 193

NAMES: JOSEPH HOWSER TO NANCY ANDERSON
DATE: MAY 4, 1826
BONDSMAN: JAMES ARTHUR
DATE PER: MAY 4, 1826
BY: DAVID NELSON, J.P.
WITNESS: WM. SWAN
REFERENCE: C.A; O.M.R. PG. 103

NAMES: PHILIP P. HOWSER TO JANE MORROW
DATE: MAY 1, 1826
BONDSMAN: JAMES KENNEDY
DATE PER: MAY 4, 1826
BY: R. HOUSTON, J.P.
REFERENCE: O.A; O.M.R. PG. 103

NAMES: ELIPHU HUNTER TO PEGGY BEANE
DATE: DEC. 6, 1826
DATE PER: DEC. 6, 1827
BY: J. JOHNSON, J.P.
REFERENCE: C.A; O.M.R. PG. 204

NAMES: CLAIBORN JOHNSTON TO POLLY NICHOLS
DATE: JANY. 25, 1826
DATE PER: JANY. 25, 1826
BY: JAMES MCMILLAN, J. P.
REFERENCE: C.A; O.M.R. PG. 100

NAMES: WILLIAM KEYS TO PEGGY WEADEN
DATE: AUG. 8, 1826
BONDSMAN: LOYD BEALL
REFERENCE: C.A.

NAMES: JOHN LAMB TO MARTHA GILLESPIE
DATE: JANY. 3, 1826
BONDSMAN: EMANUEL LAMON
REFERENCE: C.A.

NAMES: JOSEPH LAREW TO JANE PARKER
DATE: OCT. 17, 1826
DATE PER: OCT. 17, 1826
BY: ROBT. TINDELL, J.P.
REFERENCE: C.A; O.M.R. PG. 105

NAMES: PHILIP LETSINGER TO SUSAN EDMONDSON
DATE: JANY. 30, 1826
DATE PER: FEBY. 2, 1826
BY: GEO. ATKIN, M.G.
REFERENCE: O.M.R. PG. 100

NAMES: DAVID LONES TO LETITIA BROWNING
DATE: DEC. 5, 1826
DATE PER: DEC. 5, 1826
BY: WM. P. SEXTER
REFERENCE: C.A; O.M.R. PG. 106

NAMES: GEO. LOWDERMILK TO POLLY MCNUTT
DATE: JUNE 9, 1826
DATE PER: JUNE 11, 1826
BY: W.B.A. RAMSEY, J.P.
REFERENCE: C.A; O.M.R. PG. 103

NAMES: HUGH B. MAGGET TO JANE MEEK
DATE: FEBY. 20, 1826
DATE PER: FEBY. 21, 1826
BY: JAMES MCMILLAN, J.P.
REFERENCE: C.A; O.M.R. PG. 101

NAMES: WM. H. MANWARING TO MARGARET MCCARN
DATE: NOV. 20, 1826
BONDSMAN: JOEL RUDDER
DATE PER: NOV. 30, 1826
BY: WM. EAGLETON, M.G.
WITNESS: WM. SWAN
REFERENCE: C.A; O.M.R. PG. 106

NAMES: JESSE MASON TO POLLY BLAKELY
DATE: JULY 25, 1826
BONDSMAN: THOS. GIBSON
DATE PER: JULY 25, 1826
BY: ELI KING, J.P.
WITNESS: WM. SWAN
REFERENCE: C.A; O.M.R. PG. 103

NAMES: JOSEPH MICLES TO SALLY DANNEL
DATE: FEBY. 24, 1826
BONDSMAN: FREDERICK MICHAELS
DATE PER: FEBY. 24, 1826
BY: DAVID NELSON, J.P.
REFERENCE: C.A; O.M.R. PG. 101

NAMES: JAMES P. MILLER TO CHARLOTTE LOVE
DATE: JANY. 5, 1826
BONDSMAN: ROBERT BELL
DATE PER: JANY. 5, 1826
BY: JAMES Y. CRAWFORD, M.G.
REFERENCE: C.A; O.M.R. PG. 100

NAMES: JAMES M. MONTGOMERY TO SARAH KILBURN
DATE: SEPT. 23, 1826
BONDSMAN: WM. S. MONTGOMERY
DATE PER: SEPT. 24, 1826
BY: J. JOHNSON, J.P.
REFERENCE: C.A; O.M.R. PG. 105

NAMES: THOS. MOTLEY TO POLLY ORE
DATE: NOV. 10, 1826
BONDSMAN: WM. MCMILLAN
WITNESS: WM. SWAN
REFERENCE: C.A.

NAMES: REUBEN G. MUNDAY TO ANN BROWN
DATE: OCT. 26, 1826
DATE PER: NOV. 2, 1826
BY: JAMES ALLDREDGE, J.P.
REFERENCE: C.A; O.M.R. PG. 105

Names: Joseph Mynatt to Margaret Pursley
Date: Dec. 21, 1826
Bondsman: John Mynatt
Reference: C.A.

Names: George F. Reynolds to Elizabeth Gentry
Date: Jany. 24, 1826
Date Per: Jany. 25, 1826
By: J. Y. Crawford, M.G.
Reference: C.A; O.M.R. Pg. 100

Names: Aquilla Rhodes to Mary Hickle
Date: July 29, 1826
Bondsman: Lorenza D. Hamilton
Reference: C.A.

Names: Peter Rhody to Betsy Nichodemus
Date: Mar. 2, 1826
Bondsman: Jesse Nichodemus
Witness: Wm. Swan
Reference: C.A.

Names: John Rule to Nancy Hood
Date: Aug. 3, 1826
Bondsman: Jno. Husong
Date Per: Aug. 3, 1826
By: Sam. Flenniken
Witness: Wm. Swan
Reference: C.A; O.M.R. Pg. 104

Names: Aaron Smith to Letty Smith
Date: Oct. 12, 1826
Reference: C.A; O.M.R. Pg. 105

Names: Chas. Smith to Polly Wilkins
Date: Feby. 28, 1826
Date Per: Mar. 21, 1826
By: Wm. Morris, J.P.
Reference: C.A; O.M.R. Pg. 101

Names: Henry Smith to Nancy Bunday
Date: Aug. 18, 1826
Date:Per: Aug. 20, 1826
By: Wm. B. Carns, J.P.
Reference: C.A; O.M.R. Pg. 104

Names: Jacob Spore to Nancy Wade
Date: Sept. 23, 1826 – Witness: Wm. Swan
Bondsman: Wm. Honeymaker
Date Per: Sept. 1, 1826
By: Julian Frazier, J.P.
Reference: C.A; O.M.R. Pg. 105

Names: William Stephenson to Nelly Kirkpatrick
Date: Oct. 24, 1826
Date Per: Nov. 8, 1826
By: Wm. B. Carns, J.P.
Reference: C.A; O.M.R. Pg. 105

Names: Also Taylor to Nancy Simpson
Date: July 26, 1826
Bondsman: Michael Ault
Date Per: July 27, 1826
By: R. Houston, J.P.
Witness: Wm. Swan
Reference: C.A; O.M.R. Pg. 104; T.H.M. Vol. 6, Pg. 193

Names: Jeremiah Temple to Nancy Wilkins
Date: Aug. 15, 1826
Bondsman: Geo. Shetterly
Reference: C.A.

Names: James Thompson to Frances Yarnell
Date: Oct. 31, 1826
Bondsman: M. Yarnell
Date Per: Nov. 2, 1826
By: Wm. Morris, J.P.
Witness: W. C. Mynatt,
Reference: C.A; O.M.R. Pg. 106; T.H.M. Vol. 6, Pg. 193

Names: John Tillery to Rebecka Yarnell
Date: Feby. 24, 1826
By: Wm. Morris, J.P. – Date Per: Feby. 26, 1826
Reference: C.A; O.M.R. Pg. 101

Names: Wm. Wall to Jane Wolf
Date: Nov. 10, 1826
Bondsman: Jno. Wall
Date Per: Nov. 10, 1826
By: James Alldredge, J.P.
Witness: Wm. Swan
Reference: C.A; O.M.R. Pg. 106

Names: Samuel Watkins to Lucy Binly (or Birely)
Date: Mar. 16, 1826
Bondsman: Jno. Neely
Date Per: Mar. 16, 1826
By: John A. Swan, J.P.
Witness: Wm. Swan
Reference: C.A; O.M.R. Pg. 102; T.H.M. Vol. 6, Pg. 193

NAMES: GEORGE WEBB TO NANCY CALLOWAY
DATE: SEPT. 18,
REFERENCE: T.H.M. VOL. 6, PG. 193

NAMES: JAMES M. M. WHITE TO ELIZA H. CRAIGHEAD
DATE: SEPT. 19, 1826
DATE PER: SEPT. ____, 1826 (NOT LEGIBLE)
REFERENCE: O.M.R. PG. 105

NAMES: JNO. WHITE TO MARY HUMES
DATE: JUNE 29, 1826 - DATE PER: JUNE 29, 1826
BY: THO. H. NELSON, M.G.
REFERENCE: O.M.R. PG. 103

NAMES: JOHN L. WHITE TO POLLY CASH
DATE: JANY. 31, 1826
DATE PER: JANY. 31, 1826
BY: GEO. ATKIN, M. G.
REFERENCE: C.A; O.M.R. PG. 100

NAMES: WILLIAM WHITE TO POLLY WIDNER
DATE: APR. 4, 1826
BONDSMAN: JACOB WIDNER
DATE PER: APR. 4, 1826
BY: J. CUNNINGHAM
WITNESS: WM. SWAN
REFERENCE: C.A; O.M.R. PG. 102

NAMES: SIMON WHITE TO ELIZABETH VICKARS
DATE: JULY 29, 1826
BONDSMAN: JNO. T. SMITH
REFERENCE: C.A.

NAMES: SOLOMON WILSON TO JUDA MORGAN
DATE: MAR. 11, 1826
BONDSMAN: JAMES SKAGGS
DATE PER: MAR. ? 1826
BY: JOSEPH WOOD, ESQ.
REFERENCE: C.A; O.M.R. PG. 102

NAMES: JNO. WRIGHT JR. TO MIMA HILL
DATE: APR. 26, 1826
BONDSMAN: B. M. WALLACE - SPENCER JARNAGIN - WM. SWAN & GEO. M. WHITE
BY: DAVID NELSON, J.P. - DATE PER: APR. 26, 1826
WITNESS: WM. SWAN
REFERENCE: C.A; O.M.R. PG. 109

1827

NAMES: SAMUEL AILOR TO SALLY WARWICK
DATE: MAR. 14, 1827
DATE PER: MAR. 15, 1827
BY: GEO. GRAVES, J.P.
REFERENCE: C.A; O.M.R. PG. 109

NAMES: JAMES ANDERSON TO RHODA CHUMLEA
DATE: JANY. 25, 1827
DATE PER: JANY. 25, 1827
BY: WM. A. MCCAMPBELL
REFERENCE: C.A; O.M.R. PG. 108

NAMES: EDMON ATHEAN TO RELAY LONGWITH
DATE: AUG. 16, 1827
BONDSMAN: WM. PACKETT
REFERENCE: C.A; T.H.M. VOL. 6, PG. 193

NAMES: WM. J. BAKER TO MARY ANN CASE (OR COX)
DATE: DEC. 13, 1827
DATE PER: DEC. 13, 1827
BY: THO. H. NELSON
REFERENCE: C.A; O.M.R. PG. 116

NAMES: JAMES BALLINGER TO ANNE DOVE (OR LOVE)
DATE: OCT. 25, 1827
BONDSMAN: ABSALOM RUTHERFORD
DATE PER: OCT. 25, 1827
BY: WM. SAWYERS, J.P.
WITNESS: WM. SWAN
REFERENCE: C.A; O.M.R. PG. 114

NAMES: SAMUEL BAYLESS TO NANCY LISTER
DATE: MAR. 9, 1827
BONDSMAN: ISAAC BAYLESS
DATE PER: MAR. 15, 1827
BY: SAMUEL LOVE, M.G.
REFERENCE: C.A; O.M.R. PG. 109

NAMES: PHILIP D. BELL TO HARRIET JANE MURPHY
DATE: AUG. 21, 1827
BONDSMAN: HUGH M. MURPHY
REFERENCE: C.A.

NAMES: ISAAC BENTON TO NANCY INGRAM
DATE: NOV. 22, 1827
DATE PER: NOV. 22, 1827
BY: E. M. EAGLETON, M.G.
REFERENCE: O.M.R. PG. 115

Names: Hugh L. Berry to Anne Parker
Date: Feby. 14, 1827
Bondsman: Jno. Brown
Date Per: Feby. 15, 1827
By: Sam Flenniken, J.P.
Reference: C.A; O.M.R. Pg. 108

Names: William Bivens to Rebecka Raigan
Date: July 5, 1827
Date Per: July 5, 1827
By: Geo. Atkin, M. G.
Reference: C.A; O.M.R. Pg. 111

Names: Nathan Bolin to Nancy Lister
Date: Mar. 12, 1827
Bondsman: Robt. T. Lyles
Witness: Wm. Swan
Reference: C.A.

Names: M. Boring to Elizabeth McCullough
Date: Mar. 14, 1827
Date Per: Mar. 15, 1827
By: J.A. Mabry, J.P.
Reference: C.A; O.M.R. Pg. 109

Names: Gabriel R. Brown to Elizabeth King
Date: Janyl 2, 1827
Date Per: Jany. 3, 1827
By: John Brown, J.P.
Reference: C.A; O.M.R. Pg. 107

Names: Samuel Burnett to Rowena Page
Date: Oct. 17, 1827
By: J.A. Swan, J.P.
Reference: C.A; O.M.R. Pg. 114

Names: Isaac Burton to Nancy Ingram
Date: Nov. 22, 1827
Date Per: Nov. 22, 1827
By: Elijah M. Eagleton, M.G.
Reference: C.A; O.M.R. Pg. 115

Names: Henry Burum to Nancy F. King
Date: May 31, 1827
Date Per: May 31, 1827
By: Sam Flenniken, J.P.
Reference: C.A; O.M.R. Pg. 110

Names: John C. Cannon to Caroline Nelson
Date: Oct. 25, 1827
Bondsman: Andrew McMillan
Date Per: Oct. 25, 1827
By: Tho. H. Nelson,
Reference: C.A; O.M.R. Pg. 114

Names: Edmond Catham to Betsy Longwutt
Date: Aug. 16,
Reference: T.H.M. Vol. 6, Pg. 193

Names: Wm. W. Chumlee to Jane E. Anderson
Date: Dec. 20, 1827
Date Per: Dec. 27, 1827
By: W. A. McCampbell, V.D.A.
Reference: C.A; O.M.R. Pg. 115 & 116

Names: Hugh M. Clark to Mary Smith
Date: Mar. 5, 1827
Date Per: Mar. 6, 1827
By: Wm. Morris, J.P.
Reference: C.A; O.M.R. Pg. 108; T.H.M. Vol. 6, Pg. 193

Names: Thomas Cole to Margaret Tillery -
Date: Sept. 27, 1827
Date Per: Sept. 27, 1827
By: Mordecai Yarnell, J.P.
Reference: C.A; O.M.R. Pg. 113

Names: Berry Coley to Jane Frisby
Date: July 27, 1827
Bondsman: Jno. McDonough
Date Per: July 27, 1827
By: J.A. Swan, J.P.
Reference: C.A; O.M.R. Pg. 111

Names: John Coward to Sally Yarnell
Date: May 22, 1827
By: Wm. Morris, J.P.
Reference: C.A; O.M.R. Pg. 110

Names: Hugh Crawford to Catharine Mynatt
Date: Aug. 27, 1827
Reference: C.A.

Names: Hugh Crawford to Catharine Mynatt
Date: Aug. 28, 1827
Date Per: Aug. 30, 1827
By: Geo. Graves, J.P.
Reference: O.M.R. Pg. 112

NAMES: JESSE CUNNINGHAM TO BETSY NEWMAN
DATE: JULY 18, 1827
BONDSMAN: JOHN CUNNINGHAM
DATE PER: JULY 20, 1827
BY: J. CUNNINGHAM, M.G.
WITNESS: WM. SWAN
REFERENCE: C.A; O.M.R. PG. 111

NAMES: RICHARD J. DEARMOND TO LUCY MASTERSON
DATE: OCT. 24, 1827
DATE PER: OCT. 25, 1827
BY: SAM FLENNIKEN, J.P.
REFERENCE: C.A; O.M.R. PG. 114

NAMES: JAMES DOWLIN TO ELIZABETH LACEY
DATE: MAR. 29, 1827
DATE PER: MAR. 29, 1827
BY: MORDECAI YARNELL
REFERENCE: C.A; O.M.R. PG. 109

NAMES: SOLOMON DRAPER TO ISABELLA HINDS
DATE: SEPT. 6, 1827
DATE PER: SEPT. 6, 1827
BY: SAM'L LOVE, M.G.
REFERENCE: O.M.R. PG. 113

NAMES: WILLIAM DYER TO POLLY MCDANIEL
DATE: JANY. 1, 1827
DATE PER: JANY. 4, 1827
BY: JOHN BAYLESS, J.P.
REFERENCE: C.A; O.M.R. PG. 107; T.H.M. VOL. 6, PG. 193

NAMES: SAMUEL EDMONDSON TO REBECKA WHITE
DATE: FEBY. 7, 1827
DATE PER: FEBY. 8, 1827
BY: MORDECAI YARNELL, J.P.
REFERENCE: C.A; O.M.R. PG. 108

NAMES: JAMES ERWIN TO SARAH RODGERS
DATE: SEPT. 24, 1827
BONDSMAN: JOSEPH RODGERS
DATE PER: SEPT. 24, 1827
BY: J. A. SWAN, J.P.
WITNESS: CHAS. MCCLUNG
REFERENCE: C.A; O.M.R. PG. 113

NAMES: BYRD EZEL TO SALLY WADE
DATE: SEPT. 13, 1827
DATE PER: SEPT. 13, 1827
BY: WM. B. CARNS, J.P.
REFERENCE: C.A; O.M.R. PG. 113

NAMES: ROBERT F. G. FLEMING TO JANE MAILER
DATE: DEC. 5, 1827
DATE PER: DEC. 6, 1827
BY: WM. MORRIS, J.P.
REFERENCE: C.A; O.M.R. PG. 116

NAMES: WASHINGTON S. FLEMING TO RUTH BROWN
DATE: APR. 21, 1827
BONDSMAN: WM. B. CARNS
DATE PER: APR. 22, 1827
BY: WM. B. CARNS, J.P.
REFERENCE: C.A; O.M.R. PG. 110

NAMES: DANIEL FOUST TO MARTHA WILLS
DATE: MAR. 22, 1827
DATE PER: MAR. 22, 1827
BY: GEO. GRAVES, J.P.
REFERENCE: C.A; O.M.R. PG. 109

NAMES: LEWIS FOUST TO ELIZABETH L. WILLS
DATE: AUG. 29, 1827
BONDSMAN: JOHN FOUST
REFERENCE: C.A.

NAMES: PETER FRENCH JR. TO MALINDA ELLISON
DATE: DEC. 19, 1827
REFERENCE: C.A; O.M.R. PG. 116

NAMES: JOSEPH GOODMAN TO REBECKA NICHODEMUS
DATE: OCT. 1, 1827
BONDSMAN: WIATT WARWICK
DATE PER: OCT. 16, 1827
BY: GEO. GRAVES, J.P.
WITNESS: WM. SWAN
REFERENCE: C.A; O.M.R. PG. 113

NAMES: HENRY GRAMMER TO BETSY BOHAN
DATE: DEC. 28, 1827
BONDSMAN: JAMES GRAMMER
DATE PER: DEC. 30, 1827
BY: JOHN WINTON, J.P.
WITNESS: CHAS. MCCLUNG
REFERENCE: C.A; O.M.R. PG. 116

NAMES: GEORGE GRAVES, TO MARTHA SKAGGS
DATE: OCT. 30, 1827
BY: GEO. GRAVES, J.P.
REFERENCE: C.A. O.M.R. PG. 114

NAMES: GIBSON HARDIN TO MARGARET ALVIRA COBB
DATE: JANY. 2, 1827
BONDSMAN: JACOB M. BUTLER
REFERENCE: C.A.

NAMES: JACOB HARDING TO LOVE NELSON
DATE: JUNE 27, 1827
DATE PER: JUNE 28, 1827
BY: SAMUEL LOVE, M.G.
REFERENCE: C.A; O.M.R. PG. 111

NAMES: WM. HENDERSON TO CATY GIDDEON
DATE: DEC. 24, 1827
BONDSMAN: DANIEL BRANDON
REFERENCE: C.A.

NAMES: WM. HICKLE TO NANCY RUTHERFORD
DATE: JUNE 7, 1827
DATE PER: JUNE 7, 1827
BY: WM. SAWYERS, J.P.
REFERENCE: C.A; O.M.R. PG. 110

NAMES: BENJAMIN HINON TO NANCY GRAY
DATE: FEBY. 16, 1827
DATE PER: FEBY. 17, 1827
BY: SAM'L S. MCCAMPBELL, J.P.
REFERENCE: C.A; O.M.R. PG. 108

NAMES: WILLIAM HON TO SALLY FORD
DATE: NOV. 23, 1827
BONDSMAN: JACOB HON
DATE PER: NOV. 27, 1827
BY: EDWARD R. DAVIS, J.P.
WITNESS: C.A; O.M.R. PG. 115

NAMES: HYRAM HONEYCUTT TO DICE ISREAL
DATE: MAY 30, 1827
DATE PER: MAY 31, 1827
BY: JOHN BAYLESS, J.P.
REFERENCE: C.A; O.M.R. PG. 110; T.H.M. VOL. 6, PG. 193

NAMES: ROBERT HOOD TO CHRISTIANA RULE
DATE: OCT. 30, 1827
BONDSMAN: JACOB RULE
DATE: NOV. 1, 1827
BY: ELIJAH JOHNSON, J.P.
REFERENCE: C.A; O.M.R. PG. 114

NAMES: ELIJAH HUMPHREY TO MARGARET HUMPHREY
DATE: AUG. 30, 1827
REFERENCE: C.A; O.M.R. PG. 112

NAMES: WM. HUMPHREY TO AMY WEAVER
DATE: DEC. 22, 1827
BONDSMAN: RICHARD CASE
REFERENCE: C.A.

NAMES: WILLIAM KING TO MAHALA ANDERSON
DATE: NOV. 21, 1827
BONDSMAN: JAMES ANDERSON
DATE PER: NOV. 22, 1827
BY: JNO. BROWN, J.P.
WITNESS: WM. SWAN
REFERENCE: C.A; O.M.R. PG. 115

NAMES: WM. L. LARGE TO JANE MCFARLAND
DATE: NOV. 23, 1827
BONDSMAN: THOS. CANNON
WITNESS: WM. SWAN
REFERENCE: C.A.

NAMES: JNO. LETSINGER TO BETSY EDMISTON
DATE: MAR. 8, 1827
DATE PER: MAR. 8, 1827
BY: MORDECAI YARNELL, J.P.
REFERENCE: C.A; O.M.R. PG. 109

NAMES: THOMAS LIVELY TO BEDA GIBSON
DATE: JANY. 27, 1827
BONDSMAN: SHADRACK CASH
DATE PER: APR. 1, 1827
BY: JESSE CUNNINGHAM, M.G.
WITNESS: WM. SWAN
REFERENCE: C.A; O.M.R. PG. 108

NAMES: DAVID LOW TO MARGARET CURRIER
DATE: DEC. 5, 1827
BONDSMAN: R. G. FLEMING
DATE PER: DEC. 6, 1827
BY: WM. EAGLETON, M.G.
REFERENCE: C.A; O.M.R. PG. 116

NAMES: JOHN LOW TO MALVINA MCDONOUGH
DATE: NOV. 14, 1827
DATE PER: NOV. 14, 1827
BY: GEO. DONNELL, M.G.
REFERENCE: C.A; O.M.R. PG. 115

Names: Jackson Luttrell to Sally Fisher
Date: Oct. 23, 1827
Bondsman: Wm. McLamore
Witness: Wm. Swan
Reference: C.A.

Names: Robt. H. Luttrell to Harrell Monday
Date: Dec. 27, 1827
Bondsman: Jas. W. Monday
Reference: C.A.

Names: Robt. H. Luttrell to Harriett Monday
Date: Dec. 27, 1827
Date Per: Dec. 27, 1827
By: R. Houston, J.P.
Reference: O.M.R. Pg. 116; T.H.M. Vol. 6, Pg. 193

Names: John Lyons to Margaret Meek
Date: Jany. 31, 1827
Bondsman: Wm. Davis
Reference: C.A.

Names: Wm. Mason to Cynthia Plumley
Date: Sept. 1, 1827
Date Per: Sept. 2, 1827
By: Edward R. Davis, J.P.
Reference: C.A; O.M.R. Pg. 112

Names: Wm. Matthews to Jane Chevis
Date: Nov. 29, 1827
Date Per: Nov. 29, 1827
By: D. Nelson, J.P.
Reference: C.A; O.M.R. Pg. 115

Names: John McCall to Mary Ann Rentfro
Date: Jany. 2, 1827
Bondsman: Lewis Acree
Reference: C.A; T.H.M. Vol. 6, Pg. 193

Names: Isaac McCampbell to Elizabeth Crumley
Date: June 18, 1827
Date Per: June 18, 1827
By: Isaac Anderson, M.G.
Reference: C.A; O.M.R. Pg. 111

Names: Sam'l McCormack to Marion Burnett
Date: Mar. 14, 1827
Bondsman: Geo. Shetterly
Date Per: Mar. 14, 1827
By: Henry Soward, M.G.
Reference: C.A; O.M.R. Pg. 109; T.H.M. Vol. 6, Pg. 193

Names: James McHaffie to Polly Holbert
Date: Nov. 5, 1827
Bondsman: Joseph Adkins
Date Per: Nov. 8, 1827
Reference: C.A; O.M.R. Pg. 115

Names: John A. McKinney to Rebecka Skaggs
Date: Sept. 24, 1827
Bondsman: James Skaggs
Date Per: Sept. 28, 1827
By: Daniel Graves, J.P.
Reference: C.A; O.M.R. Pg. 113

Names: Greene McLamore to Nelly Cunningham
Date: June 13, 1827
Bondsman: Jacob Hackney
Date Per: June 13, 1827
By: P. Davis, J.P.
Witness: Wm. Swan
Reference: C.A; O.M.R. Pg. 111
Names: Henry Mingo to Rachael Husong
Date: Apr. 4, 1827
Bondsman: Frederick French
Reference: C.A; O.M.R. Pg. 109

Names: Ebenezer Minton to Darcus Baldwin
Date: Aug. 13, 1827
Date Per: Aug. ? 1827
By: Wm. Morris, J.P.
Reference: C.A; O.M.R. Pg. 112

Names: John Missimon to Birly (or Betsy) Minton
Date: Apr. 24, 1827
Date Per: Apr. ? 1827
By: Wm. Morris, J.P.
Reference: C.A; O.M.R. Pg. 110

Names: John Mulvaney to Mary Callen
Date: Oct. 4, 1827
Date Per: Oct. 4, 1827
By: Jesse Cunningham, M.G.
Reference: C.A; O.M.R. Pg. 113

Names: Alexander Murphy to Margaret Johnston
Date: June 20, 1827
Bondsman: Hugh M. Murphy
Date Per: June 20, 1827
By: Wm. T. Senter
Reference: C.A; O.M.R. Pg. 111

NAMES: JOSEPH MYNATT TO ELIZA TINDELL
DATE: OCT. 30, 1827
DATE PER: NOV. 2, 1827
BY: SAMUEL LOVE, M.G.
REFERENCE: C.A; O.M.R. PG. 115

NAMES: WM. B. OLIVER TO PROVIDENCE LOW
DATE: DEC. 25, 1827
BONDSMAN: THOS. DICKEY
WITNESS: CHAS. MCCLUNG
REFERENCE: C.A.

NAMES: ISAAC PAGE TO RACHEL COSBY
DATE: OCT. 29, 1827
DATE PER: OCT. 29, 1827
BY: SAM'L FLEMING, J.P.
REFERENCE: C.A; O.M.R. PG. 114

NAMES: JOHN PETERSON TO PEGGY RUTHERFORD
DATE: JANY. 31, 1827
DATE PER: FEBY. 1, 1827
BY: GEO. GRAVES, J.P.
REFERENCE: C.A; O.M.R. PG. 108

NAMES: JAMES PORTER TO PHEBE MERRIMAN
DATE: FEBY. 6, 1827
DATE PER: FEBY. 6, 1827
BY: SAM'L FLEMING, J.P.
REFERENCE: C.A; O.M.R. PG. 108

NAMES: HEZEKIAH RHODES TO NANCY ADAIR
DATE: NOV. 5, 1827
DATE PER: NOV. 14, 1827
BY: WM. B. CARNS, J.P.
REFERENCE: C.A; O.M.R. PG. 115

NAMES: GEO. W. RIGNEY TO MARY B. COUNSEL
DATE: JULY 10, 1827
DATE PER: AUG. 2, 1827
BY: MORDECAI YARNELL, J.P.
REFERENCE: C.A; O.M.R. PG. 111

NAMES: JOSEPH RUSSELL TO MILLY SCOTT
DATE: AUG. 22, 1827
DATE PER: AUG. 23, 1827
BY: J.A. MABRY, J.P.
REFERENCE: C.A; O.M.R. PG. 112

NAMES: PETER SCOTT TO POLLY FRISBEY
DATE: SEPT. 3, 1827
DATE PER: SEPT. 5, 1827
BY: J.A. MABRY, J.P.
REFERENCE: C.A; O.M.R. PG. 112

NAMES: WM. P. SCOTT TO MENOA TAYLOR
DATE PER: SEPT. 28, 1827
BY: J. A. SWAN, J.P.
REFERENCE: C.A; O.M.R. PG. 113

NAMES: WM. SIMPSON TO SUSAN LUTTRELL
DATE: APR. 11, 1827
DATE PER: APR. 12, 1827
BY: J. JOHNSON, J.P.
REFERENCE: O.M.R. PG. 109; T.H.M. VOL. 6, PG. 193

NAMES: JOHN SMITH TO CASA HADLEY
DATE: JULY 2, 1827
BONDSMAN: EDWARD ROUTH
DATE PER: JULY 2, 1827
BY: JNO. MCMILLAN, J.P.
WITNESS: WM. SWAN
REFERENCE: C.A; O.M.R. PG. 111

NAMES: ULYSSES G. SMITH TO ROSANA MCAFFEY
DATE: JANY. 31, 1827
DATE PER: FEBY. 1, 1827
BY: WM. T. SENTER
REFERENCE: C.A; O.M.R. PG. 108

NAMES: SOLOMON STANSBERRY TO FANNY GIBSON
DATE: JUNE 11, 1827
DATE PER: JANY. 12, 1827 (?)
BY: J. JOHNSON, J.P.
REFERENCE: O.M.R. PG. 110

NAMES: GEORGE STANWICK (?) TO FRANCES ENGLAND
DATE: AUG. 24, 1827
DATE PER: AUG. 26, 1827
BY: JAMES CUMMINS, ELDER
REFERENCE: C.A; O.M.R. PG. 112

NAMES: ALEXANDER STORMER TO ANNE TEENOR
DATE: JANY. 18, 1827
DATE PER: JANY. 23, 1827
BY: J.A. MABRY, J.P.
REFERENCE: C.A; O.M.R. PG. 107

NAMES: GEO. STOWMER TO FRANCES ENGLAND
DATE: AUG. 24, 1827
DATE PER: AUG. 26, 1827
BY: JAS. CUNNINGHAM
REFERENCE: O.M.R. PG. 112

NAMES: WM. SWAN TO POLLY L. WHITE
DATE: SEPT. 5, 1827
DATE PER: SEPT. 6, 1827
BY: CHARLES COFFIN, V.D.M.
REFERENCE: O.M.R. PG. 112

NAMES: SAML. THATCHER TO HANNAH M. CRAIGHEAD
DATE: SEPT. 13, 1827
DATE PER: SEPT. 13, 1827
BY: THO. H. NELSON, M. G.
REFERENCE: O.M.R. PG. 113

NAMES: HENRY VARNER TO ELIZA BROWN
DATE: OCT. 30, 1827
DATE PER: OCT. 31, 1827
BY: DAVID NELSON, J.P.
REFERENCE: C.A; O.M.R. PG. 114

NAMES: FLEMING WADE TO POLLY MCCLAIN
DATE: MAY 15, 1827
DATE PER: MAY 15, 1827
BY: SAML. FLEMING, J.P.
REFERENCE: C.A; O.M.R. PG. 110

NAMES: JAMES E. WALKER TO LOCKY THORNHILL
DATE: DEC. 24, 1827
BONDSMAN: ELIJAH JOHNSON
DATE PER: DEC. 27, 1827
BY: ELIJAH JOHNSON, J.P.
REFERENCE: C.A; O.M.R. PG. 116

NAMES: WM. W. WEBBER TO JANE MCMILLAN
DATE: OCT. 20, 1827
DATE PER: OCT. 25, 1827
BY: JNO. MCMILLAN, J.P.
REFERENCE: C.A. O.M.R. PG. 114; T.H.M. VOL. 6, PG. 193

NAMES: LARKIN WILLIAMS TO CATHARINE COONTZ
DATE: OCT. 24, 1827
BONDSMAN: BERRY WILLIAMS
DATE PER: OCT. 25, 1827
BY: WM. B. CARNS, J.P.
REFERENCE: C.A; O.M.R. PG. 114

1828

NAMES: LUKE AILER TO EDY WOOD
DATE: SEPT. 24, 1828
DATE PER: SEPT. 25, 1828
BY: DANIEL GRAVES, J.P.
REFERENCE: C.A; O.M.R. PG. 125

NAMES: JOHN ALLEN TO SOPHIA ALEXANDER
DATE: FEBY. 14, 1828
BONDSMAN: WM. WALL
REFERENCE: C.A.

NAMES: JNO. ALLEN TO SOPHIA ALEXANDER
DATE: FEBY. 14, 1828
DATE PER: FEBY. 15, 1828
BY: W. A. MCCAMPBELL, M.G.
REFERENCE: O.M.R. PG. 118; T.H.M. VOL. 6, PG. 193

NAMES: DANIEL ANDERSON TO POLLY HUMPHRY
DATE: AUG. 27, 1828
DATE PER: AUG. 28, 1828
BY: ELIJAH JOHNSON, J.P.
REFERENCE: C.A; O.M.R. PG. 123

NAMES: WM. PRESTON AYLER TO LUCRETIA CHANDLER
DATE: DEC. 17, 1828
BONDSMAN: SAML. R. RODGERS
DATE PER: DEC. 18, 1828
BY: SAM'L S. MCCAMPBELL
REFERENCE: C.A; O.M.R. PG. 127; T.H.M. VOL. 6, PG. 193

NAMES: WILLIAM PORTER (?) AYLESLTO LUCINDA CHAMBERS
DATE: DEC. 17,
REFERENCE: T.H.M. VOL. 6, PG. 193

NAMES: THOMAS BALL TO BETSY FERGUSON
DATE: SEPT. 24, 1828
DATE PER: OCT. 1, 1828
BY: WM. SAWYERS, J.P.
REFERENCE: C.A; O.M.R. PG. 125

NAMES: SAMUEL B. BOYD TO SUSAN H. MASON
DATE: DEC. 4, 1828
BONDSMAN: SAM'L R. RODGERS
DATE PER: WM. S. KENNEDY
REFERENCE: C.A.

Names: Saml. B. Boyd to Susan H. Mason
Date: Dec. 4, 1828
Date Per: Dec. 4, 1828
By: Tho. H. Nelson, M.G.
Reference: O.M.R. Pg. 127

Names: Elijah Bradley to Emily Munday
Date: Aug. 16, 1828
Date Per: Aug. 16, 1828
By: Robt. Tindell, J.P.
Reference: C.A; O.M.R. Pg. 122

Names: Phineas Brantley to Rachel Graham
Date: Mar. 28, 1828
Date Per: Mar. 28, 1828
By: E. R. Davis, J.P.
Reference: C.A; O.M.R. Pg. 120

Names: Joseph A. Brooks to Margaret A. McMillan
Date: Sept. 9, 1828
Date Per: Sept. 9, 1828
By: Tho. H. Nelson
Reference: O.M.R. Pg. 124; T.H.M. Vol. 6, Pg. 193

Names: Edward Brown to Joanna Hill
Date: Feby. 25, 1828
Bondsman: Wm. Horn
Date Per: Feby. 26, 1828
By: J. Lewis
Reference: C.A; O.M.R. Pg. 118; T.H.M. Vol. 6, Pg. 193

Names: Hugh Brown to Clarissa Browning
Date: Nov. 10, 1828
Date Per: Nov. 11, 1828
By: Wm. A. McCampbell
Reference: C.A; O.M.R. Pg. 126

Names: Joseph Burnett to Sally Brown
Date: May 31, 1828
Bondsman: Benj. Burnett
Reference: C.A.

Names: John S. Campbell to Nancy Smith
Date: Feby. 2, 1828
Bondsman: Jno. T. Smith
Date Per: Feby. 7, 1828
By: Wm. Eagleton, M.G.
Reference: C.A; O.M.R. Pg. 117; T.H.M. Vol. 6, Pg. 193

Names: Benj. B. Cannon to Eliza Tunnell
Date: Mar. 31, 1828
Date Per: Apr. 3, 1828
By: Sam'l. Fleming, J.P.
Reference: C.A; O.M.R. Pg. 120

Names: James Carpenter to Elizabeth Crank
Date: Jany. 30, 1828
Bondsman: Andrew McMillan
Date Per: Feby. 7, 1828
By: Wm. Sawyers, J.P.
Reference: C.A; O.M.R. Pg. 117

Names: Andrew Cassidy to Barbara Miltebarger
Date: Oct. 1, 1828
Date Per: Oct. 1828
By: Wm. Sawyers, J.P.
Reference: C.A; O.M.R. Pg. 125

Names: Thos. H. Chapman Jr. to Ann Crabb
Date: Aug. 7, 1828
Bondsman: Joseph Crabb
Reference: C.A.

Names: John Chumlea to Susanah Legg
Date: Aug. 11, 1828
Bondsman: Thos. G. Cardwell
Date Per: Aug. 14, 1828
By: Sam'l Love, M.G.
Reference: C.A; O.M.R. Pg. 122

Names: Milton Cobb to Jane H. Dickey
Date: Sept. 11, 1828
Bondsman: James Godfrey
Reference: C.A; T.H.M. Vol. 6, Pg. 193

Names: Leonard Coker to Elizabeth Williams
Date: Feby. 26, 1828
Bondsman: James Coker
Date Per: Feby. 28, 1828
By: Wm. Lyon, J.P.
Reference: C.A; O.M.R. Pg. 119

Names: Elisha Cox to Malinda Coker
Date: Apr. 1, 1828
Bondsman: James H. Edington
Reference: C.A; T.H.M. Vol. 6, Pg. 193

NAMES: JAMES W. CRAIG TO REBECKA LOW
DATE: FEBY. 9, 1828
BONDSMAN: JAMES H. COWAN
DATE PER: FEBY. 14, 1828
BY: GEO. DONNELL, M.G.
REFERENCE: C.A; O.M.R. PG. 118; T.H.M. VOL. 6, PG. 193

NAMES: ROBERT CRAIG TO ELIZABETH JONES
DATE: AUG. 13, 1828
BONDSMAN: ARCHIBALD WELLS
REFERENCE: C.A.

NAMES: ROB'T. CRAIG TO ELIZABETH JONES
DATE: AUG. 13, 1828
DATE PER: AUG. 14, 1828
BY: GEO. DONNELL, M.G.
REFERENCE: O.M.R. PG. 122

NAMES: THOS. G. CRAIGHEAD TO RUTGLID ARMSTRONG
DATE: AUG. 18, 1828
BONDSMAN: JNO. CAMPBELL
DATE PER: AUG. 19, 1828
BY: ELIJAH M. EAGLETON
REFERENCE: C.A; O.M.R. PG. 123

NAMES: THOMAS CROW TO RHODA JACKSON
DATE: SEPT. 22, 1828
BONDSMAN: WM. JACKSON
DATE PER: SEPT. 22, 1828
BY: SAMUEL LOVE, M.G.
WITNESS: WM. SWAN
REFERENCE: C.A; O.M.R. PG. 124

NAMES: HYRAM F. DELANEY TO NANCY FARQUHARSON
DATE: FEBY. 12, 1828
DATE PER: FEBY. 12, 1828
BY: THO. H. NELSON
REFERENCE: C.A; O.M.R. PG. 118

NAMES: JOSEPH DORAN TO CATHARINE C. CARMICHAEL
DATE: OCT. 15, 1828
BONDSMAN: JAMES MCCAMPBELL
DATE: OCT. 16, 1828
BY: ELIJAH M. EAGLETON
REFERENCE: C.A; O.M.R. PG. 126

NAMES: BENJ. DUNCAN TO HARRIET NANCE
DATE: MAY 19, 1828
DATE PER: MAY 20, 1828
BY: ISAAC ANDERSON, V.D.M.
REFERENCE: C.A; O.M.R. PG. 121

NAMES: FRANCIS EDMONSON TO JANE GRAYSON
DATE: FEBY. 1, 1828
DATE PER: FEBY. 3, 1828
BY: WM. MORRIS, J.P.
REFERENCE: C.A; O.M.R. PG. 117

NAMES: ISAAC EDMONDSON TO ANNE WHEELER
DATE: AUG. 20, 1828
DATE PER: AUG. 21, 1828
BY: WM. MORRIS, J.P.
REFERENCE: C.A; O.M.R. PG. 123

NAMES: JAMES EDMONDSON TO FRANCES MONDAY
DATE: DEC. 26, 1828
DATE PER: JANY. 1, 1829
BY: ROBT. TINDELL, J.P.
REFERENCE: C.A; O.M.R. PG. 127

NAMES: WILLIAM EDMONSON TO LILEY HOLT
DATE: FEBY. 1, 1828
BONDSMAN: JNO. M. HAVRON - FRANCIS EDMONSON
REFERENCE: C.A.

NAMES: DAVID ELKINS TO LETTY GAULY
DATE: MAR. 25, 1828
BONDSMAN: JNO. CALDWELL
DATE PER: MAR. 26, 1828
BY: JNO. BAYLESS, J.P.
REFERENCE: C.A; O.M.R. PG. 120

NAMES: BYRD F. EVERETT TO SUSANAH HAYNES
DATE: MAR. 1, 1828
DATE PER: MAR. 20, 1828
BY: B. H. MERRIMAN
REFERENCE: C.A; O.M.R. PG. 119

NAMES: JOHN FINDLEY TO SALLY M. WATSON
DATE: MAR. 29, 1828
DATE PER: APR. 10, 1828
BY: ELI KING, J.P.
REFERENCE: C.A; O.M.R. PG. 120

NAMES: DANIEL FLOOD TO PATSY WIDNER
DATE: NOV. 28, 1828
DATE PER: DEC. 2, 1828
BY: E. R. DAVIS, J.P.
REFERENCE: O.M.R. PG. 127

NAMES: JOHN FOUST TO POLLY HUMPHREYS
DATE: SEPT. 9, 1828
DATE PER: SEPT. 11, 1828
BY: WM. SAWYERS, J.P.
REFERENCE: C.A; O.M.R. PG. 124

NAMES: THOMAS GAULT TO MARIA MURPHY
DATE: AUG. 26, 1828 - BONDSMAN: HUGH MURPHY
BY: SAMUEL LOVE - DATE PER: AUG. 26, 1828
REFERENCE: C.A; O.M.R. PG. 123

NAMES: GIMERL GOOD TO JULIA ANN STEPHENSON
DATE: APR. 29, 1828
BONDSMAN: S. D. JACOBS
REFERENCE: C.A.

NAMES: GIMERL GOOD TO JULIA ANN STEPHENSON
DATE: APR. 29, 1828
DATE PER: APR. 29, 1828
BY: THO. H. NELSON
REFERENCE: O.M.R. PG. 121

NAMES: ASA GRAHAM TO SALLY SWINK
DATE: FEBY. 23, 1828
BONDSMAN: JACOB HAGAN
DATE PER: FEBY. 26, 1828
BY: EDWARD R. DAVIS, J.P.
WITNESS: WM. SWAN
REFERENCE: C.A; O.M.R. PG. 118

NAMES: WILLIAM GREYSON TO MARTHA MCCAHAN
DATE: MAR. 11, 1828
BONDSMAN: DANIEL MCMULLEN
DATE PER: MAR. 11, 1828
BY: DAVID NELSON, J.P.
REFERENCE: C.A; O.M.R. PG. 119

NAMES: PEYTON HENRY TO GUTHREY TO MARY EARLEY
DATE: DEC. 31, 1828
BONDSMAN: WM. GILBREATH
REFERENCE: C.A.

NAMES: JOHN HADLEY TO PATSY SMITH
DATE: OCT. 7, 1828
BONDSMAN: JACOB MULYANY
DATE PER: OCT. 10, 1828
BY: ELI KING, J.P. - WITNESS: WM. SWAN
REFERENCE: C.A; O.M.R. PG. 125

NAMES: JAMES HAIR TO ELIZABETH W. MCCAMPBELL
DATE: JANY. 8, 1828
DATE PER: JANY. 8, 1828
BY: ISAAC ANDERSON, V.D.M.
REFERENCE: C.A; O.M.R. PG. 117; T.H.M. VOL. 6, PG. 193

NAMES: JNO. W. HAMBRIGHT TO SARAH C. CALLOWAY
DATE: SEPT. 18, 1828
BONDSMAN: JNO. SMITH
DATE PER: SEPT. 18, 1828
BY: WM. MORRIS, J.P.
REFERENCE: C.A; O.M.R. PG. 124

NAMES: HIRAM HARMON TO SALLY YORK
DATE: OCT. 25, 1828
BONDSMAN: A. T. JONES
REFERENCE: C.A.

NAMES: JAMES HENSON TO ELLENDER HOPE
DATE: APR. 19, 1828
BONDSMAN: PLEASANT HENSON
REFERENCE: C.A.

NAMES: JAMES HINTON TO POLLY WILLIAMS
DATE: AUG. 27, 1828
DATE PER: AUG. 28, 1828
BY: ELIJAH JOHNSON, J.P.
REFERENCE: C.A; O.M.R. PG. 123

NAMES: CHARLES B. HODGES TO SARAH D. COBB
DATE: JUNE 28, 1828
DATE PER: JULY 5, 1828
BY: JAS. H. GASS (OR GOSS), M.G.
REFERENCE: O.M.R. PG. 121

NAMES: ISAAC HOOD TO ELIZABETH CASTEEL
DATE: JANY. 31, 1828
DATE PER: JANY. 31, 1828
BY: ELIJAH JOHNSON, J.P.
REFERENCE: C.A; O.M.R. PG. 117; T.H.M. VOL. 6, PG. 193

NAMES: SAMUEL HOWARD TO DIANAH GRUBB
DATE: APR. 1, 1828
BONDSMAN: TANDY MONDAY
DATE PER: APR. 1, 1828
BY: JAMES ALLDREDGE, J.P.
WITNESS: WM. SWAN
REFERENCE: C.A; O.M.R. PG. 120

NAMES: DUKE HOWELL TO MARY YOAST
DATE: OCT. 16, 1828
BONDSMAN: DAVID BELL
DATE PER: OCT. 16, 1828
BY: W. P. KINDRICK
REFERENCE: C.A; O.M.R. PG. 126

NAMES: AUSTIN JENKINS TO ABIGAIL LUCAS
DATE: APR. 3, 1828
BONDSMAN: JNO. W. HARKEN
DATE PER: APR. 24, 1828
BY: MORDECAI YARNELL, J.P.
REFERENCE: C.A; O.M.R. PG. 120

NAMES: WM. JENKINS TO PATSY MONTGOMERY
DATE: MAR. 31, 1828
BONDSMAN: GREEN CRISTENBERRY
DATE PER: APR. 4, 1828
BY: THOS. GALLAHER, J.P.
WITNESS: CHAS. MCCLUNG
REFERENCE: C.A.

NAMES: JEFFERSON JETT TO SARAH FLENNIKEN
DATE: SEPT. 25, 1828
BONDSMAN: WM. SWAN
DATE PER: SEPT. 25, 1828
BY: W.P. KINDRICK, T.E.
REFERENCE: C.A; O.M.R. PG. 125

NAMES: SAMUEL JONES TO ISABELLA LEISTER
DATE: AUG. 13, 1828
BY: G. HORNE
REFERENCE: C.A; O.M.R. PG. 122

NAMES: JACOB B. KEENER TO SALLY BOOTH
DATE: NOV. 28, 1828
BONDSMAN: ULERY KEENER - JACOB VARNER
REFERENCE: C.A.

NAMES: JAMES KENNEDY TO JANE COX
DATE: JUNE 25, 1828
BONDSMAN: F.H . MORGAN
REFERENCE: C.A:

NAMES: JAMES KENNEDY TO JANE COX
DATE: JUNE 25, 1828
DATE PER: JUNE 25, 1828
BY: CHARLES COFFIN, V.D.M.
REFERENCE: O.M.R. PG. 121

NAMES: RANSOM R. LAREW TO SALLIE CRAWFORD
DATE: JULY 3,
REFERENCE: T.H.M. VOL. 6, PG. 193

NAMES: JAMES LEDGERWOOD TO NANCY LEWIS
DATE: SEPT. 18, 1828
DATE PER: SEPT. 18, 1828
BY: DANIEL GRAVES, J.P.
REFERENCE: C.A; O.M.R. PG. 124

NAMES: SAMUEL LEDGERWOOD TO LINA RUTHERFORD
DATE: JULY 30, 1828
BY: WM. SAWYERS, J.P.
REFERENCE: C.A; O.M.R. PG. 122

NAMES: ISAAC LONES TO ANNE STOUT
DATE: JULY 31, 1828
DATE PER: JULY 31, 1828
BY: SAM'L FLEMING, J.P.
REFERENCE: C.A; O.M.R. PG. 122

NAMES: JACKSON LUTTRELL TO SALLY FISHER
DATE: OCT. 23,
REFERENCE: T.H.M. VOL. 6, PG. 193

NAMES: ANDREW LYLE TO CLARISSA CRUTCHFIELD
DATE: FEBY. 27, 1828
DATE PER: FEBY. 28, 1828
BY: CHARLES COFFIN, V.D.M.
REFERENCE: C.A; O.M.R. PG. 119

NAMES: WM. MARTIN TO MARY LISBEY
DATE : DEC. 8, 1828
BONDSMAN: JUBAL CLIBORNE
WITNESS: WM. SWAN
REFERENCE: C.A.

NAMES: WM. MARTIN TO MARY LISBY (?)
DATE: DEC. 8, 1828
DATE PER: DEC. 9, 1828
BY: SAM'L LOVE, M.G.
REFERENCE: O.M.R. PG. 127

NAMES: SHERWOOD MASSEY TO LUCINDA FORGUSON
DATE: JULY 17, 1828
BONDSMAN: PAUL CUNNINGHAM
REFERENCE: C.A.

Names: John W. Masterson to Drusilla Varner
Date: Apr. 11, 1828
Date Per: Apr. 12, 1828
By: Elijah Johnson, J.P.
Reference: C.A; O.M.R. Pg. 120

Names: Thomas W. Masterson to Mary C. Varner(or Conner)
Date: Apr. 30, 1828
Bondsman: Jno. Masterson
Date Per: May 1, 1828
By: Elijah Johnson, J.P.
Witness: Wm. Swan
Reference: C.A; O.M.R. Pg. 121

Names: John McDonough to Minty Scott
Date: July 26, 1828
Bondsman: Joseph Scott
Dat e Per: July 29, 1828
By: Geo. Donnell, M.G.
Reference: C.A; O.M.R. Pg. 122

Names: Andrew McMillan to Mary Littleford
Date: May 8, 1828
Bondsman: F.H. Morgan
Date Per: May 8, 1828
By: Charles Coffin, V.D.M.
Witness: Wm. Swan
Reference: C.A; O.M.R. Pg. 121; T.H.M. Vol. 6, Pg. 193

Names: Daniel McMullin to Catharine McCaughan
Date: Aug. 28, 1828
Bondsman: James Dardis
Date Per: Aug. 28, 1828
By: James Dardis, J.P.
Witness: William & Charles Bowen
Reference: C.A; O.M.R. Pg. 123

Names: Peter McNutt to Eleanor Callum
Date: Feby. 6, 1828
Bondsman: Charles Smith
Date Per: Feby. 7, 1828
By: E. R. Davis, J.P.
Reference: C.A; O.M.R. Pg. 118

Names: John Miles to Selina Farr
Date: Nov. 24, 1828
Bondsman: Thos. C. Smith
Reference: C.A.

Names: Pleasant Miller to Ruth Draper
Date: Sept. 17, 1828
Bondsman: Chesley Mitchell
Reference: C.A.

Names: Pleasant Miller to Ruth Draper
Date: Sept. 17, 1828
Date Per: Sept. 18, 1828
By: Jno. Bayless, J.P.
Reference: O.M.R. Pg. 124

Names: Henry T. Mitchell to Mary B. McCampbell
Date: Aug. 28, 1828
Bondsman: Daniel McMullan
Date Per: Aug. 28, 1828
By: Wm. A. McCampbell, J.P.
Reference: C.A; O.M.R. Pg. 123

Names: James W. Monday to Amelia Sharp
Date: Feby. 7, 1828
Bondsman: James Young
Date Per: Feby. 7, 1828
By: R. Houston, J.P.
Reference: C.A; O.M.R. Pg. 118

Names: Talifaro Monday to Betsy Gibson
Date: Jany. 30, 1828
Bondsman: James Wilhite
Reference: C.A.

Names: Wm. D. Moore to Susan Crush
Date: May 30, 1828
Bondsman: Wm. Turdeville
Reference: C.A.

Names: Samuel Nail to Betsy Barclay
Date: Oct. 1, 1828
Bondsman: John Naill
Date Per: Oct. 3, 1828
By: Eli King, J.P.
Reference: C.A; O.M.R. Pg. 125

Names: John M. Nelson to Nancy Holbert
Date: Mar. 10, 1828
Bondsman: Martin L. Nelson
Date Per: Mar. 13, 1828
By: Wm. B. Carns, J.P.
Reference: C.A; O.M.R. Pg. 119

NAMES: CHRISTIAN OLINGER TO SARAH GIDEON
DATE: MAR. 15, 1828
DATE PER: MAR. 15, 1828
BY: ROBT. TINDELL, J.P.
REFERENCE: C.A; O.M.R. PG. 119

NAMES: WILSON PARHAM TO MALVINA TAYLOR
DATE: JANY. 15, 1828
BY: J.A. SWAN, J.P.
REFERENCE: O.M.R. PG. 117

NAMES: HIRAM G. PARKS TO NANCY MCGHEE
DATE: APR. 22, 1828
DATE PER: APRL 22, 1828
BY: I. LEWIS
REFERENCE: O.M.R. PG. 121

NAMES: AUDLEY PAUL TO POLLY VICKERS
DATE: JULY 28, 1828
DATE PER: AUG. 2, 1828
BY: B. H. MERRIMAN, M.G.
REFERENCE: C.A; O.M.R. PG. 122

NAMES: ALLEN PERRY TO MATILDA DEARMOND
DATE: SEPT. 3, 1828
BONDSMAN: SAM'L R. RODGERS
DATE PER: SEPT. 3, 1828
BY: ISAAC LEWIS
REFERENCE: C.A; O.M.R. PG. 123

NAMES: SAMUEL PICKLE TO SALLY DOWELL
DATE: FEBY. 14, 1828
DATE PER: FEBY. 14, 1828
BY: J. JOHNSON, J.P.
REFERENCE: C.A; O.M.R. PG. 118

NAMES: JOHN PUGH TO CATHARINE SMITH
DATE: JANY, 23, 1828
BONDSMAN: JAMES STEPHENSON
DATE PER: JAN. 24, 1828
BY: JOHN BAYLESS, J P.
REFERENCE: C.A; O.M.R. PG. 117

NAMES: SHERWOOD RABY TO SARAH STRANGE
DATE: NOV. 26, 1828
BONDSMAN: J. A. MABRY
DATE PER: AUG. 8, 1828 (?)
BY: J. MABRY, J.P.
REFERENCE: C.A; O.M.R. PG. 127

NAMES: JOHN REED TO MARY HUNTER
DATE: SEPT. 11, 1828
BONDSMAN: ANDREW MCMILLAN
DATE PER: SEPT. 16, 1828
BY: JOHN MCMILLAN, J.P.
REFERENCE: C.A; O.M.R. PG. 124

NAMES: WM. REYNOLDS TO NANCY FORGEY
DATE: MAR. 1, 1828
DATE PER: MAR. 6, 1828
BY: ELIJAH M. EAGLETON
REFERENCE: C.A; O.M.R. PG. 119

NAMES: HENRY ROBERTS TO REBECKA HARRIS
DATE: OCT. 9, 1828
DATE PER: OCT. 1828
BY: WM. SAWYERS, J.P.
REFERENCE: C.A; O.M.R. PG. 126

NAMES: JAMES ROBERTS TO MINERVA HITE
DATE: DEC. 13, 1828
BONDSMAN: JNO. F. PATE
DATE PER: DEC. 23, 1828
BY: GEORGE GRAVES, J.P.
REFERENCE: C.A; O.M.R. PG. 127

NAMES: MOSES RODDY TO HETTY LOONEY
DATE: FEB. 22, 1828
REFERENCE: T.H.M. VOL. 6, PG. 193

NAMES: EDWARD RUDDER TO MAHALA NANCE
DATE: JANY. 5, 1828
DATE PER: JANY. 5, 1828
BY: WM. LYON, J.P.
REFERENCE: C.A; O.M.R. PG. 117

NAMES: JAMES RUTHERFORD TO ELIZABETH KEARNS
DATE: SEPT. 19, 1828
BONDSMAN: GEORGE GRAVES
DATE PER: SEPT. 23, 1828
BY: WM. SAWYERS, J.P.
REFERENCE: C.A; O.M.R. PG. 124

NAMES: JOSEPH RUTHERFORD TO REBECKA CLINE
DATE: OCT. 27, 1828
DATE PER: OCT. 30, 1828
BY: GEO. GRAVES, J.P.
REFERENCE: C.A; O.M.R. PG. 126

NAMES: WM. SAWYERS TO BETSY CASSADY
DATE: FEBY. 25, 1828
DATE PER: FEBY. 26, 1828
BY: ELIJAH M. EAGLETON
REFERENCE: C.A; O.M.R. PG. 119

NAMES: JOSEPH SCOTT TO MARY LOW
DATE: OCT. 27, 1828
BY: J. A. MABRY, J.P.
DATE PER: OCT. 28, 1828
REFERENCE: C.A; O.M.R. PG. 126

NAMES: WM. SIMMONS TO SUSAN KOONS
DATE: APR. 4, 1828
BY: JNO. BAYLESS, J.P.
REFERENCE: O.M.R. PG. 120

NAMES: CHARLES SMITH TO ANNE TABLER
DATE: OCT. 29, 1828
BY: W.B. KINDRICK, T.E.
REFERENCE: C.A; O.M.R. PG. 126

NAMES: THOS. C. SMITH TO BETSY MILES
DATE: OCT. 27, 1828
DATE PER: OCT. 30, 1828
BY: GEO. GRAVES, J.P.
REFERENCE: C.A; O.M.R. PG. 126

NAMES: HENDERSON STEPHENSON TO POLLY PEW
DATE: OCT. 1, 1828
BONDSMAN: JOHN PUGH
DATE PER: OCT. 2, 1828
BY: WM. B. CARNS, J.P.
REFERENCE: C.A; O.M.R. PG. 125

NAMES: WESTLEY STURGESS TO SALLY KILLINGSWORTH
DATE: FEBY. 4, 1828
BONDSMAN: ANDERSON KILLINGSWORTH
DATE PER: FEBY. 7, 1828
BY: JAMES ALLDREDGE, J.P.
REFERENCE: C.A; O.M.R. PG. 118

NAMES: ALEXANDER SWAN TO NANCY O'DELL
DATE: NOV. 19, 1828
BONDSMAN: WM. H. SWAN
DATE PER: NOV. 20, 1828
BY: WILLIAM EAGLETON, M.G.
REFERENCE: C.A; O.M.R. PG. 127

NAMES: RANSOM R. TARVER TO SALLY CRAWFORD
DATE: JULY 3, 1828
BONDSMAN: HENRY CLAPP
DATE PER: JULY 3, 1828
BY: SAM'L S. MCCAMPBELL, J.P.
REFERENCE: C.A; O.M.R. PG. 122

NAMES: WM. TAYLOR TO LUCINDA GEREN
DATE: SEPT. 4, 1828
DATE PER: SEPT. 10, 1828
BY: JNO. BAYLESS, J.P.
REFERENCE: C.A; O.M.R. PG. 124

NAMES: ABNER TINDELL TO RHODA GAULT
DATE: MAR. 6, 1828
BONDSMAN: SAM'L GEORGE
DATE PER: MAR. 11, 1828
BY: JNO. BAYLESS, J.P.
REFERENCE: C.A; O.M.R. PG. 119

NAMES: BERIAH TINDELL TO SALLY COX
DATE: APR. 8, 1828
DATE PER: APR. 10, 1828
BY: THOS. ALLDREDGE, J.P.
REFERENCE: C.A; O.M.R. PG. 120

NAMES: JONATHON TIPTON TO ELIZABETH JOHNSON
DATE: NOV. 6, 1828
DATE PER: NOV. 6, 1828
BY: ELIJAH JOHNSON, J.P.
REFERENCE: C.A; O.M.R. PG. 126

NAMES: JNO. TROUT TO ELIZABETH LUTTRELL
DATE: OCT. 2, 1828
DATE PER: OCT. 9, 1828
BY: GEO. GRAVES, J.P.
REFERENCE: C.A; O.M.R. PG. 125

NAMES: GEO. J. WASHAM (OR WORSHAM) TO MARTHA ANN CARTER
DATE: AUG. 18, 1828
BONDSMAN: CHAS. G. BOWEN
DATE PER: AUG. 27, 1828
BY: SAM'L LOVE, M.G.
REFERENCE: C.A; O.M.R. PG. 123

NAMES: JOSEPH WATT TO JANE LUTTRELL
DATE: JUNE 9, 1828
BONDSMAN: WM. MCMILLAN
REFERENCE: C.A; T.H.M. VOL. 6, PG. 193

NAMES: HENRY WIDNER TO REBECKA KING
DATE: NOV. 21, 1828
BONDSMAN: WM. WIDNER
DATE PER: NOV. 21, 1828
BY: J. JOHNSON, J.P.
WITNESS: WM. SWAN,
REFERENCE: C.A; O.M.R. PG. 127

NAMES: HENRY D. WOMACK TO ASENA CHAPMAN
DATE: SEPT. 30, 1828
DATE PER: SEPT. 30, 1828
BY: SAM'L LOVE, M.G.
REFERENCE: C.A; O.M.R. PG. 125

NAMES: JOHN WOODS TO PATSY FROST
DATE: JANY. 19, 1828
DATE PER: JANY. 24, 1828
BY: WM. SAWYERS, J.P.
REFERENCE: C.A; O.M.R. PG. 117

NAMES: JOSEPH WOOD TO GILLY MUNDAY
DATE: AUG. 16, 1828
DATE PER: AUG. 16, 1828
BY: ROBT. TINDELL, J.P.
REFERENCE: C.A; O.M.R. PG. 123; T.H.M. VOL. 6, PG. 193

NAMES: DAVID WRINKLE TO RACHEL JOHNSTON
DATE: MAR. 15, 1828
BONDSMAN: JOSEPH ABBOTT
WITNESS: WM. SWAN
REFERENCE: C.A.

NAMES: JNO. ZACHERY TO SALLY COOK
DATE: FEBY. 13, 1828
BONDSMAN: WM. ZACHERY
DATE PER: FEBY. 14, 1828
BY: WM. SAWYERS, J.P.
REFERENCE: C.A; O.M.R. PG. 118

1829

NAMES: EBENEZER ALEXANDER TO MARGARET ANN WHITE
DATE: OCT. 15, 1829
BONDSMAN: HU L. MCCLUNG
REFERENCE: C.A.

NAMES: EBENEZER ALEXANDER TO MARGARET ANN WHITE
DATE: OCT. 15, 1829
DATE PER: OCT. 15, 1829
BY: CHARLES COFFIN, V.D.M.
REFERENCE: O.M.R. PG. 136

NAMES: SOLOMON ALY (?) TO MARIA W. LUTTRELL
DATE: DEC. 29, 1829
BONDSMAN: GEO. J. JONES
DATE PER: JANY. 5, 1830
BY: J. LEWIS
WITNESS: WM. SWAN
REFERENCE: C.A; O.M.R. PG. 138; T.H.M. VOL. 6, PG. 194

NAMES: JAMES ARNOLD TO POLLY MCCALL
DATE: FEBY. 11, 1829
BONDSMAN: ANGUS MCCALL
REFERENCE: C.A.

NAMES: WM. ARTHUR TO LYDIA HOWSER
DATE: NOV. 2, 1829
BONDSMAN: JOHN WRIGHT
WITNESS: WM. SWAN
REFERENCE: C.A.

NAMES: LEWIS BABER (OR BAKER) TO LUCINDA ISREAL
DATE: JANY. 7, 1829
DATE PER: JANY. 8, 1829
BY: WM. B. CARNS, J.P.
REFERENCE: C.A; O.M.R. PG. 128

NAMES: ROBERT D. BADGETT TO MARY FERGUSON
DATE: MAR. 23, 1829
DATE PER: MAR. 27, 1829
BY: W. LYON, J.P.
REFERENCE: C.A; O.M.R. PG. 130

NAMES: LEONIDAS W. BAKER TO SUSAN WELLS PARK
DATE: APR. 9, 1829
BONDSMAN: W.B.A. RAMSEY
REFERENCE: C.A.

NAMES: LEONIDAS W. BAKER TO SUSAN M. PARK
DATE: APR. 9, 1829
DATE PER: APR. 9, 1829
BY: THO. H. NELSON
REFERENCE: O.M.R. PG. 131

NAMES: HENRY BALDWIN TO CHARLOTTE ARMSTRONG
DATE: FEBY. 9, 1829
BONDSMAN: JOSEPH A. BROOKS
DATE PER: FEBY. 10, 1829
BY: R. HOUSTON, J.P.
REFERENCE: C.A; O.M.R. PG. 129

Names: Thomas Bandy to Elizabeth Yarnell
Date: Aug. 17, 1829
Bondsman: David Hooks - James Harris
Date Per: Aug. 17, 1829
By: Wm. Morris, J.P.
Witness: Wm. Swan
Reference: C.A; O.M.R. Pg. 134

Names: William Barry to Ann B. Councell
Date: Jany. 22, 1829
Bondsman: Lloyd Rutherford
Date Per: Jany. 22, 1829
By: T. H. Nelson
Reference: C.A; O.M.R. Pg. 129

Names: Jno. Bearden to Caroline O'Dell
Date: Sept. 14, 1829
Bondsman: B. M. Wallace
Date Per: Sept. 15, 1829
By: Wm. S. McCampbell, J.P.
Reference: C.A; O.M.R. Pg. 135; T.H.M. Vol. 6, Pg. 194

Names: John S. Berry to Susan Fleshart
Date: Jany. 3, 1829
Bondsman: David Bell
Date Per: Jany. 3, 1829
By: Thos. H. Nelson
Reference: C.A; O.M.R. Pg. 128

Names: James Blackburn to Nancy Reynolds
Date: Dec. 2, 1829
Bondsman: Sam'l. Hinds
Date Per: Dec. 2, 1829
By: E. Nelson, J.P.
Reference: C.A; O.M.R. Pg. 137

Names: Salathial Blackburn to Elizabeth Mitchell
Date: Jany. 3, 1829
Date Per: Jany. 6, 1829
By: E. Nelson,
Reference: O.M.R. Pg. 128

Names: Thomas Bookout to Nancy Lumpkin
Date: Jany. 30, 1829
Bondsman: Jno. M. Bookout
Date Per: Feby. 4, 1829
By: E. Nelson
Reference: C.A; O.M.R. Pg. 129

Names: John W. Bound to Polly Carter
Date: Mar. 30, 1829
Bondsman: C.G. Bowen
Date Per: Mar. 31, 1829
By: Wm. A. McCampbell, J.P.
Reference: C.A; O.M.R. Pg. 131; T.H.M. Vol. 6, Pg. 194

Names: Langdon Bowie to Eliza Coffin
Date: July 21, 1829
Bondsman: W.B.A. Ramsey
Reference: C.A.

Names: Langdon Bowie to Eliza Coffin
Date: July 21, 1829
Date Per: July 21, 1829
By: Charles Coffin, V.D.M.
Reference: O.M.R. Pg. 134

Names: Carter Bowman to Francis Badgett
Date: Dec. 1, 1829
Bondsman: Alexander Williams
Date:Per: Dec. 13, 1829
By: Elijah Johnson, J.P.
Reference: C.A; O.M.R. Pg. 137; T.H.M. Vol. 6, Pg. 194

Names: Samuel Boyd to Dorcas E. McNutt
Date: Aug. 31, 1829
Bondsman: Edward R. Davis
Date Per: Sept. 3, 1829
By: Edward R. Davis, J.P.
Reference: C.A; O.M.R. Pg. 135

Names: Reuben Breeden to Levina Murry
Date: July 18, 1829
Date Per: July 19, 1829
By: Edward R. Davis, J.P.
Reference: C.A; O.M.R. Pg. 133

Names: James Brown to Casandra Norman
Date: Jany. 5, 1829
Bondsman: Theron Norman
Date Per: Jany. 7, 1829
By: Jno. Bayless, J.P.
Reference: C.A; O.M.R. Pg. 128

Names: James W. Campbell to Susan C. Morgan
Date: May 21, 1829
Bondsman: Wm. Swan
Reference: C.A.

NAMES: JNO. CAMPBELL TO ELIZABETH ARMSTRONG
DATE: JUNE 29, 1829
DATE: JUNE 29, 1829
BY: B. MCNUTT, J.P.
REFERENCE: C.A; O.M.R. PG. 133; T.H.M. VOL. 6, PG. 194

NAMES: LEEROY CARPENTER TO PRUDENCE WALKER
DATE: DEC. 7, 1829
DATE PER: DEC. 7, 1829
BY: JOHN MCMILLAN, J.P.
REFERENCE: C.A; O.M.R. PG. 137

NAMES: SHADRACK CASH TO ELIZABETH SHRINK
DATE: APR. 7, 1829
DATE PER: APR. 14, 1829
BY: ELI KING, J.P.
REFERENCE: C.A; O.M.R. PG. 131; T.H.M. VOL. 6, PG. 194

NAMES: WM. CATES TO AMANDA MISSIMON
DATE: JUNE 25, 1829
BONDSMAN: JOEL NANCE & JNO. MISSIMON
DATE PER: JUNE 25, 1829
BY: WM. MORRIS, J.P.
REFERENCE: C.A; O.M.R. PG. 133

NAMES: JOHN CHAPMAN TO ELLEN LEGG
DATE: JANY. 3, 1829
DATE PER: JANY. 6, 1829
BY: W. A. MCCAMPBELL, M.G.
REFERENCE: C.A; O.M.R. PG. 128; T.H.M. VOL. 6, PG. 194

NAMES: THOMAS CLARK TO ELIZABETH CRAIG
DATE: JUNE 18, 1829
DATE PER: JUNE 30, 1829
BY: WM. MORRIS, J.P.
REFERENCE: C.A; O.M.R. PG. 133

NAMES: HENDERSON CLIBURN TO MARTHA WILKES (OR WELKER)
DATE: JULY 23, 1829
DATE PER: JULY 23, 1829
BY: SAMUEL LOVE, M.G.
REFERENCE: C.A; O.M.R. PG. 134

NAMES: JAMES (OR JONES) CLIBURN TO BETSY DORAN
DATE: MAR. 7, 1829
DATE PER: MAR. 8, 1829
BY: WM. A. MCCAMPBELL, J.P.
REFERENCE: C.A; O.M.R. PG. 130

NAMES: JOHN CLIBURN TO SARAH LUSBY
DATE: JULY 23, 1829
DATE PER: JULY 27, 1829
BY: SAMUEL LOVE, M.G.
REFERENCE: C.A; OM.R. PG. 134; T.H.M. VOL. 6, PG. 194

NAMES: MALINDER CLIBURN TO SALLY BROWN
DATE: JANY. 6, 1829
REFERENCE: C.A; O.M.R. PG. 128

NAMES: RICHARD CONLEY TO ROSANAH STOUT
DATE: JANY. 26, 1829
BONDSMAN: JOHN THREEWITTS
DATE PER: JANY. 26, 1829
BY: JAMES SUTON, J.P.
WITNESS: CHAS. MCCLUNG
REFERENCE: C.A; O.M.R. PG. 129; T.H.M. VOL. 6, PG. 194

NAMES: DANIEL CONNER TO JANE HOLDEN
DATE: MAY 28, 1829
BONDSMAN: JOSIAH MULLINS
DATE PER: MAY 28, 1829
BY: W. LYON, J.P.
WITNESS: WM. SWAN
REFERENCE: C.A; O.M.R. PG. 132

NAMES: JNO. M. CONNER TO POLLY HASKEW
DATE: SEPT. 21, 1829
BONDSMAN: R. COX
DATE PER: SEPT. 24, 1829
BY: ROBT. TINDELL, J.P.
REFERENCE: C.A; O.M.R. PG. 135

NAMES: SAMUEL COTTRELL TO ELIZA SUMMERS
DATE: OCT. 8, 1829
BONDSMAN: GEO. C. BERRY
WITNESS: WM. SWAN
REFERENCE: C.A.

NAMES: SAM'L. COTTRELL TO ELIZA SUMMERS
DATE: OCT. 8, 1829
DATE PER: OCT. 9, 1829
BY: JNO. BROWN, J.P.
REFERENCE: O.M.R. PG. 136

NAMES: THOS. B. COX TO CAROLINE CALLOWAY
DATE: APR. 12, 1829
DATE PER: APR. 12, 1829
BY: MORDECAI YARNELL, J.P.
REFERENCE: C.A; O.M.R. PG. 131

NAMES: JESSE CRANK TO ELIZA GEORGE
DATE: JANY. 30, 1829
BONDSMAN: STEPHEN GEORGE
DATE PER: FEBY. 5, 1829
BY: JNO. BAYLESS, J.P.
WITNESS: WM. SWAN
REFERENCE: C.A; O.M.R. PG. 129; T.H.M. VOL. 6, PG. 194

NAMES: ARTHUR CRAWFORD TO NANCY TARVER
DATE: NOV. 24, 1829
DATE PER: NOV. 26, 1829
BY: ELIJAH M. EAGLETON
REFERENCE: C.A; O.M.R. PG. 137

NAMES: MOSES CREVAT TO NANCY WEST
DATE: JANY. 15, 1829
DATE PER: JANY. 15, 1829
BY: JNO. TINDELL, M.G.
REFERENCE: C.A.

NAMES: THOS. H. DAVENPORT TO SALLY THOMAS
DATE: DEC. 16, 1829
BONDSMAN: JAMES ALLISON
DATE PER: DEC. 17, 1829
BY: JNO. BROWN, J.P. - WITNESS: WM. SWAN
REFERENCE: C.A; O.M.R. PG. 138

NAMES: EDMUND DAVIS TO SALLY HANNON
BONDSMAN: ALEXANDER DAVIS
DATE: NOV. 16, 1829
DATE PER: NOV. 17, 1829
BY: ELIJAH JOHNSON, J.P.
WITNESS: C.A; O.M.R. PG. 137

NAMES: STEPHEN DAY TO ELIZA BLAIR
DATE: JULY 15, 1829
BONDSMAN: HUGH H. LUTTRELL - WM. LUTTRELL
DATE PER: JULY 16, 1829
BY: JNO. MCMILLAN, J.P.
WITNESS: WM. SWAN
REFERENCE: C.A; O.M.R. PG. 133

NAMES: DAVID D. DICKEY TO MARGARET ELLIS
DATE: JANY. 20, 1829
BONDSMAN: ROBT. DAVIDSON
REFERENCE: C.A.

NAMES: FRANCIS N. B. DUDLEY TO NANCY MYERS
DATE: NOV. 10, 1829
DATE PER: NOV. 1829
BY: STEPHEN FOSTER
REFERENCE: C.A; O.M.R. PG. 137

NAMES: HOLSTON EDINGTON TO POLLY ANN FORD
DATE: MAY 20, 1829
BONDSMAN: GEO. C. BERRY
DATE PER: MAY 26, 1829
BY: ELIJAH JOHNSON, J.P.
WITNESS: WM. SWAN
REFERENCE: C.A; O.M.R. PG. 132

NAMES: JOHN H. FLEMING TO JANE HARDIN
DATE: AUG. 17, 1829
BONDSMAN: ROBERT MARLEY
DATE PER: AUG. 17, 1829
BY: WM. MORRIS, J.P.
REFERENCE: C.A; O.M.R. PG. 134

NAMES: DANIEL FOUST TO POLLY FOUST
DATE: FEBY. 10, 1829
DATE PER: FEBY. 12, 1829
BY: WM. SAWYERS, J.P.
REFERENCE: C.A; O.M.R. PG. 129

NAMES: JOHN GIBSON TO ISABELLA KENNEDY
DATE: APR. 6, 1829
BONDSMAN: SAM'L KENNEDY
REFERENCE: C.A.

NAMES: BENJ. H. GIDDENS TO NANCY WARREN
DATE: NOV. 19, 1829
BONDSMAN: ALEX CAIN
DATE PER: NOV. 21, 1829
BY: ROBT. TINDELL, J.P.
REFERENCE: C.A; O.M.R. PG. 137

NAMES: JAMES F. GWIN TO SALLY ROBERTS
DATE: JUNE 10, 1829
BONDSMAN: JNO. BOYD
DATE PER: JUNE 14, 1829
BY: ELI KING, J.P.
REFERENCE: C.A; O.M.R. PAGE 132

NAMES: ABSALOM HANKINS TO CELIA GEREN
DATE: OCT. 31, 1829
BONDSMAN: LEVI HANKINS
DATE PER: NOV. 5, 1829
BY: JOHN BAYLESS, J.P.
REFERENCE: C.A; O.M.R. PG. 136

NAMES: WM. C. HANSARD TO RACHEL GRAHAM
DATE: JUNE 15, 1829
BONDSMAN: NATHAN BOWLING
REFERENCE: C.A; T.H.M. VOL. 6, PG. 194

NAMES: WM. C. HANSARD TO RACHEL GRIMES
DATE: JUNE 15, 1829
DATE PER: JUNE 18, 1829
BY: WM. B. CARNS, J.P.
REFERENCE: O.M.R. PG. 132

NAMES: JOSEPH HARDIN TO ALEY CALLOWAY
DATE: JANY. 1, 1829
BONDSMAN: ROBERT GALLAHER
DATE PER: JANY. 1, 1829
BY: WM. MORRIS, J.P.
REFERENCE: C.A; O.M.R. PG. 128

NAMES: JAMES HAVENS TO POLLY ANN HAMILTON OWEN
DATE: JULY 15, 1829
DATE PER: JULY 16, 1829
BY: E. NELSON, J.P.
REFERENCE: C.A; O.M.R. PG. 139

NAMES: EDWARD HERNDON TO SOPHIA ANNE PATTERSON GIVENS
DATE: APR. 29, 1829
BONDSMAN: J. A. MABRY
DATE PER: APR. 30, 1829
BY: W. A. MCCAMPBELL, M.V.D.
REFERENCE: C.A; O.M.R. PG. 131

NAMES: WM. HILL TO MARGARET LOW
DATE: NOV. 9, 1829
DATE PER: NOV. 10, 1829
BY: SAM'L FLEMING, J.P.
REFERENCE: C.A; O.M.R. PG. 136

NAMES: WALKER A. HOFFAR TO MARY R. WALKER
DATE: FEBY. 3, 1829
DATE PER: FEBY. 6, 1829
BY: THO. H. NELSON
REFERENCE: C.A; O.M.R. PG. 129

NAMES: JAMES HUBBARD TO ANN DUNN
DATE: OCT. 29, 1829
DATE PER: OCT. 29, 1829
BY: ISAAC LEWIS
REFERENCE: C.A; O.M.R. PG. 136

NAMES: HENRY HUFFAKER TO MARY FRENCH
DATE: SEPT. 8, 1829
DATE PER: SEPT. 10, 1829
BY: ABRAHAM MURPHY
REFERENCE: C.A; O.M.R. PG. 135

NAMES: CASPER HUNTER TO JUDY PRICE
DATE: DEC. 21, 1829
BONDSMAN: CHARLES DAVIS
REFERENCE: C.A; O.M.R. PG. 138

NAMES: WM. JENKINS TO PATSY MONTGOMERY
DATE: MAR. 31, 1829
DATE PER: APR. 4, 1829
BY: THO. GALLAHER, J.P.
REFERENCE: O.M.R. PG. 131

NAMES: JOAB JOHNSON TO ELIZABETH SMITH
DATE: NOV. 9, 1829
DATE PER: NOV. 10, 1829
BY: DANIEL GRAVES, J.P.
REFERENCE: C.A; O.M.R. PG. 136

NAMES: JAMES H. JOHNSTON TO BETSY CURRIER
DATE: DEC. 2, 1829
BONDSMAN: W. H. SWAN
DATE PER: DEC. 4, 1829
BY: W. A. MCCAMPBELL, M.V.D.
REFERENCE: C.A; O.M.R. PG. 137

NAMES: SAM'L JOHNSTON TO ANN FARMER
DATE: SEPT. 4, 1829
BONDSMAN: THOS. P. DIDDEP
BY: WM. SAWYERS, J.P.
REFERENCE: C.A; O.M.R. PG. 135

NAMES: JESSE G. JONES TO A. MORGAN
DATE: OCT. 13, 1829
BONDSMAN: GEO. J. JONES
WITNESS: WM. SWAN
REFERENCE: C.A.

NAMES: JOHN KEARNS TO NANCY RUTHERFORD
DATE: FEBY. 2, 1829
DATE PER: FEBY. 5, 1829
BY: WM. SAWYERS, J.P.
REFERENCE: C.A; O.M.R. PG. 129

NAMES: GEORGE LEGG TO LEAH LINK
DATE: FEBY. 14, 1829
BONDSMAN: DAVID WILLS
DATE PER: FEBY. 18, 1829
BY: WM. SAWYERS, J.P.
WITNESS: WM. SWAN
REFERENCE: C.A; O.M.R. PG. 130

Names: Isaac Lewis to Ellen Thatcher
Date: Jany. 8, 1829
Bondsman: Pleasant Crew
Date Per: Jany. 8, 1829
By: E. F. Sevier, M.G.
Reference: C.A; O.M.R. Pg. 128

Names: Robert Loyd to Sarah Gibbs
Date: Oct. 2, 1829
Date Per: Oct. 8, 1829
By: Samuel Love, M.G.
Reference: C.A; O.M.R. Pg. 135

Names: Abraham Mann to Eleanor Nance
Date: May 27, 1829
Date Per: May 28, 1829
By: S. S. McCampbell
Reference: O.M.R. Pg. 132

Names: John Marley to Elizabeth Ayres
Date: Feby. 2, 1829
Bondsman: R. F. G. Fleming
Date Per: Feby. 5, 1829
By: Mordecai Yarnell, J.P.
Reference: C.A; O.M.R. Pg. 129

Names: Stephen Marshall to Frances Thompson
Dec. 22, 1829, Date Issued
Bondsman: Richard Marshall
Date Per: Dec. 29, 1829
By: Wm. Morris, J.P.
Reference: C.A; O.M.R. Pg. 138

Names: Abraham Mason to Eleanor Nance
Date: May 27, 1829
Date Per: May 28, 1829
By: Sam'l. S. McCampbell
Reference: C.A.

Names: Edward Maxey to Malinda Williams
Date: Apr. 16, 1829
Bondsman: Joel Williams
Date Per: Apr. 16, 1829
By: Elijah Johnson, J.P.
Reference: C.A; O.M.R. Pg. 131

Names: James McBath to Serena Littleford
Date: July 30, 1829
Bondsman: D. P. Armstrong
Date Per: July 30, 1829
By: Stephen Foster
Reference: C.A; O.M.R. Pg. 134

Names: James McClain to Polly Hutcheson
Date: Dec. 5, 1829
Bondsman: Jno. McClain
Date Per: Dec. 6, 1829
By: Robt. Tindell, J.P.
Reference: C.A; O.M.R. Pg. 137

Names: James McLemore to Hetty McDonald
Date: June 3, 1829
Bondsman: Allen Perry
Date Per: June 4, 1829
By: Sam'l Fleming, J.P.
Reference: C.A; O.M.R. Pg. 132

Names: John McNutt to Hanna Gibson
Date: Mar. 17, 1829
Bondsman: Wm. Dowlen
By: Wm. Swan
Reference: C.A;

Names: Samuel Merrit to Elizabeth Wolfenbarger
Date: Mar. 9, 1829
Bondsman: Robt. Bell
Date Per: Mar. 9, 1829
By: Jno. Craig, M.G.
Reference: C.A; O.M.R. Pg. 130

Names: Jacob Mikels to Mary Ann Murphy
Date: Apr. 14, 1829
Bondsman: Wm. Miles
Date Per: Apr. 14, 1829
By: Elijah Johnson, J.P.
Witness: Wm. Swan
Reference: C.A; O.M.R. Pg. 131

Names: Freeman Miller to Margaret Palmer
Date: Nov. 25, 1829
Bondsman: Wm. Palmer
Witness: Wm. Swan
Reference: C.A.

Names: Peyton Molden to Eliza Sharp
Date: Aug. 12, 1829
Bondsman: Matthew Simpson
Date Per: [illegible]
Reference: C.A; O.M.R. Pg. 134
By: Edward R. Davis, J.P.

NAMES: JOSEPH MOORE (OR MOON) TO JANE PAYE
DATE: JULY 6, 1829
BONDSMAN: JAMES MOON
DATE PER: AUG. 19, 1829
BY: GEO. GRAVES, J.P.
REFERENCE: C.A; O.M.R. PG. 133

NAMES: WM. MORRIS TO FRANCES LEA
DATE: SEPT. 12, 1829
DATE PER: SEPT. 13, 1829
BY: JNO. CRAIG, M.G.
REFERENCE: C.A; O.M.R. PG. 135

NAMES: PETER MOWRY TO SOPHIA CLAPP
DATE: MAY 4, 1829
BONDSMAN: JNO. FOUST
BY: WM. SAWYERS, J.P.
WITNESS: WM. SWAN
REFERENCE: C.A; O.M.R. PG. 132

NAMES: JOSIAH MULLINS TO ALZIRA LOONEY
DATE: NOV. 26, 1829
BONDSMAN: JNO. LOONEY
WITNESS: WM. SWAN
REFERENCE: C.A.

NAMES: ALEXANDER MURPHY TO MARGARET JOHNSTON
DATE: JUNE 20, 1829
WITNESS: HUGH A. MURPHY
REFERENCE: T.H.M. VOL. 6, PG. 194

NAMES: JAMES D. MURRAY TO REBECKA BELL
DATE: APR. 27, 1829
BONDSMAN: JNO. HILLSMAN
DATE PER: APR. 28, 1829
BY: THO. H. NELSON
REFERENCE: C.A.

NAMES: RICHARD MYNATT TO SARAH PURSLEY
DATE: JANY. 8, 1829
BONDSMAN: JAMES HAIR
DATE PER: JANY. 8, 1829
BY: JOHN MCMILLAN, J.P.
REFERENCE: C.A; O.M.R. PG. 128

NAMES: WM. MYNATT TO JANE WALKER
DATE: JUNE 29, 1829
BONDSMAN: JNO. HILLSMAN
BY: OSCAR JOHNSTON
REFERENCE: C.A; O.M.R. PG. 133

NAMES: ABRAHAM NELSON TO FRANCES HOLBERT
DATE: JUNE 13, 1829
BONDSMAN: THOS. J. NELSON
DATE PER: JUNE 18, 1829
BY: WM. B. CARNS, J.P.
WITNESS: WM. SWAN
REFERENCE: C.A; O.M.R. PG. 132

NAMES: JAMES NELSON TO BETSY BOLTON
DATE: OCT. 7, 1829
BONDSMAN: ISAAC GENTRY
DATE PER: OCT. 8, 1829
BY: ISAAC LONG, M.G.
REFERENCE: C.A; O.M.R. PG. 136

NAMES: BROWN NORRIS TO LINDA ROCKARD
DATE: MAR. 26, 1829
DATE PER: MAR. 27, 1829
BY: WM. SAWYERS, J.P.
REFERENCE: C.A; O.M.R. PG. 130

NAMES: JESSE QUALLS TO RUTH YOUNG
DATE: JULY 11, 1829
DATE PER: JULY 16, 1829
BY: SAM'L S. MCCAMPBELL, J.P.
REFERENCE: C.A; O.M.R. PG. 134

NAMES: JNO. M. A. RAMSEY TO POLLY ROBISON
DATE: OCT. 5, 1829
BONDSMAN: S.K. KING
WITNESS: WM. SWAN
REFERENCE: C.A.

NAMES: JNO. M. A. RAMSEY TO POLLY ROBISON
DATE: OCT. 5, 1829
DATE PER: OCT. 6, 1829
BY: ELI KING, J.P.
REFERENCE: O.M.R. PG. 136

NAMES: GEO. W. REEVES TO BETSY HOOD
DATE: APR. 28, 1829
BONDSMAN: ISAAC COUNCIL
REFERENCE: C.A.

NAMES: CORNELIUS ROBERTSON TO NANCY BRANNUM
DATE: DEC. 1, 1829
BONDSMAN: WM. MCCULLOUGH
REFERENCE: C.A.

NAMES: TANDY SCOTT TO AMY YARNELL
DATE: SEPT. 28, 1829
BONDSMAN: JOHN GRAYSON
DATE PER: SEPT. 28, 1829
BY: WM. MORRIS, J.P.
WITNESS: WM. SWAN
REFERENCE: C.A; O.M.R. PG. 135

NAMES: WM. SIMMONS TO SUSAN KOONS
DATE: APR. 4, 1829
BY: JNO. BAYLESS, J.P.
REFERENCE: C.A.

NAMES: ELI SKAGGS TO MARY SHIPE
DATE: FEBY. 28, 1829
BONDSMAN: HENRY SHIPE
DATE PER: MAR. 5, 1829
BY: SAMUEL LOVE, M.G.
REFERENCE: C.A; O.M.R. PG. 130

NAMES: JAMES R. SMART TO MARTHA COBB
DATE: JULY 4, 1829
BONDSMAN: JOSEPH SCOTT
DATE PER: JULY 9, 1829
BY: SAMUEL LOVE, M.G.
REFERENCE: C.A; O.M.R. PG. 139

NAMES: BANISTER SMITH TO ELIZA COKER
DATE: AUG. 15, 1829
BONDSMAN: ELI MOURFIELD
DATE PER: AUG. 16, 1829
BY: WILL LYON, J.P.
WITNESS: WM. SWAN
REFERENCE: C.A; O.M.R. PG. 134

NAMES: DEMARCUS G. STACKS TO MARGARET DARDIS
DATE: APR. 14, 1829
DATE PER: APR. 14, 1829
BY: I. LEWIS
REFERENCE: O.M.R. PG. 131

NAMES: ALFRED STANDIFER TO JANE YARNELL
DATE: FEBY. 21, 1829
DATE PER: FEBY. 1829
BY: WM. MORRIS, J.P.
REFERENCE: C.A; O.M.R. PG. 130

NAMES: CLAIBORNE SWAGERTY TO HARRIETT DYKES
DATE: MAR. 27, 1829
DATE PER: MAR. 27, 1829
BY: J. JOHNSON, J.P.
REFERENCE: C.A; O.M.R. PG. 131

NAMES: ANDREW TAYLOR TO JANE EVANS
DATE: MAR. 12, 1829
BONDSMAN: WM. SHIELDS
DATE PER: MAR. 12, 1829
BY: JOHN MCCAMPBELL, V.D.M.
REFERENCE: C.A; O.M.R. PG. 130

NAMES: BARCKLY WALKER TO PEGGY ANNE DOUGLASS
DATE: DEC. 7, 1829
DATE PER: DEC. 10, 1829
BY: JOHN MCMILLAN, J.P.
REFERENCE: C.A; O.M.R. PG. 138; T.H.M. VOL. 6, PG. 194

NAMES: WILLIAM WARNACK TO NANCY MORROW
DATE: OCT. 7, 1829
BONDSMAN: P.P. HOUSER
DATE PER: OCT. 8, 1829
BY: THO. H. NELSON
REFERENCE: C.A; O.M.R. PG. 136

NAMES: WM. WARREN TO HANNAH SMITH
DATE: MAY 16, 1829
BONDSMAN: JAMES WILLIAMS
WITNESS: CHAS. MCCLUNG
REFERENCE: C.A.

NAMES: ROBERT WEBB TO DRUSILLA ANDERSON
DATE: MAR. 16, 1829
BONDSMAN: HYRAM BARRY
DATE PER: MAR. 17, 1829
BY: ISAAC ANDERSON, M.G.
REFERENCE: C.A; O.M.R. PG. 130

NAMES: JOHN WEST TO JENNY WEST
DATE: SEPT. 10,
REFERENCE: T.H.M. VOL. 6, PG. 194

NAMES: BENJ. WILLIAMS TO NANCY ISREAL
DATE: DEC. 8, 1829
BONDSMAN: ALEXANDER CAIN
DATE PER: DEC. 9, 1829
BY: E. NELSON, J.P.
WITNESS: WM. SWAN
REFERENCE: C.A; O.M.R. PG. 138; T.H.M. VOL. 6, PG. 194

NAMES: HENRY WRINKLE TO MARGARET E. WHITE
DATE: AUG. 17, 1829
DATE PER: AUG. 27, 1829
BY: B. MCNUTT, J.P.
REFERENCE: C.A; O.M.R. PG. 135

1830

NAMES: SAMUEL ALEXANDER TO JANE CLARKE
DATE: OCT. 11, 1830
BONDSMAN: JNO. CLARK
DATE PER: OCT. 12, 1830
BY: WM. MORRIS, J.P.
REFERENCE: C.A; O.M.R. PG. 147

NAMES: WILLIS ANDERSON TO ELIZABETH KERBY
DATE: APR. 7, 1830
BONDSMAN: SAM'L ANDERSON
DATE PER: APR. 8, 1830
BY: ELIJAH JOHNSON, J.P.
WITNESS: WM. SWAN
REFERENCE: C.A; O.M.R. PG. 142; T.H.M. VOL. 6, PG. 194

NAMES: JOHN O. ANTHONY TO MARY ANN DOUTY
DATE: MAR. 27, 1830
BONDSMAN: DAVID BELL
DATE PER: MAR. 28, 1830
BY: I. LEWIS
REFERENCE: C.A; O.M.R. PG. 141; T.H.M. VOL. 6, 194

NAMES: JAMES ARNOLD TO NANCY GLASS
DATE: JANY. 18, 1830
DATE PER: JANY. 19, 1830
BY: JOHN MCMILLAN, J.P.
REFERENCE: C.A; O.M.R. PG. 139

NAMES: OLIVER F. ARNOLD TO HANNAH MELTON
DATE: SEPT. 28, 1830
BONDSMAN: JAS. WRIGHT & JOHN DEARMOND
DATE PER: SEPT. 28, 1830
BY: ISAAC LEWIS
WITNESS: WM. SWAN
REFERENCE: C.A; O.M.R. PG. 146

NAMES: JACOB AULT TO SALLY GRIFFY
DATE: FEBY. 3, 1830
BONDSMAN: JOHN AULT
WITNESS: WM. SWAN
REFERENCE: C.A.

NAMES: RANSOM BAGGETT TO SOMYRA HUNTER
DATE: JUNE 8, 1830
BONDSMAN: JNO. GARNER
DATE PER: JUNE 8, 1830
BY: J. JOHNSON, J.P.
WITNESS: WM. SWAN
REFERENCE: C.A; O.M.R. PG. 142

NAMES: CHRISTIAN BAKER TO ELIZABETH HENDRIXON (OR HENDERSON)
DATE: MAY 5, 1830
BONDSMAN: THOMAS JONES
DATE PER: MAY 6, 1830
BY: MICHAEL DAVIS, J.P.
REFERENCE: C.A; O.M.R. PG. 142

NAMES: CHRISTOPHER BAKER TO REBECKA BOLTON
DATE: OCT. 6, 1830
BONDSMAN: JAMES H. COWAN
DATE PER: OCT. 10, 1830
BY: E. NELSON, J.P.
REFERENCE: C.A; O.M.R. PG. 147

NAMES: JOHN BAKER TO ELLEN GRAVES
DATE: JULY 28, 1830
BONDSMAN: JESSE LEWIS
DATE PER: AUG. 5, 1830
BY: E. NELSON, J.P.
WITNESS: WM. SWAN
REFERENCE: C.A; O.M.R. PG. 144; T.H.M. VOL. 6, PG. 194

NAMES: WM. L. BARNWELL TO SARAH TURBEVILLE
DATE: OCT. 2L, 1830
DATE PER: OCT. 21, 1830
BY: ISAAC LEWIS
REFERENCE: C.A; O.M.R. PG. 147

NAMES: REESE BAYLESS TO FRANCIS DRAPER
DATE: OCT. 29, 1830
BONDSMAN: WM. CRIPPEN
DATE:PER: NOV. 4, 1830
BY: E. NELSON, J.P.
WITNESS: WM. SWAN
REFERENCE: C.A; O.M.R. PG. 147

NAMES: JO. D. BERRY TO ELIZABETH KINNAMON
DATE: NOV. 2, 1830
BONDSMAN: MICHAEL DAVIS
DATE PER: NOV. 2, 1830
BY: MICHAEL DAVIS, J.P.
REFERENCE: C.A; O.M.R. PG. 148

NAMES: GEO. C. BEST TO LACKY (OR LOCKY) HOWELL
DATE: NOV. 8, 1830
BONDSMAN: SYLVANUS HOWELL
REFERENCE: C.A.

NAMES: LEWIS BISHOP TO SUSAN MYNATT
DATE: SEPT. 29, 1830
BONDSMAN: MOSES LINDSAY
DATE PER: SEPT. 23, 1830
BY: SAMUEL LOVE, M.G.
REFERENCE: C.A; O.M.R. PG. 146; T.H.M. VOL. 6, PG. 194

NAMES: JAMES M. BOSWORTH TO JULIA A. M. DUDLEY
DATE: JULY 27, 1830
DATE PER: JULY 27, 1830
BY: ISAAC LEWIS
REFERENCE: C.A; O.M.R. PG. 144

NAMES: WM. BRADEN TO JULIA ANN MCHAFFIE
DATE: SEPT. 20, 1830
BONDSMAN: DAVID MCHAFFIE
DATE PER: SEPT. 23, 1830
BY: E. NELSON, J.P.
REFERENCE: C.A; O.M.R. PG. 146; T.H.M. VOL. 6, PG. 194

NAMES: SAMUEL BRIGGS TO MARY JOHNSTON
DATE: JULY 19, 1830
BONDSMAN: JAMES H. CARDWELL
DATE PER: JULY 21, 1830
BY: MARTIN B. CARTER, J.P.
REFERENCE: C.A; O.M.R. PG. 143

NAMES: ANDERSON BURNETT TO ALLEY MANEY
DATE: AUG. 7, 1830
BONDSMAN: SAM'L ANDERSON
DATE PER: AUG. 8, 1830
BY: ELIJAH JOHNSON, J.P.
WITNESS: WM. SWAN
REFERENCE: C.A; O.M.R. PG. 144

NAMES: ZACHARIAH BURNETT TO MARY FORD
DATE: SEPT. 20, 1830
BONDSMAN: JOSEPH BURNETT
DATE PER: SEPT. 23, 1830
BY: ELIJAH JOHNSON, J.P.
REFERENCE: C.A; O.M.R. PG. 146

NAMES: JAMES BYERLY TO HALLALUJAH YARNELL
DATE: DEC. 7, 1830
BONDSMAN: JAMES WATKINS
DATE PER: DEC. 9, 1830
BY: WM. MORRIS, J.P.
WITNESS: WM. SWAN
REFERENCE: C.A; O.M.R. PG. 148

NAMES: WEST WALKER CAPSHAW TO MARY MAGDEYNE SENSEBAUGH
DATE: OCT. 28, 1830
DATE PER: OCT. 28, 1830
BY: B. B. CANNON, J.P.
REFERENCE: C.A; O.M.R. PG. 147

NAMES: JNO. M. CHAPMAN TO CATHARINE ANN CARNS
DATE: JANY. 2, 1830
BONDSMAN: WM. BARNWELL
DATE PER: JANY. 5, 1830
BY: W. A. MCCAMPBELL, M.V.D.
REFERENCE: C.A; O.M.R. PG. 139

NAMES: ROBT. L. CHILDRESS TO LEAH COX
DATE: FEBY. 16, 1830
DATE PER: FEBY. 16, 1830
BY: ROBT. TINDELL, J.P.
REFERENCE: C.A; O.M.R. PG. 140

NAMES: WM. CHILDRESS TO ELIZABETH WADE
DATE: SEPT. 29, 1830
BONDSMAN: WM. BROWN
DATE PER: SEPT. 29, 1830
BY: ELIJAH JOHNSON, J.P.
WITNESS: WM. SWAN
REFERENCE: C.A; O.M.R. PG. 146

NAMES: JOHN COLLINS TO MINERVA CHAPMAN
DATE: FEBY. 13, 1830
DATE PER: FEBY. 16, 1830
BY: WM. A. MCCAMPBELL, M.V.D.
REFERENCE: C.A; O.M.R. PG. 140

NAMES: ABRAM CONLEY TO SALLY HOSKINS
DATE: AUG. 28, 1830
BONDSMAN: RICHARD CONLEY
DATE PER: AUG. 29, 1830
BY: B. B. CANNON, J.P.
WITNESS: WM. SWAN
REFERENCE: C.A; O.M.R. PG. 145

NAMES: JAMES H. COWAN TO LUCINDA DICKERSON
DATE: NOV. 25, 1830
BONDSMAN: B. M. WALLACE
REFERENCE: C.A.

NAMES: JAMES H. COWAN TO LUCINDA DICKENSON
DATE: NOV. 25, 1830
DATE PER: NOV. 26, 1830
BY: ISAAC ANDERSON, V.D.M.
REFERENCE: O.M.R. PG. 149

NAMES: JOHN CRUSH TO LYDIA BALES
DATE: JUNE 5, 1830
DATE PER: JUNE 6, 1830
BY: ISAAC LEWIS
REFERENCE: C.A; O.M.R. PG. 142

NAMES: WM. DOWLER TO SUSAN MCCAUGHEN
DATE: MAR. 1, 1830
BONDSMAN: N. M. SWAN
DATE PER: MAR. 1, 1830
BY: SAM'L FLEMING, J.P.
REFERENCE: C.A; O.M.R. PG. 141

NAMES: JOEL DYER (OR DYKE) TO RACHEL ADKINS
DATE: AUG. 24, 1830
BONDSMAN: ISAAC JOHNSON
DATE PER: AUG. 26, 1830
BY: WM. A. MCCAMPBELL, J.P.
WITNESS: WM. SWAN
REFERENCE: C.A; O.M.R. PG. 144

NAMES: GEORGE EDDY TO LUCY TAYLOR
DATE: MAY 4, 1830
BONDSMAN: WM. MCDANIEL
REFERENCE: C.A.

NAMES: A. W. ELDER TO SUSAN J. CAMPBELL
DATE: AUG. 26, 1830
BONDSMAN: MAT. M. GAINES
DATE PER: AUG. 26, 1830
BY: THO. H. NELSON
REFERENCE: C.A; O.M.R. PG. 144

NAMES: JOHN ENGLAND TO REBECKA EDMONDSON
DATE: MAR. 1, 1830
BONDSMAN: ISAAC EDMONDSON
DATE PER: MAR. 2, 1830
BY: MORDECAI YARNELL, J.P.
WITNESS: WM. SWAN
REFERENCE: C.A; O.M.R. PG. 141

NAMES: JOHN EWING TO MARY SEABOLT
DATE: MAY 11, 1830
BONDSMAN: ANDERSON HILL
REFERENCE: C.A.

NAMES: WM. FERGUSON TO SALLY HARVEY
DATE: OCT. 20, 1830
DATE PER: OCT. 21, 1830
BY: MARTIN B. CARTER, J.P.
REFERENCE: C.A; O.M.R. PG. 143

NAMES: MICHAEL FRAKER TO WINNEFRED GILLUM
DATE: AUG. 26, 1830
BONDSMAN: JOHN MURPHY
DATE PER: AUG. 26, 1830
BY: ISAAC LEWIS
REFERENCE: C.A; O.M.R. PG. 144; T.H.M. VOL. 6, PG. 194

NAMES: MATTHEW M. GAINES TO MARGARET C. LUTTRELL
DATE: NOV. 11, 1830
BONDSMAN: C. WALLACE & SACKFIELD MOLIN
REFERENCE: C.A.

NAMES: JNO. H. R. G. GARDNER TO SUSAN EVANS
DATE: FEBY. 23, 1830
BONDSMAN: WM. M. SMITH
DATE PER: FEBY. 23, 1830
BY: HENRY BOWARD, M.G.
REFERENCE: C.A; O.M.R. PG. 141

NAMES: STEPHEN GEORGE TO ALVIRA QUALLS
DATE: NOV. 13, 1830
BONDSMAN: JOHN QUALLS
DATE PER: NOV. 14, 1830
BY: M. B. CARTER, J.P.
WITNESS: MARY A. SWAN
REFERENCE: C.A; O.M.R. PG. 148

NAMES: DAVID GLASS TO BURNATTA EDMONDSON
DATE: JUNE 29, 1830
BONDSMAN: WM. ARNOLD
DATE PER: JULY 6, 1830
BY: W. A. MCCAMPBELL, M.V.D.
REFERENCE: C.A; O.M.R. PG. 143

NAMES: JNO. GRADY TO SARAH DORAN
DATE: NOV. 23, 1830
BONDSMAN: JOSEPH KING
DATE PER: NOV. 24, 1830
BY: SAM'L LOVE, M.G.
WITNESS: WM. SWAN
REFERENCE: C.A; O.M.R. PG. 148

NAMES: JACOB GRAVES TO SOPHIANNA GRAVES
DATE: FEBY. 1, 1830
BONDSMAN: JOHN GRAVES
DATE PER: JANY. 4, 1830
BY: E. NELSON, J.P.
REFERENCE: C.A; O.M.R. PG. 140

NAMES: JOSEPH GRAY TO ELIZABETH WALKER
DATE: APR. 3, 1830
BONDSMAN: DAVID MCNEIL
DATE PER: APR. 6, 1830
BY: JNO. BAYLESS, J.P.
REFERENCE: C.A; O.M.R. PG. 142

NAMES: WM. HAGGARD TO JANE OGLESBY
DATE: MAR. 16, 1830
BONDSMAN: ROBERT OGLESBY
BY: JAS. SEATON, J.P.
REFERENCE: C.A; O.M.R. PG. 141

NAMES: BERRY HANCOCK TO CLARISSA SKAGGS
DATE: MAR. 12,1830
BONDSMAN: WM. HANKINS
WITNESS: WM. SWAN
REFERENCE: C.A.

NAMES: WILLIAM HANKINS TO SALLY JONES
DATES: MAR. 9, 1830
BONDSMAN: ABEL HANKINS
DATE PER: MAR. 11, 1830
BY: M. B. CARTER, J.P.
WITNESS: WM. SWAN
REFERENCE: C.A; O.M.R. PG. 141

NAMES: JOHN G. HARDIN TO SARAH GALLAHER
DATE: SEPT. 21, 1830
BONDSMAN: GEO. GALLIHER
DATE PER: SEPT. 28, 1830
BY: WM. MORRIS, J.P.
REFERENCE: C.A; O.M.R. PG. 146

NAMES: JESSE HAWTHORNE TO HANNAH BARNETT
DATE: JANY. 20, 1830
BONDSMAN: JNO. HAWTHORN
DATE PER: JANY. 21, 1830
BY: EDWARD R. DAVIS, J.P.
REFERENCE: C.A; O.M.R. PG. 139

NAMES: BAZEL HEDGECOTH TO REBECKA BROWN
DATE: OCT. 28, 1830
BONDSMAN: JOHN ANDERSON
DATE PER: OCT. 28, 1830
BY: ELIJAH JOHNSON, J.P.
REFERENCE: C.A; O.M.R. PG. 147

NAMES: ANDERSON HILL TO NANCY W. SEAY
DATE: NOV. 18, 1830
BONDSMAN: WM. MITCHELL
DATE PER: NOV. 18, 1830
BY: ISAAC LEWIS
WITNESS: WM. SWAN
REFERENCE: C.A; O.M.R. PG. 148

NAMES: DAVID L. HOPE TO MARY E. WELSH
DATE: JANY. 21, 1830
DATE PER: JANY. 21, 1830
BY: THO. H. NELSON
REFERENCE: C.A; O.M.R. PG. 139

NAMES: JOSEPH HUNTER TO REBECKA THOMPSON
DATE: OCT. 18, 1830
DATE PER: OCT. 19, 1830
BY: M. B. CARTER, J.P.
REFERENCE: C.A; O.M.R. PG. 147

NAMES: PRESLY JOHNSTON TO POLLY SMITH
DATE: AUG. 30, 1830
BONDSMAN: WM. SMITH
DATE PER: AUG. 30, 1830
BY: GEO. GRAVES, J.P.
REFERENCE: C.A; O.M.R. PG. 145

NAMES: WM. JOHNSON TO NANCY CHILDRESS
DATE: NOV. 17, 1830
BONDSMAN: ABEDNEGO CASTEEL
DATE PER: NOV. 19, 1830
BY: ELIJAH JOHNSON, J.P.
REFERENCE: C.A; O.M.R. PG. 148

NAMES: WILLIS JORDAN TO ALEE ARENCE CLIFT
DATE: JANY. 9, 1830
BONDSMAN: JACOB ADAMSON
DATE PER: JANY. 14, 1830
BY: ELI KING, J.P.
REFERENCE: C.A; O.M.R. PG. 139

NAMES: JOHN KEYHILL TO NANCY TARWATER
DATE: NOV. 27, 1830
BONDSMAN: WM. BROWN
DATE PER: DEC. 2, 1830
BY: ELIJAH JOHNSON, J.P.
WITNESS: WM. SWAN
REFERENCE: C.A; O.M.R. PG. 148

NAMES: SAMUEL KING TO MARY WALKER
DATE: MAY 15, 1830
BONDSMAN: JOSEPH M. FORD
REFERENCE: C.A.

NAMES: ANDREW KNOTT TO SARAH LONAS
DATE: JANY. 18, 1830
BONDSMAN: SAM'L LONAS
DATE PER: JANY. 19, 1830
BY: THO. H. NELSON
REFERENCE C.A; O.M.R. PG. 139

NAMES: DAVID KOONS TO SALLY MCCLANNAHAN
DATE: JULY 20, 1830
BONDSMAN: JOHN KOONS
WITNESS: WM. SWAN
REFERENCE: C.A; O.M.R. PG. 143

NAMES: WM. B. LEROY TO EMELINE KEITH
DATE: SEPT. 15, 1830
DATE PER: SEPT. 16, 1830
BY: SAML. FLEMING, J.P.
REFERENCE: O.M.R. PG. 145

NAMES: DAVID LETSINGER TO POLLY SHINPATH
DATE: NOV. 16, 1830
DATE PER: NOV. 18, 1830
BY: B. B. CANNON, J.P.
REFERENCE: C.A; O.M.R. PG. 148

NAMES: JNO. LOONEY TO ISABELLA COLEMAN
DATE: NOV. 11, 1830
DATE PER: NOV. 11, 1830
BY: ISAAC LEWIS
REFERENCE: C.A; O.M.R. PG. 148

NAMES: GEORGE LOVE TO NANCY JONES
DATE: NOV. 18, 1830
BONDSMAN: REUBEN EMMETT
DATE PER: NOV. 18, 1830
BY: MICHAEL DAVIS, J.P.
WITNESS: WM. SWAN
REFERENCE: C.A; O.M.R. PG. 148

NAMES: WM. B. LUCY TO EVELINE KEITH
DATE: SEPT. 15, 1830
DATE PER: SEPT. 15, 1830
BY: SAM'L. FLEMING, J.P.
REFERENCE: C.A.

NAMES: HUGH LUTTRELL TO AMELIA RUTHERFORD
DATE: DEC. 9, 1830
BONDSMAN: JNO. TROUT
WITNESS: WM. SWAN
REFERENCE: C.A; T.H.M. VOL. 6, PG. 194

NAMES: WM. MAGGETT TO NANCY LITTLE
DATE: SEPT. 6, 1830
BONDSMAN: ANDREW TAYLOR
DATE PER: SEPT. 7, 1830
BY: ELI KING, J.P.
REFERENCE: C.A; O.M.R. PG. 145

NAMES: WM. P. MCAFFEY TO POLLY BOND
DATE: FEBY. 3, 1830
BONDSMAN: B. M. WALLACE
DATE PER: FEBY. 3, 1830
BY: ISAAC LEWIS
REFERENCE: C.A; O.M.R. PG. 140

NAMES: ROBT. MCBATH TO SALLY DUNLAP
DATE: FEBY. 12, 1830
BONDSMAN: JAMES WILSON
DATE PER: FEBY. 12, 1830
BY: MORDECAI YARNELL, J.P.
REFERENCE: C.A; O.M.R. PG. 140

NAMES: JAMES MCCLAIN TO PATSY ELLIOTT
DATE: MAR. 20, 1830
BONDSMAN: WM. MCLAIN
DATE PER: MAR. 23, 1830
BY: ROBT. TINDELL, J.P.
REFERENCE: C.A; O.M.R. PG. 141

NAMES: JOHN MCCLAIN (OR MCLAIN) TO JANE WADE
DATE: SEPT. 11, 1830
BONDSMAN: JOSEPH MCLAIN
BY: ROBT. TINDELL, J.P.
REFERENCE: C.A; O.M.R. PAGE 145

NAMES: WM. MCCLOUD TO POLLY CONWAY
DATE: MAR. 17, 1830
BONDSMAN: THOS. G. BRITT
DATE PER: APR. 1, 1830
BY: M. B. CARTER, J.P.
REFERENCE: C.A; O.M.R. PG. 141

NAMES: JOHN McDOWEL TO SUSSANA GREEN
DATE: SEPT. 18, 1830
REFERENCE: C.A; O.M.R. PG. 145

NAMES: WM. MISSIMON TO NANCY COATS
DATE: JULY 14, 1830
BONDSMAN: WM. COATS
DATE:PER: JULY 15, 1830
BY: WM. MORRIS, J.P.
REFERENCE: C.A; O.M.R. PG. 143

NAMES: NICHOLAS MURRAY TO ELIZABETH JOHNSTON
DATE: JULY 24, 1830
BONDSMAN: WM. HEATH
DATE PER: JULY 30, 1830
BY: S. DICKEY, J.P.
WITNESS: WM. SWAN
REFERENCE: C.A; O.M.R. PG. 143

NAMES: SAM'L NEATHERING TO MAHALA COKER
DATE: DEC. 21, 1830
BONDSMAN: JNO. HICKEY
WITNESS: WM. SWAN
REFERENCE: C.A; T.H.M. VOL. 6, PG. 194

NAMES: ANDREW PARK TO AMANDA M. MORGAN
DATE : APR. 22, 1830
BONDSMAN: WM. PARK
WITNESS: MILLER TRAVIS
REFERENCE: C.A.

NAMES: ANDREW PARK TO AMANDA M. MORGAN
DATE: APR. 22, 1830
DATE PER: APR. 22, 1830
BY: THO. H. NELSON
REFERENCE: O.M.R. PG. 142

NAMES: JAMES S. PAUL TO BETSY ROBISON
DATE: JANY. 14, 1830
BONDSMAN: BENJ. ROBISON
DATE PER: JANY. 21, 1830
BY: W. LYONS J.P.
WITNESS: WM. SWAN
REFERENCE: C.A; O.M.R. PG. 139

NAMES: JOHN PAUL TO REBECKA FERGUSON
DATE: MAR. 3, 1830
BONDSMAN: JNO. AIKEN
DATE PER: MAR. 4, 1820
BY: W. LYON, J.P.
REFERENCE: C.A; O.M.R. PG. 141

NAMES: JOSEPH PITTMAN TO JANE PUCKETT
DATE: APR. 16, 1830
BONDSMAN: ANDREW PUCKETT
DATE PER: APR. 23, 1830
BY: S. DICKEY, J.P.
REFERENCE: C.A; O.M.R. PG. 142

NAMES: NICHOLAS POWELL TO POLLY HOWARD
DATE: NOV. 4, 1830
BONDSMAN: GEO. HICKEY
WITNESS: WM. SWAN
REFERENCE: C.A.

NAMES: RICHARD PRICE TO SARAH EPPS
DATE: SEPT. 11, 1830
DATE PER: SEPT. 16, 1830
BY: M. B. CARTER, J.P.
REFERENCE: C.A; O.M.R. PG. 145

NAMES: ROBT. REED TO CATHARINE FERGUSON
DATE: MAR. 15, 1830
BONDSMAN: JOHN COKER
DATE PER: MAR. 15, 1830
BY: J. JOHNSON, J.P.
WITNESS: WM. SWAN
REFERENCE: C.A; O.M.R. PG. 141

NAMES: JNO. L. ROBINSON TO POLLY HENSON
DATE: OCT. 6, 1830
BONDSMAN: HEZEKIAH KIDD
REFERENCE: C.A.

NAMES: JOSEPH ROGERS JR. TO ADELINE SCOTT
DATE: SEPT. 23, 1830
BONDSMAN: PETER SCOTT
DATE PER: SEPT. 23, 1830
BY: SAML. FLEMING, J.P.
REFERENCE: C.A; O.M.R. PG. 146

NAMES: PETER ROGERS TO SALLY NEWMAN
DATE: JUNE 8, 1830
BONDSMAN: JESSE CUNNINGHAM
DATE PER: JUNE 10, 1830
BY: B. McNUTT, J.P.
REFERENCE: C.A; O.M.R. PG. 142

NAMES: JOSEPH SCHOOLFIELD TO EMILY PARKER
DATE: AUG. 10, 1830
REFERENCE: C.A; O.M.R. PG. 144

NAMES: GEORGE SHETTERLY TO NANCY MADARIS
DATE: DEC. 1, 1830
BONDSMAN: MATTHEW MCCOWN
DATE PER: DEC. 2, 1830
BY: B. B. CANNON, J.P.
REFERENCE: C.A; O.M.R. PG. 149

NAMES: WILLIS SHIPP TO MARTHA BARNWELL
DATE: SEPT. 28, 1830
BONDSMAN: THOMAS BELL
DATE PER: SEPT. 29, 1830
BY: ISAAC LEWIS
REFERENCE: C.A; O.M.R. PG. 146

NAMES: MATTHEW SIMPSON TO ELLEN CRAWFORD
DATE: JULY 26, 1830
BONDSMAN: C. G. BOWEN
DATE PER: JULY 27, 1830
BY: W. A. MCCAMPBELL, M.V.D.
REFERENCE: C.A; O.M.R. PG. 143

NAMES: WM. SIMPSON TO SARAH HAMILTON
DATE: JUNE 9, 1830
BONDSMAN: JNO. SIMPSON
DATE PER: JUNE 9, 1830
BY: M. B. CARTER, J.P.
~~WITNESS: W. B. CARTER, J.P.~~
REFERENCE: C. A; O.M.R. PG. 143

NAMES: PLEASANT SMITH TO CASA LANE
DATE: SEPT. 9, 1830
BONDSMAN: JOHN MONTGOMERY
DATE PER: SEPT. 9, 1830
BY: J. JOHNSON, J.P.
WITNESS: WM. SWAN
REFERENCE: C.A; O.M.R. PG. 145

NAMES: JAMES STEPHENSON TO LEVINA (?) CRANK
DATE: JUNE 21, 1830
DATE PER: JUNE 24, 1830
BY: THOS. FRAZIER, J.P.
REFERENCE: O.M.R. PG. 143

NAMES: WM. SWAN TO MARY ANN SCOTT
DATE: JANY. 20, 1830
BONDSMAN: SPENCER JARNAGIN
REFERENCE: C.A.

NAMES: WM. SWAN TO MARY ANN SCOTT
DATE: JANY. 20, 1830
DATE PER: JANY. 20, 1830
BY: THO. H. NELSON, M.G.
REFERENCE: O.M.R. PG. 139

NAMES: WM. THOMPSON TO POLLY WOTTON
DATE: JANY. 6, 1830
DATE PER: JANY. 7, 1830
BY: SAMUEL DICKEY, J.P.
REFERENCE: C.A; O.M.R. PG. 139

NAMES: WILLIAM TROUT TO BETSEY HENDERSON
DATE: OCT. 14, 1830
DATE PER: OCT. 21, 1830
BY: SAM'L. S. MCCAMPBELL, J.P.
REFERENCE: C.A; O.M.R. PG. 147

NAMES: MILES C. VERNON TO CATHARINE KARNS
DATE: SEPT. 29, 1830
DATE PER: SEPT. 30, 1830
BY: ISAAC LEWIS
REFERENCE: C.A; O.M.R. PG. 146

NAMES: WILLIAM WALKER TO MARGARET SEETON
DATE: FEBY. 17, 1830
DATE PER: FEBY. 18, 1830
BY: W. A. MCCAMPBELL, M.V.D.
REFERENCE: C.A; O.M.R. PG. 140

NAMES: ROBERT WEAVER TO ELIZABETH LUMPKIN
DATE: JANY. 5, 1830
DATE PER: JANY. 5, 1830
BY: E. NELSON, J.P.
REFERENCE: C.A; O.M.R. PG. 139

NAMES: WM. B. WEBB TO SARAH G. COLE
DATE: JUNE 12, 1830
DATE PER: JUNE 12, 1830
BY: ISAAC LEWIS
REFERENCE: C.A; O.M.R. PG. 143

NAMES: JAMES WILEY TO ELMIRA UNDERWOOD
DATE: OCT. 20, 1830
BY: S. DICKEY, J.P. - DATE PER: OCT. 23, 1830
REFERENCE: C.A; O.M.R. PG. 147

NAMES: JNO. WILKERSON TO TABITHA HARRIS
DATE: FEBY. 18, 1830
BONDSMAN: J. C. VEALE
DATE PER: FEBY. 18, 1830.
BY: W. LYON, J.P.
WITNESS: WM. SWAN
REFERENCE: C.A; O.M.R. PG. 140; T.H.M. VOL. 6, PG. 194

NAMES: MAJOR WM. WILKERSON TO ELIZABETH JOHNSTON
DATE: AUG. 10, 1830
BONDSMAN: JNO. D. EDMONDSON
DATE PER: AUG. 10, 1830
BY: M. B. CARTER, J.P.
REFERENCE: C.A; O.M.R. PG. 144

NAMES: ALEXANDER WILLIAMS TO FANNY BOWMAN
DATE: SEPT. 7, 1830
DATE PER: SEPT. 7, 1830
BY: ELIJAH JOHNSON, J.P.
REFERENCE: C.A; O.M.R. PG. 145

NAMES: FRANCIS T. WILSON TO BETSY L. THOMPSON
DATE: OCT. 16, 1830
BONDSMAN: MATTHEW THOMPSON
DATE PER: OCT. 19, 1830
BY: WM. MORRIS, J.P.
REFERENCE: C.A; O.M.R. PG. 147; T.H.M. VOL. 6, PG. 194

NAMES: PETER WILSON TO OBEDIENT FERGUSON
DATE: FEBY. 4, 1830
BONDSMAN: SAM'L FERGUSON
DATE PER: FEBY. 7, 1830
BY: THOS. GALLAHER, J.P.
REFERENCE: C.A; O.M.R. PG. 140

NAMES: THOMAS WOLSEY TO RUTH HUBBS
DATE: AUG. 11, 1830
BONDSMAN: JOHN HUBBS
DATE PER: AUG. 12, 1830
BY: GEO. GRAYES, J.P.
REFERENCE: C.A; O.M.R. PG. 144

NAMES: GEORGE WRIGHT TO HANNAH HILL
DATE: FEBY. 16, 1830
DATE PER: FEBY. 18, 1830
BY: JAS. BOOTHE, J.P.
REFERENCE: C.A; O.M.R. PG. 140

1831

NAMES: ABEDNEGO ADAMS TO MARY E. CANNON
DATE: 1831
BONDSMAN: A. E. CANNON
REFERENCE: C.A.

NAMES: WM. H. ALLBRIGHT TO LYDIA BOWLING
DATE: MAR. 30, 1831
BONDSMAN: JNO. GARNER
WITNESS: WM. SWAN
REFERENCE: C.A.

NAMES: JAMES ANDERSON TO MARY SIMPSON
DATE: DEC. 20, 1831
BONDSMEN: WM. BROWN
DATE PER: DEC. 22, 1831
BY: MICHAEL DAVIS, J.P.
WITNESS: WM. SWAN
REFERENCE: C.A; O.M.R. PG. 156

NAMES: MICAJAH B. BALEW TO POLLY BROOKS
DATE: AUG. 3, 1831
DATE PER: AUG. 5, 1831
BY: MICHAEL DAVIS, J.P.
REFERENCE: O.M.R. PG. 154

NAMES: JAMES G. BELL TO PHEBE LACEY
DATE: NOV. 16, 1831
DATE PER: NOV. 20, 1831
BY: LINDSAY CHILDRESS, J.P.
REFERENCE: C.A; O.M.R. PG. 155

NAMES: JAMES D. BENNETT TO DORCAS IRWIN
DATE: JANY. 1, 1831
DATE PER: JANY. 1, 1831
BY: SAM'L. FLEMING, J.P.
REFERENCE: C.A; O.M.R. PG. 149

NAMES: JOHN BOOKOUT TO STACY BRUMMETT
DATE: FEBY. 16, 1831
BONDSMAN: ELIJAH NELSON
BY: ELIJAH NELSON, J.P.
REFERENCE: C.A; O.M.R. PG. 150

NAMES: EDWARD L. BROWN TO ELIZABETH B. RUSSELL
DATE: MAY 26, 1831
DATE PER: 1831, MAY 26
BY: ABNER W. LANSDEN, V.D.M.
REFERENCE: C.A; O.M.R. PG. 153

NAMES: JAMES CAMP TO LENORA GRAHAM
DATE: APR. 18, 1831
BONDSMAN: JOSEPH JACKSON
DATE PER: APR. 21, 1831
BY: W. LYON, J.P.
REFERENCE: C.A; O.M.R. PG. 152

NAMES: JOHN D. CANNON TO REBECKA WILKENSON
DATE: MAR. 4, 1831
BONDSMAN: B. B. CANNON
DATE PER: MAR. 8, 1831
BY: SAM'L. FLEMING, J.P.
REFERENCE: C.A.

NAMES: WM. CHUMNEY TO MATILDA BURNETT
DATE: DEC. 19, 1831
BONDSMAN: JNO. MCCULLOUGH
REFERENCE: C.A.

NAMES: WM. COTTRELL TO NANCY WILLIAMS
DATE: JUNE 14, 1831
BONDSMAN: EDWARD MANEY
DATE PER: JUNE 14, 1831
BY: ELIJAH JOHNSON, J.P.
WITNESS: WM. SWAN
REFERENCE: C.A; O.M.R. PG. 153

NAMES: WM. COULSON TO MARGARET SLATERY
DATE: DEC. 18, 1831
BONDSMAN: JOHN HERNDON
DATE PER: DEC. 29, 1831
BY: MICHAEL DAVID, J.P.
WITNESS: WM. SWAN
REFERENCE: C.A; O.M.R. PG. 157

NAMES: DAVID A. DEADERICK TO ELIZABETH JANE CROZIER
DATE: JULY 21, 1831
BONDSMAN: W.B.A. RAMSEY
REFERENCE: C.A.

NAMES: DAVID DEADERICK TO E. JANE CROZIER
DATE: JULY 21, 1831
DATE PER: JULY 21, 1831
BY: THO. H. NELSON
REFERENCE: O.M.R. PG. 153

NAMES: ARCHIBALD DOOLIN TO MALINDA HASKEW
DATE: APR. 8, 1831
BONDSMAN: RICHARD MARSHALL
DATE PER: APR. 9, 1831
BY: SAM'L. LOVE, M.G.
REFERENCE: C.A; O.M.R. PG. 152

NAMES: NATHANIEL ERWIN TO BETSY MILLER
DATE: MAR. 8, 1831
DATE PER: MAR. 9, 1831
BY: DANIEL GRAVES, J.P.
REFERENCE: C.A; O.M.R. PG. 151

NAMES: WM. EVERETT TO JANE BELEW
DATE: JUNE 7, 1831
BONDSMAN: WM. M. SMITH
REFERENCE: C.A.

NAMES: ELIJAH FADGETT TO SALLY UNDERWOOD
DATE: NOV. 8, 1831
DATE PER: NOV. 9, 1831
BY: RUSSELL BIRDWELL, M. G.
REFERENCE: C.A; O.M.R. PG. 155

NAMES: FREDERICK FORD TO RHODA MAXEY
DATE: FEBY. 24, 1831
BONDSMAN: HIRAM HARRIS
DATE PER: FEBY. 27, 1831
BY: EDWARD R. DAVIS, J.P.
WITNESS: WM. SWAN
REFERENCE: C.A; O.M.R. PG. 151

NAMES: JAMES V. (OR P.) FORD TO SUSAN HAINES
DATE: JANY. 14, 1831
BONDSMAN: JNO. KING
DATE PER: JANY. 16, 1831
BY: ELIJAH JOHNSON, J.P.
REFERENCE: C.A; O.M.R. PG. 149

NAMES: STEPHEN FOSTER TO ANN A. DAVIS
DATE: JUNE 30, 1831
BONDSMAN: WM. SWAN
DATE PER: JUNE 30, 1831
BY: JOHN MCCAMPBELL, V.D.M.
REFERENCE: C.A; O.M.R. PG. 153

NAMES: ARMSTRONG GAINS TO POLLY SWAGERTY
DATE: FEBY. 22, 1831
DATE PER: FEBY. 24, 1831
BY: EDWARD R. DAVIS, J.P.
REFERENCE: C.A; O.M.R. PG. 150

NAMES: JNO. P. GARNER TO PERMELIA NANCE
DATE: JANY. 22, 1831
BONDSMAN: JNO. GARNER
DATE PER: JANY. 25, 1831
BY: W. LYON, J.P.
WITNESS: WM. SWAN
REFERENCE: C.A; O.M.R. PG. 149

Names: Geo. W. Gibbs to Elizabeth Bayless
Date: Oct. 5, 1831
Bondsman: Wm. D. Gibbs
Date Per: Oct. 9, 1831
By: Sam'l. Love, M.G.
Reference: C.A; O.M.R. Pg. 155

Names: Jno. H. Gibbs to Susan McDaniel
Date: June 28, 1831
Bondsman: Geo. W. Gibbs
Date Per: June 28, 1831
By: Wm. Sawyers, J.P.
Reference: C.A; O.M.R. Pg. 153

Names: Robert Gordon to Elizabeth Ferguson
Date: Feby. 8, 1831
Bondsman: Ro. D. Badgett
Date Per: Feby. 23, 1831
By: Elijah Johnson, J.P.
Reference: C.A; O.M.R. Pg. 150

Names: Wm. Harmon to Sarah Gibbs
Date: May 17, 1831
Bondsman: Wm. McDonald
Date Per: May 17, 1831
By: Wm. Sawyers, J.P.
Reference: C.A; O.M.R. Pg. 152

Names: Samuel Hashbarger to Elizabeth Foust
Date: Mar. 2, 1831
Bondsman: Abram Foust
Date Per: Mar. 3, 1831
By: John Bayless, J.P.
Witness: Wm. Swan
Reference: C.A; O.M.R. Pg. 151

Names: John G. Haskins to Barsheba Larew
Date: May 25, 1831
Date Per: May 28, 1831
By: Jas. Seeton, J.P.
Reference: C.A; O.M.R. Pg. 153

Names: Wm. Henson (or Hixon) to Susan Forkner
Date: Aug. 15, 1831
Bondsman: Adam Little
Date Per: Aug. 17, 1831
By: Martin B. Carter, J.P.
Reference: C.A; O.M.R. Pg. 154

Names: John Herndon to Charity Coffett
Date: Aug. 3, 1831
Date Per: Aug. 3, 1831
By: Elijah Johnson, J.P.
Reference: C.A; O.M.R. Pg. 154

Names: John Hill to Sally Hickle
Date: Oct. 10, 1831
Bondsman: John Roberts
Date Per: Oct. 10, 1831
By: Wm. Sawyers, J.P.
Witness: Wm. Swan
Reference: C.A; O.M.R. Pg. 155

Names: John Hill to Ursula Skaggs
Date: Dec. 30, 1830
Bondsman: Abel Hill
Date Per: Jany. 6, 1831
By: Geo. Graves, J.P.
Witness: Wm. Swan
Reference: C.A; O.M.R. Pg. 157

Names: Wm. Horner (or Homer) to Elizabeth Newman
Date: Nov. 29, 1831
Bondsman: Henry Ault
Date Per: Nov. 29, 1831
By: Isaac Lewis
Reference: C.A; O.M.R. Pg. 156

Names: Jonathan Houser to Elizabeth Dorse
Date: Dec. 13, 1831
Bondsman: A. W. Elder
Reference: C.A.

Names: George Huffer to Nancy Karnes
Date: May 31, 1831
Date Per: May 31, 1831
By: Abraham Murphy
Reference: C.A; O.M.R. Pg. 153

Names: Allen Johnson to Matilda Looney
Date: Dec. 15, 1831
Bondsman: Joseph M. Looney
Reference: C.A.

Names: Benoni Johnson to Nancy Suttle
Date: Aug. 6, 1831
Date Per: Aug. 7, 1831
By: Elijah Johnson, J.P.
Reference: C.A/ O.M.R. Pg. 154

Names: Geo. M. C. Jones to Mary Mira Martin
Date: Apr. 25, 1831
Bondsman: Solomon Aley
Witness: Wm. Swan
Reference: C.A.

Names: Reuben Jones to Betsy Weeden
Date: Mar. 1, 1831
Bondsman: Wm. Hankins
Date Per: Mar. 3, 1831
By: Martin B. Carter, J.P.
Witness: Wm. Swan
Reference: C.A; O.M.R. Pg. 151

Names: Jacob Koons to Nancy Bayless
Date: Jany. 22, 1831
Date Per: Jany. 24, 1831
By: Sam'l Love, M.G.
Reference: C.A; O.M.R. Pg. 149

Names: George W. Larew to Tabitha Emerine Gammon
Date: Jany. 18, 1831
By: Robt. Tindall, J.P.
Reference: C.A; O.M.R. Pg. 149

Names: Seth Lea to Maria Bearden
Date: Mar. 29, 1831
Date Per: Apr. 3, 1831
By: J. A. Mabry, J.P.
Reference: C.A; O.M.R. Pg. 151

Names: Lewis Letsinger to Margaret Thornton
Date: Sept. 26, 1831
Bondsman: Daniel Letsinger
Date Per: Sept. 27, 1831
By: Abraham Murphy
Reference: C.A; O.M.R. Pg. 155

Names: Pleasant Love to Dialtha P. Armstrong
Date: Dec. 27, 1831
Bondsman: Henry Waggoner
Date Per: Dec. 28, 1831
By: W. A. McCampbell, M.V.D.
Reference: C.A; O.M.R. Pg. 156

Names: Hugh Luttrell to Ruth Graves
Date: Apr. 11, 1831
Bondsman: Wm. Troutt
Date Per: Apr. 14, 1831 – By: George Graves, J.P.
Witness: Wm. Swan
Reference: C.A; O.M.R. Pg. 152; T.H.M. Vol. 6, Pg. 194

Names: James Luttrell to Dick Murphy
Date: Nov. 28, 1831
Bondsman: Mat. M. Gaines
Date Per: Dec. 1, 1831
By: W. A. McCampbell, M.V.D.
Reference: C.A; O.M.R. Pg. 156; T.H.M. Vol. 6, Pg. 194

Names: Winsor Mason to Alze Smith
Date: Apr. 5, 1831
Bondsman: Sam'l Bowman
Date Per: Apr. 5, 1831
By: J. Johnson, J.P.
Reference: C.A; O.M.R. Pg. 152

Names: James J. Matthew (or Mathis) to Sarah R. Foust
Date: June 1, 1831
Bondsman: David Foust
Date Per: June 2, 1831
By: Wm. Sawyers, J.P.
Reference: C.A; O.M.R. Pg. 153; T.H.M. Vol. 6, Pg. 194

Names: Shadrac Maxey to Polly Hains
Date: Feby. 22, 1831
Bondsman: Gideon Crews
Date Per: Feby. 22, 1831
By: Elijah Johnson, J.P.
Reference: C.A; O.M.R. Pg. 151

Names: Wm. G. McClain to Rebecka Russell
Date: Apr. 20, 1831
Bondsman: Jno. E. S. Blackwell
Date Per: Apr. 21, 1831
By: Isaac Lewis
Reference: C.A; O.M.R. Pg. 152

Names: Dewitt McNutt to Mary Williams
Date: Mar. 29, 1831
Date Per: Mar. 19, 1831
By: Tho. H. Nelson
Reference: C.A; O.M.R. Pg. 151

Names: Wm. Mickles to Margery Slatery
Date: Feby. 23, 1831
Bondsman: Jno. Hendron
Date Per: Feby. 24, 1831
By: Elijah Johnson, J.P.
Witness: Wm. Swan
Reference: C.A; O.M.R. Pg. 151

NAMES: JAMES MONTGOMERY TO SARAH S. COLE
DATE: DEC. 23, 1831
BONDSMAN: WM. MOREFIELD
DATE PER: DEC. 27, 1831
BY: WM. MORRIS, J.P.
WITNESS: WM. SWAN
REFERENCE: C.A; O.M.R. PG. 156

NAMES: SAMUEL MOORE TO CAROLINE WILKISON
DATE: MAY 23, 1831
BONDSMAN: B. M. RUSSELL
DATE PER: MAY 26, 1831
BY: SAM'L. FLEMING, J.P.
REFERENCE: C.A; O.M.R. PG. 152

NAMES: JOHN MOORE TO CATHARINE EVERETT
DATE: MAY 6, 1831
BONDSMAN: WM. SWAN
DATE PER: MAY 10, 1831
BY: ABRAHAM MURPHY
REFERENCE: C.A; O.M.R. PG. 152

NAMES: WM. MYNATT TO ELIZABETH BISHOP
DATE: AUG. 23, 1831
BONDSMAN: JNO. M. HAVRON
DATE PER: SEPT. 14, 1831
BY: SAM'L. LOVE, M.G.
REFERENCE: C.A; O.M.R. PG. 154; T.H.M. VOL. 6, PG. 194

NAMES: WM. OAR TO ANNE WEBB
DATE: DEC. 19, 1831
BONDSMAN: ROBT. OGLESBY
DATE PER: DEC. 20, 1831
BY: JOHN MCMILLAN, J.P.
WITNESS: WM. SWAN
REFERENCE: C.A; O.M.R. PG. 156

NAMES: WM. O'CONNELL TO POLLY BALES
DATE: APR. 28, 1831
DATE PER: MAY 19, 1831
BY: DANIEL LYLE, L.E.
REFERENCE: C.A; O.M.R. PG. 152

NAMES: WM. PRIOR TO LAVINA KENNEDY
DATE: SEPT. 1, 1831
BONDSMAN: JOSEPH HOUSER
WITNESS: WM. SWAN
REFERENCE: C.A.

NAMES: WM. PRIOR TO LAVINIA KENNEDY
DATE: SEPT. 1, 1831
DATE PER: SEPT. 1, 1831
BY: ELIJAH JOHNSON, J.P.
REFERENCE: O.M.R. PG. 154

NAMES: ENO ROBERTS TO LUCINDA COLE
DATE: JANY. 24, 1831
DATE PER: JANY. 25, 1831
BY: LINDSAY CHILDRESS, J.P.
REFERENCE: C.A; O.M.R. PG. 150

NAMES: DANIEL ROGAN JR. TO CATHARINE WEBB
DATE: OCT. 10, 1831
BONDSMAN: JEFFERSON E. MONTGOMERY
REFERENCE: C.A.

NAMES: WILLIAM SHIELDS TO MARY ANN TAYLOR
DATE: JANY. 26, 1831
BONDSMAN: HENRY EVANS
DATE PER: FEBY. 10, 1831
BY: THOMAS WILKERSON
WITNESS: WM. SWAN
REFERENCE: C.A; O.M.R. PG. 150

NAMES: CHARLES SKAGGS TO ELIZABETH BOOKER
DATE: DEC. 20, 1831
DATE PER: FEBY. 1832
BY: GEO. GRAVES, J.P.
REFERENCE: C.A; O.M.R. PG. 156

NAMES: ELI SKAGGS TO ADALINE MCPHERIN
DATE: FEBY. 12, 1831
BONDSMAN: CHARLES SKAGGS
DATE PER: FEBY. 13, 1831
BY: SAM'L LOVE, M.G.
REFERENCE: C.A; O.M.R. PG. 150

NAMES: DAVID SMITH TO MARY ANN GALBREATH
DATE: DEC. 14, 1831
BONDSMAN: M. B. FLEMING
REFERENCE: C.A.

NAMES: WILLIAM SMITH TO NANCY DUNCAN
DATE: JULY 21, 1831
DATE PER: JULY 22, 1831
BY: THOMAS FRAZIER, J.P.
REFERENCE: C.A; O.M.R. PG. 154

NAMES: ABRAHAM STUFFLE TO ELIZABETH MCCABE
DATE: JANY. 24, 1831
DATE PER: FEBY. 3, 1831
BY: M. B. CARTER, J.P.
REFERENCE: C.A; O.M.R. PG. 150

NAMES: THOS. S. TEMPLE TO POLLY FROST
DATE: JANY. 5, 1831
DATE PER: JANY. 6, 1831
BY: B. B. CANNON, J.P.
REFERENCE: C.A; O.M.R. PG. 149

NAMES: JOHN THOMAS TO SUSAN SNAPP
DATE: DEC. 5, 1831
BONDSMAN: REUBEN EMMETT
DATE PER: DEC. 6, 1831
BY: THOS H. NELSON
WITNESS: WM. SWAN
REFERENCE: C.A; O.M.R. PG. 156

NAMES: JAMES A. THORNTON TO AMELIA A. MCMILLAN
DATE: AUG. 19,
REFERENCE: T.H.M. VOL. 6, PG. 194

NAMES: PETER VARNER TO MARY R. SUMMERS
DATE: OCT. 8, 1831
BONDSMAN: DANIEL HOUSER
DATE PER: OCT. 9, 1831
BY: ELIJAH JOHNSON, J.P.
WITNESS: WM. SWAN
REFERENCE: C.A; O.M.R. PG. 155

NAMES: DAVID WEAVER TO MARGOA JANE VARNER
DATE: MAR. 3, 1831
BONDSMAN: DANIEL HOWSER
DATE PER: MAR. 8, 1831
BY: ELIJAH JOHNSON, J.P.
WITNESS: WM. SWAN
REFERENCE: C.A; O.M.R. PG. 151

NAMES: JNO. WEBB TO ELIZABETH BELEW
DATE: DEC. 21, 1831
DATE PER: DEC. 24, 1831
BY: JNO. MCMILLAN, J.P.
REFERENCE: C.A; O.M.R. PG. 156

NAMES: JAMES WEBSTER TO AMY RHEA
DATE: SEPT. 10, 1831
BONDSMAN: SANDERS WEBSTER
REFERENCE: C.A.

NAMES: JAMES WEBSTER TO AMY RHEA
DATE: SEPT. 10, 1831
DATE PER: SEPT. 13, 1831
BY: M. B. CARTER, J.P.
REFERENCE: O.M.R. PG. 155

NAMES: SANDERS WEBSTER TO SARAH STAUNTON
DATE: SEPT. 5, 1831
DATE PER: SEPT. 6, 1831
BY: M. B. CARTER
REFERENCE: C.A; O.M.R. PG. 154

NAMES: BENJ. WILLIAMS TO FANNY MEADOWS
DATE: FEBY. 11, 1831
DATE PER: FEBY. 17, 1831
BY: LINDSAY CHILDRESS, J.P.
REFERENCE: C.A; O.M.R. PG. 150

NAMES: EPHRAIM WILLIAMS TO NANCY JOHNSTON
DATE: OCT. 1, 1831
DATE PER: OCT. 2, 1831
BY: ELIJAH JOHNSON, J.P.
REFERENCE: C.A; O.M.R. PG. 155

NAMES: HARDIN WILLIS TO MARIA COOPER
DATE: JANY. 25, 1831
BONDSMAN: GILBERT ZACHARY
DATE PER: JANY. 27, 1831
BY: WM. SAWYERS, J.P.
REFERENCE: C.A; O.M.R. PG. 150; T.H.M. VOL. 6, PG. 194

NAMES: RICHARD YARDLEY TO ANNY FOSTER
DATE: JULY 7, 1831
BONDSMAN: ADDISON W. ARMSTRONG
REFERENCE: C.A.

1832

NAMES: ISAAC BAKER TO SARAH HICKEY
DATE: OCT. 16, 1832
BONDSMAN: HUGH MCCALL
WITNESS: WM. SWAN
REFERENCE: C.A.

NAMES: NATHAN BALES TO SARAH MOORE
DATE: JANY. 9, 1832
DATE PER: JANY. 10, 1832
BY: ISAAC LEWIS
REFERENCE: C.A; O.M.R. PG. 157

NAMES: RICHARD BEARDEN TO CATHARINE SCOTT
DATE: JANY. 16, 1832
BONDSMAN: SETH LEA
DATE PER: JANY. 19, 1832
BY: G. BIRDWELL, M.G.
WITNESS: WM. SWAN
REFERENCE: C.A; O.M.R. PG. 157

NAMES: NEBUCHADNEZAR S. BELL TO EMELIN FUTHY
DATE: JUNE 5, 1832
DATE PER: JUNE 7, 1832
BY: W. A. MCCAMPBELL, M.V.D.
REFERENCE: C.A; O.M.R. PG. 160

NAMES: WASHINGTON WM. BOUNDS TO REBECKA FISHER
DATE: SEPT. 27, 1832
DATE PER: SEPT. 27, 1832
BY: B. M NUTT, J.P.
REFERENCE: C.A; O.M.R. PG. 163

NAMES: HENRY R. BROWNING TO ELIZA CLIBOURNE
DATE: OCT. 9, 1832
BONDSMAN: MILENDER CLIBOURNE
DATE PER: OCT. 16, 1832
BY: C. FLEMING, M.G.
REFERENCE: C.A; O.M.R. PG. 163

NAMES: HENRY BURAM TO NANCY F. BADGETT
DATE: DEC. 18, 1832
BONDSMAN: JNO. T. KING
REFERENCE: C.A.

NAMES: JOSEPH CARR TO REBECKA M. YATES
DATE: DEC. 30, 1832
BONDSMAN: THOMAS MILLER
DATE PER: DEC. 31, 1832
BY: THO. H. NELSON
REFERENCE: C.A; O.M.R. PG. 166

NAMES: GEO. CARRELL TO BECKY SHOOK
DATE: APR. 30, 1832
REFERENCE: O.M.R. PG. 159

NAMES: JOHN CASSADA TO MARGARET CALDWELL
DATE: DEC. 19, 1832
DATE PER: DEC. 20, 1832
BY: JOSEPH ANDERSON, J.P.
REFERENCE: C.A; O.M.R. PG. 165

NAMES: ROBT. L. CHILDRESS JR. TO HANNAH LACEY
DATE: OCT. 12, 1832
DATE PER: OCT. 18, 1832
BY: LINDSAY CHILDRESS, J.P.
REFERENCE: C.A; O.M.R. PG. 163

NAMES: WM. T. CHRISTY TO ELLEN P. MORGAN
DATE: JULY 12, 1832
BONDSMAN: WILLIAM PARK
DATE PER: JULY 12, 1832
BY: THO. H. NELSON
REFERENCE: C.A; O.M.R. PG. 161; T.H.M. VOL. 6, PG. 194

NAMES: JOHN CONNELLY TO ELIZA JANE DAVIS
DATE: DEC. 25, 1832
BONDSMAN: JNO. HILL & ISAAC HAYNES
REFERENCE: C.A.

NAMES: WM. R. CONNER TO MARTHA GAMMON
DATE: FEBY. 28, 1832
DATE PER: MAR. 1, 1832
BY: THOMAS FRAZIER
REFERENCE: C.A; O.M.R. PG. 158

NAMES: HUGH S. COPELAND TO FRANCIS BIBBS
DATE: MAR. 28, 1832
DATE PER: MAR. 29, 1832
BY: THOMAS FRAZIER, J.P.
REFERENCE: C.A; O.M.R. PG. 159

NAMES: URIAH CUMMINGS TO TALITHA SMITH
DATE: DEC. 24, 1832
BONDSMAN: JAS. S. WHITEMAN
WITNESS: WM. SWAN
REFERENCE: C.A; T.H.M. VOL. 6, PG. 194

NAMES: ABRAM DABNEY TO MARTINA PIN
DATE: SEPT. 4, 1832
BONDSMAN: HENRY AULT
DATE PER: SEPT. 5, 1832
BY: M. B. CARTER, J.P.
REFERENCE: C.A; O.M.R. PG. 162

NAMES: JAMES L. DAVIS TO EVELINA JANE MCMILLAN
DATE: NOV. 15, 1832
DATE PER: NOV. 15, 1832
BY: THO. H. NELSON
REFERENCE: C.A; O.M.R. PG. 164

NAMES: WM. DAVIS TO SUSAN GRAVES (OR GROVES)
DATE: DEC. 7, 1832
DATE PER: DEC. 11, 1832
BY: M. B. CARTER, J.P.
REFERENCE: C.A; O.M.R. PG. 165

NAMES: J. M. DOTSON TO HANNAH KARNS (OR KIMES)
DATE: NOV. 21, 1832
BONDSMAN: JESSE J. PARSLEY
DATE PER: NOV. 22, 1832
BY: J. JOHNSON, J.P.
REFERENCE: C.A; O.M.R. PG. 164

NAMES: REUBEN DOUGHTY TO MARGARET R. COOKE
DATE: DEC. 15, 1832
BONDSMAN: THOS. MARTIN
REFERENCE: C.A.

NAMES: HENRY EVANS TO SALLY TAYLOR
DATE: JUNE 30, 1832
DATE PER: JUNE 5, 1832 (?)
BY: THOS. WILKERSON
REFERENCE: C.A; O.M.R. PG. 160

NAMES: GEORGE FINK TO NANCY SMITH
DATE: DEC. 24,
REFERENCE: T.H.M. VOL. 6, PG. 194

NAMES: WILLIAM FORTNER TO CAROLINE HANCOCK
DATE: FEBY. 28, 1832
DATE PER: MAR. 1832
BY: WM. SAWYERS, J.P.
REFERENCE: C.A; O.M.R. PG. 158

NAMES: ABRAM FOUST TO LYDIA HASHBARGER
DEC. 12, 1832 - DATE ISSUED
DATE PER: DEC. 16, 1832
BY: GEORGE GRAVES, J.P.
REFERENCE: C.A; O.M.R. PG. 165

NAMES: SAMUEL FRAZIER TO TINSEY CRAIGHEAD
DATE: FEBY. 7, 1832
BONDSMAN: WM. G. FRAZIER
DATE PER: FEBY. 8, 1832
BY: SAM'L. LOVE, M.G.
REFERENCE: C.A; O.M.R. PG. 158

NAMES: WM. C. FRAZIER TO MELINDA GOLLIHER
DATE: JULY 4, 1832 - DATE PER: JULY 12, 1832
BY: ABNER W. LANDSDEN, V.D.M.
REFERENCE: C.A; O.M.R. PG. 161

NAMES: HARRIS GAMMON TO ELIZABETH BOOKOUT
DATE: NOV. 17, 1832
DATE PER: NOV. 18, 1832
BY: ROBT. TINDELL, J.P.
REFERENCE: C.A; O.M.R. PG. 164

NAMES: DAVID GIBBS TO SARAH MCLAIN
DATE: APR. 18, 1832
DATE PER: APR. 19, 1832
BY: SAMUEL LOVE, M.G.
REFERENCE: C.A; O.M.R. PG. 159

NAMES: WM. D. GIBBS TO ELIZABETH JANE JOHNSTON
DATE: NOV. 19, 1832
DATE PER: NOV. 20, 1832
BY: GEORGE GRAVES, J.P.
REFERENCE: C.A; O.M.R. PG. 164

NAMES: THOMAS GRAVES (OR GRAVIT) TO MARY OZBORNE
DATE: DEC. 31, 1832
REFERENCE: C.A; O.M.R. PG. 166

NAMES: JEFFERSON GRIFFIN TO POLLY SIMPSON
DATE: JANY. 23, 1832
DATE PER: JANY. 26, 1832
BY: MICHAEL DAVIS, J.P.
REFERENCE: C.A; O.M.R. PG. 158

NAMES: SAM'L. H. HANSARD TO A. WEAR
DATE: DEC. 3, 1832
DATE PER: DEC. 4, 1832
BY: ISAAC LEWIS
REFERENCE: C.A; O.M.R. PG. 165

NAMES: CALVIN S. HARRIS TO MARTHA M. MURPHY
DATE: MAY 30, 1832
DATE PER: MAY 31, 1832
BY: M. B. CARTER, J.P.
REFERENCE: C.A; O.M.R. PG. 160

NAMES: NATHAN HARRIS TO REBECKA GIBBS
DATE: OCT. 27, 1832
BONDSMAN: REUBEN ROGERS
DATE PER: OCT. 30, 1832
BY: SAM'L. LOVE, M.G.
WITNESS: CHAS. SCOTT
REFERENCE: C.A; O.M.R. PG. 164

Names: Stephen Haynes to Susan Dunn
Date: Jany. 4, 1832
Date Per: Jany. 4, 1832
By: Isaac Lewis
Reference: C.A; O.M.R. Pg. 157

Names: Alanson Heathcock (or Hithcoth) to Isabella McMillan
Date: June 28, 1832
Bondsman: John Nelson
Date Per: June 29, 1832
By: J. Johnson, J.P.
Witness: Wm. Swan
Reference: C.A; O.M.R. Pg. 160; T.H.M. Vol. 6, Pg. 194

Names: Etheldred Henderson to Emeline Felts
Date: Jany. 2, 1832
Date Per: Jany. 3, 1832
By: Isaac Lewis
Reference: C.A; O.M.R. Pg. 157

Names: Alfred Henley to Mary Casteel
Date: Nov. 12, 1832
Date Per: Nov. 15, 1832
By: Elijah Johnson, J.P.
Reference: C.A; O.M.R. Pg. 164

Names: Eli Hill to Susana Seabolt
Date: Sept. 21, 1832
Date Per: Sept. 21, 1832
By: Isaac Lewis
Reference: C.A; O.M.R. Pg. 163

Names: James Hinan to Polly Coffman
Date: Aug. 25, 1832
Date Per: Aug. 26, 1832
By: M. B. Carter, J.P.
Reference: C.A; O.M.R. Pg. 162

Names: Charles B. Hodge to Sarah D. Cobb
Date: June 28, 1832
Date Per: July 5, 1832
By: Jas. H. Gass, M.G.
Reference: C.A.

Names: James Humphrey to Sally Ozborne
Date: May 17, 1832
Date Per: May 17, 1832
By: Elijah Johnson, J.P.
Reference: C.A; O.M.R. Pg. 159

Names: Casper Hunyer to Matilda Price
Date: July 14, 1832
Date Per: July 15, 1832
By: M. B. Carter, J.P.
Reference: C.A; O.M.R. Pg. 161

Names: Geo. Washington Hutcheson to Delphia Coats
Date: Oct. 11, 1832
Reference: C.A; O.M.R. Pg. 163

Names: Geo. Hutson to Martha Hobbs
Date: July 23, 1832
Date Per: Aug. 3, 1832
By: J. A. McSwan, J.P.
Reference: C.A; O.M.R. Pg. 161

Names: James Johnston to Martha Watt
Date: June 9, 1832
Date Per: Aug. 30, 1832
By: Eli King, J.P.
Reference: C.A; O.M.R. Pg. 160

Names: Jno. F. Johnson to Patsy Ann Chumley
Date: Nov. 5, 1832
Bondsman: Wm. W. Chumley
Date Per: Nov. 6, 1832
By: J. Anderson, J.P.
Witness: Chas. Scott
Reference: C.A; O.M.R. Pg. 164

Names: Wm. Julian to Margaret Houk
Date: July 7, 1832
Date Per: July 8, 1832
By: J. Johnson, J.P.
Reference: C.A; O.M.R. Pg. 161

Names: Charles Karnes to Ann Tindall
Date: July 31, 1832
Date Per: July 31, 1832
By: Lindsay Childress, J.P.
Reference: C.A; O.M.R. Pg. 161

Names: Philip Karns to Elizabeth Conner
Date: Nov. 26, 1832
Date Per: Nov. 26, 1832
By: Robt. Tindell, J.P.
Reference: C.A; O.M.R. Pg. 164

NAMES: RICHARD KELLY TO CAROLINE ELIZA ANN BURKHART
DATE: SEPT. 27, 1832
BONDSMAN: PETER BURKHART
REFERENCE: C.A.

NAMES: ALEXANDER C. KEYES TO MARY ADELINE LOVE
DATE: JANY. 10, 1832
BONDSMAN: A. G. JACKSON
REFERENCE: C.A.

NAMES: HENRY KIRBY TO ELIZABETH WEYLAND
DATE: NOV. 8, 1832
DATE PER: NOV. 8, 1832
BY: ELIJAH JOHNSON, J.P.
REFERENCE: C.A; O.M.R. PG. 164

NAMES: ROBERT KIRKPATRICK TO BETSY SMITH
DATE: FEBY. 27, 1832
DATE PER: MAR. 1, 1832
BY: JNO. MYNATT, J.P.
REFERENCE: C.A; O.M.R. PG. 158

NAMES: ALEXANDER LEAK TO DICE LEAK
DATE: AUG. 8, 1832
BONDSMAN: SYLVANUS HOWELL
DATE PER: AUG. 9, 1832
BY: B. MCNUTT, J.P.
WITNESS: WM. SWAN
REFERENCE: C.A; O.M.R. PG. 162

NAMES: JNO. MARK LEAK TO BETSY ANN STEWART
DATE: NOV. 12, 1832
BONDSMAN: A. ARMSTRONG
REFERENCE: C.A.

NAMES: LEVI LINEBERRY TO POLLY ANN BALDWIN
DATE: MAR. 2, 1832
BONDSMAN: FRANCIS J. BALDWIN
DATE PER: MAR. 5, 1832
BY: WM. MORRIS, J.P.
REFERENCE: C.A; O.M.R. PG. 158

NAMES: RICHARD LITTLE TO POLLY SLATER
DATE: MAY 9, 1832
BONDSMAN: JAMES H. EDINGTON
DATE PER: MAY 10, 1832
BY: ELIJAH JOHNSON, J.P.
REFERENCE: C.A; O.M.R. PG. 159

NAMES: ROBERT LOVE TO CATHARINE MCFARLAND
DATE: AUG. 2, 1832
BONDSMAN: BENJ. B. BOYD
DATE PER: AUG. 2, 1832
BY: THO. H. NELSON
REFERENCE: C.A; O.M.R. PG. 162

NAMES: SAMUEL H. LOVE TO MARGARET C. ARMSTRONG
DATE: JUNE 26, 1832
BONDSMAN: THOMAS RODGERS
DATE PER: JUNE 26, 1832
BY: W. A. MCCAMPBELL, M.V.D.
REFERENCE: C.A; O.M.R. PG. 160

NAMES: RICHARD LUTTRELL TO JANE MYNATT
DATE: DEC. 3, 1832
BONDSMAN: AMOS CARTER
DATE PER: DEC. 9, 1832
BY: M. B. CARTER, J.P.
REFERENCE: C.A; O.M.R. PG. 165; T.H.M. VOL. 6, PG. 194

NAMES: SAMUEL LYONS TO DICE HIGHTOWER
DATE: JULY 4, 1832
BONDSMAN: S. M. SKAGGS
DATE PER: JULY 5, 1832
BY: M. B. CARTER, J.P.
WITNESS: WM. SWAN
REFERENCE: C.A; O.M.R. PG. 161

NAMES: PHILIP MAHONEY TO MARY WRIGHT
DATE: DEC. 5, 1832
DATE PER: DEC. 6, 1832
BY: B. MCNUTT, J.P.
REFERENCE: C.A; O.M.R. PG. 165

NAMES: ROBERT MARLEY TO ELIZA ANN MARTIN
DATE: SEPT. 17, 1832 - BONDSMAN: R.F.G. FLEMING
DATE PER: SEPT. 18, 1832
BY: SAM'L. FLEMING, J.P.
REFERENCE: C.A.

NAMES: TERRENCE MCAFFRY TO SELINA STANNER
DATE: OCT. 23, 1832
BONDSMAN: F. N. B. DUDLEY
REFERENCE: C.A.

NAMES: JOHN MC MCCAMPBELL TO ELIZABETH ANN REYNOLDS
DATE: JUNE 13, 1832
BONDSMAN: PLEASANT R. GRILLS
REFERENCE: C.A.

NAMES: JOHN MCCAMPBELL TO ELIZABETH ANN REYNOLDS
DATE: JUNE 13, 1832
DATE PER: JUNE 19, 1832
BY: LINDSAY CHILDRESS, J.P.
REFERENCE: O.M.R. PG. 161

NAMES: DAVID MCHAFFIE TO CATHARINE SHERRODD
DATE: MAR. 3, 1832
BONDSMAN: GEO. W. SHERRODD
DATE:PER: MAR. 8, 1832
BY: THOMAS FRAZIER, J.P.
REFERENCE: C.A; O.M.R. PG. 159

NAMES: ISAAC MCLAIN(OR MCCLAIN) TO ELIZABETH HOLLOWAY
DATE: SEPT. 13, 1832
BONDSMAN: E. HICKEY
DATE PER: SEPT. 13, 1832
BY: ROBT. TINDELL, J.P.
REFERENCE: C.A; O.M.R. PG. 162

NAMES: WM. MCMUNN TO REBECCA BROWNING
DATE: DEC. 24, 1832
DATE PER: DEC. 27, 1832
BY: J. ANDERSON, J.P.
REFERENCE: C.A; O.M.R. PG. 166 & 177

NAMES: ISAAC MORRIS TO ANNE WILSON
DATE: MAY 21, 1832
BONDSMAN: JOHN JONES
DATE PER: MAY 22, 1832
BY: GEO. GRAVES, J.P.
WITNESS: WM. SWAN
REFERENCE: C.A; O.M.R. PG. 159

NAMES: RICHARD S. MURPHY TO MARIA J. KING
DATE: JANY. 11, 1832
BONDSMAN: BOZE FORD
DATE PER: JANY. 12, 1832
BY: ELIJAH JOHNSON, J.P.
REFERENCE: C.A; O.M.R. PG. 157; T.H.M. VOL. 6, PG. 194

NAMES: WESTLEY NEELY TO SARAH LOWE
DATE: JUNE 5, 1832
DATE PER: JUNE 7, 1832
BY: JAMES SEETON, J.P.
REFERENCE: C.A; O.M.R. PG. 160

NAMES: DAVID W. NELSON TO MARIAH WELKER
DATE: SEPT. 16, 1832
DATE PER: SEPT. 16, 1832 - BY: JACOB NUTTY, M. G.
REFERENCE: O.M.R. PG. 162

NAMES: JACOB NUTTY TO SUSAN CARDWELL
DATE: OCT. 23, 1832
DATE PER: OCT. 25, 1832
BY: D. FLEMING, M.G.
REFERENCE: C.A; O.M.R. PG. 163

NAMES: SAM'L. W. O'DELL TO SARAH P. ARNOLD
DATE: AUG. 28, 1832
DATE PER: AUG. 30, 1832
BY: RUSSELL BIRDWELL, J.P.
REFERENCE: C.A; O.M.R. PG. 162

NAMES: EDWIN PARHAM TO MARY DUNN
DATE: JANY 21, 1832
BONDSMAN: WM. MITCHELL
WITNESS: WM. SWAN
REFERENCE: C.A.

NAMES: EDWIN PARHAM TO MARY DUNN
DATE: JANY. 21, 1832
DATE PER: JANY. 22, 1832
BY: ISAAC LEWIS
REFERENCE: O.M.R. PG. 158

NAMES: WM. PARKER TO PATSY TINKER (OR TUCKER)
DATE: DEC. 4, 1832
DATE PER: DEC. 11, 1832
DATE PER: DEC. 11, 1832
BY: JAMES SEETON, J.P.
REFERENCE: C.A; O.M.R. PG. 165

NAMES: JNO. F. PATE TO MARGARET MARLEY
DATE: APR. 2, 1832
DATE PER: APR. 3, 1832
BY: SAM'L. FLEMING, J.P.
REFERENCE: C.A; O.M.R. PG. 159

NAMES: JAMES W. PAXTON TO PATSY CAMPBELL
DATE: NOV. 27, 1832
BONDSMAN: JO. SCOTT
REFERENCE: C.A; T.H.M. VOL.6, PG. 194

NAMES: JOHN PLUMLEY TO MAHALA RHODY
DATE: OCT. 24, 1832
DATE PER: OCT. 25, 1832
BY: B. MCNUTT, J.P.
REFERENCE: C.A; O.M.R. PG. 163

NAMES: JAMES RABY TO PEGGY WILLIAMSON
DATE: SEPT. 22, 1832
BONDSMAN: THOS. B. COX
DATE PER: SEPT. 22, 1832
BY: WM. MORRIS, J.P.
WITNESS: CHAS. SCOTT
REFERENCE: C.A; O.M.R. PG. 163

NAMES: JOSEPH RICHEY TO NANCY LEDGERWOOD
DATE: MAY 23, 1832
BONDSMAN: JACOB SHERRICK
DATE PER: MAY 25, 1832
BY: GEO. GRAVES, J.P.
WITNESS: WM. SWAN
REFERENCE: C.A; O.M.R. PG. 160

NAMES: JOHN ROBERTS TO SARAH RUTHERFORD
DATE: MAR. 6, 1832
DATE PER: MAR. 9, 1832
BY: GEO. GRAVES, J.P.
REFERENCE: C.A; O.M.R. PG. 159

NAMES: HENRY SHINPACK TO SUSAN LETSINGER
DATE: JULY 21, 1832
BONDSMAN: DANIEL LETSINGER
DATE PER: JULY 24, 1832
BY: ROBERT WILLIAMS, M.G.
REFERENCE: C.A; O.M.R. PG. 161

NAMES: BEVERLEY SMITH TO REBECCA HUBBARD
DATE: NOV. 5, 1832
BONDSMAN: JACOB REED
WITNESS: CHAS. SCOTT
REFERENCE: C.A.

NAMES: JAMES H. SMITH TO POLLY ANN KIRKPATRICK
DATE: OCT. 1, 1832
BONDSMAN: MATTHEWS RHODES
DATE PER: OCT. 2, 1832
BY: JOHN MYNATT, J.P.
WITNESS: WM. SWAN
REFERENCE: C.A; O.M.R. PG. 163

NAMES: WILLIAM SNOW TO EMILY MONGER
DATE: OCT. 10, 1832
BONDSMAN: HYRAM BARRY
REFERENCE: C.A.

NAMES: WM. STEEL TO BETSY DUDLEY
DATE: OCT. 23, 1832
BONDSMAN: WM. M. LOWRY
DATE PER: OCT. 23, 1832
BY: THO. H. NELSON,
REFERENCE: C.A; O.M.R. PG. 163

NAMES: GEORGE STEPHENS TO SUSAN W. MALABY (COLORED)
DATE: JULY 17, 1832
DATE PER: JULY 17, 1832
BY: THO. H. NELSON
REFERENCE: C.A. O.M.R. PG. 161

NAMES: DAVID THOMAS TO BETHANA JONES
DATE: DEC. 19, 1832
BONDSMAN: WM. JONES
DATE PER: DEC. 25, 1832
BY: JAMES SEETON
WITNESS: WM. SWAN
REFERENCE: C.A; O.M.R. PG. 165

NAMES: MATTHEW THOMPSON TO MAHANA KIDD
DATE: AUG. 22, 1832
BONDSMAN: ELIJAH HICKEY
DATE PER: AUG. 23, 1832
BY: RUSSELL BIRDWELL, M.G.
REFERENCE: C.A; O.M.R. PG. 162

NAMES: JAMES TINDELL TO LEVINA WILLIAMS
DATE: OCT. 15, 1832
BONDSMAN: THOMAS FROST
REFERENCE: C.A.

NAMES: GEO. W. TURK TO NANCY SMITH
DATE: DEC. 24, 1832
BONDSMAN: JAS. S. WHITEMAN
WITNESS: WM. SWAN
REFERENCE: C.A; O.M.R. PAGE 166

NAMES: JOHN WAGGONER TO REBECKA NELSON
DATE: JUNE 12, 1832
BONDSMAN: JACOB HARDING
DATE PER: JUNE 12, 1832
BY: THO. H. NELSON
REFERENCE: C.A; O.M.R. PG. 160

NAMES: LINDSAY WALLACE TO CHARITY HOLLBERT
DATE: FEBY. 18, 1832
DATE PER: FEBY. 23, 1832
BY: ISAAC LONG, M.G.
REFERENCE: C.A; O.M.R. PG. 158

NAMES: THOMAS WALLACE TO RUTH HAVEN
DATE: AUG. 8, 1832
BONDSMAN: JNO. HAVEN
DATE PER: AUG. 8, 1832
BY: JNO. MYNATT, J.P.
WITNESS: WM. SWAN
REFERENCE: C.A; O.M.R. PG. 162

NAMES: SAM'L. WATT TO PEGGY FARGUSON
DATE: FEBY. 6, 1832
BONDSMAN: JAMES WATT
REFERENCE: C.A.

NAMES: JEREMIAH WILLIAMS TO MINNIE CHILES
DATE: MAY 3,
REFERENCE: T.H.M. VOL. 6, PG. 194

NAMES: DANIEL M. WOOD TO SARAH CHILDRESS
DATE: JANY. 7, 1832
DATE PER: JANY. 8, 1832
BY: ROBT. TINDELL, J.P.
REFERENCE: C.A; O.M.R. PG. 157

NAMES: EDWARD L. WOODWARD TO MALINDA J. FRANCIS ∠
DATE: NOV. 29, 1832
DATE PER: NOV. 29, 1832
BY: ISAAC LEWIS
REFERENCE: C.A; O.M.R. PG. 165

1833

NAMES: EBENEZER ALEXANDER TO MARGARET A. M. MCCLUNG
DATE: JANY. 31, 1833
DATE PER: JANY. 31, 1833
BY: THOS. H. NELSON, M.G.
REFERENCE: O.M.R. PG. 166

NAMES: JOHN H. ALEXANDER TO BARBARA SMITH
DATE: APR. 30, 1833
BONDSMAN: ROBT. SMITH
REFERENCE: C.A.

NAMES: OLIVER ARNOLD TO HANNAH MELTON
DATE: SEPT. 28,
REFERENCE: T.H.M. VOL. 6, PG. 194

NAMES: JACOB BARGER TO EVELINE SMITH
DATE: MAY 22, 1833
DATE PER: MAY 23, 1833
BY: WM. LYONS, J.P.
REFERENCE: C.A; O.M.R. PG. 170

NAMES: JOSEPH BARTHOLMEW TO NANCY WILLIS
DATE: OCT. 31, 1833
BONDSMAN: JOEL READ
DATE PER: OCT. 31, 1833
BY: MICHAEL DAVIS, J.P.
REFERENCE: C.A; O.M.R. PG. 175

NAMES: ALEXANDER BLACKBURN TO HARRIET CAMPBELL
DATE: DEC. 12, 1833
BONDSMAN: ANDREW SCOTT
DATE PER: DEC. 12, 1833
BY: J. H. GASS, M.G.
REFERENCE: C.A; O.M.R. PG. 176; T.H.M. VOL. 6, PG. 194

NAMES: HENRY BOGGES TO HARRIET C. GODDARD
DATE: APR. 29, 1833
DATE PER: APR. 29, 1833
BY: J. JOHNSON, J.P.
REFERENCE: C.A; O.M.R. PG. 170

NAMES: JAMES BOOKER TO BETSY ZACHARY
DATE: MAR. 4, 1833
DATE PER: MAR. 7, 1833
BY: WM. SAWYERS, J.P.
REFERENCE: C.A; O.M.R. PG. 169

NAMES: JNO. BROWN TO POLLY GOSSETT
DATE: JULY 24, 1833
DATE PER: JULY 25, 1833
BY: CHAS. HALL, J.P.
REFERENCE: C.A; O.M.R. PG. 172

NAMES: MICHAEL BURNETT TO ROSY ALEXANDER
DATE: SEPT. 10, 1833
DATE PER: SEPT. 11, 1833
BY: B. MCNUTT, J.P.
REFERENCE: C.A; O.M.R. PG. 173

NAMES: JOHN BUSH TO ELLEN HOMMEL
DATE: JUNE 6, 1833
DATE PER: JUNE 6, 1833
BY: G. FLEMING
REFERENCE: C.A; O.M.R. PG. 170

NAMES: ENGLISH CALDWELL TO AMELIA RUTHERFORD
DATE: OCT. 12, 1833
DATE PER: OCT. 17, 1833
BY: JOSEPH MEEK, J.P.
REFERENCE: C.A; O.M.R. PG. 174

NAMES: JAMES M. CARTER TO REBECKA JOHNSTON
DATE: JULY 24, 1833
BONDSMAN: M. B. CARTER
DATE PER: JULY 30, 1833
BY: THOS. STRINGFIELD
REFERENCE: C.A; O.M.R. PG. 172

NAMES: JAMES CASTEEL TO SUSANNAH UNDERWOOD
DATE: AUG. 7, 1833
BONDSMAN: ISAAC BOND
WITNESS: CHAS. SCOTT
REFERENCE: C.A.

NAMES: RICHARD M. CHINN TO SARAH ANN CREW (OR CRUISE)
DATE: NOV. 23, 1833
BONDSMAN: H. T. SCOTT
REFERENCE: C.A; T.H.M. VOL. 6, PG. 194

NAMES: DAVID CLAYTON TO CAROLINE MASON
DATE: JUNE 6, 1833
BONDSMAN: WM. FIELDS, JR.
DATE PER: JUNE 6, 1833
BY: D. FLEMING
REFERENCE: C.A; O.M.R. PG. 171

NAMES: ROBERT CLAYTON TO ELIZABETH HOMMEL
DATE: AUG. 16, 1833
DATE PER: AUG. 22, 1833
BY: MICHAEL DAVIS, J.P.
REFERENCE: C.A; O.M.R. PG. 173

NAMES: JAMES CLIFT/SEN., TO PATSY KNIPPER
DATE: SEPT. 28, 1833
BONDSMAN: CHAS. W. PRICE
DATE PER: SEPT. 29, 1833
BY: ELI KING, J.P.
REFERENCE: C.A; O.M.R. PG. 174

NAMES: RADFORD R. CLOWDIS TO CATHARINE MARLEY
DATE: MAR. 19, 1833
DATE PER: MAR. 21, 1833
BY: WM. MORRIS, J.P.
REFERENCE: C.A; O.M.R. PG. 169

NAMES: JAMES COFFMAN TO SARAH CHUMBLEY
DATE: MAY 23,
REFERENCE: T.H.M. VOL. 6, PG. 195

NAMES: AARON COMER (CONNER) TO LEVINA BELL
DATE: FEBY. 27, 1833
BONDSMAN: FRANCIS G. BROWN
DATE PER: FEBY. 28, 1833 - BY: MORDECAI ---J.P.
REFERENCE: C.A; O.M.R. PG. 168

NAMES: JAMES COURTNEY TO ELIZABETH HENSON
DATE: JANY. 2, 1833
BONDSMAN: ARTHUR ROBERTSON
DATE PER: JANY. 3, 1833
BY: WM. LYONS, J.P. - WITNESS: CHAS. SCOTT
REFERENCE: C.A; O.M.R. PG. 166
NAMES:
NAMES: ABRAHAM COX TO MARY W. CALLOWAY
DATE: JULY 10, 1833
BONDSMAN: THOS. F. CALLOWAY
DATE PER: JULY 11, 1833
BY: WM. MORRIS, J.P.
REFERENCE: C.A; O.M.R. PG. 171

NAMES: ADAM CRAWFORD TO CATHRINA SCOTT
DATE: JAN. 18,
REFERENCE: T.H.M. VOL. 6, PG. 6, 195

NAMES: EDWIN CRAWFORD TO POLLY WEBSTER
DATE: MAR. 9, 1833
BONDSMAN: HUGH JONES
DATE PER: MAR. 9, 1833
BY: M. B. CARTER, J.P.
REFERENCE: C.A; O.M.R. PG. 169

NAMES: WM. H. CRAWFORD TO ELIZABETH BARGER
DATE: MAR. 21, 1833
BONDSMAN: NICHOLAS BARGER
DATE PER: MAR. 24, 1833
BY: SAM'L. WHITE, J.P.
WITNESS: WM. SWAN
REFERENCE: C.A; O.M.R. PG. 169

NAMES: WM. P. CRIPPENS TO DICE TINDELL
DATE: NOV. 21, 1833
DATE PER: NOV. 21, 1833
BY: LEWIS LUTTRELL, J.P.
REFERENCE: C.A; O.M.R. PG. 176

NAMES: JAMES CURRIER TO SARAH BEARDEN
DATE: JULY 14, 1833
BONDSMAN: SETH LEA
DATE PER: JULY 14, 1833
BY: SAM'L. WHITE, J.P.
WITNESS: CHARLES MCCLUNG
REFERENCE: C.A; O.M.R. PG. 172; T.H.M. VOL. 6, PG. 195

NAMES: CLIBORNE DAVIS, TO LAVISTA (?) DAMEWOOD
DATE: DEC. 14, 1833 - DATE PER: DEC. 26, 1833
BY: ISAAC BAYLESS, J.P.
REFERENCE: O.M.R. PG. 177

Names: Jno. R. Davis to Polly McCarrell
Date: Oct. 23, 1833
Bondsman: Michael Davis
Date Per: Oct. 24, 1833
By: Elijah Johnson, J.P.
Reference: C.A; O.M.R. Pg. 175

Names: Matthew B. Donald to Isabella D. Douglass
Date: Feby. 12, 1833
Reference: C.A; O.M.R. Pg. 167

Names: Tandy Dowell to Elizabeth Childress
Date: Feby. 14, 1833
Date Per: Feby. 17, 1833
By: Elijah Johnson, J.P.
Reference: C.A; O.M.R. Pg. 168

Names: James P. Doyle to Mahala Childress
Date: Aug. 29, 1833
Date Per: Aug. 29, 1833
By: Elijah Johnson, J.P.
Reference: C.A; O.M.R. Pg. 173

Names: Geo. W. English to Mary Park
Date: Aug. 24, 1833
Bondsman: Wm. Williams
Reference: C.A.

Names: Geo. W. English to Mary Park
Date: Aug. 24, 1833
Date Per: Oct. 13, 1833
By: Jacob Nutty, M.G.
Reference: O.M.R. Pg. 173

Names: Ezekiel Fortner to Sarah Balinger
Date: Feby. 21, 1833
Date Per: Feby. 21, 1833
By: Wm. Sawyers, J.P.
Reference: C.A; O.M.R. Pg. 168

Names: Hugh Fulton to Elizabeth Nichols
Date: Feby. 27, 1833
Date Per: Feby. 28, 1833
By: Eli King, J.P.
Reference: C.A; O.M.R. Pg. 168

Names: Aaron Gentry to Elizabeth Reynolds
Date: Feby. 13, 1833
Date Per: Feby. 14, 1833
By: Mordecai Yarnell, J.P.
Reference: O.M.R. Pg. 167

Names: Josiah George to Minerva King
Date: Oct. 7, 1833
Date Per: Oct. 8, 1833
By: D. Fleming, M.G.
Reference: C.A; O.M.R. Pg. 174

Names: Samuel Gill to Diana Cobb
Date: Sept. 6, 1833
Date Per: Sept. 10, 1833
By: J. H. Gass, M.G.
Reference: C.A.

Names: John Goddard to Martha Johnson
Date: June 19, 1833
Date Per: June 20, 1833
By: Elijah Johnson, J.P.
Reference: C.A; O.M.R. Pg. 171; T.H.M. Vol. 6, Pg. 195

Names: Pleasant R. Grill to Margaret R. Gentry
Date: Oct. 2, 1833
Bondsman: Henry Graves,
Date Per: Oct. 3, 1833
By: Jacob Nutter, M.G.
Reference: C.A; O.M.R. Pg. 174

Names: Wm. Hall to Polly Dowell
Date: Dec. 16, 1833
Date Per: Dec. 17, 1833
By: Jno. Mynatt, J.P.
Reference: C.A; O.M.R. Pg. 176

Names: Joseph A. M. Harrison to Leona Crippin
Date: Apr. 13, 1833
Reference: T.H.M. Vol. 6, Pg. 195

Names: Solomon Harris to Patsy Pierce (or Pinn)
Date: Feby. 13, 1833
Date Per: Mar. 6, 1833
By: Elijah Johnson, J.P.
Reference: C.A; O.M.R. Pg. 168

Names: John Hendrixson (or Henderson) to Nancy Williams
Date: May 1, 1833
Reference: C.A; O.M.R. Pg. 170

Names: John Hill to Ann McNutt
Date: Sept. 23, 1833
Bondsman: James Boyd
Date Per: Sept. 24, 1833
By: Tho. H. Nelson
Reference: C.A; O.M.R. Pg. 173

NAMES: Wm. Hogshead to Margaret Ann R. Veals
DATE: Oct. 22, 1833
BONDSMAN: Isaac B. Havely
DATE PER: Oct. 22, 1833
BY: I. Lewis
REFERENCE: C.A; O.M.R. Pg. 175

NAMES: Philip Houser to Mary Ann French
DATE: Oct. 16, 1833
DATE PER: Oct. 17, 1833
BY: John Russom, M.G.
REFERENCE: C.A; O.M.R. Pg. 175

NAMES: Amos Huffaker to Mary Pickle
DATE: Sept. 30, 1833
DATE PER: Oct. 31, 1833
BY: B. McNutt, J.P.
REFERENCE: C.A; O.M.R. Pg. 174

NAMES: Alexander Humphreys to Isabella M. Johnston
DATE: Jany. 11, 1833
DATE PER: Jany. 17, 1833
BY: W. A. McCampbell, M.V.D.
REFERENCE: C.A; O.M.R. Pg. 166

NAMES: Sam'l A. Hunt to Eliza Hall
DATE: June 22, 1833
BONDSMAN: Wm. Nelson
REFERENCE: C.A.

NAMES: Geo. W. Hutchison to Susan Weaver
DATE: Nov. 7, 1833
BONDSMAN: Wm. Weaver
DATE PER: Nov. 7, 1833
BY: Lewis Luttrell, J.P.
REFERENCE: C.A; O.M.R. Pg. 176

NAMES: James Isbell to Rutelia Houston
DATE: Mar. 19, 1833
BONDSMAN: James D. Houston
DATE PER: Mar. 19, 1833
BY: Tho. H. Nelson
REFERENCE: C.A; O.M.R. Pg. 169

NAMES: Samuel Johnston to Elizabeth Gibbs
DATE: Jany. 19, 1833
BONDSMAN: Archer Hansard
DATE PER: Jany. 31, 1833
BY: Joseph Meeks, J.P.
REFERENCE: C.A; O.M.R. Pg. 167

NAMES: Lewis Jorcon to Mary Jones
DATE: Nov. 2, 1833
DATE PER: Nov. 3, 1833
BY: Tho. H. Nelson
REFERENCE: C.A; O.M.R. Pg. 176

NAMES: William S. Kennedy to Elizabeth G. Cox
DATE: Oct. 15, 1833
BONDSMAN: C.W. Crozier
REFERENCE: C.A.

NAMES: Edward Laverty (or Lanerty) to Minerva Veals
DATE: May 27, 1833
DATE PER: May 28, 1833
BY: D. Fleming, M.G.
REFERENCE: C.A; O.M.R. Pg. 170

NAMES: Wm. Ledgerwood to Mary Ann Duran
DATE: Sept. 26, 1833
DATE PER: Sept. 26, 1833
BY: J. Anderson, J.P.
REFERENCE: C.A; O.M.R. Pg. 174

NAMES: Jacob Like to Rebecca Pratt
DATE: May 25,
REFERENCE: T. H.M. Vol. 6, Pg. 195

NAMES: Daniel Lyon to Zabilla Lonas
DATE: Aug. 15, 1833
DATE PER: Aug. 15, 1833
BY: Tho. H. Nelson
REFERENCE: C.A; O.M.R. Pg. 172

NAMES: Wm. McCammon to Eliza E. E. Pickle
DATE: Sept. 25, 1833
DATE PER: Sept. 26, 1833
BY: B. McNutt, J.P.
REFERENCE: C.A; O.M.R. Pg. 174

NAMES: Jno./McCampbell (Mc written above) to Elizabeth Ann Reynolds
DATE: June 13, 1833
DATE PER: June 19, 1833
BY: Lindsay Childress, J.P.
REFERENCE: O.M.R. Pg. 171

NAMES: Archibald McNeill to Margaret Chapman
DATE: Mar. 26, 1833
DATE PER: Mary 27, 1833
BY: W. A. McCampbell, M.V.D.
REFERENCE: C.A; O.M.R. Pg. 169

NAMES: JNO. MCPHERRIN TO LAVINA WHITECOTTON
DATE: JULY 4, 1833
DATE PER: JULY 9, 1833
BY: ISAAC BAYLESS, J.P.
REFERENCE: C.A; O.M.R. PG. 171

NAMES: THOS. H. MILLER TO ELIZABETH CARR
DATE: JUNE 16, 1833
BONDSMAN: ISAAC B. HAVELY
DATE PER: JUNE 17, 1833
BY: THOS. H. NELSON
REFERENCE: C.A; O.M.R. PG. 171; T.H.M. VOL. 6, PG. 195

NAMES: WM. MILLS TO MARTHA RUTH
DATE: JULY 15, 1833
BONDSMAN: MOSES RUSSELL
DATE PER: JULY 18, 1833
BY: ELI KING, J.P.
REFERENCE: C.A; O.M.R. PG. 172

NAMES: EDWIN MONDAY TO MILLY BRADLEY
DATE: DEC. 3, 1833
DATE PER: DEC. 5, 1833
BY: LINDSAY CHILDRESS, J.P.
REFERENCE: C.A; O.M.R. PG. 176

NAMES: JEREMIAH MONDAY TO LUCINDA MCNUTT
DATE: JANY. 4, 1833
BONDSMAN: ROBT. SHIELDS
REFERENCE: C.A.

NAMES: JAMES H. MORRIS TO REBECCA E. CALLOWAY
DATE: JULY 2, 1833
DATE PER: JULY 1833
BY: SAM'L. LOVE, M.G.
REFERENCE: C.A; O.M.R. PG. 171

NAMES: WM. MOULDEN TO NANCY DAVIS
DATE: OCT. 3, 1833
BONDSMAN: WM. SWAN
REFERENCE: C.A.

NAMES: WM. MOLDEN TO NANCY DAVIS
DATE: OCT. 3, 1833
DATE PER: OCT. 3, 1833
BY: THOS. STRINGFIELD, M.G.
REFERENCE: O.M.R. PG. 174

NAMES: GARVAN MYNATT TO MARY G. HILLSMAN
DATE: APR. 5, 1833 – DATE PER: APR. 11, 1833
BY: SAM'L. LOVE, M.G.
REFERENCE: C.A; O.M.R. PG. 170

NAMES: HARDIN W. MYNATT TO MARY FROST
DATE: FEBY. 9, 1833
DATE PER: FEBY. 10, 1833
BY: WM. SAWYERS, J.P.
REFERENCE: C.A; O.M.R. PG. 167

NAMES: PRYOR NANCE TO CHARLOTTE TIPTON
DATE: APR. 15, 1833
DATE PER: APR. 15, 1833
BY: ELIJAH JOHNSON, J.P.
REFERENCE: C.A; O.M.R. PG. 170

NAMES: SPRILL NANKINS TO MARGARET MADRAS
DATE: NOV. 11, 1833
BONDSMAN: JOSEPH DAVENPORT
REFERENCE: C.A.

NAMES: SAMUEL NEELY TO BETSY MILES
DATE: SEPT. 6, 1833
DATE PER: SEPT. 8, 1833
BY: SAM'L. WHITE, J.P.
REFERENCE: C.A; O.M.R. PG. 173

NAMES: JAMES NELSON TO ELIZABETH HINES
DATE: JUNE 18, 1833
DATE PER: JUNE 18, 1833
BY: J. JOHNSON, J.P.
REFERENCE: C.A.

NAMES: JOHN NELSON TO NANCY THOMPSON
DATE: OCT. 15, 1833
DATE PER: OCT. 22, 1833
BY: B. MCNUTT, J.P.
REFERENCE: C.A; O.M.R. PG. 175

NAMES: J. C. C. PARK TO MINERVA YARNELL
DATE: OCT. 22, 1833
DATE PER: OCT. 22, 1833
BY: WM. MORRIS, J.P.
REFERENCE: C.A; O.M.R. PG. 175

NAMES: JONATHAN PARKER TO SELINA NORMAN
DATE: JANY. 30, 1833
BONDSMAN: JO. SCHOOLFIELD
DATE PER: JANY. 30, 1833
BY: SAM'L. LOVE, M.G.
REFERENCE: C.A; O.M.R. PG. 167

NAMES: FRANCIS A.R. PATTON TO ROSANA BELL
DATE: JULY 30, 1833
BONDSMAN: SAM'L. BELL
REFERENCE: C.A.

NAMES: JAMES POE TO MALINDA HENSLEY
DATE: NOV. 16, 1833
DATE PER: NOV. 20, 1833
BY: SAM'L. WHITE, J.P.
REFERENCE: C.A; O.M.R. PG. 176

NAMES: ROBERT PORTER TO POLLY EASTERLY
DATE: FEBY. 13, 1833
DATE PER: FEBY. 14, 1833
BY: ELIJAH JOHNSON, J.P.
REFERENCE: C.A; O.M.R. PG. 168

NAMES: WM. PRATT TO CHARITY RHODES
DATE: JANY. 9, 1833
DATE PER: JANY. 9, 1833
BY: WM. CRAIGHEAD, J.P.
REFERENCE: C.A; O.M.R. PG. 166

NAMES: WILLIAM PRICE TO JUDA JONES
DATE: FEBY. 23, 1833
DATE PER: FEBY. 24, 1833
BY: M. B. CARTER, J.P.
REFERENCE: C.A; O.M.R. PG. 168

NAMES: ADDISON PURSLEY TO LUCINDA LUSSEY
DATE: DEC. 17, 1833
DATE PER: DEC. 17, 1833
BY: SAM'L LOVE, M.G.
REFERENCE: C.A; O.M.R. PG. 176

NAMES: ALEXANDER L. PURSLEY TO JANE LUSSEY
DATE: OCT. 14, 1833
BONDSMAN: DAN'L MCMULLAN
DATE PER: NOV. 15, 1833
BY: JOSEPH MEEK, J.P.
REFERENCE: C.A; O.M.R. PG. 175

NAMES: SHERWOOD RABY TO LUCINDA HORD
DATE: JULY 24, 1833
DATE PER: JULY 25, 1833
BY: JAS. SEETON, ESQ.
REFERENCE: O.M.R. PG. 172

NAMES: WM. S. RAMSEY TO VINEY JACKSON
DATE: SEPT. 16, 1833
DATE PER: SEPT. 16, 1833
BY: JACOB NUTTY, M.G.
REFERENCE: O.M.R. PG. 173

NAMES: JEHU REED TO SUSAN O. THOMPSON
DATE: SEPT. 4, 1833
BONDSMAN: ELIJAH HICKEY
DATE PER: SEPT. 5, 1833
BY: ISAAC LEWIS
REFERENCE: C.A; O.M.R. PG. 173

NAMES: NATHANIEL L. RODY TO ELIZA PLUMLEY
DATE: DEC. 2, 1833
BONDSMAN: JOSIAH RODY
REFERENCE: C.A.

NAMES: MOSES RUSSELL TO ANN RUTH
DATE: JULY 15, 1833
DATE PER: JULY 18, 1833
BY: ELI KING, J.P.
REFERENCE: C.A; O.M.R. PG. 172

NAMES: MARK RUTHERFORD TO CHARLOTTE SKAGGS
DATE: AUG. 9, 1833
DATE PER: AUG. 12, 1833
BY: JACOB NATTY
REFERENCE: C.A; O.M.R. PG. 172

NAMES: RUSSELL SEABOTT TO JANE HILL
DATE: MAR. 25, 1833
BONDSMAN: JO. SCOTT
REFERENCE: C.A;

NAMES: NATHANIEL SHIELDS TO REBECCA EVANS
DATE: MAR. 9, 1833
DATE PER: MAR. 26, 1833
BY: THOS. WILKERSON
REFERENCE: C.A; O.M.R. PG. 169

NAMES: ALEXANDER SMITH TO CATHARINE J. TINSLEY
DATE: FEBY. 11, 1833
DATE PER: FEBY. 11, 1833
BY: THO. H. NELSON
REFERENCE: C.A; O.M.R. PG. 167

NAMES: THOS. F. SMITH TO FRANCES BRANNER
DATE: DEC. 24, 1833
DATE PER: DEC. 24, 1833
BY: JAS. D. MURRAY, J.P.
REFERENCE: C.A; O.M.R. PG. 177

NAMES: JOHN N. SNIDER TO MARTHA CLINE
DATE: MAR. 4, 1833
DATE PER: MAR. 5, 1833
BY: GEO. GRAVES, J.P.
REFERENCE: C.A; O.M.R. PG. 169

NAMES: JOSEPH L. SWAN TO LUCINDA MARTIN
DATE: JANY. 25, 1833
DATE PER: JANY. 29, 1833
BY: W. A. MCCAMPBELL, M.N.D.
REFERENCE: C.A; O.M.R. PG. 167

NAMES: JAMES M. TAYLOR TO ANN MASON
DATE: FEBY. 18, 1833
BONDSMAN: A. G. JACKSON
WITNESS: WM. SWAN
REFERENCE: C.A.

NAMES: ROBERT S. TAYLOR TO ELIZABETH COBB
DATE: OCT. 24, 1833
DATE PER: NOV. 14, 1833
BY: ABNER W. LANSDEN, V.D.M.
REFERENCE: C.A; O.M.R. PG. 175

NAMES: ADAM THOMAS TO LYDIA YEAROUT
DATE: JUNE 12, 1833
DATE PER: JUNE 13, 1833
BY: MICHAEL DAVIS, J.P.
REFERENCE: C.A; O.M.R. PG. 171

NAMES: ANDREW THOMAS TO JANE PRICE
DATE: MAR. 4, 1833
BONDSMAN: JNO. GARNER
DATE PER: MAR. 14, 1833
BY: WM. LYON, J.P.
WITNESS: WM. SWAN
REFERENCE: C.A; O.M.R. PG. 169

NAMES: THOS. D. THORNTON TO ELIZABETH MCMILLAN
DATE: SEPT. 17, 1833
DATE PER: SEPT. 19, 1833
BY: THOS. STRINGFIELD, M.G.
REFERENCE: C.A; O.M.R. PG. 173

NAMES: MARTIN TINDELL TO SALLY CONNER
DATE: JULY 16, 1833
BONDSMAN: ABNER TINDELL
DATE PER: JULY 17, 1833
BY: THOS. FRAZIER, J.P.
REFERENCE: C.A; O.M.R. PG. 167

NAMES: WM. C. TIPTON TO REBECCA JANE DOYLE
DATE: JULY 18, 1833
BONDSMAN: DAVID B. TIPTON
DATE PER: JULY 18, 1833
BY: ELIJAH JOHNSON, J.P.
REFERENCE: C.A; O.M.R. PG. 172

NAME: BARTLEY TOVEREA TO MATILDA LOW
DATE: JANY. 2, 1833
BONDSMAN: WM. OLIVER
DATE PER: JAN. 3, 1833
BY: S. DICKEY, J.P.
WITNESS: CHAS. SCOTT
REFERENCE: C.A; O.M.R. PG. 166

NAMES: ISAAC TROUT TO NANCY LUTTRELL
DATE: SEPT. 17, 1833
BONDSMAN:C JNO. TROUT
DATE PER: SEPT. 24, 1833
BY: M. B. CARTER, J.P.
WITNESS: W. C. MYNATT
REFERENCE: C.A; O.M.R. PG. 174; T.H.M. VOL. 6, PG. 195

NAMES: JOHN VANCE TO MARGARET KENNEDY
DATE: DEC. 31, 1833
DATE PER: JANY. 9, 1834 (?)
BY: JAMES H. GASS, M.G.
REFERENCE: C.A; O.M.R. PG. 177

NAMES: SAM'L VANCE TO MARY J. KENNEDY
DATE: OCT. 25, 1833
DATE PER: OCT. 31, 1835
BY: JAS. H. GASS, M.G.
REFERENCE: C.A; O.M.R. PG. 175

NAMES: JAMES E. WALKER TO MARY ANN WRIGHT
DATE: FEBY. 25, 1833
DATE PER: FEBY. 28, 1833
BONDSMAN: JOHN KING
BY: MICHAEL DAVIS, J.P.
REFERENCE: C.A; O.M.R. PG. 168

NAMES: ELIJAH WALLACE TO ALVINA MANLEY
DATE: MAR. 18, 1833
DATE PER: MAR. 21, 1833
BY: JNO. MYNATT, J.P.
REFERENCE: C. A; O.M.R. PG. 169

NAMES: JAMES WHITE TO NANCY RHEA
DATE: JANY. 28, 1833
DATE PER: JANY. 29, 1833
BY: M. B. CARTER, J.P.
REFERENCE: O.M.R. PG. 167

NAMES: BENJ. WILKERSON TO MARY CUMMINS (?)
DATE: DEC. 21, 1833
BONDSMAN: URIAH CUMMINS
WITNESS: WM. SWAN
REFERENCE: C.A;

NAMES: JNO. WILLOUGHBY TO MARY M. MAXWELL
DATE: SEPT. 3, 1833
BONDSMAN: JAMES MAXWELL
REFERENCE: C.A.

NAMES: THOMAS WILLSON TO NANCY BUMMITT
DATE: JULY 3,
REFERENCE: T.H.M. VOL. 6, PG. 195

NAMES: JAMES WILSON TO ELIZABETH HINES
DATE: JUNE 18, 1833
DATE PER: JUNE 18, 1833
BY: J. JOHNSON, J.P.
REFERENCE: O.M.R. PG. 171

NAMES: JNO. A. S. WOOD TO SALLY KIRKPATRICK
DATE: DEC. 18, 1833
BONDSMAN: LUKE AILER
DATE PER: DEC. 19, 1833
BY: ISAAC BAYLESS, J.P.
WITNESS: WM. SWAN
REFERENCE: C.A; O.M.R. PG. 176; T.H.M. VOL. 6, PG. 195

NAMES: WILLIAM WRIGHT TO ISABELLA KING
DATE: APR. 1, 1833
BONDSMAN: JAS. CALDWELL
REFERENCE: C.A.

NAMES: MARTIN W. YARNELL TO HARRIET JANE BELL
DATE: DEC. 31, 1833
BONDSMAN: NATHAN ALLDREDGE
BY: SAM'L. LOVE, M.G.
REFERENCE: C.A; O.M.R. PG. 177

1834

NAMES: CALVIN ADKINS TO ELENOR MITCHELL
DATE: SEPT. 29, 1834
DATE PER: OCT. 6, 1834
BY: ISAAC LONG, M.G.
REFERENCE: C.A; O.M.R. PG. 182

NAMES: ALEXANDER ARMSTRONG TO MARTHA MERRYMAN
DATE: JULY 17, 1834
DATE PER: JULY 1834
BY: WM. CRAIGHEAD, J.P.
REFERENCE: C.A; O.M.R. PG. 181

NAMES: WM. ARNOLD TO REBECKA MCNUTT
DATE: MAR. 27, 1834
DATE PER: MAR. 27, 1834
BY: ROBT. H. SNODDY, M.G.
REFERENCE: C.A; O.M.R. PG. 178

NAMES: ROBT. H. BARNWELL TO ELIZA JANE WHITE
DATE: SEPT. 25, 1834
DATE PER: SEPT. 25, 1834
BY: J. ANDERSON, J.P.
REFERENCE: C.A; O.M.R. PG. 182

NAMES: JAMES BEAN TO MARY DORSE
DATE: SEPT. 11, 1834
DATE PER: SEPT. 11, 1834
BY: ZAC. BOOTHE, J.P.
REFERENCE: C.A; O.M.R. PG. 182

NAMES: EDMUND G. BELL TO MARTHA COMER
DATE: APR. 3, 1834
DATE PER: APR. 3, 1834
BY: TANDY MONDAY, J.P.
REFERENCE: O.M.R. PG. 179

NAMES: ROBT. W. BLAIR (OR BLAIN) TO AMANDA MYNATT
DATE: JULY 14, 1834
DATE PER: JULY 17, 1834
BY: WM. HICKLE, M.G.
REFERENCE: C.A; O.M.R. PG. 180

NAMES: ISAAC BYERLY TO POLLY HOBBS
DATE: FEBY. 25, 1834
BONDSMAN: JAMES COURTNEY
REFERENCE: C.A.

NAMES: JAMES H. CARDWELL TO CLARISSA GRAVES
DATE: JANY. 14, 1834
BONDSMAN: A. G. JACKSON
DATE PER: JANY. 15, 1834
BY: JACOB NUTTY, M.G.
REFERENCE: C.A; O.M.R. PG. 177

NAMES: ALEXANDER C. CARNS TO ELIZABETH ISRAEL
DATE: JUNE 19, 1834
DATE PER: JUNE 22, 1834
BY: JNO. MYNATT, J.P.
REFERENCE: C.A; O.M.R. PG. 180

NAMES: REUBEN CLOUD TO ELIZABETH STOUT
DATE: JULY 15, 1834
BONDSMAN: JOSEPH SCOTT
REFERENCE: C.A.

NAMES: REUBEN CLOUD TO ELIZABETH STOUT
DATE: JULY 15, 1834
DATE PER: JULY 17, 1834
BY: WM. RODGERS, J.P.
REFERENCE: O.M.R. PG. 180; T.H.M. VOL. 6, PG. 195

NAMES: WM. CRASSAN TO ELIZABETH SPILLMAN
DATE: FEBY. 10, 1834
DATE PER: FEBY. 10, 1834
BY: SAML. WHITE, J.P.
REFERENCE: O.M.R. PG. 178

NAMES: EPHRAIM DANIEL TO MARTHA JOHNSON
DATE: DEC. 18, 1834
DATE PER: DEC. 22, 1834
BY: RICHARD KEYHILL, J.P.
REFERENCE: C.A; O.M.R. PG. 184

NAMES : JAMES DAVIS TO SARAH KIMBRO
DATE: DEC. 27, 1834
BONDSMAN: JEFFERSON GIFFIN
DATE PER: DEC. 28, 1834
BY: ROBT. H. SNODDY, M.G.
WITNESS: GEO. M. WHITE
REFERENCE: C.A; O.M.R. PG. 185

NAMES: WM. CEARMOND TO JANE CAMPBELL
DATE: DEC. 16, 1834
BONDSMAN: ALLEN PERRY
DATE PER: DEC. 17, 1834
BY: RICHARD TINDELL, J.P.
REFERENCE: C.A; O.M.R. PG. 184; T.H.M. VOL. 6, PG. 195

NAMES: JOHN DOYLE TO POLLY THOMAS
DATE: DEC. 16, 1834
BONDSMAN: JNO. BROWN
REFERENCE: C.A.; O.M.R. PG. 184

NAMES: GEO. J. G. DUNN TO EDY STOW
DATE: NOV. 29, 1834
DATE PER: NOV. 30, 1834
BY: MICHAEL DAVIS, J.P.
REFERENCE: C.A; O.M.R. PG. 184

NAMES: DAVID FORTNER TO SARAH WHITE
DATE: MAR. 27, 1834
BONDSMAN: NICHOLAS GIBBS
DATE PER: MAR. 31, 1834
BY: JAMES CRIPPEN, J.P.
REFERENCE: C.A; O.M.R. PG. 178

NAMES: WM. S. GIBBS TO MALINDA CLAPP
DATE: JANY. 2, 1834
BONDSMAN: DANIEL GIBBS
DATE PER: JANY. 5, 1834
BY: JO. MEEK, J.P.
REFERENCE: C.A; O.M.R. PG. 177

NAMES: JEPTHA GINN TO SARAH C. DAVIS
DATE: JUNE 16, 1834
DATE PER: JUNE 22, 1834
BY: WM. BILLUE, M.G.
REFERENCE: C.A; O.M.R. PG. 180

NAMES: JOHN GODFREY TO LUCINDA CHILDRESS
DATE: JUNE 14, 1834
DATE PER: JUNE 15, 1834
BY: ELIJAH JOHNSON, J.P.
REFERENCE: C.A; O.M.R. PG. 179

NAMES: THOS. O. HALL TO TELITHA WEIR
DATE: JULY 29, 1834
DATE PER: JULY 29, 1834
BY: THOS. STRINGFIELD, M.G.
REFERENCE: C.A; O.M.R. PG. 181

NAMES: WM. HARRISON TO MARY TINDELL
DATE: AUG. 30, 1834
DATE PER: AUG. 31, 1834
BY: JOSEPH MEEK, J.P.
REFERENCE: C.A; O.M.R. PG. 181

NAMES: SAM'L. D. HARPER TO MATILDA FELTS
DATE: SEPT. 20, 1834
DATE PER: SEPT. 21, 1834
BY: ISAAC LEWIS
REFERENCE: C.A; O.M.R. PG. 182

NAMES: STEPHEN HARRIS TO CATHARINE PRICE
DATE: APR. 16, 1834
DATE PER: SEPT. 17, 1834
BY: SAM'L. LOVE, M.G.
REFERENCE: C.A; O.M.R. PG. 179

NAMES: ABSALOM HART TO FANNY QUALS
DATE: OCT. 18, 1834
DATE PER: OCT. 22, 1834
BY: M. B. CARTER, J.P.
REFERENCE: C.A; O.M.R. PG. 183

NAMES: SAMUEL HARVEY TO MAHALY FALKNER
DATE: AUG. 16, 1834
DATE PER: AUG. 21, 1834
BY: JOSEPH MEEK, J.P.
REFERENCE : C.A.

NAMES: WM. HARVEY TO MARY A. H. BELL
DATE: DEC. 23, 1834
DATE PER: DEC. 27, 1834
BY: JACOB NUTTY
REFERENCE: C.A; O.M.R. PG. 184

NAMES: WM. HATCHER TO MARIA NEWMAN
DATE: APR. 7, 1834
DATE PER: APR. 7, 1834
BY: WM. CRAIGHEAD
REFERENCE: C. A; O.M.R. PG. 179

NAMES: AUSTIN H. HENDRIX TO SUSAN M. REED
DATE: SEPT. 20, 1834
DATE PER: SEPT. 23, 1834
BY: WM. MORRIS, J.P.
REFERENCE: C.A; O.M.R. PG. 182

NAMES: MATTHEW HILLSMAN TO ANN ELIZA MYNATT
DATE: JANY. 25, 1834
DATE PER: JANY. 1834
BY: SAM'L. LOVE, M.G.
REFERENCE: C.A; O.M.R. PG. 177

NAMES: JAMES HINDS TO SALLY PAYNE
DATE: SEPT. 24, 1834
BONDSMAN: JOHN N. GAMBLE
REFERENCE: C.A; O.M.R. PG. 182

NAMES: HENRY HOMMEL TO AMANDA M. WALKER
DATE: JUNE 19, 1834
DATE PER: JUNE 19, 1834
BY: DAVID ADAMS, M.G.
REFERENCE: C.A; O.M.R. PG. 180

NAMES: WM. HORNER TO MARGARET NEWMAN
DATE: MAR. 11, 1834
DATE PER: MAR. 11, 1834
BY: DAVID ADAMS, M.G.
REFERENCE: C.A; O.M.R. PG. 178

NAMES: SAM'L. HOWRY TO MAHALY FALKNER
DATE: AUG. 16, 1834
DATE PER: AUG. 21, 1834
BY: JOSEPH MEEK, J.P.
REFERENCE: O.M.R. PG. 181

NAMES: PLEASANT JOHNSON TO FRANCIS GRAVES
DATE: OCT. 15, 1834
BONDSMAN: JOSEPH OAKS
DATE PER: OCT. 16, 1834
BY: ISAAC BAYLESS, J.P.
REFERENCE: C.A; O.M.R. PG. 183

NAMES: WM. JONES TO NANCY WISE
DATE: NOV. 26, 1834
DATE PER: NOV. 27, 1834
BY: W. A. CAMPBELL, M.N.D.
REFERENCE: C.A; O.M.R. PG. 183

NAMES: JOSEPH KING TO SALLY FORD
DATE: JULY 4, 1834
DATE PER: JULY 9, 1834
BY: RICHARD KEYHILL, J.P.
REFERENCE: C.A; O.M.R. PG. 180

NAMES: JOHN LITTLE TO NANCY HICKEY
DATE: SEPT. 9, 1834
DATE PER: SEPT. 11, 1834
BY: J. D. MURRAY, J.P.
REFERENCE: C.A; O.M.R. PG. 182

NAMES: MATTHEW LOW TO PATIENCE MABRY
DATE: JULY 11, 1834
DATE PER: JULY 15, 1834 - BY: WM. MORRIS, J.P.
REFERENCE: O.M.R. PG. 180

NAMES: JOSEPH LUSTER TO ELIZABETH MYNATT
DATE: NOV. 21, 1834
DATE PER: DEC. 7, 1834
BY: WM. HICKLE, M.G.
REFERENCE: C.A; O.M.R. PG. 183

NAMES: GEO. HAINES TO CATHARINE GODDARD
DATE: JUNE 12, 1834
BONDSMAN: MICHAEL DAVIS
DATE PER: JUNE 12, 1834
BY: MICHAEL DAVIS, J.P.
REFERENCE: C.A; O.M.R. PG. 179

NAMES: JNO. MCCARROLL TO PARMELA MURPHY
DATE: DEC. 1, 1834
DATE PER: DEC. 2, 1834
BY: MICHAEL DAVIS, J.P.
REFERENCE: C.A; O.M.R. PG. 184

NAMES: AUSTIN D. MCCLAIN TO POLLY REAGAN
DATE: FEBY. 5, 1834
BONDSMAN: JNO. WEAVER
DATE PER: FEBY. 6, 1834
BY: WM. MORRIS, J.P.
REFERENCE: C.A; O.M.R. PG. 178

NAMES: PLUMLEE MCGREW TO SERINA LAWRENCE
DATE: OCT. 22, 1834
BONDSMAN: ABRAHAM PLUMLEE
REFERENCE: C.A;

NAMES: GAVIN MILLER TO MARTHA HILL
DATE: AUG. 15, 1834
BONDSMAN: TRAVIS GEORGE
DATE PER: OCT. 14, 1834
BY: ISAAC BAYLESS, J.P.
REFERENCE: C.A; O.M.R. PG. 181

NAMES: WM. T. MONTGOMERY TO MARY JANE WEBB
DATE: FEBY. 20, 1834
BONDSMAN: J. E. MONTGOMERY
REFERENCE: C.A.

NAMES: WM. NASH TO CATHARINE SIMMONS
DATE: JULY 28, 1834
DATE PER: JULY 28, 1834
BY: M. B. CARTER, J.P.
REFERENCE: C.A; O.M.R. PG. 181

NAMES: DAVID W. NELSON TO MARIAH WILKES
DATE: SEPT. 16, 1834
BONDSMAN: FRANCIS H. BOUNDS
REFERENCE: C.A.

NAMES: DAVID W. NELSON TO MARIAH WILKES
DATE: SEPT. 16, 1834
DATE PER: SEPT. 16, 1834
BY: JACOB NUTTY, M.G.
REFERENCE: O.M.R. PG. 182

NAMES: GUILFORD NESTER TO SARAH ANN HOOD
DATE: DEC. 17, 1834
BONDSMAN: E. HICKEY
DATE PER: DEC. 18, 1834
BY: ELIJAH JOHNSON, J.P.
REFERENCE: C.A; O.M.R. PG. 184

NAMES: GEORGE NEWMAN TO MALINDA MONDAY
DATE: MAR. 21, 1834
BONDSMAN: JNO. A. WAGGONER
DATE PER: MAR. 21, 1834
BY: ISAAC LEWIS
WITNESS: WM. SWAN
REFERENCE: C.A; O.M.R. PG. 178

NAMES: BENJ. W. PARHAM TO SALLEY TAYLOR
DATE: MAY 5, 1834
BONDSMAN: EDWIN N. PARHAM
REFERENCE: C.A.

NAMES: BENJ. W. PARHAM TO SALLY TAYLOR
DATE: MAY 5, 1834
DATE PER: MAY 5, 1834
BY: WM. MORRIS, J.P.
REFERENCE: O.M.R. PG. 179

NAMES: ALFRED PARONS TO SUSAN READER
DATE: JULY 10, 1834
BONDSMAN: WASHINGTON BRANDON
WITNESS: GEO. M. WHITE
REFERENCE: C.A.

NAMES: WILEY POTTS TO EMOLINE ROBISON
DATE: NOV. 13, 1834
DATE PER: NOV. 13, 1834
BY: ZAC. BOOTHE, J.P.
REFERENCE: C.A; O.M.R. PG. 183

NAMES: JAMES PRICE TO MAHALA MAYFIELD
DATE: MAR. 8, 1834
BONDSMAN: BENJ. FERGUSON
DATE PER: MAR. 8, 1834
BY: SAM'L. WHITE, J.P.
REFERENCE: C.A; O.M.R. PG. 178

NAMES: ISAAC QUALS TO NANCY THOMPSON
DATE: JULY 15, 1834
DATE PER: JULY 22, 1834
BY: M. B. CARTER, J.P.
REFERENCE: C.A; O.M.R. PG. 180

NAMES: W. B. A. RAMSEY TO ELIZA H.C. WHITE
DATE: OCT. 30, 1834
BONDSMAN: E. ALEXANDER
REFERENCE: C.A.

NAMES: WM. B.B. RAMSEY TO ELIZA H.C. WHITE
DATE: OCT. 30, 1834
DATE PER: OCT. 30, 1834
BY: THO. H. NELSON, M.G.
REFERENCE: O.M.R. PG. 183

NAMES: ISAIAH RICE TO RUTH BALES
DATE: APR. 4, 1834
BONDSMAN: NICHOLAS FRYE
DATE PER: APR. 4, 1834
BY: JACOB NUTTY, M.G.
WITNESS: WM. SWAN
REFERENCE: C.A; O.M.R. PG. 179

NAMES: THOMAS ROADY TO POLLY HOWELL
DATE: JULY 21, 1834
BONDSMAN: NATHANIEL ROADY
DATE PER: JULY 21, 1834
BY: WM. CRAIGHEAD, J.P.
REFERENCE: C.A; O.M.R. PG. 181

NAMES: HENRY ROBERTS TO NANCY TROUT
DATE: SEPT. 30, 1834
BONDSMAN: WM. TROUT
DATE PER: SEPT. 30, 1834
BY: JOSEPH MEEK, J.P.
REFERENCE: C.A; O.M.R. PG. 182

NAMES: HENRY RULE TO NANCY J. TARWATER
DATE: JULY 31, 1834
DATE PER: JULY 31, 1834
BY: ELIJAH JOHNSON, J.P.
REFERENCE: C. A; O.M.R. PG. 181

NAMES: LLOYD RUTHERFORD TO ELIZABETH HILL
DATE: AUG. 19, 1834
BONDSMAN: H. B. NEWMAN
REFERENCE: C.A.

NAMES: THOMAS SCOTT TO MARGARET UNDERWOOD
DATE: NOV. 13, 1834
BONDSMAN: J. C. YEALE
DATE PER: NOV. 17, 1834
BY: RICHARD KEYHILL
REFERENCE: C.A; O.M.R. PG. 183

NAMES: JAMES N. SEATON TO RACHEL CRAIG
DATE: NOV. 18, 1834
BONDSMAN: SAM'L. R. RODGERS
REFERENCE: C.A.

NAMES: JAMES SHARP TO NANCY WARWICK
DATE: AUG. 9, 1834
BONDSMAN: ORANGE WARRICK
DATE PER: AUG. 14, 1834
BY: WM. HICKLE, M.G.
REFERENCE: C.A; O.M.R. PG. 181

NAMES: OSWELL SHARP TO ELIZABETH MEEK
DATE: JULY 16, 1834
BONDSMAN: DANIEL MCMULLEN
REFERENCE: C.A.

NAMES: JOSEPH SUTTLE TO MARY KIMBRO
DATE: DEC. 26, 1834
BONDSMAN: HENRY ARNOLD
REFERENCE: C.A.

NAMES: DAVID TARWATER TO EMOLINE SUMMERS
DATE: DEC. 16, 1834
DATE PER: DEC. 18, 1834
BY: MICHAEL DAVIS, J.P.
REFERENCE: C.A; O.M.R. PG. 184

NAMES: LOYAL B. THOMPSON TO NANCY ROADY
DATE: JUNE 11, 1834
DATE PER: JUNE 17, 1834
BY: WM. CRAIGHEAD, J.P.
REFERENCE: C.A; O.M.R. PG. 179

NAMES: RICHARD W. THOMPSON TO ELIZABETH McCLOUD
DATE: OCT. 20, 1834
DATE PER: DEC. 2, 1834
BY: JNO. MCMILLAN, J.P.
REFERENCE: C.A; O.M.R. PG. 189

NAMES: ALFRED TINDELL TO SARAH GRAY
DATE: JUNE 18, 1834
DATE PER: JUNE 19, 1834
BY: MORDECAI YARNELL, J.P.
REFERENCE: C.A; O.M.R. PG. 180

NAMES: HIRAM TINDELL TO MARY HARBISON
DATE: DEC. 16, 1834
BONDSMAN: JNO. GIBBS
DATE PER: DEC. 18, 1834
BY: LEWIS LUTTRELL, J.P.
REFERENCE: C.A; O.M.R. PG. 184

NAMES: THOS. UNDERWOOD TO ELIZABETH JOHNSON
DATE: OCT. 25, 1834
DATE PER: OCT. 30, 1834
BY: B. MCNUTT, J.P.
REFERENCE: C.A; O.M.R. PG. 183

NAMES: JAMES VANCE TO MARGARET KING
DATE: SEPT. 13, 1834
BONDSMAN: WM. WALKER
DATE PER: SEPT. 23, 1834
BY: JOHN MCMILLAN, J.P.
REFERENCE: C.A; O.M.R. PG. 182

NAMES: HENRY WAGGONER TO JANE BOOTHE
DATE: AUG. 12, 1834
BONDSMAN: JOHN A. WAGGONER
DATE PER: AUG. 12, 1834
BY: JACOB NUTTY, M.G.
REFERENCE: C.A; O.M.R. PG. 181

NAMES: ALEXANDER WILLIAMS TO SALLY McCLINE (OR McCLURE)
DATE: MAR. 27, 1834
BONDSMAN: BENJ. FERGUSON
REFERENCE: C.A; T.H.M. VOL. 6, PG. 195

NAMES: GILBERT ZACHARY TO SUSAN DAMEWOOD
DATE: SEPT. 4, 834
BONDSMAN: JUBEL CLIBOURN
REFERENCE: C.A.

1835

NAMES: JOSEPHUS ALEXANDER TO CYNTHIA ROBERTS
DATE: APR. 6, 1835
BONDSMAN: JOSEPH PLUMLEE
DATE PER: APR. 12, 1835
BY: B. MCNUTT, J.P.
REFERENCE: C.A; O.M.R. PG. 187; T.H.M.VOL. 6, PG. 195

NAMES: ALLEN ANDERSON TO LETTY McCAMMON
DATE: DEC. 21, 1835
BONDSMAN: ANDREW J. BROWN
DATE PER: DEC. 22, 1835
BY: RICHARD KAYHILL, J.P.
REFERENCE: C.A; O.M.R. PG. 193; T.H.M. VOL. 6, PG. 195

NAMES: WM. J. ANDERSON TO MARY B. CHILDRESS
DATE: DEC. 24, 1835
BONDSMAN: ANDERSON BURNETT
DATE PER: DEC. 26, 1835
BY: H. LINDSAY, M.G.
REFERENCE: C.A; O.M.R. PG. 193; T.H.M. VOL. 6, PG. 195

NAMES: SOLOMON BALES TO BARBARY STEWART
DATE: JANY. 27, 1835
BONDSMAN: WM. HORNER
DATE PER: JANY. 27, 1835
BY: JACOB NUTTY, M.G.
REFERENCE: C.A; O.M.R. PG. 185

NAMES: ANDREW BEAN TO CYNTHIA PEDIGO
DATE: NOV. 25, 1835
BONDSMAN: JNO. DAWSON
REFERENCE: C.A.

NAMES: ANDREW BEAN TO CYNTHIA PEDIGO
DATE: NOV. 25, 1835
DATE PER: NOV. 12, 1835 (?)
BY: R. H. SNODDY, M.G.
REFERENCE: O.M.R. PG. 192; T.H.M. VOL. 6, PG. 195

NAMES: SAMUEL N. BELL TO CHARLOTT HAMMER
DATE: APR. 13, 1835
BY: J. M. KELLEY, M.G.
REFERENCE: C.A; O.M.R. PG. 187

NAMES: THOMAS BIRD TO MALVINA GOINS
DATE: APR. 11, 1835
REFERENCE: T.H.M. VOL. 6, PG. 195

NAMES: THOS. BRANCH TO MARY HENDERSON
DATE: SEPT. 28, 1835
BONDSMAN: WM. D. MOORE
WITNESS: GEO. M. WHITE
REFERENCE: C.A.

NAMES: JOHN BRIGHT JR. TO SUSAN PUGH
DATE: AUG. 13, 1835
BONDSMAN: TERRENCE W. MCAFFRY
DATE PER: AUG. 18, 1835
BY: JAMES CRIPPEN, J.P.
REFERENCE: C.A; O.M.R. PG. 190; T.H.M. VOL. 6, PG. 195

NAMES: WM. BROWN TO MARY ANN LYLES
DATE: NOV. 3, 1835
BONDSMAN: LEWIS LYLES
WITNESS: GEO. M. WHITE
REFERENCE: C.A; T.H.M. VOL. 6, PG. 195

NAMES: SHADRACK CALLOWAY TO MARY HENDRIX
DATE: JUNE 20, 1835
BONDSMAN: THOS. CALLOWAY
DATE PER: JUNE 21, 1835
BY: WM. MORRIS, J.P.
REFERENCE: C.A; O.M.R. PG. 189

NAMES: GEO. W. CHENOWITH TO NANCY NESTER
DATE: AUG. 26, 1835
BONDSMAN: SAM'L P. BELL
DATE PER: AUG. 27, 1835
BY: SAM'L. WHITE, J.P.
REFERENCE: C.A; O.M.R. PG. 190; T.H.M. VOL. 6, PG. 195

NAMES: WILLIAM CHILDRESS TO EVALINE CHILDRESS
DATE: MAY 1, 1835
DATE PER: MAY 10, 1835
BY: TANDY MUNDAY, J.P.
REFERENCE: C.A; O.M.R. PG. 188

NAMES: LEONARD CLAIBORNE TO EMELINE CLAIBORNE
DATE: NOV. 9, 1835
DATE PER: NOV. 10, 1835
BY: JOSEPH MEEK, J.P.
REFERENCE: C.A; O.M.R. PG. 192

NAMES: GREENBERRY COOK TO PHEBY OLINGER
DATE: MAR. 11, 1835
BONDSMAN: WM. ARTS
DATE PER: MAR. 11, 1835
BY: MICHAEL DAVIS, J.P.
REFERENCE: C.A; O.M.R. PG. 186; T.H.M. VOL. 6, PG. 195

NAMES: DANIEL COVINGTON TO NARCISSA PITNER
DATE: MAY 7, 1835
BONDSMAN: JNO. T. PALM
DATE PER: MAY 7, 1835
BY: J. JOHNSON, J.P.
REFERENCE: C.A; O.M.R. PG. 188; T.H.M. VOL. 6, PG. 195

NAMES: C. C. COX TO NANCY LACY
DATE: SEPT. 21, 1835
DATE PER: OCT. 1, 1835
REFERENCE: C.A; O.M.R. PG. 191

NAMES: WM. CRAIG TO ANN A. G. SEATON
DATE: NOV. 24, 1835
DATE PER: NOV. 26, 1835
BY: W. A. MCCAMPBELL, M.V.D.
REFERENCE: O.M.R. PG. 192

NAMES: PLEASANT CREW TO ROBERTA S. PARHAM
DATE: OCT. 8, 1835
BONDSMAN: SAM'L. R. RODGERS
REFERENCE: C.A.

NAMES: WM. B. CUTHBERTSON TO LUCY CARLASS
DATE: OCT. 9, 1835
BONDSMAN: WM. PRYOR
DATE PER: OCT. 9, 1835
BY: MICHAEL DAVIS, J.P.
REFERENCE: C.A; O.M.R. PG. 192; T.H.M. VOL. 6, PG. 195

NAMES: SAMUEL DAVIDSON TO ELIZABETH RUSSELL
DATE: JUNE 10, 1835
BONDSMAN: HENRY LONAS
DATE PER: JUNE 11, 1835
BY: SAM'L. DICKEY, J.P.
REFERENCE: C.A; O.M.R. PG. 185 (& PG. 189); T.H.M. VOL. 6, PG. 195

NAMES: GEORGE DICKSON TO ANNY NIPPER
DATE: MAY 6, 1835
BONDSMAN: WM. MCMILLAN
DATE PER: MAY 14, 1835
BY: ELI KING, J.P.
WITNESS: GEO. M. WHITE
REFERENCE: C.A; O.M.R. PG. 188

NAMES: STEPHEN DICKSON TO MARGARET BUN
DATE: APR. 14, 1835
BONDSMAN: WM. DUNN
DATE PER: APR. 16, 1835 - BY: ELI KING, J.P.
WITNESS: GEO. M. WHITE
REFERENCE: C.A; O.M.R. PG. 187; T.H.M. VOL. 6, PG. 195

NAMES: JOHN DRAKE TO FANNY DAMEWOOD
DATE: AUG. 27, 1835
BONDSMAN: WM. RUTHERFORD
DATE PER: AUG. 27, 1835
BY: JAMES CRIPPEN, J.P.
REFERENCE: O.A; O.M.R. PG. 190; T.H.M. VOL. 6, PG. 195

NAMES: WILLIAM DUNN TO SARAH CUMMINGS
DATE: JANY. 5, 1835
DATE PER: FEBY. 5, 1835
BY: WM. LINDSAY, J.P.
REFERENCE: C.A; O.M.R. PG. 185

NAMES: WM. C. DUNN TO LYDIA BALES
DATE: MAY 23, 1835
BONDSMAN: GEO. J. G. DUNN
REFERENCE: C.A; O.M.R. PG. 188

NAMES: NICHOLAS EDDINGTON TO PATIENCE WRIGHT
DATE: MAR. 12, 1835
BONDSMAN: JAS. H. EDDINGTON
DATE PER: MAR. 12, 1835
BY: RICHARD KEYHILL
REFERENCE: C.A; O.M.R. PG. 186; T.H.M. VOL. 6, PG. 195

NAMES: ANDREW FERGUSON TO CATHERINE ZACHERY
DATE: OCT. 17,
REFERENCE: T.H.M. VOL. 6, PG. 195

NAMES: SAMUEL W. FRAZIER TO LYDIA JULIAN
DATE: MAR. 6, 1835
BONDSMAN: ROBT. B. REYNOLDS
DATE PER: MAR. 1835
BY: SAM'L. LOVE, M.G.
REFERENCE: O.A; O.M.R. PG. 186; T.H.M. VOL. 6, PG. 195

NAMES: NEWEL C. FRY TO LUCINDA HARRISON
DATE: NOV. 10, 1835
BONDSMAN: JNO. R. ORR
DATE PER: NOV. 10, 1835
BY: JAMES CRIPPEN, J.P.
REFERENCE: C.A; O.M.R. PG. 192

NAMES: ROBERT GAMBLE TO ANN YARNELL
DATE: MAY 18, 1835
BONDSMAN: R. GALLAHER
DATE PER: MAY 26, 1835
BY: WM. MORRIS, J.P.
REFERENCE: C.A; O.M.R. PG. 188; T.H.M. VOL. 6, PG. 195

NAMES: SAMUEL GEORGE TO ELIZA H. KARNS
DATE: SEPT. 21, 1835
DATE PER: SEPT. 22, 1835
BY: W. A. MCCAMPBELL, M.N.D.
REFERENCE: C.A; O.M.R. PG. 191; T.H.M. VOL. 6, PG. 195

NAMES: SAM'L. M. GODDARD TO HARRIET JONES
DATE: AUG. 20, 1835
DATE PER: AUG. 20, 1835
BY: SAM'L. WHITE, J.P.
REFERENCE: C.A; O.M.R. PG. 190; T.H.M. VOL. 6, PG. 195

NAMES: WILLIAM GOLDEN TO MARGARET SMITH
DATE: APR. 14, 1835
BONDSMAN: WM. SMITH
REFERENCE: O.A.

NAMES: HENRY GRAVES TO JANE DAMEWOOD
DATE: SEPT. 12, 1835
BONDSMAN: JNO. GRAVES
REFERENCE: C.A; T.H.M. VOL. 6, PG. 195

NAMES: BENJAMIN GRIFFIN TO SARAH CULSON
DATE: NOV. 17,
REFERENCE: T.H.M. VOL. 6, PG. 195

NAMES: WM. D. GRILL TO HULDY JULIAN
DATE: APR. 1, 1835
DATE PER: APR. 2, 1835
BY: JACOB NUTTY, M.G.
REFERENCE: C.A; O.M.R. PG. 187

NAMES: LARKIN HAIR TO CYNTHIA MILLER
DATE: SEPT. 1, 1835
BONDSMAN: ADAM FORMWALT
DATE PER: SEPT. 4, 1835
BY: JOHN PRYOR
REFERENCE: C.A; O.M.R. PG. 190; T.H.M. VOL. 6, PG. 195

NAMES: ARON HARBISON TO DICY ADKINS
DATE: MAY 30, 1835 - DATE PER: JUNE 4, 1835
BY: JOHN MYNATT, J.P.
REFERENCE: O.A; O.M.R. PG. 189; T.H.M. VOL. 6, PG. 195

NAMES: GIDEON M. HAZEN TO MARY STRONG
DATE: MAR. 19, 1835
DATE PER: MAR. 19, 1835
BY: THO. H. NELSON
REFERENCE: O.M.R. PG. 186

NAMES: THOS. HENDERSON TO ELIZA JANE GIFFEN
DATE: DEC. 8, 1835
DATE PER: DEC. 8, 1835
BY: RICHARD KEYHILL, J.P.
REFERENCE: O.M.R. PG. 193

NAMES: ALBRED (?) E. HILL TO ELIZABETH CROZIER (OR CROSS)
DATE: APR. 11, 1835
BONDSMAN: JAMES PRYOR
DATE PER: APR. 16, 1835
BY: SAM'L WHITE, J.P.
REFERENCE: C.A; O.M.R. PG. 187

NAMES: WILLIAM HIXON TO MARGARET DEVAULT
DATE: SEPT. 17, 1835
DATE PER: SEPT. 23, 1835
BY: M. B. CARTER, J.P.
REFERENCE: C.A; O.M.R. PG. 191; T.H.M. VOL. 6, PG. 195

NAMES: DANIEL R. HOOD TO MARGARET L. J. SWAN
DATE: FEBY. 21, 1835
BONDSMAN: WM. P. DYER
DATE PER: FEBY. 26, 1835
BY: W. A. MCCAMPBELL, M.V.D.
REFERENCE: C.A; O.M.R. PG. 186; T.H.M. VOL. 6, PG. 195

NAMES: EPHRAIM JOHNSON TO JANE WATT
DATE: AUG. 18, 1835
BONDSMAN: JNO. DAVIS
DATE PER: AUG. 20, 1835
BY: ELI KING, J.P.
REFERENCE: C.A; O.M.R. PG. 190

NAMES: NATHAN JOHNSON TO CYNTHIA MILES
DATE: JANY. 28, 1835
BONDSMAN: JACOB RIDGE
WITNESS: GEO. W. WHITE
REFERENCE: C.A; T.H.M. VOL. 6, PG. 195

NAMES: STEPHEN JOHNSON TO MARY ANN HILLSMAN
DATE: AUG. 13, 1835
REFERENCE: T.H.M. VOL. 6, PG. 195

NAMES: WM. D. JOHNSON TO ELIZA HINTON
DATE: NOV. 20, 1835
BONDSMAN: STEPHEN JOHNSON
REFERENCE: C.A; O.M.R. PG. 192; T.H.M. VOL. 6, PG. 195

NAMES: R. D. JOUROLMAN TO MARIAH W. CARDWELL
DATE: FEBY. 26, 1835
BONDSMAN: A. G. JACKSON
DATE PER: FEBY. 26, 1835
BY: JACOB NUTTY, M.G.
REFERENCE: C.A; O.M.R. PG. 186; T.H.M. VOL. 6, PG. 195

NAMES: JOHN T. KING TO ELIZABETH WELLS
DATE: SEPT. 3, 1835
BONDSMAN: CHRISTOPHER HANBY
REFERENCE: C.A; T.H.M. VOL. 6, PG. 195

NAMES: ROBERT LUCAS TO MARY COX
DATE: SEPT. 12, 1835
BONDSMAN: EDWARD LUCAS
DATE PER: SEPT. 17, 1835
BY: LINDSAY CHILDRESS, J.P.
REFERENCE: C.A; O.M.R. PG. 191; T.H.M. VOL. 6, PG. 195

NAMES: JOHN MAJOR TO MARY GAULT
DATE: JUNE 27, 1835
BONDSMAN: WM. MAJOR
DATE PER: JULY 7, 1835
BY: JAMES CRIPPEN, J.P.
REFERENCE: C.A; O.M.R. PG. 189; T.H.M. VOL. 6, PG. 195

NAMES: WM. MANNON TO NANCY LONG
DATE: DEC. 9, 1835
BONDSMAN: JOB LONG
WITNESS: GEO. W. WHITE
REFERENCE: C.A.

NAMES: WM. MANNON TO NANCY LONG
DATE: DEC. 9, 1835
DATE PER: DEC. 10, 1835
BY: ELI KING, J.P.
REFERENCE: O.M.R. PG. 193; T.H.M. VOL. 6, PG. 196

NAMES: WM. A. MARLEY TO NANCY GAMBLE
DATE: JULY 16, 1835
BONDSMAN: JNO. HAGARD
REFERENCE: C.A; T.H.M. VOL. 6, PG. 196

NAMES: JNO. MAXWELL TO LEVINA MOORE
DATE: DEC. 10, 1835
BONDSMAN: ALLEN ANDERSON
DATE PER: DEC. 12, 1835
BY: R. H. SNIDDY, M.G.
REFERENCE: C.A; O.M.R. PG. 193; T.H.M. VOL. 6, PG. 196

NAMES: DUNCAN MCCALL TO MARY HICKEY
DATE: JUNE 20, 1835
BONDSMAN: CHAS. M. MURRAY
DATE PER: JUNE 21, 1835
BY: JAS. D. MURRAY, J.P.
REFERENCE: C.A; O.M.R. PG. 189; T.H.M. VOL. 6, PG. 195

NAMES: DANIEL MCCOLLUM TO MARY AYERS
DATE: DEC. 30, 1835
BONDSMAN: THOS. F. CALLOWAY
DATE PER: DEC. 31, 1835
BY: MORDECAI YARNELL, J.P.
REFERENCE: C.A; O.M.R. PG. 194; T.H.M. VOL. 6, PG. 195

NAMES: WM. MCCULLOUGH TO ELIZA R. GROUNDS (OR GOUNDS)
DATE: APR. 6, 1835
DATE PER: APR. 16, 1835
BY: GEO. RUSSELL
REFERENCE: C.A; O.M.R. PG. 187

NAMES: JACKSON MCMILLAN TO AVERY CATES
DATE: SEPT. 26, 1835
BONDSMAN: ROBERT TALLEY
DATE PER: OCT. 22, 1835
BY: ELI KING, J.P.
REFERENCE: C.A; O.M.R. PG. 191; T.H.M. VOL. 6, PG. 195

NAMES: C. A. MCPHETRIDGE TO ELIZA LEVY (OR SEAY)
DATE: MAR. 11, 1835
BONDSMAN: JOHN BOYD
DATE PER: MAR. 16, 1835
BY: JOHN PRYOR
REFERENCE: C.A; O.M.R. PG. 186; T.H.M. VOL. 6, PG. 195

NAMES: ADAM C. MEEK TO SARAH L. DOUGLASS
DATE: DEC. 1, 1835
BONDSMAN: ISAAC M. MCBEE
DATE PER: DEC. 3, 1835
BY: JAMES H. GASS, M.G.
REFERENCE: C.A; O.M.R. PG. 193; T.H.M. VOL. 6, PG. 196

NAMES: WM. MILTEBARGER TO SARAH FOUST
DATE: JANY. 6, 1835
BONDSMAN: HENRY GRAVES
REFERENCE: C.A; T.H.M. VOL. 6, PG. 196

NAMES: PRESTON MINTON TO ELIZABETH MCALLISTER
DATE: MAR. 28, 1835
BONDSMAN: ISAAC BUFALO
REFERENCE: C.A; T.H.M. VOL. 6, PG. 196

NAMES: JOSHUA E. MONDAY TO SARAH E. LITTLE
DATE: JANY. 27, 1835
BONDSMAN: JO. L. LITTLE
WITNESS: GEO. W. WHITE
REFERENCE: C.A; T.H.M. VOL. 6, PG. 196

NAMES: WM. MORRISON TO NANCY LONG
DATE: DEC. 9, 1835
DATE PER: DEC. 10, 1835
BY: ELI KING, J.P.
REFERENCE: C.A.

NAMES: DAVID S. MOURFIELD TO REBECKAH LUCY
DATE: AUG. 10, 1835
BONDSMAN: NICHOLAS BARGER
REFERENCE: C.A; T.H.M. VOL. 6, PG. 196

NAMES: JACKSON MOWERY TO LEAH COFFMAN (OR COFFIN)
DATE: AUG. 7, 1835
BONDSMAN: JAMES M. CARTER
REFERENCE: C.A; T.H.M. VOL. 6, PG. 196

NAMES: A. J. D. MURPHY TO REBECKA FORD
DATE: FEBY. 9, 1835
BONDSMAN: ABNER DYKES
DATE PER: FEBY. 10, 1835
BY: LEWIS JONES, T. E.
REFERENCE: C.A; O.M.R. PG. 186; T.H.M. VOL. 6, PG. 196

NAMES: JOSEPH MYNATT TO MINERVA TINDELL
DATE: JANY. 5, 1835
BONDSMAN: HENRY G. ROBERTS
DATE PER: JANY. 9, 1835
BY: JOSEPH MEEK, J.P.
REFERENCE: C.A; O.M.R. PG. 185; T.H.M. VOL. 6, PG. 196

NAMES: RUFUS M. MYNATT TO ELIZABETH HILLSMAN
DATE: JUNE 2, 1835.
BONDSMAN: MAT. HILLSMAN
DATE PER: JUNE 2, 1835
BY: SAM'L. LOVE, M.G.
REFERENCE: C.A; O.M.R. PG. 189; T.H.M. VOL. 6, PG. 196

NAMES: LEONARD C. NANCE TO NANCY TIPTON
DATE: JANY. 20, 1835
BONDSMAN: W. W. CRAWFORD
DATE PER: JANY. 20, 1835
BY: ELIJAH JOHNSON, J.P.
REFERENCE: C.A; O.M.R. PG. 185; T.H.M. VOL. 6, PG. 196

NAMES : THOS. D. PARHAM TO CATHARINE RUDDER
DATE: SEPT. 24, 1835
BONDSMAN: THOS. MITCHELL
REFERENCE: C.A.

NAMES: THOS. D. PARHEM TO CATHARINE RUDDER
DATE: SEPT. 24, 1835
BY: W. LYON, J.P.
REFERENCE: O.M.R. PG. 191; T.H.M. VOL. 6, PG. 196

NAMES: JNO. PERRY TO ALVIRA MADERIS
DATE: AUG. 3, 1835
BONDSMAN: HALL L. WILKERSON
DATE PER: AUG. 1835
BY: J. M. KELLEY, M.G.
REFERENCE: C.A; O.M.R. PG. 190; T.H.M. VOL. 6, PG. 196

NAMES: ROBT. PERRY TO MARGARET M. CAMPBELL (OR MCCAMPBELL)
DATE: OCT. 2, 1835
BONDSMAN: JAMES CAMPBELL
DATE PER: OCT. 2, 1835
BY: GEO. RUSSELL, M.G.
REFERENCE: C.A; O.M.R. PG. 192; T.H.M. VOL. 6, PG. 196

NAMES: JOHN PICKETT TO MARTHA H. HOWELL
DATE: JUNE 25, 1835
BONDSMAN: SAM'L. R. RODGERS
REFERENCE: C.A; T.H.M. VOL. 6, PG. 196

NAMES: JAMES PRIOR TO LUCY CRUSE
DATE: JULY 30, 1835
BONDSMAN: JACOB KENNEDY & WM. PRIOR
REFERENCE: C.A; O.M.R. PG. 189; T.H.M. VOL. 6, PG. 196

NAMES: JOHN PRYOR TO ANN L. TRIGG
DATE: JULY 7, 1835
BONDSMAN: L. S. MARSHALL
DATE PER: NOV. 26, 1835
BY: W. PATTON, M. G.
REFERENCE: C.A; O.M.R. PG. 189; T.H.M. VOL. 6, PG. 196

NAMES: SAMUEL B. RALSTON TO ELIZABETH HARMON (OR HANNA)
DATE: APR. 21, 1835
BONDSMAN: ROBT. B. REYNOLDS
DATE PER: APR. 24, 1835
BY: THO. H. NELSON
REFERENCE: C.A; O.M.R. PG. 187; T.H.M. VOL. 6, PG. 196

NAMES: JACOB REED TO ELIZABETH MCCALL
DATE: DEC. 9, 1835
BONDSMAN: ROBT. REED
DATE PER: DEC. 17, 1835
BY: SAM'L. WHITE, J.P.
REFERENCE: C.A; O.M.R. PG. 193; T.H.M. VOL. 6, PG. 196

NAMES: THOMAS REEDER TO MALVINA GROVES
DATE: APR. 11, 1835
BONDSMAN: JAMES REEDER
DATE PER: APR. 16, 1835
BY: JAS. KENNERS, M.G.
REFERENCE: C.A; O.M.R. PG. 187

NAMES: JOHN P. RUSSELL TO MARY ANN SMITH
DATE: MAY 14, 1835
BONDSMAN: S. D. W. LOW
DATE PER: MAY 21, 1835
BY: GEO. RUSSELL, M.G.
REFERENCE: C.A; O.M.R. PG. 188; T.H.M. VOL. 6, PG. 196

NAMES: CLARK SARTIN TO SARAH ANDERSON
DATE: MAY 7, 1835
BONDSMAN: JNO. RHEA
REFERENCE: C.A; T.H.M. VOL. 6, PG. 196

NAMES: JOSIAH SCRUGGINS TO MARTHA HARVEY
DATE: SEPT. 20, 1835
BONDSMAN: JOHN R. HARVEY
WITNESS: GEO. M. WHITE
REFERENCE: C.A; T.H.M. VOL. 6, PG. 196

NAMES: GEORGE SHANABERRY TO RACHEL ADAIR
DATE: DEC. 19, 1835
BONDSMAN: S. H. LOVE
DATE PER: DEC. 24, 1835
BY: G. S. WHITE, M.G.
REFERENCE: C.A; O.M.R. PG. 193

NAMES: WM. SHERERTZ TO SARAH MILLER
DATE: DEC. 31, 1835
BONDSMAN: DAVID BENNETT
DATE PER: DEC. 31, 1835
BY: G. S. WHITE, M.G.
WITNESS: GEO. W. WHITE
REFERENCE: C.A; O.M.R. PG. 194; T.H.M. VOL. 6, PG. 196

NAMES: WM. SIMPSON TO JANE W. DAVIS
DATE: FEBY. 3, 1835
BONDSMAN: THOS. H. WALKER
DATE PER: FEBY. 3, 1835
BY: ROBT. H. SNODDY, M.G.
REFERENCE: C.A; O.M.R. PG. 185; T.H.M. VOL. 6, PG. 196

NAMES: JNO. W. SINGLETON TO FANNY BADGETT
DATE: MAY 19, 1835
BONDSMAN: WM. PRYOR
DATE PER: MAY 19, 1835
BY: MICHAEL DAVIS, J.P.
REFERENCE: C.A; O.M.R. PG. 188; T.H.M. VOL. 6, PG. 196

NAMES: WILLIAM SMEDLEY TO LOUISA WHITEMAN
DATE: OCT. 1, 1835
BONDSMAN: JAMES CALDWELL
DATE PER: OCT. 1, 1835
BY: ISAAC LEWIS
REFERENCE: C.A; O.M.R. PG. 192

NAMES: JAMES H. SMITH TO SUSAN MAJORS
DATE: OCT. 1, 1835
BONDSMAN: WM. D. F. SMITH
DATE PER: OCT. 1, 1835
BY: THOS. FRAZIER, J.P.
REFERENCE: C.A; O.M.R. PG. 192; T.H.M. VOL. 6, PG. 196

NAMES: JESSE R. SMITH TO REBECKA BOND
DATE: DEC. 30, 1835
BONDSMAN: HIRAM MILLER
DATE PER: DEC. 31, 1835
BY: WM. RODGERS, J.P.
WITNESS: GEO. M. WHITE
REFERENCE: C.A; O.M.R. PG. 194; T.H.M. VOL. 6, PG. 196

NAMES: JOHN H. SMITH TO CATHARINE LOW
DATE: MAR. 23, 1835
BONDSMAN: JNO. F. RUSSELL
REFERENCE: C.A; T.H.M. VOL. 6, PG. 196

NAMES: ROBERT SMITH TO ANNY ELKINS
DATE: APR. 6, 1835
DATE PER: APR. 7, 1835
BY: ISAAC BAYLESS, J.P.
REFERENCE: C.A; O.M.R. PG. 187

NAMES: WM. H. SMITH TO MARTHA L. ANDERSON
DATE: DEC. 30, 1835
BONDSMAN: JAMES ANDERSON
DATE PER: DEC. 31, 1835 - BY: G. S. WHITE, M.G.
REFERENCE: C.A; O.M.R. PG. 194; T.H.M. VOL. 6, PG. 196

NAMES: NICHOLAS TROUT TO PHOEBY QUALS
DATE: MAR. 2, 1835
BONDSMAN: WM. RUTHERFORD
REFERENCE: C.A.

NAMES: ARCHIBALD WALDROP TO CHANEY ARNOLD
DATE: SEPT. 17, 1835
BONDSMAN: JAMES S. BOYD
DATE PER: SEPT. 17, 1835
BY: ROBT. H. SNODDY
REFERENCE: C.A; O.M.R. PG. 191

NAMES: SAM'L. K. WALKER TO SARAH NAVE
DATE: APR. 25, 1835
BONDSMAN: HARVEY WALKER
DATE PER: MAY 7, 1835
BY: WM. RODGERS, J.P.
REFERENCE: C.A; O.M.R. PG. 188

NAMES: FRANCIS WALSH TO ELLEN CALVERTT
DATE: AUG. 28, 1835
BONDSMAN: FREDERICK BARGER
WITNESS: GEO. M. WHITE
REFERENCE: C.A; T.H.M. VOL. 6, PG. 196

NAMES: REUBEN WEBB TO JANE BAKER
DATE: APR. 23, 1835
BONDSMAN: THOS. H. DAVENPORT
DATE PER: APR. 23, 1835
BY: JOHN RUSSOM, M.G.
REFERENCE: C.A; O.M.R. PG. 188

NAMES: CASPER WEBBER TO KISSY ISRAEL
DATE: JUNE 17, 1835
DATE PER: JUNE 17, 1835
BY: JNO. MYNATT
REFERENCE: C.A; O.M.R. PG. 189

NAMES: SANDERS WEBSTER TO SARAH STAUNTON
DATE: SEPT. 5, 1835
BONDSMAN: ISAIAH WILSON
REFERENCE: C.A; T.H.M. VOL. 6, PG. 196

NAMES: JESSE WELLS TO MATILDA PARKER
DATE: AUG. 25, 1835
BONDSMAN: NATHANIEL PARKER
DATE PER: AUG. 25, 1835
BY: I. LEWIS
REFERENCE: C.A; O.M.R. PG. 190

Names: Hall L. Wilkerson to Elizabeth Conner
Date: Sept. 25, 1835
Bondsman: Sam'l. R. Rodgers
Reference: C.A.

Names: Samuel Wilkes to Martha Jane Smith
Date: Dec. 23, 1835
Bondsman: M. Clibourne
Date Per: Dec. 1835
By: Sam'l. Love, M.G.
Reference: C.A; O.M.R. Pg. 193

Names: Joseph Williams to Elizabeth McCloud
Date: Sept. 20, 1835
Bondsman: John Seabolt
Date Per: Sept. 22, 1835
By: Wm. Lindsay, J.P.
Witness: Geo. M. White
Reference: C.A; O.M.R. Pg. 191

Names: David S. Wills to Sarah Lovelace
Date: Jany. 16, 1835
Bondsman: Andrew McMillan
Date Per: Feby. 3, 1835
By: M. B. Carter, J.P.
Reference: C.A; O.M.R. Pg. 185

Names: Tobias Wyner to Mirna Horner
Date: Dec. 2, 1835
Bondsman: Washington Brannum
Reference: C.A.

Names: Henry J. Yarnell to Ellen Murray
Date: Dec. 10, 1835
Bondsman: Wm. Dunlap
Reference: C. A.

Names: Lewis C. Yarnell to Catharine Julian
Date: Feby. 11, 1835
Date Per: Feby. 19, 1835
By: Mordecai Yarnell, J.P.
Reference: C.A; O.M.R. Pg. 186

Names: Andrew Yost to Margaret McKinley
Date: Sept. 15, 1835
Bondsman: Henry Lonas
Date Per: Sept. 17, 1835
By: Tho. H. Nelson
Reference: C.A; O.M.R. Pg. 191

1836

Names: Alexander Adair to Sarah A. M. C. Thompson
Date: Feby. 1, 1836
Bondsman: Lewis Foust
Date Per: Feby. 4, 1836
By: G. S. White, M.G.
Reference: C.A; O.M.R. Pg. 195; T.H.M. Vol. 6, Pg. 196

Names: Joseph Ayres to Lotty Shelton
Date: Aug. 23, 1836
Date Per: Aug. 25, 1836
By: James C. England
Reference: C.A; O.M.R. Pg. 201; T.H.M. Vol. 6, Pg. 196

Names: Robert Bell to Mary Wood
Date: Jany. 12, 1836
Bondsman: Alfred Wood
Date Per: Jany. 20, 1836
By: Tandy Monday, J.P.
Reference: C.A; O.M.R. Pg. 195; T.H.M. Vol. 6, Pg. 196

Names: Alexander Blaine to Mary Childress
Date: Aug. 27, 1836
Bondsman: Chas. P. Chapman
Date Per: Aug. 27, 1836
By: G. S. White, M.G.
Reference: C.A; O.M.R. Pg. 201

Names: P. L. Blanc to Sarah Ann Bell
Date: Jany. 8, 1836
Bondsman: Adam Formwalt
Date Per: Jany. 8, 1836
By: J. Nutty, M.G.
Reference: C.A; O.M.R. Pg. 194; T.H.M. Vol. 6, Pg. 196

Names: Lea Branham to During Lingo
Date: Dec. 22, 1836
Bondsman: Yearly Thompson
Reference: C.A.

Names: James Brittingham to Louisa Boyer
Date: Nov. 21, 1836
Bondsman: Sims Crawford
Reference: C.A; T.H.M. Vol. 6, Pg. 196

Names: Peter Buckhart to Anna Gillum
Date: Aug. 10, 1836
Bondsman: Thos. Frazier
Date Per: Aug. 14, 1836
By: Jno. Mynatt, J.P.
Reference: C.A; O.M.R. Pg. 200; T.H.M. Vol. 6, Pg. 196

Names: Martin Byerley to Polly Roop
Date: Nov. 19, 1836
Bondsman: Wm. Watkins
Date Per: Dec. 6, 1836
By: Jas. Rodgers, J.P.
Reference: C.A; O.M.R. Pg. 204

Names: Nathaniel Byrd to Mary Lea
Date: Nov. 7,
Reference: T.H.M. Vol. 6, Pg. 196

Names: Wm. Cole to Mathiah Ashley
Date: Apr. 2, 1836
Bondsman: Wm. Mourfield
Witness: Geo. M. White
Reference: C.A.

Names: Joseph Cheatham to Nancy Hines
Date: Aug. 10, 1836
Bondsman: D. F. Dearmond
Date Per: Aug. 16, 1836
By: J. Johnson, J.P.
Reference: C.A; O.M.R. Pg. 201

Names: Nathaniel Chesney to Sally Rodgers
Date: Dec. 16, 1836
Bondsman: Jno. Seabolt
Date Per: Dec. 20, 1836
By: Thos. Annwood, J.P.
Witness: M. M. Swan
Reference: C.A; O.M.R. Pg. 205

Names: Geo. W. Churchwell to Sophia N. Park
Date: Sept. 14, 1836
Bondsman: And. R. Humes
Reference: C.A.

Names: Geo. W. Churchwell to Sophia M. Park
Date: Sept. 14, 1836
Date Per: Sept. 15, 1836
By: Tho. H. Nelson
Reference: O.M.R. Pg. 202

Names: Wm. J. Clark to Mary S. Ralston
Date: June 2, 1836
Date Per: June 2, 1836
By: J. D. Bennett, J.P.
Reference: C.A; O.M.R. Pg. 199

Names: Geo. Clouse to Nancy McInterf
Date: Dec. 29, 1836
Bondsman: Jesse Sherrod
Reference: C.A; T.H.M. Vol. 6, Pg. 196

Names: Jno. P. Coker to Bertha (or Rutha) Caldwell
Date: June 16, 1836
Bondsman: Leonard Coker
Date Per: June 16, 1836
By: Jas. D. Murray, J.P.
Reference: C.A; O.M.R. Pg. 199

Names: John Cole to Lucy Parker
Date: June 23, 1836
Bondsman: Joseph Parker
Date Per: June 23, 1836
By: B. McNutt, J.P.
Reference: C.A; O.M.R. Pg. 199

Names: James M. Conley to Nancy Coker
Date: July 21, 1836
Date Per: July 21, 1836
By: R. H. Lindsay, M.G.
Reference: C.A; O.M.R. Pg. 200

Names: James Conway to Jane Nipper
Date: Mar. 13, 1836
Date Per: Mar. 22, 1836
By: Eli King, J.P.
Reference: C.A; O.M.R. Pg. 196

Names: Joseph Cooper to Beth (or Elizabeth) Chiles
Date: Oct. 27, 1836
Date Per: Oct. 27, 1836
By: Wm. Lindsay, J.P.
Reference: C.A; O.M.R. Pg. 203

Names: Gilbert C. Craig to Eliza Swan
Date: Mar. 1, 1836
Bondsman: Robt. Carns
Reference: C. A.

Names: Thos. Craig to Susan Graves
Date: Sept. 28, 1836
Bondsman: Nathaniel Byrd
Date Per: Sept. 29, 1836
By: Duerrett Everett, Esq.
Witness: Geo. M. White
Reference: C.A; O.M.R. Pg. 202

Names: Henry Crawford to Betsy Hickson
Date: Nov. 9, 1836
Date Per: Nov. 10, 1836
By: Martin L. Mynatt, J.P.
Reference: C.A; O.M.R. Pg. 203

Names: Archibald Crews to Margaret Brown
Date: Feby. 8, 1836
Bondsman: A. J. Brown
Date Per: Feby. 8, 1836
By: Richard Keyhill, J.P.
Reference: C.A; O.M.R. Pg. 195

Names: Jno. Cunningham to Mary Ann Wilson
Date: Apr. 30, 1836
Date Per: May 30, 1836
By: T. G. Craighead, J.P.
Reference: C.A; O.M.R. Pg. 198

Names: Ephraim Daniel to Polly Wright
Date: Mar. 12, 1836
Date Per: Mar. 12, 1836
By: Richard Keyhill, J.P.
Reference: C.A; O.M.R. Pg. 196

Names: Jno. M. D'Efriese to Sarah Parmer
Date: Sept. 28, 1836
Date Per: Sept. 29, 1836
By: D. Everett, Esq.
Reference: C.A; O.M.R. Pg. 203

Names: Henry Dick to Rebecca McMond
Date: Nov. 10, 1836
Bondsman: Hugh L. Brown
Date Per: Nov. 10, 1836
By: Eli King, J.P.
Reference: C.A; O.M.R. Pg. 204

Names: Jno. Douglass to Margaret King
Date: Apr. 5, 1836
Date Per: Apr. 7, 1836
By: James H. Gass, M.G.
Reference: C.A; O.M.R. Pg. 197

Names: Francis N. B. Dudley to Polly Murphy
Date: Dec. 16, 1836
Bondsman: Wm. F. Edmonds
Date Per: Dec. 27, 1836
Reference: C.A; O.M.R. Pg. 205 (R.H.F. Moss(?) M.G.)

Names: Wm. Dunn to Sarah Cummings
Date: Jany. 5, 1836
Bondsman: Geo. Cheata
Reference: C.A; T.H.M. Vol. 6, Pg. 196

Names: John C. Elikson to Polly Watts
Date: Aug. 29, 1836
Bondsman: Wm. C. Barnes
Reference: C.A; T.H.M. Vol. 6, Pg. 196

Names: Wm. Elliott to Lucinda R. Landrum
Date: June 19, 1836
Bondsman: Thos. M. Landrum
Reference: C.A.

Names: Wm. Elliott to Lucinda R. Landrum
Date: June 19, 1836
Date Per: June 19, 1836
By: Jas. D. Murray, J.P.
Reference: O.M.R. Pg. 199; T.H.M. Vol. 6, Pg. 196

Names: Joseph Elsey to Eliza Simpson
Date: Mar. 12, 1836
Reference: C.A.

Names: Joseph Elsey to Eliza Simpson
Date: Mar. 12, 1836
Date Per: Mar. 13, 1836
Reference: O.M.R. Pg. 196; T.H.M. Vol. 6, Pg. 196

Names: Enisley (or Ensley) Fisher to Sarah McNutt
Date: Feby. 25, 1836
Bondsman: W. M. Bounds
Date Per: Feby. 25, 1836
By: B. McNutt, J.P.
Witness: Geo. M. White
Reference: C.A; O.M.R. Pg. 196; T.H.M. Vol. 6, Pg. 196

Names: George Fisher to Eliza Cable
Date: July 22, 1836
Reference: T.H.M. Vol. 6, Pg. 196

Names: Geo. W. Fitzgerald to Betsy Proctor
Date: Apr. 29, 1836
Bondsman: Jno. Fitzgerald
Date Per: May 5, 1836
By: M. L. Mynatt, J.P.
Witness: Geo. M. White
Reference: C.A; O.M.R. Pg. 198; T.H.M. Vol. 6, Pg. 196

NAMES: DAVID FORTNER TO MELINDA BARNES
DATE: AUG. 27, 1836
REFERENCE: T.H.M. VOL. 6, PG. 196

NAMES: JOHN FORTNER TO ELIZABETH RUTHERFORD
DATE: APR. 21, 1836
BONDSMAN: WM. McDOWEL
REFERENCE: C.A.

NAMES: HENRY FOUST TO CARRY HASHBARGER
DATE: FEBY. 29, 1836
BONDSMAN: P. H. SKAGGS
REFERENCE: C.A.

NAMES: JOHN FOUST TO JUDY SHINBERRY
DATE: AUG. 31, 1836
DATE PER: SEPT. 1, 1836
BY: G. S. WHITE, M.G.
REFERENCE: C.A; O.M.R. PG. 201; T.H.M. VOL. 6, PG. 196

NAMES: GEO. FRAKER TO ELIZA GRAYBILL
DATE: JULY 22, 1836
DATE PER: JULY 24, 1836
BY: JOHN MYNATT, J.P.
REFERENCE: C.A; O.M.R. PG. 200

NAMES: SAMUEL FRANKLIN TO LIVIA RUDDER
DATE: JULY 21, 1836
BONDSMAN: SIMS CRAWFORD
DATE PER: JULY 21, 1836
BY: J. D. BENNETT, J.P.
REFERENCE: C.A; O.M.R. PG. 200

NAMES: ISAAC FRITS TO FRANKY FORTNER
DATE: APR. 11,
REFERENCE: T.H.M. VOL. 6, PG. 196

NAMES: WM. GALLAHER TO MARY KING
DATE: AUG. 15, 1836
BONDSMAN: E. S. TEMPLE
REFERENCE: C.A.

NAMES: REUBEN GARRETT TO SUSAN ATKINS
DATE: AUG. 12, 1836
DATE PER: AUG. 28, 1836
BY: M. L. MYNATT, J.P.
REFERENCE: C.A; O.M.R. PG. 201

NAMES: JNO. GIBBS TO SUSANNAH GEORGE
DATE: JULY 30, 1836
BONDSMAN: A. G. JACKSON
BY: JOSEPH MEEK, J.P.
REFERENCE: C.A; O.M.R. PG. 200

NAMES: NICHOLAS GIBBS TO ELIZABETH PARKER
DATE: MAR. 22, 1836
DATE PER: MAR. 31, 1836
BY: LEWIS LUTTRELL, J.P.
REFERENCE: C.A; O.M.R. PG. 197

NAMES: MARK GILLISPY TO ELIZA JANE SIMPSON
DATE: JULY 11, 1836
BONDSMAN: ALEXANDER SIMPSON
DATE PER: JULY 14, 1836
BY: DUERETT EVERETT, J.P.
REFERENCE: C.A; O.M.R. PG. 200; T.H.M. VOL. 6, PG. 196

NAMES: WILLIAM GUNN (OR GUINN) TO SARAH HOOD
DATE: SEPT. 19, 1836
DATE PER: SEPT. 19, 1836
BY: WM. BALLUE, M.G.
REFERENCE: C.A; O.M.R. PG. 202

NAMES: CLINTON HAINES TO MARGARET HENRY
DATE: FEB. 1,
REFERENCE: T.H.M. VOL. 6, PG. 196

NAMES: MAJOR L. HALL TO ADALINE McCAMPBELL
DATE: JANY. 28, 1836
BONDSMAN: WIATT HALL
DATE PER: FEBY. 4, 1836
BY: G. S. WHITE, M.G.
REFERENCE: C.A; O.M.R. PG. 195; T.H.M. VOL. 6, PG. 196

NAMES: ABRAHAM HANKINS TO ANNA SHERROD
DATE: MAY 300, 1836
BONDSMAN: ELI HANKINS
DATE PER: MAY 30, 1836
BY: HENRY GRAVES, J.P.
REFERENCE: C.A; O.M.R. PG. 198; T.H.M. VOL. 6, PG. 197

NAMES: CALVIN B. HANSARD TO HANNAH AILOR
DATE: SEPT. 8, 1836
BONDSMAN: JNO. CHUMLEA
DATE PER: SEPT. 13, 1836
BY: HENRY GRAVES, J.P.
REFERENCE: C.A; O.M.R. PG. 202; T.H.M. VOL. 6, PG. 197

NAMES: JACOB HARRIS TO ELIZABETH MYNATT
DATE: NOV. 25, 1836
BONDSMAN: L. P. ROBERTS
DATE PER: NOV. 29, 1836
BY: G. S. WHITE, M.G.
REFERENCE: C.A; O.M.R. PG. 204; T.H.M. VOL. 6, PG. 197

NAMES: BENJ. HARTLEY TO ELIZABETH KIRKPATRICK
DATE: SEPT. 1, 1836
DATE PER: SEPT. 15, 1836
BY: P. C. I. HALL, J.P.
REFERENCE: C.A; C.M.R. PG. 202

NAMES: ISAAC HEDRICK TO LYDIA LANE
DATE: MAR. 26, 1836
BONDSMAN: JOHN FINGER
WITNESS: GEO. M. WHITE
REFERENCE: C.A.

NAMES: THOMAS HENDERSON TO JANE GIFFEN
DATE: DEC. 8, 1836
DATE PER: DEC. 8, 1836
BY: RICHARD KEYHILL, J.P.
REFERENCE: C.A; C.M.R. PG. 204

NAMES: JAMES E. HICKS TO NANCY HARRALSON
DATE: JANY. 2, 1836
DATE PER: JANY. 3, 1836
BY: LINDSAY CHILDRESS, J.P.
REFERENCE: C.A; C.M.R. PG. 194

NAMES: ISAAC HINDS, JR. TO CYNTHIA ANN HOUSEHOLDER
DATE: FEBY. 19, 1836
DATE PER: FEBY. 19, 1836
BY: J. JOHNSON, J.P.
REFERENCE: C.A; C.M.R. PG. 196

NAMES: PAYTON HOOD TO CATHERINE DAVIS
DATE: JULY 4,
REFERENCE: T.H.M. VOL. 6, PG. 197

NAMES: CHRISTIAN HOUSELY TO RACHEL MILLER
DATE: DEC. 16, 1836
DATE PER: DEC. 22, 1836
BY: HENRY GRAVES, J.P.
REFERENCE: C.A; C.M.R. 205

NAMES: GEO. HUFFAKER, JR. TO MARY LONES
DATE: FEBY. 10, 1836
DATE PER: FEBY. 11, 1836
BY: J. JOHNSON, J.P.
REFERENCE: C.A; C.M.R. PG. 195; T.H.M. VOL. 6, PG. 197

NAMES: ROBERT HUNTER TO JANE THOMPSON
DATE: MAR. 26, 1836
DATE PER: MAR. 31, 1836
BY: M. B. CARTER, J.P.
REFERENCE: C.A; C.M.R. PG. 197; T.H.M. VOL. 6, PG. 197

NAMES: JEFFERSON JETT TO SARAH WEBB
DATE: MAY 28, 1836
DATE PER: MAY 29, 1836
BY: JAS. D. MURRAY, J.P.
REFERENCE: C.A; C.M.R. PG. 198; T.H.M. VOL. 6, PG. 197

NAMES: SOLOMON (OR LABOURN) JOHNSON TO ANN BROWN
DATE: JANY. 20, 1836
DATE PER: JANY. 21, 1836
BY: RICHARD KEYHILL, J.P.
REFERENCE: C.A; C.M.R. PG. 195; T.H.M. VOL. 6, PG. 197

NAMES: STEPHEN JOHNSON TO NANCY HILLSMAN
DATE: JUNE 19, 1836
BONDSMAN: RICHARD KEYHILL
DATE PER: JUNE 19, 1836
BY: RICH'D KEYHILL, J.P.
REFERENCE: C.A; C.M.R. PG. 199; T.H.M. VOL. 6, PG. 197

NAMES: GEO. W. JONES TO ELIZABETH WALKER
DATE: SEPT. 28, 1836
DATE PER: SEPT. 29, 1836
REFERENCE: C.A; C.M.R. PG. 203

NAMES: JOHN JONES TO MATILDA HALL (OR HOLT)
DATE: FEBY. 15, 1836
DATE PER: FEBY. 16, 1836
BY: SAM'L. DICKEY, J.P.
REFERENCE: C.A; C.M.R. PG. 195; T.H.M. VOL. 6, PG. 197

NAMES: JOHN JONES TO NANCY BUCKHART
DATE: NOV. 7,
REFERENCE: T.H.M. VOL. 6, PG. 197

NAMES: JOHN JONES TO VINEY WILHITE
DATE: NOV. 7, 1836
DATE PER: DEC. 22, 1836
BY: J. JOHNSON, J.P.
REFERENCE: C.A; C.M.R. PG. 203

NAMES: BENJ. KING TO PRISCY CATES
DATE: FEBY. 29, 1836
BONDSMAN: JAMES UNDERWOOD
DATE PER: MAR. 10, 1836
BY: ELI KING, J.P.
REFERENCE: C.A; C.M.R. PG. 196; T.H.M. VOL. 6, PG. 197

NAMES: ROBERT KIRKPATRICK TO MELINDA HARTLEY
DATE: NOV. 4,
REFERENCE: T.H.M. VOL. 6, PG. 197

NAMES: JACOB LACEY TO CATHERINE BOYD
DATE: AUG. 4, 1836 (OR 1833 ?)
REFERENCE: T.H.M. VOL. 6, PG. 197

NAMES: HENRY LAMAR TO ELIZA ANN KENNEDY
DATE: AUG. 12, 1836
DATE PER: AUG. 18, 1836
BY: JAMES H. GASS, M.G:
REFERENCE: O.M.R. PG. 201; T.H.M. VOL. 6, PG. 197

NAMES: DUNCAN LEA TO OLIVIA NANCE
DATE: FEBY. 13, 1837
BONDSMAN: GEORGE WRIGHT
WITNESS: M. M. SWAN
REFERENCE: C.A.

NAMES: JOHN LEA TO REBECCA COATS
DATE: JULY 30, 1836
BONDSMAN: WM. CLARK
WITNESS: M. M. SWAN
REFERENCE: C.A; T.H.M' VOL. 6, PG. 197

NAMES: WM. LEDGERWOOD TO AILCY KARNS
DATE: JULY 15, 1836
BONDSMAN: M. M. GAINES
DATE PER: JULY 20, 1836
BY: HENRY GRAVES, J.P.
REFERENCE: C.A; O.M.R. PG. 200

NAMES: WM. LETHCO TO MALINDA STOUT
DATE: JUNE 20, 1836
DATE PER: JUNE 21, 1836
BY: WM. RODGERS, J.P.
REFERENCE: C.A; O.M.R. PG. 199; T. H.M. VOL. 6, PG. 197

NAMES: ANDREW LIKE TO SOPHIA ROBERTS
DATE: APR. 13, 1836
DATE PER: APR. 19, 1836
BY: B. McNUTT, J.P.
REFERENCE: C.A.

NAMES: ADAM LITTLE TO MARY McCAMPBELL
DATE: MAR. 16, 1836
DATE PER: MAR. 17, 1836
BY: G. S. WHITE, M.G.
REFERENCE: C.A; O.M.R. PG. 197; T.H.M. VOL. 6, PG. 197

NAMES: GEORGE W. LONES TO ELIZABETH WATKINS
DATE: SEPT. 28,
REFERENCE: T. H.M. VOL. 6, PG. 197

NAMES: HUGH F. LUTTRELL TO ELIZA BOUNDS
DATE: MAR. 7, 1836
BONDSMAN: JNO. CHUMLEA, JR.
REFERENCE: C.A.

NAMES: HUGH F. LUTTRELL TO ELIZA BOUNDS
DATE: MAR. 7, 1836
DATE PER: MAR. 9, 1836
BY: ISAAC LEWIS
REFERENCE: O.M.R. PG. 196; T.H.M. VOL. 6, PG. 195

NAMES: LEWIS LYLE TO IVY ROARK
DATE: SEPT. 7, 1836
DATE:PER: SEPT. 7, 1836
BY: JAMES RODGERS, J.P.
REFERENCE: C.A; O.M.R. PG. 202; T.H.M. VOL. 6, PG. 197

NAMES: CALVIN LYON TO BETSY DAVIS
DATE: JULY 2, 1836
BONDSMAN: HUGH JONES
REFERENCE: C.A.

NAMES: JOHN MATLOCK TO SARAH HOLOWAY
DATE: DEC. 24, 1836
REFERENCE: T.H.M. VOL. 6, PG. 197

NAMES: JOHN McCARTY TO JANE WRIGHT
DATE: SEPT. 5, 1836
DATE PER: SEPT. 5, 1836
BY: THO. H. NELSON, M.G.
REFERENCE: O.M.R. PG. 202

NAMES: JOHN McHAFFIE TO SUSAN SHERROD
DATE: MAR. 16, 1836
BONDSMAN: DAVID McHAFFIE
DATE PER: MAR. 17, 1836
BY: P.C.I. HALL, J.P.
REFERENCE: C.A; O.M.R. PG. 197; T.H.M. VOL. 6, PG. 197

NAMES: STEPHEN McLAIN TO MALINDA NESTER
DATE: DEC. 26, 1836
REFERENCE: C.A.

NAMES: STEPHEN MCLAIN TO MALINDA NESTER
DATE: DEC. 26, 1836
DATE PER: DEC. 28, 1836
BY: G. S. WHITE, M.G.
REFERENCE: O.M.R. PG. 205

NAMES: JOHN MCTWIFFS TO MARY ANN PRICE
DATE: MAR. 19, 1836
BONDSMAN: JOHN DAVIS
DATE PER: MAR. 20, 1836
BY: ELI KING, J.P.
REFERENCE: C.A; O.M.R. PG. 197; T.H.M. VOL. 6, PG. 197

NAMES: JNO. MEDLOCK TO MARIAH HOLLOWAY
DATE: DEC. 24, 1836
BONDSMAN: ISAAC MCLAIN
DATE PER: DEC. 25, 1836
BY: JNO. NESTER, ESQ.
REFERENCE: C.A; O.M.R. PG. 205

NAMES: ISAAC MICHAELS TO SALLY DAVIS
DATE: AUG. 25, 1836
REFERENCE: O.M.R. PG. 201

NAMES: PAYTON MITCHELL TO CATHARINE DAVIS
DATE: JULY 4, 1836
DATE PER: JULY 4, 1836
BY: S. H. JOHNSON, J.P.
REFERENCE: C.A; O.M.R. PG. 200

NAMES: ELIJA MOON TO MARY BEADLEY
DATE: MAY 18,
REFERENCE: T.H.M. VOL. 6, PG. 197

NAMES: JOSHUA MOON TO ISABELLA DUNN
DATE: MCH. 24,
REFERENCE: T.H.M. VOL. 6, PG. 197

NAMES: JAMES C. MOORE TO ELIZA EDDINGTON
DATE: DEC. 19, 1836
BONDSMAN: WM. GODDARD
DATE PER: DEC. 19, 1836
BY: J. T. KING, J.P.
REFERENCE: C.A; O.M.R. PG. 205; T.H.M. VOL. 6, PG. 197

NAMES: JOSHUA MOORE TO MALINDA DUNN
DATE: MAR. 24, 1836
BONDSMAN: CHAS. ROBERTS
DATE PER: MAR. 24, 1836 - BY: JOHN PRYOR
WITNESS: GEO. M. WHITE
REFERENCE: C.A; O.M.R. PG. 197; T.H.M. VOL. 6, PG. 197

NAMES: ELIJAH MORSE TO MARY BRADLY
DATE: MAY 18, 1836
BONDSMAN: WM. F. SEAY
DATE PER: MAY 19, 1836
BY: JOHN PRYOR
WITNESS: M. M. SWAN
REFERENCE: C.A; O.M.R. PG. 198; T.H.M. VOL. 6, PG. 197

NAMES: CHARLES MUNDAY TO BIDDY LIVELY
DATE: FEBY. 21, 1836
BONDSMAN: GEO. B. HOUSTON
DATE PER: FEBY. 22, 1836
BY: J. JOHNSON, J.P.
REFERENCE: C.A; O.M.R. PG. 196; T.H.M. VOL. 6, PG. 197

NAMES: ROBERT M. MURPHY TO MARY C. HARRIS
DATE: DEC. 28, 1836
BONDSMAN: SAM'L. B. BRIGGS
DATE PER: DEC. 28, 1836
BY: G. S. WHITE, M.G.
REFERENCE: C.A; O.M.R. PG. 205

NAMES: WM. A. MYNATT TO AMANDA FOUST
DATE: AUG. 29, 1836
DATE PER: SEPT. 8, 1836
BY: ISAAC CONDRAY, J.P.
REFERENCE: C.A; O.M.R. PG. 201

NAMES: CHARLES W. NELSON TO CYNTHY HALBERT
DATE: NOV. 14, 1836
BONDSMAN: JNO. M. NELSON
DATE PER: NOV. 17, 1836
BY: P.C.I. HALL, J.P.
REFERENCE: C.A; O.M.R. PG. 204; T.H.M. VOL. 6, PG. 197

NAMES: DAVID NELSON TO CHARLOTTE LONES
DATE: JANY. 6, 1836
BONDSMAN: NICHOLAS NELSON
DATE PER: JANY. 9, 1836
BY: JAS. D. MURRAY, J.P.
REFERENCE: C.A; O.M.R. PG. 194; T.H.M. VOL. 6, PG. 197

NAMES: HENRY M. NELSON TO MAHALA KIDD
DATE: MAR. 13, 1836
BONDSMAN: STEPHEN MCLAIN
DATE PER: MAR. 17, 1836
BY: SAM'L. WHITE
REFERENCE: C.A; O.M.R. PG. 197; T.H.M. VOL. 6, PG. 197

Names: James Nelson to Mary Lones
Date: Sept. 17, 1836
Date Per: Sept. 18, 1836
By: Jas. D. Murray, J.P.
Reference: C.A; O.M.R. Pg. 202; T.H.M. Vol. 6, Pg. 197

Names: Holland Osbourn to Martha Nelson
Date: Nov. 29, 1836
Bondsman: Wm. Gravitt
Date Per: Nov. 29, 1836
Reference: C.A; O.M.R. Pg. 204; T.H.M. Vol. 6, Pg. 197

Names: Christian Owsley to Rachel Miller
Date: Dec. 17, 1836
Bondsman: L. P. Roberts
Reference: C.A.

Names: William Page to Margaret Rice
Date: Oct. 3, 1836
Bondsman: Isiah Rice
Date Per: Oct. 3, 1836
By: I. Lewis
Reference: C.A; O.M.R. Pg. 203

Names: William N. Rice to Margaret Rice
Date: Oct. 5,
Reference: T.H.M. Vol. 6, Pg. 197

Names: James Perry to Elizabeth Hudson
Date: Sept. 11,
Reference: T.H.M. Vol. 6, Pg. 197

Names: Benj. Powell to Patsy Buffalow
Date: Sept. 10, 1836
Bondsman: Joel Reed
Date Per: Sept. 22, 1836
By: Jas. D. Murray, J.P.
Reference: C.A; O.M.R. Pg. 202; T.H.M. Vol. 6, Pg. 197

Names: Squire Raby to Nancy Mourfield
Date: Oct. 24, 1836
Date Per: Oct. 24, 1836 - Bondsman: Jno. Raby
By: James Rodgers, J.P.
Reference: C.A; O.M.R. Pg. 203; T.H.M. Vol. 6, Pg. 197

Names: Lloyd Riggin to Ruth Ann Israel
Date: Jany. 10, 1836
Bondsman: James Weaver
Date Per: Jany. 10, 1836 - By: Jno. Mynatt, J.P.
Witness: Geo. M. White
Reference: C.A; O.M.R. Pg. 195; T.H.M. Vol. 6, Pg. 197

Names: Charles Roberts to Charlotte Mitchell
Date: July 5, 1836
Bondsman: Geo. M. White
Reference: C.A; T.H.M. Vol. 6, Pg. 197

Names: Joel Rudder to Sarah A. Camp
Date: Apr. 6, 1896
Bondsman: Wm. Doss
Date Per: Apr. 6, 1836
By: W. Lyon, J.P.
Witness: Geo. M. White
Reference: C.A; O.M.R. Pg. 197; T.H.M. Vol. 6, Pg. 197

Names: George Rule to Mary Ann Capps
Date: Nov. 17, 1836
Bondsman: Peter Rule
Date Per: Nov. 17, 1836
By: Wm. Billue, M. G.
Reference: C.A; O.M.R. Pg. 204; T.H.M. Vol. 6, Pg. 197

Names: Houston L. Rutherford to Mary Miltisarger
Date: Nov. 12, 1836
Bondsman: Wm. Trout
Date Per: Nov. 13, 1836
By: Isaac Condray, J.P.
Reference: C.A; O.M.R. Pg. 204; T.H.M. Vol. 6, Pg. 197

Names: Westley Shannon to Susan Davis
Date: Jany. 30, 1836
Bondsman: Bartley ______ (?)
Date Per: Jany. 31, 1836
By: S. Dickey, J.P.
Reference: C.A; O.M.R. Pg. 195; T.H.M. Vol. 6, Pg. 197

Names: Elijah Shelby to Margaret Lowdermilk
Date: Jany. 20, 1836
Bondsman: Wm. Goddard
Reference: C.A; T.H.M. Vol. 6, Pg. 197

Names: Philip Sherrod to Elizabeth McMillan
Date: Dec. 20, 1836
Bondsman: Alexander McMillan
Date Per: Dec. 29, 1836
By: Eli King, J.P.
Reference: C.A; O.M.R. Pg. 205; T.H.M. Vol. 6, Pg. 197

Names: Jesse Simpson Jr. to Margaret Coker
Date: Jany. 4, 1836
Bondsman: Matthew Simpson
Date Per: Jany. 7, 1836 - By: R. H. Snoddy, M. G.
Reference: C.A; O.M.R. Pg. 194; T.H.M. Vol. 6, Pg. 197

NAMES: PRESTON H. SKAGGS TO PRICILLA W. WILSON
DATE: FEBY. 18, 1836
DATE PER: MAR. 3, 1836
BY: JOSEPH MEEK, J.P.
REFERENCE: C.A; O.M.R. PG. 196

NAMES: THOS. SLATERY TO ELIZABETH KENNEDY
DATE: NOV. 30, 1836
BONDSMAN: WM. PRYOR
REFERENCE: C.A.

NAMES: ANDREW SMITH TO SARAH RICHARDS
DATE: JANY. 8, 1836
BONDSMAN: JAMES SCOTT
DATE PER: JANY. 10, 1836
BY: JAS. CRIPPEN, J.P.
REFERENCE: C.A; O.M.R. PG. 194; T.H.M. VOL. 6, PG. 197

NAMES: JOHN SMITH TO RUTHA MURPHY
DATE: JUNE 16, 1836
BONDSMAN: JOEL COKER
DATE PER: JUNE 23, 1836
BY: JOHN T. KING, J.P.
REFERENCE: C.A; O.M.R. PG. 199; T.H.M. VOL. 6, PG. 197

NAMES: WM. H. SMITH TO MARY SMITH
DATE: SEPT. 17, 1836
BONDSMAN: ROBT. SMITH
DATE PER: SEPT. 22, 1836
BY: GEO. RUSSELL, M.G.
REFERENCE: C.A; O.M.R. PG. 202

NAMES: THOMAS STATTEN TO ELIZABETH KENNEDY
DATE: NOV. 30,
REFERENCE: T.H.M. VOL. 6, PG. 197

NAMES: JESSE TAYLOR TO REBECCA SLAGLE
DATE: DEC. 15, 1836
BONDSMAN: MICHAEL SLAGLE
DATE PER: DEC. 18, 1836
BY: ISAAC CONDRAY, J.P.
WITNESS: M. M. SWAN
REFERENCE: C.A; O.M.R. PG. 205

NAMES: JONATHAN THOMPSON TO ELIZA HALL
DATE: NOV. 7, 1836
BONDSMAN: OBEDIAH HALL
DATE PER: NOV. 10, 1836
BY: JNO. MYNATT
WITNESS: M. M. SWAN
REFERENCE: C.A; O.M.R. PG. 203

NAMES: CALVIN TINDLE TO CATHARINE JULIAN
DATE: OCT. 27, 1836
BONDSMAN: JNO. BROWN
DATE PER: OCT. 27, 1836
BY: TANDY MUNDAY, J.P.
REFERENCE: C.A; O.M.R. PG. 203

NAMES: CAMPBELL TUCKER TO PHEBE BROWN
DATE: MAY 22, 1836
BONDSMAN: JNO. M. ALEXANDER
DATE PER: MAY 25, 1836
BY: D. EVERETT, ESQ.
REFERENCE: C.A; O.M.R. PG. 198

NAMES: JAMES WEAVER TO JANE WHITEHEAD
DATE: APR. 13, 1836
BONDSMAN: JNO. WHITEHEAD
DATE PER: APR. 14, 1836
BY: JOSEPH MEEK, J.P.
WITNESS: GEO. M. WHITE
REFERENCE: C.A; O.M.R. PG. 198

NAMES: LUKE WILES TO PATSY ANN LISBY
DATE: JUNE 20, 1836
BONDSMAN: JNO. PARKER
DATE PER: JUNE 1836
BY: SAM'L. LOVE, M.G.
REFERENCE: C.A; O.M.R. PG. 199; T.H.M. VOL. 6, PG. 197

NAMES: THOS. WHITEHEAD TO SUSAN WARREN
DATE: MAY 22, 1836
DATE PER: MAY 26, 1836
BY: LEWIS LUTTRELL, J.P.
REFERENCE: O.M.R. PG. 198

NAMES: WILLIAMSON TUCKER TO MARY LOUISE PAYNE
DATE: AUG. 5, 1836
BONDSMAN: RUSSELL TUCKER
DATE PER: AUG. 6, 1836
BY: GEO. RUSSELL, M. G.
REFERENCE: C.A; O.M.R. PG. 200

1837

NAMES: HENRY G. ANDERSON TO DRUCILLA C. MCCAMPBELL
DATE: MAR. 6, 1837
DATE:PER: MAR. 7, 1837
BY: G. S. WHITE, M.G.
REFERENCE: C.A; O.M.R. PG. 208; T.H.M. VOL. 6, PG. 197

NAMES: CHARLES W. ATKINS TO MARY HENRY
DATE : JULY 8, 1837
BONDSMAN: P. A. WATERS
DATE PER: JULY 9, 1837
BY: T. SULLINS
REFERENCE: C.A; O.M.R. PG. 210; T.H.M. VOL. 6, PG. 197

NAMES: ANDREW J. AULT TO MARY RUTHERFORD
DATE: SEPT. 21, 1837
BONDSMAN: JOSIAH RODDY
DATE PER: SEPT. 21, 1837
BY: JAMES MCNUTT, J.P.
REFERENCE: C.A; O.M.R. PG.212; T.H.M. VOL. 6, PG. 197

NAMES: JOHN BABRING TO BETSY SMITH
DATE: MAY 22,
REFERENCE: T.H.M. VOL. 6, PG. 198

NAMES: ANDREW J. BALLARD TO NANCY FRANKLIN
DATE: APR. 22, 1837
DATE PER: APR. 25, 1837
BY: JAMES RODGERS, J.P.
REFERENCE: C.A; O.M.R. PG. 209

NAMES: NEWMAN BASKETT (OR BARKETT) TO PHEBE ANN FRANKLIN
DATE: JANY. 16, 1837
DATE PER: JANY. 17, 1837
BY: J. D. BENNETT, J.P.
REFERENCE: C.A; O.M.R. PG. 206

NAMES: JOHN I. BEAN TO SARAH CARROLL
DATE: JULY 26,
REFERENCE: T.H.M. VOL. 6, PG. 197

NAMES: JNO. J. BEARD TO JANE MCCARROLL
DATE: JULY 26, 1837
BONDSMAN: JNO. R. DAVIS
DATE PER: JULY 27, 1837
BY: JOHN NESTER, ESQ.
WITNESS: M. M. SWAN
REFERENCE: C.A; O.M.R. PG. 211

NAMES: WM. R. BOWEN TO MATILDA E. SPRENKLES
DATE: DEC. 27, 1837
BONDSMAN: WM. DUNLAP
DATE PER: DEC. 28, 1837
BY: J. M. KELLEY, M.G.
REFERENCE: C.A; O.M.R. PG. 216; T.H.M. VOL. 6, PG. 197

NAMES: AUGUSTIAN BRADLY TO RACHEL HAZLEWOOD
DATE: JANY. 24, 1837
DATE PER: JANY. 29, 1837
BY: T. G. CRAIGHEAD, J.P.
REFERENCE: C.A; O.M.R. PG. 206

NAMES: JUBILEE BRADLY TO NANCY GAINS (OR GOINGS)
DATE: APR. 10, 1837
DATE PER: APR. 13, 1837
BY: JAS. D. MURRAY, J.P.
REFERENCE: C.A; O.M.R. PG. 208

NAMES: HUGH BROWN TO SARAH WOOD
DATE: APR. 20, 1837
DATE:PER: APR. 20, 1837
BY: RICHARD KEYHILL, J.P.
REFERENCE: C.A; O.M.R. PG. 209

NAMES: CALVIN E. BRYANT TO ANN KEITH
DATE: NOV. 17, 1837
DATE PER: NOV. 17, 1837
BY: JOHN PRYOR
REFERENCE: C.A; O.M.R. PG. 214

NAMES: ABSALOM BURNETT TO SARAH CATHERINE ROBERTS
DATE: APR. 27, 1837
BONDSMAN: JOSEPHUS ALEXANDER
DATE PER: APR. 27, 1837
BY: WM. LINDSAY, J.P.
REFERENCE: C.A; O.M.R. PG. 209

NAMES: ROBERT CALDWELL TO ELIZABETH CLAPP
DATE: OCT. 30, 1837
BONDSMAN: DANIEL GRAVES
REFERENCE: C.A; T.H.M. VOL. 6, PG. 198

NAMES: THOS. F. CALLOWAY TO POLLY COX
DATE: NOV. 22, 1837
BY: J. C. ENGLAND - DATE PER: NOV. 3, 1837
REFERENCE: C.A; O.M.R. PG. 215

NAMES: WILLIAM CARSON TO ANN MCCALLUM
DATE: JAN. 15,
REFERENCE: T.H.M. VOL. 6, PG. 198

NAMES: CHARLES P. CHAPMAN TO MARY B. THOMPSON
DATE: MAR. 4, 1837
BONDSMAN: JAMES DUNLAP
DATE PER: MAR. 9, 1837
BY: G. S. WHITE, M.G.
REFERENCE: C.A; O.M.R. PG. 208; T.H.M. VOL. 6, PG. 198

NAMES: GEORGE CHASTIN TO BETSY LISBY
DATE: MCH. 10,
REFERENCE: T.H.M. VOL. 6, PG. 198

NAMES: GEO. CHEATHAM TO ELIZA BUNCH
DATE: DEC. 12, 1837
BONDSMAN: WM. HICKMAN
WITNESS: M. M. SWAN
REFERENCE: C.A.

NAMES: LINDSAY CHILDRESS TO MARY M. KARNES
DATE: NOV. 21, 1837
BONDSMAN: WM. DUNLAP
DATE PER: NOV. 21, 1837
BY: NATHAN ALLDRIDGE, J.P.
REFERENCE: C.A; O.M.R. PG. 214

NAMES: REUBEN CHINN TO LOTTIE EDDINGTON
DATE: FEB. 16,
REFERENCE: T.H.M. VOL. 6, PG. 198

NAMES: MILTON CHRISTIAN TO JANE PERRY
DATE: DEC. 26, 1837
DATE PER: JANY. 2, 1837
BY: JOSEPH MEEK, J.P.
REFERENCE: C.A; O.M.R. PG. 216

NAMES: WILLIAM CLARK TO SUSAN CLARK
DATE: JANY. 3, 1837
BONDSMAN: JNO. NEAL
DATE PER: JANY. 5, 1837
BY: JAMES C. ENGLAND, J.P.
REFERENCE: C.A; O.M.R. PG. 206; T.H.M. VOL. 6, PG. 198

NAMES: CHAS. A. COFFIN TO ELIZA PARK
DATE: JANY. 3, 1837
BONDSMAN: A. R. HUMES
REFERENCE: C.A.

NAMES: CHARLES H. COFFIN TO ELIZA PARK
DATE: JANY. 3, 1837
DATE PER: JANY. 4, 1837
BY: T. H. NELSON, M.G.
REFERENCE: O.M.R. PG. 206

NAMES: JAMES R. COKER TO MARGARET MCTEER
DATE: JANY. 3, 1837
BONDSMAN: CHAS. LONES
DATE PER: JANY. 3, 1837
BY: WM. BILLUE, M. G.
REFERENCE: C.A; O.M.R. PG. 206

NAMES: JOSEPH M. COX TO DELILA MAY
DATE: FEBY. 15, 1837
BONDSMAN: THOS. B. COX
DATE PER: FEBY. 16, 1837
BY: JOHN MYNATT, J.P.
REFERENCE: C.A; O.M.R. PG. 207; T.H.M. VOL. 6, PG. 198

NAMES: BARNES CRAWFORD TO AMANDA(LOUISE, LAVIN)OR LONES
DATE: DEC. 4, 1837
BONDSMAN: DAVID LYON
DATE PER: DEC. 5, 1837
BY: J. M. KELLEY, M.G.
REFERENCE: C.A; O.M.R. PG. 215; T.H.M. VOL. 6, PG. 198

NAMES: MICAJAH CRAWFORD TO MARY F. JACKSON
DATE: NOV. 20, 1837
BONDSMAN: G. M. HAZEN
DATE PER: NOV. 20, 1837
BY: JACOB NUTTY, T. D.
REFERENCE: C.A; O.M.R. PG. 214

NAMES: TIMOTHY CUNNINGHAM TO VITON COOLY
DATE: FEBY. 13, 1837
BONDSMAN: DANIEL MCMULLEN
DATE PER: FEBY. 15, 1837
BY: JNO. T. KING, J.P.
REFERENCE: C.A; O.M.R. PG. 207

NAMES: ADAM CURRIER TO MARY LETHCO
DATE: NOV. 15, 1837
BONDSMAN: JONATHAN MARLEY
DATE PER: NOV. 16, 1837
BY: WM. RODGERS, J.P.
WITNESS: M. M. SWAN
REFERENCE: C.A; O.M.R. PG. 214

NAMES: JOHN DIGS TO RACHEL WELKER
DATE: AUG. 19, 1837
BONDSMAN: GEO. G. HARDIN
REFERENCE: C.A.

NAMES: JAMES DUNLAP TO SARAH A. LEGG
DATE: AUG. 21, 1837
BONDSMAN: M. M. SWAN
REFERENCE: C.A.

NAMES: ISAAC ELLEDGE TO JANE MORROW
DATE: SEPT. 15, 1837
REFERENCE: C.A; O.M.R. PG. 212; T.H.M. VOL. 6, PG. 198

NAMES: THOMAS A. EPPES TO SARAH A. WESTERFIELD
DATE: OCT. 18, 1837
DATE PER: OCT. 19, 1837
BY: G. S. WHITE, M.G.
REFERENCE: C.A; O.M.R. PG. 213

NAMES: ROBERT C. EVANS TO ELIZABETH SHEROD
DATE: AUG. 29, 1837
BONDSMAN: WM. MCMILLAN
DATE PER: AUG. 31, 1837
BY: WM. MCMILLAN, J.P.
REFERENCE: C.A; O.M.R. PG. 211; T.H.M. VOL. 6, PG. 198

NAMES: SAM'L. FERGUSON TO LUCY HINDS
DATE: OCT. 7, 1837
DATE PER: OCT. 7, 1837
BY: T. SULLINS
REFERENCE: C.A; O.M.R. PG. 213

NAMES: THOMAS W. FLEMING TO CATHERINE WALLAND
DATE: DEC. 27
REFERENCE: T.H.M. VOL. 6, PG. 198

NAMES: WILLIAM FORD TO MARGARET TARWATER
DATE: JAN. 16,
REFERENCE: T.H.M. VOL. 6, PG. 198

NAMES: ADAM FORMWALT TO MARY MCAFFREY
DATE: MAY 11, 1837
REFERENCE: T.H.M. VOL. 6, PG. 198

NAMES: JOHN FRANKLIN TO ANNA LUSTER
DATE: APR. 19, 1837
DATE PER: APR. 23, 1837
BY: M. L. MYNATT, J.P.
REFERENCE: C.A; O.M.R. PG. 209; T.H.M. VOL. 6, PG. 198

NAMES: ETHELDRED FUTERELL TO _____ MARTIN
DATE: SEPT. 19, 1837
BONDSMAN: WM. LINDSAY
REFERENCE: C.A; T.H.M. VOL. 6, PG. 198

NAMES: ETHELDRED FUTRIL TO SARAH NICHODEMUS
DATE: SEPT. 19, 1837
DATE PER: SEPT. 19, 1837
BY: WM. LINDSAY, J.P.
REFERENCE: C.A; T.H.M. VOL. 6, PG. 198

NAMES: WILLIAM GOLDSON TO MARGARET SMITH
DATE: APR. 14,
REFERENCE: T.H.M. VOL. 6, PG. 198

NAMES: WILLIAM GRAVES TO MAHALA GRAVES
DATE: OCT. 3, 1837
BONDSMAN: M. M. GAINES
DATE PER: OCT. 3, 1837
BY: WM. C. GRAVES, M.G.
REFERENCE: C.A; O.M.R. PG. 212; T.H.M. VOL. 6, PG. 198

NAMES: ALLEN HENDERSON TO MARY GORDON
DATE: OCT. 24, 1837
BONDSMAN: ROBT. CAMPBELL
REFERENCE: C.A; T.H.M. VOL. 6, PG. 198

NAMES: ANDREW A. HENDERSON TO MARY CAMPBELL
DATE: AUG. 24, 1837
BONDSMAN: JOHN CAMPBELL
DATE PER: AUG. 24, 1837
BY: O. F. CUNNINGHAM
REFERENCE: C.A; O.M.R. PG. 211; T.H.M. VOL. 6, PG. 198

NAMES: WILLIAM HENDERSON TO MARY GOLDEN
DATE: OCT. 21,
REFERENCE: T.H.M. VOL. 6, PG. 198

NAMES: RICHARD HENSON TO EVELINE COWAN
DATE: OCT. 12, 1837
BONDSMAN: JAMES COURTNEY
DATE PER: OCT. 12, 1837
BY: D. B. TIPTON, J.P.
WITNESS: M. M. SWAN
REFERENCE: C.A; O.M.R. PG. 213; T.H.M. VOL. 6, PG. 198

NAMES: JAMES HOOD TO NANCY RABY
DATE: OCT. 7, 1837
BY: D. EVERETT, J.P. - DATE PER: OCT. 10, 1837
REFERENCE: C.A; O.M.R; PG. 213; T.H.M. VOL. 6, PG. 198

NAMES: HARDIN HOPE TO NANCY GODDARD
DATE: APR. 11, 1837
BONDSMAN: J. D. BENNETT
DATE PER: APR. 11, 1837 - BY: J. D. BENNETT, J.P.
REFERENCE: C.A; O.M.R. PG. 208; &.209

NAMES: WILLIAM S. HOWELL TO MINERVA CRUZE
DATE: JAN. 11,
REFERENCE: T.H.M. VOL. 6, PG. 198

NAMES: JOSEPH HOWSER TO POLLY ANN BUCHKORD
DATE: NOV. 11, 1837
DATE PER: NOV. 14, 1837
BY: D. B. TIPTON, J.P.
REFERENCE: C.A; O.M.R. PG. 214; T.H.M. VOL. 6, PG. 198

NAMES: ELLET HUFFERMAN TO NANCY BUND
DATE: JAN. 11,
REFERENCE: T.H.M. VOL. 6, PG. 198

NAMES: LEWIS ISRAEL TO TILDA WEBBER (OR WEBB)
DATE: JANY. 25, 1837
BONDSMAN: WM. WEAVER
DATE PER: JANY. 25, 1837
BY: MICHAEL SMITH, J.P.
WITNESS: GEO. M. WHITE
REFERENCE: C.A; O.M.R. PG. 206; T.H.M. VOL. 6, PG. 198

NAMES: HUGH JACKSON TO HULDAH WILSON
DATE: AUG. 14, 1837
DATE PER: AUG. 18, 1837
BY: SAM'L. LOVE, M.G.
REFERENCE: C.A; O.M.R. PG. 211; T.H.M. VOL. 6, PG. 198

NAMES: JESSE B. JACOBS TO PATSY ANN COZART
DATE: MAY 17, 1837
DATE PER: MAY 19, 1837
BY: LEWIS LUTTRELL
REFERENCE: C.A; O.M.R. PG. 210; T.H.M. VOL. 6, PG. 198

NAMES: FREDERICK JOHNSTON TO DORTHULA LEDGERWOOD
DATE: SEPT. 8, 1837
DATE PER: SEPT. 12, 1837
BY: HENRY GRAVES, J.P.
REFERENCE: C.A; O.M.R. PG.212; T.H.M. VOL. 6, PG. 198

NAMES: HENRY KARNS TO JAMIMA CONNER
DATE: SEPT. 21, 1837
DATE PER: SEPT. 21, 1837
BY: JNO. MYNATT, J.P.
REFERENCE: C.A; O.M.R. PG. 212; T.H.M. VOL. 6, PG. 198

NAMES: HENRY KARNES TO CHARLOTTE MCLAIN
DATE: MCH. 22,
REFERENCE: T.H.M. VOL. 6, PG. 198

NAMES: EDMUND KIDD TO MELINDA GIFFIN
DATE: OCT. 20, 1837
DATE PER: OCT. 22, 1837
BY: DAVID B. TIPTON, J.P.
REFERENCE: O.M.R. PG. 213; T.H.M. VOL. 6, PG. 198

NAMES: JOHN KING TO POLLY MILLS
DATE: NOV. 25, 1837
DATE PER: NOV. 1837
BY: WM. MCMILLAN, J.P.
REFERENCE: C.A; O.M.R. PG. 215; T.H.M. VOL. 6, PG. 198

NAMES: MATTHEW KING TO M. M. FORD
DATE: OCT. 17, 1837
BONDSMAN: JNO. ANDERSON
REFERENCE: C.A; T.H.M. VOL. 6, PG. 198

NAMES: GEO. W. KIRBY TO LETTY MCCAMMON
DATE: NOV. 28, 1837
BONDSMAN: BENONI JOHNSON
WITNESS: M. M. SWAN
REFERENCE: C.A; O.M.R. PG. 215

NAMES: GEORGE KOONS TO SALLY EZELL
DATE: FEBY. 25, 1837
DATE PER: FEBY. 26, 1837
BY: MICHAEL SMITH, J.P.
REFERENCE: C.A; O.M.R. PG. 207; T.H.M. VOL. 6, PG. 198

NAMES: ELKANS LASTLY TO ELIZABETH TAYLOR
DATE: DEC. 12, 1837
DATE PER: DEC. 14, 1837
BY: M. L. MARTIN, J.P.
REFERENCE: C.A; O.M.R. PG. 215

NAMES: DUNCAN LEA TO OLIVIA NANCE
DATE: FEBY. 13, 1837
DATE PER: JULY 1, 1837
BY: DUERRETT EVERETT, J.P.
REFERENCE: C.A; O.M.R. PG. 207; T.H.M. VOL. 6, PG. 198

NAMES: ANDREW LIKE TO SOPHIA ROBERTS
DATE: MAR. 13, 1837
BY: B. MCNUTT, J.P. - DATE PER: APR. 18, 1837
REFERENCE: O.M.R. PG. 208; T.H.M. VOL. 6, PG. 198

NAMES: JAMES LISBY TO MAHALA HARRIS
DATE: DEC. 27, 1837
DATE PER: DEC. 28, 1837
BY: JOSEPH MEEK, J.P.
REFERENCE: C.A; O.M.R. PG. 216; T.H.M. VOL. 6, PG. 198

NAMES: CHRISTOPHER LITTLE TO MARY S. MCCAMPBELL
DATE: NOV. 15, 1837
BONDSMAN: CHAS. MCMILLAN
DATE PER: NOV. 16, 1837
BY: G. S. WHITE, M.G.
REFERENCE: C.A; O.M.R. PG. 214; T.H.M. VOL. 6, PG. 198

NAMES: GEORGE LONG TO REBECCA JOHNSON
DATE: DEC. 19, 1837
DATE PER: DEC. 21, 1837
BY: HENRY GRAVES, J.P.
REFERENCE: C.A; O.M.R. PG. 216; T.H.M. VOL. 6, PG. 198

NAMES: THOMAS LUCY TO MARY MCDANIEL
DATE: JULY 27
REFERENCE: T.H.M. VOL. 6, PG. 198

NAMES: GEO. MARTIN TO BETSY LISBY
DATE: MAR. 10, 1837
BONDSMAN: ALLEN LETSINGER
REFERENCE: C.A.

NAMES: JACOB L. MASSEY TO ANN JANE GRAY
DATE: JULY 26, 1837
BONDSMAN: THOS. A. MASSEY
DATE PER: JULY 27, 1837
BY: JAS. D. MURRAY, J.P.
REFERENCE: C.A; O.M.R. PG. 211; T.H.M. VOL. 6, PG. 198

NAMES: THOS. MCCALLAY TO AMANDA A. BOUNDS
DATE: SEPT. 19, 1837
DATE PER: SEPT. 19, 1837
BY: ________ NUTTY, T. D.
REFERENCE: C.A; O.M.R. PG. 212

NAMES: HUGH MCCANN TO MARGARET ANN PRICE
DATE: AUG. 17, 1837
DATE PER: AUG. 17, 1837
BY: JAMES RODGERS, J.P.
REFERENCE: C.A; O.M.R. PG. 211; T.H.M. VOL. 6, PG. 198

NAMES: CHAS. A. MCCLURE TO ELIZABETH L. KEITH
DATE: APR. 25, 1837
DATE PER: APR. 25, 1837
BY: W. J. KEITH
REFERENCE: C.A; O.M.R. PG. 209; T.H.M. VOL. 6, PG. 198

NAMES: SAMUEL MCKINLEY TO PEGGY MITCHELL
DATE: APR. 11,
REFERENCE: T.H.M. VOL. 6, PG. 198

NAMES: JOSEPH MCLAIN TO MARGARET ANN SHOOKEY
DATE: MAR. 1, 1837
BONDSMAN: AUSTIN D. MCLAIN
REFERENCE: C.A; T.H.M. VOL. 6, PG. 198

NAMES: THOMAS MCMILLAN TO JANE M. C. MEEK
DATE: JANY. 25, 1837
DATE PER: JANY. 26, 1837
BY: G. S. WHITE, M.G.
REFERENCE: C.A; O.M.R. PG. 206

NAMES: WILSON F. MEDARIS TO EVELINE YOUNG
DATE: DEC. 13, 1837
BONDSMAN: THOS. PEARSON
DATE PER: DEC. 14, 1837
BY: HENRY SOWARD, M.G.
REFERENCE: C.A; O.M.R. PG. 216; T.H.M. VOL. 6, PG. 198

NAMES: WESLEY MIKLES TO MARGARET GADDIS
DATE: JULY 7, 1837
BONDSMAN: JNO. N. MILLS
DATE PER: JULY 7, 1837
BY: RICHARD KEYHILL, J.P.
REFERENCE: C.A; O.M.R. PG. 210; T.H.M. VOL. 6, PG. 198

NAMES: THOS. M. MITCHELL TO ROSSANNA SMITH
DATE: APR. 6, 1837
BONDSMAN: ADAM R. FORMWATT
DATE PER: APR. 6, 1837
BY: T. SULLINS, M.G.
REFERENCE: C.A; O.M.R. PG. 209; T.H.M. VOL. 6, PG. 198

NAMES: REUBEN MOORE TO LOTTY EDDINGTON
DATE: FEBY. 16, 1837
BONDSMAN: ANDREW J. BROWN
DATE PER: FEBY. 16, 1837
BY: JNO. T. KING, J.P.
REFERENCE: C.A; O.M.R. PG. 207

NAMES: WESLEY MOURFIELD TO MAJORY THOMPSON
DATE: OCT. 27, 1837
BONDSMAN: JEHU REED
DATE PER: OCT. 28, 1837
BY: J. C. ENGLAND
WITNESS: M. M. SWAN
REFERENCE: C.A; O.M.R. PG. 214; T.H.M. VOL. 6, PG. 198

NAMES: JOHN MULVENY TO BETSY SMITH
DATE: MAY 22, 1837
BONDSMAN: JNO. HICKMAN
REFERENCE: C.A.

NAMES: JNO. MELVINY TO BETSY SMITH
DATE: MAY 22, 1837
DATE PER: MAY 23, 1837
BY: JNO. DOUGLASS, J.P.
REFERENCE: O.M.R. PG. 210

NAMES: THOS. MURPHY TO SARAH LUTTRELL
DATE: OCT. 25, 1837
DATE PER: OCT. 26, 1837
BY: J. ANDERSON, J.P.
REFERENCE: O.M.R. PG. 213; T.H.M. VOL. 6, PG. 198

NAMES: JAMES M. NANCE TO ELIZABETH LITOW
DATE: DEC. 27,
REFERENCE: T.H.M. VOL. 6, PG. 198

NAMES: WILLIAM NEAL TO ELIZABETH SMITH
DATE: MAY 4, 1837
BONDSMAN: JESSE GRONER
REFERENCE: C.A; T.H.M VOL. 6, PG. 198

NAMES: FREDERICK NICHODEMUS TO UNIA BARBER
DATE: MAY 19, 1837
BONDSMAN: JAMES A. MURPHY
DATE PER: MAY 25, 1837
BY: WM. MCMILLAM, J.P.
REFERENCE: C.A; O.M.R. PG. 210; T.H.M. VOL. 6, PG. 198

NAMES: JNO. OLIVER TO MALINDA B. COBB
DATE: OCT. 12, 1837
BONDSMAN: R. B. REYNOLDS
DATE PER: OCT. 12, 1837
BY: L. S. MARSHALL
REFERENCE: C.A; O.M.R. PG. 213; T.H.M VOL. 6, PG. 198

NAMES: WILLIAM PALMER TO JANE SMITH
DATE: FEBY. 10, 1837
BONDSMAN: ROBERT ARMSTRONG
DATE PER: FEBY. 10, 1837
BY: T. G. CRAIGHEAD, J.P.
REFERENCE: C.A; O.M.R. PG. 207; T.H.M. VOL. 6, PG. 199

NAMES: WM. F. PARHAM TO NELLY ANN TAYLOR
DATE: MAR. 24, 1837
BONDSMAN: THOS. D. PARHAM
WITNESS: M. M. SWAN
REFERENCE: C.A; T.H.M. VOL. 6, PG. 199

NAMES: THOS. PEARSON TO ELIZABETH HASHBARGER
DATE: JUNE 22, 1837
BONDSMAN: MICHAEL SLAGLE
WITNESS: M. M. SWAN
REFERENCE: C.A; T.H.M. VOL. 6, PG. 199

NAMES: ALLEN PERRY TO ELIZA JANE OAR
DATE: MAR. 28, 1837
BONDSMAN: DANIEL MCMULLEN
REFERENCE: C.A; T.H.M. VOL. 6, PG. 199

NAMES: WM. PETREE TO MYRA COX
DATE: OCT. 26, 1837
BONDSMAN: C. COX
DATE PER: OCT. 26, 1837
BY: LINDSAY CHILDRESS, J.P.
REFERENCE: C.A; O.M.R. PG. 213

NAMES: WILLIAM PETTY TO AGNES CON
DATE: OCT. 26, 1837
REFERENCE: T.H.M. VOL. 6, PG. 199

NAMES: ROBT. PILANT TO SUSANNA RUTH
DATE: DEC. 2, 1837
BONDSMAN: MOSES RUSSELL
DATE PER: DEC. 3, 1837
BY: LAYMAN JONES
REFERENCE: C.A; O.M.R. PG. 215; T.H.M. VOL. 6, PG. 199

NAMES: DAVID PRATT TO SARAH MITCHELL
DATE: NOV. 2, 1837
BONDSMAN: CHARLES MITCHELL
BY: M. M. GAINES
REFERENCE: C.A; O.M.R. PG. 214; T.H.M. VOL. 6, PG. 199

NAMES: JAMES PRATT TO REBECCA CUNNINGHAM
DATE: NOV. 21, 1837
BONDSMAN: ANDREW CUNNINGHAM
DATE PER: NOV. 21, 1837
BY: J. LEWIS
WITNESS: M. M. SWAN
REFERENCE: C.A; O.M.R. PG. 215; T.H.M. VOL. 6, PG. 199

NAMES: JOHN C. RABY TO JOANNA NAVE
DATE: AUG. 7, 1837
BONDSMAN: SQUIRE RABY
DATE PER: AUG. 22, 1837
BY: JAMES RODGERS, J.P.
REFERENCE: C.A; O.M.R. PG. 211; T.H.M. VOL. 6, PG. 199

Names: Wm. Rash to Sally Hains (or Harris)
Date: Feby. 9, 1837
Bondsman: James M. Nance
Date Per: Feby. 9, 1837
By: I. Lewis.
Reference: C.A; O.M.R. Pg. 207; T.H.M. Vol. 6, Pg. 199

Names: Thos. B. Reed to Martha J. Cobb
Date: Mar. 6, 1837
Bondsman: Wm. R. Bowen
Date Per: Mar. 9, 1837
By: G. S. White, M.G.
Reference: C.A; O.M.R. Pg. 208; T.H.M. Vol. 6, Pg. 199

Names: Martin L. Reynolds to Polly (or Mary) Nester
Date: Apr. 17, 1837
Bondsman: James O. Gentry
By: J. D. Bennett, J.P.
Reference: C.A; O.M.R. Pg. 209; T.H.M. Vol. 6, Pg. 199

Names: John Rose to Eliza Wrinkle
Date: May 25; 1837
Bondsman: Sam'l. Widener
Reference: C.A; T.H.M. Vol. 6, Pg. 199

Names: Jno. Scarbury to Anna J. Hollinsworth
Date: Mar. 7, 1837
Bondsman: Jno. T. Wells
Reference: C.A.

Names: Jno. Scarbury to Anna J. Hollinsworth
Date: Mar. 7, 1837
Date Per: Mar. 7, 1837
By: Sam'l. Vickey, J.P.
Reference: O.M.R. Pg. 208; T.H.M. Vol. 6, Pg. 199

Names: Nelson M. Scisson to Mahuldah Roark
Date: Jany. 24, 1837
Bondsman: Lewis Grannon
Witness: M. M. Swan
Reference: C.A.

Names: Thomas Seay to Mary McDaniel
Date: July 27, 1837
Date Per: July 27, 1837
By: T. Sullins
Reference: C.A; O.M.R. Pg. 211

Names: Elija Shelby to Amanda Lane
Date: Aug. 21, 1837
Bondsman: Edward Haynes
Witness: M. M. Swan
Reference: C.A; T.H.M. Vol. 6, Pg. 199

Names: Nelson Shipe to Nancy Johnson
Date: Nov. 28, 1837
Bondsman: Orange Warick
Date Per: Nov. 28, 1837
By: Henry Graves, J.P.
Reference: C.A; O.M.R. Pg. 215; T.H.M. Vol. 6, Pg. 199

Names: Alexander Simpson to Elizabeth Gillespie
Date: Mar. 6, 1837
Bondsman: Mark Gillespie
Date Per: Mar. 9, 1837
By: G. Everett, Esq.
Witness: M. M. Swan.
Reference: C.A; O.M.R. Pg. 208

Names: Jno. G. Smith to Martha O. Evans
Date: Dec. 26, 1837
Reference: O.M.R. Pg. 216

Names: Jno. N. Smith to Sarah Nicholson
Date: Jany. 4, 1837
Bondsman: Dennis Dozier
Date Per: Jany. 5, 1837
By: J. D. Bennett, J.P.
Witness: M. M. Swan
Reference: C.A; O.M.R. Pg. 206; T.H.M. Vol. 6, Pg. 199

Names: Wm. Smith to Juliet Lane
Date: Nov. 30, 1837
Bondsman: Elijah Shelly
Date Per: Nov. 30, 1837
By: Jno. G. Humbert, M.G.
Witness: M. M. Swan
Reference: C.A; O.M.R. Pg. 215; T.H.M. Vol. 6, Pg. 199

Names: Jno. C. Sawyer to Susan Frost
Date: July 28, 1837
Bondsman: H. W. Mynatt
Reference: C.A.

NAMES: PETER TARWATER TO SALLY BEAN
DATE: SEPT. 2, 1837
BONDSMAN: JESSE SIMPSON
DATE PER: SEPT. 7, 1837
BY: J. JOHNSON, J.P.
WITNESS: JAMES DUNLAP
REFERENCE: C.A; O.M.R. PG. 212

NAMES: PLEASANT J. TEMPLE TO MARY J. GILBREATH
DATE: JUNE 23, 1837
BONDSMAN: E. ALEXANDER
REFERENCE: C.A; T.H.M. VOL. 6, PG. 199

NAMES: JACOB THOMAS TO SARAH BARNETT
DATE: APR. 27, 1837
BONDSMAN: ADAM THOMAS
DATE PER: APR. 27, 1837
BY: JNO. T. KING, J.P.
REFERENCE: C.A; O.M.R. PG. 209; T.H.M. VOL. 6, PG. 199

NAMES: JAMES H. THOMPSON TO ANN MARIAH HICKEY
DATE: JUNE 28, 1837
BONDSMAN: ELIJAH HICKEY
DATE PER: JUNE 28, 1837
BY: J. C. ENGLAND
REFERENCE: C.A; O.M.R. PG. 210; T.H.M. VOL. 6, PG. 199

NAMES: WILEY Y. TINCH (OR LINCH) TO PENINA ROBESON
DATE: OCT. 14, 1837
DATE PER: OCT. 19, 1837
BY: LINDSAY CHILDRESS, J.P.
REFERENCE: C.A; O.M.R. PG.213

NAMES: ALEXANDER TURNER TO HANNA A. STERLING
DATE: SEPT. 9, 1837
BONDSMAN: DANIEL LYON
DATE PER: SEPT. 19, 1837
BY: G. S. WHITE, M.G.
REFERENCE: C.A; O.M.R. PG. 212; T.H.M. VOL. 6, PG. 199

NAMES: JAMES K. WALKER TO MARY MCMILLAN
DATE: DEC. 16, 1837
BONDSMAN: HARVEY WALKER
DATE PER: DEC. 1837
BY: WM. MCMILLAN, J.P.
REFERENCE: C.A; O.M.R. PG. 216; T.H.M. VOL. 6, PG. 199

NAMES: JAMES M. WALLIN TO SARAH B. ROSE
DATE: AUG. 29, 1837
BONDSMAN: C. H. KEITH
REFERENCE: C.A.

NAMES: ORANGE WARWICK TO DORCAS JOHNSTON
DATE: OCT. 10, 1837
BONDSMAN: STEPHEN M. SKAGGS
DATE PER: OCT. 10, 1837
BY: JOHN WOODS, ESQ.
REFERENCE: C.A; O.M.R. PG. 213

NAMES: NEWTON WHEELER TO MARY JOHNSON
DATE: FEBY. 1, 1837
BONDSMAN: THOS. CUNDIFF
DATE PER: FEBY. 5, 1837
BY: JOHN T. KING, J.P.
REFERENCE: C.A; O.M.R. PG. 207

NAMES: HUGH L. WHITE TO MARY ANN LAREW
DATE: MAR. 16, 1837
DATE PER: APR. 16, 1837
BY: WM. RODGERS, J.P.
REFERENCE: O. M. R. PG. 208

NAMES: JNO. M. WING TO BETSY SMITH
DATE: MAY 22, 1837
DATE PER: MAY 23, 1837
BY: JOHN DOUGLASS, J.P.
REFERENCE: C.A.

NAMES: CLEMENT WOOD TO NANCY DOBBINS
DATE: NOV. 3, 1837
BONDSMAN: HENDERSON DOBBINS
REFERENCE: C.A.

NAMES: CLEMENT WOODS TO NANCY DOBBINS
DATE: NOV. 3, 1837
DATE PER: NOV. 9, 1837
BY: TANDY MUNDAY, J.P.
REFERENCE: O.M.R. PG. 214

NAMES: JAMES YOUNG TO NERCISA MOSELY
DATE: JUNE 29, 1837
BONDSMAN: ROBERT ROSS
DATE PER: JUNE 28, 1837
BY: JAMES C. ENGLAND
REFERENCE: C.A.

www.ingramcontent.com/pod-product-compliance
Lightning Source LLC
Chambersburg PA
CBHW080420270326
41929CB00018B/3094
* 9 7 8 0 7 8 8 4 8 8 0 8 5 *